Aspen Coursebook Series

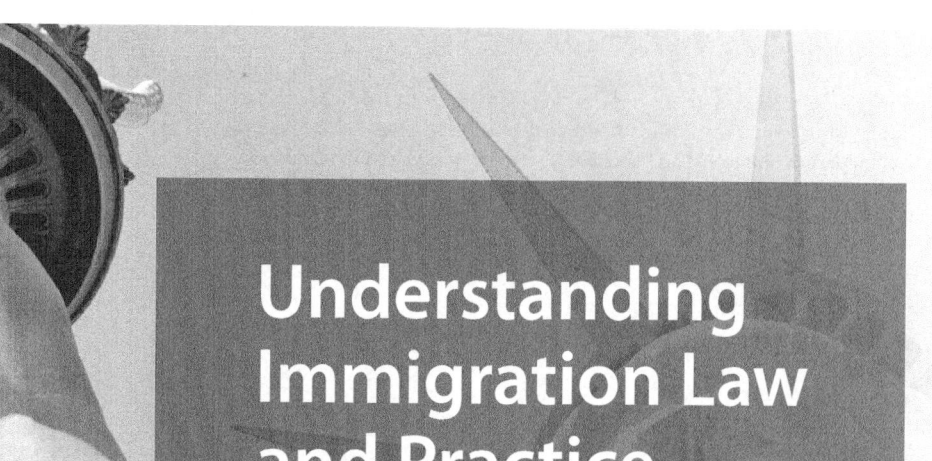

Understanding Immigration Law and Practice

Ayodele Gansallo, Esq., LLM

HIAS Pennsylvania, *and*
Adjunct Faculty
University of Pennsylvania School of Law

Judith Bernstein-Baker, M.S.W., Esq.

Executive Director,
HIAS Pennsylvania, *and*
Adjunct Professor
Community College Philadelphia

Copyright © 2017 CCH Incorporated.

Published by Wolters Kluwer in New York.

Wolters Kluwer Legal & Regulatory US serves customers worldwide with CCH, Aspen Publishers, and Kluwer Law International products. (www.WKLegaledu.com)

No part of this publication may be reproduced or transmitted in any form or by any means, electronic or mechanical, including photocopy, recording, or utilized by any information storage or retrieval system, without written permission from the publisher. For information about permissions or to request permissions online, visit us at www.WKLegaledu.com, or a written request may be faxed to our permissions department at 212-771-0803.

To contact Customer Service, e-mail customer.service@wolterskluwer.com, call 1-800-234-1660, fax 1-800-901-9075, or mail correspondence to:

Wolters Kluwer
Attn: Order Department
PO Box 990
Frederick, MD 21705

Printed in the United States of America.

1 2 3 4 5 6 7 8 9 0

ISBN 978-1-4548-5038-0

Names: Gansallo, Ayodele. | Bernstein-Baker, Judith.
Title: Understanding immigration law and practice / Ayodele Gansallo, Esq., LLM, HIAS Pennsylvania, and Adjunct Faculty, University of Pennsylvania School of Law ; Judith Bernstein-Baker, M.S.W., Esq., Executive Director, HIAS Pennsylvania, and Adjunct Professor Community College, Philadelphia.
Description: New York : Wolters Kluwer, [2016] | Series: Aspen coursebook series | Includes index.
Identifiers: LCCN 2016029479 | ISBN 9781454850380
Subjects: LCSH: Emigration and immigration law—United States.
Classification: LCC KF4819 .G36 2016 | DDC 342.7308/2—dc23 LC record available at https://lccn.loc.gov/2016029479

Understanding Immigration Law and Practice

Dear Wale,

I share this book as I share my love, unwaveringly! Kudos to you, as our family's first author. I only seek to share the podium. Enjoy the fruits of my labour!

Much love,

Ayo xoxo

About Wolters Kluwer Legal & Regulatory US

Wolters Kluwer Legal & Regulatory US delivers expert content and solutions in the areas of law, corporate compliance, health compliance, reimbursement, and legal education. Its practical solutions help customers successfully navigate the demands of a changing environment to drive their daily activities, enhance decision quality and inspire confident outcomes.

Serving customers worldwide, its legal and regulatory portfolio includes products under the Aspen Publishers, CCH Incorporated, Kluwer Law International, ftwilliam.com and MediRegs names. They are regarded as exceptional and trusted resources for general legal and practice-specific knowledge, compliance and risk management, dynamic workflow solutions, and expert commentary.

This book is in memory of my mother, Rebecca Masler Bernstein, who fled Poland with her family in 1921, and of my father, Joseph M. Bernstein, who was the first in his immigrant family to attend college—Yale—after his father came to the United States from Lithuania. Through them I learned about the determination and courage of parents and grandparents who come to the United States so their children can have better lives and, in some cases, by escaping persecution and war, can have life itself. Like my co-author, Ayodele Gansallo, I also pay homage to the immigrants and refugees I have been privileged to serve, who have shared their stories and culture with me, broadening my world immeasurably.

—Judith Bernstein-Baker

This book is dedicated to the many clients who have entrusted me to help them resolve their immigration issues. To each and every one, I am deeply honored. It is also dedicated to my parents, Ashabi Soboyejo Shokoya-Eleshin and Olubayode Shokoya-Eleshin, first generation immigrants to the United Kingdom from Nigeria, whose immigrant experiences and struggles have directed and inspired the lives of my brothers and me; and to my son, Noah, who, because of their sacrifices, can write his own chapter in our continuing immigrant family history.

—Ayodele Gansallo

Brief Contents

Contents xi ■ Figures xxxiii ■ Tables xxxv ■ Preface xxxvii

1	Historical Background and Introduction to the U.S. Immigration System	1
2	Nonimmigrant Visas for Brief Stays, Studies, and Cultural Exchange	43
3	Nonimmigrant Visas for Intracompany Transferees, Trade and Investment, and Professional Employment	93
4	Nonimmigrant Visas for Extraordinary Ability, Religious Workers, and Ancillary Activities	139
5	Asylum and Other Related Humanitarian Relief	181
6	Family Sponsored Immigration and Permanent Resident Status	245
7	Employment-Based and Self-Sponsored Immigration	305
8	Immigration Relief for Vulnerable Populations	383
9	Grounds of Inadmissibility and Deportation	455
10	Immigration Court Practice and Relief from Removal	505
11	Citizenship and Naturalization	569
12	Managing an Immigration Practice	617

Glossary 651

Index 667

Contents

Figures xxxiii ■ Tables xxxv ■ Preface xxxvii

1 Historical Background and Introduction to the U.S. Immigration System 1

A.	INTRODUCTION TO THE STUDY OF IMMIGRATION LAW	2
	A.1. Key Definitions	2
B.	A BRIEF HISTORY OF IMMIGRATION LAW AND POLICY	4
	B.1. 1776 to 1875: Migration from a Policy of Open Borders	5
	B.2. 1875 to 1902: Restrictions Begin Through Federal Control of Immigration	6
	B.3. 1903 to 1952: Quotas and Restrictionism	7
	B.4. 1952 to 1986: The Cold War and Elimination of Quotas	8
	B.5. 1986 to 1996: Enforcement and Legalization	9
	B.6. 1996 to 2001: Increased Enforcement and Economic Limitations	11
	B.7. 2001 to Present: September 11, 2001, and Its Aftermath	12
C.	THE IMMIGRATION SYSTEM TODAY	13
D.	SOURCES OF IMMIGRATION LAW	16
	D.1. Immigration and the U.S. Constitution	16
	Case for Discussion 1.1	*17*
	D.2. Primary Sources	17
	D.2.a. Statutes	17
	D.2.b. Regulations	18
	D.2.c. Case Law	18
	D.3. Secondary Sources	18
	D.3.a. Websites	19
	Case for Discussion 1.2	*19*
	D.3.b. Other Agency Guidance	19

Contents

D.3.c. International Law		20
D.3.d. Treatises and Casebooks		20

E. UNDERSTANDING BASIC IMMIGRATION DOCUMENTS AND FORMS — 20

- E.1. A Nonimmigrant Visa — 20
- E.2. I-94 Arrival/Departure Record Card — 20
- E.3. An Immigrant Visa — 24
- E.4. A Resident Alien Card — 25
- E.5. Employment Authorization Card — 27
- E.6. Other Immigration Forms and Correspondence — 27
- E.7. Representation Forms: G-28 — 30
- E.8. Receipts — 30
- E.9. Request for Evidence — 36
- E.10. Notice of Action — 36

F. DETERMINING IMMIGRATION STATUS — 36

Case for Discussion 1.3 — 41

G. CONCLUSION — 41

2 Nonimmigrant Visas for Brief Stays, Studies, and Cultural Exchange 43

A. DIFFERENCES BETWEEN NONIMMIGRANT AND IMMIGRANT VISAS — 45

B. THE VISA APPLICATION PROCESS — 48

Case for Discussion 2.1 — 49

- B.1. Nonimmigrant Waivers — 50

C. OBTAINING A NONIMMIGRANT VISA STAMP — 51

D. CHANGING OR EXTENDING NONIMMIGRANT STATUS — 54

Case for Discussion 2.2 — 57

- D.1. The Application Process — 57

E. NONIMMIGRANT VISAS THAT DO NOT AUTOMATICALLY GRANT EMPLOYMENT AUTHORIZATION — 60

- E.1. Sources of Law — 60
- E.2. Temporary Visitors to The United States for Business (B-1) and Pleasure (B-2): INA § 101(a)(15)(B); 8 C.F.R. § 214.2(b); 9 FAM 402.2 — 61

		Case for Discussion 2.3	63
	E.2.a.	Requirements for Entry	64
	E.2.b.	Reasons for Seeking B-1 Classification	66
		Case for Discussion 2.4	69
	E.2.c.	Compiling the B1/B2 Nonimmigrant Visa Application	69
	E.2.d.	Related Visa Classification, Transit (C-1) and Crew (D) Visas: INA § 101(a)(15)(C); 8 C.F.R. § 214.2(c); 9 FAM 402.4-6; INA § 101(a)(15)(D); 8 C.F.R. § 214.2(d); FAM 402.8-3	70
E.3.		Visas for Study (F-1 and M-1): INA § 101(a)(15)(F); 8 C.F.R. § 214.2(f); INA § 101(a)(15)(M); 8 C.F.R. § 214.2(m); 9 FAM 402.5	70
	E.3.a.	Application Procedure and Requirements	71
	E.3.b.	Compiling the F-1 or M-1 Nonimmigrant Visa Application	75
	E.3.c.	Duration	75
	E.3.d.	Employment Eligibility	76
		Case for Discussion 2.5	79
	E.3.e.	Spouses and Dependent Children	79
	E.3.f.	Travel Considerations for Those in F-1 Status	79
	E.3.g.	Reinstatement of Status	80
E.4.		Visas for Exchange Visitors (J-1): INA § 101(a)(15)(J); INA § 212(e); 8 C.F.R. § 214.2(j); 22 C.F.R. § 62; 9 FAM 402.5	81
	E.4.a.	Cultural Exchange Visitor Requirements for Specific J-1 Programs	83
		Case for Discussion 2.6	85
	E.4.b.	Two-Year Residence Requirement	85
		Case for Discussion 2.7	88
	E.4.c.	Spouses and Minor Children	89
E.5.		Visas for Related Cultural Exchange Visa (Q): INA § 101(a)(15)(Q); 8 C.F.R. § 214.2(q); 9 FAM 402.15	89
E.6.		Visas for Special Education Exchange Visitors and Trainees (H-3): INA § 101(a)(15)(H); 8 C.F.R. § 214.2(h)(7); 9 FAM 402.10-4(F)	90
F. VISA SUMMARY CHART			91
G. CONCLUSION			92

3. Nonimmigrant Visas for Intracompany Transferees, Trade and Investment, and Professional Employment 93

- A. VISAS BASED ON QUALIFYING TREATIES OF COMMERCE AND NAVIGATION FOR TREATY TRADERS (E-1) AND TREATY INVESTORS (E-2): 8 INA § 101(a)(15)(E); 8 C.F.R. § 214.2(e); 9 FAM 402.9 — 95
  - A.1. Sources of Law — 95
  - A.2. Specific E Visa Requirements — 97
    - A.2.a. Shared Requirements for Both E-1 and E-2 Visa Classification — 97
    - A.2.b. Requirements for E-1 Treaty Trader — 98
      - *Case for Discussion 3.1* — *100*
    - A.2.c. Requirements for E-2 Treaty Investor — 100
  - A.3. Using the E Visa for Principal Investors, Executive Employees, Supervisory Employees, and Essential Skills Employees — 102
      - *Case for Discussion 3.2* — *104*
  - A.4. Compiling the E Nonimmigrant Visa Application — 104
  - A.5. Duration of Stay — 106
  - A.6. Spouses and Children — 106
- B. VISAS FOR INTRACOMPANY TRANSFEREES OF MULTINATIONAL CORPORATIONS, MANAGERS AND EXECUTIVES (L-1A) AND SPECIALIZED KNOWLEDGE (L-1B): INA § 101(a)(15)(L); 8 C.F.R. § 214.2(l); 9 FAM 402.12 — 107
  - B.1. Sources of Law — 107
  - B.2. Specific Requirements — 108
    - B.2.a. Qualifying Organization — 108
    - B.2.b. Qualifying Employment — 110
      - *Case for Discussion 3.3* — *113*
      - *Case for Discussion 3.4* — *115*
  - B.3. Duration of Stay for L Visa Holders — 115
  - B.4. New Office L Classification — 117
  - B.5. Blanket L Status — 117
  - B.6. Compiling the L Nonimmigrant Visa Application — 118
  - B.7. Spouses and Children — 120

C. PROFESSIONAL SPECIALTY OCCUPATIONS (H-1B) AND SPECIALTY WORKERS FROM SINGAPORE AND CHILE (H-1B1): INA § 101(a)(15)(H); 8 C.F.R. § 214.2(h); 20 C.F.R. § 655; 9 FAM 402.10-4; INA § 101(a)(15)(H)(I)(B1); 9 FAM 402.10-5 — 120

   C.1. H-1B: Introduction and Sources of Law — 120
   C.2. H-1B Requirements — 122
      C.2.a. Qualifying Employer for H-1B Classification Purposes — 122
      C.2.b. Qualifying Position — 123
      C.2.c. Beneficiary's Qualifications for H-1B Classification — 123
         Case for Discussion 3.5 — *125*
      C.2.d. The Department of Labor's Labor Condition Application Requirement — 125
         Case for Discussion 3.6 — *126*
      C.2.e. Actual and Prevailing Wage Rate — 127
         Case for Discussion 3.7 — *128*
      C.2.f. Similar Working Conditions — 128
   C.3. Numerical Limitation: The H-1B Cap — 129
   C.4. Duration of Stay — 130
   C.5. Changes in Employment, Job Flexibility, and Transition from Student to Professional Worker — 130
   C.6. Compiling the H-1B Nonimmigrant Visa Application — 131
   C.7. Termination of Status — 132
   C.8. Spouses and Children — 133
         Case for Discussion 3.8 — *133*
   C.9. Specialty Workers from Singapore and Chile (H-1B1) — 133

D. CERTAIN SPECIALITY OCCUPATION PROFESSIONALS FROM AUSTRALIA (E-3): INA § 101(a)(15)(E)(III); 9 FAM 402.9-8 — 134

E. TN NAFTA PROFESSIONALS (TN): INA § 214(e); 8 C.F.R. § 214.6; 9 FAM 402.17 — 135
   E.1. Requirements for TN Classification — 135
   E.2. Application Procedure and Duration — 136
         Case for Discussion 3.9 — *137*

F. VISA SUMMARY CHART — 137

G. CONCLUSION — 138

 **4 Nonimmigrant Visas for Extraordinary Ability, Religious Workers, and Ancillary Activities 139**

A. VISAS FOR INDIVIDUALS WITH EXTRAORDINARY ABILITY IN THE SCIENCES, EDUCATION, BUSINESS, OR ATHLETICS (O-1A) AND ARTS, MOTION PICTURE, OR TELEVISION INDUSTRY (O-1B): INA § 101(a)(15)(O); 8 C.F.R. § 214.2(o)	140
A.1. Specific O Nonimmigrant Visa Requirements	141
A.1.a. Shared Requirements for Both O-1A and O-1B Nonimmigrant Visa Classifications	141
A.1.b. Evidentiary Criteria	142
Case for Discussion 4.1	*143*
A.1.c. Consultation or Peer Advisory Opinion	143
A.1.d. Itineraries	144
A.1.e. Contract Between Petitioner and Beneficiary	145
A.1.f. Duration	147
A.2. Proving the Merits for O-1A Nonimmigrant Classification: Demonstrating Extraordinary Ability in the Field of Sciences, Education, Business, or Athletics	147
Case for Discussion 4.2	*149*
A.3. Proving the Merits for O-1B Nonimmigrant Classification: Demonstrating Extraordinary Ability in the Arts, and Extraordinary Achievement in the Motion Picture or Television Industry	149
Case for Discussion 4.3	*151*
A.4. Compiling the O Nonimmigrant Petition	152
A.5. Changes in Employment and Permanent Residency	153
A.6. Visas for Derivatives of the Principal O-1 Foreign National	154
A.6.a. O-2 Visa Holders: Essential Support of O-1 Foreign Nationals	154
Case for Discussion 4.4	*155*
A.6.b. O-3 Nonimmigrant Visa Holders: Spouse and Children of O-1 Beneficiary	155
B. VISAS FOR ATHLETES (P-1) AND ARTISTS AND ENTERTAINERS (P-2 AND P-3): INA § 101(a)(15)(P); 8 C.F.R. § 214.2(p)	156
B.1. Shared Requirements for All P Classifications and Similarities to the O-1 Classification	157

Contents

	B.2.	Evidentiary Criteria for P-1 Athlete Classification	159
		Case for Discussion 4.5	*160*
	B.3.	Evidentiary Criteria for P-1B Nonimmigrant Classification: Members of an Internationally Recognized Entertainment Group	161
		Case for Discussion 4.6	*162*
	B.4.	Evidentiary Criteria for P-2 Nonimmigrant Artists or Entertainers Under a Reciprocal Exchange Program	163
	B.5.	Evidentiary Criteria for P-3 Nonimmigrant Artists or Entertainers Under a Culturally Unique Program	164
		Case for Discussion 4.7	*165*
	B.6.	Compiling the P Nonimmigrant Visa Petition	165
	B.7.	P-4 Nonimmigrant Visa Holders: Spouse and Children of P Beneficiary	165
C.	**VISAS FOR RELIGIOUS WORKERS (R-1): INA § 101(a)(15)(R); 8 C.F.R. § 214.2(r)**		**166**
	C.1.	Types of Religious Workers Eligible for R-1 Nonimmigrant Classification	166
	C.2.	Compensation for R-1 Nonimmigrant Workers	167
	C.3.	Site Inspections	168
	C.4.	Duration of Stay and Derivatives	168
	C.5.	Compiling the R Nonimmigrant Visa Petition	169
		Case for Discussion 4.8	*169*
D.	**VISAS FOR INFORMATION MEDIA REPRESENTATIVES (I): INA § 101(a)(15)(I); 8 C.F.R. § 214.2(i); 9 FAM 402.11**		**170**
	Case for Discussion 4.9		*171*
E.	**VISAS FOR TEMPORARY NONIMMIGRANT WORKERS (H-2): INA § 101(a)(15)(H); 8 C.F.R. § 214.2(h)**		**171**
	E.1.	Visas for Agricultural Work of a Temporary or Seasonal Nature (H-2A): INA § 101(a)(15)(H)(ii)(a); 8 C.F.R. § 214.2(h)(5)	172
		Case for Discussion 4.10	*174*
	E.2.	Visas for Non-Agricultural Work of a Temporary or Seasonal Nature (H-2B): INA § 101(a)(15)(H); 8 C.F.R. § 214.2(h)(6)	174
	E.3.	Compiling the Petitions for H-2A and H-2B Nonimmigrant Classifications	176

Contents

F.	VISA SUMMARY CHART	176
G.	VISAS FOR FOREIGN GOVERNMENT OFFICIALS (A): INA § 101(a)(15)(A); 8 C.F.R. § 214.2(a)	178
H.	VISA FOR EMPLOYEES OF INTERNATIONAL ORGANIZATIONS AND NATO (G): INA § 101(a)(15)(G); 8 C.F.R. § 214.2(g)	179
I.	CONCLUSION	179

5 Asylum and Other Related Humanitarian Relief 181

A.	OVERVIEW AND SOURCES OF LAW FOR ASYLUM	182
	A.1. Sources of Law: INA § 101(a)(42); INA § 208; INA § 209; 8 C.F.R. § 208; 8 C.F.R. § 1208; 8 C.F.R. § 1209	182
	A.2. Definitions	183
	A.2.a. Persecution	184
	Case for Discussion 5.1	*186*
	A.2.b. Agents of Persecution	187
	A.2.c. Past Persecution	187
	Case for Discussion 5.2	*188*
	A.2.d. Well-Founded Fear of Future Persecution	189
	Case for Discussion 5.3	*190*
	A.3. The Enumerated Grounds	190
	A.3.a. Race	191
	A.3.b. Religion	191
	A.3.c. Nationality	192
	A.3.d. Membership in a Particular Social Group	192
	Case for Discussion 5.4	*193*
	A.3.e. Political Opinion	195
	Case for Discussion 5.5	*195*
	Case for Discussion 5.6	*196*
	A.4. Standard of Proof and Credibility	196
	A.5. Bars to Asylum Eligibility	197
	A.5.a. One-Year Deadline	198
	A.5.b. Persecutors	199
	Case for Discussion 5.7	*200*

	A.5.c. Convicted of an Aggravated Felony or Particularly Serious Crime	200
	A.5.d. Firm Resettlement	200
	Case for Discussion 5.8	*201*
	A.5.e. Safe Third Country	201
	A.5.f. Terrorism and Danger to U.S. Security	202
	A.5.g. Multiple Asylum Applications	202
A.6.	Denial, Revocation, or Termination of Asylum	202
B.	**ASYLUM PROCEDURE**	**203**
B.1.	Building the Asylum Case	203
B.2.	Compiling the Affirmative Asylum Request	216
B.3.	Defensive Asylum Claims	221
B.4.	Frivolous Asylum Applications	226
B.5.	Asylum Applicants and Employment Authorization	228
C.	**CREDIBLE AND REASONABLE FEAR INTERVIEWS: INA § 235(b); 8 C.F.R. §§ 208.30-31; 8 C.F.R. §§ 1208.30-31**	**229**
D.	**BENEFITS OF ASYLUM GRANT**	**230**
	Case for Discussion 5.9	*230*
E.	**WITHHOLDING OF REMOVAL: INA § 241(B)(3); 8 C.F.R. § 208.16, 8 C.F.R. § 1208.16**	**231**
F.	**CONVENTION AGAINST TORTURE: 8 C.F.R. §§ 208.16-18, 8 C.F.R. §§ 1208.16-18**	**232**
G.	**TEMPORARY PROTECTED STATUS AND DEFERRED ENFORCED DEPARTURE: INA § 244; 8 C.F.R. § 244; 8 C.F.R. § 1244**	**235**
H.	**REFUGEES: INA § 101(A)(42); INA § 207; INA § 209; 8 C.F.R. § 201; 8 C.F.R. § 1207; 8 C.F.R. § 209; 8 C.F.R. § 1209**	**237**
H.1.	Determination of Refugees to the United States	237
H.2.	Family Reunification	239
H.3.	Adjustment of Status	240
H.4.	Refugee Resettlement Program	241
I.	**COMPARISON OF REFUGEE AND ASYLUM STATUS**	**241**
J.	**HUMANITARIAN PAROLE: INA § 212(D)(5)(A)**	**243**
K.	**CONCLUSION**	**243**

6 Family Sponsored Immigration and Permanent Resident Status 245

A.	**PART I: FAMILY RELATIONSHIPS AND THE PETITIONING PROCESS**	**246**
	A.1. Sources of Law and Quotas: INA §§ 201-4; 8 C.F.R. § 204	246
	A.2. Family Preference Categories	247
	Case for Discussion 6.1	*248*
	A.3. Chargeability Issues	250
B.	**FAMILY RELATIONSHIPS UNDER IMMIGRATION LAW**	**251**
	B.1. Preferential Treatment of Immediate Relatives	252
C.	**THE RELATIVE PETITION**	**252**
	C.1. Petitions for Spouses	253
	Case for Discussion 6.2	*253*
	C.2. Petitions for Children and Siblings	257
	Case for Discussion 6.3	*258*
	C.3. Adam Walsh Child Protection and Safety Act	259
	C.4. Documenting the Relationship	260
	Case for Discussion 6.4	*262*
	C.5. Benefits of the Child Status Protection Act	262
	C.5.a. CSPA Benefits for Children of U.S. Citizens	262
	C.5.b. CSPA Benefits for Children of Lawful Permanent Residents	263
D.	**TERMINATION AND REVOCATION OF IMMIGRANT VISAS: INA § 205; 8 C.F.R. § 205**	**264**
	Case for Discussion 6.5	*266*
E.	**IMMIGRATION BENEFITS AVAILABLE WHEN A PETITIONER DIES: 8 C.F.R. § 204.2**	**266**
	E.1. Immigration Benefits Available to Widow(er)s When Spouse Dies Before Petition Filed	266
	Case for Discussion 6.6	*268*
	E.2. Immigration Benefits Available When Petitioner Dies After Petition Filed	268
F.	**COMPILING THE APPLICATION PACKAGE FOR A RELATIVE PETITION**	**269**

G. PART II: BECOMING A LAWFUL PERMANENT RESIDENT THROUGH ADJUSTMENT OF STATUS IN THE UNITED STATES OR CONSULAR PROCESSING ABROAD: INA § 245; 8 C.F.R. § 245 — 270
- G.1. Adjustment of Status in the United States — 271
- G.2. Compiling the Adjustment Application — 273
  - G.2.a. Form I-485, Application to Register Permanent Residence or Adjust Status — 274
  - G.2.b. Form G-28, Notice of Entry of Appearance as Attorney or Accredited Representative — 274
    - *Case for Discussion 6.7* — *275*
  - G.2.c. Form G-325A, Biographic Information — 276
  - G.2.d. Form I-94 Arrival/Departure Record — 276
  - G.2.e. Birth Certificates and Immigration Medical Examination — 276
  - G.2.f. Form I-864, Affidavit of Support — 278
    - *Case for Discussion 6.8* — *280*
  - G.2.g. Certified Dispositions — 282
  - G.2.h. Form I-765, Application for Employment Authorization — 282
  - G.2.i. Form I-131, Application for a Travel Document — 283
  - G.2.j. Photographs and Fees — 284
- G.3. Inadmissibility Issues and Waivers — 284
  - G.3.a. Unlawful Presence and Provisional Waiver — 284
  - G.3.b. Section 245(i) of the Immigration and Nationality Act — 287
- G.4. Submitting the Application — 290

H. CONSULAR PROCESSING — 290

I. POST INTERVIEW — 295
- I.1. Conditional Residency: INA § 216; 8 C.F.R. § 216 — 295
  - *Case for Discussion 6.9* — *298*

J. FIANCÉ(E)S: INA § 101(A)(15)(K) — 298
- *Case for Discussion 6.10* — *300*

K. CONCLUSION — 303

7 Employment-Based and Self-Sponsored Immigration 305

A. OVERVIEW AND SOURCES OF LAW — 306

B. SHARED REQUIREMENTS FOR PERMANENT RESIDENCY CATEGORIES — 311

C. PRIORITY WORKERS, ALIENS WITH EXTRAORDINARY ABILITY, OUTSTANDING PROFESSORS AND RESEARCHERS, AND CERTAIN MULTINATIONAL EXECUTIVES AND MANAGERS (EB-1): INA § 203(b)(1)(A), 8 C.F.R. § 204.5(h); 8 C.F.R. § 204.5(i); 8 C.F.R. § 204.5(j) ... 313

    C.1. EB-1A Aliens with Extraordinary Ability in the Sciences, Arts, Education, Business, or Athletics ... 314
        Case for Discussion 7.1 ... *316*
        Case for Discussion 7.2 ... *317*
    C.2. EB-1B for Outstanding Researchers and Professors ... 317
        Case for Discussion 7.3 ... *320*
        Case for Discussion 7.4 ... *321*
    C.3. EB-1C for Certain Multinational Executives and Managers ... 322
        Case for Discussion 7.5 ... *324*
    C.4. Compiling the EB-1 Priority Worker Petition ... 325

D. ADVANCED DEGREE PROFESSIONALS (EB-2) AND SKILLED WORKERS, PROFESSIONALS, AND OTHER WORKERS (EB-3), AND THE PERM LABOR CERTIFICATION APPLICATION PROCESS: INA § 203(b)(2); INA § 203(b)(3); 8 C.F.R. § 204.5(k); 8 C.F.R. § 204.5(l); 20 C.F.R. § 656 ... 327

    D.1. EB-2 for Advanced Degree Professionals ... 327
    D.2. EB-3 for Skilled Workers, Professionals, and Other Workers ... 328
        Case for Discussion 7.6 ... *329*
    D.3. Labor Certification Application: The PERM process ... 329
        D.3.a. Step 1: Identify Minimum Requirements and Draft the Job Description ... 330
        D.3.b. Step 2: Confirm that the Foreign National Satisfies the Employer's Minimum Requirements ... 336
        D.3.c. Step 3: Prevailing Wage Determination ... 337
        D.3.d. Step 4: Recruitment ... 344
            Case for Discussion 7.7 ... *349*
        D.3.e. Step 5: PERM Filing Procedure and Document Retention Requirements ... 351
    D.4. Determinations ... 352

E. PROCEDURE FOR EB-2 AND EB-3 LABOR CERTIFICATION CASES ... 363

    E.1. Compiling an EB-2 and EB-3 Petition Based on Labor Certification ... 364

F. EXCEPTIONS TO THE PERM LABOR CERTIFICATION APPLICATION PROCESS, NATIONAL INTEREST WAIVERS (EB-2), AND EB-2 OR EB-3 SCHEDULE A LABOR CERTIFICATION: INA § 203(b)(2)(A); 8 C.F.R. § 204.5(k); 8 C.F.R. § 204.12 — 365

- F.1. EB-2 National Interest Waiver for Advanced Degree Professionals, Those with Exceptional Abilities, and for Physicians Working in Shortage Areas or Veterans Facilities — 365
   - *Case for Discussion 7.8* — 366
- F.2. Schedule A Occupations — 367

G. CERTAIN SPECIAL IMMIGRANTS, INCLUDING RELIGIOUS WORKERS (EB-4): INA § 101(a)(27)(C); 8 C.F.R. § 204.5(m) — 368
   Case for Discussion 7.9 — 370
- G.1. Compiling the EB-4 Religious Worker Petition — 372
   Case for Discussion 7.10 — 375

H. INVESTOR VISA (EB-5): INA § 203(b)(5); 8 C.F.R. § 204.6 — 375
- H.1. Compiling the EB-5 Petition — 379

I. OTHER CATEGORIES: INA § 203(c); 22 C.F.R. § 42.33 — 380
- I.1. Diversity Visa Lottery — 380
   - I.1.a. Procedure for DV Immigrants — 381

J. CONCLUSION — 381

8 Immigration Relief for Vulnerable Populations 383

A. OVERVIEW AND SOURCES OF LAW PROTECTING IMMIGRANT VICTIMS OF DOMESTIC ABUSE AND CRIMES: INA § 204; 8 C.F.R. § 204.2 — 385
- A.1. Petitions Based on Marriage — 385
   - A.1.a. Validity of the Marriage and Residency Requirements — 385
       Case for Discussion 8.1 — 387
   - A.1.b. Proof of Immigration Status of the Abuser — 388
- A.2. Petitions by Children — 389
   Case for Discussion 8.2 — 391
- A.3. Parents — 391

B. QUALIFYING CRITERIA FOR RELIEF — 391
- B.1. Battery or Extreme Cruelty — 391
- B.2. Good Moral Character — 392
   Case for Discussion 8.3 — 393

Contents

C.	COMPILING THE VAWA PETITION	397
D.	PROCESSING THE VAWA SELF-PETITION	401
	D.1. Prima Facie Finding	401
	D.2. Deferred Action Status	401
	D.3. Inadmissibility Issues	402
	D.4. Affirmative Petitions vs. Defensive Applications	403
	D.5. Confidentiality	403
E.	REMOVAL OF CONDITIONS FOR ABUSED CONDITIONAL LAWFUL PERMANENT RESIDENTS: INA § 216; 8 C.F.R. § 216	403
	E.1. Compiling the Removal of Conditions Petition	404
F.	U NONIMMIGRANT STATUS, VICTIMS OF ENUMERATED CRIMES: INA § 101(a)(15)(U); 8 C.F.R. § 214.14	405
	F.1. Eligibility for the U Nonimmigrant Status	405
	F.2. Certification for Qualifying or Enumerated Crimes	406
	Case for Discussion 8.4	*407*
	F.3. Substantial Physical or Emotional Abuse	408
	F.4. Identifying the Victim	409
	Case for Discussion 8.5	*410*
G.	COMPILING THE U NONIMMIGRANT STATUS PETITION	410
	G.1. Petitions for Qualifying Derivative Family Members	417
H.	U NONIMMIGRANT STATUS BENEFITS	417
I.	U NONIMMIGRANT PETITIONERS IN REMOVAL PROCEEDINGS	421
J.	ADJUSTMENT OF STATUS FOR U NONIMMIGRANT STATUS RECIPIENTS: INA § 245(m); 8 C.F.R. § 245.24	422
	J.1. Compiling the Application for U Nonimmigrant Adjustment of Status	423
K.	T NONIMMIGRANT STATUS, SEVERE FORMS OF HUMAN TRAFFICKING: INA § 101(a)(15)(T); 8 C.F.R. § 214.11	427
	K.1. Eligibility for T Nonimmigrant Status	428
	Case for Discussion 8.6	*428*
	K.2. Protection for Victims in the United States	429
	K.2.a. Continued Presence and Eligibility for Public Benefits	429
L.	APPLYING FOR T NONIMMIGRANT STATUS	430
	L.1. Compiling the T Nonimmigrant Status Application Package	431
	L.2. Applications for Qualifying Derivative Family Members	437

M.	T NONIMMIGRANT STATUS BENEFITS	438
N.	T NONIMMIGRANT APPLICANTS IN REMOVAL PROCEEDINGS	438
O.	ADJUSTMENT OF STATUS FOR T NONIMMIGRANT STATUS RECIPIENTS: INA § 245(l); 8 C.F.R. § 245.23	439
	O.1. Compiling the Application for T Nonimmigrant Adjustment of Status	441
P.	DIFFERENCES AND SIMILARITIES BETWEEN U AND T NONIMMIGRANT ADJUSTMENT OF STATUS APPLICATIONS	441
Q.	SPECIAL IMMIGRANT JUVENILE STATUS: INA § 101(a)(27)(J); 8 C.F.R. § 204.11	443
	Q.1. Obtaining a Dependency Order	443
R.	FILING THE SIJ APPLICATION AFTER THE STATE COURT ORDER IS ISSUED	444
	R.1. Affirmative Applications	445
	Case for Discussion 8.7	*447*
	R.2. Defensive Applications	447
S.	CHILDREN IN THE CUSTODY OF THE DEPARTMENT OF HEALTH AND HUMAN SERVICES, OFFICE OF REFUGEE RESETTLEMENT	448
T.	DEFERRED ACTION FOR CHILDHOOD ARRIVALS, OR DACA	449
	Case for Discussion 8.8	*451*
U.	CENTRAL AMERICAN MINORS REFUGEE/PAROLE PROGRAM, OR CAM	451
V.	CONCLUSION	453

9 Grounds of Inadmissibility and Deportation 455

A.	THE CONCEPTS OF ADMISSION AND DEPORTATION	456
	A.1. Admission and Admitted	457
	Case for Discussion 9.1	*459*
	A.2. Deportation	460
	Case for Discussion 9.2	*460*

B. GROUNDS OF INADMISSIBILITY — 461

- B.1. Health-Related Grounds: INA § 212(a)(1) — 461
  - *Case for Discussion 9.3* — 462
- B.2. Criminal Grounds: INA § 212(a)(2) — 464
  - B.2.a. Definition of Conviction — 464
    - *Case for Discussion 9.4* — 466
  - B.2.b. Inadmissibility Based on Specific Criminal Offenses — 466
    - *Case for Discussion 9.5* — 468
- B.3. Security and Related Grounds: INA § 212(a)(3) — 472
  - *Case for Discussion 9.6* — 473
- B.4. Public Charge: INA § 212(a)(4) — 474
  - *Case for Discussion 9.7* — 475
- B.5. Labor Certification and Qualifications for Certain Immigrants: INA § 212(a)(5) — 475
- B.6. Illegal Entrants and Other Immigration Violators: INA § 212(a)(6) — 476
  - B.6.a. Aliens Present Without Permission or Parole: INA § 212(a)(6)(A) — 476
  - B.6.b. Failure to Attend a Removal Proceeding: INA § 212(a)(6)(B) — 477
  - B.6.c. Misrepresentation: INA § 212(a)(6)(C) — 477
    - *Case for Discussion 9.8* — 478
- B.7. Documentation Requirements: INA § 212(a)(7) — 480
- B.8. Ineligible for Citizenship: INA § 212(a)(8) — 480
- B.9. Aliens Previously Removed: INA § 212(a)(9) — 480
  - B.9.a. Departing the United States After Being Unlawfully Present: INA § 212(a)(9)(B) — 481
    - *Case for Discussion 9.9* — 484
- B.10. Miscellaneous Grounds: INA § 212(a)(10) — 487
- B.11. Waiver to Facilitate Temporary Admission of Nonimmigrants: INA § 212(d)(3) — 487

C. GROUNDS OF DEPORTATION: INA § 237 — 488

- C.1. Inadmissible at Time of Entry or Adjustment of Status or Violates Status: INA § 237(a)(1) — 489
- C.2. Criminal Offenses: INA § 237(a)(2)(A) — 490
  - C.2.a. General Crimes: INA § 237(a)(2)(A) — 490
  - C.2.b. Controlled Substances: INA § 237(a)(2)(B) — 493
  - C.2.c. Firearms Offenses: INA § 237(a)(2)(C) — 493
  - C.2.d. Miscellaneous Crimes: INA § 237(a)(2)(D) — 494

	C.2.e. Domestic Violence Crimes: INA § 237(a)(2)(E)	494
	Case for Discussion 9.10	*494*
C.3.	Failure to Register and Falsification of Documents: INA § 237(a)(3)	495
	C.3.a. Change of Address: INA § 237(a)(3)(A)	495
	C.3.b. False Documents: INA § 237(a)(3)(B)	495
C.4.	Security Related Grounds: INA § 237(a)(4)	495
C.5.	Public Charge: INA § 237(a)(5)	495
C.6.	Unlawful Voters: INA § 237(a)(6)	496

D.	**INADMISSIBILITY VS. DEPORTATION**	**496**
E.	**AGENCIES INVOLVED IN INADMISSIBILITY AND DEPORTATION DECISION MAKING**	**500**
	E.1. The Decision Makers	501
	E.1.a. U.S. Consulates	501
	E.1.b. Enforcement Agencies	501
	E.1.c. Executive Office for Immigration Review	502
	E.2. Comparison of the Grounds	502
F.	**CONCLUSION**	**503**

10   Immigration Court Practice and Relief from Removal   505

A.	**OVERVIEW OF THE REMOVAL PROCESS**	**506**
	A.1. Notice to Appear	507
	Case for Discussion 10.1	*511*
	A.2. Notice of Hearing	514
	A.3. Authorized Legal Representatives	517
B.	**IMMIGRATION COURT HEARINGS**	**517**
	B.1. The Master Calendar Hearing	517
	B.1.a. Obtaining a Copy of the Immigration File	521
	B.1.b. Pleadings	521
	B.1.c. Pre-Hearing Voluntary Departure	526
	Case for Discussion 10.2	*527*
	B.2. The Individual Hearing	527
	B.2.a. Case Preparation	529
	B.2.b. Case Proceedings	531

	B.3. Evidence Rules in Immigration Court	532
	B.4. Decision of the Immigration Judge	533
	B.5. Post-Hearing Voluntary Departure	533
C.	EXPEDITED REMOVAL PROCEEDINGS	537
	Case for Discussion 10.3	*539*
D.	DETENTION	539
	D.1. Mandatory Detention	541
E.	MOTIONS PRACTICE IN IMMIGRATION COURT	543
	E.1. Motion to Reopen	543
	Case for Discussion 10.4	*543*
	E.2. Motion to Reconsider	544
	E.3. Motion to Change Venue	544
F.	ADMINISTRATIVE CLOSURE	546
G.	APPEALS PRACTICE	549
H.	FEDERAL COURT PRACTICE	551
I.	RELIEF AVAILABLE IN REMOVAL PROCEEDINGS	552
	I.1. Adjustment of Status	553
	I.2. Cancellation of Removal	553
	Case for Discussion 10.5	*555*
	I.3. Cancellation of Removal for LPRs	556
	I.4. Non-LPR Cancellation of Removal	558
	I.5. Cancellation of Removal Under the Violence Against Women Act, or VAWA	561
	Case for Discussion 10.6	*565*
J.	NACARA AND OTHER FORMS OF CANCELLATION OF REMOVAL	567
K.	CONCLUSION	567

11 Citizenship and Naturalization 569

A.	OVERVIEW OF CITIZENSHIP	570
	A.1. Sources of law	570
	A.2. Advantages of Citizenship	571

B.	**CITIZENSHIP BASED ON BIRTH IN THE UNITED STATES**	**572**
	Case for Discussion 11.1	*573*
C.	**CITIZENSHIP THROUGH NATURALIZATION**	**573**
	C.1. The Applicant Must Be at Least 18-Years Old	573
	C.2. The Applicant Must Be a Lawful Permanent Resident for a Continuous Period	574
	Case for Discussion 11.2	*574*
	Case for Discussion 11.3	*575*
	C.3. Absences from the United States: Continuous Residence and Physical Presence Requirements	576
	C.3.a. Continuous Residence	576
	Case for Discussion 11.4	*577*
	C.3.b. Physical Presence	579
	Case for Discussion 11.5	*580*
	C.4. Good Moral Character	580
	C.4.a. Individuals on Probation or Parole	584
	Case for Discussion 11.6	*584*
	C.4.b. Selective Service	584
	C.4.c. Payment of Taxes	585
	C.4.d. Dependent Support	585
	Case for Discussion 11.7	*585*
	C.4.e. Voting	586
	C.4.f. Marriage Fraud	586
	C.4.g. Evidence to Demonstrate Good Moral Character	587
	C.4.h. Literacy and Civics	587
	C.5. Exemptions, Waivers, and Reasonable Accommodation	588
	Case for Discussion 11.8	*588*
	C.6. Bars to Naturalization and the Oath of Allegiance	596
D.	**THE NATURALIZATION APPLICATION PROCESS**	**597**
	D.1. Compiling the Application for Naturalization	597
	D.2. The Final Steps of the Naturalization Application	599
	Case for Discussion 11.9	*600*
E.	**DERIVATIVE CITIZENSHIP: INA § 320**	**601**
	Case for Discussion 11.10	*601*
	E.1. Compiling the Application for Proof of Derivation	603
F.	**CITIZENSHIP BY ACQUISITION: INA § 301**	**604**
	Case for Discussion 11.11	*605*

G. ACQUISITION OF CITIZENSHIP FOR CHILDREN WHOSE
   PARENTS REGULARLY LIVE ABROAD: INA § 322 609
   Case for Discussion 11.12 .... *611*

H. LOSS OF CITIZENSHIP 611
   H.1. Expatriation 611
       Case for Discussion 11.13 .... *613*
   H.2. Denaturalization 613
       Case for Discussion 11.14 .... *614*

I. CONCLUSION 614

12 Managing an Immigration Practice   617

A. TYPES OF IMMIGRATION PRACTICES 618
   A.1. The Private Immigration Law Firm and Corporate Offices 618
   A.2. Nonprofit Organizations Recognized by the Board of Immigration Appeals and Accredited Representatives 618

B. CASE ASSESSMENT 620
   Case for Discussion 12.1 .... *621*
   B.1. Filing a FOIA 623
   B.2. Obtaining Criminal Records 623
       Case for Discussion 12.2 .... *624*

C. CONDUCTING THE INTAKE OR INITIAL CONSULTATION 624

D. RETAINER OR REPRESENTATION AGREEMENTS 627
   D.1. Payment of Fees 632

E. GATHERING EVIDENCE FOR SUBMISSION 632
   Case for Discussion 12.3 .... *635*

F. EXAMINING IMMIGRATION OPTIONS 636
   Case for Discussion 12.4 .... *637*
   Case for Discussion 12.5 .... *637*

G. MANAGING AN IMMIGRATION CASE AND RESPONDING
   TO REQUESTS FROM THE USCIS 638
   G.1. Responding to USCIS Requests for Evidence or Notices of Intent to Deny 638
       Case for Discussion 12.6 .... *639*

H. FILING SYSTEMS	640
I. ETHICAL ISSUES ARISING DURING THE COURSE OF REPRESENTATION	640
J. CONFLICT OF INTEREST	644
K. SPECIAL PROFESSIONAL CONDUCT RULES FOR PRACTITIONERS OF IMMIGRATION LAW	646
Case for Discussion 12.7	*648*
Case for Discussion 12.8	*648*
Case for Discussion 12.9	*649*
L. CONCLUSION	649

Glossary 651

Index 667

Figures

Figure 1.1.	Government Entities Involved in Implementing and Interpreting Immigration Laws	13
Figure 1.2.	Government Agencies Involved in the Administration of Immigration Laws	15
Figure 1.3.	Nonimmigrant Visa Document	21
Figure 1.4.	New I-94 Document	23
Figure 1.5.	Old I-94 Arrival/Departure Record Document	24
Figure 1.6.	Immigrant Visa Document	25
Figure 1.7.	Temporary I-551 Stamp	25
Figure 1.8.	Previous Sample Permanent Resident Card	27
Figure 1.9	Current Permanent Resident or I-551 Card, Front and Back	28
Figure 1.10.	Employment Authorization Card, Front and Back	29
Figure 1.11.	Form G-28, Notice of Entry of Appearance as Attorney or Accredited Representative	31
Figure 1.12.	Form I-797C, Notice of Action Receipt Notice	35
Figure 1.13.	Request for Evidence	37
Figure 1.14.	Sample Form I-797, Notice of Action Approval	39
Figure 1.15.	Sample Form I-797A, Notice of Action Approval Status Grant	40
Figure 2.1.	Form I-20, Certificate of Eligibility for Nonimmigrant Student Status	72
Figure 3.1.	E Visa Acquisition Map	96
Figure 3.2.	L-Visa Acquisition Map	108
Figure 3.3.	Qualifying Corporate Relationships for L-Visa Purposes	109
Figure 3.4.	H-1B Acquisition Map	121
Figure 5.1.	Sample Form I-589, Application for Asylum and for Withholding of Removal	204
Figure 5.2.	Sample Asylum Application Receipt Notice	218
Figure 5.3.	Sample Form I-797C, Notice of Action for Biometrics Appointment	220
Figure 5.4.	Typical Route of an Affirmative Asylum Application	222
Figure 5.5.	Instructions for Submitting Certain Applications in Immigration Court	224

Figures

Figure 5.6.	Typical Route of a Defensive Asylum Application	226
Figure 5.7.	Sample Frivolous Application Warning	227
Figure 6.1	Typical Route of an Adjustment Application	273
Figure 6.2	Typical Route of Immigrant Visa Consular Processing	294
Figure 7.1.	Department of Labor's Five Job Zones: Information and Specific Vocational Preparation	332
Figure 7.2.	Sample Prevailing Wage Determination	339
Figure 7.3.	Sample Notice of Filing	346
Figure 7.4.	Sample PERM Application	353
Figure 8.1.	Sample Notice of Extension of Status	426
Figure 9.1	Grounds of Inadmissibility and Deportation	458
Figure 10.1	Notice to Appear	508
Figure 10.2	Notice of Hearing	515
Figure 10.3	Notice of Entry of Appearance as Attorney or Representative Before the Immigration Court	518
Figure 10.4	Sample Written Pleading	522
Figure 10.5	Sample Proof or Certificate of Service	530
Figure 10.6	Sample Minute Order	534
Figure 10.7	Post-Order Instructions for Individuals Granted Relief or Protection from Removal by Immigration Court	536
Figure 10.8	Sample Proposed Order	547
Figure 10.9	Sample Notice of Intent to Offer Evidence in Cancellation of Removal Case	562
Figure 11.1	Sample Form N-648, Medical Certification for Disability Exceptions	590
Figure 11.2	USCIS Chart 3 on Derivative Citizenship: INA § 320	602
Figure 11.3	USCIS Chart 1 on Acquisition of Citizenship for Children Born in Wedlock: INA § 301	606
Figure 11.4	USCIS Chart 1 on Acquisition of Citizenship for Children Born Out of Wedlock: INA § 301	608
Figure 11.5	USCIS Chart on the Acquisition of Citizenship for Children Whose Parents Regularly Live Abroad: INA § 322	610
Figure 12.1	Form I-797C, Notice of Action Receipt with Electronic Tracking	625
Figure 12.2	Sample Engagement Letter Used in Employment-Based Immigration Cases	628
Figure 12.3	Sample Service Fee Agreement Used by a NonProfit Organization	630

Tables

Table 1.1.	Selection of Nonimmigrant Visa Categories	21
Table 1.2.	Selection of Immigrant Visa Categories	26
Table 2.1.	Chart of Nonimmigrant Visas	46
Table 2.2.	Visa Reciprocity Table for China	53
Table 2.3.	Current Visa Waiver Program Designated Countries	65
Table 2.4.	Some Sample Valid Uses of the B-1 Visa Classification with FAM Citation	66
Table 2.5.	Exchange Visitor Programs	81
Table 2.6.	Summary of Major Nonimmigrant Status Classifications	91
Table 3.1.	Comparison of Nonimmigrant Visas	137
Table 4.1.	Summary Comparison of Nonimmigrant Visas	176
Table 5.1.	Comparison of Asylum, Withholding, and Convention Against Torture Reliefs	233
Table 5.2.	Immigration Forms for TPS and DED	237
Table 5.3.	Comparison Chart of Refugee and Asylum Status	242
Table 6.1.	State Department Visa Bulletin, July 2015	248
Table 6.2.	State Department Visa Bulletin May 2016: Application Final Action Dates for Family-Sponsored Preference Cases	249
Table 6.3.	State Department Visa Bulletin May 2016: Dates for Filing Family-Sponsored Visa Applications	250
Table 7.1.	State Department Visa Bulletin, July 2015	309
Table 7.2.	State Department Visa Bulletin May 2016: Application Final Action Dates for Employment-Based Preference Cases	310
Table 7.3.	State Department Visa Bulletin May 2016: Dates for Filing Employment-Based Visa Applications	311
Table 8.1.	Comparison Between U and T Nonimmigrants Applying for Adjustment of Status	442

Table 9.1.	General Categories of Crimes Involving Moral Turpitude (CIMTs)	467
Table 9.2.	Comparison of Inadmissibility and Deportation Statutory Provisions	496
Table 9.3.	Waivers to Ameliorate Inadmissibility or Deportation	498
Table 9.4.	General Comparison of Inadmissibility and Deportation	502
Table 11.1.	Conditional Bars to Good Moral Character for Acts Committed in Statutory Period	582

Preface

Today, the population of foreign-born residents living in the United States on a long-term basis is the highest it has ever been in the history of the nation. According to the Migration Policy Institute, in 2013 the United States had 41.3 million foreign-born residents, representing 13 percent of the total U.S. population of 316.1 million people.[1] Since almost all foreign-born residents interact at some point with the U.S. immigration system, immigration law and policy is a growing field with dramatic impact on the foreign-born, their family members, and the U.S. workforce.

Applying immigration law in a particular case can work to protect refugees, bring needed workers to the U.S, and reunite families, but it can also result in family separation or forced return of a foreign national to that person's home country. Given the high stakes involved in an immigration case, all practitioners have an obligation to be well informed and to work within the legal and ethical scope of their profession.

Between us, we have more than 25 years of immigration law experience in nonprofit organizations. Working from this experience, we sought to offer a book that would be easily accessible to both students and teachers, recognizing that, in today's world, both are engaged in busy lives. Because we lacked extensive knowledge of working with those seeking immigration benefits through employment, we turned to wonderful colleagues in the immigration bar to assist us. Their contributions regarding employment-based immigration law issues have been invaluable. Through our combined efforts, we sought to provide a comprehensive textbook covering most aspects of immigration law today. We hope that *Understanding Immigration Law and Practice* goes some way toward achieving that goal. Our hope is that the book can be used in college-level courses exploring immigration law, while also teaching paralegals and others fundamental substantive law and procedure. It can also be used outside the classroom by paralegals, legal practitioners, and attorneys who, new to the field of immigration, may wish to refer to it as a guide and resource while they learn to navigate this complex area of law.

In this text, we sought to condense the complicated laws and regulations that make up our immigration system into user-friendly yet comprehensible chapters. It has been a challenge to decide what to include and what to leave out. The book

---

[1] J. Zong and J. Batalov, *Frequently Requested Statistics on Immigrants and Immigration in the United States* (February 26, 2015), available at http://www.migrationpolicy.org/article/frequently-requested-statistics-immigrants-and-immigration-united-states.

could easily have been three times in length, but that would not have achieved our objective. We have focused on what we considered to be the most important areas to cover. For the more complex issues dealing with those with criminal convictions, we have chosen not to delve too deeply, as more often than not, these cases require the expertise of a lawyer with a criminal law background or access to someone whose practice focuses on this companion area of law. Rather, we have tried to focus more on issue spotting so that the practitioner might know when to seek assistance from others.

In order to make the book accessible, we offer various scenarios as examples, placing information in contexts that illuminate the lives of those needing representation. Because we believe that posing questions is an invaluable aid to test comprehension and creates a gateway for deeper exploration of the material, we have included numerous "Cases for Discussion," with answers deliberately omitted from the text but available in the online Instructor's Manual. These and the examples used throughout the text emanate from cases we have been involved in through our client interactions and, therefore, offer real-world problems for beginning practitioners to consider. We have included a glossary of terms and acronyms, which are in boldface when they appear in the text for the first time. Other tools for students include learning objectives, marginal notes clarifying key vocabulary, which are in boldface and italicized, and numerous documents and other illustrative materials generated in the course of actual practice.

The last item points to a central aspect of this text. The facts behind many of the examples and cases for discussion are based on real-life situations on which we have advised over the years in the course of direct client representation, although clients' names have been changed to protect their privacy. We have found in our classes that using real cases brings to life the myriad experiences of and problems faced by those who come into contact with the U.S. immigration system. They assist students in translating legal rules and theory into practice. With that necessity in mind, we have sought to balance coverage of statutory and procedural rules with insights into practical information.

We have chosen to use the words "foreign national" rather than "alien" or "illegal alien" when addressing those who are neither U.S. citizens or lawful permanent residents, or who are here temporarily. We also use this term for those who, for various reasons, may not have permission to be in the United States and are therefore undocumented. We chose this terminology for both the text and for reproduced statutory and regulatory language. Those seeking the unaltered language will need to refer to the original source, which is good practice in any event.

A companion Instructor's Manual is available online to assist those wishing to teach substantive or procedural immigration law or both. As noted, it includes what we consider appropriate responses to the text's numerous "Cases for Discussion." As with immigration law broadly, these suggested responses take into account the many variables involved in reaching a satisfactory solution. The Manual also contains sample PowerPoint slides, tested in the classroom, that can be used in whole or in part, as well as sample lesson plans. Additional Cases for Discussion, entire class or small group exercises for enhanced learning, and ideas for homework assignments calling for analyzing fact patterns and applying legal principles are also included. Finally, suggestions for in-class computer-based exercises provide teachers with tools to familiarize students with techniques for researching the information necessary to corroborate an application.

Today, much of the practice of immigration law depends on the Internet, which is used extensively by the government agencies responsible for implementing the laws in this area. Readers should always check relevant websites and other source material to ensure they have the latest information.

Immigration law is never static. As an instrument of public policy, it is always changing as societal goals and public priorities change. New immigration benefits can be created, and others eliminated; forms are updated and new procedures announced. We have done our best to incorporate significant changes through March 2016, but urge readers to do their own due diligence with respect to keeping abreast of possible changes as they use this text. Providing complete and definitive information on this fluctuating area of law would not be possible. Rather, our goal for this text has been to provide readers with the tools they will need to conduct their own analysis and research and, more importantly, to spark their interest in a field we find both challenging and rewarding.

ACKNOWLEDGMENTS

The process of writing a book is never an easy endeavor. In fact, many times along the way, we found ourselves relating to George Orwell who once wrote, "[w]riting a book is a horrible, exhausting struggle, like a long bout of some painful illness." For two lawyers with no experience of book writing, we received moral, intellectual, and sustaining support during those difficult times from many people who assisted or provided guidance along the way. First and foremost, we wish to thank our two contributors, Jonathan Grode, of Green and Spiegel LLC, and Wendy Hess, of Landau, Hess, Simon, and Choi, our business immigration gurus who wrote Chapters 2 through 4 and Chapter 7, respectively. Without their expertise and insights, this book would not be complete. We would also like to thank, with great gratitude, the Goldblum and Pollins team of Maria Fritzinger Elias (for the many hours she devoted to answering our questions, sometimes late into the night!), and Karen Pollins and Yuah Jessica Choi of Landau, Hess, Simon, and Choi, three exceptional attorneys without whom Chapter 7 would never have been written. To the team at Green and Spiegel, we thank Andrew Rodgers, Lindsay Parnell, John Rowan, and Marc Kaplan for their assistance in writing, editing, and reviewing Chapters 2 through 4.

A hearty "thank you" to our colleagues at HIAS Pennsylvania, from whom we have learned so much over the years. Their commitment to excellence in practice and to the immigrants and refugees we serve is without equal. In particular, we wish to thank Lori Alexander, whose almost 40 years of working in the immigration field has made her an invaluable asset; she reviewed a number of our chapters and always offered helpful suggestions, from the perspective of someone who could recite much of the information in this book in her sleep. Our deepest thanks as well to Elizabeth Yaeger and Stephanie Costa, who were always willing to offer anecdotal information, statutory analysis, and legal procedure when requested.

Thank you to our friends in the Philadelphia Immigration Bar who offered their assistance, in particular Wayne Sachs of the Sachs Law Group, LLC, who reviewed and offered critical suggestions for improving Chapter 10, and Thomas Griffin of Surin & Griffin, P.C., who did likewise for Chapter 6; your critiques were always constructive, and we thank you. Our thanks also to William Stock, of Klasko Immigration Law Partners, LLP, and current President of the American Immigration Lawyers Association, for the business-based sample retainer agreement used in Chapter 12. Thank you to Kelsey Logar, a recent law graduate of the Thomas R. Kline School of Law at Drexel University, who fact-checked our citations and kept us on track. We would also like to take this opportunity to recognize a stellar Philadelphia immigration lawyer, Lisa Baird, the first attorney to join the staff of HIAS PA and who mentored us both early in our careers, but sadly passed away too soon.

Many thanks to the staff at Wolters Kluwer, particularly Susan Boulanger, who provided guidance and encouragement in equal measure. Your assistance saw us through when there appeared to be no end in sight. To Sarah Hains of The Froebe Group, who shepherded two rookies through a complex maze that is the book production process, but made sure we made it to the other side unscathed and full of new and useful information. You did a great job of teaching us what we needed to know, all the while being patient, firm, and amusing! We definitely appreciated your professionalism. And, to the many who reviewed the book and offered suggestions that have greatly improved our original drafts, we thank you.

Finally, we thank our many friends and our families—particularly Karl Baker, Kira Baker-Doyle, Akil Dasan Baker, Noah Gansallo, Obafemi Shokoya, Adekunle Shokoya, and Adewale Shokoya—who have encouraged us all along the way. Without your support, this book might never have been completed.

—**Ayodele Gansallo and Judith Bernstein-Baker**

Understanding Immigration Law and Practice

Historical Background and Introduction to the U.S. Immigration System

Key Terms and Acronyms

Board of Immigration Appeals (BIA)
Chinese Exclusion Cases
Customs and Border Protection (CBP)
Department of Homeland Security (DHS)
Department of Justice (DOJ)
Department of Labor (DOL)
Department of State (DOS)
Executive Office for Immigration Review (EOIR)
Federal Register
Immigration and Customs Enforcement (ICE)
Immigration and Nationality Act (INA)
Immigration Status
Inadmissible
Lawful Permanent Resident (LPR)
Precedent Decisions
Quotas
Regulations
Unauthorized/Undocumented Foreign National
U.S. Citizenship and Immigration Service (USCIS)
Visa

Chapter Objectives

- Provide a historical overview of U.S. Immigration Policy
- Explain the evolution of federal authority in immigration matters
- Describe current agencies and decision-maker roles in the immigration system
- Examine sources of immigration law

In its simplest form, immigration law addresses three questions: which foreign nationals are permitted to enter the United States; who is allowed to stay, and for how long; and who must leave. Current answers to these questions are rooted in the history of immigration law, developed over centuries and which may or may not be relevant to the needs of the country today. In trying to understand these complex questions, it may be helpful to visualize the opening and closing of a gate. At times, the gate is open widely, allowing many foreign-born individuals to visit and remain permanently in the United States; at other times, the gate is closed and as a result, those wanting to immigrate are shut out.

Immigration law is constantly in flux and practitioners often need to research the current state of the law or procedures as they relate to a particular set of facts. This chapter outlines sources of immigration law and policy that are important to utilize in understanding the law and keeping up-to-date. It briefly discusses the evolution of immigration policy and explains the key decision makers and agencies today, an important foundation for any practitioner who may interact with the immigration system.

A. Introduction to the Study of Immigration Law

Today, Congress has the primary authority to decide immigration policy. There is a complex set of agencies in the Executive Branch, including agencies within the **Department of Homeland Security**, or **DHS**, the **Department of State**, or **DOS**, and the **Department of Labor**, or **DOL**, that implements congressional legislation and regulates immigration. These agencies and policies developed over time in response to the evolving needs of the country.

The United States began as a nation with open borders and no controls, and progressed to what exists now, a highly regulated system that endeavors to manage the inflow of people within its borders. How we arrived at this position and where we move from here are always interesting topics of debate. While we do not intend to address future immigration policy, a survey of the past may be a useful starting point from which to look forward.

A.1. Key Definitions

There are some key terms that must be introduced at this point in order to understand the historical background and current structure of our immigration system:

- **Immigration status** refers to a person's status with respect to our immigration laws. This can include either a legal or unlawful status here. There are five general categories of immigration status covered in this text, which are:
    - ☐ A **United States citizen** refers to a person who obtains his or her citizenship either by birth, adoption, or naturalization.

- ☐ A **lawful permanent resident**, abbreviated as **LPR**, refers to a foreign national who has immigrated here; that is, the person intends and is authorized to reside permanently and indefinitely in the United States. Individuals who are LPRs have a document as evidence of their immigration status. Formally, it is known as an I-551 Permanent Resident card or stamp and is referred to colloquially as a "**green card**."
- ☐ A **nonimmigrant** refers to a foreign national who is in the United States for a specific purpose such as tourism, temporary work, or study. Most nonimmigrants require a **nonimmigrant visa,** which enables the holder to present him or herself at a port of entry so that a request to enter and remain in the United States in a particular immigration category can be determined by a **Customs and Border Protection**, or **CBP**, officer, who decides whether to approve the application or not. If granted, the foreign national may remain in the country legally for a specific length of time in order to pursue the particular purpose attributed to the visa category. There are many types of nonimmigrant visas and they are usually described by a letter and a number. For instance, tourists are issued B-2 visas, temporary skilled workers receive an H-1B visa, and students receive an F-1 visa.
- ☐ A **refugee** refers to a foreign national who faces persecution in his or her home country and has been granted protection so that s/he does not have to return there. Those who enter the United States as refugees receive their status while outside the country; individuals already physically present in the United States who seek protection apply for asylum and, if granted, are known as **asylees.** Refugees and asylees are expected to apply for lawful permanent resident status after one year of the grant of their protective status and eventually can apply to become citizens. A foreign national who is not otherwise eligible to enter the United States as a refugee may be allowed to enter on a temporary basis, known as parole. Granted by an official from the DHS, it is based on an assessment of an emergency, humanitarian concern, or because it is in the public interest. A foreign national granted this status is known as a **parolee.**
- ☐ An **undocumented or unauthorized foreign national** refers to a person who entered the United States without being inspected by U.S. immigration authorities or who entered lawfully but remains here in violation of the law. This may be because the foreign national has remained beyond any period of authorized stay or because s/he has breached any of the terms of the stay granted to him or her. Those who enter the United States without permission are referred to as having **Entered Without Inspection,** or **EWI.**

> - **Lawful Status** refers to a foreign national who is in the country with the permission of the United States government, either on a temporary or permanent basis. For example, a foreign national granted **Temporary Protected Status**, or **TPS**,[1] for eighteen months is in lawful status during that period.
> - A *Visa* is an official document permitting a person to travel to a United States border in order to request permission to enter the country in a specific category.

Visa: An official U.S. government-issued document placed in a foreign national's passport that allows him or her to travel to and apply for admission to the United States at a designated border or a port of entry.

B. A Brief History of Immigration Law and Policy

To help understand how immigration laws have changed over time, let us examine a family for a snap shot. Adrianna is a fifty-nine-year-old U.S. citizen. Her great-great grandfather, Pio, was from Italy and entered the United States in 1874. Pio had no visa, job offer, or any family members in the United States. When he arrived at the Port of Philadelphia, Pio was briefly inspected by a customs officer appointed by the Commonwealth of Pennsylvania who determined that Pio was young and healthy and likely a strong worker. Accordingly, Pio was permitted to enter the United States to seek employment and stay for as long as he wanted. Pio entered, worked as a bricklayer, and eventually became a U.S. citizen.

Fast forward to 2016 when Adrianna's son, Paul, meets a friend, Domenic, while studying in Italy. Domenic wants to come to the United States to work for a few years and perhaps remain permanently. While there are some exceptions, in general Domenic must have a visa to be able to come to the United States to work, whether temporarily or permanently. He will need a sponsor — either a family member or an employer — to help him apply for that visa. Intricate rules governing which family member can sponsor Domenic or the types of jobs and employers required for sponsorship exist today to restrict movement that did not exist in Pio's time. Those rules are discussed in detail in Chapters two through four and six and seven.

As the nation matured, many laws were passed that addressed immigration and determined the ability of people like Pio or Domenic to enter lawfully and/or remain permanently in the United States. Presenting a complete survey on immigration law and policy is beyond the scope of this textbook. Rather, we have chosen to include some key pieces of legislation that are representative of a particular period. The history of immigration shows that Congress may enact laws to restrict movement during one period but later may pass legislation to loosen those very restrictions. What follows is a brief summary of certain laws leading up to our current system.

---

[1] The concept of Temporary Protected Status is discussed further in Section G of Chapter 5, Asylum and Other Related Humanitarian Relief.

B.1. 1776 to 1875: Migration from a Policy of Open Borders

Prior to 1798, there were few restrictions on immigration to the United States, although Congress did enact legislation to regulate *naturalization*.

Naturalization: The process by which a foreign national can apply to become a citizen of the United States.

The Naturalization Act of 1790 established procedures for free white persons to achieve citizenship after just two years of residency, which later became five.

In 1798, in response to perceived threats by foreign powers, particularly France, Congress passed a series of individual laws — together known as The Alien and Sedition Acts, which included The Naturalization Act of 1798, the Alien Friends Act, the Alien Enemies Act, and the Sedition Act, which permitted the President to deport foreign nationals perceived to be "dangerous to the peace and safety of the United States,"[2] including noncitizens from countries with which the United States was at war. The Alien and Sedition Acts also made it more difficult for immigrants to become U.S. citizens by increasing the residency requirement to 14 years.[3] These Acts were the beginning of federal controls imposed on immigration. Domestically, they also restricted the ability to criticize the U.S. government, either in print or in speech, by making it a crime to utter statements that were "false, scandalous, or malicious."[4]

The role of the federal government in regulating immigration was supported by the United States Supreme Court in the Passenger Cases, 48 U.S. 283 (1849), which challenged state laws in New York and Massachusetts that empowered localities to tax vessels and individual foreign-born passengers arriving at their ports. Finding that such laws prevented the uniform governing of commerce by the federal government, the Supreme Court declared them unconstitutional because they violated the commerce clause of the United States Constitution.

The American Civil War brought about changes to our citizenship laws and enlarged the rights of all individuals in the United States, whether or not they were citizens, through the passage of the **Fourteenth Amendment** to the U.S. Constitution. Designed to protect the newly freed slave, this Amendment declared that "all persons born or naturalized in the United States and subject to the jurisdiction thereof" were full United States citizens. It further mandated that no state may deprive any person, citizen, or noncitizen, of "life, liberty, or property without due process of law" or deny any person within its jurisdiction the "equal protection" of the law.[5] This language, known as the **due process clause**, means that even noncitizens have certain protections under the Constitution. The scope of these protections, particularly for those who lack immigration status, is often a source of federal litigation.

---

[2] The Alien Friends Act, 1798, § 1.
[3] The Naturalization Act, 1798, § 1.
[4] The Sedition Act, 1798, § 2.
[5] United States Constitution, amend. XIV § 1.

B.2. 1875 to 1902: Restrictions Begin Through Federal Control of Immigration

By 1875, restrictions based on the characteristics of immigrants and their ethnicity and nationality began to appear. In 1882, the Immigration Act was passed that excluded "idiots, lunatics, convicts, and persons likely to be a public charge." Of great significance in that year was the first major effort to restrict immigration based on race, targeting Chinese immigrants. Previously, the United States and the government of China had enacted the Burlingame-Seward Treaty in 1868, which promoted legal emigration from China to the United States. Under this agreement and another that promoted commerce, Chinese nationals arrived to work in gold mines, agriculture, or to build the western railroads and were considered legal residents. However, economic, cultural, and racial tensions related to the success and number of Chinese immigrants began to build, culminating in the Chinese Exclusion Act of 1882, which created a ten-year moratorium on Chinese labor immigration. It also denied citizenship to Chinese citizens already in the United States.

The legality of this law was challenged by Chae Chan Ping who, pursuant to the Burlingame-Seward Treaty, had lived legally in the United States for many years and had traveled back to China for a visit. The changes in the law created by the Chinese Exclusion Act meant that he was prevented from returning to the United States to resume his residency, even though his trip abroad was for a short period. Ping challenged his exclusion all the way to the United States Supreme Court, which ruled that, despite the terms of the Burlingame-Seward Treaty that should have facilitated his return, Congress had the power to overrule the agreement and therefore exclude Ping.[6]

The Geary Act of 1892[7] extended the Chinese Exclusion Act by providing that Chinese nationals already in the United States who could not obtain a certificate of residency signed by a white citizen — required as a condition of remaining in the United States — could be deported. Fong Yue Ting, a Chinese resident, failed to get a white citizen to certify that he was here legally and was detained and placed into deportation proceedings. Ting had a number of witnesses willing to testify that he was in the country legally, but since they were all of Chinese descent, their testimony carried little weight. His case was also reviewed by the United States Supreme Court in 1893, which held that Congress had the right to both admit and expel foreign born residents and could overrule previous treaties or legislation.[8]

Through the cases challenging the legitimacy of the laws excluding the Chinese, the doctrine that Congress has the primary power to regulate immigration was established. The exclusion of Chinese immigrants remained in effect until 1943 when, in an effort to recognize Chinese alliance with the United States during the Second World War, the United States Congress passed the Magnuson

---

[6] *See Chae Chan Ping v. U.S.*, 130 U.S. 581 (1889).
[7] An Act to Prohibit the Coming of Chinese Persons into the United States of May 1892 (27 Stat. 25).
[8] *Fong Yue Ting v. United States*, 149 U.S. 698 (1893).

Act, which repealed legislation designed to exclude immigration of Chinese people to the United States.[9]

In addition to the Chinese Exclusion Acts, federal regulation of immigration was also strengthened through the Immigration Act of 1891, which gave the federal government direct control of inspecting, admitting, excluding, and processing all immigrants who sought entry to the United States. The Act created the Office of the Superintendent of Immigration within the Department of Treasury. This Office supervised United States' immigration inspectors and created immigration stations that had hearing and detention rooms, administrative offices, medical facilities, and railroad ticket offices. Perhaps the best known of these stations was Ellis Island, located in New York Bay.

B.3. 1903 to 1952: Quotas and Restrictionism

During the late 1800s until the 1920s, the United States experienced a great wave of immigration when over 22 million immigrants entered the country at a time of major industrial growth. As immigrant populations from eastern and southern Europe swelled, resistance to new groups considered to be inferior, uneducated, and economic competitors, also grew.

Between 1903 and 1907, the category of immigrants excluded from entering the United States was enlarged to include anarchists, polygamists, epileptics, beggars, individuals with physical or mental defects, those infected with tuberculosis, and children unaccompanied by parents.

In 1907, the Dillingham Commission, a bi-partisan congressional group, was formed to study the impact of immigration on the United States. The commission's work, which was completed in 1911, concluded that immigrants from eastern and southern Europe were a major threat to the United States economy and culture and proposed limiting immigrants from these regions. One vehicle to achieve this was a new literacy requirement that was enacted into law in the Immigration Act of 1917.[10] Known as the Literacy Act, the law required that all individuals, sixteen and older, have the ability to read thirty to forty words in their own language, thereby preventing the immigration of illiterate individuals. Interestingly, it did not require the ability to read in English.

Congress passed the Emergency Quota Act in 1921,[11] which provided that the number of immigrants from any region be limited to three percent of the population already living in the United States by 1910, thereby favoring Northern and Western Europeans who were present in the largest numbers at that time. These groups benefitted further from quotas contained in the National Origins Act of 1924,[12] which based the number of immigrants permitted to enter on two percent of those already living in the United States in 1890.

---

[9] *See* The Magnuson Act 1943, Pub. L. 78-199, 57 Stat. 600 (1943), also known as the Chinese Exclusion Repeal Act of 1943.
[10] Pub. L. 301; 39 Stat. 874 (1917), § 3.
[11] Pub. L. 67-5; 42 Stat. 5 (1921), § 2(a).
[12] Pub. L. 68-139; 43 Stat. 153 (1924).

By 1906, the government created the Bureau of Immigration and Naturalization, which was initially under the control of the Treasury Department. Through this agency, uniform standards for achieving naturalization were developed. The Bureau was later placed within the DOL in 1913. At the same time, it was divided into two separate divisions: the Bureau of Immigration and the Bureau of Naturalization. They were reunited again in 1933 as the **Immigration and Naturalization Service**, or **INS**, which was later transferred to the jurisdiction of the **Department of Justice**, or **DOJ**, in 1940. It had responsibility to both grant benefits and enforce immigration law against violators.

Immigration was significantly curtailed from the time of the Great Depression of 1929 through the beginning of World War II. However, the war caused labor shortages in the agricultural sector, prompting President Roosevelt to negotiate a series of bilateral agreements with Mexico to enable Mexican farm workers to enter the United States as temporary workers. Known as the Bracero Program, hundreds of thousands of Mexican nationals were invited to work in the United States after its initiation in 1942, marking a period where immigration was encouraged. Under pressure from reports of poor living conditions and exploitation in the program and from the United States labor movement anxious to create more jobs for American workers, the program was eventually ended in 1964.

Immediately after World War II, restrictive immigration quotas were overlooked as the country sought to get back on its feet. Following the war, some 250,000 Europeans made **stateless** or uprooted from their country of origin because of the conflict, were permitted to enter the United States as refugees. Congress then passed its first refugee legislation, the Displaced Persons Act of 1948,[13] which allowed for an additional 400,000 refugees to enter over a two-year period. "War brides" and fiancées of army personnel also added to this number.

B.4. 1952 to 1986: The Cold War and Elimination of Quotas

In 1952, Congress passed the **Immigration and Nationality Act**, or **INA**, also known as the McCarran-Walter Act.[14] The INA was a partial response to those concerned about communists in the United States, permitting the exclusion or deportation of noncitizens deemed to be subversive and engaged in activities that were prejudicial to the public interest. At the same time, the INA collected and organized many existing statutes into one comprehensive document governing immigration and nationality law. The statute was passed over a veto exercised by President Truman, who viewed it as discriminatory.

The INA maintained the quota system based on the national origin of intending immigrants, thereby continuing to favor immigration from countries in the western hemisphere. The Act tightened screening of applicants and security provisions, especially in relation to those from countries the United States

---

[13] Pub. L. 80-774; 62 Stat. 1009 (1948).
[14] The McCarran Walter Act, Pub. L. 82-414, 66 Stat. 163 (1952).

fought against in World War II and those associated with Communism. It established a preference system, favoring skilled workers and certain relatives of United States citizens and lawful permanent residents, all of which are still in place today.

The discriminatory national origins quotas came to an end through the Immigration and Nationality Act of 1965,[15] which established quotas for those from the eastern or western Hemispheres instead. During the signing ceremony for the legislation, President Lyndon Johnson remarked that the new law "corrects a cruel and enduring wrong in the conduct of the American nation." The law paved the way for profound and unintended demographic shifts in the make-up of America today. Rather than maintain the status quo with regards to the ethnic groups who were already in the United States as many had predicted and sought, the 1965 Act inadvertently opened the door for foreign nationals from all over the world and different backgrounds to immigrate here. The Act's primary purpose of reuniting families became the driving force for increasing ethnic diversity as more non-European groups left their home countries to resettle in the United States. This created a process referred to by some as "chain migration." In addition, the Act permitted immigration based on artistic and special work related skills and refugee status, all contributing to the current make-up of the country. This law is the centerpiece of a policy that continues to generate ethnic and cultural diversity in populations who immigrate to the United States today.

In the wake of the ad hoc entry of large numbers of refugees from Southeast Asia following the end of the Vietnamese war in 1975, Congress sought to provide a more organized system to protect those who were escaping persecution and deserving of protection in the United States. This led to the passing of the Refugee Act of 1980,[16] which was a comprehensive set of laws intended to permit the United States to meet its obligations under international law. The Act created a uniform method to admit and support new refugees, while also creating a system for individuals already in the United States to apply for asylum and thereby seek protection from persecution.

B.5. 1986 to 1996: Enforcement and Legalization

Partially as a result of the Bracero Program, which allowed millions of Mexican men to come to the United States to work as short term agricultural contract laborers, large farms grew to depend on immigrant labor. Following the termination of the program in 1964, many recent migrant farm laborers no longer had permission to be in the country, nor did they have authorization for employment. The continuing need for farm workers, however, resulted in the presence of large numbers of undocumented migrants who were unable to secure legal status in the United States or permission to work legally. Sensitive to the needs of

---

[15] Pub. L. 89-236; 79 Stat. 911 (1965).
[16] Pub. L. 96-212; 94 Stat. 102 (1980).

the farming community for agricultural workers and the problems created by large numbers of undocumented migrants while also concerned about employers hiring migrants who were unauthorized to work, Congress passed the Immigration Reform and Control Act of 1986 or IRCA.[17] This was an attempt to address the need for legalization of certain migrants, while developing sanctions for employers of undocumented workers to deter growth in this population.

IRCA created an opportunity for unauthorized migrants who entered the United States before January 1, 1982, and had not been convicted of a felony or three misdemeanors, to legalize their immigration status. It established a procedure by which all employers were required to check the immigration status of their employees, including citizens, to ensure each person was authorized to work. IRCA also created a unit in the DOJ to deal with possible discrimination claims arising from increased scrutiny of immigration status by employers. Another section of the statute allowed nationals of certain countries to enter the United States without a visa for a brief stay, under a program known as the visa waiver program.[18]

Stricter control of immigration was also the subject of the **Immigration Marriage Fraud Amendments Act of 1986**, or **IMFA**.[19] Previously, any person applying to become an LPR based on marriage would be granted this status indefinitely. However, due to concerns that people were engaging in fraudulent marriages in order to obtain immigration benefits, the IMFA limited the grant of status from indefinite to a conditional two-year period, if the marriage occurred less than two years prior to the date of adjudication of the application for status. This requirement, intended to limit **marriage fraud**, obligates couples to remain together for at least two years before jointly petitioning to lift the conditions on the foreign national who is then able to receive LPR status indefinitely. For example, if a couple appears for the marriage adjustment interview 1 year, 11 months, and 29 days after the marriage took place, the adjudicating immigration officer who approves the application can only grant LPR status to the foreign national for a conditional period of two years, requiring a further application to be filed two years later in order for the status to be granted indefinitely. However, if the couple has been married two years and one day at the time of the interview, then the officer must grant LPR status to the foreign national indefinitely.[20] Engaging in marriage fraud became a ground of deportation for the first time in this statute and also a crime for which either party could be criminally charged.

In contrast to the sustained increased controls on immigration, the early 1990s saw a period of openness and reform. The Immigration Act of 1990, or

---

[17] Pub. L. 99-603, 100 Stat. 3359 (1986).
[18] This is discussed in detail in Section E.2.a of Chapter 2, Nonimmigrant Visas for Brief Stays, Studies, and Cultural Exchange.
[19] Pub. L. 99-639, 100 Stat. 3537 (1986).
[20] This is discussed in detail in Section I.1 of Chapter 6, Family Sponsored Immigration and Permanent Resident Status.

IMMACT 90,[21] increased the level of permanent legal immigration to 700,000 per year, an increase of 35 percent. Immigrants sponsored by family members and employers benefited most from this change. While the world-wide limit later decreased to 675,000 after three years, it still remained higher than previous levels.

B.6. 1996 to 2001: Increased Enforcement and Economic Limitations

Sentiments against immigrants began to rise again in the mid-1990s as the economy of the United States contracted. Security concerns were also a factor, as there was the first bombing of the World Trade Center in 1993 by foreign nationals. To deal with perceived anti-immigrant attitudes, Congress passed three major laws in 1996: the Antiterrorism and Effective Death Penalty Act, or AEDPA;[22] the Personal Responsibility and Work Opportunity Reconciliation Act, known colloquially as the Welfare Reform Act;[23] and the **Illegal Immigration Reform and Immigration Responsibility Act, or IIRAIRA**.[24]

AEDPA created special deportation procedures for persons considered a threat to national security, expanded expedited removal procedures for certain immigrants, and limited **judicial review** of many decisions made by immigration courts. The Welfare Reform Act, among other things, denied most **means-tested federal public benefits** to legal immigrants for a period of five years after entry, and in some cases until a person naturalizes.[25] Undocumented immigrants were denied completely, unless they secured legal status.

IIRAIRA is a significant piece of immigration legislation enacted to better control the borders, and established new procedures governing admission, deportation, and legalization. One major change was the introduction of the concept of **inadmissibility,** described more fully in Chapter 9, Grounds of Inadmissibility and Deportation. Prior to IIRAIRA, a foreign national who physically entered the United States was subject to deportation proceedings, which meant the government had the burden to prove the person was deportable. A person caught at the border trying to enter the country who did not have a basis to be admitted to the United States was subject to be excluded; in other words, refused permission to enter altogether, and placed in exclusion proceedings before an **immigration judge** who would determine if any **exclusion grounds** applied to her entry into the United States. After the passage of IIRAIRA, that same person is now considered **inadmissible** and referred to as an arriving alien.[26] The foreign national is now placed into removal rather than deportation proceedings,

---

[21] Pub. L. 101- 649, 140 Stat. 4978 (1990).
[22] Pub. L. 104-132, 110 Stat. 1214 (1996).
[23] Pub. L. 104-193, title IV; 110 Stat. 2105 (1996).
[24] Pub. L. 104-208, div. C: 110 Stat. 3009 (1996).
[25] The relationship between eligibility for public benefits and legal status is extremely complex and beyond the scope of this text. Readers are advised to review the website of the various benefit granting agencies for more details.
[26] *See* Section C of Chapter 10, Immigration Court Practice and Relief from Removal.

even though the final determination will be as to whether s/he leaves the country or stays. While the proper technical term for deportation is removal, many immigration practitioners still use the old language.

IIRAIRA further expanded the grounds that would make a person inadmissible to or deportable from the United States, introduced border systems to track those entering and leaving the country, made it more difficult for the long-term unauthorized person to legalize, and further limited judicial review by federal courts of certain decisions of immigration authorities. While the major thrust of this period was in heightened enforcement, there were also laws to address specific vulnerable populations. The 1997 Nicaraguan Adjustment and Central American Relief Act, or NACARA,[27] and the Haitian Refugee Immigration Fairness Act of 1998, or HRIFA,[28] allowed Salvadorans, Guatemalans, some Eastern Europeans, and Haitians to apply for lawful permanent resident status under the standards of the less stringent pre-1996 law.[29]

In order to encourage immigrants to cooperate with law enforcement and to escape both sexual and labor trafficking, the Victims of Trafficking and Violence Protection Act of 2000, or VTVPA,[30] created new immigration benefits for victims of certain enumerated crimes. The relief is known as U Nonimmigrant Status. The law also sought to protect victims of severe forms of trafficking through the availability of T Nonimmigrant Status. Both of these reliefs are discussed in Sections F.1 and K of Chapter 8, Immigration Relief for Vulnerable Populations. Children of U.S. citizens were afforded additional protections under the Child Citizenship Act 2000, which permitted LPR children under 18 and in the legal and physical custody of a citizen parent to automatically acquire U.S. citizenship immediately upon fulfilment of these criteria.[31]

B.7. 2001 to Present: September 11, 2001, and Its Aftermath

The terrorist acts of September 11, 2001 ushered in a period where security concerns significantly influenced immigration policy. The Uniting and Strengthening America by Providing Appropriate Tools Required to Intercept and Obstruct Terrorism Act, or USA Patriot Act, of 2001[32] and the Enhanced Border Security and Visa Entry Reform Act of 2002[33] increased the number of border patrol agents threefold and implemented a stricter screening system, including the collection of ***biometrics***, for those entering the United States or seeking most types of immigration benefits.

Biometrics: The digital capturing of an individual's fingerprints, photograph, eye scan, and signature for submission and search through several government databases for background security checks and identity verification.

---

[27] Pub. L. 105-100, title II, 111 Stat. 2160, 2193-2201 (1997).
[28] Pub. L. 105-277, div. A title IX; 112 Stat. 2681-538 to 2681-542 (1998).
[29] Suspension of deportation, which was the relief previously available, is discussed in Section J of Chapter 10, Immigration Court Practice and Relief from Removal.
[30] 2000 Pub. L. 106-386, 114 Stat. 1464 (2000).
[31] Pub. L. 106-395, 114 Stat. 1631 (2000).
[32] Pub. L. 107-56, 115 Stat. 272. 26 (2001).
[33] Pub. L. No. 107-173, 116 Stat. 543 (2002).

A further major change in the structure of immigration control occurred with the passage of the Homeland Security Act,[34] which dismantled the INS on March 1, 2003, with responsibility for its immigration functions assumed by the DHS. The former agency was now separated into three components: CBP, which is responsible for protecting U.S. borders; **Immigration and Customs Enforcement,** or **ICE**, which is strictly an enforcement body; and the **United States Immigration and Citizenship Service,** or **USCIS**, which is responsible for granting immigration benefits. These agencies are housed within DHS, under the control of the Executive Branch. The statute also mandated that an unaccompanied minor child should be cared for by the **Office of Refugee Resettlement**, or **ORR**, under the **Department of Health and Human Services**, or **HHS**.[35]

The REAL ID Act of 2005[36] heightened the legal standards necessary to gain asylum in the United States and further limited judicial review of decisions made by an immigration judge or the **Board of Immigration Appeals**, or **BIA**. It also set a federal standard for the issuance of drivers' licenses, where applicants must prove they are in lawful immigration status before they are eligible to obtain one.

C. The Immigration System Today

As the history of immigration laws reveal, the legislative branch, through Congress, has major authority in determining immigration policy. While Congress has considerable power to create the framework and standards that govern immigration policy, most of the authority to decide which particular foreign nationals get approved for a visa or can remain in the United States rests with the Executive Branch agencies that interpret and implement the laws. The federal courts also play a role in reviewing a statute, regulation, or decision and determining whether it should be modified, explained, or discarded. The role of these government entities is depicted in Figure 1.1.

Congressional Branch	Executive Branch	Judicial Branch
• Passes laws	• Formulates regulations • Implements laws	• Reviews regulations, statutes, and lower-court decisions

Figure 1.1

Government Entities Involved in Implementing and Interpreting Immigration Laws

---

[34] Pub. L. 107-296, title IV, subtitle C-F; 116 Stat. 2135, 2177-2212 (2002).
[35] *Id.* at § 462.
[36] Pub. L. 109-13, 119 Stat. 302 (2005).

DHS implements immigration laws. Designed to secure the nation from any threats it might face, DHS has seven major agencies under its authority of which three — USCIS, CBP, and ICE — are relevant to immigration law. ICE is divided into two sections: **Enforcement and Removal Operations,** or **ERO**, which is responsible for detaining and removing those who have violated U.S. immigration laws; and **Homeland Security Investigations**, or **HSI**, which is responsible for investigating cross-border criminal activity.

In addition to the immigration agencies under the aegis of DHS, there are three other federal agencies that play a direct role in immigration decision making:

- The **Department of State**, or DOS, which maintains consular offices in countries throughout the world where foreign nationals can apply to obtain visas to enter the United States on a temporary or permanent basis. It also regulates the entry of refugees into the United States through the **Bureau of Population, Refugee, and Migration,** or **PRM**, which is described by the DOS as the entity that "provides aid and sustainable solutions for refugees, victims of conflict, and stateless people around the world, through repatriation, local integration, and resettlement in the United States."[37]
- The DOL, which is responsible for reviewing and approving certain employment-based applications for the benefit of foreign workers. It must certify that the position to be filled by the foreign worker is one that does not undercut the wages of or displace a capable and available American worker, thus acting as a gatekeeper to protect American jobs.
- The **Executive Office for Immigration Review,** or **EOIR**, which is charged with interpreting and administering the nation's immigration laws and adjudicates the immigration cases of those in **removal proceedings** to determine if a foreign national can stay in the United States or must leave. It is part of the DOJ and, under delegated authority from the Attorney General of the United States, conducts immigration court proceedings and engages in appellate review of decisions made by immigration judges.

The ORR, within the Administration for Children and Families, HHS, has an indirect role with respect to the foreign-born. It administers programs that support refugees, and minors who arrive in the United States without parents.

Figure 1.2 depicts the myriad agencies that have any role in overseeing immigration laws. Because so many of them are involved in administering immigration laws, each independent from the other, it is often necessary for the immigration practitioner to determine which agency or agencies are handling a case and review procedures and requirements of each of these individual entities. An immigrant may interface with multiple agencies in any one case or situation.

---

[37] *See* the website for this agency at http://www.state.gov/j/prm/.

C: The Immigration System Today   15

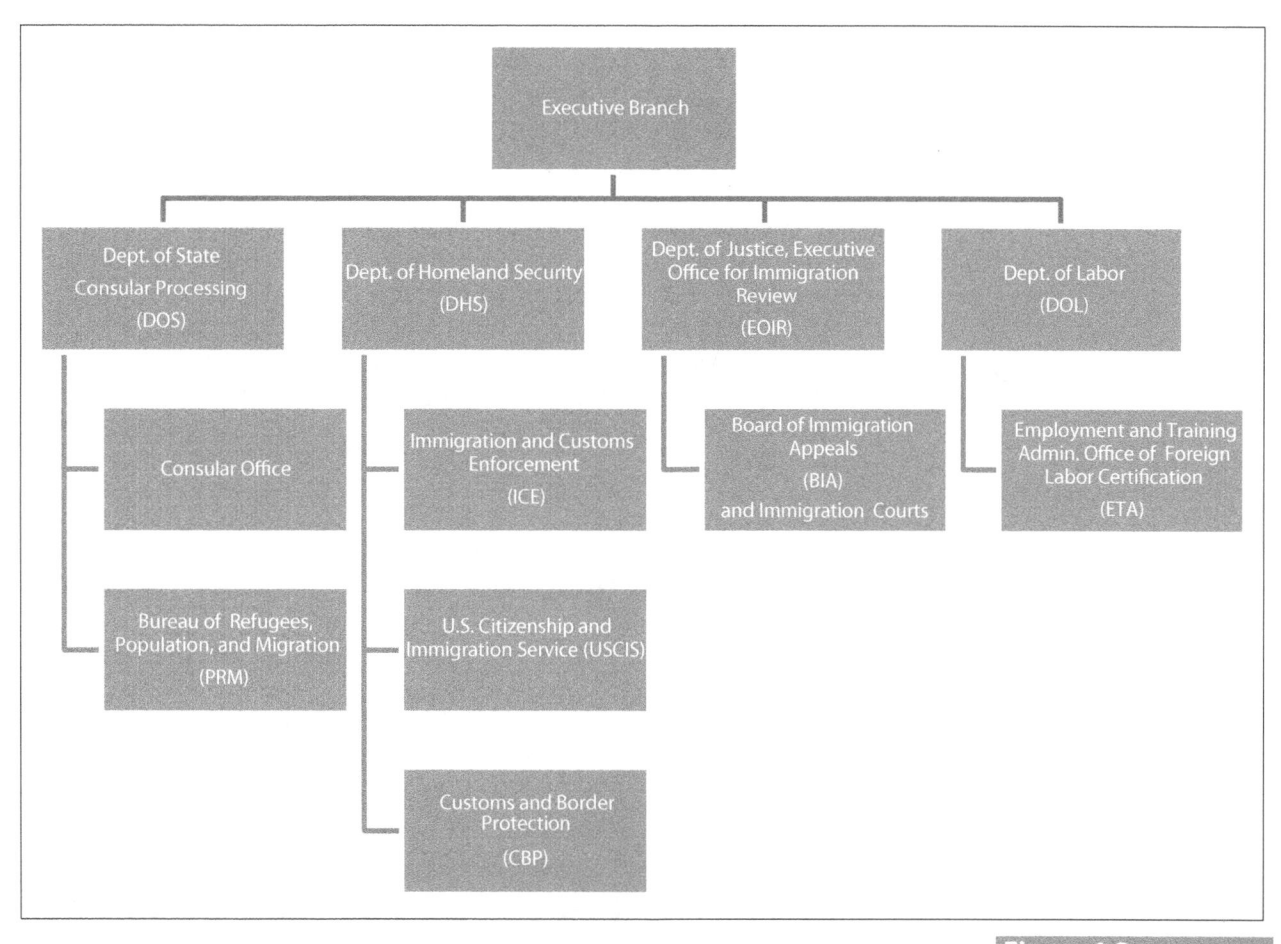

```
                          Executive Branch
       ┌──────────────┬──────────────┬──────────────┐
  Dept. of State   Dept. of      Dept. of Justice,   Dept. of Labor
  Consular         Homeland      Executive Office    (DOL)
  Processing       Security      for Immigration
  (DOS)            (DHS)         Review (EOIR)

  Consular Office  Immigration   Board of            Employment and Training
                   and Customs   Immigration         Admin. Office of Foreign
                   Enforcement   Appeals (BIA)       Labor Certification
                   (ICE)         and Immigration     (ETA)
                                 Courts

  Bureau of        U.S. Citizenship
  Refugees,        and Immigration
  Population,      Service (USCIS)
  and Migration
  (PRM)

                   Customs and Border
                   Protection (CBP)
```

Figure 1.2

Government Agencies Involved in the Administration of Immigration Laws

● **EXAMPLE**

Domenic, from Italy, has been accepted to attend college in the United States. He needs to go to the U.S. consulate in Italy, under the jurisdiction of the DOS, to obtain a student visa[38] to enter the country. The consular officer will review his application and approve or deny his request, depending on whether or not he meets the relevant criteria. If Domenic receives a visa, he will be able to board a plane and arrive at a U.S. airport where an officer from CBP will inspect him. The CBP officer will view Domenic as an applicant for admission to the United States and review his request to enter in order to decide, ultimately, if Domenic can enter the United States. This will depend on whether the officer discovers discrepancies in his application or has security or other concerns about his reason for being here. Once Domenic enters the country, he is expected to attend classes, since this is the purpose for which he was issued a visa. If he fails to attend, the school can report

---

[38] *See* Section E.3 of Chapter 2, Nonimmigrant Visas for Brief Stays, Studies, and Cultural Exchange, for further discussion of this visa category.

him to ICE, which may place him in removal or deportation proceedings where a U.S. immigration judge will decide in immigration court if he should have to leave the country. The court is part of the DOJ's EOIR. If Domenic can show he had a good reason for not attending class — perhaps he was very ill — he can apply to the USCIS to ask that it reinstate his student status. Once reinstated, Domenic can explain this to the immigration judge and ask him or her to terminate his proceedings so that he will no longer be subject to deportation.

In this example, Domenic interfaced with five different government departments or agencies: the DOS, CBP, ICE, the EOIR, and the USCIS. In such a scenario, an immigration practitioner must make sure s/he files the correct application, petition, or document with the correct agency and that the different decision makers are aware of decisions made by another agency involved in the case.

D. Sources of Immigration Law

Immigration law is governed by a variety of laws, from the U.S. Constitution and primary sources of law such as statutes, regulations, and case law, to secondary sources that can include internal memoranda interpreting these documents. All of these sources are important when seeking to understand immigration law in general or a specific provision and its application in particular. We examine both the primary and secondary sources of law.

D.1. Immigration and the U.S. Constitution

The U.S. Supreme Court has looked to the Constitution in conferring Congress the power to regulate immigration law and policy. In particular, in the Passenger Cases discussed earlier, the Court found that the Commerce Clause in U.S. Constitution Art. I, § 8 cl. 3, which authorizes Congress to "regulate commerce with foreign nations," provides a basis to establish Congressional power. The Naturalization Clause contained in U.S. Constitution Art. I, § 8, cl. 4 grants Congress the power to "establish a uniform rule of naturalization." Other powers in the Constitution include the right of Congress to declare war, close our borders, and remove enemy foreign nationals. In maintaining that Congress has the ultimate power to control immigration policy, the Supreme Court found that the power to exclude the foreign-born was an "incident of sovereignty."[39] The Constitution limits governmental authority when any person, including a noncitizen, is deprived of his or her liberty or property without the "due process of law" as

---

[39] *See Chae Chan Ping v. U.S.*, 130 U.S. 581 (1889), *supra*.

proscribed in the Fourteenth Amendment.[40] For immigration purposes, therefore, no one within the United States can be deported without some form of adjudication to determine whether the removal decision is appropriate.

Under the Supremacy Clause,[41] the federal government's laws supersede state laws when there is a conflict. This is particularly important when it comes to immigration laws. The scope of federal regulation of immigration law has often been the subject of litigation related to the concept known as **preemption**, which means when there is a conflict between federal law and state or local law, the federal law governs. When a state or local statute presents an obstacle to the accomplishment of a federal purpose, or when a person or entity cannot comply with both the state and federal law, preemption requires that the latter govern. Federal case law continues to be invoked to determine the division of power between federal and state authorities with respect to immigration enforcement.

Case for Discussion 1.1

Due to a significant increase in its Latino population, the City Council of Harmony believes there are more unauthorized immigrants who are moving there. The Harmony City Council and Mayor want to limit the number of such immigrants who reside in Harmony. It has passed a law requiring landlords to verify the immigration status of prospective tenants.

- Does this law raise any constitutional issues?

D.2. Primary Sources

Since immigration is federal law, primary sources include federal statutes, regulations, and federal case law.

D.2.a. Statutes

The basic source of immigration laws emanate from statutes passed by Congress. Most statutes related to immigration law are incorporated in the Immigration and Nationality Act, or INA, contained in Title 8 of the U.S. Code, Aliens and Nationality, referred to as 8 U.S.C. Typically, the INA is referenced when dealing with government agencies and courts governed by the EOIR, while 8 U.S.C. is referenced in cases before federal and district courts. Throughout this book, we reference only the INA when we cite to a particular statute.

---

[40] U.S. Constitution amend. XIV § 1.
[41] *See* U.S. Constitution art. VI, cl. 2.

D.2.b. Regulations

After a statute is passed, the agency responsible for implementing it develops regulations that describe in more detail the rules and procedures that they will follow in order to carry out the intent of Congress as reflected in the statute. Therefore, statutes and regulations work in tandem, with the former providing the framework and the latter the flesh. Regulations are published in the **Federal Register**, usually allowing for public comment, and then republished at a later date as a final rule. The regulations pertaining to immigration are generally found at Title 8 of the **Code of Federal Regulations**, or 8 C.F.R. The numbering for the sections of the Code will generally mirror the section numbers for the statute it interprets, in this case, the INA. However, 8 C.F.R. is divided into two sections, one that relates to the DHS — numbered 1-499 — and one that relates to the Executive Office for Immigration Review — numbered 1001-1337. While the different sections usually contain the same content, it is probably wise to cross check just to be certain. Since the DOS plays a major role regarding applications to come to the United States made abroad, it is also important to be familiar with the regulations that govern its functions which can be found at Title 22 of the C.F.R. There are also regulations related to the DOL's role in immigration matters in other sections of the Code.

D.2.c. Case Law

Case law is a fundamental source of immigration law as it interprets statutes, regulations, and procedures to ensure they express the intent of Congress, are consistent with other laws, and do not violate the U.S. Constitution. When a decision is meant to create a principle or rule that should apply to similar situations, it is called a precedent decision. Both judicial and administrative cases guide immigration law. Judicial case law derives from the federal courts, including the United States Supreme Court and the circuit courts. Decisions made by the Supreme Court bind all courts around the country, whereas a decision of a circuit court is binding only within the jurisdiction of the court that issued it. Administrative case law includes decisions made by the BIA, the appellate division of the EOIR. The decision of the BIA is binding on all immigration courts around the country. Other administrative case law can be found as published opinions of the **Administrative Appeals Office**, or **AAO**, the appeals division of USCIS, and the **Board of Alien Labor Certification Appeals**, or **BALCA**, which hears appeals of denials by the DOL of employment-based sponsored applications.

D.3. Secondary Sources

Secondary sources help to interpret and analyze primary source materials. In immigration law, there is an array of options. We discuss just some in the following sections.

D.3.a. Websites

Each key federal agency has a website that lists procedures, forms, and other components of immigration practice for which it is responsible. The USCIS' website, at www.uscis.gov, provides instructions on various applications it adjudicates, as well as eligibility and procedure with respect to achieving LPR status and citizenship. It also provides access to relevant forms for applications, which it constantly updates. Before completing any form from a source other than the USCIS' website, it is prudent to check that it is the most up to date version because using an old form could result in an application being rejected and an important deadline being missed. The DOS, Bureau of Consular Affairs, also has an extensive website describing forms and procedures for obtaining nonimmigrant visas.[42]

Case for Discussion 1.2

Tran was born in Vietnam and is now a lawful permanent resident in the United States, living in Pennsylvania. She comes into an immigration law office requesting assistance to apply for citizenship. She meets all the legal requirements. Practitioner Judy is asked to find the correct form, the cost of the application, and the address where it should be mailed. Judy knows that, since Tran is applying for a benefit, the correct agency that Tran will interface with is the USCIS.

- How should Judy find the correct form and the other information requested?
- Will Judy use primary or secondary sources in her search?

D.3.b. Other Agency Guidance

Agencies publish handbooks, guidance, and manuals to be used both by their staff in determining procedures and by those in the general public to make sure applicable eligibility criteria is met. Many of these are also available on the specific website for the agency in question. The USCIS website has a special section devoted to manuals and guidance.[43] The **Department of State Foreign Affairs Manual**, abbreviated as **FAM**, contains directives and interpretations of immigration law available to **consular officers** and the public and is a very useful source.[44]

---

[42] See http://travel.state.gov/content/visas/english.html.
[43] See http://www.uscis.gov/laws/immigration-handbooks-manuals-and-guidance.
[44] See https://fam.state.gov.

D.3.c. International Law

International law is also a source that can be used as guidance or authority to pursue a certain course of action, particularly in areas that concern human rights, including asylum cases. Of particular note is the 1951 Convention Relating to the Status of Refugees, a multilateral treaty developed by the United Nations, which was followed by the 1967 Protocol Relating to the Status of Refugees. The United States has ratified the latter but not the former.

D.3.d. Treatises and Casebooks

Treatises, casebooks, and journals explain various aspects of immigration laws and procedures. In researching a matter, practitioners often begin with a treatise and casebook and then investigate the primary sources cited in the material.

E. Understanding Basic Immigration Documents and Forms

There are many documents and forms used in immigration law and practitioners must develop an understanding of how to recognize and interpret them. We review some in the following sections.

E.1. A Nonimmigrant Visa

This nonimmigrant visa, as shown in Figure 1.3, contains the name and date of birth of the holder and the country and particular consular office where the visa was issued. In addition, we can learn the date and the purpose for which the visa was issued and the length of the visa's validity. It is stamped B1/B-2 visa, denoting a tourist visa, issued for the purpose of traveling temporarily to the United States. It was issued on April 8, 2003 in Seoul, South Korea and is a multi-entry visa, valid for ten years. This means the holder can travel back and forth between her home country and the United States using this visa to gain entry as a tourist theoretically for as many times as she likes in that ten-year period. If, instead of an M for "multiple entries," the figure 1 appeared under Entries, then the visa would only be valid for a single visit to the United States. However, the actual time the foreign national can remain in the country in this category will be determined by the CBP officer at the border, who will enter a stamp in the person's passport to indicate this period. A selection of nonimmigrant visa categories is shown in Table 1.1.

E.2. I-94 Arrival/Departure Record Card

Prior to April, 2013, foreign nationals entering the United States as nonimmigrants, immigrants, or refugees were given a small white or green card, called an I-94

E: Understanding Basic Immigration Documents and Forms

Figure 1.3
Nonimmigrant Visa Document
Source: U.S. Department of State.

Check that your ppt number is correct.

Check that your name is spelled correctly.

Where your visa was issued.

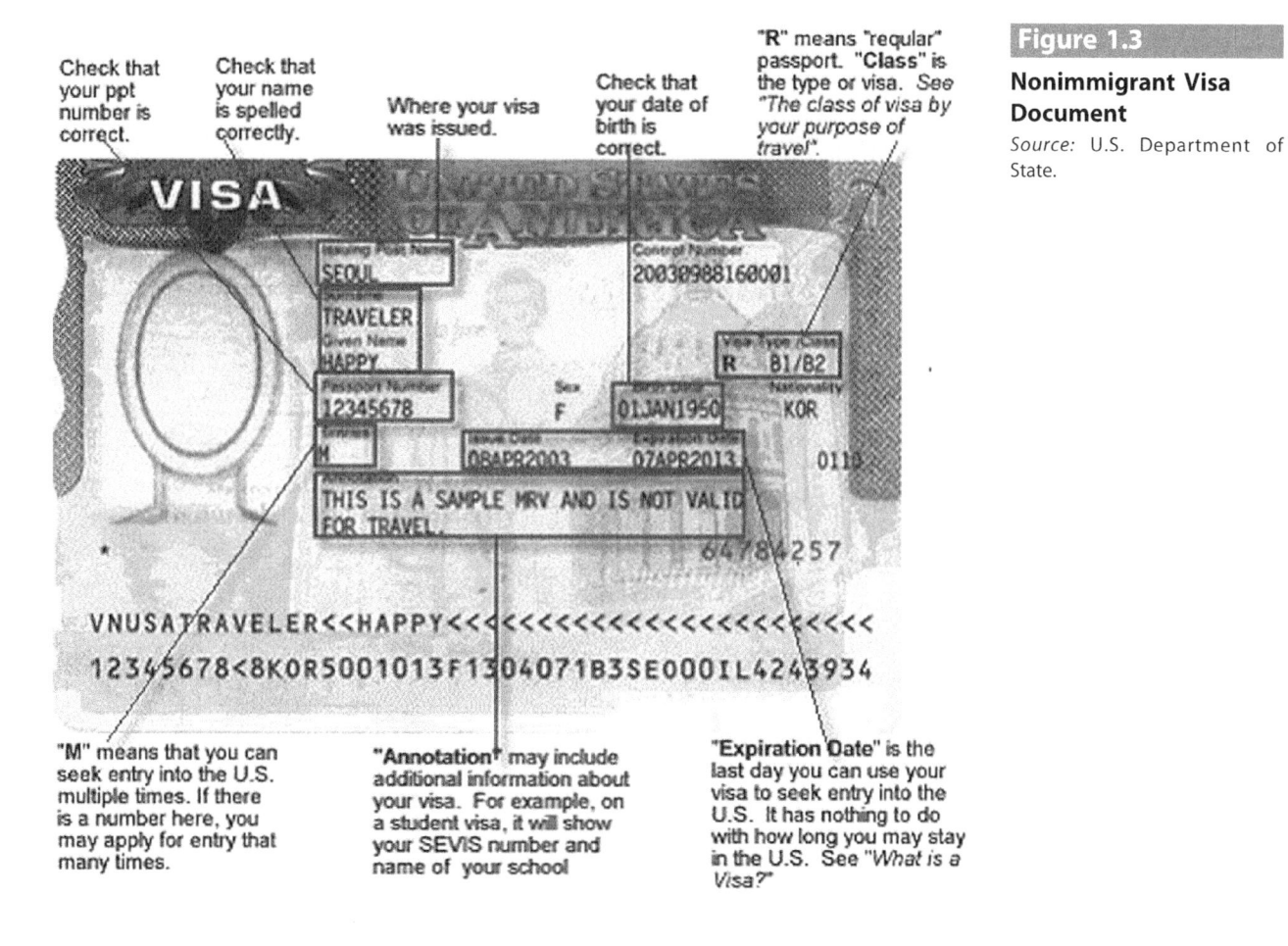

Check that your date of birth is correct.

"R" means "regular" passport. "**Class**" is the type or visa. See "The class of visa by your purpose of travel".

"M" means that you can seek entry into the U.S. multiple times. If there is a number here, you may apply for entry that many times.

"Annotation" may include additional information about your visa. For example, on a student visa, it will show your SEVIS number and name of your school

"Expiration Date" is the last day you can use your visa to seek entry into the U.S. It has nothing to do with how long you may stay in the U.S. See "What is a Visa?"

Table 1.1 Selection of Nonimmigrant Visa Categories

Purpose of Travel	Visa Category
Athlete, amateur or professional (competing for prize money only)	B-1
Au pair (exchange visitor)	J
Australian professional specialty	E-3
Border Crossing Card: Mexico	BCC
Business visitor	B-1
CNMI-only transitional worker	CW-1
Crewmember	D
Diplomat or foreign government official	A
Domestic employee or nanny — must be accompanying a foreign national employer	B-1

Table 1.1 (continued)

Purpose of Travel	Visa Category
Employee of a designated international organization or NATO	G1-G5, NATO
Exchange visitor	J
Foreign military personnel stationed in the United States	A-2?NATO1-6
Foreign national with extraordinary ability in Sciences, Arts, Education, Business, or Athletics	O
Free Trade Agreement (FTA) Professional: Chile, Singapore	H-1B1 — Chile H-1B1 — Singapore
International cultural exchange visitor	Q
Intra-company transferee	L
Medical treatment, visitor for	B-2
Media, journalist	I
NAFTA professional worker: Mexico, Canada	TN/TD
Performing athlete, artist, entertainer	P
Physician	J, H-1B
Professor, scholar, teacher (exchange visitor)	J
Religious worker	R
Specialty occupations in fields requiring highly specialized knowledge	H-1B
Student: academic, vocational	F, M
Temporary agricultural worker	H-2A
Temporary worker performing other services or labor of a temporary or seasonal nature	H-2B
Tourism, vacation, pleasure visitor	B-2
Training in a program not primarily for employment	H-3
Treaty trader/treaty investor	E
Transiting the United States	C
Victim of criminal activity	U
Victim of human trafficking	T
Nonimmigrant (V) Visa for Spouse and Children of a Lawful Permanent Resident (LPR)	V

Source: U.S. Department of State.

Arrival/Departure Record card, which would be stamped and stapled into their passports. The card was evidence of lawful admission into the United States, the expiration date of the individual's authorized stay (in some cases "D/S," or "duration of stay,"[45] was noted in lieu of a date), and the nonimmigrant classification under which entry was granted. It was not issued to immigrants returning to the United States. In order to streamline the admission process and reduce costs, however, CBP phased out the I-94 card. Now, all nonimmigrants arriving by air or sea no longer receive a card. Rather, the information is collected electronically and can be accessed online at a later time by the foreign national.[46] Those arriving by land and certain humanitarian immigrants such as refugees, still receive a paper I-94 Arrival/Departure Record card. Those that do not receive one will be given an admission stamp in his or her passport or ***travel document*** instead, annotated with the date of admission, the admission classification, and the date the period of stay expires. A sample of the electronic card is in Figure 1.4.

Even though the Form I-94 Arrival/Departure Record card is no longer being issued, it may be helpful to review what the old cards looked like because many foreign nationals still have them. A sample of the old I-94 document is shown in Figure 1.5.

Travel Document: A document used to facilitate the international travel of individuals that can include a passport or other government-issued identity document authorizing travel.

Figure 1.4

New I-94 Document
Source: USCIS.

---

[45] This allows a foreign national to remain in the United States for an undesignated period of time, so long as s/he maintains the purpose for which the visa and permission to enter was granted. It is discussed further in the student context in Section E.3.c of Chapter 2, Nonimmigrant Visas for Brief Stays, Studies, and Cultural Exchange.
[46] Access online is available at https://i94.cbp.dhs.gov/I94/request.html.

Figure 1.5

Old I-94 Arrival/Departure Record Document

Source: USCIS.

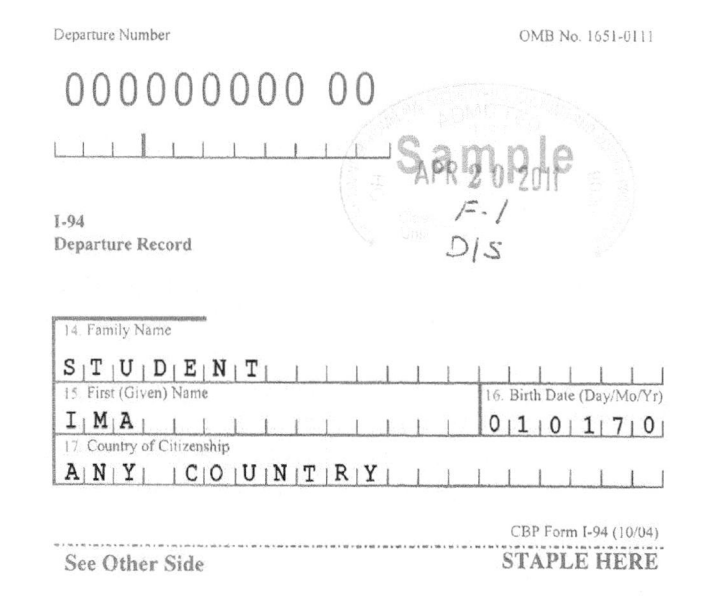

This I-94 Arrival/Departure Record was issued to a foreign national entering as a student, or in F-1 status. The stamp shows the date of entry and that s/he has been given permission to remain here so long as the student status is maintained, or D/S.

E.3. An Immigrant Visa

We previously discussed that visas can be for temporary or permanent purposes. The visa in Figure 1.3 is issued to someone who is coming to the United States for a temporary reason, such as to visit or study. The sample visa in Figure 1.6 is issued to someone coming to the United States to live here indefinitely.

This visa is issued at a U.S. consular post abroad and given to someone who will be entering the United States as an LPR. This status does not limit the length of time a foreign national can remain in the country, so long as the person does not commit certain crimes or live outside of the United States for more than six months with no intent to return and reside here.[47] The person with this visa may also have been given an I-551 stamp in his or her passport on entry, indicating that the foreign national has been approved for LPR status but is awaiting receipt of the document that confirms this status has been granted. That document is known as the I-551 or permanent resident card — known colloquially as a "green card" — and should arrive in the mail soon after entry into the United States. Immigration officers at the local office also used to place this stamp in a foreign national's passport following a successful adjustment interview, as evidence of the change in immigration status before s/he received the green card. A sample of the stamp placed in the passport is in Figure 1.7.

---

[47] Exceptions to this rule exist for those who live temporarily abroad for valid purposes, such as study or United States government related work, and can demonstrate they did not have an intent to abandon their residency in the United States.

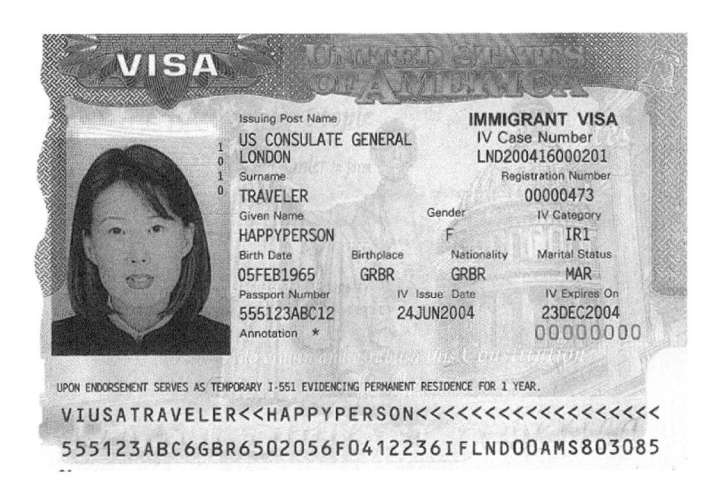

Figure 1.6

Immigrant Visa Document
Source: USCIS.

Figure 1.7

Temporary I-551 Stamp

With changes in USCIS processing procedures, it is less likely that a foreign national will receive this stamp, since it now only takes a few weeks for him or her to receive the Permanent Resident card. Table 1.2 shows a selection of immigrant visas that may be issued by a consular officer abroad.

E.4. A Resident Alien Card

This card was issued to those authorized to live and work in the United States permanently and contained little information about the foreign national. It originally had no security features, and has been modified more than 15 times since its initial production. Prior versions of the card are still in circulation today,

Table 1.2 Selection of Immigrant Visa Categories

Immediate Relative & Family Sponsored	Visa Category
Spouse of a U.S. Citizen	IR1, CR1
Spouse of a U.S. Citizen awaiting approval of an I-130 immigrant petition	K-3 *
Fiancé(e) to marry U.S. Citizen & live in U.S.	K-1 *
Intercountry Adoption of Orphan Children by U.S. Citizens	IR3, IH3, IR4, IH4
Certain Family Members of U.S. Citizens	IR2, CR2, IR5, F1, F3, F4
Certain Family Members of Lawful Permanent Residents	F2A, F2B
Employer Sponsored — Employment	
Employment-Based Immigrants, including (preference group): Priority workers [First] Professionals Holding Advanced Degrees and Persons of Exceptional Ability [Second] Professionals and Other Workers [Third] Employment Creation/Investors [Fifth] Certain Special Immigrants [Fourth]	E1 E2 E3, EW3 C5, T5, R5, I5 S (many**)
Religious Workers	SD, SR
Iraqi and Afghan Translators/Interpreters	SI
Iraqis Who Worked for/on Behalf of the U.S. Government	SQ
Afghans Who Worked for/on Behalf of the U.S. Government	SQ
Other Immigrants	
Diversity Immigrant Visa	DV
Returning Resident	SB

Source: U.S. Department of State.

although there has been a push by the USCIS to encourage its replacement for the newer, more secure machine-readable documents. A sample of an Alien Resident Card appears in Figure 1.8.

In December 1997, the first I-551 Permanent Resident card was issued. The card in Figure 1.9 shows the holder received her LPR status because she entered as the child of a refugee.[48] This is the I-551 card issued by the USCIS currently.[49]

---

[48] Refugees are discussed in Section H of Chapter 5, Asylum and Other Related Humanitarian Relief.
[49] A full list of the various cards and codes issued and used by the USCIS can be found at http://www.dhs.state.mn.us/main/idcplg?IdcService=GET_FILE&RevisionSelectionMethod=LatestReleased&Rendition=Primary&allowInterrupt=1&noSaveAs=1&dDocName=dhs16_159911.

Figure 1.8

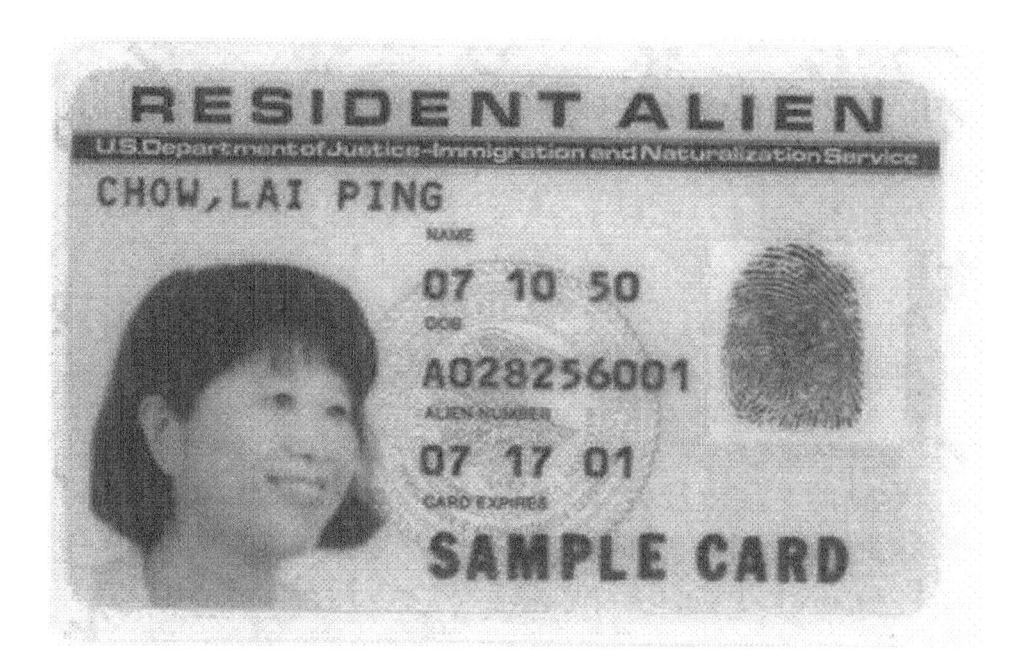

Previous Sample Permanent Resident Card
Source: USCIS.

E.5. Employment Authorization Card

This card is issued to any foreign national who applies for and is given permission to work in the United States. Not all nonimmigrant categories automatically grant permission to work incidental to the status. Therefore, those who do wish to work must apply for and receive permission first, and only if, the law allows it. In contrast, all immigrant and refugee categories do automatically have permission and so do not require an employment authorization card to be issued. Even so, some of these foreign nationals, such as asylees and refugees, choose to apply for the card because it may be their only form of government issued identity document. Additionally, nonimmigrants who arrive as temporary workers usually do not require an employment authorization document because their visa or I-94 Arrival/Departure Record card will clearly state that they are eligible to work in the United States, and, in any event, their employment is tied to a particular employer who filed a petition for them. A sample employment authorization card appears in Figure 1.10.

E.6. Other Immigration Forms and Correspondence

There are many additional documents and forms used in immigration applications. One of the main tasks of a practitioner is to determine the proper form, how it is to be completed, and where it is to be sent or filed. Most forms associated with the USCIS begin with the prefix "G," "I," or "N," while most forms or applications issued by the Department of State begin with the prefix "DS." Forms

Chapter 1: Historical Background and Introduction to the U.S. Immigration System

Figure 1.9

Current Permanent Resident or I-551 Card, Front and Back

Source: USCIS.

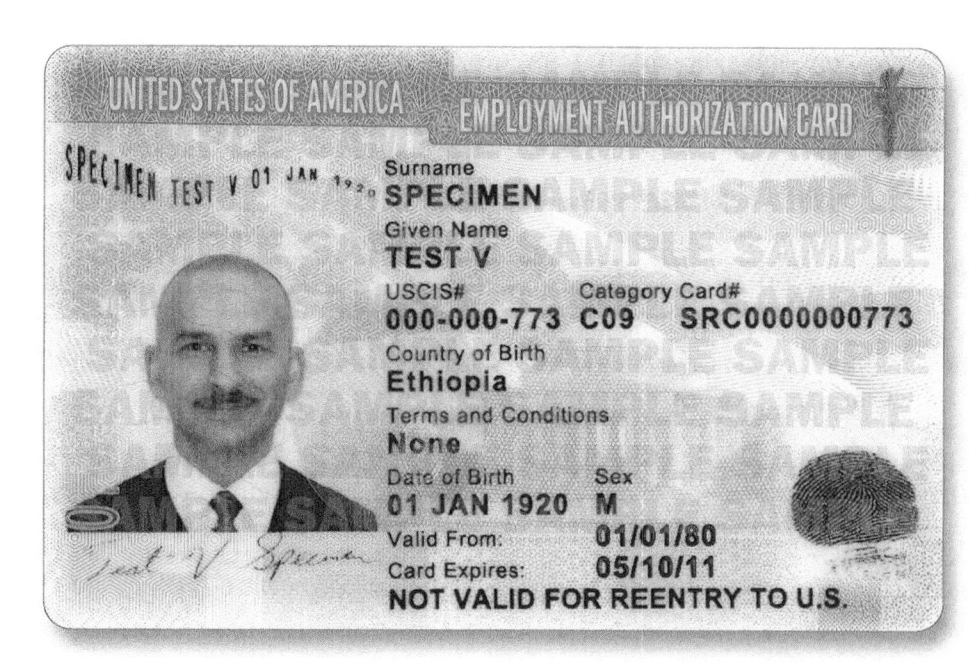

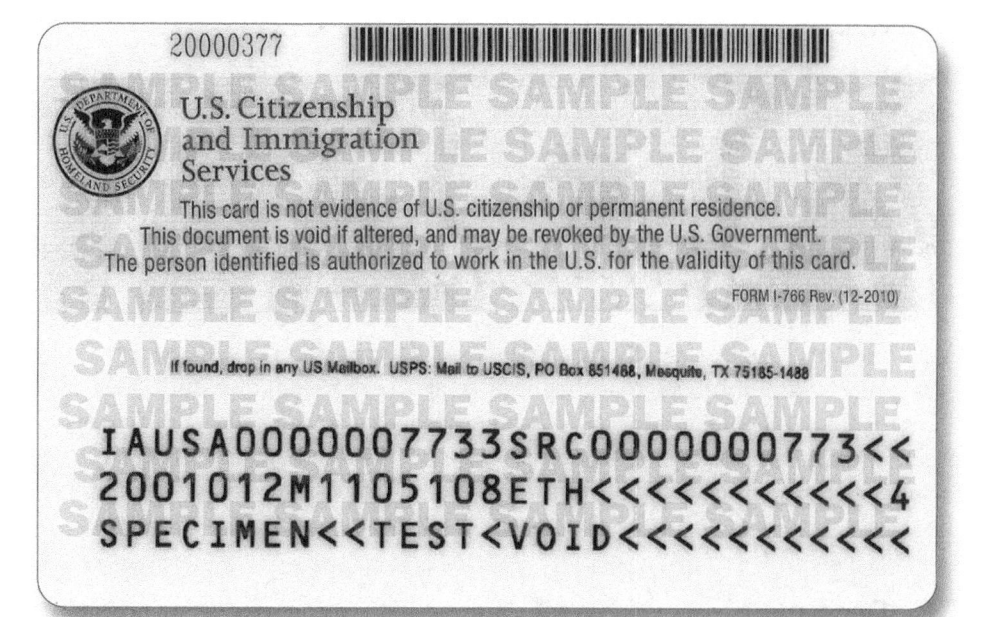

E: Understanding Basic Immigration Documents and Forms

Figure 1.10

Employment Authorization Card, Front and Back
Source: USCIS.

associated with immigration court and the BIA begin with "EOIR," while Forms associated with the DOL begin with "ETA." Immigration agencies are increasing the use of electronic submissions of forms in an effort to phase out paper versions. Practitioners must confirm with the relevant agency if it accepts only paper, electronic, or both types of forms.

> ● **EXAMPLE**
>
> Victor Rojas, from Panama, would like to visit his sister in the United States for three months to see her new baby. In order to do so he must apply for a visitor's visa. Victor's sister comes to your immigration office to ask how he can apply. Practitioner Philippe explains that since this is a temporary visa which must be applied for from abroad, the application must be made on a form created by the Department of State. The form, DS 160, Online Nonimmigrant Visa Application, must be completed online. Philippe shows Victor's sister the DOS website,[50] which contains instructions about applying for a tourist visa, links to the form, and information about the consulate in Panama City where Victor will be interviewed to see if he will be approved for a B-2 visitor's visa.

E.7. Representation Forms: G-28

Form G-28, Notice of Entry of Appearance as Attorney or Accredited Representative, is used by an attorney or authorized individual to enter an appearance on behalf of the foreign national before DHS agencies. A sample form appears in Figure 1.11. Where more than one application is being filed for an individual, the form must indicate each one where representation is provided. Individuals authorized to provide representation include attorneys, accredited staff members of charitable organizations recognized by the EOIR, and law students working under the supervision of an attorney.[51] Paralegals who are not **accredited representatives** cannot sign a Form G-28, but often prepare them for the attorney's signature. After receiving a Form G-28, DHS agencies are on notice that they must mail the representative duplicates of all items mailed to the foreign national. This may not always happen, however. The better practice would be for both the practitioner and the client to inform each other whenever correspondence is received in relation to the case to ensure nothing gets missed.

E.8. Receipts

Petition: An application filed with the USCIS that must first be approved before a foreign national can apply for a visa to enter the United States or seek particular immigration benefits.

Immigration procedures often involve filing an application or *petition* to a specific government agency.

---

[50] *See* http://panama.usembassy.gov/howtoapply.html.
[51] *See* Section A.3 of Chapter 10, Immigration Court Practice and Relief from Removal.

E: Understanding Basic Immigration Documents and Forms

Figure 1.11

Form G-28, Notice of Entry of Appearance as Attorney or Accredited Representative

---

Notice of Entry of Appearance as Attorney or Accredited Representative
Department of Homeland Security

DHS Form G-28
OMB No. 1615-0105
Expires 03/31/2018

Part 1. Information About Attorney or Accredited Representative

1. USCIS ELIS Account Number *(if any)*

Name and Address of Attorney or Accredited Representative

- 2.a. Family Name *(Last Name)*: Torney
- 2.b. Given Name *(First Name)*: Attentive
- 2.c. Middle Name:
- 3.a. Street Number and Name: 2100 Yellow Brick Road
- 3.b. Apt. ☐ Ste. ☐ Flr. ☒ 3rd
- 3.c. City or Town: Wichita
- 3.d. State: KS
- 3.e. ZIP Code: 45100
- 3.f. Province:
- 3.g. Postal Code:
- 3.h. Country: USA
- 4. Daytime Telephone Number: 2155555555
- 5. Fax Number: 2155555556
- 6. E-Mail Address *(if any)*: attorney@happylawfirm.com
- 7. Mobile Telephone Number *(if any)*:

Part 2. Notice of Appearance as Attorney or Accredited Representative

This appearance relates to immigration matters before *(Select only one box)*:

- 1.a. ☒ USCIS
- 1.b. List the form numbers: I-485 I-131 I-864 G-325A I-765
- 2.a. ☐ ICE
- 2.b. List the specific matter in which appearance is entered:
- 3.a. ☐ CBP
- 3.b. List the specific matter in which appearance is entered:

I enter my appearance as attorney or accredited representative at the request of:

4. Select **only one** box:
   ☒ Applicant ☐ Petitioner ☐ Requestor
   ☐ Respondent (ICE, CBP)

Information About Applicant, Petitioner, Requestor, or Respondent

- 5.a. Family Name *(Last Name)*: Doe
- 5.b. Given Name *(First Name)*: Dorothy
- 5.c. Middle Name:
- 6. Name of Company or Organization *(if applicable)*:

Form G-28 03/04/15 N

Figure 1.11 (Continued)

Part 2. Notice of Appearance as Attorney or Accredited Representative *(continued)*

Information About Applicant, Petitioner, Requestor, or Respondent (continued)

7. USCIS ELIS Account Number *(if any)*
   ▶ [   ]

8. Alien Registration Number (A-Number) or Receipt Number
   [203030303]

9. Daytime Telephone Number
   [   ]

10. Mobile Telephone Number *(if any)*
    [   ]

11. E-Mail Address *(if any)*
    [   ]

Mailing Address of Applicant, Petitioner, Requestor, or Respondent

NOTE: Provide the mailing address of the applicant, petitioner, requestor, or respondent. If the applicant, petitioner, requestor, or respondent has used a safe mailing address on the application, petition, or request being filed with this Form G-28, provide it in these spaces.

12.a. Street Number and Name: [2 Second Street]

12.b. Apt. ☐ Ste. ☐ Flr. ☐ [   ]

12.c. City or Town: [Wichita]

12.d. State: [KS] 12.e. ZIP Code: [67227]

12.f. Province: [   ]

12.g. Postal Code: [   ]

12.h. Country: [USA]

Part 3. Eligibility Information for Attorney or Accredited Representative

Select **all applicable** items.

1.a. ☒ I am an attorney eligible to practice law in, and a member in good standing of, the bar of the highest courts of the following states, possessions, territories, commonwealths, or the District of Columbia. *(If you need additional space, use Part 6.)*

   Licensing Authority
   [Court of Appeals New York]

1.b. Bar Number *(if applicable)*
   [   ]

1.c. Name of Law Firm
   [Happy Law Firm LLP]

1.d. I *(choose one)* ☒ **am not** ☐ **am** subject to any order of any court or administrative agency disbarring, suspending, enjoining, restraining, or otherwise restricting me in the practice of law. If you are subject to any orders, explain in the space below. *(If you need additional space, use Part 6.)*
   [   ]

2.a. ☐ I am an accredited representative of the following qualified nonprofit religious, charitable, social service, or similar organization established in the United States, so recognized by the Department of Justice, Board of Immigration Appeals, in accordance with 8 CFR 292.2. Provide the name of the organization and the expiration date of accreditation.

2.b. Name of Recognized Organization
   [   ]

2.c. Date accreditation expires
   (mm/dd/yyyy) ▶ [   ]

Form G-28 03/04/15 N

Part 3. Eligibility Information for Attorney or Accredited Representative (continued)

3. ☒ I am associated with

   [_____],

   the attorney or accredited representative of record who previously filed Form G-28 in this case, and my appearance as an attorney or accredited representative is at his or her request.

   NOTE: If you select this item, also complete **Item Numbers 1.a. - 1.b. or Item Numbers 2.a. - 2.c.** in **Part 3.** *(whichever is appropriate).*

4.a. ☐ I am a law student or law graduate working under the direct supervision of the attorney or accredited representative of record on this form in accordance with the requirements in 8 CFR 292.1(a)(2)(iv).

4.b. Name of Law Student or Law Graduate

Part 4. Applicant, Petitioner, Requestor, or Respondent Consent to Representation, Contact Information, and Signature

Consent to Representation and Release of Information

1. I have requested the representation of and consented to being represented by the attorney or accredited representative named in **Part 1.** of this form. According to the Privacy Act of 1974 and DHS policy, I also consent to the disclosure to the named attorney or accredited representative of any record pertaining to me that appears in any system of records of USCIS, ICE or CBP.

   When you (the applicant, petitioner, requestor, or respondent) are represented, DHS will send notices to both you and your attorney or accredited representative either through mail or electronic delivery.

   DHS will also send the Form I-94, Arrival Departure Record, to you **unless** you select **Item Number 2.a.** in **Part 4.** All secure identity documents and Travel Documents will be sent to you (the applicant, petitioner, requestor, or respondent) unless you ask us to send those documents to your attorney of record or accredited representative.

If you do not want to receive original notices or secure identity documents directly, but would rather have such notices and documents sent to your attorney of record or accredited representative, please select **all applicable** boxes below:

2.a ☒ I request DHS send any notice (including Form I-94) on an application, petition, or request to the business address of my attorney of record or accredited representative as listed in this form. I understand that I may change this election at any future date through written notice to DHS.

2.b. ☒ I request that DHS send any secure identity document, such as a Permanent Resident Card, Employment Authorization Document, or Travel Document, that I am approved to receive and authorized to possess, to the business address of my attorney of record or accredited representative as listed in this form. I consent to having my secure identity document sent to my attorney of record or accredited representative and understand that I may request, at any future date and through written notice to DHS, that DHS send any secure identity document to me directly.

3.a. Signature of Applicant, Petitioner, Requestor, or Respondent

3.b. Date of Signature *(mm/dd/yyyy)* ▶

Part 5. Signature of Attorney or Accredited Representative

I have read and understand the regulations and conditions contained in 8 CFR 103.2 and 292 governing appearances and representation before the Department of Homeland Security. I declare under penalty of perjury under the laws of the United States that the information I have provided on this form is true and correct.

1. Signature of Attorney or Accredited Representative

2. Signature of Law Student or Law Graduate

3. Date of Signature *(mm/dd/yyyy)* ▶

Figure 1.11 (Continued)

Figure 1.11 (Continued)

Part 6. Additional Information

Use the space below to provide additional information pertaining to **Part 3., Item Numbers 1.a. - 1.d.**

E: Understanding Basic Immigration Documents and Forms

Figure 1.12
Form I-797C, Notice of Action Receipt Notice

Department of Homeland Security
U.S. Citizenship and Immigration Services

Form I-797C, Notice of Action

THIS NOTICE DOES NOT GRANT ANY IMMIGRATION STATUS OR BENEFIT.

RECEIPT NUMBER		CASE TYPE	I485 APPLICATION TO REGISTER PERMANENT RESIDENCE OR ADJUST STATUS
EAC-15-			
RECEIVED DATE June 8, 2015	PRIORITY DATE	APPLICANT A	
NOTICE DATE June 10, 2015	PAGE 1 of 2		

3501 SANSOM STREET
PHILADELPHIA PA 19104

Notice Type: Receipt Notice
Amount received: $1,070.00 U.S.
Section: Other basis for adjustment

This notice is to advise you of action taken on this case. The official notice has been mailed according to the mailing preferences noted on the Form G-28, Notice of Entry of Appearance as Attorney or Accredited Representative. Any relevant documentation was mailed according to the specified mailing preferences.

Receipt Notice- This notice confirms that USCIS received your application or petition ("this case") as shown above. If any of the above information is incorrect, please immediately call 800-375-5283 to let us know. This will help avoid future problems.

This notice does not grant any immigration status or benefit, nor is it evidence that this case is still pending. It only shows that the application or petition was filed on the date shown.

Processing time - Processing times vary by case type. You can check our website at www.uscis.gov for our current "processing times" for this case type at the particular office to which this case is or becomes assigned. On our website's "case status online" page, you can also view status or sign up to receive free e-mail updates as we complete key processing steps on this case. During most of the time this case is pending, however, our systems will show only that the case has been received, and the processing status will not have changed, because we will be working on other cases that were filed earlier than this one. We will notify you by mail, and show in our systems, when we make a decision on this case or if we need something from you. If you do not receive an initial decision or update from us within our current processing time, check our website or call 800-375-5283. Please save this notice, and any other notice we send you about this case, and please make and keep a copy of any papers you send us by any means, along with any proof of delivery to us. Please have all these papers with you if you contact us about this case.

If this case is an I-130 Petition - Filing and approval of a Form I-130, Petition for Alien Relative, is only the first step in helping a relative immigrate to the United States. The beneficiaries of a petition must wait until a visa number is available before they can take the next step to apply for an immigrant visa or adjustment of status to lawful permanent residence. To best allocate resources, USCIS may wait to process I-130 forms until closer to the time when a visa number will become available, which may be years after the petition was filed. Nevertheless, USCIS processes I-130 forms in time not to delay relatives' ability to take the next step toward permanent residence once a visa number does become available. If, before final action on the petition, you decide to withdraw your petition, your family relationship with the beneficiary ends, or you become a U.S. citizen, call 800-375-5283.

Applications requiring biometrics- In some types of cases USCIS requires biometrics. In such cases, USCIS will send you a SEPARATE appointment notice with a specific date, time and place for you to go to a USCIS Application Support Center (ASC) for biometrics processing. You must WAIT for that separate appointment notice and take it (NOT this receipt notice) to your ASC appointment along with your photo identification. Acceptable kinds of photo identification are: a passport or national photo identification issued by your country, a drivers license, a military photo identification, or a state-issued photo identification card. If you receive more than one ASC appointment notice, even for different cases, take them both to the first appointment.

If your address changes- If your mailing address changes while your case is pending, call 800-375-5283 or use the "Online Change of Address" function on our website. Otherwise, you might not receive notice of our action on this case.

NOTICE: Pursuant to the terms of the United States Immigration & Nationality Act (INA), the information provided on and in support of applications and petitions is submitted under penalty of perjury. USCIS and the U.S. Department of Homeland Security reserve the right to verify this information before and/or after adjudication to ensure conformity with applicable laws, rules, regulations, and other authorities. Methods used for verifying information may include, but are not limited

---

Please see the additional information on the back. You will be notified separately about any other cases you filed.
U.S. CITIZENSHIP & IMMIGRATION SVCS
VERMONT SERVICE CENTER
75 LOWER WELDEN STREET
SAINT ALBANS   VT   05479-0001
Customer Service Telephone: (800) 375-5283

If this is an interview or biometrics appointment notice, please see the back of this notice for important information.   Form I-797C 07/11/14 Y

For example, Tran, the applicant for citizenship discussed in Case for Discussion 1.2 earlier, will mail the appropriate immigration form to the proper location with the requisite documentation and fee. Once the form is received, the USCIS will send Tran a **Form I-797C, Notice of Action receipt notice,** depicted in Figure 1.12, listing the date the application was received and the date that the notice was sent to the applicant. A copy of the notice will also be sent to the authorized representative.

E.9. Request for Evidence

When a key item is missing from an application, preventing its adjudication, the USCIS will issue a **Request for Evidence**, also known as an RFE, which will explain what items or facts are missing and a deadline for their submission. Failure to mail the requested information by this time will allow the USCIS to determine the case based on information before it, which may result in the denial of the application or petition for lack of sufficient evidence. The sample request for further evidence in Figure 1.13 requests additional documents needed to verify the identity of an applicant for immigration relief.

E.10. Notice of Action

Once an application or petition filed with the USCIS is approved, either the foreign national or a petitioner who made the request will be notified through receipt of Form I-797, Notice of Action. Depending on the type of application or petition, the notice will either simply acknowledge approval and constitute evidence that can be used in the next stage of an application process (either at a consular office abroad or with the USCIS in the United States), or evidence any new status granted. In some instances, the USCIS will also issue a new I-94 Arrival/Departure Record that is different from that issued at the border by CBP. It will state the immigration classification granted and its period of validity. Figure 1.14 is a sample of a Notice of Action Approval Notice. Figure 1.15 is a Notice of Action granting an immigration status with a new I-94 Arrival/Departure Record attached.

F. Determining Immigration Status

Assessing a foreign national's immigration status is a fundamental and frequent task requested of an immigration practitioner. Such an assessment should not be based only on what is represented by the client, but rather confirmed through any documentation that may be available. This is because a foreign national may not know his or her immigration status, especially if the person has lived in the United States for many years and no longer has documents or believes s/he may be a citizen simply because of the length of time spent here. One method that may be used in order to obtain documents that the foreign national no longer has

Figure 1.13
Request for Evidence

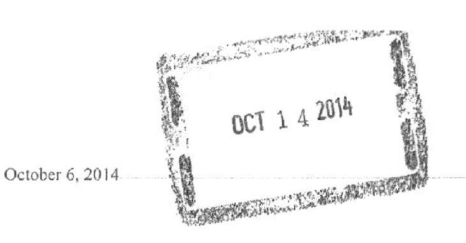

October 6, 2014

OCT 1 4 2014

U.S. Department of Homeland Security
U.S. Citizenship and Immigration Services
P.O. Box 82521
Lincoln, NE 68501-2521

U.S. Citizenship and Immigration Services

HIAS PENNSYLVANIA
2100 ARCH STREET
PHILADELPHIA, PA 19103
US

RE: M
I-821 D, Deferred Action for Childhood Arrivals

REQUEST FOR EVIDENCE

The documentation submitted is not sufficient to warrant favorable consideration of your request.

See Letter for Details
Your response must be received in this office by December 29, 2014

Your case is being held in this office pending your response. Within this period you may:

1. Submit all of the evidence requested;
2. Submit some or none of the evidence requested and ask for a decision based upon the record; or
3. Withdraw the request. (Please note that if the request is withdrawn, the filing fee cannot be refunded.)

You must submit all of the evidence at one time. Submission of only part of the evidence requested will be considered a request for a decision based on the record. No extension of the period allowed to submit evidence will be granted. If the evidence submitted does not establish that your case was approvable at the time it was filed, it can be denied. If you do not respond to this request within the time allowed, your case will be considered abandoned and denied. Evidence received in this office after the due date may not be considered.

If you submit a document in any language other than English, it must be accompanied by a full **complete** English translation. The translator must certify the translation is accurate and he or she is competent to translate. Note: You must submit the requested foreign language document along with the translation.

For deferred action for childhood arrivals, **affidavits or sworn statements generally are not satisfactory evidence.** Affidavits will only be considered as evidence in two situations: 1. When there is a shortcoming in documentation to explain brief, casual, and innocent departures during the period of continuous residence in the United States; and 2. To explain a minor gap in documentation showing you meet the continuous residence requirement. If you submit affidavits for these two reasons, you should provide two or more affidavits, sworn to or affirmed by people other than yourself who have direct, personal knowledge of the information.

Figure 1.13 (Continued)

IDENTITY

The evidence you submitted with your Form I-821D, Consideration of Deferred Action for Childhood Arrivals, to prove your identity is insufficient. You submitted your birth certificate to prove your identity; however, it was not accompanied by photo identification. You may still submit evidence, which may include, but is not limited to, copies of:

- Passport;
- Birth certificate accompanied by photo identification;
- Any national identity documents from your country of origin bearing your photo and/or fingerprint;
- Any U.S.-government immigration or other document bearing your name and photograph (e.g., Employment Authorization Documents (EADs), expired visas, driver's licenses, non-driver cards, etc.);
- Any school-issued form of identification with photo;
- Military identification document with photo;
- State issued photo ID showing date of birth; or
- Any other document that you believe is relevant.

Expired documents are acceptable.

PLACE THIS ENTIRE LETTER ON TOP OF YOUR RESPONSE. SUBMISSION OF EVIDENCE WITHOUT THIS LETTER WILL DELAY PROCESSING OF YOUR CASE AND MAY RESULT IN A DENIAL. PLEASE USE THE ENCLOSED ENVELOPE TO MAIL THE ADDITIONAL EVIDENCE REQUESTED BACK TO THIS OFFICE.

Sincerely,

Mark J. Hazuda
Director
Officer: 0042

Figure 1.14

Sample Form I-797, Notice of Action Approval

```
Department of Homeland Security         JAN 2 5 2016                    I-797, Notice of Action
U.S. Citizenship and Immigration Services

                       THE UNITED STATES OF AMERICA

RECEIPT NUMBER                        CASE TYPE  I130 PETITION FOR ALIEN RELATIVE
EAC-

RECEIPT DATE        PRIORITY DATE     PETITIONER  AO
September 23, 2014  September 22, 2014

NOTICE DATE         PAGE              BENEFICIARY A200
January 15, 2016    1 of 1

                                      Notice Type: Approval Notice
    HIAS PENNSYLVANIA                 Section: Husband or wife of U.S. Citizen,
    2100 ARCH STREET                  201(b) INA
    PHILADELPHIA PA 19103
```

This notice is to advise you of action taken on this case. The official notice has been mailed according to the mailing preferences noted on the Form G-28, Notice of Entry of Appearance as Attorney or Accredited Representative. Any relevant documentation was mailed according to the specified mailing preferences.

The above petition has been approved. The petition indicates that the person for whom you are petitioning is in the United States and will apply for adjustment of status. He or she should contact the local USCIS office to obtain Form I-485, Application for Permanent Residence. A copy of this notice should be submitted with the application.

If the person for whom you are petitioning decides to apply for a visa outside the United States based on this petition, the petitioner should file Form I-824, Application for Action on an Approved Application or Petition, to request that we send the petition to the Department of State National Visa Center (NVC).

The NVC processes all approved immigrant visa petitions that require consular action. The NVC also determines which consular post is the appropriate consulate to complete visa processing. It will then forward the approved petition to that consulate.

The approval of this visa petition does not in itself grant any immigration status and does not guarantee that the alien beneficiary will subsequently be found to be eligible for a visa, for admission to the United States, or for an extension, change, or adjustment of status.

This courtesy copy may not be used in lieu of official notification to demonstrate the filing or processing action taken on this case.

THIS FORM IS NOT A VISA AND MAY NOT BE USED IN PLACE OF A VISA.

NOTICE: Although this application/petition has been approved, USCIS and the U.S. Department of Homeland Security reserve the right to verify the information submitted in this application, petition and/or supporting documentation to ensure conformity with applicable laws, rules, regulations, and other authorities. Methods used for verifying information may include, but are not limited to, the review of public information and records, contact by correspondence, the internet, or telephone, and site inspections of businesses and residences. Information obtained during the course of verification will be used to determine whether revocation, rescission, and/or removal proceedings are appropriate. Applicants, petitioners, and representatives of record will be provided an opportunity to address derogatory information before any formal proceeding is initiated.

Please see the additional information on the back. You will be notified separately about any other cases you filed.
USCIS
VERMONT SERVICE CENTER
75 LOWER WELDEN STREET
SAINT ALBANS   VT   05479-0001
Customer Service Telephone: (800) 375-5283

Form I-797 (Rev. 01/31/05) N

Chapter 1: Historical Background and Introduction to the U.S. Immigration System

Figure 1.15

Sample Form I-797A, Notice of Action Approval, Status Grant

Department of Homeland Security
U.S. Citizenship and Immigration Services

I-797A, Notice of Action

THE UNITED STATES OF AMERICA

RECEIPT NUMBER: EAC*220250184 OCT 0 7 2014	CASE TYPE: I-918 Petition for U Nonimmigrant Status
RECEIPT DATE: July 17, 2012	PRIORITY DATE	Principal Applicant:
NOTICE DATE: October 02, 2014	PAGE: 1 of 1	Principal A#: A0█

HIAS PENNSYLVANIA
2100 ARCH STREET 3RD FLOOR
PHILADELPHIA PA 19103

Notice Type: Approval
Class: U1
Valid From: October 01, 2014   To: September 30, 2018

Your Petition for U Nonimmigrant Status has been approved. Attached below please find a completed Form I-94, Arrival-Departure Record, indicating that you have been granted U nonimmigrant status for a period of 4 years.

EMPLOYMENT AUTHORIZATION:

You are authorized to work in the United States for the validity period of your U nonimmigrant status. Your Employment Authorization Document will be mailed to you separately.

ADJUSTMENT OF STATUS:

Federal law provides that you may be eligible to adjust your status to that of a lawful permanent resident. A U-1 nonimmigrant may submit an application for adjustment of status after he/she has been physically present in the United States for a continuous period of at least 3 years after the date he/she was admitted as a U-1 nonimmigrant.

DERIVATIVE U NONIMMIGRANT CLASSIFICATION:

You may request derivative U nonimmigrant status for qualifying family members. To request derivative status, you must submit a Form I-918 with Supplement A in accordance with the instructions printed on the form. If you included qualifying family members on your original application, a notice of decision on the derivative petition(s) will be mailed to you separately.

DEPARTING FROM THE UNITED STATES:

Aliens with U nonimmigrant status may travel outside the United States. However, in order to return to the United States, you must obtain a U nonimmigrant visa for re-entry to the United States unless you are visa exempt or obtain a waiver. Also, if you accrued "unlawful presence" prior to obtaining U nonimmigrant status, you may be unable to re-enter the United States and may need to obtain a waiver of inadmissibility prior to or upon your return to the United States.

Contact the Vermont Service Center if you would like to be provided a list of nongovernmental organizations that may be of assistance to you.

Please see attached additional information on the back. You will be notified separately about other cases you filed.

U. S. Citizenship and Immigration Services
Vermont Service Center
75 Lower Welden Street
St. Albans, VT 05479
VAWA Customer Service Hotline: 1-802-527-4888

For Official Use Only

PLEASE TEAR OFF FORM I-94 PRINTED BELOW AND STAPLE TO ORIGINAL I-94 IF AVAILABLE

Detach This Half for Personal Records	Receipt Number: EAC
Receipt # EAC	U. S. Citizenship and Immigration Services
I-94 #	I-94 Departure Record
NAME	
CLASS U1	14. Family Name
VALID FROM 10/01/2014 UNTIL 09/30/2018	
	15. First (Given) Name	16. Date of Birth 03/04/197█
	17. Country of Citizenship NIGERIA

in his or her possession is to request a copy of the person's immigration file from the USCIS using a Freedom of Information Act request, known as a FOIA. This is done on a form issued by the USCIS called a Form G-639, Freedom of Information Act/Privacy Act Request, accompanied by a completed Form G-28, Notice of Entry of Appearance as Attorney or Accredited Representative, which will inform the government where the documents should be sent once retrieved.

> **Case for Discussion 1.3**
>
> Practitioner Lori has been asked to do an initial interview of the Coulter family to determine the immigration status of each of them. Sam Coulter, born in Trinidad, states he is a lawful permanent resident and has a Resident Alien card. Two years ago Sam met Anne, who arrived in the United States from Trinidad as a visitor on a B-2 single entry visa to compete in an athletic event. Anne's I-94 Arrival/Departure Record card shows she had permission to remain in the United States for six months but she met Sam, fell in love, and never left. They recently married and now have one daughter, Sheri, born in the United States.
>
> - What documents would you use to determine or confirm each family member's immigration status?

G. Conclusion

Now that we have discussed the development of immigration law and policy, identified important resources, and reviewed some key concepts, documents, and procedures, we are ready for a more detailed examination of the various types of nonimmigrant visas issued to foreign nationals under immigration law.

Nonimmigrant Visas for Brief Stays, Studies, and Cultural Exchange

Key Terms and Acronyms

8 C.F.R.
Change of Status
Consular Processing
ESTA
Foreign Affairs Manual
Form DS-160
Form DS-2019
Form I-20
Form I-539
Nonimmigrant Intent
Nunc pro tunc
SEVIS
STEM
Visa Exempt
Visa Waiver Program

Chapter Objectives

- Understand the difference between nonimmigrant and immigrant visas
- Review the differences between consular processing and changing status
- Explain the procedure for filing Form DS-160 and Form I-539
- Analyze and understand the criteria for nonimmigrant visas that do not automatically grant employment authorization
- Analyze the benefits and drawbacks of the nonimmigrant visas discussed in this chapter

Chapter 2: Nonimmigrant Visas for Brief Stays, Studies, and Cultural Exchange

According to the Department of State, or DOS, between 2010 and 2013, over 32 million foreign nationals entered the United States on temporary visas, which permitted them to remain here for varying periods depending on the purpose of their stay. These temporary visas are known as nonimmigrant visas. Considering that many entrants stay more than a year, at any one time there may be more than 20 million foreign nationals in the United States in a temporary capacity.[1]

There are volumes of laws and regulations that provide detailed guidance on the many ways in which a foreign national can enter the United States on a temporary basis. A list of temporary visas and their purposes is contained in the definitions section of the Immigration and Nationality Act at INA § 101(a)(15). The letters of the subsections correspond to those that denote a specific visa category. For example, INA § 101(a)(15)(F) describes the F visa used for students, and INA § 101(a)(15)(B) describes the B visa used for business or pleasure. Visas are also designated by letter and number, such as: H-1B; J-1; TN; and R.

While at first glance it may seem that these categorizations are similar to an alphabet soup of legal jargon, once there is an understanding as to the purpose for each visa, the lettering system becomes second nature. To mirror this concept, this chapter and the two that follow, which cover the most common nonimmigrant visa classifications, do not follow alphabetical order. Instead, Chapters 2, 3, and 4 proceed by examining the underlying purpose behind each nonimmigrant visa class designation. This chapter reviews and analyzes visas for business and pleasure visitors, called B-1 and B-2 visas respectively; academic and vocational students, called F-1 and M visas respectively; and cultural exchange visitors and trainees, called J-1, Q, and H-3 visas respectively. Chapter 3, Intracompany Transferees, Trade, and Investment and Professional Employment, covers employment-based nonimmigrant visas including visas for treaty investors, intracompany managers, and professionals. Chapter 4, Nonimmigrant Visas for Extraordinary Ability, Religious Workers, and Ancillary Activities, covers the remaining nonimmigrant visa classifications that range from temporary seasonal workers to extraordinary ability athletes and entertainers.

These three chapters provide a basic understanding of the overarching system for legal immigration and guidance regarding the use of visas that allow for temporary admission to the United States. By analyzing the substantive issues regarding the law and regulations related to nonimmigrant visas, they provide a framework for understanding the factors necessary to create a successful nonimmigrant visa filing. This chapter continues with a comparison of consular processing or obtaining a visa abroad in contrast to changing from one nonimmigrant classification to another or extending a current stay without leaving the United States. It then analyzes the specific nonimmigrant visa classifications that, in most instances, provide for visiting the United States, allowing cultural exchanges and study, but do not inherently carry the ability to work in the

---

[1] *See* http://travel.state.gov/content/dam/visas/Statistics/AnnualReports/FY2013AnnualReport/FY13Annual Report-TableIA.pdf.

country. The H-1B visa,[2] which is the most common temporary visa for professional specialty workers, is described in detail in Chapter 3, but as it is one of the most widely accessible nonimmigrant visas, it is often referenced here.

While reading these three chapters, consider each nonimmigrant visa category as a specific tool to solve a problem where, to achieve a particular objective, sometimes more than one visa is necessary.

A. Differences Between Nonimmigrant and Immigrant Visas

A nonimmigrant visa is simply permission that allows a foreign national to present himself or herself at a border for entry to the United States and, if given permission, remain for a temporary period, depending on the reason the visa was granted.

A foreign national who does not intend to remain permanently in the United States possesses what is known as ***nonimmigrant intent***. In most visa applications, the intent of the foreign national becomes a critical component of the application process, as many of these temporary visas require an applicant to demonstrate 100 percent nonimmigrant intent.

Nonimmigrant Intent: Proven intent to return to the country of origin following expiration of the period of stay.

If a foreign national obtains permission to remain permanently in the United States, then s/he receives lawful permanent resident, or LPR, status, referred to as having a green card. In order to obtain LPR status, in most instances, either a person or a company has to sponsor the foreign national by filing an immigrant visa petition for his or her benefit. When seeking LPR status, the foreign national must possess immigrant intent or intend to remain permanently in the United States. Chapter 6, Family Sponsored Immigration and Permanent Resident Status, discusses the immigrant visa process through family sponsorship and Chapter 7, Employment-Based and Self-Sponsored Immigration, discusses the immigrant visa process through employment sponsorship.

Once a foreign national receives LPR status, s/he can work for most employers, open a business, or attend any schools of higher education without restriction. In contrast, the activity that the foreign national will engage in while in the United States in nonimmigrant classification is of the utmost importance. Each nonimmigrant visa classification has a specific purpose, often a specific duration, and a variety of U.S. government agencies that are responsible for administering the benefit.

---

[2] The H-1B visa provides employment authorization for foreign nationals who possess a baccalaureate level education or higher in a specific field and are providing services to an employer in a position that requires that type of education. It is subject to numerical limitations on an annual basis and the demand for those numbers often outstrips supply. For example, in the USCIS fiscal year 2016, 233,000 H-1B petitions were filed for the available 85,000 H-1B visa numbers during the first week the category became available. For more information on the H-1B visa classification, refer to Section C of Chapter 3, Nonimmigrant Visas for Intracompany Transferees, Trade and Investment, and Professional Employment.

It is also worth noting that there is currently no equal protection or other constitutional safeguards afforded to nonimmigrants seeking temporary status in the United States from abroad. This aspect of immigration law means that if there is a problem with a nonimmigrant visa application and it is denied, or if a foreign national feels a consular officer treated him or her unfairly during a nonimmigrant visa application process, there is little that can be done to challenge the decision.[3] However, once inside the United States, foreign workers are entitled to due process of the law with protection from discriminatory and unfair labor practices by a number of state and federal laws, including, but not limited to, Title VII of the Civil Rights Act of 1964.

Table 2.1 serves as a good checklist when deciding which visa is best for a given fact pattern. It lists all of the nonimmigrant visa classifications, and provides the corresponding chapters in the book where they are discussed, giving their associated purpose:

Table 2.1 Chart of Nonimmigrant Visas

Visas for Temporary Visits (Chapter 2)	
B	Temporary stays for business and pleasure visits
C	Transit
D	Crewmen
Visas for Students (Chapter 2)	
F	Students in academic institutions and language training programs
M	Students in vocational and other nonacademic institutions
Visas for Cultural Exchange (Chapter 2)	
J	Exchange programs
Q	Cultural exchange programs
Visas for Trainees (Chapter 2)	
H-3	Trainees
Visas for Intracompany Transferees (Chapter 3)	
L	Executive, managerial, and specialized knowledge employees of international companies

---

[3] *See Kerry v. Din*, 576 U.S. __, 135 S. Ct. 2128 U.S. (2015).

A: Differences Between Nonimmigrant and Immigrant Visas

Visas for Professionals (Chapter 3)	
H-1B	Professional specialty workers
H-1B1	Professional specialty workers from Singapore and Chile
TN	NAFTA treaty workers (available for citizens of Canada and Mexico only)
E-3	Professional specialty workers based on international treaty (available for citizens of Australia only)
Visas for Seasonal and Short-Term Need Workers (Chapter 4)	
H-2A	Temporary agricultural workers
H-2B	Temporary non-agricultural workers
Visas for Artists, Entertainers, Athletes, and Those at the Top of Their Field (Chapter 4)	
O	Aliens of extraordinary ability
P	Artists, athletes, and entertainers
Visas for Diplomats and Representatives to International Organizations (Chapter 4)	
A	Foreign government officials
G	Representatives to international organizations
Visas for Representatives of Information Media (Chapter 4)	
I	Representatives of information media
Visas for Religious Workers (Chapter 4)	
R	Religious workers

It is important to remember that while each visa classification has a specific designation and objective, there might be more than one visa category that will work for a given purpose to enter the United States temporarily. Sometimes the choice of nonimmigrant visa is obvious. However, when faced with a situation where the foreign national could engage in multiple activities while in the United States, understanding what alternative visas classification might apply may be helpful.

● EXAMPLE

Nick is a dual national from Canada and Australia. He is hired by a university in the United States to serve as a Professor of Engineering. Nick has a Ph.D. in electrical engineering. Therefore, referring to the categories in Table 2.1, he might qualify for the TN or NAFTA classification because he has Canadian nationality, the E-3 classification because he has Australian nationality, and the H-1B classification because his job is a professional specialty occupation.

Nonimmigrant visas are especially useful for employment purposes. Often, multinational companies need to transfer foreign nationals from one entity to another to share knowledge, provide managerial services, or perform specialized work. In addition, many of the nonimmigrant visas granted are advantageous to U.S. businesses as they allow these companies to fill vacancies where there may not be available U.S. professionals with equivalent backgrounds. This fact is particularly true for occupations in science, technology engineering, and mathematics, or **STEM**, fields where there is a perceived shortage of available workers. In response to this demand for foreign talent, there are varieties of nonimmigrant visa classifications that provide temporary entry to fulfill these specific purposes.

At the same time, the U.S. government maintains an interest in protecting U.S. workers and their working conditions. It does this through agencies such as the U.S. Immigration and Customs Enforcement, or ICE; sub-agencies, such as the Fraud Detection and National Security Directorate, or FDNS, of the United States Citizenship and Immigration Service, or USCIS; and the Wage and Hour Division of the Department of Labor, or DOL. Through worksite visits that ensure employers are hiring individuals legally allowed to work here and ***U.S. worker*** wages are not undercut by foreign national employment, these agencies help curtail visa abuse and fraud.

Therefore, there is a balance built into the framework for nonimmigrant visas that encourages temporary immigration that benefits the economy, while discouraging immigration that harms U.S. workers. This desire for balance is found within all nonimmigrant visa classifications, whether those that automatically grant employment authorization or those that do not.

U.S. Worker:
A U.S. citizen, lawful permanent resident, asylee, refugee, or any other person granted permission to work by the USCIS.

Consular Processing:
Applying for an immigrant or nonimmigrant visa from abroad.

Visa Waiver Program:
Allows citizens of designated countries to travel to the United States without a visa for stays of ninety days or less, when they meet certain eligibility requirements.

B. The Visa Application Process

Most foreign nationals from around the world must have permission to enter the United States in the form of a visa from a U.S. embassy or consular office abroad. This can be for either a temporary or nonimmigrant purpose or to remain here permanently. The DOS controls Embassies and Consulate General offices abroad. Each has a consular section where consular officers decide whether a particular visa application should be approved through a process called ***consular processing***.

In most instances, in order to enter the United States for a particular purpose, the foreign national must obtain a visa. However, for some seeking to enter as *bona fide* visitors, this requirement is waived because they may enter on the ***Visa Waiver Program***, or VWP.[4] In addition, Canadians and

---

[4]INA § 217.

Bermudians are *visa exempt*, which means, except for a few very specific nonimmigrant visa classifications, nationals from visa exempt countries do not need a visa at all to enter the United States as nonimmigrants.[5] Regardless of whether a need for a visa is waived or the foreign national is exempt from obtaining a visa, everyone seeking admission to the United States is required to have a valid passport.

A visa[6] to enter the United States is a colorful stamp placed in the foreign national's passport that provides the following important information:

- Biographical information
- Visa type
- Duration of visa validity

The best way to remember how a visa functions is to think of it like a window of time in which a foreign national may present him or herself for entry to the United States. It does not dictate whether s/he will ultimately be allowed in or for how long a foreign national can remain in the country, as a Customs and Border Protection, or CBP, officer determines this when the foreign national actually arrives at a designated U.S. port of entry. Therefore, even though a consular officer has examined the foreign national before issuance of the visa, there is no guarantee of entry as a different agency makes this decision.

Visa Exempt: The ability to enter the United States without the need for a foreign national to obtain a visa stamp.

Case for Discussion 2.1

Alberto is a foreign national from Brazil. He obtains a B-2 visa to come to the United States as a visitor for pleasure in 2012. However, since the time his visa was issued, Alberto started doing some work for a distributor located in Miami, Florida. Alberto has business cards listing his job as an importer and it carries the Miami company's contact information. When showing his B-2 visa to the CBP officer at the Miami airport on a recent trip, one of Alberto's business cards falls out of his wallet and the CBP officer picks it up and examines it, noticing the address in the United States.

- What types of questions do you think the CBP officer will ask?
- Do you think Alberto will be admitted to the United States as a B-2 visitor?

Different visa classifications allow for different periods of admission that have no relationship to the duration provided on the visa stamp. For example, a visitor visa may be valid for a ten-year period. However, a foreign national

---

[5] 8 C.F.R. § 212.1(a).
[6] A sample nonimmigrant visa is available at Fig. 1.3, in Section E.1 of Chapter 1, Historical Background and Introduction to the U.S. Immigration System.

entering the United States in that category can remain for a maximum period of six months on any one entry unless an extension application is timely filed.[7]

Prior to April 2013, when a foreign national entered the United States for a temporary purpose, s/he would be given an ink stamp in the passport denoting the place, date, and nonimmigrant classification of entry. In addition, there would also be a small white card issued, called an I-94 Arrival/Departure Records card, that would be stapled into the foreign national's passport. The card was evidence of the foreign national's lawful admission into the United States, how long s/he could remain, and under which nonimmigrant classification. A sample of the old I-94 card is available in Figure 1.5 of Chapter 1, Historical Background and Introduction to the United States Immigration System.

However, in order to streamline the admission process and save on costs, CBP phased out the I-94 Arrival/Departure Records card, with the information now entered digitally by a CBP officer and maintained on a website. Now all that is provided to the foreign national at the time of admission is the ink stamp confirming the immigration classification granted and the permitted length of stay.[8] In addition to being able to retrieve I-94 card information electronically, it is also possible to obtain the foreign nationals recent travel history. This information is beneficial when applying for immigration benefits.

B.1. Nonimmigrant Waivers

Many nonimmigrant visa applicants require approval of an underlying petition or application first by the USCIS at one of its benefits processing centers in the United States before making an application at the consular section abroad for the corresponding nonimmigrant or immigrant visa. However, an approval of an application or petition does not guarantee the issuance of a visa. For example, a foreign national can have an approved benefit petition but still be deemed inadmissible to the United States because of a previous immigration violation or criminal conviction.[9] Therefore, it is important to obtain a full history from the foreign national before starting any immigration benefit process. Most law firms conduct this analysis by having the foreign national complete an intake questionnaire that covers all grounds of inadmissibility.

● EXAMPLE

Frances is an Austrian national who just received an approval notice for a petition her employer filed. When applying for the visa stamp in her passport at the U.S. Embassy in Vienna, Frances disclosed that she has a conviction for aggravated assault that occurred 15 years ago. Frances' visa application was denied because the seriousness of her offense renders her inadmissible to the United States.

---

[7] 8 C.F.R. § 214.2(b)(2).
[8] A foreign national can retrieve his or her I-94 Arrival/Departure Record entry records by visiting https://i94.cbp.dhs.gov/I94/request.html.
[9] A more detailed discussion of inadmissibility issues is in Chapter 9, Grounds of Inadmissibility and Deportation.

For those seeking nonimmigrant visas who are inadmissible, it is possible to obtain a ***nonimmigrant waiver*** under INA § 212(d)(3).[10] While not applicable to all grounds of inadmissibility, it is particularly useful for foreign nationals with minor criminal convictions and those who have previously violated immigration laws. Unlike an immigrant visa waiver, which requires the foreign national to have a qualifying family relationship to a lawful permanent resident or citizen of the United States based on humanitarian or hardship grounds,[11] the nonimmigrant waiver can be issued for almost any purpose tied to a nonimmigrant visa classification. When deciding whether to grant a waiver, the embassy or consulate will consider:

Nonimmigrant Waiver: A waiver that allows a foreign national to overcome a ground of inadmissibility for temporary stays in the United States.

- The risk of harm in admitting the foreign national,
- The serious nature of the acts that caused the inadmissibility issue, and
- The importance of the foreign national's reason for seeking entry to the United States.[12]

If the consular officer recommends granting the waiver, the application will be forwarded to the Admissibility Review Office, based in Washington D.C., for a final decision. A similar process exists for visa exempt Canadians who have not processed an application at an embassy or consular office and instead choose to obtain a waiver through a U.S. port of entry. If a foreign national is unable to obtain an immigrant visa due to a ground of inadmissibility, it is worth exploring whether a temporary entry to the United States can be obtained through a nonimmigrant waiver under INA § 212(d)(3).

● **EXAMPLE**

Roger, a British National, has a conviction for possessing more than 30 grams of marijuana over 25 years ago. He paid a large fine and performed 200 hours of community service. Since that time, Roger graduated from university with a Ph.D. in Economics and is now a college professor. He receives an invitation to give a lecture in the United States but is inadmissible because of this conviction. He may, however, be a strong candidate for a nonimmigrant waiver under INA § 212(d)(3).

C. Obtaining a Nonimmigrant Visa Stamp

While the visa process does vary slightly for each consular section, the Department of State in recent years has moved to systemize the process across the entire world. However, a recommended first-step in assisting any foreign national applying for a nonimmigrant visa is to check the specific requirements and procedures in the

---

[10] *See* Section B.11 of Chapter 9, Grounds of Inadmissibility and Deportation for further discussion.
[11] *See* Sections B.2.b and B.6.c of Chapter 9, Grounds of Inadmissibility and Deportability.
[12] *See Matter of Hranka*, 16 I&N Dec. 491 (BIA 1978). *See also* 22 C.F.R. § 40.301.

country where the individual will be submitting the visa application. This can be done by visiting the website for the U.S. embassy or Consulate General office where the application will be made. Each consular section maintains its own website that details the application process as well as any specific requirements for a given visa that might not be standard in all jurisdictions. In most instances, nonimmigrant visa applicants who are between the ages of 14 and 79 must appear in person for a visa interview through a pre-arranged appointment. However, for second or subsequent visa applications, some consular sections will waive the need to appear in person.

Visas for studying or working temporarily in the United States generally require a pre-approved application or petition before the foreign national applies for a visa at a United States consular office. For example, the school where students will study must accept them and produce a document to show future enrollment in the course. This is discussed further in Section E.3. In general, foreign nationals who will be working in the United States require the USCIS approval of an employer sponsor, accomplished by submitting a petition from the employer for the nonimmigrant worker. Chapter 3, Intracompany Transferees, Trade and Investment, and Professional Employment, discusses this process. In contrast, those who seek to enter as visitors do not need a pre-approved application or petition when they apply abroad for a temporary visa at the consulate office.

Regardless of whether a pre-approved petition is needed, foreign nationals seeking to obtain a visa stamp at a consular section abroad must complete Form DS-160, Online Nonimmigrant Visa Application, which can only be completed electronically and is used for all nonimmigrant visa classifications. When completing the form, the foreign national is able to select which visa classification s/he is seeking and then the form automatically adds additional questions that are relevant to that particular category. A key part of Form DS-160 is answering a series of questions that will assist the consular officer in determining whether the foreign national is admissible to the United States. The foreign national will also be required to upload a recent passport style photograph of him or herself. Once completed and submitted, the applicant will receive a confirmation page.

Thereafter, the foreign national will be directed to visit a country-specific website that provides information on how to pay the visa application fee locally and to schedule an interview. Some consular offices also provide a call-in number to accomplish this step. Each visa application carries a different fee and, in some instances, additional charges are levied depending on the visa type and the nationality of the applicant. These additional fees are called ***reciprocity fees***.

Reciprocity Fee: An additional fee a visa applicant must pay depending on the visa classification and nationality of the applicant.

The DOS' Bureau of Consular Affairs dictates the reciprocity fee, based on reciprocal charges levied by the foreign national's home country for Americans who wish to enter that nation for similar purposes.[13] It is also important to note that the country-specific reciprocity table dictates the length of issuance of a particular visa classification for a particular nationality. By way of example, Table 2.2 shows an excerpt of the visa reciprocity table for Chinese nationals for December 2014.

---

[13] Country specific information pertaining to reciprocity fees can be found at http://travel.state.gov/content/visas/english/fees/reciprocity-by-country.html.

C: Obtaining a Nonimmigrant Visa Stamp

Table 2.2 Visa Reciprocity Table for China

Visa Classification	Fee	Number of Applications	Validity Period
B-1	None	Multiple	120 Months
B-2	None	Multiple	120 Months
B-1/B-2	None	Multiple	120 Months
F-1	None	Multiple	60 Months
F-2	None	Multiple	60 Months
H-1B	None	Multiple	12 Months
H-4	None	Multiple	12 Months
I	None	One	3 Months
J-1	None	Multiple	60 Months
J-2	None	Multiple	60 Months
L-1	$120.00	Multiple	24 Months
L-2	$120.00	Multiple	24 Months
O-1	None	One	3 Months

Source: Adapted from the Department of State's Visa Reciprocity Schedule for China.

The final step in the application process is to appear at the embassy or consular office for the visa application interview itself. It is important to note that for most visa classifications, evidence in support of the application should be provided at the time of interview. What needs to be submitted for consular officer review is specific to the type of nonimmigrant visa classification sought and will be discussed in detail as each classification is explored.

If the consular officer reviewing the application and performing the interview is confident that the foreign national meets the criteria for visa issuance, the consular section will place a visa sticker[14] inside the foreign national's passport. The foreign national may then present himself or herself at a port of entry so that a CBP officer can decide whether to grant permission to enter and for how long. If the inspecting CBP officer is unsure whether a foreign national is admissible to the United States, the officer will refer him or her to an area of the airport or port of entry known as Secondary Inspection. There, another CBP officer will

---

[14] *See* Visa in Fig. 1.3 in Section E.1 of Chapter 1, Historical Background and Introduction to the U.S. Immigration System.

examine the individual's admissibility in greater detail. Sometimes, the foreign national is permitted to enter the United States for a few days in order to obtain additional documentation before returning for a follow up interview where s/he will have the opportunity to demonstrate his or her admissibility.

> ● **EXAMPLE**
>
> **Kuramoto is a Japanese national seeking to enter the United States as a student via a flight from Tokyo that arrived on a Saturday at Los Angeles International Airport. He has a valid F-1 visa, but forgot to bring with him Form I-20, Certificate of Eligibility for Nonimmigrant Student Status, issued by the university. This important document proves he has been accepted to study at an educational facility in the United States. Without it, the CBP officer could not confirm his enrollment in school. After further examination at Secondary Inspection, a supervising officer granted Kuramoto permission to enter the United States for five days so he could get another copy of Form I-20 and present it in order to prove that he is a *bona fide* student. If he does this, he will be given permission to enter as a F-1 student.**

Obtaining a visa is important for another reason. Many airlines now operate as the first line of immigration control because they will not allow a foreign national to get on a plane if s/he does not have the appropriate nonimmigrant or immigrant documents that would demonstrate a likelihood of a grant of permission to enter the United States. This is because, if a person is denied entry, the airlines are fined a substantial amount of money for allowing him or her to travel.[15] Having the visa will satisfy the airline that it is in compliance with its obligations with respect to checking that the foreign national passenger is traveling with an unexpired visa, where required by law.

D. Changing or Extending Nonimmigrant Status

While the DOS adjudicates initial visa applications, the USCIS is responsible for deciding applications to change or extend nonimmigrant status for those foreign nationals already in the United States.

Once a foreign national is present in the country for a temporary purpose, it is possible for him or her to change from one nonimmigrant classification to another or to extend his or her stay in the current class of admission. Exceptions to this rule include those who entered the United States under the VWP. Foreign nationals present under this special admission cannot change to another

---

[15] INA § 273(a)(1): "It shall be unlawful for any person, including any transportation company, or the owner, master, commanding officer, agent, charterer, or consignee of any vessel or aircraft, to bring to the United States from any place outside thereof (other than from foreign contiguous territory) any [foreign national] who does not have a valid passport and an unexpired visa, if a visa was required under this Act or regulations issued thereunder."

nonimmigrant status or extend their stay, but in limited circumstances can apply to adjust their status to an immigrant for permanent residency.[16]

For example, if a foreign national enters the United States as a visitor to backpack across the country and wants to stay longer for *bona fide* tourist reasons, s/he can file an application to extend his or her stay. The application is filed on Form I-539, Application to Extend/Change Nonimmigrant Status, and submitted to the appropriate USCIS Service Center with jurisdiction over the particular type of change or extension request. If that same foreign national entered under the VWP, however, it would not be possible for him or her to file an extension of stay. Rather, s/he would need to leave the United Sates and reapply for admission in the particular category sought. In extreme humanitarian circumstances, such as severe illness, it is possible to extend a VWP entry for a 30-day period.[17] Section E.2.a discusses the VWP in detail.

For a foreign national currently present in the United States, the process for changing or extending status can often be viewed as less significant than obtaining the visa itself because there is no interview process. However, the importance of accurately completing the application or petition form, providing the correct supporting material for a change or extension filing, and ensuring that it is timely filed cannot be overstated.

An important consideration when deciding to change status in the United States is timing. When a foreign national either applies for a visa at a consular office, requests admission at a port of entry, or enters on the VWP, the assumption is that s/he is being truthful with respect to all aspects of that application. If once in the United States, s/he seeks to change status to another category, for either a non- or immigrant classification, or does some act which violates the conditions of the category in which s/he entered, the timing of that application or act may raise a presumption about his or her true intent.

The DOS applies a 30/60 Day Rule[18] to those who enter as visitors but violate the conditions of their stay either by:

- Actively seeking unauthorized employment and, subsequently, becoming engaged in such employment;
- Enrolling in a full course of academic study without the benefit of the appropriate change of status;
- Marrying and taking up permanent residence; or
- Undertaking any other activity for which a change of status or an adjustment of status would be required, without the benefit of such a change or adjustment.

There is a presumption that a foreign national engaging in any of these activities within 30 days of arrival misrepresented his or her intent when applying

---

[16] Chapter 6, Family Sponsored Immigration and Permanent Resident Status, discusses this further.
[17] 8 C.F.R. § 217.3(a).
[18] 9 FAM 302.9-4(B)(3)(g).

for a visa.[19] This would then lead to initiating removal proceedings so that an immigration judge can decide whether s/he can stay or will be deported.[20] Those who do so within 30 but less than 60 days of entering the United States will trigger a rebuttable presumption, which may be overcome, based on the facts of the case.[21] No such presumption arises after 60 days without more information.[22]

A foreign national seeking to extend or change status must do so while s/he still has permission to be here. In order for an application to change or extend status to be deemed timely filed, it must be *received* by USCIS on or before the date the foreign national's current stay expires. Overstaying a period of admission or having an application to change or extend status denied can have serious and long-ranging impact on a foreign national's ability to visit the United States in the future or remain here for the length of time needed. In addition, if the deadline for applying is missed, then the original visa granting permission to enter in a particular category could be cancelled and/or the foreign national could face being barred from entering the United States in the future for a specified period.[23] At a bare minimum, overstaying a period of admission will always require the foreign national to report the violation on future immigration-benefit applications and petitions.

● EXAMPLE

Kelvar is a national of Georgia who is present in the United States on a B-2 visa. His six-month stay expires on June 1. On May 20, Kelvar makes a new friend who suggests that they take a two-week trip to the Grand Canyon. Kelvar, forgetting that his stay is about to expire, eagerly agrees. On June 3, Kelvar realizes that he overstayed his visa. Kelvar quickly files an application on Form I-539, *Application to Extend/Change Nonimmigrant Status*. However, because the application was filed after his stay expired, Kelvar is out of status and so cannot file his application in the United States and so cannot be granted the extension he wants.

If a foreign national is not able to timely submit an application or petition to change or extend status, there is only one way to deem a late filing as timely submitted. This requires a request for forgiveness, called a *nunc pro tunc* filing, which is a legal Latin term that literally means *now for then*. Essentially, the USCIS requires evidence to show that the delay was due to circumstances beyond the foreign national's control. 8 C.F.R. § 214.1(c)(4) lists the factors the USCIS will consider when adjudicating a *nunc pro tunc* request, which include:

- The delay was due to extraordinary circumstances beyond the control of the applicant or petitioner, and the USCIS finds the delay commensurate with the circumstances;

---

[19] 9 FAM 302.9-4(B)(3)(g)(3).
[20] *See* Section B.6.c of Chapter 9, Grounds of Inadmissibility and Deportation for further discussion on misrepresentation.
[21] 9 FAM 302.9-4(B)(3)(g)(4).
[22] 9 FAM 302.9-4(B)(3)(g)(5).
[23] *See* Section B.9.b of Chapter 9, Grounds of Inadmissibility and Deportation for a review of the unlawful presence bars.

- The [foreign national] has not otherwise violated his or her nonimmigrant status;
- The [foreign national] remains a *bona fide* nonimmigrant; and
- The [foreign national] is not subject to removal procedures.[24]

Case for Discussion 2.2

Seema, a foreign national from India, entered the United States as a visitor to take a six-month tour of the entire country. She is an avid hiker and climber and spent the majority of her trip visiting various national parks throughout the country. During the last week of her tour, she suffered a severely broken leg and several broken ribs while climbing Mount Rainier in Washington. She was airlifted to the nearest medical facility and spent the next three weeks in traction. Seema's doctors informed her that she should not travel for at least thirty days. Seema suddenly remembered that her stay in the United States expired while she was in the hospital. Seema would like to extend her visit so that she can fully recover.

- Do you think that Seema would be eligible for *nunc pro tunc* relief?

D.1. The Application Process

There are two separate and distinct processes to change or extend a nonimmigrant visa classification depending on the type of status sought. For the most part, if the foreign national is seeking a benefit that does not provide an automatic grant of employment authorization, the foreign national will file a Form I-539, Application to Change/Extend Nonimmigrant Status. However, if the foreign national is seeking a benefit that *does* provide an automatic grant of employment authorization, a petitioner — usually a company seeking to employ the foreign national — will file a Form I-129, Petition for a Nonimmigrant Worker, on the foreign national's behalf.

Examples of when Form I-539, Application to Change/Extend Nonimmigrant Status, is used include:

- Extending a stay as a visitor
- Changing from visitor to student classifications

---

[24] These are proceedings instituted to decide whether a person who is not a U.S. citizen should be deported or not and is discussed further in Chapter 10, Immigration Court Practice and Relief from Removal.

Examples of when Form I-129, Petition for a Nonimmigrant Worker, is used include:

- Changing from student status to professional specialty worker
- Extending status when there has been a transfer of a manager from a foreign branch office to one inside the United States

The visa classification sought and the location of where the foreign national resides in the United States will dictate which USCIS Service Center will process the application filed using Form I-539 or the petition filed using Form I-129. This information is readily available by visiting www.uscis.gov. The Forms tab on the USCIS website contains specific instructions on how to use every available USCIS form, the fee applicable, and the relevant address for submission. Note that the USCIS is currently moving to a process for electronic filings.

Unlike Form I-539, Application to Change/Extend Nonimmigrant Status, where a single fee covers all applications, using Form I-129, Petition for a Nonimmigrant Worker, is much more complicated as each visa petition carries a different set of filing fees. In addition to the base Form I-129, there is also a supplement contained in the form that is specific to the visa classification sought.

● **EXAMPLE**

Sophie is a French national who entered the United States on a visa to study. She just completed a Master's degree in psychology. She has received an offer of a job as a staff psychologist at a teaching hospital. Sophie needs to obtain a specialty worker classification to work for her new employer. The teaching hospital would submit a petition on Form I-129, Petition for a Nonimmigrant Worker, and the corresponding particular classification supplement, to the designated USCIS Service Center to obtain the classification needed for Sophie to be able to work for it.

While it is often confusing to know when to call a particular process an application or a petition, it is easiest to remember the distinction by thinking about the purpose of the visa classification. In general, an application is used when a foreign national files for a benefit on his or her own behalf and where the right to work is not automatically conferred. A petition is used when an employer or family member files for a benefit on behalf of the foreign national that will allow him or her to work.[25] Remembering that most work-based nonimmigrant classifications require sponsorship should help to recall that filing a petition on Form I-129, Petition for a Nonimmigrant Worker, is necessary.

When changing or extending a nonimmigrant status, evidence that the foreign national meets the criteria required for the requested classification is essential, in a way similar to applying for the visa from abroad. For example,

---

[25] *See* Section C of Chapter 6, Family Sponsored Immigration and Permanent Resident Status, for a discussion of when a family based petition can be used to secure permission to work on behalf of the foreign national through achieving permanent residency status.

if a foreign national wants to change from B-2 visitor status to student status, the application must include proof that a college or university has accepted the foreign national. S/he must also show that the current stay as a visitor will not expire before the date the course is due to begin. If there is a gap between when the visitor status expires and when the student status is due to commence, the application to change status will be denied, as the foreign national must remain in lawful status in order to be granted permission to change to F-1 status.

This requirement is specific to those seeking to change to students. Any other request to extend or change status is possible if the foreign national files the application before current leave expires, even if a decision whether to grant or deny is made *after* that date. Since some applications and petitions can take several months to be adjudicated by the USCIS, a foreign national may need to make a strategic decision about how long to stay and wait to learn if the application will be granted or not. If the application or petition is denied, then the foreign national may have accrued a substantial period of ***unlawful presence***. that might cause problems for any future attempts to apply for visas to travel to the United States. Essentially, anyone who has been present in the United States without lawful status for more than 180 days but less than one year and who voluntarily leave the country is barred from reentry for a period of three years, while anyone present without lawful status for a year or more and who leaves is barred for ten years. A foreign national seeking to enter the United States earlier than these periods must request and receive a waiver first, unless s/he is reentering with advanced parole. This is discussed in detail in Section B.9.b of Chapter 9, Grounds of Inadmissibility and Deportation.

Another issue that might arise while waiting for a decision on an extension of stay application is if the time waiting for a decision is longer than the maximum time the USCIS can grant a period of stay in a particular category. In this instance, filing a second application for an extension will be necessary *before* the putative date of the first extension request expires, assuming that it is granted. In such a situation, a foreign national could have more than one application with the USCIS awaiting adjudication at the same time.

Unlawful Presence: Present in the United States without permission, which can include someone who entered without being admitted, inspected, or paroled, or someone who entered legally but remained beyond the admission period initially granted.

● EXAMPLE

Hyacinth from Jamaica is in the United States visiting relatives when she discovers that she has colon cancer. She is receiving treatment that requires her to stay beyond the six months initially granted to her that will expire in March. A week before this period ends, she files an application for a further six months so that she can continue treatment. If granted, it would give Hyacinth permission to be here until September. By August, she still has not heard from the USCIS on her application. However, she is now receiving chemotherapy and needs to stay until that treatment is completed. She therefore has to file a new application for an extension before the date that the current application, if granted, would expire. As a result, she will have two applications for extension of stay outstanding with the USCIS. If granted, her stay will be extended until the following March.

By keeping in mind these basic components of processing nonimmigrant visas from abroad as well as changing and extending visa classification from within the United States, it will be easier to work through the specific requirements of a given classification. Table 2.6 at the end of this chapter may help to summarize the most important features of each nonimmigrant visa classification.

E. Nonimmigrant Visas That Do Not Automatically Grant Employment Authorization

After having discussed the process for obtaining a nonimmigrant visa to enter the United States, we now survey the various types of nonimmigrant visas available to foreign nationals. While the previous sections mention these classifications to provide illustrative examples of visa processing concepts, the following provides an in-depth overview.

E.1. Sources of Law

As noted in Chapter 1, Historical Background and Introduction to the U.S. Immigration System, regulations provide guidance to agencies charged with implementing a statute. They are particularly important in helping to interpret immigration law. The relevant regulatory sections for the adjudication of nonimmigrant visa classification by the USCIS are found in Title 8 of the Code of Federal Regulations, or 8 C.F.R. Additionally, Title 20 C.F.R. deals with the employment of foreign nationals in the United States and often requires the involvement of the DOL.

While the regulations can be lengthy, it is useful to review them when analyzing a particular visa classification. It is also helpful to consult the ***Department of State Foreign Affairs Manual***, or FAM, which is essentially a handbook for the DOS consular officers, providing guidance and, in some cases, interpretation of laws that affect the way in which consular offices operate.[26]

The DOS reorganized the FAM in 2015 and currently has sixteen volumes in all, each referred to as a Title. Guidance on the nuances of specific visa classifications are found in Title 9. The handbook is a particularly good source because it uses plain language that is easier to understand than the statutes or regulations and it is broken down into well-defined subject headers. In addition, when a foreign national applies for a visa classification abroad with the assistance of a legal representative, citation to the FAM is common because consular officers use it as their reference, receive training on it, and are very familiar with this resource.

Unlike other areas of immigration law, such as asylum, case law does not play a major role as a source of law for nonimmigrant visa classification for two major reasons:

- Denials of nonimmigrant visa applications made abroad cannot be appealed,[27] and

Department of State Foreign Affairs Manual: Statutory authority detailing the Department of State's regulations and policies on its organizational structure and operations.

---

[26] The Foreign Affairs Manual (FAM) can be found at at https://fam.state.gov.
[27] *Kerry v. Din*, 576 U.S. __, 135 S. Ct. 2128 U.S. (2015).

- For applications and petitions made in the United States when review is possible, it is often more cost effective and expeditious for foreign nationals and employers to file new applications or petitions addressing any deficiency in a prior application or petition, rather than go through the lengthy appellate process.

Decisions by consular officers are subject to the ***Doctrine of Consular Nonreviewability.*** When a consular section denies an application, the only option available for obtaining the nonimmigrant classification sought is submission of a new application. Of course, this new application can serve as an appeal of sorts as the foreign national will often include additional evidence and argue why the grant of the visa is appropriate. There is still no official judicial review mechanism, however.

Doctrine of Consular Nonreviewability: The doctrine that a decision by a consular officer is final and cannot be appealed.

● **EXAMPLE**

Amalgamated Technology, or AT, is a company with offices in the United States and a manufacturing plant in Bangladesh. Raj is a manager for AT abroad. AT filed a petition for Raj to work in one of the company's offices in Texas, but forgot to include evidence of Raj's previous managerial experience. Rather than filing an appeal, AT filed a new petition on behalf of Raj with the additional evidence.

Instead of case law driving changes to the adjudication of nonimmigrant visas, legal representatives should look to the USCIS interpretations and current guidance available via policy memoranda or changes to the regulations. While announcement of policy memoranda can occur without notice, the federal courts hear challenges to them if they are in violation of statutory law.[28] Note that while policy memoranda are enforceable, they do not carry as much legal weight as the regulations themselves or decisions from the Administrative Appeals Office, or AAO.

E.2. Temporary Visitors to The United States for Business (B-1) and Pleasure (B-2): INA § 101(a)(15)(B); 8 C.F.R. § 214.2(b); 9 FAM 402.2

The visitor visa B classification is one of the most versatile nonimmigrant visa classifications available to foreign nationals. It permits entry for a number of varied purposes, such as to attend business meetings, conferences, or to vacation in the United States. While limited in duration and scope, the B visa is a powerful tool to assist both individuals and businesses that want to engage the U.S. market. One of the hallmarks of the business visitor classification is that it is not available to conduct ***productive work*** in the United States, except in very limited circumstances.

Productive Work: Duties or activities that would normally be performed by a U.S. worker and/or activities that result in financial gain for the U.S. employer.

---

[28] Current and valid policy memoranda are available for review on the USCIS website, accessed at http://www.uscis.gov/laws/policy-memoranda (searchable by date and subject).

The best way to remember that the B visa is for visitors is to think of it as the "Bystander" visa classification. It is divided into two categories: B-1 for business and B-2 for visitors. The visa given is usually identified as B1/B2, although in some limited circumstances, either category can be given on its own.

The B visa is far more versatile for business purposes as opposed to tourism. Yet, the basic requirements regarding eligibility are the same for both sub-classifications. The overarching factors that a consular officer must consider when determining whether the foreign national meets the criteria for B visitor visa status are listed in 9 FAM 402.2-2(B), which states:

1. In determining whether visa applicants are entitled to temporary visitor classification, you (the consular officer) must assess whether the applicants:
   a. Have a residence in a foreign country, which they do not intend to abandon;
   b. Intend to enter the United States for a period of specifically limited duration; and
   c. Seek admission for the sole purpose of engaging in legitimate activities relating to business or pleasure.
2. If an applicant for a B1/B2 visa fails to meet one or more of the above criteria, you must refuse the applicant . . .

Out of all of the factors listed above, the one that causes the most problems for applicants for tourism is proving that they will return to their home country after entering as a visitor. This is the essence of proving nonimmigrant intent. Certain nationalities in particular struggle to overcome this requirement if they are from countries where there has been a high rate of individuals who enter the United States and remain by overstaying the period of stay or admission granted to them. For example, according to the DOS, in fiscal year 2013, 47.7 percent of the approximate 4,000 B Visa applications made by nationals of Mali were refused, indicating the U.S. government is concerned that those entering from Mali will violate their permission to stay by not returning home after the period given to them. In contrast, in the same period, there was a refusal rate of 2.8 percent of approximately 24,000 B Visa applications filed for nationals of Uruguay, because the U.S. government found it very likely those from Uruguay would return to their country before their permission to stay expired.[29]

For a foreign national wishing to demonstrate nonimmigrant intent, some of the best evidence that can be provided to support a visitor visa application include:

- A letter from the individual's employer abroad, if any;
- Evidence of the existence of a business, for those who are self-employed;
- Proof of property or land ownership in the applicant's home country; and

---

[29] *See* http://travel.state.gov/content/dam/visas/Statistics/Non-Immigrant-Statistics/RefusalRates/FY13.pdf.

- Evidence of family members that the foreign national will return to following his or her visit to the United States.

For a foreign national to demonstrate that s/he intends to enter the United States for a specific duration only, the best evidence of this is an itinerary of activities that clearly list where the foreign national will be and when, along with a copy of his or her return ticket home. If any of the events on the itinerary require registration or cost money, such as attending a concert or seeing a show, a receipt for the purchase of those tickets will help alleviate a consular officer's concerns regarding what the foreign national will be doing in the United States.

Case for Discussion 2.3

Raisa, a Russian national, is applying for a B-1/B-2 visitor visa for the United States. During her interview, the consular officer asks Raisa why she wants to go to the United States. Raisa states: "I love the United States, ever since I was a child, I have dreamed of coming to the United States. There is nothing more that I would like in this world than to go to the United States. It is the greatest country in the world."

- Based on this response, do you think the consular officer will determine that Raisa possesses 100 percent nonimmigrant intent?

Visitors for pleasure receive B-2 classification for a variety of reasons, including but not limited to:

- Tourism or family visits
- To seek medical treatment
- Participating in a social event
- Short courses of study
- Performing as an amateur entertainer, where no compensation is provided
- Co-habiting partners of foreign nationals present in other nonimmigrant visa classifications

Visitors for business have a wide range of activities that they can engage in while in the United States. A business visitor, for example, can come for meetings, to attend seminars, or conduct initial sales calls. The list in Section E.2.b details the most common uses of the visitor visa for business related reasons.

It is critical to remember that visitors for business cannot engage in productive work in the United States. Productive work in this context refers to duties or activities normally performed by a U.S. worker and/or activities that result in financial gain for the U.S. employer. There are limited situations that allow a foreign national to conduct some work on behalf of a foreign employer with business interests in the United States, such as after-sales service pursuant to a contract for goods. Under no circumstances, however, can a foreign national undertake such efforts on behalf of a U.S. employer while s/he is in the United States in B-1 classification. Violation of this rule could result in the levying of fines against the U.S. employer. In addition to a company facing fines, the foreign national may be determined inadmissible to the United States in the future because of a finding of visa fraud.

● **EXAMPLE**

Silvio is an Italian national who works for a large multinational employer as a Network Engineer in Germany. The United States subsidiary of Silvio's employer writes a letter inviting him to come for a series of meetings in California, scheduled to last a week. Silvio enters the United States as a business visitor in B-1 classification. While here, the entire company's network fails. Silvio stays three weeks longer than expected, helping the company fix their network. Fixing the network would be considered productive work in violation of the visitor visa classification. In contrast, if Silvio were entering to fulfill a sales obligation to a U.S. client of the foreign company, he might be able to do work in the United States, categorized as aftersales service.

E.2.a. Requirements for Entry

A foreign national seeking to visit the United States for business purposes has two avenues to facilitate entry to the United States, unless s/he is from a visa-exempt country. The foreign national may apply for a B-1 visa through consular processing at the Embassy or Consular Office abroad, or may enter using his or her passport via the VWP that allows citizens from designated countries to enter the United States without obtaining a visa first. In return for this benefit, VWP foreign nationals agree to the curtailment of certain rights, discussed later.

The list of countries eligible to participate in the Visa Waiver Program rarely change and the designation is maintained by the DOS.[30] As part of the 2016 federal budget appropriations, some limitations were placed on the VWP in light of terrorist attacks that occurred around the world in 2015. Such restrictions include not allowing foreign nationals who visit Iraq, Syria, Iran, or the Sudan after March 1, 2011, or who are dual nationals of a VWP country and one of these countries, to use the program.[31]

---

[30] The list of participating countries is available on the DOS website at https://travel.state.gov/content/visas/en/visit/visa-waiver-program.html.
[31] *See* Visa Waiver Program Improvement and Terrorist Travel Prevention Act of 2015, available at https://www.govtrack.us/congress/bills/114/hr158/text.

E: Nonimmigrant Visas That Do Not Automatically Grant Employment Authorization

Table 2.3 Current Visa Waiver Program Designated Countries

Andorra	Denmark	Iceland	Luxembourg	San Marino	Taiwan
Australia	Estonia	Ireland	Monaco	Singapore	United Kingdom
Austria	Finland	Italy	Netherlands	Slovakia	
Belgium	France	Japan	New Zealand	South Korea	
Brunei	Germany	Latvia	Norway	Spain	
Chile	Greece	Liechtenstein	Portugal	Sweden	
Czech Republic	Hungary	Lithuania	Republic of Malta	Switzerland	

In order to use the VWP, the foreign national must apply and obtain permission via the Electronic System for Travel Authorization, or ESTA, if s/he is a national of a designated country that is included in the program.[32]

Table 2.3 displays the countries that are currently included in the Visa Waiver Program.

In some instances, the B-1 visa can be more advantageous than using the VWP as it provides entry for up to six months per visit and is extendable. In contrast, a foreign national can only remain in the United States under the VWP for up to ninety days with extension possible only for emergencies. In addition, once in the United States, a foreign national in B-1 classification can change his or her status to a different category or extend his or her status while the VWP strictly prohibits such actions in most circumstances.[33] Finally, when attempting to gain admission in B-1 classification, it is beneficial for a consular officer to have approved and possibly annotated a visa stamp for a specific entry, rather than relying on presenting justification for entry at the border, as would be necessary for someone entering in the VWP. That said, for most business visitors entering for a short stay in the United States, often the ease of the VWP and avoiding the nonimmigrant application process at an embassy or consular office far outweighs these benefits.

---

[32] The ESTA application process is monitored by CBP and may be accessed at https://esta.cbp.dhs.gov/esta/application.html?execution=e1s1.
[33] The only changes of status permitted for a VWP is to LPR based on marriage (*see* Chapter 6, Family Sponsored Immigration and Permanent Resident Status) or because the foreign national has been granted asylum protection (*see* Chapter 5, Asylum and Other Related Humanitarian Relief).

● EXAMPLE

Monica is a foreign national from Norway. Her employer asks her to attend a trade show in the United States that will last a week. Given the fact that Norway is a visa waiver country and Monica is coming for such a short period of time, using the VWP is likely to be the best means of entering the United States to achieve this purpose.

E.2.b. Reasons for Seeking B-1 Classification

The threshold issue for the business visitor in obtaining a B-1 visa is demonstrating a legitimate business purpose for gaining admission to the United States. Again, the FAM, and specifically 9 FAM 402.2-5, is particularly helpful in determining whether a specific reason for entering the United States is possible using a B-1 visa. Business purposes specifically permitted include, but are not limited to, those contained in Table 2.4.

Table 2.4 Some Sample Valid Uses of the B-1 Visa Classification with FAM Citation

Purpose	9 FAM 402.2-5
Commercial Transaction (e.g. order for goods manufactured abroad)	9 FAM 402.2-5(B)(1)
Negotiating Contracts	9 FAM 402.2-5(B)(2)
Consulting with Business Associates	9 FAM 402.2-5(B)(3)
Litigation	9 FAM 402.2-5(B)(4)
Participating in Scientific, Educational, Professional, or Business Conventions, etc.	9 FAM 402.2-5(B)(5)
Participating in Voluntary Service Programs	9 FAM 402.2-5(C)(2)
Members of Board of Directors of U.S. Corporations	9 FAM 402.2-5(C)(3)
Personal / Domestic Employees	9 FAM 402.2-5(D)
Professional Athletes Competing in Competitions Where Compensation Is Prize Money	9 FAM 402.2-5(C)(4)(a)
Investors Seeking Investment in the U.S.	9 FAM 402.2-5(C)(7)
Horse Races	9 FAM 402.2-5(C)(8)
Commercial or Industrial Workers Coming to the U.S. for Installation, Service, Repairs	9 FAM 402.2-5(E)(1)
Short-Term Professional Work on Behalf of Foreign Employer (B-1 in lieu of H-1B)	9 FAM 402.2-5(F)
Short-Term Training (B-1 in lieu of H-3)	9 FAM 402.2-5(F)(9)

On the other end of the spectrum, 9 FAM 402.2-5 specifically prohibits the following activities as valid reasons to enter the United States as a visitor:

- To participate in a course of long term study
- To perform work that would be considered gainful employment
- To engage in paid performances, or any professional performance before a paying audience
- To work as a foreign press, radio, or film journalist, etc.

Note that, for these specifically prohibited activities, there are other nonimmigrant visa classifications available that allow a foreign national to enter the United States as indicated in Table 2.1. The process for these classifications are more robust, time consuming, and costly to obtain, however. As indicated in Table 2.4, there are a few uses of the B-1 classification that seem to blur the line between purely visiting and working in the United States. An example of this might be Commercial or Industrial Workers coming to the United States for Installation, Service, Repairs, and Short-Term Professional Work on Behalf of Foreign Employer, using B-1 in lieu of H-1B. These uses are sometimes underutilized and often overlooked, but are powerful tools in conducting international business and therefore are examined in detail.

B-1 in lieu of H-1B

The B-1 in lieu of H-1B is useful when a U.S. employer is interested in bringing an employee of a foreign affiliate to the U.S. for a job requiring a short term commitment that will directly benefit the overseas employer. "*In lieu of*" simply means "instead of." Therefore, this sub-classification is essentially for a situation where an H-1B visa would be appropriate but for the fact that it is a short-term assignment. Here, a foreign national can enter the United States as a business visitor *instead of* obtaining H-1B classification. The H-1B classification is for professional specialty occupations, described in detail in Section C of Chapter 3, Nonimmigrant Visas for Intracompany Transferees, Trade and Investment, and Professional Employment. The base requirements for the B-1 *in lieu* of H-1B classification require that the foreign national:

- Hold the equivalent of a U.S. bachelor's degree,
- Plan to perform H-1B caliber work or training,
- Will be paid only by the foreign employer, except for travel reimbursement, and
- Will maintain a position as a permanent employee (not a contractor) of the foreign employer.[34]

---

[34] 9 FAM 402.2-5(F).

Because there is a significant shortage in the number of H-1B visas available for distribution, this version of the business-visitor visa classification receives a high degree of scrutiny to ensure it is not being used to circumvent the H-1B process. Therefore, applications for this version of the B-1 visa require extensive documentation not only because of the temporary and discrete nature of the project, but also the qualifications of the foreign national.

Commercial or Industrial Workers

A foreign national "coming to the United States to install, service, or repair commercial or industrial equipment or machinery purchased from a company outside the United States, or to train U.S. workers to perform such services," is permitted to enter in B-1 classification.[35] The key to obtaining a visitor visa for this purpose lies in the wording of the contract between the entity in the United States purchasing the equipment and the foreign company that manufactured it. Specifically, the contract must specifically require the foreign company to provide these services or training. In addition, the foreign national entering the United States to perform such services must be able to demonstrate that s/he possesses knowledge that is essential to achieving this goal.

● **EXAMPLE**

A U.S. pharmaceutical company purchases an Italian made packaging machine for a new product line. The specialized foreign national employees of the Italian Company may enter the United States as business visitors in B-1 classification to set up the new packaging equipment, service and repair it only if such efforts are specifically delineated in the purchase agreement.

Investors Seeking Investment in the United States

The B-1 visa classification also has a special provision to support investors seeking investment in the United States. This use of the business visitor visa is highly advantageous to individuals and companies seeking to commence operations in the United States. It is unlikely that a foreign national would want to invest thousands of dollars without being able to first visit and secure a proper location for the enterprise, meet with legal and accounting professionals to discuss the structure of the business, and interview potential candidates for future hire. In fact, such business-visitor visa activities are often necessary in order to ultimately qualify for an investor or E-2 classification.[36]

---

[35] 9 FAM 402.2-5(E)(1).
[36] 9 FAM 402.2-5(C)(7). *See* Section A of Chapter 3, Nonimmigrant Visas for Intracompany Transferees, Trade and Investment, and Professional Employment, for a discussion of the E Visa.

| Case for Discussion | 2.4 |

Jorge is the marketing manager for a small software company located in Madrid, Spain and is entering the United States for a series of meetings and congresses across the country. He expects to be in the country for approximately two months. His schedule is as follows:

(a) Meet with a small U.S. software company about working together to translate and customize Jorge's product for sale in the U.S. market;
(b) Attend a small convention for medical software, where he will man the booth and answer questions about the company's products and services, possibly taking orders as well;
(c) Meet with a larger software company that is interested in purchasing the entire business of Jorge's company;
(d) Investigate the possibility of opening a U.S. subsidiary of the European business, including looking at property and meeting with a corporate lawyer;
(e) Meet with a current client about some issues they are having with the software they purchased; and
(f) Review and modify the marketing materials for a former employer of his in the US who is interested in selling his product in Spain.
- [ ] Does Jorge come from a country that makes him eligible for VWP admission?
- [ ] Do you have concerns or questions about the schedule or any of the activities Jorge will be engaged in?

E.2.c. Compiling the B1/B2 Nonimmigrant Visa Application

In order to gain admission to the United States, a business visitor must adhere to the overarching admission criteria for all B visa applicants listed earlier, to demonstrate a nonimmigrant intent and unrelinquished residence abroad. For most business visitors who do not often travel to the United States and only remain for a short period, however, a ticket showing return air transportation is often sufficient to gain admission. A letter of invitation from a client for a sales visit or a business meeting from a colleague can also prove beneficial.

It is also worth noting that a business visitor must have sufficient funds to cover his or her expenses in the United States. This is often not an issue as most business visitors have their expenses covered by an employer. If a U.S. business is to pay the expenses or travel, they should be commensurate to the actual cost and should not in any way be mistakable for financial compensation. Regarding compensation, the business visitor must receive all remuneration from his or her foreign employer, except reimbursement for travel expenses such as per diem payments and lodging.

A typical B-1/B-2 visitor visa application should include the following:

- Form DS-160, Online Nonimmigrant Visa Application
- Receipt of payment of filing fee
- Proof of valid visitor visa purpose of travel to the United States (e.g., invitation letter)
- Proof of funds to cover the trip
- Itinerary outlining the activities associated with the trip if it is for a business purpose

All requests are filed with a consular office abroad, which does not have to be a post based in the applicant's country of nationality as any consular post has jurisdiction to consider the application. Table 2.6 at the end of this chapter may help to summarize the most important features of the B-1/B-2 nonimmigrant visa classification.

E.2.d. Related Visa Classification, Transit (C-1) and Crew (D) Visas: INA § 101(a)(15)(C); 8 C.F.R. § 214.2(c); 9 FAM 402.4-6; INA § 101(a)(15)(D); 8 C.F.R. § 214.2(d); FAM 402.8-3

The C-1 and D visa classifications are for foreign nationals traveling in transit through the United States or working on international airlines or sea vessels. For the D classification, the foreign national must be providing services that support the normal operations of the airline or sea vessel, such as a ship captain, and must intend to depart the United States within 29 days of arriving in the country. Similar to the VWP, those that enter the United States in C-1 or D classification cannot change status under any circumstances. These visas are purely for the purpose of entry into the United States and do not confer employment eligibility for any other purpose.

E.3. Visas for Study (F-1 and M-1): INA § 101(a)(15)(F); 8 C.F.R. § 214.2(f); INA § 101(a)(15)(M); 8 C.F.R. § 214.2(m); 9 FAM 402.5

To facilitate cultural and educational exchange, the United States allows foreign nationals to enter the country for the purposes of study. The type of visa required will depend on the course of study, the type of school, and whether the individual is participating in a certified exchange program.

The F-1 student classification is available to foreign nationals wishing to enroll in academic or language studies in a private primary, secondary, or a public or private post-secondary school verified by the Department of State as authorized to support international students.[37] The M-1 student classification is available to foreign nationals wishing to pursue a vocational education in the

---

[37] 8 C.F.R. § 214.2(f).

United States, such as a trade school. The requirements for the M-1 visa classification are very similar to those associated with the F-1 classification.[38]

Generally, students wishing to enter the United States for the purposes of receiving an education under the F-1 or M-1 classification must be accepted to an approved institute with a full-time course load of at least 12 credit hours, possess sufficient funds for their stay, and intend to depart the United States at the conclusion of their course of study.[39] A requirement of the F-1 and the M-1 classifications that is similar to the B classification is that the foreign national must possess nonimmigrant intent.

The F-1 and M-1 classifications require admission to an educational institution as a first step before submitting a visa application. The institution must provide the foreign national with evidence of admission to the school on a Form I-20, Certificate of Eligibility for Nonimmigrant Student Status. A sample of the form appears in Figure 2.1.

E.3.a. Application Procedure and Requirements

The first step for foreign nationals wishing to pursue an education in the United States is choosing an educational institution for study that must be on a list of approved schools issued by the **Student and Exchange Visitor Program,** or **SEVP**, a branch of ICE.[40] Each school has a *Designated School Official,* or **DSO**, whose role is to guide the foreign student through the visa application process. The SEVP also manages the **Student and Exchange Visitor Information System**, or **SEVIS**, a database used to track student information such as enrollment, graduation, changes to programs, maintenance of required course load, etc.

Designated School Official: A responsible employee of an educational institution that is charged with assisting students in obtaining and maintaining F-1 and M-1 status as well as entering student information into SEVIS.

Once the student applies to and is accepted by a SEVP approved institution, the DSO will issue the student a Form I-20, Certificate of Eligibility for Nonimmigrant Student Status, generated through the online SEVIS system. The Form I-20 functions like an approval notice and provides strong evidence to a consular officer that the foreign national is eligible for F-1 or M-1 classification. Foreign nationals that are from visa exempt countries do not need to make an application for F-1 or M-1 classification through consular processing and can instead apply at a U.S. port of entry. They must still possess Form I-20, Certificate of Eligibility for Nonimmigrant Student Status, when seeking entry, in order to enter the United States as students and comply with the terms of these visas.

After obtaining Form I-20, Certificate of Eligibility for Nonimmigrant Student Status, from their chosen school, foreign nationals who are not visa exempt and are seeking F-1 or M-1 status must go through consular processing and complete and submit Form DS-160, Online Nonimmigrant Visa Application, prior to their visa interview. Applicants should be prepared to bring their

---

[38] 8 C.F.R. § 214.2(m).
[39] INA § 101(a)(15)(F)(i); INA § 101(a)(15)(M)(i); 8 CFR § 214.2(f); 8 C.F.R. § 214.2(m).
[40] A full list of SEVP-approved schools are on DHS' website, available at http://studyinthestates.dhs.gov/school-search.

Figure 2.1

Form I-20, Certificate of Eligibility for Nonimmigrant Student Status

---

U.S. Department of Justice
Immigration and Naturalization Service

Certificate of Eligibility for Nonimmigrant (F-1) Student Status - For Academic and Language Students (OMB NO. 1115-0051)

Page 1

SEVIS
Student's Copy

Please read Instructions on Page 2
This page must be completed and signed in the U.S. by a designated school official.

1. Family Name (surname): ▇▇▇
   First (given) Name: ▇▇▇   Middle Name: ▇▇▇
   Country of birth: INDIA
   Date of birth (mo/day/year): ▇▇▇
   Country of citizenship: INDIA
   Admission number: ▇▇▇

   For Immigration Official User
   Visa issuing post | Date Visa Issued
   Reinstated, extension granted to:

2. School (School district) name:
   University of Bridgeport
   University of Bridgeport

   School Official to be notified of student's arrival in U.S. (Name and Title):
   Rosalie Schwarz
   Secretary, International Admissions

   School address (include zip code):
   International Affairs Office
   126 Park Ave., G-level
   Bridgeport, CT 06601

   School code (including 3-digit suffix, if any) and approval date:
   BOS214F10145000   approved on 01/02/2003

3. This certificate is issued to the student named above for:
   Initial attendance at this school.

4. Level of education the student is pursuing or will pursue in the United States:
   MASTER'S

5. The student named above has been accepted for a full course of study at this school, majoring in Electrical, Electronics and Communicati
   The student is expected to report to the school no later than 01/17/2004 and complete studies not later than 12/31/2005. The normal length of study is 24 months.

6. English proficiency:
   This school requires English proficiency.
   The student has the required English proficiency.

7. This school estimates the student's average costs for an academic term of 9 (up to 12) months to be:
   a. Tuition and fees $ 10,450.00
   b. Living expenses $ 4,400.00
   c. Expenses of dependents (0) $ 0.00
   d. Other (specify): Insurance $ 508.00
      Total $ 15,358.00

8. This school has information showing the following as the student's means of support, estimated for an academic term of 9 months (Use the same number of months given in item 7).
   a. Student's personal funds $ 0.00
   b. Funds from this school $ 0.00
      Specify type:
   c. Funds from another source $ 15,358.00
      Specify type: Family Funds
   d. On-campus employment $ 0.00
      Total $ 15,358.00

9. Remarks: Semester costs must be paid at registration.

10. School Certification: I certify under penalty of perjury that all information provided above in items 1 through 9 was completed before I signed this form and is true and correct; I executed this form in the United States after review and evaluation in the United States by me or other officials of the school of the student's application, transcripts, or other records of courses taken and proof of financial responsibility, which were received at the school prior to the execution of this form; the school has determined that the above named student's qualifications meet all standards for admission to the school; the student will be required to pursue a full course of study as defined by 8 CFR 214.2(f)(6); I am a designated official of the above named school and am authorized to issue this form.

    Rosalie Schwarz | [signature] | Secretary, International Admissions | 12/18/2003 | Bridgeport, CT
    Name of School Official | Signature of Designated School Official | Title | Date Issued | Place Issued (city and state)

11. Student Certification: I have read and agreed to comply with the terms and conditions of my admission and those of any extension of stay as specified on page 2. I certify that all information provided on this form refers specifically to me and is true and correct to the best of my knowledge. I certify that I seek to enter or remain in the United States temporarily, and solely for the purpose of pursuing a full course of study at the school named on page 1 of this form. I also authorize the named school to release any information from my records which is needed by the INS pursuant to 8 CFR 214.3(g) to determine my nonimmigrant status.

    Name of Student | Signature of Student | Date

    Name of parent or guardian | Signature of parent or guardian | Address (city) | (State or Province) (Country) | (Date)
    If student under 18

Form I-20 A-B (Rev. 04-27-88)N

For Official Use Only
Microfilm Index Number

E: Nonimmigrant Visas That Do Not Automatically Grant Employment Authorization 73

Page 2

Figure 2.1 (Continued)

Authority for collecting the information on this and related student forms is contained in 8 U.S.C. 1101 and 1184. The information solicited will be used by the Department of State and the Immigration and Naturalization Service to determine eligibility for the benefits requested.

INSTRUCTIONS TO DESIGNATED SCHOOL OFFICIALS
1. The law provides severe penalties for knowingly and willfully falsifying or concealing a material fact or using any false document in the submission of this form. Designated school officials should consult regulations pertaining to the issuance of Form I-20 A-B at 8 CFR 214.3 (K) before completing this form. Failure to comply with these regulations may result in the withdrawal of the school approval for attendance by foreign students by the Immigration and Naturalization Service (8 CFR 214.4).

2. ISSUANCE OF FORM I-20 A-B. Designated school officials may issue a Form I-20 A-B to a student who fits into one of the following categories, if the student has been accepted for full-time attendance at the institution: a) a prospective F-1 nonimmigrant student; b) an F-1 transfer student; c) an F-1 student advancing to a higher educational level at the same institution; d) an out of status student seeking reinstatement. The form may also be issued to the dependent spouse or child of an F-1 student for securing entry into the United States.

When issuing a Form I-20 A-B, designated school officials should complete the student's admission number whenever possible to ensure proper data entry and record keeping.

3. ENDORSEMENT OF PAGE 3 FOR REENTRY. Designated school officials may endorse page 3 of the Form I-20 A-B for reentry if the student and/or the F-2 dependents is to leave the United States temporarily. This should be done only when the information on the Form I-20 remains unchanged. If there have been substantial changes in item 4, 5, 7, or 8, a new Form I-20 A-B should be issued.

4. REPORTING REQUIREMENT. Designated school officials should always forward the top page of the form I-20 A-B to the INS data processing center at P.O. Box 140, London, Kentucky 40741 for data entry except when the form is issued to an F-1 student for initial entry or reentry into the United States, or for reinstatement to student status. (Requests for reinstatement should be sent to the Immigration and Naturalization Service district office having jurisdiction over the student's temporary residence in this country.)

The INS data processing center will return this top page to the issuing school for disposal after data entry and microfilming.

5. CERTIFICATION. Designated school officials should certify on the bottom part of page 1 of this form that the Form I-20 A-B is completed and issued in accordance with the pertinent regulations. The designated school official should remove the carbon sheet from the completed and signed Form I-20 A-B before forwarding it to the student.

6. ADMISSION RECORDS. Since the Immigration and Naturalization Service may request information concerning the student's immigration status for various reasons, designated school officials should retain all evidence which shows the scholastic ability and financial status on which admission was based, until the school has reported the student's termination of studies to the Immigration and Naturalization Service.

INSTRUCTIONS TO STUDENTS
1. Student Certification. You should read everything on this page carefully and be sure that you understand the terms and conditions concerning your admission and stay in the United States as a nonimmigrant student before you sign the student certification on the bottom part of page 1. The law provides severe penalties for knowingly and willfully falsifying or concealing a material fact, or using any false document in the submission of this form.

2. ADMISSION. A nonimmigrant student may be admitted for duration of status. This means that you are authorized to stay in the United States for the entire length of time during which you are enrolled as a full-time student in an educational program and any period of authorized practical training plus sixty days. While in the United States, you must maintain a valid foreign passport unless you are exempt from passport requirements.

You may continue from one educational level to another, such as progressing from high school to a bachelor's program or a bachelor's program to a master's program, etc., simply by invoking the procedures for school transfers.

Form I-20 A-B (Rev. 04-27-88)N

3. SCHOOL. For initial admission, you must attend the school specified on your visa. If you have a Form I-20 A-B from more than one school, it is important to have the name of the school you intend to attend specified on your visa by presenting a Form I-20 A-B from that school to the visa issuing consular officer. Failure to attend the specified school will result in the loss of your student status and subject you to deportation.

4. REENTRY. A nonimmigrant student may be readmitted after a temporary absence of five months or less from the United States, if the student is otherwise admissible. You may be readmitted by presenting a valid foreign passport, a valid visa, and either a new Form I-20 A-B or a page 3 of the Form I-20 A-B (the I-20 ID Copy) properly endorsed for reentry if the information on the I-20 form is current.

5. TRANSFER. A nonimmigrant student is permitted to transfer to a different school provided the transfer procedure is followed. To transfer schools, you should first notify the school you are attending of the intent to transfer, then obtain a Form I-20 A-B from the school you intend to attend. Transfer will be effected only if you return the Form I-20 A-B to the designated school official within 15 days of beginning attendance at the new school. The designated school official will then report the transfer to the Immigration and Naturalization Service.

6. EXTENSION OF STAY. If you cannot complete the educational program after having been in student status for longer than the anticipated length of the program plus a grace period in a single educational level, or for more than eight consecutive years, you must apply for extension of stay. An application for extension of stay on a Form I-538 should be filed with the Immigration and Naturalization Service district office having jurisdiction over your school at least 15 days but no more than 60 days before the expiration of your authorized stay.

7. EMPLOYMENT. As an F-1 student, you are not permitted to work off campus or to engage in business without specific employment authorization. After your first year in F-1 student status, you may apply for employment authorization on Form I-538 based on financial needs arising after receiving student status, or the need to obtain practical training.

8. Notice of Address. If you move, you must submit a notice within 10 days of the change of address to the Immigration and Naturalization Service. (Form AR-11 is available at any INS office.)

9. Arrival/Departure. When you leave the United States, you must surrender your Form I-94 Departure Record. Please see back side of Form I-94 for detailed instructions. You do not have to turn in the I-94 if you are visiting Canada, Mexico, or adjacent islands other than Cuba for less than 30 days.

10. Financial Support. You must demonstrate that you are financially able to support yourself for the entire period of stay in the United States while pursuing a full course of study. You are required to attach documentary evidence of means of support.

11. Authorization to Release Information by School. To comply with requests from the United States Immigration & Naturalization Service for information concerning your immigration status, you are required to give authorization to the named school to release such information from your records. The school will provide the Service your name, country of birth, current address, and any other information on a regular basis or upon request.

12. Penalty. To maintain your nonimmigrant student status, you must be enrolled as a full-time student at the school you are authorized to attend. You may engage in employment only when you have received permission to work. Failure to comply with these regulations will result in the loss of your student status and subject you to deportation.

AUTHORITY FOR COLLECTING. Authority for collecting the information on this and related student forms is contained in 8 U.S.C. 1101 and 1184. The information solicited will be used by the Department of State and the Immigration and Naturalization Service to determine eligibility for the benefits requested. The law provides severe penalties for knowingly and willfully falsifying or concealing a material fact, or using any false document in the submission of this form.

REPORTING BURDEN. Public reporting burden for this collection of information is estimated to average 30 minutes per response, including the time for reviewing instructions, searching existing data sources, gathering and maintaining the data needed, and completing and reviewing the collection or information. Send comments regarding this burden estimated or any other aspect of this collection of information, including suggestions for reducing this burden, to: U.S Department of Justice, Immigration and Naturalization Service (Room 2011), Washington, D.C. 20536; and to the Office of Management and Budget, Paperwork Reduction Project, OMB No. 1115-0051, Washington, D.C. 20503.

74 **Chapter 2:** Nonimmigrant Visas for Brief Stays, Studies, and Cultural Exchange

Figure 2.1 (Continued)

Page 3

IF YOU NEED MORE INFORMATION CONCERNING YOUR F-1 NONIMMIGRANT STUDENT STATUS AND THE RELATING IMMIGRATION PROCEDURES, PLEASE CONTACT EITHER YOUR FOREIGN STUDENT ADVISOR ON CAMPUS OR A NEARBY IMMIGRATION AND NATURALIZATION SERVICE OFFICE.

SEVIS
Student's Copy

FAMILY NAME: _____ FIRST NAME: _____

Student Employment Authorization:

Employment Status: _____   Type: _____

Duration of Employment - From (Date): _____   To (Date): _____
Employer Name:
Employer Location:

Comments:

Event History (Past two years):
Event Name: Event Date: Name of Official: Title of Official:

This page when properly endorsed, may be used for reentry of the student to attend the same school after a temporary absence from the United States. Each certification signature is valid for one year.

Name of School:

Name of School Official	Signature of Designated School Official	Title	Date Issued	Place Issued (city and state)
Rosalie Schwarz		Secretary, International Admissions	12/18/2003	Bridgeport, CT
Name of School Official	Signature of Designated School Official	Title	Date Issued	Place Issued (city and state)
Name of School Official	Signature of Designated School Official	Title	Date Issued	Place Issued (city and state)
Name of School Official	Signature of Designated School Official	Title	Date Issued	Place Issued (city and state)

Form I-20 A-B (Rev. 04-27-88)N

DS-160 confirmation of receipt of application page along with the Form I-20 to their visa interview. Additional documentation may be required, including evidence of prior education, proof of intent to depart the United States at the end of the course of study, and proof of sufficient funds to pay the costs of the travel.

While it is possible to change status while in the United States from another nonimmigrant visa classification to F-1 or M-1 classification, it is generally not advisable for a foreign national to attempt to change from the B visitor visa classification to F-1 status. As discussed in Sec D.1, it is hard to complete the student admissions process and obtain approval of an application filed on Form I-539, Application to Extend/Change Nonimmigrant Status, within the limited time visitors have to remain in the United States. That said, if at the time of applying for a visa the foreign national indicates a desire to visit various schools to determine which to attend at the time s/he is interviewed for a B-2 visa, changing to F-1 status from within the United States may become somewhat easier if the consular officer annotates the B-2 visa and indicates that the foreign national is a "prospective student."

E.3.b. Compiling the F-1 or M-1 Nonimmigrant Visa Application

Foreign nationals seeking F-1 or M-1 status who are not visa-exempt should provide the following to the appropriate consular section:

- Form DS-160 Online Nonimmigrant Visa Application,
- Proof of payment of visa application fee,
- Form I-20, Certificate of Eligibility for Nonimmigrant Student Status,
- Proof of funds to pay for tuition, room, and board, and
- Potentially proof of ties to home country as well as relevant educational qualifications.

The application is then processed by a consular officer at a consular post abroad.

E.3.c. Duration

Unlike the visitor visa classification and most other nonimmigrant classifications that allow foreign nationals to remain for a specified period, F-1 and M-1 students are admitted for **Duration of Status,** or **D/S**, as indicated on their entry stamps.[41] Duration of status means that as long as the student preserves a valid Form I-20, Certificate of Eligibility for Nonimmigrant Student Status, is pursuing a full course of study and has up-to-date records in SEVIS, s/he can continue to remain in the United States. Essentially, the foreign national must remain in valid student status. The flexibility of a D/S admission is important as often a course of study may run longer or shorter than intended due to modifications to course

Duration of Status, or D/S: Admission to the United States for an unspecified duration so long as underlying nonimmigrant status is maintained.

---

[41] 8 C.F.R. § 214.2(f)(5)(i), 8 C.F.R. § 214.2(m)(5).

load and changes in primary fields of study, especially while attending colleges or universities. In addition, some students enter the United States for a specific course of study, for example a baccalaureate degree, and then decide to pursue further education, such as a master's degree. A D/S admission allows these students to remain and seamlessly continue their education without having to depart and reapply for a new visa and admission.

Once a course of study is completed and the foreign national is no longer in possession of a valid Form I-20, Certificate of Eligibility for Nonimmigrant Student Status, s/he is provided a grace period of additional time to remain in valid status to prepare to leave the United States. For F-1 students, the grace period is 60 days[42] and for M-1 students the grace period is 30 days.[43] The foreign national should leave the United States before the grace period expires. However, it is possible to stay beyond these periods by changing into a different visa classification or obtaining employment authorization through Optional Practical Training, or OPT,[44] discussed later.

● EXAMPLE

Omar, an Iraqi national, has completed his studies in the United States, earning a B.S. in Computer Science. He plans to return to Iraq after taking a short holiday. On day 30 of the 60-day F-1 grace period, Omar receives an email from a small University about taking a job opportunity to work in their IT department as a network administrator. Because Omar is still within the 60-day grace period, he is considered to be in status and can seek a period of OPT to take the job with the university. Omar is not required to depart the United States to achieve this.

E.3.d. Employment Eligibility

Unlike the visitor visa classification which strictly prohibits employment in the United States, foreign nationals in F-1 classification are given some latitude to work while completing their education and afterwards. In fact, Post-Completion Optional Practical Training is viewed as a key component to most foreign student's education in the United States. Students graduating in the STEM fields are favored in immigration law and have permission from both Congress and the Executive branch[45] to extend their post-graduate employment. The primary employment options for F-1 students are:

---

[42] 8 C.F.R. § 214.2(f)(5)(iv).
[43] 8 C.F.R. § 214.2(m)(5).
[44] 8 C.F.R. § 214.2(f)(10)(ii).
[45] At the time of this writing, a rule has been published in the Federal register extending OPT for STEM graduates from 17 months to 24 months. *See* Federal Register Vol. 81, No. 48, Friday, March 11, 2016, effective May 10, 2016. This means that STEM graduates can work a total of 36 months in a STEM field after completing their course of study.

E: Nonimmigrant Visas That Do Not Automatically Grant Employment Authorization

- *On-Campus Employment,*[46] which is automatically available to all foreign national students from the date the course of study begins and allows for up to 20 hours per week of employment. During the period of time when school is not in session, F-1 students can work up to 40 hours per week. Students do not need to make a separate application to the USCIS to gain permission to do this type of work.
- *Off-Campus Employment,*[47] which is available only after the first academic year has been completed and is based on a demonstration to the USCIS of severe economic necessity by the foreign national. Such employment authorization provides more flexibility as to where employment can occur, but carries a much higher burden of proof and still only allows up to 20 hours per week of employment. To qualify, a student must demonstrate that s/he is in good academic standing and is experiencing severe economic hardship that was unforeseen at the time of the visa interview for F-1 classification.[48] This can include death of a benefactor abroad, excessive medical bills, rapid currency exchange rates making payment of fees difficult, and similar events. An application for permission to work must be filed on Form I-765, Application for Employment Authorization,[49] with the USCIS and the **Employment Authorization Document,** or **EAD**, must be issued and received by the foreign national before s/he can commence employment. A significant benefit of a successful application under this provision is that the time worked off-campus does not count against the time permitted for future use of the Optional Practical Training period.
- *Curricular Practical Training,* or CPT,[50] which is a temporary grant of employment authorization that occurs while the student is in the process of completing his or her degree. The employment must be directly associated with the foreign national's major or primary course of study. CPT encourages industry experience through internships in order to give a real world application to the theoretical lessons received on campus. It envisages internships that grant university credit and can be issued for full or part-time employment. An EAD application is not necessary and a grant of CPT is possible simply by securing employment and having the DSO annotate Form I-20, Certificate of Eligibility for Nonimmigrant Student Status, accordingly. The foreign national is not required to deduct time spent in CPT from the time allowable for post-completion OPT. However, if a CPT holder exceeds 364 days of employment authorization under this provision, s/he cannot receive post-completion OPT as well.[51]

Employment Authorization Document: A document issued by the USCIS that confirms the ability of a foreign national to work in the United States.

---

[46] 8 C.F.R. § 214.2(f)(9)(i).
[47] 8 C.F.R. § 214.2(f)(9)(ii).
[48] 8 C.F.R. § 214.2(f)(9)(ii)(C).
[49] 8 C.F.R. § 214.2(f)(9)(ii)(F).
[50] 8 C.F.R. § 214.2(f)(10)(i).
[51] *Id.*

- *Optional Practical Training*, or OPT,[52] which can be obtained either while the foreign national is enrolled in school, known as pre-completion OPT, or after being granted a degree, which is post-completion OPT. In general, students are afforded a total of 12 months of OPT time. Any pre-completion OPT time is subtracted from the permitted 12 months of optional practical training. If a student has a degree in a STEM field and his or her employer participates in *E-Verify*, OPT status can be extended to 36 months in total.[53] Applicants for both pre and post-completion OPT must obtain an EAD by filing an application on Form I-765, Application for Employment Authorization, with the USCIS. There is a prohibition against accepting employment before the EAD is issued to and received by the foreign national. Post-completion OPT applications can be submitted to the USCIS from 90 days prior to graduation and up to 60 days after graduation. Employment for both pre- and post-completion OPT must be related to the foreign national's field of study.[54] If a foreign national is unemployed for a consecutive period of 90 days during post-completion OPT, the student is deemed to be out of status.
- *International Organizations*[55] recognized by the DOS, such as the Red Cross and the World Health Organization, that provide opportunities for student employment through internships. An EAD application is required in order to commence employment that does not detract from the grant of OPT status for a full 12 months in either a pre-completion or post-completion context.

E-Verify: An optional pilot program offered by the U.S. Department of Homeland Security to assist employers in ensuring the employment eligibility of new hires.

M-1 vocational students are only eligible for employment considered practical training in a related field of study that takes place after the student's graduation.[56] M-1 students must apply to the USCIS for an EAD on Form I-765, Application for Employment Authorization, no later than the date of completion of the program as listed in the Form I-20, Certificate of Eligibility for Nonimmigrant Student Status. M-1 students must receive approval of the practical training from their school's DSO on Form I-538, Certification by Designated School. The student may only begin employment on receipt of the EAD. The maximum period of employment for an M-1 is six months.[57]

---

[52] 8 C.F.R. § 214.2(f)(10)(ii).
[53] 81 FR 13039, effective May 10, 2016.
[54] 8 C.F.R. § 214.2(f)(10)(ii)(A).
[55] 8 C.F.R. § 214.2(f)(9)(iii).
[56] 8 C.F.R. § 214.2(m)(14).
[57] 8 C.F.R. § 214.2(m)(14)(iii).

> **Case for Discussion 2.5**
>
> Kimiko is a foreign national from Japan currently in valid F-1 classification studying at a large U.S. state university. Kimiko is a chemical engineer major and a number of local employers want her to work for them during the summer. While only a sophomore, Kimiko has published a paper in an industry-leading journal and is already considered an up and coming star in her field. ChemEngPlus, a local industrial solvent company, has offered Kimiko a position in their summer leadership development program that will be good for her career.
>
> - What options does Kimiko have for accepting this summer employment?
> - Do you see any potential issues for Kimiko in working for ChemEngPlus?

E.3.e. Spouses and Dependent Children

Spouses and minor children of F-1 and M-1 visa holders can apply for F-2 and M-2 visa status respectively,[58] each carrying the same requirements regarding intent as the principal F-1 or M-1 visa. Each must produce his or her own SEVIS Form I-20, Certificate of Eligibility for Nonimmigrant Student Status, listing him or her as a dependent. Regardless of whether the F-2 or M-2 application is made via consular processing or a change of status application, the dependents must establish that the principal foreign national is in valid student status, which can be demonstrated by presenting a current copy of the Form I-20, along with proof of the familial relationship, such as a marriage or birth certificate. F-2 and M-2 spouses and minor children do not have permission to work while in the United States.[59] They can engage in less than a full course of study[60] or, for minor children, in a full course of study in elementary or secondary school.[61] To engage in studies full time, a spouse or minor child must apply for and receive his or her own F-1 status.[62]

E.3.f. Travel Considerations for Those in F-1 Status

In most cases, a foreign national will be issued an F-1 visa that allows entry to the United States multiple times on the visa so long as s/he is pursuing a course of study. In some instances, the visa is valid for a single entry to the United States. If the student wishes to travel outside the country, s/he will need to obtain a new F-1 visa stamp, which will require going through consular processing again,

---

[58] 8 C.F.R. § 214.2(f)(3); 8 C.F.R. § 214.2(m)(3).
[59] 8 C.F.R. § 214.2(f)(15)(i); 8 C.F.R. § 214.2(m)(17)(i).
[60] 8 C.F.R. § 214.2(f)(15)(ii)(A)(1); 8 C.F.R. § 214.2(m)(17)(ii).
[61] 8 C.F.R. § 214.2(f)(15)(ii)(A)(1); 8 C.F.R. § 214.2(m)(17)(ii).
[62] 8 C.F.R. § 214.2(f)(15)(ii)(B); 8 C.F.R. § 214.2(m)(17)(ii)(A).

showing not only that F-1 status has been maintained through SEVIS, but also that s/he still possesses nonimmigrant intent. Proving nonimmigrant intent can be difficult for some foreign nationals who have been in the United States for an extended period while engaging in academic study.

There is one exception to the requirement to have a valid F-1 stamp to travel outside the United States. If the foreign national takes a trip to Canada, Mexico, or one of the designated lists of adjacent islands for not more than 30 days, a new visa stamp is not necessary and results in automatic visa revalidation so long as other criteria are satisfied.[63] It is also possible to travel while on OPT, but this does require the foreign national to obtain a new F-1 visa. In order to do this, s/he must be able to provide an employment confirmation letter from the employer.

E.3.g. Reinstatement of Status

A designated official is required to notify ICE in the event that a student falls out of status. There are many reasons why this may occur, for instance because of a serious illness or financial difficulties. Despite this, a foreign national can make a request to the USCIS to be reinstated to student status again. In order for this to happen, a foreign national must file an application on Form I-539, Application to Extend/Change Nonimmigrant Status, together with a newly issued Form I-20, Certificate of Eligibility for Nonimmigrant Student Status, indicating the DSO's recommendation for reinstatement.[64] 8 C.F.R. § 214.2(f)(16)(i) requires the student to establish that s/he:

> (A) Has not been out of status for more than 5 months at the time of filing the request for reinstatement (or demonstrates that the failure to file within the 5-month period was the result of exceptional circumstances and that the student filed the request for reinstatement as promptly as possible under these exceptional circumstances);
> (B) Does not have a record of repeated or willful violations of Service regulations;
> (C) Is currently pursuing, or intending to pursue, a full course of study in the immediate future at the school which issued the Form I-20;
> (D) Has not engaged in unauthorized employment;
> (E) Is not deportable on any ground other than § 237(a)(1)(B) or (C)(i) of the [Immigration and Nationality] Act; and
> (F) Establishes to the satisfaction of the [U.S. Citizenship and Immigration] Service, by a detailed showing, either that:

---

[63] 22 C.F.R. § 41.112(d).
[64] 8 C.F.R. § 214.2(f)(16); 8 C.F.R. § 214.2(m)(16).

(1) The violation of status resulted from circumstances beyond the student's control. Such circumstances might include serious injury or illness, closure of the institution, a natural disaster, or inadvertence, oversight, or neglect on the part of the DSO, but do not include instances where a pattern of repeated violations or where a willful failure on the part of the student resulted in the need for reinstatement; or

(2) The violation relates to a reduction in the student's course load that would have been within a DSO's power to authorize, and that failure to approve reinstatement would result in extreme hardship to the student.

The provisions for M-1 students contained in 8 C.F.R. 214.2(m)(16)(i) are identical. Table 2.6 at the end of this chapter may help to summarize the most important features of the F-1/M-1 nonimmigrant visa classifications.

E.4. Visas for Exchange Visitors (J-1): INA § 101(a)(15)(J); INA § 212(e); 8 C.F.R. § 214.2(j); 22 C.F.R. § 62; 9 FAM 402.5

The J-1 visa classification, second to maybe the B-1 visa classification, is the most versatile nonimmigrant visa category. The purpose of the J-1 visa is to facilitate educational and cultural exchange programs that promote the interchange of persons, knowledge, and skills in the field of education, arts, and sciences.[65] The DOS operates the Exchange Visitor Program. As a result, it follows a unique scheme for obtaining permission to apply for a J-1 visa.

There are currently 14 broad-exchange visitor programs accepting applications from foreign nationals. Table 2.5 provides a list.[66]

Table 2.5 **Exchange Visitor Programs**

Programs	
Au Pair	Through the Au Pair program, participants and host families take part in a mutually rewarding, intercultural opportunity. Participants can continue their education while experiencing everyday life with an American family, and hosts receive reliable and responsible childcare from individuals who become part of the family.
Camp Counselor	The Camp Counselor Program enables post-secondary students, youth workers, and teachers to share their culture and ideas with the people of the United States in camp settings throughout the country.

---

[65] 8 C.F.R. § 214.2(j); 22 C.F.R. § 62; 9 FAM 402.5-6.
[66] The list is maintained by the DOS and is available at j1visa.state.gov/programs.

Table 2.5 (continued)

Programs	
College and University Students	Foreign students have the opportunity to study at American degree-granting post-secondary accredited academic institutions, or participate in a student internship program that will fulfill the educational objectives of the student's degree program in her or his home country.
Government Visitors	Through the Government Visitor program, distinguished international visitors develop and strengthen professional and personal relationships with their American counterparts in U.S. federal, state, or local government agencies.
Intern	Internship programs are designed to allow foreign college and university students or recent graduates to come to the United States to gain exposure to U.S. culture and to receive hands-on experience in U.S. business practices in their chosen occupational field.
International Visitor	The International Visitor category is for people-to people programs, which seek to develop and strengthen professional and personal ties between key foreign nationals and Americans and American institutions.
Physician	Through the Alien Physician program, foreign physicians participate in U.S. graduate medical education programs or training at accredited U.S. schools of medicine.
Professor and Research Scholars	The exchange of professors and research scholars promotes the exchange of ideas, research, mutual enrichment, and linkages between research and academic institutions in the United States and foreign countries.
Secondary School Students	Secondary school students travel to the United States to study at an accredited public or private high school and live with an American host family or at an accredited boarding school.
Short-Term Scholars	Professors, research scholars, and other individuals with similar education or accomplishments travel to the United States on a short-term visit to lecture, observe, consult, train, or demonstrate special skills at research institutions, museums, libraries, post-secondary accredited academic institutions, or similar types of institutions.
Specialists	Specialists are experts in a field of specialized knowledge or skills who provide opportunities to increase the exchange of ideas with American counterparts.
Summer Work Travel	College and University students enrolled full time and pursuing studies at post-secondary accredited academic institutions located outside the United States come to share their culture and ideas through temporary work and travel opportunities.
Teacher	Foreign teachers have the opportunity to teach in accredited primary and secondary schools in the United States.
Trainee	Training programs are designed to allow foreign professionals to come to the United States to gain exposure to U.S. culture and to receive training in U.S. business practices in their chosen occupational field.

Source: J-1 Visa website.

It is important to note that each J-1 visa program carries separate and distinct requirements with issuance for different durations. Some of these programs are discussed in the following sections. Of particular note is the fact that the J-1 can be used for study in the United States. Most schools make the decision to issue the J-1 instead of the F-1 if a government agency or a non-governmental organization or NGO is providing funding to the foreign national. Students rarely have the opportunity to choose between the two classifications.

In addition, an organization designated by the DOS as a *Cultural Exchange Program Sponsor* must sponsor the J-1 visa holder.[67] The organizations can be third-party independent for-profit or nonprofit organizations, educational institutions, or even private employers.

Cultural Exchange Program Sponsor: A legal entity designated by the Secretary of State to conduct an exchange visitor program.

In order to gain designation as a sponsoring organization, there is a robust application process conducted by DOS which then closely monitors those organizations approved as program sponsors to curtail abuse and track the number of international exchange visitors that enter the United States on an annual basis.

While the Program Sponsor is responsible for the foreign national's stay in the United States, in most instances a host organization is designated to oversee the day-to-day activities of the exchange visitor. For example, a foreign national in a trainee program will be issued authorization for J-1 status so that s/he can receive training at a predetermined sponsoring corporation that serves as the host organization. Both the foreign national and the host organization report to the J-1 Program Sponsor on a regular basis to ensure compliance with the Exchange Visitor Program.

● EXAMPLE

Umut is a Turkish national who just finished a degree in business administration. While looking for jobs, Umut came across an article about a tech company in the United States that is looking to expand operations to Turkey over the next two years. Umut contacts the company and it decides it would be beneficial to train Umut in United States business practices in case it would like to hire him later to assist in launching its enterprise in Turkey. Umut agrees to take the training position and the company contacts a Program Sponsor to facilitate the J-1 visa under the intern provision.

E.4.a. Cultural Exchange Visitor Requirements for Specific J-1 Programs

Like the B1/B2, F-1, and M-1 categories, the J-1 classification requires that the foreign national possess nonimmigrant intent in order to gain admission to the United States. In addition, the foreign national must have sufficient funds or have a scholarship or stipend to ensure the ability to cover the expenses associated with his or her stay here. A primary difference between the F-1 or M-1 classifications and the J-1 category is that approval for participation in a J-1 program must occur through a DOS approved cultural exchange program and is demonstrated by Form DS-2019, Certificate of Eligibility for Exchange Visitor (J-1)

---

[67] 22 C.F.R. § 62.1(b).

Status, as opposed to Form I-20, Certificate of Eligibility for Nonimmigrant Student Status.[68]

Intern and Trainee Programs

The intern and trainee programs are very similar in purpose and orientation.[69] Both classifications are used to provide the foreign national with skills related to his or her education and experience that will prove beneficial when the foreign national ultimately returns home.

Most often, corporate hosts who gain permission from a Program Sponsor to train foreign nationals at their work location use these programs. The host company must provide a very detailed training program for the foreign national by completing and submitting Form DS-7002, Training/Internship Placement Plan, to the Program Sponsor, who then uses the SEVIS system to register the internship or training program with the DOS. J-1 trainee and intern programs may not substitute for ordinary employment or work purposes; nor may they be used under any circumstances to displace American workers.[70]

In order to qualify for the J-1 intern program, the foreign national must be currently enrolled and pursuing a baccalaureate or higher degree, or studying with a certificate granting institution outside of the United States.[71] In addition, foreign nationals who graduated from one of these institutions less than 12 months prior to the start of the exchange visitor program may also qualify as an intern.[72] The maximum duration for a J-1 intern program is 12 months while a trainee program is 18 months.[73]

In order to qualify for the J-1 trainee program, the foreign national must have a degree or certificate from a post-secondary institution and at least 12 months of related work experience outside the United States.[74] *In lieu* of such education and experience, a foreign national can still qualify for the trainee program if s/he possesses five years of related work experience outside of the United States in the occupation or field in which the foreign national will be receiving training.[75] J-1 interns must be currently enrolled full time and pursuing studies in their advanced chosen career field at a degree- or certificate-granting post-secondary academic institution outside the United States, or have graduated from such an institution no more than 12 months prior to their exchange visitor program start date.[76] Once the program is complete, all J-1 visa holders, regardless of the type of program they are

---

[68] 8 C.F.R. § 214.2(j)(1)(i).
[69] 22 C.F.R. § 62.22(a).
[70] 22 C.F.R. § 62.22(b)(ii).
[71] 22 C.F.R. § 62.22(b)(2).
[72] *Id.*
[73] 22 C.F.R. § 62.22(k).
[74] 22 C.F.R. § 62.22(d)(2).
[75] *Id.*
[76] 22 C.F.R. § 62.22(d)(3).

in, are allowed a 30-day grace period to leave the United States at the end of their authorized stay in the United States.[77]

The J-1 intern or trainee programs and the F-1 grant of OPT are similar in purpose because they both provide the opportunity for foreign nationals to receive practical work-related experience in the United States. However, as highlighted previously, the J-1 intern or trainee programs are only for foreign nationals that have earned or are in the process of earning a degree or post-secondary certificate or have gained five years of relevant experience abroad. In most instances, a foreign national cannot convert from F-1 OPT to a J-1 visa. In addition, a foreign national cannot complete successive J-1 intern or trainee programs if each corresponds to the maximum period of stay allowed in the United States. The foreign national must return abroad for two years in order to be eligible for a new J-1 training program.[78]

Case for Discussion 2.6

Robert is a 24-year-old U.K. national who dropped out of University about six months ago. For the past five years, he was seeking a degree in psychology, but realized that his true calling in life is entertainment promotion. While at university, Robert worked for a few local nightclubs promoting various events and since dropping out has been running his own small business doing the same thing. Robert feels that the only way to take his business to the next level is to get some practical training in New York City, which, in his opinion, is the best place to learn the business. Through persistence, a famous club in New York has agreed to provide Robert with a 12-month training program in entertainment marketing.

- Can Robert get a J-1 visa to train at the club in New York City?
- If yes, which version of the J-1 visa is most appropriate and why?
- If no, explain why Robert is ineligible for the J-1 visa.

E.4.b. Two-Year Residence Requirement

Because the J-1 programs are based on the notion of a cultural and educational exchange, some J-1 holders ultimately become subject to what is known as the *two-year home residency requirement*.[79] Determining whether a J-1 visa holder

Two-Year Home Residency Requirement: The requirement that J-1 visa holders return to their home country or place of last residence abroad for a two-year period after completing a J-1 program before seeking other immigration benefits in the United States.

---

[77] 8 C.F.R. § 214.2(j)(1)(ii).
[78] 22 C.F.R. § 62.22(n)(2). The H-3 visa classification also allows for training and is discussed briefly in Chapter 4, Nonimmigrant Visas for Extraordinary Ability, Religious Workers, and Ancillary Activities.
[79] INA § 212(e).

is subject to this requirement is based on the type of J-1 program pursued and the individual's nationality. Those who are subject to the requirement must return to their country of nationality or place of last residence for a period of two years before applying for most nonimmigrant visa classifications or immigrant status.

J-1 visitors who have received funding for their program of study or research from a government source, either in whole or in part, are automatically subject to the home residence requirement.[80] In addition, those that receive clinical medical training are always subject to the two-year home residency requirement.[81] However, the analysis is slightly more complicated when dealing with skills that are gained primarily through the J-1 Trainee and Intern Programs. When the foreign national receives training or gains experience in a skill that his or her home country has determined is in demand, the two-year home residency requirement is mandated. The list of needed knowledge and ability subject to two-year home residency requirement must be publically available and designated by a foreign country on its ***skills list*** that the DOS electronically manages and publishes.[82]

Skills List: A list of skills cited by a foreign country that subject a J-1 visa holder to the two-year home residency requirement.

● **EXAMPLE**

Paola has come to the United States to study Mechanical Engineering from her native Brazil, a skill that is much needed there. On completing her studies, Paola will be required to return to Brazil for at least two years before she can return to the United States in an employment-based category because mechanical engineering is listed as a needed skill in Brazil on the DOS website.

In most instances, it can be determined if the foreign national is subject to the two-year home residency requirement by looking at his or her J-1 visa stamp, which will indicate under the annotation section whether the consular officer has deemed the requirement applicable. For example, the annotation might state that INA § 212(e) does NOT apply. In addition, the determination may also be listed on the Form DS-2019, Certificate of Eligibility for Exchange Visitor (J-1) Status. If a foreign national is in doubt as to whether the residency requirement is applicable to his or her J-1 program, it is possible to make a request to the Department of State for an ***advisory opinion***.

Advisory Opinion: An opinion providing guidance on legal interpretation regarding a point of law requested from and issued by the government before an application or petition for a benefit is submitted and adjudicated.

The DOS advisory opinion is one of the few instances where a foreign national can proactively ask the government to make a determination as to whether s/he is entitled to an immigration benefit before actually filing the application.[83] Once the advisory opinion has been provided, the foreign national will be in a better position to decide as to whether the application should proceed.

---

[80] INA § 212(e)(i).
[81] INA § 212(e)(iii).
[82] The skills list by country can be accessed on the DOS website by visiting http://travel.state.gov/content/visas/english/study-exchange/exchange/exchange-visitor-skills-list.html.
[83] *See* http://travel.state.gov/content/visas/english/general/advisory-opinions.html.

Waiver of the Two-Year Home Residence Requirement

Notwithstanding the fact that certain J-1 visa holders are subject to the two-year home residency requirement, the DOS in conjunction with the USCIS, has a mechanism to waive the two-year home residency requirement. A waiver can be granted under the following broad categories:[84]

- Receipt of a **No Objection Statement** from the foreign national's home country
- Exceptional hardship to a United States citizen or lawful permanent resident spouse or child
- Fear of **persecution**
- **Interested Government Agency**, or **IGA**

The No Objection Statement is probably the easiest waiver to obtain, but is only available to J-1 visa holders for whom the home residence requirement is necessary because of the skills their country may require. Therefore, J-1 visa holders who have received government financing or are receiving medical training in the United States may not use this less onerous means of getting the home residency requirement waived. The No Objection Statement is simply a letter stating that the country from which the foreign national last resided does not object to the exchange visitor *not* returning abroad in order to fulfill the two-year residency obligation. It is obtained through the foreign national's home country embassy or Consulate General in the United States. The letter is then forwarded to the DOS and becomes the primary evidence in support of removing the home residency requirement and granting the waiver.

To obtain the exceptional hardship waiver, the foreign national must demonstrate the harm the J-1 visa holder's U.S. citizen or LPR spouse or child under 21 would suffer if the J-1 visa holder were required to depart the United States for a period of two years.[85] This is a considerably harder waiver to obtain than the No Objection Statement because there are more factors at play and the standard for granting the waiver is much higher. For example, a qualifying basis for filing an exceptional hardship waiver might be when a program participant's U.S. citizen spouse has a serious medical condition that the J-1 visa holder's home country is not able to treat. The mere separation of husband and wife, with no other compelling factors, would not qualify as exceptional hardship.

The **persecution waiver** is also sometimes referred to as the asylum waiver,[86] even though it is a modified standard for J-1 visa holders. Essentially, the foreign national must show that returning to his or her home country would result in him or her being subject to persecution on account of race, religion or political opinion. These are the only grounds of persecution that can be considered for this waiver, whereas there are five asylum enumerated grounds.[87] Additionally, the J-1 visa holder must show that s/

---

[84] INA § 212(e).
[85] 8 C.F.R. § 212.7(c)(5).
[86] *Id. See* also Chapter 5, Asylum and Other Related Humanitarian Relief, for further discussion of this immigration benefit.
[87] *Id.*

he "*will be* subject to" persecution (emphasis added).[88] This is a higher standard than that required for asylum filed by any other foreign national, who only has to demonstrate a "reasonable possibility of suffering such persecution if he or she were to return to [the country where persecution is feared]."[89]

Finally, the foreign national may petition a U.S. government agency for an Interested Government Agency waiver.[90] Typically, this waiver is most often used by researchers who received government funding for their J-1 program, but now have made such significant contributions to their field of endeavor that it would be contrary to the interest of the United States to send the foreign national back to his or her home country for the two-year period. Each government agency tends to have its own process for determining whom it will recommend for the IGA waiver. The U.S. Department of Health and Human Services is one of the many agencies that will often entertain this type of J-1 two-year home-residency requirement waiver.

Within the IGA waiver category, there is a separate process for medical professionals seeking to remain continuously in the United States, called a Conrad 30 waiver,[91] because each state is allowed to issue 30 such waivers a year. Here, a state will recommend a waiver to the DOS on the basis that it is in the public interest to keep a physician in a certain region due to a lack of medical professionals practicing in that area. Typically, health professionals who will be serving in one of four types of designated areas receive these waivers. The areas are:

- Medically Underserved Area, or MUA
- Health Professional Shortage Area, or HPSA
- Mental Health Professional Shortage Area, or MHPSA
- Veteran Affairs, or VA

Case for Discussion 2.7

Harra is from Laos and has been in the United States in J-1 status for the past 18 months, training on industrial engineering with a well-known manufacturer. The manufacturer now wishes to hire Harra on a long-term basis because their business needs have changed. Harra is subject to the J-1 two-year home residency requirement because his training appears on Laos's skills list. Harra contacted his local Laos consular section and was told they do not mind if he stays in the United States.

- Which would be the best type of waiver to try to get and why?

---

[88] 8 C.F.R. § 212.7(c)(5).
[89] 8 C.F.R. § 208.13(b)(2)(i)(B). Section A.4 of Chapter 5, Asylum and Other Related Humanitarian Relief, discusses the applicable standard.
[90] 22 C.F.R. § 41.63(c)(1).
[91] INA § 214(l).

E.4.c. Spouses and Minor Children

Spouses and minor children of J-1 visa holders can apply for J-2 visa status.[92] For this dependent visa, the J-1 Program Sponsor will issue the J-2 applicant his or her own Form DS-2019, Certificate of Eligibility for Exchange Visitor (J-1) Status. However, the dependents must still show proof of the family relationship when going through consular processing. One of the benefits of being a J-2 over an F-2 visa holder is that the J-2 dependent spouse can work in the United States, following application for and receipt of an EAD from the USCIS.[93] J-2 visa holders who are dependents of J-1 visa holders who are subject to the home residency requirement are also subject to it and will need their own waiver in order to remain continuously in the United States.[94]

Table 2.6 at the end of this chapter may help to summarize the most important features of the J-1 nonimmigrant visa classification.

E.5. Visas for Related Cultural Exchange Visa (Q): INA § 101(a)(15)(Q); 8 C.F.R. § 214.2(q); 9 FAM 402.15

Founded on the concept of cultural exchange, the Q visa is similar to the J-1 visa. While the J-1 is a program run through the DOS, the USCIS administers this program.[95] As the Q classification is a USCIS process, it does not vary from program to program like the J-1 sponsorship process. Here, the sponsoring organization will file a Form I-129, Petition for Nonimmigrant Worker, with the USCIS and prove that it maintains an established international cultural exchange program. The employer must also show that the program activities occur in a setting where the foreign national's culture can be shared with the American public.[96] Finally, the employer must show that the wages and working conditions provided to the foreign national will be the same as those provided to similarly situated U.S. workers[97] and that the employer has the ability to pay the offered wages.[98]

A foreign national in Q visa classification can remain in the United States for up to 15 months.[99] The foreign national must be at least 18 years old in order to obtain the Q visa and must have the ability to communicate "effectively about the cultural attributes of his or her country of nationality to the American Public."[100] Similar to the J-1 visa, Q visa holders are allowed a 30-day grace period to depart the United States at the end of their cultural exchange program.[101] Unlike the F or J visa classifications however, spouses and dependents cannot apply to enter as

---

[92] 8 C.F.R. § 214.2(j)(i).
[93] 8 C.F.R. § 214.2(j)(1)(v).
[94] 8 C.F.R. § 212.7(c)(4).
[95] 8 C.F.R. § 214.2(q).
[96] 8 C.F.R. § 214.2(q)(3)(iii)(A).
[97] 8 C.F.R. § 214.2(q)(4)(i)(D).
[98] 8 C.F.R. § 214.2(q)(4)(i)(E).
[99] 8 C.F.R. § 214.2(q)(7)(iii).
[100] 8 C.F.R. § 214.2(q)(3)(iv).
[101] 8 C.F.R. § 214.2(q)(3)(ii).

dependents of the **principal applicant** but rather must seek their own visa, most often a B-2, in order to accompany the principal foreign national to the United States.

E.6. Visas for Special Education Exchange Visitors and Trainees (H-3): INA § 101(a)(15)(H); 8 C.F.R. § 214.2(h)(7); 9 FAM 402.10-4(F)

The H-3 visa classification is similar to the J-1 visa in that it is centered on the concept of providing training to foreign nationals who wish to further their careers abroad by spending time in the United States in a professional setting.[102] However, like the J-1 visa, the H-3 visa program is adjudicated by the USCIS and all requests for this classification are filed on Form I-129, Petition for Nonimmigrant Worker.

One of the main differences between the H-3 and the J-1 is that under the H-3 classification a petitioner can file for multiple beneficiaries using one single filing. This option is particularly advantageous for large international companies seeking to train a "class" of foreign workers. In the past, adjudication of H-3 visa petitions occurred with greater scrutiny than J-1 applications. In recent years, as the DOS has enforced the J-1 regulations with greater vigor, the H-3 classification has gained in popularity. One of the detriments of this visa classification however, is that spouses have no avenue for employment authorization, except in limited circumstances.[103]

In order to obtain H-3 approval, a petitioner must show:

- The proposed training is not available in the [foreign national's] own country;
- The beneficiary will not be placed in a position which is in the normal operation of the business and in which citizens and resident workers are regularly employed;
- The beneficiary will not engage in productive employment unless such employment is incidental and necessary to the training; and
- The training will benefit the beneficiary in pursuing a career outside the United States.[104]

The emphasis is on the requirement that any productive work performed must be incidental to the training, because the H-3 cannot be used as a substitute for a true working visa classification such as an H-1B. Successful H-3 petitions will contain detailed training programs as well as attestations regarding the benefit the training will provide not only the petitioner, but more importantly

---

[102] 8 C.F.R. § 214.2(h)(1)(ii)(E).
[103] 8 C.F.R. § 214.2(h)(9)(iv).
[104] 8 C.F.R. § 214.2(h)(7)(ii)(A).

the foreign national once the trainee returns to his or her home country. Issuance of the visa can be for up to two years in duration[105] but cannot be renewed or extended.

F. Visa Summary Chart

Table 2.6 reviews each major visa classification discussed in this chapter.

Table 2.6 Summary of Major Nonimmigrant Status Classifications

Maximum Duration of Visa	Maximum Duration of Each Entry	Maximum Duration Classification Can Be Held Without Departing the United States	Intent Requirement	Available for Spousal Employment Authorization
B-1/B-2 Visa				
Up to 10 years — be sure to check reciprocity	6 months	6 months — but extensions are possible	100 percent nonimmigrant intent	No
Visa Waiver Program — ESTA				
Visa requirement waived	90 days	No extensions permitted — except for limited circumstance	100 percent nonimmigrant intent	No
F-1 / M-1 Visas				
Varies — be sure to check reciprocity	D/S	Indefinite	100 percent nonimmigrant intent	No
J-1 Visa				
Varies — be sure to check reciprocity	D/S	Varies based on J-1 sub-classification	100 percent nonimmigrant intent	Yes

---

[105] 8 C.F.R. § 214.2(h)(9)(iii)(C)(1).

G. Conclusion

Throughout this chapter, we explored the broad concepts and nuances associated with the nonimmigrant visa system. It is far more important to understand the function of a particular nonimmigrant visa classification as opposed to memorizing the letter or number combination by which it is designated.

The following two chapters explore the remaining nonimmigrant visa classification where employment authorization is integrated. The regulatory requirements for these categories are often more robust than the classifications discussed in this chapter, and may involve additional government agencies such as the DOL. The framework for analyzing all nonimmigrant visas remains the same, however: identifying the purpose of the visa; determining whether pre-approval is necessary; factoring the length of time permitted by the visa; and addressing employability of the spouse of the visa holder.

3

Nonimmigrant Visas for Intracompany Transferees, Trade and Investment, and Professional Employment

Key Terms and Acronyms

Beneficiary
Dual Intent
Dual Representation
Intracompany Transferee
Labor Condition Application (LCA)
Petitioner
Portability

Premium Processing
Prevailing Wage Rate
Public Access File
Specialized Knowledge
Specialty Occupation
Treaty Investor
Treaty Trader

Chapter Objectives

- Analyze criteria for employment-based nonimmigrant visa classifications
- Review sources of law for nonimmigrant visa classifications
- Enhance understanding of consular processing for nonimmigrant visas
- Explain the procedure for filing a Petition for a Nonimmigrant Worker for each particular visa classification
- Analyze the benefits and drawbacks of particular nonimmigrant visa classifications

In order to perform productive work in the United States on a temporary basis, a foreign national must obtain a nonimmigrant visa that authorizes employment. In Chapter 2, Nonimmigrant Visas for Brief Stays, Studies, and Cultural Exchange, we explored the various nonimmigrant visas that are available for visitors (B-1/B-2), students (F-1/M-1), and exchange programs (J-1). While each of these visa classifications contains provisions that allow for some work in the United States in limited circumstances, for the most part, they focus on temporary stays that do not include a grant of employment authorization. In this chapter and the next, the focus is exclusively on the nonimmigrant visa classifications that allow for employment in the United States and the manner in which a foreign national obtains them.

The nonimmigrant visa classifications explored here cover those most often used by companies seeking to hire foreign nationals on a temporary basis, such as the E-1/E-2 visas for treaty traders and investors; the L visa classification for intracompany transferees; and the H-1B classification for workers in professional specialty occupations. In addition, this chapter explores the related nonimmigrant visa classifications created by bi-lateral and tri-lateral free trade agreements such as the North American Free Trade Agreement, or NAFTA.

As with the visa classifications covered in Chapter 2, it is easier to think about the purpose associated with the classification rather than the alphanumeric designation. Using this methodology allows for easier selection and recognition of the best nonimmigrant visa options available for a given situation. In addition, when working with an employer or **petitioner** looking to sponsor a foreign national or **beneficiary** to work in the United States, such employers are often less concerned with the name of the visa and more focused on the following factors:

Petitioner: U.S. citizen, lawful permanent resident relative, or employer who seeks to sponsor a foreign national family member or employee.

Beneficiary: The foreign national family member or employee who will receive an immigration benefit from a family sponsored or employee-based petition.

- Cost — How expensive is it going to be to obtain employment authorization?
- Duration — How long is the visa valid for and is renewal available?
- Delay — How long is it going to take to secure employment authorization?
- Ease — How much effort is required on the part of the company to secure the employment authorization?

Of course, when preparing an application for an employment-based nonimmigrant visa through consular processing abroad or filing a petition in the United States, it is important to apply the specific requirements associated with each classification. Table 3.1 at the end of this chapter may help to summarize the most important features of each nonimmigrant visa as we explore the legal standards in detail.

A. Visas Based on Qualifying Treaties of Commerce and Navigation for Treaty Traders (E-1) and Treaty Investors (E-2): 8 INA § 101(a)(15)(E); 8 C.F.R. § 214.2(e); 9 FAM 402.9

Throughout the majority of the history of the United States, the federal government has entered into treaties with foreign countries to establish stronger relationships, primarily for economic purposes. Born from these treaties is the reciprocal ability to enter each other's country to conduct business. The visa classification that facilitates this purpose is the E visa that is available to persons, including corporate entities, from treaty countries that qualify as a treaty trader, or E-1, and a treaty investor, or E-2.[1]

A.1. Sources of Law

The statute that created the E nonimmigrant classification is found at the Immigration and Nationality Act, or INA § 101(a)(15)(E), and correspondingly further explained in the regulations at 8 C.F.R. § 214.2(e) and 22 C.F.R. § 41.51. In addition, the Foreign Affairs Manual, or FAM, entry at 9 FAM 409 provides direct guidance to consular officers when adjudicating applications for E visas. While the regulations for E visa classification are useful in discussing the key principles associated with this classification, the FAM is particularly helpful as most applications for this classification are made through consular processing. Also, the plain language used in the FAM makes understanding the E classification more accessible than reviewing the statute and regulations alone.

9 FAM 402.9-2(b) best explains the purpose behind the creation of this very useful nonimmigrant visa classification when it instructs consular officers on how to consider such applications. It states:

> As the E visa is becoming ever more popular, you should remember that the basis of this classification lies in treaties which were entered into, at least in part, to enhance or facilitate economic and commercial interaction between the United States and the treaty country. It is with this spirit in mind that cases under INA [§]101(a)(15)(E) should be adjudicated.

The key to understanding the requirements of the E nonimmigrant visa is to focus on the nationality of the ultimate owner of the U.S. entity. If s/he is a national or nationals of a country that has a qualifying treaty of commerce and navigation, it may be possible to use the E visa classification. If available, it is a great vehicle for new company start-ups and global corporations that need to transfer key individuals to the United States who share the nationality of the

---

[1] 8 C.F.R. § 214.2(e); 9 FAM 402.9.

Figure 3.1

E Visa Acquisition Map

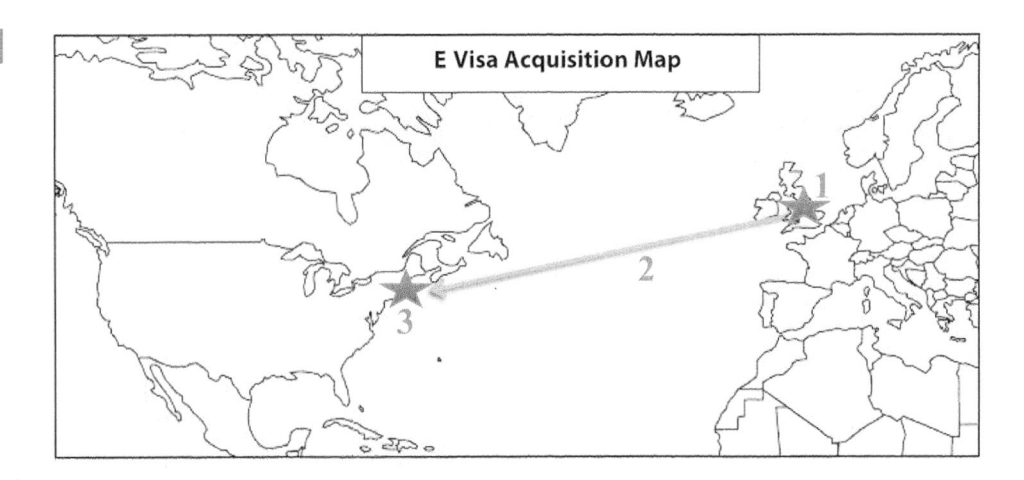

treaty country. The size of the enterprise in the United States, while important for predicting success in the E nonimmigrant visa application process, does not, in and of itself, dictate whether a given application will be approved. In fact, the E visa is very much associated with entrepreneurship.

Unlike many other employment-based nonimmigrant classifications, to obtain the E classification, the foreign national must go through consular processing at a United States embassy or consulate abroad. Bearing in mind that each consular section has different policies and procedures for consular processing, it is important to review a particular embassy or consulate's website before preparing an E nonimmigrant visa application. Because the financial relationships that form part of the E visa application can be complex, some consular sections dealing with high volumes of applications have specific E Visa Units that only adjudicate this type of visa.

To help understand how most foreign nationals obtain a particular visa classification, this chapter has various "acquisition maps," as shown in Figure 3.1, that provide illustrative examples. These maps do not show all means by which a foreign national can obtain a particular visa, just the most common. For consistency, most visa acquisition maps use the United States Embassy in London and Customs and Border Protection, or CBP, at JFK airport in New York, New York as reference points. The various steps taken by a foreign national seeking to enter the United States in E nonimmigrant classification, as depicted in Figure 3.1, are as follows:

- Step 1: Apply for E visa through embassy or consulate abroad. In this case, the U.S. Embassy in London receives the application.
- Step 2: With E visa issued by the embassy, the British National travels to the United States.
- Step 3: CBP admits the British National in New York, New York and the British National commences working for the qualifying E classification enterprise in the United States.

Because there is no specific need to first submit a petition to the United States Citizenship and Immigration Service, or USCIS, in order to secure E visa status, it is one of the fastest employment-based visas to obtain, and in many cases, one of the most cost-efficient as well. It is important to check the processing times and procedures at each consular section, however, as some posts have more rigorous requirements that can lengthen the time before the application is approved.

A.2. Specific E Visa Requirements

As a threshold issue, for a foreign national to qualify for an E visa, s/he must be a citizen of a country with which the United States has entered into a "treaty of commerce and navigation."[2] Demonstrating this requirement by referencing the actual treaty between the United States and the foreign country is simple. Either a letter of support from the enterprise in the United States, or an attorney cover letter containing the legal argument explaining why approval of the status is appropriate may be used.[3] Some countries may only be granted E-1 *or* E-2 eligibility.

It should not be assumed that a particular country has E visa designation. While most Western countries do, some countries that possess qualifying treaties might seem counterintuitive given the current global political climate. For example, Iran remained a treaty country even during the period that it was subject to economic sanctions, because of the close ties it forged with the United States during the 1950s. However, the BRIC countries of Brazil, Russia, India, and China, even though considered globally influential because of their rapid economic growth, are not eligible for E visa classification. The oldest active qualifying E visa treaty is with the United Kingdom, dating back to 1815.

A.2.a. Shared Requirements for Both E-1 and E-2 Visa Classification

In order for a foreign national to qualify for either type of E visa, s/he must establish the following shared threshold requirements:

- The foreign national who will be employed in the United States must be a citizen of the same country of citizenship as the owners of the entity.[4] Prior employment with the company is not required.
- The principal foreign national employer must be
  - ☐ A person in the United States having the nationality of the treaty country and maintaining nonimmigrant treaty trader or treaty investor status or, if not in the United States, would be classifiable as a treaty trader or treaty investor;[5] or
  - ☐ An enterprise or organization at least 50 percent owned by persons in the United States having the nationality of the treaty country and maintaining nonimmigrant treaty trader or treaty investor status or who, if not in the United States, would be classifiable as treaty traders or treaty investors.[6]

---

[2] 9 FAM 402.9-4(A).
[3] For a full list of treaty countries, visit http://travel.state.gov/content/visas/english/fees/treaty.html.
[4] 8 C.F.R. § 214.2(e)(3).
[5] 8 C.F.R. § 214.2(e)(3)(i).
[6] 8 C.F.R. § 214.2(e)(3)(ii).

Limited Liability Entity: A particular type of corporate formation with no shareholders, where the owners enjoy some protection from liability, while simultaneously gaining some benefits of profits and losses by being treated as individuals.

The 50 percent ownership rule is known as the 50 Percent Rule.[7] The individuals maintaining ownership are not included when calculating the percentage, if they are lawful permanent residents, or LPRs in, or dual-nationals of, the United States. If the entity seeking E nonimmigrant classification is a *limited liability entity* or owned by a foreign limited liability entity, the operating agreement will be sufficient evidence of ownership percentages. When dealing with corporations seeking E visa classification, a consular officer or USCIS adjudicator will review the nationality of the owners of the shares issued by the U.S. enterprise or the foreign entity that owns it. If the ultimate owner of the U.S. entity is a publicly traded company, there is a presumption that it possesses the nationality of the country where its shares are listed or traded.

While the 50 Percent Rule can become cumbersome for larger global corporations, the nationality of the ultimate owner of the U.S. enterprise can be demonstrated by providing stock certificates, excerpts from corporate registries, annual reports, and other documentation of public listings.

● EXAMPLE

Intek UK is a privately held technology company headquartered in the United Kingdom and registered as a corporation under U.K. law. Intek UK has a small subsidiary in the United States called Intek US that is 100 percent owned by Intek UK. In order to determine if Intek US can use the E nonimmigrant visa classification, a consular officer will review the nationality of the individuals who own shares of Intek UK. If at least 50 percent of those shareholders are U.K. citizens, Intek US can use the E nonimmigrant visa to transfer British nationals to the United States.

Establishing that the person seeking E nonimmigrant status is of the same nationality as the treaty country of the owner of the enterprise is simple once the ownership of the U.S. enterprise is clear. When there is an enterprise in the United States that is a 50-50 joint venture between nationals of two treaty countries, the enterprise designates one nationality for E nonimmigrant purposes.[8]

A.2.b. Requirements for E-1 Treaty Trader

The E-1 treaty trader nonimmigrant visa is based on trade and issued so that foreign nationals can facilitate international commerce between the United States and a treaty country. During FY 2013, the Department of State, or DOS, issued approximately 7,000 E-1 visas, compared to approximately 35,000 E-2 visas.[9] Although the E-1 visa may not be as popular as the E-2 visa, it still serves a vital purpose in the overall visa system.

---

[7] 9 FAM 402.9-4(B)(c).
[8] 9 FAM 402.9-4(B)(d).
[9] *See* http://travel.state.gov/content/dam/visas/Statistics/Non-Immigrant-Statistics/NIVWorkload/FY2013NIVWorkloadbyVisaCategory.pdf.

In order to qualify for E-1 classification, the enterprise employing the foreign national, or in the case of an owner/operator, must be:

- Engaged in trade that is substantial in nature,
- Principally with the United States, and
- The individual E-1 visa applicant must be a manager, executive, or *essential skills employee*.[10]

> **Essential Skills Employee:** An employee with special qualifications that make the service s/he renders essential to the efficient operation of the enterprise.

Trade, as cited at 9 FAM 402.9-5(B), contains three components that must exist in all E-1 nonimmigrant visa applications. It must be:

- An actual exchange,
- International in scope, and
- Involve qualifying activities such as the exchange of goods and services.

Any service item or good commonly traded in international commerce can qualify as valid trade for E-1 visa purposes so long as such goods are verifiably transferred between a treaty country and the United States in a commercial context. Qualifying goods for trade are wide-ranging and include manufactured goods, computer programs, and, even in limited circumstances, services such as legal and accounting services.[11]

The trade must be *substantial* and, to qualify as such, trade must be in a continuous flow, involving numerous transactions over time.[12] Exactly what constitutes a flow very much depends on the nature of the industry and the goods or services being exchanged. When adjudicating an E-1 nonimmigrant visa application, a consular officer will focus on the volume of the trade and the monetary value of each transaction.[13] There is a preference in granting E-1 visas to high-volume traders of moderately priced goods, but a low volume trader may qualify if the value of the goods is extremely high.

● EXAMPLE

SuperDuperComputer is a company in the United States owned by Mexican nationals that sells expensive automated engineering solutions for the beverage industry and only has a few very high value sales a year. The goods are made in Mexico and then sold to SuperDuperComputer in the United States for third party sales, service, and installation. The sales that the company does have are valued in the hundreds of thousands of dollars each. Therefore, the low volume of trade does not preclude the Mexican nationals from E-1 classification because the value of the trade is so high.

For trade to be "principally with the United States," more than 50 percent of the U.S. enterprise's total international trade must be between the United States

---

[10] 8 C.F.R. §§ 214(e)(1)(i) and 214(e)(3).
[11] 8 C.F.R. § 214(e)(9).
[12] 8 C.F.R. § 214(e)(10).
[13] 9 FAM 402.9-5(C).

and the treaty country.[14] The remainder of the trade can be with other countries or domestic. Demonstrating that this requirement has been met can be achieved by producing invoices, contracts, bills of lading, sales reports, bank records, or audited annual reports. As the world's economy continues to grow and companies continue to expand and trade within the global marketplace with diverse international players, it is this requirement that has become the hardest for enterprises to prove when seeking E nonimmigrant classification.

Case for Discussion 3.1

Sprzet, Inc. is a Polish owned hardware distributor in the United States that imports approximately 75 percent of its goods from Poland. Recently, the business has decided to start sourcing a number of its products from a new manufacturer in Vietnam and also start a global direct to consumer sales website. Currently, the President of the company is in the United States on an E-1 visa.

- What warnings would you give the President about the planned expansion and source of manufacturing?

A.2.c. Requirements for E-2 Treaty Investor

The E-2 treaty investor nonimmigrant visa classification is very versatile and can be used by businesses that range from small start-up enterprises to larger multinational corporations. The central focus of the E-2 visa classification is an *active, substantial* investment by a treaty investor.[15] The investment in the United States must not lead to the creation of a ***marginal enterprise***,[16] and must be overseen by the principal investor or an employee within an executive, supervisory, or essential role in the enterprise.[17]

In addition, investment for E-2 classification requires that the investor has irrevocably committed funds to the enterprise in the United States.[18] Some examples of irrevocably committed assets include:

- Loans secured by the Treaty Investor's personal assets,
- Assets in a bank account with evidence of an expense plan, and
- Equipment and property already purchased at the time of filing.[19]

Marginal Enterprise: An enterprise that does not have the present or future capacity to generate more than enough income to provide a minimal living for the treaty investor and his or her family.

---

[14] 8 C.F.R. § 214(e)(11).
[15] 8 C.F.R. § 214(e)(2)(i).
[16] 8 C.F.R. § 214(e)(15); 9 FAM 402.9-6(E).
[17] 9 FAM 402.9-6(A).
[18] 8 C.F.R. § 214(e)(12).
[19] 9 FAM 402.9-6(B)(e).

To ensure an active exchange of culture and commerce, and to constitute an active investment, the E-2 nonimmigrant visa applicant must have invested or be in the process of investing in an operating company that produces some good or service in the United States. The investment must remain in the control of the foreign national or entity of the treaty nation, for use in the ongoing operation of the business only.[20]

If the business is not yet operational, the applicant must demonstrate that there is a ***business plan*** in place with agreed contracts to carry out the investment. This requirement is far more critical for individual investors as opposed to corporate entities using the E-2 nonimmigrant visa as a means of expanding operations to the United States. This is because most corporate entities have a track record of success abroad that will provide assurances to a consular officer that such success and effort will be duplicated in the United States.

Business Plan: An outline set forth by an enterprise that explains its goals and strategy for reaching them.

Regardless of whether the enterprise in the United States is already operational or plans to be operational following issuance of the E-2 nonimmigrant visa, it is recommended that a business plan be included in the application package anyway. In addition, as the E visa can be issued in increments of up to five years, it is advisable that the business plan contain financial and hiring projections that match this maximum validity duration. Furthermore, to show the irrevocable investment of funds transferred to the United States, it is beneficial to also include receipts and bank statements demonstrating the expenditures of the enterprise.

A substantial investment does not require a minimum amount of financial capital, but it must be enough to establish the business to the point of being operational.[21] Therefore, investment of a magic dollar amount is not required to assure issuance of an E-2 visa. The purpose of the requirement is to ensure that the business is not speculative but is, or soon will be, a successful enterprise.[22] Two requirements must be met in order for an investment to be considered substantial:

- The investment must be *proportional* to the overall value of the business, or the cost of establishing such a business, and
- The investment must be an amount necessary to establish the type of business in question.[23]

The FAM suggests that the proportionality aspect of proving that an investment is substantial is best understood as a scale.[24] The smaller the amount of funds required to start the business, the higher the percentage of those funds must be placed at risk, i.e. committed to the enterprise. Correspondingly, an enterprise that requires a lot of money to begin operations necessitates a

---

[20] 8 C.F.R. § 214(e)(12).
[21] 8 C.F.R. § 214(e)(14).
[22] 9 FAM 402.9-6(D).
[23] 22 C.F.R. § 41.51(b)(9)(i).
[24] 9 FAM 402.9-6(D)(f).

lower percentage of committed funds. For example, an investment of $100,000 is substantial for a services based business, such as an accounting firm, where the typical expenses needed to commence operations might be limited to office equipment, marketing material, and specialized computer software. To be proportional, the investor should commit almost that entire amount to satisfy a consular officer's review. However, an investment of $20 million is substantial for a manufacturing business, such as a factory, where the initial expenses associated with commencing operations are much higher because specialized equipment is needed to create the goods that will be sold. To be proportional, the investor should commit a fraction of that amount, for example $5 million, to satisfy a consular officer.

As indicated earlier, in order for a foreign national to qualify for E-2 classification, the underlying investment must *not* be marginal. In short, the investment must create jobs for U.S. workers or provide a significant economic impact. An enterprise that outsources much of its production to local firms and thus indirectly creates jobs will likely be sufficient as long as the gross revenue generated by the business is related to absorbing such an expense. The projected future capacity should generally be met within five years of commencement of business operations.[25] The non-marginality requirement is another reason why a comprehensive business plan is recommended for all initial E-2 filings.

A.3. Using the E Visa for Principal Investors, Executive Employees, Supervisory Employees, and Essential Skills Employees

The E nonimmigrant visa classification can secure E-1 or E-2 status for the executive and supervisory or essential skills employees of a qualifying enterprise.[26] For treaty investors, the principal owner of the enterprise can also receive a corresponding designation in order to direct and develop the enterprise in the United States. The foreign national employee entering in E-1 or E-2 status does not have to possess previous work experience with the enterprise either in the United States or for a related entity abroad.[27] However, with respect to remuneration, the employee can be paid from a U.S. source or be paid by a related corporate entity abroad.

Additionally, the employee must intend to depart the United States when the employment in E-1 or E-2 classification no longer exists.[28] This intent to depart the United States is considered temporary nonimmigrant intent, even though the foreign national can hold E visa status for many years.

Unlike other working visa classifications, there is no specific regulatory definition that enumerates what is required for an employee to qualify for E visa

---

[25] 9 FAM 402.9-6(E).
[26] 8 C.F.R. § 214(e)(3).
[27] 9 FAM 402.9-7(C)(l).
[28] 8 C.F.R. § 214(e)(1)(ii) and 8 C.F.R. § 214(e)(2)(iii).

classification. With respect to essential skills employees, the FAM does provide some guidance by stating that the "employee must have special qualifications that make the service to be rendered essential to the efficient operation of the enterprise."[29] The FAM also provides criteria that a consular officer should consider when making a decision for an essential skills E nonimmigrant visa application. They are:

- The degree of proven expertise of the foreign national in the area of specialization,
- The uniqueness of the specific skills,
- The function of the job to which the foreign national is destined,
- The salary such special skills can command, and
- The general availability of U.S. workers to provide the service.[30]

When assembling an E visa application for a potential essential skills employee, it is important not only to address and provide evidence of the above factors, but also to demonstrate how the employment of the foreign national will be critical for the success of the enterprise in the United States.

● EXAMPLE

Rory, an Irish National, started a computer systems integration business in the United States. Based on this investment, Rory obtained E-2 nonimmigrant status. He has met a number of potential clients in the United States looking for help incorporating a very specific European systems integration software product into their existing operations. Although Rory searched for a few weeks, he could not find a U.S. worker who possessed this essential knowledge. However, he has a colleague, Ian, who is also an Irish national and is an expert in this exact type of work. Rory would be able to support Ian to obtain an E-2 essential skills visa to perform this work on behalf of his company.

The test for obtaining an executive or supervisory E visa is also not readily defined. Once again, the FAM lists a number of criteria that a consular officer should consider when determining if a foreign national will function in an executive or supervisory position in the United States.[31] For these employees, some of the factors the consular officer will consider include:

- The title of the position,
- Where the position fits within the firm's organizational structure,
- The duties of the position,
- The degree to which the applicant will have ultimate control and responsibility for the firm's overall operations or a major component thereof,
- The number and skill levels of the employees the applicant will supervise,
- The level of pay, and

---

[29] 9 FAM 402.9-7(C).
[30] 9 FAM 402.9-7(C)(f).
[31] 9 FAM 402.9-7(B).

- The applicant's history of holding qualifying executive or supervisory positions in the past.[32]

After establishing the above threshold requirements regarding either trade or investment, many consular sections and E Visa Units will allow enterprises to register their organization. Once registered, future E visa eligible employees of an enterprise in the United States need only show that they qualify for the classification as either executive, supervisory, or essential skills employees. Therefore, while an initial application for E nonimmigrant classification might take considerable time to be adjudicated based on the workload of a given E visa unit, if registration is available, subsequent applications are generally processed within a couple of weeks of submission because requisite information regarding requirements have already been established. This fact means that the E classification will be very beneficial for an enterprise that is large enough to use the E visa on a regular basis.

Case for Discussion 3.2

TigerTaleTechnologies, or TTT, manufactures a specialty foam for the automotive industry using organic materials. Currently, the business only exists in Japan and caters almost exclusively to the Japanese automotive industry. The only owner of TTT, Taiko, a Japanese national, wants to expand to the U.S. market and establish an enterprise that will first serve as a sales office. Later, Taiko hopes to manufacture the TTT foam in the United States. Taiko wants to invest around $50,000 for the initial operations of the office in the United States. Taiko wants his son Yuyai, also a Japanese national, to move to the United States to run the business. Yuyai does have a degree in agricultural engineering and is considered by most to be bright and trustworthy.

- Describe what the enterprise will need to prove in order to obtain an E-1 visa for Yuyai.
- Describe what the enterprise will need to prove in order to obtain an E-2 visa for Yuyai.
- What additional information would be helpful?

A.4. Compiling the E Nonimmigrant Visa Application

The E nonimmigrant visa process is truly unique, as most filings are submitted directly to the consular office or embassy in the foreign national's country of citizenship.

---

[32] *Id.*

In addition, many consular sections, especially those in Europe, have specific and individualized application procedures and requirements for each E visa submission. However, the following components are always required as part of an application:

- Form DS-160, Online Nonimmigrant Visa Application
- Form DS-156E, Nonimmigrant Treaty Trader/Investor Visa Application
- Form G-28, Notice of Entry of Appearance as Attorney or Accredited Representative
- Proof of a qualifying treaty between the United States and foreign country
- Proof that the owners of the enterprise share the nationality of the treaty country; a sample legal argument to address this is in Box 3.1
- Proof that the foreign national being transferred to the United States shares the nationality of the foreign treaty country
- Proof that the foreign national will be coming to the United States in a qualifying occupation and possesses the experience needed to fulfill that role
- Visa type-specific supporting material:
    - ☐ E-1
        - ☐ Business plan
        - ☐ Proof that that trade is substantial and ongoing
    - ☐ E-2
        - ☐ Business plan
        - ☐ Proof of investment
        - ☐ Proof investment has been placed at risk
        - ☐ Proof that the enterprise is real, active, and operating or near being real, active, and operating
        - ☐ Proof that the enterprise is not marginal

> **Box 3.1** **Sample Legal Argument: Owners of the Enterprise Share the Nationality of the Treaty**
>
> Spark Science, a corporation formed on June 27, 2014 pursuant to the Delaware General Corporation Law, more than meets the foreign ownership requirement necessary for E-2 classification. Specifically, Spark Science, which has approximately 48 shareholders, is 57% owned by French nationals, a group which includes Mr. Spark (the principal investor with 40.08%), as well as numerous other individual investors and two French venture capital firms. In accordance with 8 C.F.R § 214.2(e)(3)(ii), nationals of the treaty country (France) own more than the requisite 50% of the business entity. As evidence of such ownership by French nationals, please see the copies of the Certificate of Incorporation, Articles of Incorporation, shareholder chart, and corporate stock certificates appended at Exhibit E. In addition, as evidence of the French nationality of the relevant French shareholders, please reference the copies of the relevant investors' passport biographical pages, also appended at Exhibit F.

A.5. Duration of Stay

Similar to the B nonimmigrant visa for visitors or business, each entry into the United States is limited in duration. Although an E visa can be issued for up to five years, each admission is for up to two years. For larger enterprises, executive, supervisory, and essential skills employees generally receive visas for the full duration available. For the principal investors of a small enterprise, however, or the owner of a trade-based enterprise when seeking initial E classification, a consular officer might limit the duration of the visa to ensure that the business is successful and not merely idle.

Once in the United States, a foreign national may extend his or her E visa status by filing a petition on Form I-129, Petition for a Nonimmigrant Worker, with the USCIS. Filing this form allows a foreign national to change status from one category to another or extend a stay in a particular category, as discussed in Section D in Chapter 2, Nonimmigrant Visas for Brief Stays, Studies, and Cultural Exchange. This course of action is only recommended, however, if travel to the foreign national's home country in order to apply for a visa in a different category is not feasible or practical from a business perspective, since a full E nonimmigrant visa filing is required abroad in order to reenter the United States in this status. It is worth noting that even though Canadian nationals are visa exempt, they are also required to process E-2 visas through a consular section before coming to the United States in this category.

A.6. Spouses and Children

Spouses and children of E visa holders may obtain derivative E nonimmigrant visa classification.[33] There is no separate alphanumeric designation for qualified dependent family members; they are simply referred to as either E-1 or E-2 derivatives, depending on the classification of the principal family member. The duration of the E derivative visas will mirror that of the principal visa holder.

One of the key advantages of E classification is that spouses can be granted employment authorization. Once a spouse of an E visa holder enters the United States, s/he can file an application on Form I-765, Application for Employment Authorization. This process is similar to the one an F-1 or M-1 student will follow when seeking Optional Practical Training status.[34] Once employment authorization is granted, the spouse of the E visa holder is allowed to work for any employer in the United States without restriction, so long as the principal's underlying E status remains valid.

The chart in Table 3.1 at the end of this chapter may help to summarize the most important features of the L nonimmigrant status classification.

---

[33] 8 C.F.R. § 214.2(e)(4).
[34] *See* Section E.3.d in Chapter 2, Nonimmigrant Visas for Brief Stays, Studies, and Cultural Exchange.

B. Visas for Intracompany Transferees of Multinational Corporations, Managers and Executives (L-1A) and Specialized Knowledge (L-1B): INA § 101(a)(15)(L); 8 C.F.R. § 214.2(l); 9 FAM 402.12

Companies often need to transfer employees from one related overseas entity to another in the United States. Allowing for foreign corporate investment and know-how can lead to job creation within the company itself, as well as for secondary markets that benefit from the growth of the high-skill population. The L visa is one that facilitates the transfer of employees working for international companies.

B.1. Sources of Law

Using the L visa, a multinational company may temporarily transfer foreign employees to a qualifying organization in the United States for the purpose of improving management effectiveness, expanding U.S. exports, and enhancing competitiveness in markets abroad.[35] Found at INA § 101(a)(15)(L), the visa offers temporary nonimmigrant status to managers and executives, or L-1A classification, and workers with specialized knowledge, or L-1B.

Unlike the E visa where most foreign nationals enter the United States through consular processing, the L visa follows a more traditional nonimmigrant benefit route. A petition is filed in the United States and, once approved, the foreign national can apply for the visa at a consular office abroad. Canadian nationals are allowed to apply directly for L classification at a *Class A Port of Entry*.

If a multinational company is large enough and needs to transfer workers regularly, it can petition the USCIS for a Blanket L status.[36] This helps to expedite the flow of workers between the qualifying organizations because the entity can process transfers directly through consular processing as opposed to first filing a petition in the United States at a designated service center.[37] The various steps taken by a foreign national seeking to enter the United States in L nonimmigrant classification, as depicted in Figure 3.2, are as follows:

- Step 1: A **subsidiary** of a U.K. company located in Chicago, Illinois files a petition for L-1 nonimmigrant visa classification on behalf of a designated beneficiary with the USCIS California Service Center.
- Step 2: The USCIS approves the petition and returns it to the U.S. subsidiary.
- Step 3: The company sends the approval notice to the foreign national in the U.K.

Class A Port of Entry: A location where all travelers, including foreign nationals, permanent residents, and United States Citizens, can apply for entry to the United States.

---

[35] 9 FAM 402.12-2(c).
[36] 8 C.F.R. § 214.2(l)(2)(ii). *See* Section B.5 for further discussion.
[37] 8 C.F.R. § 214.2(l)(4)-(5).

Figure 3.2
L-Visa Acquisition Map

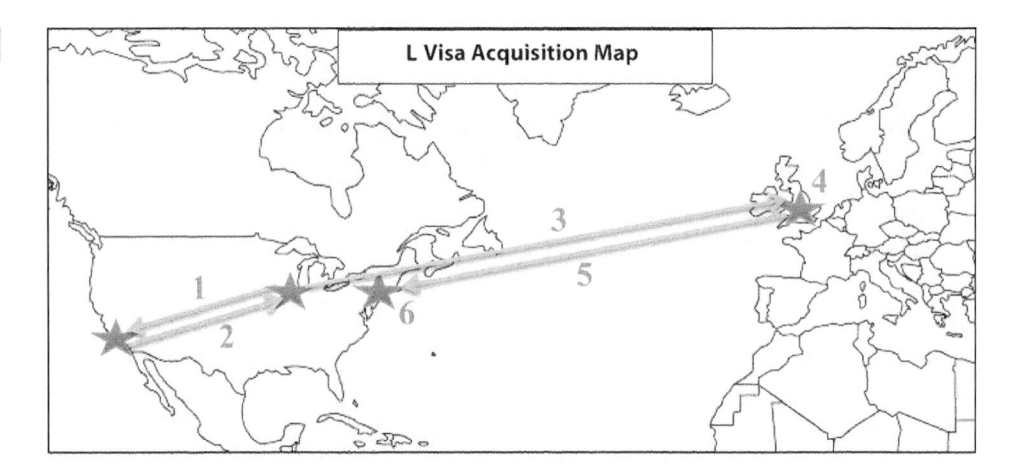

- Step 4: The beneficiary of the petition applies for an L visa through the embassy or consular office abroad. In this case, the application is made through the U.S. Embassy in London.
- Step 5: With an L visa issued by the embassy, the foreign national travels to the United States.
- Step 6: CBP admits the foreign national at the airport in New York, New York and s/he begins working as an executive, managerial, or specialized knowledge employee.

B.2. Specific Requirements

The requirements for the L classification can be split into two: the requirements for *qualifying organizations* and for *qualifying employment* in the United States.

B.2.a. Qualifying Organization

In order for an intracompany transferee to obtain an L visa, the transferee must be employed by a qualifying organization abroad,[38] or, in the case of an application to extend status, must have been employed by a qualifying organization abroad before being lawfully admitted to the United States. A qualifying organization is one that meets the following requirements:

- The organization must be a multinational company maintaining both a foreign and domestic presence,
- The U.S. and foreign entities must share a qualifying corporate relationship, and
- The multinational company must be doing business in the United States in the present or near future.[39]

---

[38] 8 C.F.R. § 214.2(l)(ii)(A).
[39] 8 C.F.R. 214.2(l)(1)(ii)(G).

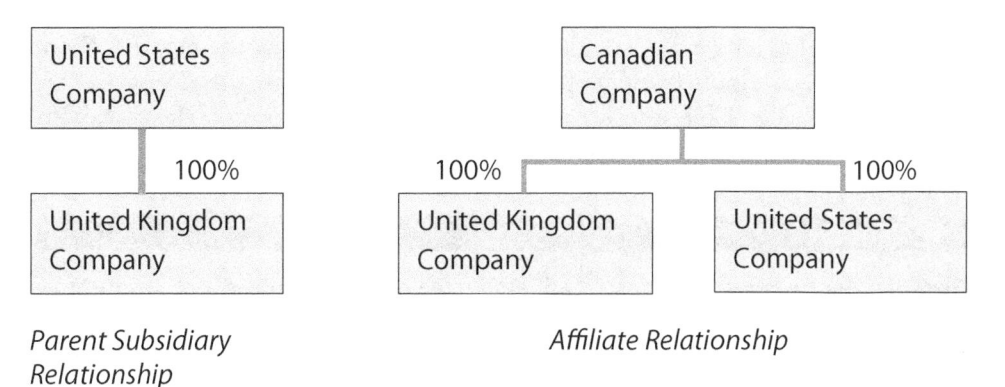

Figure 3.3

Qualifying Corporate Relationships for L-Visa Purposes

```
United States                    Canadian
Company                          Company
   |                                |
  100%                    100% ----------- 100%
   |                       |                |
United Kingdom         United Kingdom   United States
Company                Company          Company

Parent Subsidiary           Affiliate Relationship
Relationship
```

There are no company size requirements for individual L petitions, therefore allowing recently formed businesses to take advantage of the classification. However, they are subject to greater scrutiny by the USCIS because they do not have a proven track record of viability. The differential in regulatory and evidentiary requirements for L petitions filed for newly formed businesses, or "New Office L," as opposed to established businesses is discussed in detail in Section B.4.

The U.S. entity that is serving as the petitioner must "meet exactly one of the qualifying relationships specified in the definitions of parent, branch, **affiliate**, or subsidiary."[40] The FAM provides a detailed definition of each type of entity,[41] as do the regulations.[42] A **parent-subsidiary relationship** involves an entity that is directly and majority-owned by another entity. Two entities are affiliates if they are both ultimately majority-owned and controlled by the same parent entity or group of individual owners. The affiliates may have a common corporate owner or common shareholders owning at least 50 percent of the affiliates in roughly proportionate shares. Any office or operating division not established as a separate business entity is considered a **branch**. The examples in Figure 3.3 may help to illustrate this.

Under the parent subsidiary relationship, the United Kingdom company is a subsidiary of the United States company because the United States company owns 100 percent of the United Kingdom company. Under the affiliated relationship, the United Kingdom company is an affiliate of the United States company because the Canadian company owns 100 percent of both entities.

The key factor for establishing the qualifying relationship for L visa purposes is *control*. Ownership without control is insufficient to establish the qualifying relationship. In addition, an entity can still qualify as being eligible for L visa classification if there is common control between the transferring entity abroad

Control: The right and authority to direct the management and operations of a business entity.

---

[40] *Id.*
[41] 9 FAM 402.12-9(A).
[42] 8 C.F.R. § 214.2(l)(1)(ii).

and the receiving entity in the United States, notwithstanding the fact that there might not be common ownership. The L visa differs from the E visa in this important respect. While the L classification focuses on control, the E classification focuses solely on ownership.

> ● **EXAMPLE**
>
> **GlassCup Inc. wishes to transfer an employee from its subsidiary in Uruguay (GlassCup UR) to the United States. GlassCup UR is 51 percent owned by Rodrigo and 49 percent owned by GlassCup Inc. GlassCup Inc. has 49 Class A shares with two-for-one voting rights of GlassCup UR and Rodrigo has 51 Class B shares with one-for-one voting rights. Because ClassCup Inc. has majority control through its voting power, the two entities are qualified for L visa classification.**

The best way to demonstrate that there is common ownership and/or control is by presenting the USCIS with share certificates issued by corporations, operating agreements entered into by limited liability companies, or LLCs, and audited financial statements and/or corporate tax returns, which often have separate schedules detailing ownership percentages.

Finally, the qualifying organization must be one that is or will be doing business as an employer in the United States and in at least one other country directly, or through a parent, branch, affiliate, or subsidiary. International trade is not required. Doing business means the regular, systematic, and continuous provision of goods and/or services by a qualifying organization.[43] The mere presence of an agent or office of the qualifying organization in the United States and abroad is not sufficient and will not constitute doing business. Again, tax returns are often sufficient evidence to prove that a business is operating here. In addition, including printouts from the company's website is always encouraged. For smaller operations or companies which have experienced significant growth since the most recent tax return was submitted, it is generally advisable to include bank statements, service contracts, invoices, payroll records, or other similar evidence as well.

B.2.b. Qualifying Employment

The second major component of a successful L classification is proving that the foreign national will engage in a qualifying role in the United States and possesses qualifying experience gained abroad.

Employment Abroad

The intracompany transferee must have been employed abroad continuously by the foreign qualifying organization for one year within the last three in a qualifying position.[44] If the proposed transferee spent any time in the United

---

[43] 8 C.F.R. § 214.2(l)(1)(ii)(H).
[44] 8 C.F.R. § 214.2(l)(1)(ii)(A).

States during that year, those visits are not counted towards fulfillment of the one-year requirement.[45] However, the time spent in the United States, whether on business or pleasure, does not interrupt the year of continuous employment. The qualifying position can either be managerial, executive, or one involving specialized knowledge.[46] All of these qualifying positions have specific definitions and requirements and are discussed in detail later.

● EXAMPLE

Sharifa has been employed abroad for an international financial services provider for the last thirteen months. The company now wishes to transfer Sharifa to the United States in a managerial position. However, over the course of Sharifa's employment with the company abroad, she has spent a total of eight weeks in the United States in B-1 visa classification to attend meetings and conferences. Therefore, Sharifa will not be immediately eligible for an L visa transfer. She must wait until she has served at least twelve months of working for the company outside of the United States before she can file. In other words, she must wait an additional one month to qualify.

The foreign national is not required to have held the same type of position abroad as s/he is intending to hold in the United States.[47] However, it must be a logical transfer. For example, most companies will not transfer someone who holds a specialized knowledge position abroad into an executive position in the United States because it is rare that a "worker" will become an "officer" through a foreign assignment.

Qualifying Positions for L-1A Classification in the United States

In order to qualify for L-1A nonimmigrant visa status, the intracompany transferee must be coming to the United States to work in an executive or **managerial capacity**.[48] In order to be considered a manager, the foreign national employee must actively manage a division of the company and its personnel.[49] A first-line supervisor of a multinational company will not qualify if the transferee's primary duty is the provision of services or production of a product. Rather, the manager should supervise and control the work of other professional employees or lower-level managers,[50] ideally all of whom hold positions that require a bachelor's degree level education or higher.

The actual regulatory language associated with an L-1A manager is very insightful and provides far greater guidance compared to what is given for a supervisory employee for E visa classification purposes. 8 C.F.R. § 214.2(l)(1)(ii)(B) creates a four-part test, which states:

---

[45] *Id.*
[46] *Id.*
[47] *See Matter of Vaillancourt*, 13 I&N Dec. 654 (RC 1970).
[48] 8 C.F.R. § 214.2(l)(1)(ii)(A).
[49] 8 C.F.R. § 214.2(l)(1)(ii)(B)(1).
[50] 8 C.F.R. § 214.2(l)(1)(ii)(B)(2).

Managerial capacity means an assignment within an organization in which the employee primarily:

- Manages the organization, or a department, subdivision, function, or component of the organization;
- Supervises and controls the work of other supervisory, professional, or managerial employees, or manages an essential function within the organization, or a department or subdivision of the organization;
- Has the authority to hire and fire or recommend those as well as other personnel actions (such as promotion and leave authorization) if another employee or other employees are directly supervised; if no other employee is directly supervised, functions at a senior level within the organizational hierarchy or with respect to the function managed; and
- Exercises discretion over the day-to-day operations of the activity or function for which the employee has authority. A first-line supervisor is not considered to be acting in a managerial capacity merely by virtue of the supervisor's supervisory duties unless the employees supervised are professional.

The use of the word "and" in the legal standard for managerial employees in L classification is important because it links the four parts or requirements together. This is a conjunctive test, requiring all four parts to be fulfilled in order to meet the definition of a manager. Some tests within the immigration regulations use the word "or" to link the requirements together. Known as a disjunctive test, it requires that only one part of the test be satisfied in order to meet the definition. Use of either "or" or "and" makes a tremendous difference in the level of proof that needs to be demonstrated and therefore the way a case will be presented.

A good example of an L-1A manager is an Engineering Manager who has multiple engineers reporting to him or her and functions with a high degree of discretionary decision-making authority. However, not all cases are this simple and straightforward. Often, there are employees that serve as project managers and therefore carry lots of authority for particular large scale assignments, but will not carry a title that is always associated with management, such as Senior Engineer. It is important to look beyond the title of a position when determining if it is sufficiently managerial to meet the criteria for L-1A classification. What is important to consider are the duties, skills, and responsibilities associated with the position.

To support an L-1A nonimmigrant visa filing for an intracompany manager, it has become almost an unwritten mandatory requirement that the petitioner include personnel organizational charts of both the business abroad and the one in the United States so that the adjudicating officer can see how the foreign national functions within the organization. In addition, to prove that an individual was a manager in the past (if that is the qualifying employment) performance evaluations conducted by the intracompany transferee for subordinate employees will serve as strong evidence that the person exercised managerial control. It is also wise to include such evidence when filing for an extension of L-1A classification from within the United States.

A close reading of the regulation defining a manager also shows that the L-1A manager does not have to manage people, *per se*, in order to obtain

L-1A classification because the nonimmigrant visa is also available for foreign nationals who are *functional managers*.[51] As an example, a Comptroller, as manager of the key finance functions of a company, is often deemed eligible for L-1A classification.

Functional Managers: Those in charge of a key function or division in an organization, but do not have any subordinates reporting to them.

The other category of employee that is eligible for L-1A nonimmigrant classification is the executive. One easy way to think of an executive is to view these employees as one or more steps above the manger in the corporate hierarchy. Executives are managers of managers and policy setters. 8 C.F.R. § 214.2(l)(1)(ii)(C) sets out the legal standard for an executive in a conjunctive four-part test.

Executive capacity means an assignment within an organization in which the employee primarily:

- Directs the management of the organization or a major component or function of the organization,
- Establishes the goals and policies of the organization, component, or function,
- Exercises wide latitude in discretionary decision-making, and
- Receives only general supervision or direction from higher level executives, the board of directors, or stockholders of the organization.

Again, it is important to remember that an executive's title is not determinative, and the executive should in fact command a position with a high level of authority within the multinational company. Organizational charts are great evidence for this type of L-1A filing. In addition, if there are corporate governance documents, such as an operating agreement, an annual report, or contracts that list the executive's name and title, this is another good source of evidence for demonstrating to the USCIS that a foreign national is in fact an executive employee.

Case for Discussion 3.3

Limone, LLC is the U.S. subsidiary of a large lemon producer in Lebanon. Its business in the United States has been failing lately and the company wants to transfer Amir there to help correct the financial issue. Amir has worked for the parent company for the past five years as a Supply Chain Engineer. Once he arrives in the United States, Amir will be promoted to the position of Supply Chain Manager.

- Can Amir get an L-1A nonimmigrant visa for this purpose?
- If so, what additional information would be needed in order to proceed?

---

[51] 8 C.F.R. §§ 214.2(l)(1)(ii)(B)(2) and (3).

Qualifying Positions L-1B classification in the United States

For L-1B nonimmigrant status, the transferee must be engaged in work requiring ***specialized knowledge***. While specialized knowledge carries a plain meaning that immediately resonates, the term carries a special definition for immigration purposes.[52]

The L-1B intracompany transferee must have knowledge that surpasses the usual knowledge of an employee in the same field gained through "significant prior experience" with the company.[53] Theoretically, the specialized knowledge professional may be employed at any level in the company, so long as his or her specialized knowledge is not readily available in the United States. However, in practice, the USCIS does tend to look more favorably on L-1B petitions submitted on behalf of higher ranking employees within the organization.

Some examples of positions that qualify as specialized knowledge range from machine operators and technicians to engineers who possess patents assigned to the company that employs them. The key here is that, not only is the knowledge noteworthy and uncommon, but that it is so within the company as well. The L-1B standard for specialized knowledge is not as well-defined as the L-1A four-part tests for managers and executives and therefore is often a harder standard to prove. While not controlling, it is often easiest to think of the specialized knowledge standard as having to prove that the knowledge possessed by the employee is proprietary or exclusive to the company.

Specialized Knowledge: Special knowledge of a company's products, services, equipment, techniques, management, or other interests and its application in international markets, or an advanced level of knowledge or expertise in the organization's processes and procedures.

● **EXAMPLE**

Silvio is a lauded chemist working for a company in Brazil, having joined them about two years ago. The Brazilian company has an affiliate entity in the United States. Silvio was hired because he has a Ph.D in chemistry. Christino has been working for the same company as a chemist for five years and was part of the team that created some of the company's most successful products. Christino only has a bachelor's degree. Christino is the better L-1B nonimmigrant visa candidate because his knowledge can be tied directly to the company and its products whereas Silvio's knowledge is based on his understanding of the field of chemistry in general.

Over the past decade, the L-1B visa has become one of the most heavily scrutinized classifications because of a shortage of H-1B visas and concerns over fraudulent use. In fact, accordingly to a 2014 USCIS Ombudsman report, over a third of all L-1B filings are denied and over 50 percent of all filings receive Requests for Evidence, or RFEs.[54] Therefore, it is important to document how the foreign national obtained the key knowledge that is the basis of the L-1B transfer (whether it was through extensive training or extensive experience) and be able to demonstrate how the employee, in performing his or her job abroad or

---

[52] 8 C.F.R. § 214.2(l)(1)(ii)(D).
[53] 9 FAM 402.12-14(C)(b).
[54] *See* http://www.dhs.gov/sites/default/files/publications/cisomb-annual-report-2014-508compliant.pdf, and Section E.9 in Chapter 1, Historical Background and Introduction to the U.S. Immigration System.

in the United States, has used such knowledge. The evidence can include assigned patents, detailed presentations, schematic drawings of key technology, and training material authored by the foreign national. In 2015, through a policy memorandum,[55] the L-1B standard was relaxed to a certain extent, yet given the length and depth of this memorandum, specialized knowledge remains one of the most challenging legal thresholds in immigration law.

> **Case for Discussion 3.4**
>
> StoneBook, Inc. is the U.S. parent company to StoneBook, GmbH in Germany. StoneBook, Inc. owns 100 percent of StoneBook, GmbH, which currently employs Sasha in the position of Account Manager. In this position, she is responsible for managing some of the company's key European accounts. She often gives presentations regarding its proprietary technology to clients and at industry trade shows. In addition, Sasha recently wrote an article in an industry trade publication regarding StoneBook, GmbH's latest product line. Sasha supervises the work of three Junior Account Managers and is responsible for directing personnel activities for her subordinates including hire, fire, promotion, and demotion. StoneBook, Inc. now wishes to employ Sasha in a similar position in the United States.
>
> - Is Sasha eligible for L classification?
> - If so, which version of the L visa would be easier to obtain for Sasha and why?

B.3. Duration of Stay for L Visa Holders

Intracompany transferees applying for an L visa through consular processing are not subject to the presumption that they intend to immigrate to the United States, and therefore are not required to prove intent to return to their home country as part of the visa application process. Instead, this classification allows for what is known as ***dual intent.*** This is very important for those wishing to ultimately remain in the United States permanently as it allows the foreign national to pursue lawful permanent resident status without jeopardizing his or her underlying nonimmigrant classification. Most nonimmigrant classifications do not allow for dual intent.

Dual Intent. The simultaneous intent to remain either temporarily or permanently in the United States.

---

[55] *See* L-1B Adjudications Policy Memorandum, dated August 17, 2015 and accessed here: https://www.uscis.gov/sites/default/files/USCIS/Laws/Memoranda/2015/L-1B_Memorandum_8_14_15_draft_for_FINAL_4pmAPPROVED.pdf.

The initial admission period for an intracompany transferee in L-1 status is up to three years for both L-1A and L-1B classification.[56] Transferees in a managerial or executive position, or L-1A, may qualify for a two-year extension twice, for a total of seven years.[57] Specialized knowledge, or L-1B, transferees may only qualify for a single two-year extension, for a total of five years.[58]

Time spent outside of the United States is not included as time spent in a visa classification. Therefore, it can be recaptured and added back into the maximum period of time for both the L-1A and L-1B classifications.

● **EXAMPLE**

Ivan has held L-1A classification for six years. However, during his time in this classification, Ivan has travelled home to Russia every year for a month during the summer. Therefore, Ivan has eighteen months of possible L-1A time left in the United States because he is able to recapture the time he spent in Russia and complete the seven years in total allowed for those in L-1A status.

It is possible for a specialized knowledge employee who has been promoted to a managerial or executive position to convert from L-1B classification to L-1A classification while in the United States. The conversion requires that the USCIS approve a request to change positions and that the foreign national be in this new position for at least six months prior to when s/he would otherwise have reached the five-year maximum period of stay in L-1B classification.[59] This will then permit the foreign national to receive an additional two years of stay in the United States for a total of seven years, which is the maximum period of stay under the L-1A classification.

After the L visa transferee's maximum period of stay has elapsed, s/he must depart the United States and remain abroad for a full year before applying for re-entry under the L classification.[60] The U.S. entity must then file a new petition on behalf of the foreign national, who can still travel to the United States as a visitor during that year. However, any time spent in the United States will not count towards fulfilling the one-year abroad requirement.

It is also important to note that if the foreign national spends less than half of the year in the United States while in L nonimmigrant visa status, the use of the classification is deemed intermittent and therefore not subject to the duration limitations associated with this classification.[61] Theoretically, this will allow for the foreign national to hold L classification indefinitely.

---

[56] 8 C.F.R. § 214.2(l)(11).
[57] 8 C.F.R. § 214.2(l)(15)(ii).
[58] *Id.*
[59] 8 C.F.R. § 214.2(l)(15)(ii).
[60] 8 C.F.R. § 214.2(l)(12)(i).
[61] 8 C.F.R. § 214.2(l)(12)(ii).

B.4. New Office L Classification

The U.S. entity of a multinational company that has been doing business for less than one year is considered a **new office**.[62] The USCIS, through regulation, is more wary of new businesses than established enterprises in the United States and therefore requires additional evidence to be submitted to support an L visa filing of this nature. In addition, because the USCIS is concerned about the organization becoming real, active, and operating in the United States, New Office L visas are only issued for one year,[63] allowing the opportunity to review the actual activities of the company and ensure that it is actually doing business.

The primary requirement, in addition to proving qualifying employment abroad, is to show that the business is set up to become fully operational quickly. The petitioning entity must submit evidence that sufficient physical premises have been secured to house the new office. In addition, a strong business plan indicating how the business will be grown, both in terms of revenue and staff is critical to success and a key component to the New Office L visa petition.[64] Once the business is launched and successful, the foreign national can obtain an extension of the L nonimmigrant classification for two years to make up the initial three year period, and thereafter in two year increments.[65]

B.5. Blanket L Status

Larger multinational companies who would like to expedite the transfer of their managers, executives, or specialized knowledge employees may petition the USCIS for Blanket L classification.[66] Once approved, such status allows for transferees to apply via consular processing for L classification rather than first having to petition the USCIS in the United States, thus saving time.

In order to obtain approval of a Blanket L petition, the U.S. entity must demonstrate that:

- All of the business's L-qualifying organizations are engaged in commercial trade or services;
- The U.S. entity has been doing business for one year or more; and
- The petitioner has three or more domestic and foreign entities and one of the following:
    - ☐ The petitioner and other qualifying organizations have obtained approval for at least ten "L" petitions during the previous 12 months;
    - ☐ The company has U.S. subsidiaries or affiliates with combined annual sales of at least $25 million; *or*
    - ☐ The company has a U.S. work force of at least 1,000 employees.[67]

---

[62] 8 C.F.R. § 214.2(l)(1)(ii)(F).
[63] 8 C.F.R. § 214.2(l)(7)(i)(A)(3).
[64] 8 C.F.R. § 214.2(l)(3)(v).
[65] 8 C.F.R. § 214.2(l)(14)(ii).
[66] 8 C.F.R. § 214.2(l)(2)(ii).
[67] 8 C.F.R. § 214.2(l)(4).

If the Blanket L petition is approved, all transferees from organizations included within the blanket petition only need to show that they are employed in a qualifying position abroad and will be employed in a qualifying capacity in the United States when going through consular processing. In addition, those seeking Blanket L-1B classification must also possess a bachelor degree level education or equivalent work experience or higher. Therefore, obtaining Blanket L status, where feasible, is advantageous because it expedites the intracompany transferee process and makes it more cost effective.

● EXAMPLE

A large auto manufacturer headquartered in Japan has manufacturing and distribution facilities located throughout the world, including the United States. The company often needs to mobilize its global workforce for emergent technology troubleshooting, such as a recall. Rather than being subject to the longer processing times and costs associated with the regular L nonimmigrant visa petition process, the auto manufacturer obtains Blanket L status to hasten entry to the United States.

B.6. Compiling the L Nonimmigrant Visa Application

As with many other nonimmigrant employment-based classifications, the L visa classification requires a company to submit a petition on Form I-129, Petition for a Nonimmigrant Worker, to the USCIS unless Blanket L status is available. All Form I-129 petitions must also include Form I-129 Supplement L, which will allow the petitioning entity to provide information specific to the L visa request. These petitions are eligible for the USCIS' **premium processing service**, which, for an additional fee, guarantees initial adjudication of the petition in 15 calendar days. Regular processing times vary due to demand and the USCIS resources, but often run in excess of three months. Therefore, the premium processing option can be very helpful for entities looking to quickly effectuate the L classification transfer.

A complete petition for L visa classification should include:

- Form I-129, Petition for a Nonimmigrant Worker
- L Classification Supplement to Form I-129
- Form G-28, Notice of Entry of Appearance as Attorney or Accredited Representative
- Proof of qualifying corporate relationship
- Proof that the foreign national will be coming to the United States in a qualifying occupation and possesses the experience needed to fulfill that role
- Visa Type Specific Supporting Material:
    - ☐ L-1A
        - ☐ Proof of qualifying employment abroad

- [ ] Proof of the position in the United States being managerial or executive in nature; a sample legal argument is in Box 3.2
- [ ] L-1B
  - [ ] Proof of qualifying employment abroad
  - [ ] Proof of specialized knowledge being required for the position in the United States

> **Box 3.2** **Sample Legal Argument: In Support of Qualifying Managerial Position in the United States**
>
> Mr. Nespia has responsibility for improving the customer experience for our shoppers across all points of contact, including our website, product delivery, our products themselves, and advertisements for our products in the position of Vice President of User Experience (VP-UX). The VP-UX position will require coordination of multiple business units and a holistic approach to our business's brand definition and our interactions with our customers. This role requires a dedicated leader who embraces challenges, learns from criticism, and exhibits persistence and focus when overcoming obstacles. Mr. Nespia has demonstrated all of these traits during his time with our subsidiary abroad and, as a result, was a natural choice to assume the important managerial role of VP-UX.
>
> In his role as VP-UX, Mr. Nespia will report directly to our CEO and will continue to maintain responsibility for his current team of subordinates abroad. In addition to maintaining his current responsibilities, he will also be responsible for managing six additional professionals in the United States. Critically, each of these positions is professional in nature and requires at least a baccalaureate degree in the relevant field.
>
> Mr. Nespia will possess significant authority over day-to-day human resource actions for his team, including the ability to make recommendations pertaining to hiring, firing, promotion, discipline, and adjustments to benefits and compensation. Further, Mr. Nespia will continue to be responsible for providing performance reviews for subordinate employees and will have significant influence over decisions regarding their assignment for future projects.
>
> As the above duties indicate, Mr. Nespia will serve in an unequivocally managerial capacity as Vice President of User Experience. His managerial expertise, technical proficiency, and deep understanding of online usability principles are invaluable to our ongoing objectives in the United States. Therefore, based on the continued job duties outlined above, Mr. Nespia will clearly occupy a managerial position as defined under 8 C.F.R. § 214.2 (l)(1)(ii)(B).

B.7. Spouses and Children

Spouses and unmarried minor children of L visa holders may obtain derivative L-2 visa classification.[68] Similar to the E visa classification, spouses of L-1A and L-1B visa holders are eligible to receive employment authorization. Once the L-2 spouse enters the United States, s/he can file an application on Form I-765, Application for Employment Authorization. Once granted, the L-2 visa holder can work for any employer in the United States without restriction, so long as the spouse's corresponding stay in L-1A or L-1B remains valid. Similar to the E visa classifications, an L visa derivative's length of stay in the United States will mirror that of the principal.

The chart in Table 3.1 at the end of this chapter may help to summarize the most important features of the L nonimmigrant visa classification.

C. Professional Specialty Occupations (H-1B) and Specialty Workers from Singapore and Chile (H-1B1): INA § 101(a)(15)(H); 8 C.F.R. § 214.2(h); 20 C.F.R. § 655; 9 FAM 402.10-4; INA § 101(a)(15)(H)(i)(b1); 9 FAM 402.10-5

C.1. H-1B: Introduction and Sources of Law

The H-1B visa plays an important part in the United States economy because it allows companies to hire professional foreign workers on a temporary basis. The statutory provision authorizing H-1B nonimmigrant visas is at INA § 101(a)(15)(H), with the corresponding regulations at 8 C.F.R. § 214.2(h). The role that the Department of Labor, or DOL, plays in the process is outlined at 20 C.F.R. § 655. Further guidance can also be obtained from the FAM at 9 FAM 402.10-4. However, unlike the E and L visa classifications, the FAM is not as helpful because of the DOL's role in regulating the H-1B process.

The basic premise of the H-1B visa (and most of the professional specialty occupation visas) is that the position in the United States must require at least a baccalaureate-level education in a specific field and the foreign national must possesses a degree in a related field of endeavor or an equivalent amount of experience.[69] Simplified, the foreign national's education must match what the employer deems is required for the position.

In today's workforce, the H-1B classification has become an important tool in the technology industry and expansion of the program to meet the needs in this area has gained support from some of the country's most renowned business leaders. While the H-1B visa has widespread application, it is often used to

---

[68] 8 C.F.R. § 214.2(l)(7)(ii).
[69] 8 C.F.R. § 214.2(h)(4)(ii).

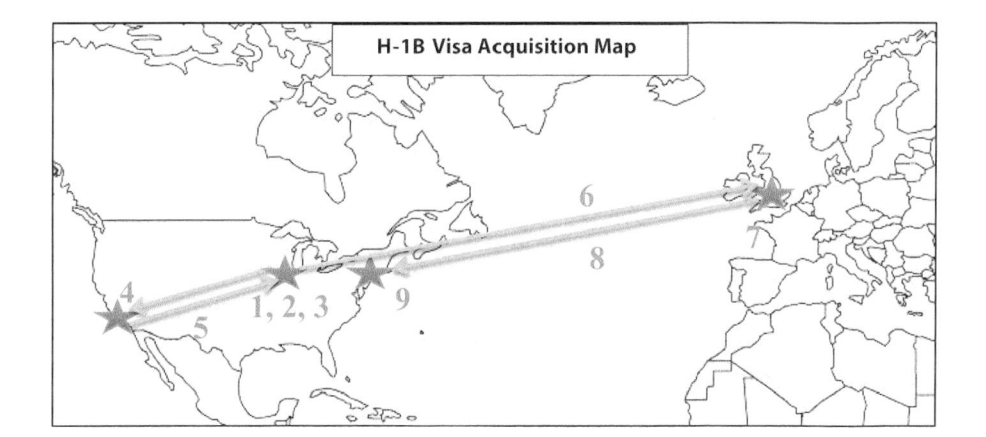

Figure 3.4

H-1B Acquisition Map

facilitate the transition of a foreign national in F-1 Optional Practical Training[70] student status to the U.S. workforce on a longer term basis.

The H-1B classification, similar to the L category, is considered a dual-intent visa, where the recipient does not need to show that s/he will return to the home country after the visa expires. It is one of the most expensive nonimmigrant visas to obtain because of the fees associated with the application. In addition to the base petition filing fee, H-1B petitioners are also required to pay a special fraud fee, as well as a fee that goes towards the training of U.S. workers called the American Competitiveness and Workforce Improvement Act, or ACWIA, fee. Unlike other visa classifications, the employer must pay all fees, including both legal and government fees, for the H-1B, as well as any visa that requires a **Labor Condition Application**, or **LCA**. It is also one of the most limited nonimmigrant visas in terms of availability because it is subject to annual quota limitations.

Furthermore, the H-1B classification is subject to increased government oversight and regulation compared to other nonimmigrant visa classifications because of the role the DOL plays in overseeing certain aspects of H-1B attainment and compliance. Notwithstanding these factors, in recent years the H-1B classification has been consistently oversubscribed and remains one of the most prominent nonimmigrant visas available. The various steps taken by a foreign national seeking to enter the United States in an H-1B nonimmigrant classification, as depicted in Figure 3.4, are as follows:

- Step 1: A company located in Chicago posts a notice informing workers of the future H-1B filing in two locations where the employment will occur for a foreign national based in the United Kingdom.
- Step 2: The Company files an LCA on Form ETA 9035 with the DOL, most often electronically via the **iCert** Portal.
- Step 3: The DOL certifies the LCA.

---

[70] *See* Section E.3.d of Chapter 2, Nonimmigrant Visas for Brief Stays, Studies, and Cultural Exchange.

- Step 4: The H-1B petition with the certified LCA is submitted to the USCIS Service Center. In this case, because the company is located in Chicago, the proper USCIS Service Center is the California Service Center.
- Step 5: The USCIS approves the petition and returns it to the Company.
- Step 6: The Company sends the approval notice to the foreign national in the United Kingdom.
- Step 7: The foreign national applies for the H-1B visa through the U.S. embassy in London.
- Step 8: With H-1B visa issued by the embassy, the foreign national travels to the United States.
- Step 9: CBP admits the foreign national at the airport in New York, New York, and s/he commences working for the company in the professional specialty occupation.

C.2. H-1B Requirements

Generally, for issuance of an H-1B nonimmigrant classification to a petitioning enterprise wishing to hire a foreign national, the petitioner must show that:

- The employer is a real, active, and operating entity;
- The occupation is a *specialty occupation*, requiring at least a baccalaureate level education or higher;
- The proposed employee is qualified for the specialty occupation; and
- The wage paid to the employee is 100 percent of the *prevailing wage rate* or the *actual wage*, whichever is higher.[71]

C.2.a. Qualifying Employer for H-1B Classification Purposes

The petitioner must be a U.S. person or entity,[72] which includes a corporation organized under the laws of the United States. The relationship between the foreign national and the sponsor must be characterized as an employee/employer relationship. This is a critical component for the H-1B petition as it precludes business owners from sponsoring themselves for H-1B status. If someone owns a business, then s/he, in most instances, cannot be considered an employee. This aspect of the qualifying employer rule effectively excludes independent contractors from obtaining H-1B classification. The final requirement for an employer is that s/he must maintain an **Employer Identification Number** (EIN), which is issued by the Internal Revenue Service, or IRS.

Specialty Occupation: A position that requires theoretical and practical application of a body of highly specialized knowledge in fields of human endeavor, and that requires the attainment of a bachelor's degree or higher in a specific specialty, or its equivalent, as a minimum for entry into the occupation in the United States.

Prevailing Wage Rate: The wage that is considered average for a given occupation in the area of intended employment, obtained either through requesting a determination from the Department of Labor, known as a Prevailing Wage Determination, or PWD, or from other legitimate sources.

Actual Wage: The wage paid to similarly qualified U.S. workers for similar work.

---

[71] 8 C.F.R. § 214.2(h) and 20 C.F.R. § 655.
[72] 8 C.F.R. § 214.2(h)(4)(ii).

C.2.b. Qualifying Position

A specialty occupation requires the theoretical or practical application of a body of highly specialized knowledge.[73] Generally, the minimum requirement for such a specialty occupation is a bachelor's degree or its equivalent. 8 C.F.R. § 214.2(h)(4)(iii)(A) sets forth the disjunctive test for proving that a position is a specialty occupation as follows:

> To qualify as a specialty occupation, the position must meet one of the following criteria:
>
> - A baccalaureate or higher degree or its equivalent is normally the minimum requirement for entry into the particular position;
> - The degree requirement is common to the industry in parallel positions among similar organizations or, in the alternative, an employer may show that its particular position is so complex or unique that it can be performed only by an individual with a degree;
> - The employer normally requires a degree or its equivalent for the position; or
> - The nature of the specific duties are so specialized and complex that knowledge required to perform the duties is usually associated with the attainment of a baccalaureate or higher degree.

While it is advisable to submit proof of all factors if such evidence is available, especially if the nature of the position is questioned by the USCIS through an RFE, most larger employers can simply attest to the fourth part in order to have the position deemed a specialty occupation. In addition, in order to satisfy the first part of this test, a review of the DOL's **Occupational Information Network**, or **O*Net**, for a particular occupational title can provide insight into the normal minimum requirements for entry into a field of endeavor.[74]

C.2.c. Beneficiary's Qualifications for H-1B Classification

In order to obtain H-1B classification, the foreign national must meet the qualifications set forth by the employer for the specialty occupation. 8 C.F.R. § 214.2(h)(4)(iii)(C) provides the test for establishing that a beneficiary qualifies for the specialty occupation as follows:

> To qualify to perform services in a specialty occupation, the [foreign national] must meet one of the following criteria:
>
> - Hold a United States baccalaureate or higher degree required by the specialty occupation from an accredited college or university;
> - Hold a foreign degree determined to be equivalent to a United States baccalaureate or higher degree required by the specialty occupation from an accredited college or university;

---

[73] 8 C.F.R. § 214.2(h)(4)(i)(A)(1).
[74] *See* www.onetonline.org.

- Hold an unrestricted state license, registration, or certification that authorizes him or her to fully practice the specialty occupation and be immediately engaged in that specialty in the state of intended employment; **or**
- Have education, specialized training, and/or progressively responsible experience that is equivalent to completion of a United States baccalaureate or higher degree in the specialty occupation, and have recognition of expertise in the specialty through progressively responsible positions directly related to the specialty.

Again, the standard for proving that a foreign national qualifies for H-1B classification is dictated by a disjunctive test. While part two allows a foreign national to show experience or education that is a foreign equivalent of a U.S. bachelor's degree, it may be difficult to show this fact without the assistance of a credentials evaluation service to prove that the foreign education is the equivalent of a United States degree. 8 C.F.R. § 214.2(h)(4)(iii)(D) describes the various avenues for credential evaluation.

The USCIS will also accept a combination of education and/or work experience as evidence that the foreign national possess the equivalent education required for the offered position,[75] as indicated by the fourth part of the test above. The standard formula for equating experience to education for H-1B purposes is that every three years of specialized training and/or work experience is equal to one year of college education.[76] This standard can be applied widely for a variety of education and experience combinations. The best way to prove progressive experience is through letters from previous employers confirming the beneficiary's experience, responsibilities, and achievements at different stages of his or her career.

● EXAMPLE

Roger, a foreign national from Canada, possesses a two year Associates Degree in electrical technology from a technical college and six years of progressive experience as an electrical engineer. This education and experience can be equated to a baccalaureate level education in Electrical Engineering because the six years of experience makes up the missing two years associated with a standard United States bachelor's degree.

● EXAMPLE

Susan, a foreign national from New Zealand, possesses 12 years of progressive experience in marketing, working for an advertising company abroad in a variety of positions of increasing importance. This experience can be equated to a baccalaureate-level education in marketing because it is considered to be the equivalent of four years of college or university level education.

---

[75] 8.C.F.R. § 214.2(h)(4)(iii)(D)(5).
[76] *Id.*

If a license is required to practice in the specialty occupation, the foreign national must provide documentation, such as a certificate, showing its acquisition.[77] This requirement must be fulfilled prior to submitting the H-1B petition to the USCIS. Issues pertaining to licensure are important when dealing with professional specialty occupations such as lawyers, physicians, and certain engineers.

Case for Discussion 3.5

PhoneClip, Inc. is an online retailer of mobile phone accessories based in the United States. The Company wants to employ Sullae, a national of Korea, in the position of Database Manager pursuant to H-1B classification. PhoneClip has never employed anyone in this position before. A few years ago, Sullae completed a three year advanced Associate's degree in Information Science. After obtaining her degree, Sullae worked as a Database Manager for four years for a company located in Korea that sold similar products.

- Is the position of Database Manager a professional specialty occupation that qualifies for H-1B classification?
- If you are not sure, what additional questions should you ask the employer?
- Does Sullae qualify for H-1B classification?
- If you feel that Sullae does qualify for H-1B classification, what steps should the employer take prior to filing the H-1B petition?

C.2.d. The Department of Labor's Labor Condition Application Requirement

The DOL plays a dual role in the H-1B process. It seeks to protect jobs of U.S. workers from undue displacement while at the same time ensures that foreign workers are not exploited by U.S. employers. To achieve this goal, the DOL requires that the DOL approves a Labor Condition Application, or LCA, before the USCIS receives an H-1B petition submission.[78] A potential employer intending to petition for a foreign national must attest to the following:

- The wage paid to the H-1B worker will be the higher of the prevailing wage rate or actual wage,[79]

---

[77] 8 C.F.R. § 214.2(h)(4)(v).
[78] INA § 212(n).
[79] 20 C.F.R. § 655.731.

- The foreign national will be working under conditions on the same basis as and that do not adversely affect the working conditions of similarly employed U.S. workers,[80]
- There is no current strike or lockout as a result of a labor dispute in that occupational classification,[81] and
- The employer has provided notice of the filing of the LCA to the bargaining representative of the employer's employees in the occupation classification that the H-1B nonimmigrant will be employed, or, if there is no bargaining representative, has posted notice of filing in the employer's location where the foreign national will be employed.[82]

Included within the LCA regulations is the obligation of an employer to maintain a ***public access file*** to show that it is compliant with the LCA process. The specific requirements for the public access file can be found at 20 C.F.R. § 655.760. The DOL's Wage and Hour Division, charged with overseeing employer compliance with the LCA process, regularly investigates complaints against employers in the H-1B process. Such investigations can lead to significant fines and possible exclusion from the use of the program. Therefore, ensuring employers follow the LCA regulations and properly maintain public access files are very important in demonstrating good faith and providing appropriate protections. The two areas that most result in fines for employers are not maintaining appropriate wages and offering poor employment conditions for the H-1B worker.

Public Access File: A file that maintains documentation pertaining to the LCA for a given foreign national employee as well as evidence of the compensation and benefits provided.

Case for Discussion 3.6

Sparkling, LP is a limited partnership located in the United States that employs fifteen people. Last year, Sparkling, LP hired its first foreign national in H-1B classification. When Sparkling LP's immigration lawyer sent over the posting notice that alerts other employees that an H-1B petition is to be submitted, Sparkling, LP became worried that existing employees would be upset when they saw the wage being offered because it was substantially lower than the regular rate. To minimize exposure, the HR Manager for Sparkling, LP posted the notice behind her desk right below a calendar and above her file cabinet.

- Has Sparkling LP complied with the LCA requirements discussed above?

---

[80] 20 C.F.R. § 655.732.
[81] 20 C.F.R. § 655.733.
[82] 20 C.F.R. § 655.734.

C.2.e. Actual and Prevailing Wage Rate

As part of the LCA, the petitioner must attest that it is paying the foreign worker the required wage rate.[83] The wage paid to the H-1B beneficiary must be the higher of: (i) the actual wage paid by the employer to employees with similar experience and qualifications within the occupation; or (ii) the prevailing wage rate for the employee's occupation in the geographic area.[84]

To determine the actual wage, the wages paid to individuals employed in the same occupational classification at that particular location by the petitioner are important.[85] Where there are other employees within the company with "substantially similar experience and qualifications in the specific employment in question," the actual wage is the wage paid to those employees.[86] If no such employees exist at that particular location, then the actual wage is simply the wage paid to the H-1B visa holder.[87]

The prevailing wage rate for the intended position is determined at the time of the filing of the LCA.[88] The prevailing wage is the rate dictated by a collective bargaining agreement if the position is unionized.[89] If it is not, then it is the wage paid to all similarly situated employees in the area of intended employment.[90] Normally, the prevailing wage rate is obtained through a government wage survey compiled by the Bureau of Labor Statistics. If an employee will be performing work at multiple locations in the United States, the prevailing wage must be met for each area where the employee will be located. There are exceptions to the prevailing wage rate requirement for short assignments, generally less than 30 days in duration.[91] However, if a foreign national is moved to a new work site for more than 30 days, then the employer must not only file a new LCA, but also must submit to the USCIS an amended petition describing the change in work location and role.[92]

While the DOL's regulations regarding the prevailing wage rate requirement offer a variety of means for proving that an employer is compliant, by far the easiest way to obtain a swift approval of the LCA is to use wage data provided by the government. The **Foreign Labor Certification Data Center**, or **FLCDC**,[93] provides an easy to navigate database of wages that is searchable by geographic area of intended employment and occupational classification. It is important to note that, for each occupation, the FLCDC Wage Search Wizard will provide four wage levels. Referencing the employer's requirements for the position, such as years of experience and educational requirements, is imperative when

---

[83] 20 C.F.R. § 655.731(a).
[84] INA § 212(n)(1)(A)(i).
[85] INA § 212(n)(1)(A)(i)(I).
[86] 20 C.F.R. § 655.731(a)(1).
[87] *Id.*
[88] 20 C.F.R. § 655.731(a)(2).
[89] 20 C.F.R. § 655.731(a)(2)(i).
[90] 20 C.F.R. § 655.731(a)(2)(ii).
[91] 20 C.F.R. § 655.735(c).
[92] *See Matter of Simeio Solutions, LLC*, 26 I&N Dec. 542 (AAO 2015).
[93] For more information, *see* www.flcdatacenter.com.

determining which wage level is applicable to a given position.[94] If the prevailing wage rate as dictated by the FLCDC exceeds the employers' offered salary by a significant margin, it might be due to a data collection deviation, and employers can look to commercially available wage surveys to show that it is paying the foreign national the prevailing wage for the intended position.

Case for Discussion 3.7

The River City Law Firm in Pittsburgh, Pennsylvania wishes to hire Paula, a German national who recently graduated college with a degree in finance, as an accountant in H-1B classification.

- Using the Foreign Labor Certification Data Center, or FLCDC, find the prevailing wage rate the firm must offer Paula.
- If Paula worked in Philadelphia, what is the prevailing wage for that location?

Benching: Failure to pay a worker his or her salary during periods when no active work is available, in violation of the DOL's regulations regarding the attestations made in the signed LCA.

It is important to note that employers are required to pay the foreign national for the duration of time s/he works in valid H-1B classification. It is common in some industries to engage in ***benching*** employees and not pay them when there are no active projects available.

H-1B workers are not allowed to be benched. An employer found liable will be required to pay back wages and other penalties if this should occur.[95]

C.2.f. Similar Working Conditions

Similar to the wage requirements discussed above, an employer must also ensure that it is not disadvantaging its workforce by treating H-1B employees differently than the rest of its employees. Therefore, when executing the LCA, the employer attests that the H-1B worker will be employed under conditions on the same basis as and that do not adversely affect other employees in the organization.[96] This requirement ensures the provision of the same benefits package to H-1B specialty workers as that enjoyed by their U.S. colleagues in similar positions. Benefits include, but are not limited to, health insurance, vacations, working hours, shifts, office conditions, and other perks that are provided to the U.S. workers. Employers should keep proof of the equitable working conditions

---

[94] For additional guidance on determining the correct wage for a given position, refer to the discussion of the Labor Certification process in Section D of Chapter 7, Employment-Based and Self-Sponsored Immigration.
[95] 20 C.F.R. § 655.731(c)(7)(i).
[96] 20 C.F.R. § 655.732(a).

through a properly maintained public access file, in case of a potential investigation by the DOL.

C.3. Numerical Limitation: The H-1B Cap

One of the most challenging aspects of dealing with the H-1B classification is the fact that there is a numerical limitation to the amount of H-1B visas that can be issued to foreign nationals each year. This limitation is known as the H-1B Cap. At the beginning of the fiscal year (which commences on October 1st for the USCIS), 65,000 H-1B visas are made available.[97] In addition, Congress passed the H-1B Visa Reform Act of 2004,[98] which created an additional allotment of 20,000 H-1B visas specifically for foreign nationals who have earned a master's or higher degree from a United States Institute of Higher Education.

Employers are permitted to file petitions for nonimmigrant visas six months in advance of the need for the particular worker.[99] This rule means that for employers seeking to obtain an H-1B visa at the start of a USCIS fiscal year, the filing window in which petitions can be accepted begins on April 1 of the preceding fiscal year.

It is important to note that the cap only applies to foreign national beneficiaries seeking H-1B classification for the first time. Therefore, if a foreign national is switching from one H-1B employer to another or seeking an extension of stay for employment with the same employer, s/he is not subject to the H-1B cap as s/he has already been counted against the figures.[100] In addition, not all employers are subject to the H-1B cap. Most notably, foreign nationals seeking H-1B classification to work on behalf of institutes of higher education are deemed to be cap exempt petitioners.[101] Spouses and children who enter as derivatives are not counted against the cap.[102]

● EXAMPLE

Dr. Lefu is a foreign national from South Africa who just completed a degree in mechanical engineering last year. For the past six months, he has been working for the Company in valid OPT status. The Company now wishes to obtain H-1B classification for Dr. Lefu to continue working. The Company and their immigration lawyer will commence the preparation of the petition as early as February, so that when the filing window opens on April 1st, Dr. Lefu's H-1B petition will be ready for submission. If Dr. Lefu is instead hired by a University, then it does not matter when the H-1B petition is filed as there is no H-1B cap for institutions of higher education.

---

[97] INA § 214(g)(1).
[98] Pub. L. 108-447, div. j, title IV, subtitle B, 118 Stat. 3353 (2004).
[99] 8 C.F.R. § 214.2(h)(9)(i)(B).
[100] INA § 214(g)(7).
[101] INA § 214(g)(5).
[102] INA § 214(g)(8)(B)(iii).

Recently, the demand for H-1B visas has far exceeded the supply. For fiscal year 2015, the USCIS received 172,500 petitions for H-1B classification for the available 85,000 spots.[103] When there are more petitions received than available visas, the USCIS holds a random lottery to determine which petitions to select for adjudication. For fiscal year 2017, the number of petitions filed jumped to 236,000,[104] meaning only 36 percent of all beneficiaries were selected. If a petition is not selected for the lottery, the petition is returned to the employer along with the filing fees.

C.4. Duration of Stay

The H-1B visa can be held for up to six years[105] and is issued in two increments of three years each. Similar to the L visa classification, to become eligible for H-1B classification after reaching the six year maximum period of stay, a foreign national must depart the United States for a full year.[106] When attempting to secure H-1B status after this period, a new petition must be filed and the foreign national once again becomes subject to the H-1B Cap.

There are two special exceptions when the six year maximum period of stay in H-1B classification can be extended, both of which were created by the American Competitiveness Act of the 21st Century,[107] or AC 21. Under § 104(c) of the statute, if the foreign national is the beneficiary of an approved employment-based immigrant visa petition leading to a grant of lawful permanent residency but cannot adjust status because the priority date has not yet been reached,[108] the H-1B visa holder can extend his or her status in three-year increments until the priority date becomes current.

AC 21 § 106(a) also permits extension of the H-1B classification when the foreign national has a labor certification application or immigrant visa petition that was filed on his or her behalf more than 365 days before s/he reached the six-year maximum period of stay in H-1B classification whether subsequently approved or currently pending. Under this provision, the foreign national can extend his or her status in one-year increments only, extending H-1B status beyond the six-year duration, until the application or petition is adjudicated.

C.5. Changes in Employment, Job Flexibility, and Transition from Student to Professional Worker

A petitioner has the responsibility to notify the USCIS whenever there is a change in the terms and conditions of a foreign national's employment that may affect his or her eligibility for H-1B status.[109] Some changes may require

---

[103] See https://www.uscis.gov/news/uscis-reaches-fy-2015-h-1b-cap-0.
[104] See https://www.uscis.gov/news/alerts/uscis-completes-h-1b-cap-random-selection-process-fy-2017.
[105] 8 C.F.R. § 214.2(h)(13)(iii).
[106] Id.
[107] Pub. L. 106-313, 114 Stat. 1251 (2000).
[108] See Section A.2 of Chapter 6, Family Sponsored Immigration and Permanent Resident Status, for a discussion on priority dates.
[109] 8 C.F.R. § 214.2(h)(11)(i)(A).

a new petition to be filed and approved in order for employment to continue. Minor changes in job duties or salary will not require a new petition. Similarly, changes in an employer's name or ownership will generally not require any additional action, so long as the new entity succeeds to the "interests and obligations of the original petitioning employer and where the terms and conditions of employment remain the same but for the identity of the petitioner."[110]

Where there are material changes, then an amended petition must be filed.[111] This would include changes in duties from one specialty occupation to another or a change in location of employment. The amended petition is filed on Form I-129, Petition for a Nonimmigrant Worker, and must be accompanied by a new labor condition application.[112]

Under AC 21 § 105(a), foreign nationals in H-1B classification are provided additional flexibility for changing employers. This provision, known as H-1B *portability*, allows H-1B workers to commence working for a new employer once the USCIS receives a non-frivolous petition for new employment, thus allowing the foreign national to begin a new job before actual approval of the petition for the new employer.

Another important provision of the H-1B classification concerns foreign students converting from F-1 status to H-1B classification. If a student graduates at the end of the spring semester, his or her Optional Practical Training or OPT status will often expire during the summer of the following year because it is only valid for 12 months. To cover the gap between when the OPT expires and when an H-1B could commence, the USCIS created a provision called **cap gap**[113] whereby employment authorization will continue if the foreign national's H-1B petition is selected for adjudication.

> **Portability:** The ability of an in-status employee to change employment after a prospective employer files non-frivolous petition for a change of status and receives proof of that filing from the USCIS, without waiting for the petition to be approved first.

● EXAMPLE

The OPT status of Pritesh, a citizen of India, will expire on July 15, 2015. On April 1, 2015, Pritesh's employer filed an H-1B petition on his behalf, which was selected in the H-1B lottery, and later approved on April 30, 2015 with a start date of October 1, 2015. Under the cap gap provision, Pritesh can continue working for his employer during the interim period when the OPT expires on July 15 and when the H-1B starts on October 1.

C.6. Compiling the H-1B Nonimmigrant Visa Application

A complete petition for H-1B visa classification should include:

- Certified Labor Condition Application issued by the DOL

---

[110] INA § 214(c)(10).
[111] 8 C.F.R. § 214.2(h)(2)(i)(E).
[112] *Id.*
[113] 8 C.F.R. § 214.2(f)(5)(vi).

Chapter 3: Nonimmigrant Visas for Intracompany Transferees

- Form I-129, Petition for a Nonimmigrant Worker
- H Classification Supplement to Form I-129
- Form G-28, Notice of Entry of Appearance as Attorney or Accredited Representative
- Proof of qualifying position in the United States (is it a professional specialty occupation?)
- Proof that the foreign national possesses a baccalaureate level education in a specific field of endeavor related to the offered position

A sample legal argument detailing a foreign national's qualifications for H-1B nonimmigrant visa purposes is in Box 3.3.

Box 3.3   **Sample Legal Argument: In Support of H1B Qualification**

Ms. L'Cavia is ideally qualified for the offered position of Marketing Manager. Indeed, as documented by the attached evaluation, she holds the equivalent of a U.S. Master of Science Degree in Marketing [Intelligence Marketing] by virtue of her Specialized Master's degree in Marketing Intelligence from a well-known and respected university in France (2015). During the course of her studies, Ms. L'Cavia took such applicable courses as Datamining, Introduction to Marketing, Marketing Research, Digital Marketing Strategy, Statistics, Strategic Marketing Strategy, Consumer Behavior, Consumer Goods Specialization, Brand Management, Marketing and Innovation, and numerous others. For more information regarding Ms. L'Cavia's qualifying educational credentials, please refer to the copies of her credentials evaluation, diploma, and transcripts attached at Exhibit C.

C.7. Termination of Status

There will occasionally be situations when an employer must terminate an H-1B employee's services, or when an H-1B employee voluntarily resigns. In this case, there are duties that the employer must fulfill. If an employer no longer employs the beneficiary, the employer must immediately notify the USCIS.[114] In addition, if the employer terminates the employment, s/he is also responsible for providing

---

[114] 8 C.F.R. § 214.2(h)(11)(i)(A).

the reasonable cost of transportation to the employee's last place of foreign residence.[115] This requirement does not extend to the employee's spouse and children who may also be here.

C.8. Spouses and Children

Spouses and children of H-1B visa holders may obtain derivative status as H-4 visa holders.[116] Unlike the E and L classifications, spouses are not permitted to work in the United States and therefore are not eligible to apply for employment authorization upon immediately entering the United States. However, if the H-1B visa holder later is the beneficiary of an approved Form I-140, Immigrant Petition for Alien Worker (so that s/he can live in the United States permanently), or has extended his or her status pursuant to AC 21 § 106(a), the H-4 dependents are able to submit an application for employment authorization using Form I-765, Application for Employment Authorization.[117]

Case for Discussion 3.8

Top of the Heap, Inc. is a recycling company in the United States. They wish to hire Jaden, a Public Relations Specialist from New Zealand, to be their newest Marketing Manager. Jaden has a degree in Psychology from abroad.

- Make an argument as to why Jaden's education is a related field to the offered position of Marketing Manager.

The chart in Table 3.1 at the end of this chapter may help to summarize the most important features of the H-1B nonimmigrant visa classification.

C.9. Specialty Workers from Singapore and Chile (H-1B1)

Each year, 6,800 visas for **professionals** from Chile and Singapore are set aside from the 65,000 H-1B visa cap. Under the H-1B1 nonimmigrant program, professionals from Chile and Singapore are not required to file a petition with the USCIS. Instead, an employee may present his or her evidence for H-1B1 classification eligibility directly to consular officials at the time of filing the visa application.[118]

The specialty occupation requirement for H-1B1 nonimmigrant visa applicants is identical to that of the normal H-1B. Likewise, professionals from

---

[115] 8 C.F.R. § 214.2(h)(4)(iii)(E).
[116] 8 C.F.R. § 214.2(h)(9)(iv).
[117] Id.
[118] 9 FAM 402.10-5; 8 C.F.R. § 214.2(h).

Singapore and Chile must have an approved LCA along with a written offer of employment at the time they are requesting status.

An essential distinction between the H-1B1 and H-1B visa classification is that individuals from Singapore and Chile cannot have any immigrant intent upon entering the United States and they must demonstrate that they intend to leave at the end of the employment term. They cannot change their status to lawful permanent residents while they are in the country in H-1B1 classification.

In addition, H-1B1 nonimmigrants are admitted for a period of only 18 months, which may be renewed indefinitely without requiring the recipient to live outside the United States for one year. While spouses of H-1B1 workers may enter as derivatives, they cannot file for employment authorization. The chart in Table 3.1 at the end of this chapter may help to summarize the most important features of the H-1B1 nonimmigrant status classification.

D. Certain Speciality Occupation Professionals from Australia (E-3): INA § 101(a)(15)(E)(iii); 9 FAM 402.9-8

The E-3 classification applies only to nationals of Australia coming to the United States to perform work in a specialty occupation.[119] Theoretically, other countries could also get E-3 status, but at the moment, only the Australian U.S. free trade agreement allows for this type of visa to be used. To be eligible to receive an E-3, an Australian national must have a legitimate offer of employment in the United States and possess the necessary academic or other qualifying credentials to fulfill their offered position in a specialty occupation. There is a 10,500 annual cap on E-3 visa issuance that has never been reached in the history of the visa classification.

While the E-3 classification shares some similarities with the E-1 and E-2 categories, it is more closely related to the H-1B nonimmigrant visa, particularly since the rubric for determining a specialty occupation and academic credentials are the same. Also, similar to the H-1B, Australians seeking to enter the United States on an E-3 must have an LCA submitted and approved on his or her behalf.[120]

E-3 beneficiaries are admitted for an initial period of two years, with unlimited two-year extensions. However, similar to the E-1/E-2 classifications, the E-3 visa holder must possess nonimmigrant intent. In addition, E-3 applications are often filed and obtained through consular processing. Spouses of E-3 classifications may apply for employment authorization through an application on Form I-765, Application for Employment Authorization. The chart in Table 3.1 at the end of this chapter may help to summarize the most important features of the E-3 nonimmigrant status classification.

---

[119] INA § 101(a)(15)(E)(iii); 9 FAM 402.9-8.
[120] 9 FAM 402.9-8(A)(c).

E. TN Nafta Professionals (TN): INA § 214(e); 8 C.F.R. § 214.6; 9 FAM 402.17

In 1992, The North American Free Trade Agreement, or NAFTA, was signed into law, creating special economic and trade relationships between Mexico, Canada, and the United States. The nonimmigrant NAFTA Professional, or TN nonimmigrant visa, allows professional citizens from Canada and Mexico to enter the United States as visitors for a temporary period of time in order to work, while receiving remuneration or a salary from a U.S. entity.[121] The application and entry procedures are slightly different for citizens of Canada and Mexico, but the requirements remain largely the same. Canadian Citizens are not required to obtain a visa beforehand, and may apply for admission at the border. Mexican citizens must apply for a visa at a U.S. embassy or consular office before traveling to the United States.

E.1. Requirements for TN Classification

The **TN Professional** must be a citizen of Mexico or Canada. Permanent Residents of either country are not eligible for a TN visa.[122] Citizens of Mexico and Canada must be employed in a qualifying profession, and the position in the United States must require a TN professional.[123] TN professionals must also have prearranged full-time or part-time work with a U.S. employer (self-employment is prohibited) in a profession for which s/he is qualified.[124]

There are 38 qualifying positions cited in NAFTA that can be used for TN classification. They include, but are not limited to: accountants; architects; computer analysts; engineers; lawyers; management consultants; scientists; teachers; and medical professionals.[125] There are 23 subgroups of scientists, and 3 subgroups of teachers.

The fact that there is a specific list of occupations for TN classification has always limited the types of workers that can enter the United States. Interestingly, because the NAFTA agreement is over 20 years old and the list of professions has never been updated, there is only one computer-related occupation on the list, Computer Systems Analyst, even though computer technology is an ever growing professional area. This means that other standard information technology positions are not able to use this visa classification. This fact is particularly troubling for common IT positions such as programmers, database administrators, and web developers. As a result, the Computer Systems Analyst Classification, while the only category available to such professionals seeking entry, is also subject to heavy scrutiny to ensure it is not being used inappropriately.

---

[121] 8 C.F.R. § 214.6(b)(4).
[122] 9 FAM 402.17-2(B).
[123] 9 FAM 402.17-4(A).
[124] 9 FAM 402.17-5(A).
[125] *See* NAFTA Appendix 1603.D.1 for a full list of positions, 8 C.F.R. § 214.6(c).

The remaining requirements for the TN Professional are very similar to the H-1B, except a **prevailing wage determination** is not required. Theoretically, therefore, a TN Professional can be paid any wage by a U.S. employer. Some theorize that this was an accidental loophole in the TN regulations and this is why subsequent free trade agreement visas with other countries contain the requirement of a labor condition application.

TN Professionals must demonstrate that they are going to perform services in a specialty occupation, requiring theoretical and practical application of a body of highly specialized knowledge. The beneficiary must also have obtained the necessary qualifications to perform in this role. Attainment of a bachelor's degree is required by most of the professions, although some will require a more **advanced degree**. Generally, experience is not an acceptable substitute for the proper degree, as is the case with the H-1B and other visas.[126] The Management Consultant occupation, one of the few specialties in which experience may substitute for education, is often heavily scrutinized for this reason. Finally, the qualifications must be in an area related to the profession.

E.2. Application Procedure and Duration

Since the TN Professional visa is only for Canadian and Mexican citizens, proof of citizenship of these countries is required.[127] The foreign national must present evidence that the position is a business activity at a professional level and that s/he meets the criteria to carry on such work.[128] This can be in the form of a support letter from the prospective employer in the United States or from the foreign employer. The TN Professional must also submit educational qualifications or appropriate credentials demonstrating professional status. Unlike the H-1B, a TN applicant does not need to obtain an independent evaluation of his or her academic credentials if they were issued by an educational institution in Canada or Mexico, although foreign degrees from other countries will require such an evaluation.[129] For occupations requiring state licenses, the beneficiary may obtain the license after entry.[130]

TN status is available for up to three years,[131] with unlimited three-year extensions.[132] Spouses and unmarried minor children may enter at the same time as the primary visa holder but may not engage in work.[133] As these are not dual intent visas, the beneficiary must prove nonimmigrant intent. The chart in Table 3.1 at the end of this chapter may help to summarize the most important features of the TN nonimmigrant status classification.

---

[126] 9 FAM 402.17-4(A)(b).
[127] 8 C.F.R. § 214.6(d)(3)(i).
[128] 8 C.F.R. § 214.6(d)(3)(ii).
[129] *Id.*
[130] 9 FAM 402.17-4(B).
[131] 8 C.F.R. § 214.6(e).
[132] 8 C.F.R. § 214.6(h).
[133] 8 C.F.R. § 214.6(j)(4).

> **Case for Discussion 3.9**
>
> Olivia is a dual national of Australia and Canada. Olivia has found an employer in New York that wants to hire her as an Accountant. Olivia has a degree in Accounting from a well-respected University in Australia. Olivia's husband wants to be able to work in the United States as well.
>
> - Which professional specialty visa will best serve Olivia and her husband's stay in the United States and why?

F. Visa Summary Chart

In order to highlight the key points described for the various nonimmigrant statuses, this chapter utilizes summary charts in Table 3.1 to review each major visa classification discussed.

Table 3.1 Comparison of Nonimmigrant Visas

\multicolumn{5}{c}{E Visa}
Maximum Duration of Visa	Maximum Duration of Each Entry	Maximum Duration Classification Can Be Held Without Departing the United States for a Year	Intent Requirement	Available for Spousal Employment Authorization
5 years	2 years	Indefinite	To depart the U.S. at the end of the employment in E-1 / E-2 status nonimmigrant	Yes
\multicolumn{5}{c}{L Visa}
L-1A: 3 years for initial filing, 2 years for extensions for a maximum of 7 years; L-1B: 3 years for initial filing, 2 years for extension for a maximum of 5 years	Matches approval notice term	L-1A: 7 years; L-1B: 5 years	Dual intent	Yes

Maximum Duration of Visa	Maximum Duration of Each Entry	Maximum Duration Classification Can Be Held Without Departing the United States for a Year	Intent Requirement	Available for Spousal Employment Authorization
H-1B Visa				
H-1B: 3 years for initial filing; 3 years for extension	Matches approval notice	6 years with ability to extend beyond under AC 21	Dual intent	No, unless H-1B holder has approved Form I-140, Immigrant Petition for Alien Worker
H-1B1 Visa				
18 months; 18-month extensions	Matches visa dates	Theoretically indefinitely	100 percent nonimmigrant intent	No
E-3 Visa				
2 years; 2-year extensions	2 years per admission	Theoretically indefinitely	100 percent nonimmigrant intent	Yes
TN Visa				
3 years for Canadians; 1 year for Mexicans (visa only); indefinite extensions available	For Canadians, period of time on I-94 card; For Mexicans, date listed on visa	Theoretically indefinite	100 percent nonimmigrant intent	No

G. Conclusion

Throughout this chapter, we explored the various visa classifications most often used by corporate entities when employing foreign nationals in the United States. As with our discussion of the other employment-based nonimmigrant categories in Chapter 2, Nonimmigrant Visas for Brief Stays, Studies, and Cultural Exchange, it is wise to think of the visa classifications in terms of purpose rather than the alpha-numeric designation. The E-1/E-2 visas are valuable tools for treaty countries when transferring supervisory and essential skills professionals. The L-1A/L-1B visas are useful for multinational corporations. Finally, the H-1B and the remaining professional specialty occupation visas — H-1B1, E-3, TN — are key in employing professionals with degrees.

In the following chapter, we explore the remaining nonimmigrant employment-based visa classifications that are less common, but still serve a very particular purpose. These visas cover foreign government workers, extraordinary ability scientists, business people, athletes and entertainers, members of the international media, and religious workers. Although these classifications are widely different than those discussed in this chapter, the information presented here remains relevant as the exploration of nonimmigrant business immigration visas continues.

Nonimmigrant Visas for Extraordinary Ability, Religious Workers, and Ancillary Activities

Key Terms and Acronyms

National or International Acclaim
Advisory Opinion
Contract
Essential Support
Extraordinary Ability
Government Official
International Media
Itinerary
Peer Group
Religious Worker
Temporary Worker

Chapter Objectives

- Review sources of law for nonimmigrant foreign nationals of extraordinary ability or O-1 classification
- Analyze and apply the criteria associated with O-1 classification
- Review sources of law for nonimmigrant artists, athletes, and entertainers
- Analyze and apply the criteria associated with P classification
- Review sources of law for nonimmigrant visa classifications R, I, H-2A, H-2B, A, and G to understand purpose and function in the overarching visa system

Foreign nationals seeking to enter the United States on a temporary basis must obtain a nonimmigrant visa that authorizes admission for a specific purpose and duration. Chapter 2, Nonimmigrant Visas for Brief Stays, Studies, and Cultural Exchange, deals with nonimmigrant visa classifications that generally do not confer employment authorization. Chapter 3, Nonimmigrant Visas for Intracompany Transferees, Trade and Investment, and Professional Employment, covers the most used nonimmigrant visa classifications for employment purposes by corporate entities in the United States. This chapter covers the remaining visa classifications that automatically grant employment authorization. It also pays particular attention to nonimmigrant classifications for individuals practicing in the top levels of their field, whether it be sciences, arts, education, business, athletics, or other certain fields. These individuals are eligible for status in the O and P nonimmigrant visa classifications.

In addition, this chapter covers religious workers, members of international media, temporary agricultural workers, and temporary non-agricultural workers. Finally, it reviews options for foreign government officials and representatives of international organizations wishing to come to the United States to work. Table 4.1 may be a helpful guide to aid in comparing the various nonimmigrant visa types that support a variety of extraordinary ability, athletic, artistic, religious, and temporary or seasonal employment needs discussed in this chapter.

In reviewing these additional visa classifications, we complete the overview of options for those seeking to enter the United States for employment-based nonimmigrant purposes.

A. Visas for Individuals with Extraordinary Ability in the Sciences, Education, Business, or Athletics (O-1A) and Arts, Motion Picture, or Television Industry (O-1B): INA § 101(a)(15)(O); 8 C.F.R. § 214.2(o)

At its very core, the design of the O-1 classification through statute and regulation[1] allows the best of the best to enter the United States for a temporary period and for a specific objective. Section 101(a)(15)(O) of the Immigration and Nationality Act, or INA, states that an eligible foreign national of **extraordinary ability** may receive authorization to enter the United States and subsequently provide services concerning either a single or a sequence of events, if petitioned for by an *authorized entity*.

Authorized Entity: An individual person, agent, or corporate organization that is permitted to file a nonimmigrant visa petition on behalf of a foreign national.

By specific designation and design, O-1 classification permits use for those who can demonstrate extraordinary ability in the field of science, arts, education, business, or athletics. Therefore, in theory, almost any area of professional endeavor imaginable can support O-1 classification. Whether it is a rock star singing to sold-out stadiums, a famous CEO of a technology company, or a former Olympic athlete who has become a renowned coach, the O-1 classification is intentionally broad. In fact, an area of employment that carries little fame, such as a worm farmer, could use the O-1 classification as long as the foreign national carries sustained international acclaim within that particular field of endeavor.

---

[1] 8 C.F.R. § 214.2(o).

While the intention of the O-1 classification remains the same for all purposes, the legal and evidentiary standard associated with different uses of the classification is varied. The two primary variations of O-1 classification are as follows:

- O-1A: individuals with extraordinary ability in the sciences, education, business, or athletics
- O-1B: individuals with an extraordinary ability in the arts or extraordinary achievement in the motion picture or television industry

Another special component of the O-1A and O-1B classifications is that essential support personnel can also enter the United States alongside the foreign national using O-2 classification. While they are subject to their own regulatory requirements and require the filing of a separate petition for them, most uses of the O-2 category are easy to assess because they must have a logical connection to the activities of the principal O-1 visa holder.

● EXAMPLE

Madam Papillon is a world famous French opera singer who was recently booked on a tour of the United States. The tour is to last six months. For decades, Madam Papillon has always worked with the same voice coach, Monsieur Chenille. Madam Papillon knows that her voice will suffer and that she will not be able to maintain the strength of her performances in the United States without Monsieur Chenille's coaching. If Madam Papillon receives O-1 classification, Monsieur should receive O-2 classification as well because his presence is a logical connection to the activities of Madam Papillon in the United States.

A.1. Specific O Nonimmigrant Visa Requirements

Similar to the L-1A and L-1B categories discussed in Section B of Chapter 3, Nonimmigrant Visas for Intracompany Transferees, Trade and Investment, and Professional Employment, the O nonimmigrant visa classifications have both shared and separate eligibility criteria. We first review the requirements they have in common.

A.1.a. Shared Requirements for Both O-1A and O-1B Nonimmigrant Visa Classifications

The mechanics of the O-1A and O-1B classifications are essentially the same. Both require filing petitions with the United States Citizenship and Immigration Service, or USCIS, and require beneficiaries to obtain a visa abroad in order to enter the United States in this category, with the exception of visa exempt nationals such as Canadians. In addition, both classifications require, where possible and feasible, an advisory opinion from a recognized ***peer group***,[2] including a labor or management group, if applicable, or a person with expertise in the beneficiary's area of

Peer Group: A group or organization comprised of practitioners of the foreign national's occupation.

---

[2] 8 C.F.R. § 214.2(o)(3)(ii).

ability, which would either support, object to, or not object to the approval of the petition.

Finally, with both the O-1A classification and O-1B classification, **_agents_**[3] (who carry a special definition under the immigration regulations), as well as direct employers, are allowed to serve as the petitioner for the beneficiary.

Agents have permission to act on behalf of foreign nationals of extraordinary ability because many of these professionals do not work for a single employer. Without an agent's assistance, the O-1 beneficiary would need to have each intended employer file a separate petition on his or her behalf, which can be cumbersome. Instead, use of an agent allows the submission of one petition on behalf of all of the potential employers.

> **Agents:** The actual employers of the beneficiary who will perform at an event, the representatives of both the employer and the beneficiary of the petition, or a person or entity authorized by an employer to act for, or in place of, the employer as its agent.

● EXAMPLE

Senior Escarabajo is a one-man classic rock tribute band from Peru that has gained worldwide fame for incorporating traditional Latin rhythms into familiar melodies from the '60s, '70s, and '80s. A number of medium-sized venues in the United States want to hire Senior Escarabajo to perform. Because each venue would have to file their own O-1 petition for Senior Escarabajo, having an agent file on his behalf would dramatically reduce the administrative burden associated with the process, as well as cut costs considerably.

A.1.b. Evidentiary Criteria

Approval of a petition for O-1 classification is based on a successful demonstration of a beneficiary's extraordinary ability through evidence of sustained national or international acclaim within his or her particular field of endeavor. Therefore, while it is important to correctly complete Form I-129, Petition for a Nonimmigrant Worker, and the O Classification supplement, more time is spent gathering evidence to support the filing itself. As mentioned earlier, what extraordinary ability means in each one of the types of O-1 visa classifications differs. These distinctions are very important because they point to the type of evidence that will lead to a successful petition process. The following definitions of extraordinary ability provided in 8 C.F.R. § 214.2(o)(3)(ii) provide a guide:

- Extraordinary ability in the fields of science, education, business, or athletics means a level of expertise indicating that the person is one of the small percentage who has risen to the very top of the field of endeavor.
- Extraordinary ability in the field of arts means distinction. Distinction means a high level of achievement in the field of the arts evidenced by a degree of skill and recognition substantially above that ordinarily encountered to the extent that a person described as prominent is renowned, leading, or well known in the field of arts.

---

[3] 8 C.F.R. § 214.2(o)(2)(iv)(E).

- Extraordinary achievement with respect to motion and television production mean . . . a degree of skill and recognition significantly above that ordinarily encountered to the extent the person is recognized as outstanding, notable, or leading in the motion picture and/or television field.

Case for Discussion 4.1

Hand-Selected Management Group, or HMG, represents artists in a variety of different fields, many of whom are foreign nationals. Some of their clients work in the motion picture industry and some are musicians. Recently, HMG signed a contract to represent a famous Austrian physicist who will be coming to the United States to consult on a new Hollywood movie about black holes and quantum mechanics.

- Based on the different meanings of extraordinary ability, which type of client does HMG have the easiest burden for demonstrating extraordinary ability; the actors, the musicians, or the scientists?
- Why?

Proof must supplement an O-1 petition, showing that the work and services provided are in the area of extraordinary ability and that the foreign national meets the corresponding evidentiary criteria.[4] Because the definition of extraordinary ability is different for each type of O-1 classification used, so too is the criteria required to prove the same. A detailed discussion of these varying criteria is discussed in Sections A.2 and A.3.

A.1.c. Consultation or Peer Advisory Opinion

Those seeking O-1 and O-2 status, regardless of whether it is in the O-1A or O-1B sub-classification, must obtain and submit a consultation or advisory opinion letter authored by the appropriate peer advisory group, such as a labor or management group, or a person who possesses expertise in the field, if one exists.[5] If there is a collective bargaining representative of an employer's employees in the occupational classification for which the foreign national will work, the representative may be considered the appropriate peer group for purposes of consultation. If there is no submission of such a letter, the petitioner bears the burden to establish that no appropriate peer group exists for the particular field of endeavor, at which point the USCIS will adjudicate the petition based on the information submitted.[6]

The advisory opinion must be in writing and signed by a certified official of the chosen association or union.[7] From a procedural perspective, this task is similar to

---

[4] 8 C.F.R. § 214.2(o)(3)(i).
[5] 8 C.F.R. § 214.2(o)(2)(ii)(D) and 8 C.F.R. § 214.2(o)(5).
[6] 8 C.F.R. § 214.2(o)(5)(i)(G).
[7] 8 C.F.R. § 214.2(o)(5)(i)(C).

obtaining a Labor Condition Application, or LCA, from the Department of Labor, or DOL, before filing an H-1B petition. While the requirements differ, both the advisory opinion and the LCA seek to protect U.S. workers by ensuring that the presence of a foreign national will not adversely affect their field of endeavor. The advisory opinion phase of the O-1 petition process can be time consuming and it is imperative to research how to complete this important step for the foreign national's field of expertise. When working with unions from an artistic field of endeavor, most require a fully assembled copy of the entire petition in order to give the opinion.

While a written and executed advisory opinion is mandatory with all O-1 petitions, there are situations where adjudication of the petition can begin without the advisory opinion accompanying the filing in the case of beneficiaries working in the fields of the arts and athletics. In addition, it is possible for the USCIS to make a decision based solely on the beneficiary's submitted evidence. The two circumstances where adjudication of this nature can occur are as follows:

- Returning Artists: The USCIS can waive the consultation requirement if the foreign national received O-1 classification in the past two years and is coming back to the United States to give similar services.[8]
- Expedited Handling: In cases where the USCIS has to adjudicate a petition quickly because of a verifiable need, but an advisory opinion is absent, it will directly communicate with the appropriate labor and/or management organization identified on the O Supplement of Form I-129, Petition for a Nonimmigrant Worker, and request the consultation. If the union does not respond in writing to the USCIS within 24 hours, the USCIS will adjudicate the petition based on the evidence already submitted.[9]

● EXAMPLE

Charlotte, an Irish actress who was recently named one of Western Europe's most exciting emergent screen artists, has been cast as an emergency replacement in an independent film that begins production in New York City in two weeks. Prior to submitting her O-1 petition, Charlotte's New York-based talent agent tried to obtain an advisory opinion from the appropriate actors' union, but there was not enough time. Because of the rush to start filming, she submitted the petition without the advisory opinion. In this case, the USCIS will try to obtain the advisory opinion from the union but will proceed with adjudication of the O-1 petition if the union does not respond within 24 hours.

> **Event**: An activity such as, but not limited to, a scientific project, conference, convention, lecture series, tour, exhibit, business project, or engagement.

A.1.d. Itineraries

While proving extraordinary ability is paramount in any O-1 filing, what is also of importance is proof of a substantial *event* in the United States that requires

---

[8] 8 C.F.R. § 214.2(o)(5)(ii)(B).
[9] 8 C.F.R. § 214.2(o)(5)(i)(E).

the presence of the foreign national. S/he can clearly be the best of the best, but if there is no proof of what the person will be doing in the United States, the O-1 petition will be denied. Therefore, it is wise to think of any O-1 filing as having two main components:

- The merits, meaning does the foreign national qualify as extraordinary in his or her particular field of endeavor?
- The itinerary, meaning what is the event[10] that the foreign national is coming to the United States to perform?

In support of the O-1, the petitioner should submit a detailed itinerary that discusses the nature of the event.[11] Also, in support of the itinerary, the petitioner should submit contracts for performances, deal memos, or other comparable proof of the veracity of the proposed schedule. Of course, for those who have regular full-time employment (such as a researcher at a university or college), an offer letter or an employment contract can satisfy the itinerary requirement.

For artists, the itinerary is of the utmost importance and should include beginning and ending dates for any and all activities the beneficiary will be required to participate in, which must mirror the validity period of the requested visa, and moreover, reflect the terms of the contract or representation agreement between the petitioner and the beneficiary. Further, it is critical that the petitioner conclusively demonstrate that the beneficiary will complete only activities and events in their field of extraordinary ability.

● **EXAMPLE**

Abby is an Australian national and is the writer, director, and lead actress of a popular web series with an enthusiastic and dedicated digital following. Abby seeks to enter the United States to pursue professional comedy writing in Los Angeles. The itinerary that her petitioner, a talent agent based in Los Angeles, California, will submit to the USCIS will be comprised of a tentative shooting and production schedule for Abby's upcoming web series, and additional promotional appearances in and around the greater Los Angeles area that should last 18 months. In this case, the O-1B petition will only be granted for that period and not the maximum three years available, since that is the length of the demonstrated need.

A.1.e. Contract Between Petitioner and Beneficiary

In order to establish the validity of the professional partnership existing between the petitioner and the beneficiary, a contract must accompany the O-1 petition.[12] However, even if a contract does not exist, the USCIS will allow the petitioner to include a summary of the oral terms of the agreement between

---

[10] 8 C.F.R. § 214.2(o)(3)(ii).
[11] 8 C.F.R. § 214.2(o)(2)(ii)(C).
[12] 8 C.F.R. § 214.2(o)(2)(ii)(B).

the parties.[13] This requirement applies regardless of whether an agent or an employer is the petitioner. The summary of the terms of the oral agreement must unequivocally articulate the conditions offered by the employer and accepted by the employee. These should include, but are not limited to:

- Responsibilities to be provided for compensation
- What the compensation will be
- Tentative timelines regarding services to be successfully executed
- Expected duration of professional partnership

Essentially, the USCIS is looking for a valid contract, which means that there is an exchange of something for the services provided.

As previously mentioned, an agent can be a petitioner for a foreign national, particularly if the intended beneficiary is self-employed, uses agents to arrange short term events, or intends to work for numerous employers.[14] However, s/he cannot be merely a friend in the industry, which was once common in the arts. The USCIS created stricter guidelines about this requirement in 2015, particularly where there might be an oral contract. Now, established proof of the existence and execution of the oral agreement may include but is not restricted to:

- Electronic correspondence between both parties,
- An authored synopsis of the terms of the agreement, or
- Any other evidence that exhibits the existence of the oral agreement.

It is critical to remember that valid O status is petitioner specific. If there is a breach in the contract between the petitioner and beneficiary, a change in employment or agent for an O-1 foreign national requires a new employer and corresponding O-1 petition.[15]

● EXAMPLE

A start-up tech company based in Santa Barbara, California recruits a Digital Marketing Executive, who is a Chinese foreign national. After working for two years in valid O-1A status as a Business Executive of Extraordinary Ability, the Digital Marketing Executive is then headhunted by a large, East Coast based advertising conglomerate serving multinational clientele. Prior to starting work for the East Coast company, the new employer must file a new and entirely separate petition on behalf of the beneficiary in order for him to maintain employment authorization.

---

[13] *Id.*
[14] 8 C.F.R. § 214.2(o)(2)(iv)(E).
[15] 8 C.F.R. § 214.2(o)(2)(iv)(C).

A.1.f. Duration

O-1 petitions can initially be granted for up to three years.[16] However, the USCIS will not grant blanket authorization for that entire duration unless the petitioner can show that the foreign national is needed in the United States for that length of time.[17] Events that merit granting O-1 classification can, in theory, be as short as one day in duration. The petitioner's requested duration of O-1 classification validity must be corroborated by the events highlighted on the beneficiary's accompanying itinerary. General guidelines for duration are field specific. The length of time needed to complete the itinerary of events should dictate the duration requested by a petitioner on behalf of a beneficiary. For example, the petitioner supporting a professional athlete who has signed a one-year contract with a performance-contingent option of a two-year extension, will undoubtedly request the maximum O-1 duration of three years. On the other hand, the petitioner of a visual artist, such as an independently run not-for-profit art gallery, may only request a 12-month validity period in order to support the running of a specific installation or exhibit. While there exists no maximum period for which a beneficiary may be sponsored in continued O-1 status, a petitioner must apply for the beneficiary in single, one-year extensions in order that s/he may continue or complete the same event or activity that qualified them for admission.[18]

A.2. Proving the Merits for O-1A Nonimmigrant Classification: Demonstrating Extraordinary Ability in the Field of Sciences, Education, Business, or Athletics

Extraordinary ability in the fields of science, education, business and athletics explicitly refers to corresponding professionals who have achieved this level of expertise, indicating that the applicant is irrefutably one of the minute percentage who has risen to the top of the field of endeavor. To demonstrate this, the petitioner must present evidence confirming the beneficiary's receipt of a major, internationally recognized award, such as a Nobel Prize, or, in its place, evidence that adheres to a minimum of three of the following eight criteria:[19]

- Receipt of nationally or internationally recognized prizes or awards for excellence in the field of endeavors;
- Membership in associations in the field for which classification is sought which require outstanding achievements, judged as such by recognized national or international experts in the field;
- Published material about the beneficiary and the beneficiary's work in the field for which classification is sought in professional or major trade publications, newspapers, or other major media;

---

[16] 8 C.F.R. § 214.2(o)(6)(iii)(A).
[17] INA § 214(a)(2)(A).
[18] 8 C.F.R. § 214.2(o)(12).
[19] 8 C.F.R. § 214.2(o)(3)(iii)(B).

- Original scientific, scholarly, or business-related contributions of major significance in the field;
- Authorship of scholarly articles in the field for which classification is sought in professional journals or other major media;
- A high salary or other remuneration for services as evidenced by contracts or other reliable sources;
- Participation on a panel, or individually, as a judge of the work of others in the same, or in a field of specialization allied to that field for which classification is sought; or
- Employment in a critical or essential capacity for organizations and establishments that have a distinguished reputation.

When reviewing the criteria listed above, proving extraordinary ability may appear to be a daunting task. However, for scientific researchers in particular, the very nature of the industry lends itself to meeting at least three of the criteria needed to demonstrate that the foreign national is truly extraordinary. For example, in most university settings, in order to become a tenured professor, an employee must publish extensively in his or her field. In accomplishing this employment goal, a foreign national will often meet many of the criteria listed above.

The published work of the foreign national as well as testimonial letters written on behalf of the foreign national by other leading members of the specific scientific community can easily demonstrate original scientific contributions. Often, a foreign national will be asked to review the work of others in his or her field of expertise. This is commonplace in the sciences through the peer review publication system and is considered judging the work of others for O-1 classification purposes.

When reviewing or assessing the strength of the published material by a foreign national, a few or even a single publication in a high-quality journal, such as one with a high-impact factor, carries more weight than numerous publications in lesser journals. In addition, where the foreign national's name falls in the order of authors listed is also important. Therefore, two or three first-listed author publications are more impressive than ten fourth- or fifth-listed author publications. Also of note is the fact that most scientific researchers will work for organizations that carry a distinguished reputation, whether it is a university or a private research facility. Therefore, demonstrating that the employee will work for such an employer in a critical or essential capacity will serve to meet one of the three required criteria.

If the aforementioned evidentiary criteria do not unequivocally pertain to the beneficiary's occupation or field of endeavor, the petitioner may also submit comparable evidence in order to successfully establish extraordinary ability.[20] This regulatory caveat is of particular importance for those in the field of

---

[20] 8 C.F.R. § 214.2(o)(3)(iii)(C).

business, where publications are not necessarily required for employment, nor are they commonplace.

● EXAMPLE

Padama is an Indian national who has been working in London for the past six years for one of Europe's most profitable hedge funds. Padama has found a new job in New York and her new employer wishes to secure O-1 classification for her. Because the techniques created by Padama and used by the hedge fund in London are considered trade secrets, there is little evidence of her extraordinary ability. In this case, the hedge fund can show Padama's portfolio profitability as other comparable evidence of her extraordinary ability even though it is not one of the listed criteria for establishing extraordinary ability in business.

Case for Discussion 4.2

Dr. Klum is a German national and renowned biochemist. For the past ten years, he has worked as a tenured professor at one of Austria's most distinguished universities. He is best known for his breakthroughs in chemotherapy medication. To his credit, Dr. Klum has been published over 50 times in leading journals and has given presentations at numerous industry conferences across the globe. Dr. Klum was also the first runner-up for a national prize for excellence in the field of science. Recently, a major publication interviewed him for a feature article. An Ivy League university is now recruiting Dr. Klum to head up their chemistry department. The position is scheduled for an indefinite term.

- Is Dr. Klum eligible for O-1A classification?
- If so, from the description above, which criteria does he meet?
- What additional information would you want before starting to draft the petition?

A.3. Proving the Merits for O-1B Nonimmigrant Classification: Demonstrating Extraordinary Ability in the Arts, and Extraordinary Achievement in the Motion Picture or Television Industry

The definition of extraordinary ability for O-1B foreign nationals carries a lower evidentiary burden than the O-1A sub-classification. Those who have demonstrated extraordinary ability in the field of arts refer to foreign nationals who have achieved honors and acclaim of distinction within the field, while extraordinary achievement in the motion picture or television industry refers to those that have achieved a level of superior accomplishment.

> **Arts**: Any field of creative activity or endeavor such as, but not limited to, fine, visual, culinary, and performing arts.

Extraordinary ability in the field of ***arts*** refers to distinction, or a high level of achievement, such that the foreign national is recognized as prominent in his or her field of endeavor.[21] A person described as prominent is renowned, leading, or well known in the field.

Extraordinary achievement in the field of Motion Picture or the Television Industry refers to a very high level of accomplishment in those industries. This includes the demonstration of a degree of skill significantly above that ordinarily encountered, to the extent that those industries recognize the person as outstanding, notable, or leading in the motion picture or television field.[22]

To qualify for an O-1 visa in the arts or the motion picture and/or television industry, O-1B beneficiaries must display extraordinary achievement demonstrated by sustained national or international acclaim and field recognition considerably greater than that typically experienced, including an acknowledgment of outstanding achievement. In the drafting and assembly of the O-1B petition, the petitioner must present evidence that the beneficiary has received or been nominated for significant national or international awards or prizes in the particular field, such as an Academy Award, Emmy, Grammy, or Director's Guild Award.[23] Alternatively, evidence of at least three of the following will also suffice:[24]

- Performed and will perform services as a lead or starring participant in productions or events that have a distinguished reputation as evidenced by critical reviews, advertisements, publicity releases, publications, contracts, or endorsement;
- Achieved national or international recognition for achievements, as shown by critical reviews or other published materials by or about the beneficiary in major newspapers, trade journals, magazines, or other publications;
- Performed and will perform in a lead, starring, or critical role for organizations and establishments that have a distinguished reputation as evidenced by articles in newspapers, trade journals, publications, or testimonials;
- A record of major commercial or critically acclaimed successes, as shown by such indicators as title, rating or standing in the field, box office receipts, motion picture or television ratings, and other occupational achievements reported in trade journals, major newspapers, or other publications;
- Received significant recognition for achievements from organizations, critics, government agencies, or other recognized experts in the field in which the beneficiary is engaged, with testimonials clearly indicating the author's authority, expertise, and knowledge of the beneficiary's achievements; or

---

[21] 8 C.F.R. § 214.2(o)(3)(iv).
[22] 8 C.F.R. § 214.2(o)(3)(v).
[23] 8 C.F.R. § 214.2(o)(3)(v)(A).
[24] 8 C.F.R. § 214.2(o)(3)(v)(B).

- A high salary or other substantial remuneration for services in relation to others in the field, as shown by contracts or other reliable evidence.

As with the criteria for proving extraordinary ability for O-1A classification, these criteria can appear daunting at first. While most foreign nationals will not possess a one-time achievement of significant national or international acclaim, however, many artists that "have a distinguished reputation" will meet at least three of the six criteria.

One area of significant concern when assembling an O-1B petition is the fact that many avenues of critical reviews have moved away from traditional print media to online publications. While online publications can and do carry significance when demonstrating the merits of a candidate for O-1B classification, it is very important to ensure the quality of the publication before submitting it to the USCIS as evidence. For example, citing a small independent film blog without additional documents might be more detrimental than beneficial to the filing because an USCIS adjudicator will not give much weight to such evidence.

When reviewing the above criteria, it is worth noting that two of the standards refer to a foreign national performing a "lead, starring, or critical role." This qualifier refers to organizations and establishments *or* productions that have a distinguished reputation. Implicitly, similar evidence can be provided to demonstrate meeting both of these standards. In addition, when proving a foreign national's "recognition for achievement," testimonial letters from other leaders in the field familiar with his or her work serve as excellent evidence.

Case for Discussion 4.3

Natasha is a Russian ballerina who has graced some of the world's finest stages. Unfortunately, a severe knee injury forced her to take two years off from performing. Before taking a leave from her field, however, Natasha was widely regarded as one of the best ballerinas in all of Russia and maybe even Europe. She has been featured in numerous online publications, has often been asked to teach master classes at leading universities, and has had her work reviewed by both local and national newspapers. Natasha has always had strong box office results. In order to herald her triumphant return to the stage, Natasha has decided to perform a two-month series with a renowned dance company in the United States. While her compensation for such artistic efforts will not be significant when compared to her previous earnings, both Natasha and her agent feel the exposure is worth the reduction in pay.

- Is Natasha eligible for O-1B classification?
- From the description above, which criteria does she meet?
- What are your primary concerns, if any, with the potential success of this petition?

A.4. Compiling the O Nonimmigrant Petition

A complete petition for O visa classification should include:

- Form I-129, Petition for a Nonimmigrant Worker
- O and P Classification Supplement to Form I-129
- Form G-28, Notice of Entry of Appearance as Attorney or Accredited Representative
- Advisory opinion
- Contracts between petitioner and beneficiary
- A valid itinerary and proof of same
- Visa type specific supporting material:
  - ☐ O-1A
    - ☐ Proof that the foreign national has sustained national or international acclaim in the fields of science, business, or athletics
  - ☐ O-1B
    - ☐ Proof that the foreign national has sustained national or international acclaim in the field of the arts *or* motion picture/television industry

A sample legal argument on the merits of a beneficiary's extraordinary ability is shown in Box 4.1.

Box 4.1 — **Sample Legal Argument: In Support of Extraordinary Ability Finding**

Ms. Tate is truly an author of extraordinary ability. As discussed earlier and as established by the documentation provided in support of this petition, Ms. Tate has garnered sustained international acclaim and generated an intense interest surrounding the release of her new novel. She has been interviewed for inclusion in leading publications, news outlets, and periodicals. In addition, her first three novels all received tremendous acclaim and financial success. Ms. Tate's presence in the United States is not just important for the upcoming promotional tour of her latest novel, but for the planned creation of a new book and the potential adaptation of her first two novels to film.

It is acknowledged that meeting three of six criteria (in the instant case five of the six criteria) does not, in itself, establish Ms. Tate as a Foreign National of Extraordinary Ability. However, it must be recognized that the quality of the evidence, taken subjectively as a whole, must be a determining factor in the adjudication of Extraordinary Ability classification. In order to truly understand the basis of Ms. Tate's petition, a final merit determination must be made on her entire body of evidentiary material. When subjectively considering the preponderance of evidence accumulated, it easily merits Ms. Tate as being far more than what is ordinarily encountered, an internationally distinguished individual who demonstrates extraordinary ability as an author.

Similar to the primary working visa classifications discussed in Chapter 3, Nonimmigrant Visas for Intracompany Transferees, Traders and Investors, and Professional Employment, Form I-129, Petition for a Nonimmigrant Worker, and its corresponding O and P Classification Supplement to Form I-129, must accompany all O visa classification petitions and be submitted to the USCIS Service Center with jurisdiction over the location of intended employment.[25] Filing cannot start more than one year before the work is to begin.[26] If the beneficiary will be providing services in multiple jurisdictions, filing of the petition should be with the Service Center with jurisdiction over the headquarters of the employer or agent. The premium processing option is available for all O-1 petitions using Form I-907, Request for Premium Processing Service, which guarantees initial adjudication of the petition within 15 calendar days.

In addition, if the beneficiary is in the United States in a valid immigration status, it is possible, in limited circumstances, to change to O-1 classification without leaving the country. However, if the foreign national is outside the United States, s/he will need to obtain the corresponding O-1 visa stamp at a United States consular section abroad in order to enter the country in this category.[27]

A.5. Changes in Employment and Permanent Residency

A petitioner has the responsibility to notify immediately the USCIS whenever there is a change in the terms and conditions of a foreign national's employment that may affect his or her eligibility for O status.[28] Some changes may require the filing and approval of a new petition in order for employment to continue. Any material change in the terms and conditions of employment or eligibility as originally specified will require filing an amended petition.[29] Additional events or engagements added for an artist or entertainer will not require an amended petition, so long as they fall within the validity period of the petition and require a foreign national of O-1 caliber.[30] If the employment relationship terminates other than through the foreign national's own volition, then the employer and petitioner (where they are different entities) are jointly and severally responsible for providing the reasonable cost of transportation to the foreign national's last place of foreign residence.[31]

Interestingly, even though foreign nationals seeking to enter in O classification are required to demonstrate that they have a residence abroad that they do not intend to abandon (*see* 8 C.F.R. § 214.2(o)(1)(i)), they may still file an application for permanent residency without negative consequence.[32]

The chart in Table 4.1 at the end of this chapter may help to summarize the most important features of the O nonimmigrant status classification.

---

[25] 8 C.F.R. § 214.2(o)(2)(i).
[26] *Id.*
[27] *See* Section B of Chapter 2, Nonimmigrant Visas for Brief Stays, Studies, and Cultural Exchange for a discussion on consular processing.
[28] 8 C.F.R. § 214.2(o)(8)(i)(A).
[29] 8 C.F.R. § 214.2(o)(2)(iv)(D).
[30] *Id.*
[31] 8 C.F.R. § 214.2(o)(16).
[32] 8 C.F.R. § 214.2(o)(13).

A.6. Visas for Derivatives of the Principal O-1 Foreign National

Foreign nationals granted O nonimmigrant visa status may apply for others to enter the United States alongside them to serve in an essential capacity. Those granted such status are given O-2 classification, which refers to those who temporarily visit the United States either exclusively to support the artistic or athletic performance by a foreign national holding valid O-1 classification,[33] or as qualified derivative family members.[34]

A.6.a. O-2 Visa Holders: Essential Support of O-1 Foreign Nationals

Eligibility for O-2 status rests on the foreign national accompanying and serving an essential purpose in order to assist an O-1 nonimmigrant visa holder. Different criteria apply depending on which O-1 classification is sought. These are:

- For those foreign nationals accompanying an O-1 artist or athlete of extraordinary ability, they must be coming to assist in the performance of the O-1 recipient, be an integral part of the actual performance, and, furthermore, hold and present critical skills and experience with the O-1 foreign national that are not of a general nature and are not possessed by U.S. workers.[35]
- With regards to those accompanying an O-1 of extraordinary achievement involved in a motion picture or television production, the O-2 must possess skills and experience specifically in collaboration with the O-1 foreign national that are not of a general nature and that are critical, either based on a pre-established and longstanding working partnership or, if in correlation with a particular performance or show, significant to production, including pre- or post-production work that will take place both in the United States and abroad, and to which the continuing contribution of the accompanying foreign national is essential to the successful completion of that production.[36]

Foreign nationals may not obtain O-2 status in order to accompany O-1 foreign nationals in the fields of science, business, or education. Instead, they must obtain status through a different visa classification such as the H-1B for skilled workers.

It is important to note that the O-2 beneficiary must file a separate petition with the USCIS, necessitating an advisory opinion, in order to obtain this status.[37] While authorized employment in the O-2 category is petitioner specific, the recipient is also required to provide support only to the specified O-1 foreign

---

[33] 8 C.F.R. § 214.2(o)(4).
[34] INA § 101(a)(15)(o)(iii); 8 C.F.R. § 214.2(o)(1)(i).
[35] 8 C.F.R. § 214.2(o)(4)(ii)(A).
[36] 8 C.F.R. § 214.2(o)(4)(ii)(B).
[37] 8 C.F.R. § 214.2(o)(4)(i).

national and no other.[38] In addition, filing of the O-2 foreign national's petition must be concurrent with the request for the services of the O-1 nonimmigrant visa holder.[39] Examples of O-2 support personnel can range from hair and make-up artists for an actor or a voice coach for a singer, to a coach or athletic trainer for a tennis player. The important factor to consider is the function the foreign national accompanying the O-1 beneficiary serves and the essential nature of the services provided.

Case for Discussion 4.4

Salizar, a foreign national from Georgia, is an expert voice coach. About three years ago, he worked with a now-famous rock star, Belinda, from the United Kingdom, when she was just getting started in the industry. Salizar wants to work in the United States. He knows that Belinda has a tour coming up there soon. Salizar calls Belinda and she says that he can join the tour for the first month or so, but after that her regular voice coach will be coming. Belinda has an O-1 visa valid for the full length of the 18-month tour.

- Can Salizar obtain O-2 status?
- If so, how long will Salizar be permitted to be in the United States in O-2 support personnel status?

A.6.b. O-3 Nonimmigrant Visa Holders: Spouse and Children of O-1 Beneficiary

Like many other nonimmigrant and immigrant visas, spouses and children of foreign nationals with valid classifications are able to obtain status as dependents.[40] In the case of dependents of an O-1 beneficiary, any accompanying spouse of either an O-1 or O-2 and/or unmarried children under the age of 21 are eligible to apply for the O-3 visa classification as an **accompanying relative**, subject to the same period of admission and limitations as the principal beneficiary.[41] While valid O-3 visa holders are not eligible to work without employment authorization, they are able to enroll in either full or part time academic study without applying for a student visa.

---

[38] Id.
[39] Id.
[40] INA § 101(a)(15)(O)(iii); 8 C.F.R. § 214.2(o)(1)(i).
[41] 8 C.F.R. § 214.2(o)(6)(iv).

B. Visas for Athletes (P-1) and Artists and Entertainers (P-2 and P-3): INA § 101(a)(15)(P); 8 C.F.R. § 214.2(p)

Under § 101(a)(15)(P) of the Immigration and Nationality Act, a foreign national that has a residence in a foreign country that s/he has no intention of abandoning can demonstrate nonimmigrant intent. Those that meet this qualification may receive authorization to come to the United States temporarily to perform services for an employer or a sponsor as an artist, athlete, or entertainer. While the P classification mirrors the O-1 category by requiring supporting documentation demonstrating a required number of criteria from an expansive list, the P nonimmigrant visa generally carries a lower threshold and is used for more specific purposes.

There are three types of P classifications:

- The P-1 is for foreign nationals coming to the United States to compete as athletes at an internationally recognized level of performance, either as an individual or as part of a group or team, or to perform as part of an entertainment group that carries an international reputation as being outstanding;[42]
- The P-2 is for foreign nationals coming to the United States to perform as artists or entertainers, either on their own or as part of a group, under a reciprocal exchange program between aligned professional organizations in the United States and abroad, e.g. trade unions;[43] or
- The P-3 is for foreign national artists or entertainers coming to the United States to perform, teach, or coach under a commercial or noncommercial program that is culturally unique.[44]

Athletes on professional sports teams, such as a National Football League or Major League Baseball player or an individual sports player such as a professional golfer often use P-1 classifications. The B-1 nonimmigrant visa classification for business can also be used for those coming to the United States as athletes to participate in competitions where the only compensation is prize money and the need to be in the United States is for a limited duration.[45] P-1 classification also allows for entertainment groups, such as foreign musical acts or performance artists, to come to the United States for a particular performance.

Performers who are members of unions that have reciprocal agreements often use the P-2 classification. Such unions include the Screen Actors Guild, or SAG, and the American Federation of Television and Radio Artists, or AFTRA, in the United States, and Alliance of Canadian Cinema, Television,

---

[42] 8 C.F.R. § 214.2(p)(1)(ii)(A).
[43] 8 C.F.R. § 214.2(p)(1)(ii)(B).
[44] 8 C.F.R. § 214.2(p)(1)(ii)(C).
[45] See Section E.2.b of Chapter 2, Nonimmigrant Visas for Brief Stays, Studies, and Cultural Exchange.

and Radio Artists, or ACTRA, in Canada. The P-3 classification is purely for cultural uniqueness, such as Mongolian throat singers and Aboriginal musicians from Australia. Detailed discussion of each of the uses of the P nonimmigrant classification follows.

Similar to the O-1 classification, given the nature of the industries that use the P classification, agents can act as petitioners.[46] In addition, P classification allows for essential support personnel to accompany the primary beneficiary to the United States, so long as individual petitions are filed and approved for them.[47] There is no special designation for P classification essential support personnel, who are comparable to the O-2 classification. Instead, they receive the same P-1, P-2, or P-3 designation as the primary beneficiary and an annotation of the visa page itself will indicate their role.

B.1. Shared Requirements for All P Classifications and Similarities to the O-1 Classification

The mechanics of the P nonimmigrant classification are largely the same as the O-1 classification. All P classifications require the filing of petitions with the USCIS on Form I-129, Petition for a Nonimmigrant Worker, along with the O and P Classification Supplement to Form I-129.[48] In addition, the P-1 classification requires the petitioner to obtain a consultation before submitting the petition.[49] However, unlike the O classification where peer groups can also serve in a consultancy capacity, the P-1 classification requires the use of a labor organization, if one exists in the field of endeavor.[50]

Similar to the O-1 classification, the P-1 nonimmigrant classification also requires filing new petitions whenever there is a change in employer or agent[51] and allows the filing of petitions no more than six months before the identified need for the foreign national's service.[52] Any material change in the terms and conditions of employment or eligibility as originally specified will require filing an amended petition.[53] Additional similar or comparable performances, engagements, or competitions added will not require an amended petition, so long as they fall within the validity period of the petition.[54]

The P-1 classification has a special provision for the trading of professional athletes from one team to another.[55] Under this circumstance, the foreign

---

[46] 8 C.F.R. § 214.2(p)(2)(iv)(E).
[47] 8 C.F.R. § 214.2(p)(2)(i).
[48] 8 C.F.R. § 214.2(p)(2).
[49] 8 C.F.R. § 214.2(p)(7).
[50] 8 C.F.R. § 214.2(p)(7)(C).
[51] 8 C.F.R. § 214.2(p)(2)(iv)(C).
[52] 8 C.F.R. § 214.2(p)(2).
[53] 8 C.F.R. § 214.2(p)(2)(iv)(D).
[54] *Id.*
[55] 8 C.F.R. § 214.2(p)(2)(iv)(C)(2).

national's employment authorization automatically continues for a period of 30 days during which time the new team is expected to file a new petition for the traded athlete and, if timely filed, the employment authorization continues until the case is adjudicated.

> ● **EXAMPLE**
>
> **Ronaldo, a foreign national from the Dominican Republic holding P-1 nonimmigrant classification, is a pitcher for a Major League Baseball team that is having a bad season. Ronaldo, however, is personally having a great season. He is finally traded to a division leader. Ronaldo can pitch for the new team immediately even though a filing for a new petition has not yet been filed on his behalf. The team will then have a 30-day grace period to do so. If it fails to file within that period, Ronaldo will lose his employment authorization and will be out of status.**

One of the unique components of the P nonimmigrant classification is the filing of a single petition for multiple beneficiaries.[56] This provision stems from the fact that entertainment groups are specifically referenced in each subclassification, and, as will be discussed in detail, the group is often assessed for P classification together rather than by examining the merits of each individual foreign national member. While it is necessary to name each beneficiary specifically on Form I-129, Petition for a Nonimmigrant Worker, it is possible to substitute beneficiaries at the consular office when obtaining the visa to enter the country if necessary.[57]

> ● **EXAMPLE**
>
> **The Jongleurs are a Swiss juggling act. The group has ten members listed individually on the initial petition for P-1 nonimmigrant classification. The P-1 petition was approved, but right before the group was to go to the consular section in Bern for their visa applications, one of the troop's performers broke her arm. Fortunately, the Jongleurs were able to find another Swiss national to replace her. In this case, the new performer can obtain P-1 status through the consular section even though his name does not appear in the original petition.**

In addition, similar to the O-1 nonimmigrant classification, essential support personnel to P classification principal beneficiaries require their own petitions and advisory opinion.[58] Another similarity between the P and the O-1 classifications is the need for a dedicated itinerary that discusses in detail the nature of the events and locations where they will take place.[59] In this respect, the P nonimmigrant visa petition can be viewed as having both a merits component and an itinerary component.

---

[56] 8 C.F.R. § 214.2(p)(2)(iv)(F).
[57] 8 C.F.R. § 214.2(p)(2)(H).
[58] 8 C.F.R. § 214.2(p)(2).
[59] 8 C.F.R. § 214.2(p)(2)(ii)(C).

If the employment relationship terminates other than through the foreign national's own volition, then the employer and petitioner (where they are different entities) are jointly and severally responsible for providing the reasonable cost of the transportation to the foreign national's last place of foreign residence.[60] Similar to those in O classifications, foreign nationals in P category are required to demonstrate that they have a residence abroad that they do not intend to abandon (see 8 C.F.R. § 214.2(p)(1)(i)) but may still file an application for permanent residency without negative consequence.[61]

B.2. Evidentiary Criteria for P-1 Athlete Classification

While many foreign national professional athletes can obtain O-1A nonimmigrant classification, the majority enter the United States in P-1 athlete, or P-1A, classification instead. This path is preferable because the evidentiary standard is lower. In addition, P-1A classification grants use for up to five years[62] instead of three and is renewable for up to an additional five-year period instead of annually.[63] However, the maximum period permitted in P-1A status is ten years.[64] While this may seem a significant difference from the O-1A classification, which has no limit, the reality is that ten years exceeds most professional sports careers and provides ample time for the foreign national to pursue lawful permanent resident status in the United States, if desired.

Professional sports teams coming to compete in the United States can use the P-1A classification. A team, for P-1A purposes, is defined as two or more individuals who function as a unit.[65] This distinction is important because O-1A classification is only for individuals.

A P-1A athlete must have acquired an internationally recognized reputation or be a member of a foreign team that is internationally recognized.[66] In order to meet the evidentiary standard, the petitioner must provide documentary evidence that the foreign national or team meet at least two of the following criteria:[67]

- Evidence of having participated to a significant extent in a prior season with a major U.S. sports league;
- Evidence of having participated in international competition with a national team;
- Evidence of having participated to a significant extent in a prior season for a U.S. college or university in intercollegiate competition;

---

[60] 8 C.F.R. § 214.2(p)(18).
[61] 8 C.F.R. § 214.2(p)(15).
[62] 8 C.F.R. § 214.2(p)(8)(iii)(A).
[63] 8 C.F.R. § 214.2(p)(14).
[64] Id.
[65] 8 C.F.R. § 214.2(p)(4)(i)(B).
[66] 8 C.F.R. § 214.2(p)(4)(i).
[67] 8 C.F.R. § 214.2(p)(4)(ii)(B)(2).

- A written statement from an official of a major U.S. sports league or an official of the governing body of the sport which details how the foreign national or team is internationally recognized;
- A written statement from a member of the sports media or a recognized expert in the sport which details how the foreign national or team is internationally recognized;
- Evidence that the individual or team is ranked if the sport has international rankings; or
- Evidence that the foreign national or team has received a significant honor or award in the sport.

When comparing this list of criteria to those for O-1 nonimmigrant classification, the most noticeable difference is that only two tests from this list need to be satisfied rather than three, making the P-1A a lower threshold. It is good practice to always submit as much evidence as possible for any P-1 petition and not rest simply on providing evidence for the benchmark criteria alone. Even when examining these criteria from a common sense perspective, it is clear as to why the P-1 is easier to obtain than the O-1 visa. For example, a world-renowned golfer can probably obtain a written statement from an official of the Professional Golf Association, or PGA, given that participation in a PGA sponsored event is what drives the need to enter the United States. In addition, most internationally recognized golfers have been interviewed by members of the sports media and therefore can approach these journalists for a testimonial letter.

Seeking entry into the United Sates for a competition requires the event to carry a distinguished reputation, such as the U.S. Tennis Open Championships or other similar competitions.[68] To demonstrate this fact, all P-1 petitions must include a contract with a major United States sports league or team, or a contract in an individual sport that is associated with international recognition.[69]

Case for Discussion 4.5

Mario is a famous jockey from Italy who has competed in numerous flat track races in Italy as well as other countries in Europe. Mario rode on the Italian National Junior Equestrian team when he was in high school and also is ranked in the top 100 in the sport. A stable in the United States recently contacted Mario, asking him if he would like to ride on their behalf for the upcoming season.

- Is Mario eligible for P-1A classification?
- From the description above, which criteria does he meet?
- What additional information would you want before starting to draft the petition?

---

[68] 8 C.F.R. § 214.2(p)(4)(ii).
[69] 8 CF.R. § 214.2(p)(4)(ii)(B)(1).

B.3. Evidentiary Criteria for P-1B Nonimmigrant Classification: Members of an Internationally Recognized Entertainment Group

Similar to the P-1A athlete, most internationally recognized entertainers can seek O-1 classification. However, the P-1 Members of Internationally Recognized Entertainment Group classification, or P-1B, has a distinct advantage since all members of the entertainment group can apply on a single petition with the merit of their eligibility driven by their collective ability rather than an assessment of each individual member's talent.[70]

To support P-1B nonimmigrant classification, the petition must include evidence that the group has been established and performing together regularly for at least one year.[71] In terms of the merits decision itself, the criteria listed in the regulation is nearly the same as the criteria listed for O-1B classification. Specifically, the group can provide proof that it has been the recipient of a major international award, such as a Grammy,[72] or satisfies at least three of the following criteria:[73]

- Evidence that the group has performed, and will perform, as a starring or lead entertainment group in productions or events that have a distinguished reputation as evidenced by critical reviews, advertisements, publicity releases, publications, contracts, or endorsements;
- Evidence that the group has achieved international recognition and acclaim for outstanding achievement in its field as evidenced by reviews in major newspapers, trade journal magazines, or other published material;
- Evidence that the group has performed, and will perform, services as a leading or starring group for organizations and establishments that have a distinguished reputation evidenced by articles in newspapers, trade journals, publications, or testimonials;
- Evidence that the group has a record of major commercial or critically acclaimed successes, as evidenced by such indicators as ratings, standing in the field, box office receipts, or video sales, and other achievements in the field as reported in trade journals, major newspapers, or other publications;
- Evidence that the group has achieved significant recognition for achievements by organizations, critics, government agencies, or other recognized experts in the field. Such testimonials must be in a form that clearly indicates the author's authority, expertise, and knowledge of the achievements; or
- Evidence that the group either has commanded a high salary or will command a high salary or other substantial remuneration for services comparable to others similarly situated in the field as evidenced by contracts or other reliable evidence.

---

[70] 8 C.F.R. § 214.2(p)(4)(i)(B).
[71] Id.
[72] 8 C.F.R. § 214.2(p)(4)(iii)(B)(3).
[73] Id.

There are some special provisions associated with the P-1B classification that are worth noting. When reviewing the composition of the group for the purposes of demonstrating the one-year establishment requirement, only 75 percent of the total members of the group are required to have been performing together for that period.[74] In addition, there is a special provision for foreign nationals who are members of a circus, an industry known for a high turnover of performers. They are not subject to the one-year membership or international recognition requirements so long as the petitioner can prove that they are coming to join a circus that has itself been recognized nationally as outstanding for a substantial and sustained period.[75]

With respect to duration of stay, P-1B nonimmigrant status can be granted for the period needed to complete the event, which cannot exceed one year,[76] yet is theoretically renewable indefinitely, so long as it is required to complete the same event or activity for which the foreign national was admitted.[77] This admission period differs greatly from the P-1A classification, where an athlete can only be granted two five-year terms, at a maximum.

Case for Discussion 4.6

Drop Kick is a heavy metal band that has been performing together to small audiences at local bars dotted throughout the United Kingdom for close to a decade. Recently, a talent agent came across one of their performances and was incredibly impressed. After a whirlwind video shoot, instant fame fell upon them. From talk show appearances to industry magazine articles, the attention is percolating. The band is comprised of four members: three United Kingdom nationals and one Irish national. In order to capitalize on the success of the band, the agent arranged a short U.S. tour that will last approximately a month in duration. A petition for P-1B nonimmigrant classification was filed with the USCIS and approved. Right before the band members headed off to the Embassy to apply for their visa stamps, the Irish national decided to quit, citing creative differences and a desire to start a solo project. The band was able to find a replacement, a Swedish national.

- Is Drop Kick still eligible for P-1B classification?
- If so, can the Swedish national obtain a visa to travel and perform with the band in the United States?

---

[74] 8 C.F.R. § 214.2(p)(4)(i)(B).
[75] 8 C.F.R. § 214.2(p)(4)(iii)(C).
[76] 8 C.F.R. § 214.2(p)(8)(iii)(B).
[77] 8 C.F.R. § 214.2(p)(14)(ii)(B).

B.4. Evidentiary Criteria for P-2 Nonimmigrant Artists or Entertainers Under a Reciprocal Exchange Program

The P-2 nonimmigrant classification provides another avenue for artists and entertainers to enter the United States.[78] Rather than being based primarily on the skills of the particular artist, the P-2 visa classification is firmly rooted in the nature of exchange agreements between artistic organizations, primarily unions. While limited in applicability, it is a useful tool especially for stage and screen acting communities. Similar to the P-1B classification, P-2 status can be issued in one-year renewable increments to complete the event or activity for which they were admitted.[79]

● EXAMPLE

Elisabeth is a Canadian stage actor who has always dreamed of performing in New York's annual Shakespeare in the Park productions. While not well known internationally, Elisabeth is a Canadian ACTRA actors' union member in good standing. ACTRA and its U.S. equivalent, SAG-AFTRA, have a reciprocal exchange agreement. After a successful audition and issuance of a contract, Elisabeth is able to obtain P-2 nonimmigrant classification even though she may not have qualified for O-1B status because she lacks a distinguished reputation.

In order to support a P-2 filing, 8 C.F.R. § 214.2(p)(5)(ii) states that the petition include the following criteria:

- A copy of the formal reciprocal exchange agreement between the U.S. organization or organizations which sponsor the [foreign nationals] and an organization or organizations in a foreign country which will receive the U.S. artist or entertainers;
- A statement from the sponsoring organization describing the reciprocal exchange of U.S. artists or entertainers as it relates to the specific petition for which P-2 classification is being sought;
- Evidence that an appropriate labor organization in the United States was involved in negotiating, or has concurred with, the reciprocal exchange of U.S. and foreign artists or entertainers; and
- Evidence that the [foreign nationals] for whom P-2 classification is being sought and the U.S. art entertainers subject to the reciprocal exchange agreement are artists or entertainers with comparable skills, and that the terms and conditions of employment are similar.

---

[78] 8 C.F.R. § 214.2(p)(1)(ii)(B).
[79] 8 C.F.R. § 214.2(p)(14)(ii)(B).

B.5. Evidentiary Criteria for P-3 Nonimmigrant Artists or Entertainers Under a Culturally Unique Program

The P-3 nonimmigrant classification provides yet another means by which artists and entertainers can enter the United States.[80] What sets this classification apart from the rest of the P categories is most certainly the culturally unique component. However, under the P-3 classification, the artist or entertainer has a wider selection of permissible activities they can engage in while in the United States. Similar to the other artists and entertainer P-1 classification, P-3 nonimmigrant visas are issued in one-year renewable increments to complete the event or activity for which the foreign national was admitted.[81] A P-3 beneficiary can enter the United States for the purpose of developing, interpreting, representing, coaching, or teaching a unique or traditional ethnic, folk, cultural, musical, theatrical, or artistic performance presentation.[82]

> **Culturally Unique**: Style of artistic expression, methodology, or medium that is unique to a particular country, nation, society, class, ethnicity, religion, tribe, or other group of persons.

Most P-3 cases turn on whether or not the activity is truly *culturally unique*.[83] For example, the art of miming was born in France but, because it has become so ubiquitous throughout numerous cultures as a common art form, it is no longer unique to that country nor to a particular subset of French culture. Therefore, it would be extremely difficult for a mime artist to obtain P-3 classification. The same analysis would also be true for certain fields of martial arts, such as Brazilian Jujutsu. At one point, this act of expression most certainly would have qualified for P-3 classification, but now that it is relatively common in the United States, obtaining this status for this art form might be more difficult. While it is safe to say that Mongolian throat singers are still eligible for this classification, careful analysis of not only art, but culture, is critical to a successful application.

The central evidence needed to demonstrate the cultural uniqueness of a particular performance is stated in 8 C.F.R. § 214.2(6)(ii) as:

- Affidavits, testimonials, or letters from recognized experts attesting to the authenticity of the [foreign national's] or the group's skills in performing, presenting, coaching, or teaching the unique or traditional art form, giving the credentials of the expert, including the basis of his or her knowledge of the [foreign national's] or group's skill; or
- Documentation that the performance of the [foreign national] or group is culturally unique, as evidenced by reviews in newspapers, journals, or other published materials; and
- Evidence that all of the performances or presentations will be culturally unique events.

---

[80] 8 C.F.R. § 214.2(p)(1)(ii)(C).
[81] 8 C.F.R. § 214.2(p)(14)(ii)(B).
[82] 8 C.F.R. § 214.2(p)(6)(i)(A).
[83] 8 C.F.R. § 214.2(p)(3).

> **Case for Discussion 4.7**
>
> While traveling the back country of the Amazon Rain Forest, Roger, an American anthropologist, came across one of the last discovered indigenous tribes in the world. While interacting with the tribe, he discovered that they had created a number of instruments never heard before by the Western World. Roger convinced a few members of the tribe to return with him to the United States to share their talents.
>
> - How would you demonstrate that the tribe musicians are eligible for P-3 nonimmigrant classification so that they can obtain a visa to travel?

B.6. Compiling the P Nonimmigrant Visa Petition

All P nonimmigrant classification filings should include:

- Form I-129, Petition for a Nonimmigrant Worker
- O and P Classification Supplement to Form I-129
- Form G-28, Notice of Entry of Appearance as Attorney or Accredited Representative
- Copies of any written contracts between the petitioner and the beneficiary, and if there is no written agreement, a summary of the oral terms of the agreement under which the foreign national(s) operate in the United States
- An explanation of the nature of the event or activities and the duration for which the foreign national(s)'s services are needed in the United States
- A written consultation from a labor organization
- Visa type specific supporting material:
    - ☐ P-1
        - ☐ Proof that the foreign national is an international athlete or performance group of merit
    - ☐ P-2
        - ☐ Proof of a valid reciprocal agreement between performance unions
        - ☐ Proof of the foreign national's artistic merit
    - ☐ P-3
        - ☐ Proof that the foreign national or foreign group is culturally unique

Similar to the O nonimmigrant classification, filings for P status can also use the premium processing service. The chart in Table 4.1 at the end of this chapter may help to summarize the most important features of the P nonimmigrant status classification.

B.7. P-4 Nonimmigrant Visa Holders: Spouse and Children of P Beneficiary

The spouse and children of foreign nationals with valid P nonimmigrant classification are able to obtain visas to enter and remain in the United States as dependents.[84] Any accompanying spouse of either the principal beneficiary or supporting personnel and/or unmarried children under the age of 21 are eligible to apply for the P-4 nonimmigrant visa classification[85] but are not eligible to work without prior employment authorization.

C. Visas for Religious Workers (R-1): INA § 101(a)(15)(R); 8 C.F.R. § 214.2(r)

The United States has always prided itself on its protection of religious freedom. Therefore, it is not surprising that there is a specific visa classification just for **religious workers**, the R-1 classification.[86] While not related to the functions that are provided by those in O or P classification, the R-1 is similar in that it can be used for a wide variety of professional purposes. It is a mistake to think that this classification is solely reserved for members of the clergy. It is also worth noting that a religious worker with extraordinary ability could qualify for O-1 classification. In addition, similar to the O and P classifications, those seeking status petition the USCIS using Form I-129, Petition for a Nonimmigrant Worker, along with the R Classification Supplement to Form I-129.[87] Premium processing for this category is only available for certain petitioners seeking R-1 classification, namely those who have previously obtained such status on behalf of a foreign national employee in the past, after a site inspection.

● **EXAMPLE**

St John's Episcopal Church is seeking a new Minister. They finally locate a qualified Canadian national to hold the position after an extensive search. With less than a month before the Christmas holiday period, St. John's files the corresponding R-1 petition via premium processing. Because it had a site visit two years ago when hiring a Youth Minister from the United Kingdom, the USCIS will accept the premium-processing request.

C.1. Types of Religious Workers Eligible for R-1 Nonimmigrant Classification

Religious Vocation: A position where the foreign national has undertaken a lifelong commitment to a religious denomination, demonstrated by the adoption of vows, such as for a nun or a monk.

To obtain R classification, the foreign national must be coming to the United States either to perform services as a minister, a person working in a **religious occupation,** or in a *religious vocation*.[88]

---

[84] INA § 101(a)(15)(P)(iv).
[85] 8 C.F.R. § 214.2(p)(8)(iii)(D).
[86] INA § 101(a)(15)(R).
[87] 8 C.F.R. § 214.2(r)(3).
[88] 8 C.F.R. § 214.2(r)(2).

In addition, the foreign national must be coming to the United States to work for at least 20 hours per week.[89] The other major requirement associated with R-1 classification is that, for the last two years, the foreign national has been a member of the same religious denomination as the petitioning religious organization that has ***bona fide nonprofit religious organization*** status.[90]

While the USCIS's definition of minister essentially falls in line with a common understanding of the term,[91] what qualifies as a religious occupation is far more complicated because there are differences based on the specific religious denomination. The central tenet is that the duties must be affiliated with furthering the religious beliefs of the denomination. The USCIS does not rely on a specific list of occupations when it comes to religious occupations, but examples of these types of jobs include religious teachers, choir leaders, missionaries, and religious broadcasters. Positions that are mostly administrative in nature and those that provide support services that do not require religious training, such as janitorial services, cannot qualify as religious workers.

***Bona Fide* Nonprofit Religious Organization:** A tax-exempt religious organization as cited in § 501(c)(3) of the Internal Revenue Code of 1986, and possessing a currently valid determination letter from the Internal Revenue Service, confirming the tax-exempt status.

● **EXAMPLE**

Hailey is an accomplished Israeli Hebrew School Teacher. A synagogue in the United States hires her to run their religious school program. Hailey would be eligible for R-1 classification as a professional religious worker.

C.2. Compensation for R-1 Nonimmigrant Workers

While there is no prevailing wage requirement for religious workers as with other classifications like the H-1B skilled worker, the petitioning organization must still provide evidence of how it is going to compensate the foreign national.[92] Specifically, the petitioner must state monetary compensation amounts as well as any additional fringe benefits such as housing or room and board. For those religious orders that cannot accept monetary compensation, the organization is still required to demonstrate how it intends to sustain the foreign national during the course of employment. The petitioner is obligated to provide evidence of previous compensation for similar positions or other evidence such as a budget that sets aside money for the religious worker.[93]

---

[89] 8 C.F.R. § 214.2(r)(1)(ii).
[90] 8 C.F.R. § 214.2(r)(1).
[91] 8 C.F.R. § 214.2(r)(2).
[92] 8 C.F.R. § 214.2(r)(11).
[93] 8 C.F.R. § 214.2(r)(11)(i).

C.3. Site Inspections

Due to concerns over fraud within the R-1 nonimmigrant classification, the USCIS mandates that all petitioners seeking to employ a religious worker be subject to at least one site inspection before the grant of this status.[94] Issuance of the R-1 nonimmigrant visa can only occur after completion of the inspection. During a site visit, the USCIS inspector will often tour the facility and interview organizational officials and staff. Once the location of the petitioner is deemed *bona fide*, the USCIS Service Center with jurisdiction over the petition will be notified and regular processing of the case will continue.

C.4. Duration of Stay and Derivatives

The initial period of admission for an R-1 visa holder is 30 months, which can be renewed once so that the maximum period of stay in R-1 nonimmigrant classification is five years.[95] However, after spending one year outside the United States, the foreign national can obtain a new grant of R-1 classification for another five years[96] If the R-1 foreign national is present in the United States less than six months a year, the need to be in the United States is deemed intermittent and the five year maximum duration rule will not apply.[97] This is similar to the L-1 nonimmigrant visa for intracompany transferees and the H-1B nonimmigrant visa for professional specialty occupations (discussed in Chapter 3, Nonimmigrant Visas for Intracompany Transferees, Trade and Investment, and Professional Employment).[98] In addition, and similar to the H-1B and L-1 classifications, any time spent outside of the United States during the visa period can be recaptured and tacked to the end of the initial five-year stay in the United States. It should also be noted that an R-1 religious worker can work for more than one employer at the same time, so long as both employers have obtained approval from the USCIS in advance of any work being performed.[99] If a religious worker wishes to remain in the United States on a permanent basis, s/he can seek immigrant visa status through another separate procedure specifically for religious workers without it negatively affecting his or her nonimmigrant status as a religious worker.[100]

Approved spouses and unmarried children under 21 of R-1 beneficiaries can obtain R-2 nonimmigrant classification, with the same length of stay as the principal foreign national.[101] However, they cannot receive permission to work.

---

[94] 8 C.F.R. § 214.2(r)(16).
[95] 8 C.F.R. §§ 214.2(r)(4)(i),(5).
[96] 8 C.F.R. § 214.2(r)(6).
[97] *Id.*
[98] *See* Sections B.3 and C.4 of Chapter 3, Nonimmigrant Visas for Intracompany Transferees, Trade and Investment, and Professional Employment.
[99] 8 C.F.R. § 214.2(r)(2).
[100] 8 C.F.R. § 214.2(r)(15). The process for applying for permanent residency as a religious worker is at Section G of Chapter 7, Employment-Based and Self-Sponsored Immigration.
[101] 8 C.F.R. § 214.2(r)(4)(ii).

C.5. Compiling the R Nonimmigrant Visa Petition

An R nonimmigrant classification filing should include:

- Form I-129, Petition for a Nonimmigrant Worker
- R Classification Supplement to Form I-129
- Form G-28, Notice of Entry of Appearance as Attorney or Accredited Representative
- Form I-539, Application to Extend/Change Nonimmigrant Status if application is to be filed in the United States, together with I-94, Arrival/Departure Record, as evidence of lawful entry
- Evidence of petitioner's tax-exempt organization status through IRS documentation
- Verifiable evidence of salaried or non-salaried compensation
- If the beneficiary is a minister, provide:
  - ☐ Copy of the beneficiary's certificate of ordination or similar documents
  - ☐ Documents reflecting acceptance of the beneficiary's qualifications as a minister in the religious denomination
- Evidence demonstrating the religious duties and responsibilities associated with the position can be helpful.
- Evidence of membership in a religious denomination having a *bona fide* non-profit religious organization in the United States for at least two years immediately preceding the filing of the petition. This can be in the form of the certificate of ordination or letters from prior employers.[102]

The chart in Table 4.1 at the end of this chapter may help to summarize the most important features of the R nonimmigrant status classification.

Case for Discussion 4.8

Simon is a Canadian citizen who is Christian and is currently going through the process of becoming ordained. He is about half way through his seminary course. Simon decided to take a break from his studies to gain some real world experience. He found a job as a Youth Coordinator and part-time administrator at a church in the same denomination in New Jersey.

- Does the offered position constitute a religious occupation?
- If so, what evidence would you provide to the USCIS to demonstrate the validity of the R-1 filing?

---

[102] A checklist of documents required for the R-1 petition filing can be found at https://www.uscis.gov/sites/default/files/files/form/m-736.pdf.

D. Visas for Information Media Representatives (I): INA § 101(a)(15)(I); 8 C.F.R. § 214.2(i); 9 FAM 402.11

Another central tenet of the United States Constitution is Freedom of the Press. Therefore, in the same way that the R classification is available for the use of religious organizations, the I nonimmigrant visa classification is used by members of the international community engaged in the work of broadcast and print communications.[103] Members of the foreign press, TV, radio productions, and publications who seek to travel to the United States on a temporary basis can obtain the I visa in order to perform professional, educational, and informational obligations vital to the operations of international media.[104] The range of occupations that can qualify for I nonimmigrant visa classification is extensive and includes journalists as well as key support personnel such as film crews, editors, producers, photographers, and directors.[105] Unlike the other nonimmigrant visa classifications described in this chapter, foreign national media representatives can submit a consular processing application for an I nonimmigrant visa without the need to first file a petition with the USCIS, making it more flexible and cost effective for the foreign media outlet.

To be eligible to receive the I nonimmigrant visa, foreign nationals must be representatives of a media outlet with a home office in a foreign country and must be travelling to the United States exclusively to further the professional goals of the respective communications agency.[106] As such, the I visa beneficiary can work only for the entity based abroad. Like all other nonimmigrant employment based visa classifications, I status is employer specific.

Those working in the media freelance may also obtain I nonimmigrant visa status, although the process is much more difficult.[107] To be successful, they should have trade and industry qualifications that demonstrate their professional merit. For example, a prospective freelancing I visa beneficiary must be the recipient of a credential distributed by a professional journalistic organization, be in contract with a media organization and lastly, publish material or news not principally intended for profit-making, entertainment, or a commercial marketing strategy.

The foreign national must participate in the defined activities for the international media organization as stated in the original filing with the consular section. The consular officer has discretion to determine whether a particular activity qualifies for the nonimmigrant visa as a media representative. Recently, the expansion of reality television has caused some concern with respect to the

---

[103] INA § 101(a)(15)(I).
[104] 9 FAM 402.11-2.
[105] 9 FAM 402.11-2&3.
[106] 9 FAM 402.11-2.
[107] 9 FAM 402.11-7(d).

applicability of the I visa classification, as the crossover between documentary and scripted productions have become blurred.

While the I nonimmigrant visa itself will be granted for a specific duration as dictated by the particular country's **reciprocity table**, I nonimmigrant visa beneficiaries are admitted for duration of status, or D/S,[108] for an unlimited period, similar to those granted F-1 student status.[109] They can remain in the United States as long as the foreign media outlet requires their presence. Derivative spouses and unmarried children under 21 may also obtain I nonimmigrant classification,[110] but cannot be authorized to work.

The chart in Table 4.1 at the end of this chapter may help to summarize the most important features of the I nonimmigrant status classification.

Case for Discussion 4.9

David is a South African photographer who has worked for numerous media outlets over the past two decades as a freelancer. Recently, he was hired on a contract basis to cover the upcoming national elections in the United States.

- Can David seek I nonimmigrant visa classification?
- What documents will he need to provide to show he meets the criteria?

E. Visas for Temporary Nonimmigrant Workers (H-2): INA § 101(a)(15)(H); 8 C.F.R. § 214.2(h)

The H-2 nonimmigrant classification offers temporary and seasonal visas that can provide year round unskilled employees in the United States labor market. It allows U.S. employers to employ foreign labor (often referred to as guest workers) on a temporary basis for short-term needs.[111] The employer must prove that the foreign national is necessary to the effective functioning of the business operations *and* that there is a shortage of U.S. workers who are capable, willing,

---

[108] Section C of Chapter 2, Nonimmigrant Visas for Brief Stays, Studies, and Cultural Exchange, for a discussion of D/S status.
[109] 8 C.F.R. § 214.2(i). *See* Section E.3.c of Chapter 2, Nonimmigrant Visas for Brief Stays, Studies, and Cultural Exchange.
[110] 9 FAM 402.11-5.
[111] INA § 101(a)(15)(H)(ii).

qualified, and available to carry out the work that needs to be done.[112] The H-2 classification is divided into H-2A for temporary agricultural workers and the H-2B for temporary non-agricultural workers.

The H-2 nonimmigrant visa classification requires the employer to file a temporary labor certification application with the DOL, which must be approved before filing the application with the USCIS in order for the foreign national to be granted H-2 classification.[113] This process involves testing the labor market by placing advertisements for the position in locations where U.S. workers typically seek out such opportunities. The employer must demonstrate that it is unable to find a capable U.S. worker following its publicity efforts and completing interviews with potential candidates. An employer can file for multiple beneficiaries at once,[114] in a similar way to the P-1, members of an internationally recognized entertainment group, or P-3, artists or entertainers under a culturally unique program, nonimmigrant visa classifications.

The H-2 nonimmigrant classification is available to nationals from a list of designated countries allowed to use the program.[115] Currently, this includes 84 countries.[116] Regardless of this, the USCIS may still grant H-2 petitions for nationals of non-listed countries, only if the approval is in the national interest of the United States.[117]

E.1. Visas for Agricultural Work of a Temporary or Seasonal Nature (H-2A): INA § 101(a)(15)(H)(ii)(a); 8 C.F.R. § 214.2(h)(5)

The H-2A nonimmigrant visa classification is specifically reserved for the agricultural industry. Generally, there are two main requirements for employers seeking H-2A classification for their foreign workers:

- The employer must show that there are no available U.S. workers at the time and place needed in order to do the job, and
- Adverse effects on wages to U.S. workers will not occur because of the hiring of foreign agricultural workers.[118]

---

[112] 20 C.F.R. § 655.100.
[113] *Id.*
[114] 8 C.F.R. § 214.2(h)(5)(i)(B).
[115] 8 C.F.R. § 214.2(h)(5)(i)(F)(1)(ii).
[116] The list of designated countries is announced in the Federal Register. The most recent announcement was made on November 18, 2015 and has been effective since January 16, 2016. Federal Register Volume 80, Number 222, November 18, 2015, 72079-72081. It is available at https://www.gpo.gov/fdsys/pkg/FR-2015-11-18/html/2015-29373.htm.
[117] 8 C.F.R. § 214.2(h)(5)(i)(F)(1)(ii); 9 FAM 402.10-4(E)(c).
[118] 20 C.F.R. § 655.1305.

The H-2A classification applies to agricultural jobs that are seasonal in nature, meaning that they are limited to a certain time of year, or temporary, meaning that the employer's need will not extend beyond one year.[119]

Employers must fulfill certain wage criteria when employing foreign nationals under this visa and must cover all transportation costs and provide accommodations to the foreign nationals.[120] The employer must also pay the area's prevailing wage as determined by the DOL, meet at least the state or federal minimum wage, or pay the ***adverse effect wage rate,*** or AEWR,[121] which is calculated by finding the average wage of non-supervisory field and livestock staff as ascertained by the United States Department of Agriculture, or USDA, findings.[122]

The foreign national beneficiary of H-2A nonimmigrant classification can extend the visa for up to three years provided that s/he finds qualifying temporary agricultural work with appropriate employers.[123] The status permits an additional period of up to one week before the beginning of the approved period to allow for travel to the worksite, and a 30-day period following the expiration of the H-2A petition for departure, or to seek an extension based on a subsequent offer of employment.[124] In order to re-establish eligibility for this visa after the maximum period is over, the holder must leave the United States for a minimum of three months, after which s/he can reapply for another three-year term.[125] If a worker in H-2A status needs to leave the country, in certain circumstances time spent outside of the United States will not count toward the three-year limit and is considered an interruption of the employment.[126]

There is no numerical limitation to the number of foreign nationals admissible in H-2A nonimmigrant status to a particular employer on an annual basis. Spouses and unmarried children under the age of 21 of H-2A visa beneficiaries can seek H-4 classification.[127] They are ineligible for work authorization, except in the limited circumstances of those who have been abused or subjected to extreme cruelty. This is a new provision under INA § 106. A policy memorandum issued by the USCIS on March 8, 2016 discusses this in more detail.[128]

An employer issued a H-2A petition has additional responsibilities in that s/he must agree to provide access to the employment site to allow inspections by immigration compliance officers.[129] In addition, the employer agrees to notify DHS within two working days if:

Adverse Effect Wage Rate: Minimum hourly wage, as determined by the Department of Labor, that must be paid by the employer to the foreign agricultural employee in a given area so that U.S. workers are not adversely affected.

---

[119] 8 C.F.R. § 214.2(h)(5)(i)(F)(1)(iv)(A).
[120] 20 C.F.R. § 655.122.
[121] 20 C.F.R. § 655.120.
[122] *See* https://www.foreignlaborcert.doleta.gov/pdf/AEWR/Adverse_Effect_Wage_Rates_2016.pdf.
[123] 8 C.F.R. § 214.2(h)(5)(i)(F)(1)(viii)(C).
[124] 8 C.F.R. § 214.2(h)(5)(i)(F)(1)(viii)(B).
[125] 8 C.F.R. § 214.2(h)(5)(i)(F)(1)(viii)(C).
[126] 8 C.F.R. § 214.2(h)(5)(i)(F)(1)(viii)(C).
[127] 8 C.F.R. § 214.2(h)(9).
[128] *See* USCIS Policy Memorandum PM-602-0130, dated March 8, 2016, *Eligibility for Employment Authorization for Battered Spouses of Certain Nonimmigrants*, accessed at https://www.uscis.gov/sites/default/files/USCIS/Laws/Memoranda/2016/2016-0308_PM-602-0130_Eligibility_for_Employment_Authorization_for_Battered_Spouses_of_Certain_Nonimmigrants.pdf.
[129] 8 C.F.R. § 214.2(h)(5)(vi)(A).

- An H-2A worker fails to report to work within 5 workdays of the employment start date on the H-2A petition or within 5 workdays of the start date established by his or her employer, whichever is later;
- The agricultural labor or services for which H-2A workers were hired is completed more than 30 days earlier than the employment end date stated on the H-2A petition; or
- The H-2A worker absconds from the worksite or is terminated prior to the completion of agricultural labor or services for which he or she was hired.[130]

Case for Discussion 4.10

Steven owns a small mushroom farm in the United States. He is very worried because his harvest season is starting in a few months, but he does not have enough workers lined up to assist him. He wants to hire some foreign nationals to do the work and wants to do so legally. However, Steven does not want to pay the legal, transportation, or housing costs associated with bringing the workers to his Farm.

- Can he achieve his goal in this way?

E.2. Visas for Non-Agricultural Work of a Temporary or Seasonal Nature (H-2B): INA § 101(a)(15)(H); 8 C.F.R. § 214.2(h)(6)

Unlike the H-2A category, which is very narrow in scope, the H-2B nonimmigrant visa classification is broad, allowing for use in most types of employment so long as they are temporary in nature. This category allows foreign nationals the ability to provide temporary non-agricultural services or to work in seasonal employment, if U.S. workers capable of performing these duties cannot be found.[131]

Temporary services or labor, as defined by the USCIS, refers to those required by the hiring company for a limited and defined period.[132] This generally entails work with a termination date in the near and predictable future. The following criteria are cited in 8 C.F.R. § 214.2(h)(6)(ii) as valid reasons for seeking H-2B classification:

- One-time occurrence. The petitioner must establish that it has not employed workers to perform the services or labor in the past and that it will not need workers to perform the services or labor in the future, or that it has an

---

[130] 8 C.F.R. § 214.2(h)(5)(vi)(B)(1).
[131] 8 C.F.R. § 214.2(h)(6)(i).
[132] 8 C.F.R. § 214.2(h)(6)(ii).

employment situation that is otherwise permanent, but a temporary event of short duration has created the need for a temporary worker.
- Seasonal need. The petitioner must establish that the services or labor is traditionally tied to a season of the year by an event or pattern and is of a recurring nature. The petitioner shall specify the period(s) of time during each year in which it does not need the services or labor. The employment is not seasonal if the period during which the services or labor is not needed is unpredictable or subject to change or is considered a vacation period for the petitioner's permanent employees.
- Peakload need. The petitioner must establish that it regularly employs permanent workers to perform the services or labor at the place of employment and that it needs to supplement its permanent staff at the place of employment on a temporary basis due to a seasonal or short-term demand and that the temporary additions to staff will not become a part of the petitioner's regular operation.
- Intermittent need. The petitioner must establish that it has not employed permanent or full-time workers to perform the services or labor, but occasionally or intermittently needs temporary workers to perform services or labor for short periods.

Jobs that may also be granted H-2B status include competitive athletes, camp counselors, artisans and crafts persons, horse and animal trainers, as well as in-home aides for people suffering from terminal illness. Unlike the H-2A category, the H-2B nonimmigrant classification is subject to an annual numerical limitation of 66,000 visas that are divided by two six-month segments to ensure that all seasonal businesses have the opportunity to use the program.[133] Spouses and unmarried minor children under 21 years old can also obtain H-4 nonimmigrant status.[134]

● EXAMPLE

Dr. Larry Waidelinski is a U.S. citizen. On a recent vacation to Poland, he visited the home of friends and fell in love with their traditionally built stone chimney. He decided that this was just the thing that was missing in the country home he is currently building. Unfortunately, there is no one in the United States with the skill set to make what Dr. Waidelinski wants. Therefore, he wants to bring some workers in from Poland to assist. These workers could qualify for H-2B classification because it is unlikely there are qualified U.S. workers available for the job and because the need is a one-time occurrence.

---

[133] 8 C.F.R. § 214.2(h)(8)(i)(C).
[134] 8 C.F.R. § 214.2(h)(9)(iv).

E.3. Compiling the Petitions for H-2A and H-2B Nonimmigrant Classifications

Compiling the application for both H-2 nonimmigrant visa categories involves the same forms but different supporting documents. The common application documents are:

- Form I-129, Petition for a Nonimmigrant worker
- H Classification Supplement to Form I-129,
- Form G-28, Notice of Entry of Appearance as Attorney or Accredited Representative
- Temporary Labor Certification from the DOL
- Evidence the applicant is a national of one of the designated countries, or for nationals of unlisted countries, evidence that granting a visa would be in the national interest of the United States

The chart in Table 4.1 at the end of this chapter may help to summarize the most important features of the I nonimmigrant status classification.

F. Visa Summary Chart

The summary chart in Table 4.1 reviews each major visa classification discussed in this chapter.

Table 4.1 Summary Comparison of Nonimmigrant Visas

Maximum Duration of Visa	Maximum Duration of Each Entry	Maximum Duration Classification Can Be Held Without Departing the United States for a Year	Intent Requirement	Available for Spousal Employment Authorization
O-1 Visa				
3 Years for initial filing and extensions of 1-year durations	Matches approval notice	Indefinite	Nonimmigrant intent, but no negative consequence if adjustment to lawful permanent resident, or LPR, status is sought	No

F: Visa Summary Chart

Maximum Duration of Visa	Maximum Duration of Each Entry	Maximum Duration Classification Can Be Held Without Departing the United States for a Year	Intent Requirement	Available for Spousal Employment Authorization
P-1 Athlete				
5 years for initial filing and renewable for another 5 years	Matches approval notice term	10 years	Nonimmigrant intent, but no negative consequence if adjustment to LPR sought	No
P-1 Artist / P-2 / P-3				
1 year with indefinite 1-year renewals	Matches approval notice	Indefinite	Nonimmigrant intent, but no negative consequence if adjustment to LPR sought	No
R-1 Visa				
30 months for initial filing; renewable for another 30 months	Matches approval notices	5 years; must leave for one year but can be admitted after the year abroad	Nonimmigrant intent, but no negative consequence if adjustment to LPR sought	No
H-2A / H-2B				
Up to 3 years, renewable annually	Matches approval notice; most uses are far less than 3 years because of seasonal nature	6 years	Nonimmigrant intent throughout	No
I Visa				
5 years renewable in 5-year increments	Duration of Stay (D/S)	Theoretically indefinite	Nonimmigrant intent, but no negative consequence if adjustment to LPR sought	No

G. Visas for Foreign Government Officials (A): INA § 101(a)(15)(A); 8 C.F.R. § 214.2(a)

The United States prides itself on its diplomatic relationships with foreign countries. As such, there is a reciprocal flow of workers and diplomats between allied countries. A foreign national seeking entry into the United States on behalf of his or her national government is eligible to apply for A-1 and A-2 nonimmigrant visa classification, if the proposed work relates only to the official actions of that government. This would include those in the diplomatic service, such as Heads of State, Ministers, Ambassadors, Consuls, and Parliamentary and Delegation Representatives, all of whom are eligible candidates for A-1 nonimmigrant status.[135] The applicant must be at least 21 years of age and have full time employment by the relevant governing body.

All Heads of State qualify for A-1 nonimmigrant visas, regardless of the purpose of their visit, and it is available for an indefinite period, as its validity is contingent upon the governmental official's recognition as a member of the diplomatic community.[136] Full time employees of foreign governments working at accredited embassies and consulates are eligible for A-2 nonimmigrant visas.[137]

There is a "90-day-rule" which stipulates that foreign government officials coming to the United States for 90 days or more will only be allowed to enter in A-2 status if their place of work is at an embassy, consulate, or other foreign government agency in the United States.[138] A notable exception, however, applies to persons within the foreign armed forces who are travelling to the United States for education or training.[139]

Spouses, unmarried children under 21, and other dependent family members of diplomats are eligible for the A nonimmigrant visa and therefore subject to the same application process.[140] An A nonimmigrant visa beneficiary can leave and return to the United States an unlimited number of times. Interestingly, children of A nonimmigrant visa beneficiaries physically born in the United States do not become U.S. citizens, since they are considered to have been born in the country of the diplomatic mission. However, they may be eligible for LPR status.[141] By contrast, the principal A nonimmigrant visa holder is not allowed to adjust to an LPR.

---

[135] 9 FAM 402-3.
[136] 8 C.F.R. § 214.2(a)(1).
[137] INA § 101(a)(15)(A)(ii).
[138] 9 FAM 402.3-5(D)(5).
[139] 9 FAM 402.3-5(D)(2).
[140] 8 C.F.R. § 214.2(a)(2).
[141] *See* Section B of Chapter 11, Citizenship and Naturalization. *See also* INA §§ 101(a)(20), 103, 262, 264 and 8 C.F.R. § 101.3(a)(1), 101.4 and 264.2.

H. VISA FOR EMPLOYEES OF INTERNATIONAL ORGANIZATIONS AND NATO (G): INA § 101(a)(15)(G); 8 C.F.R. § 214.2(g)

Foreign nationals officially employed by their governments in certain international organizations who need to travel to the United States for employment, assemblies, or visits to a designated global organization qualify for the G nonimmigrant visa category.[142] These international bodies include the United Nations, the International Monetary Fund, the Inter-American Development Bank, the Organization of American States, the World Health Organization, as well as the World Trade Organization among, many others.[143]

Those foreign nationals who are engaged in work with NATO are not eligible for G nonimmigrant status and must apply for the designated NATO Visa or NATO-1 through -7 instead.[144]

I. CONCLUSION

Chapters 2, 3, and 4 discuss all nonimmigrant visa classifications that facilitate business meetings, education, training, and employment. Again, it is always best to think about the foreign national's purpose or need to be in the United States rather than the alphanumeric designation. By doing so, the various visa options that exist for a given fact pattern or scenario are more easily discernible.

As Chapter 4 in particular demonstrates, there are nonimmigrant visas for a wide range of needs. From extraordinary ability to temporary seasonal work, the current visa system supports the U.S. economy through the legal flow of foreign talent.

---

[142] INA § 101(a)(15)(G).
[143] 9 FAM 402.3-7(N).
[144] 9 FAM 402.3-8(B).

Asylum and Other Related Humanitarian Relief

Key Terms and Acronyms

Affirmative Asylum
Asylee
Convention Against Torture
Credible Fear
Enumerated Grounds
Frivolous Application
Non-refoulement
One-Year Deadline

Persecution
Reasonable Fear
Refugee
Refugee Resettlement
Temporary Protected Status
UNHCR
Withholding of Removal

Chapter Objectives

- Review sources of law for asylum, including international and domestic law
- Analyze criteria for asylum eligibility
- Explain procedure for filing an asylum application
- Understand related forms of relief
- Analyze refugee status in comparison to asylum status

People sometimes arrive in the United States fleeing persecution or dangerous situations in their home countries. Others may already live in the United States but find the situation at home has changed and they are now afraid to return. In some cases, the United States may have a responsibility to provide short- or long-term safeguards for those in this situation. U.S. immigration law thus offers protection in the form of **asylum** and other related humanitarian relief. It is a legal status that accords eligible individuals the protection of residence in the United States, with the possibility of eventually achieving citizenship. Asylum is a discretionary relief, granted either by the United States Citizenship and Immigration Service, or USCIS, or by an immigration judge.

As with immigration law generally, asylum is a sensitive topic, about which Americans hold many differing viewpoints. Some believe the United States has an obligation to provide protection to anyone who reaches its shores seeking refuge, regardless of numbers. Others doubt that most people seeking asylum are doing so for protection reasons; rather, they believe that many of them are economic migrants looking for an opportunity to improve their lives and those of their family members remaining behind. The asylum assessment process is stringent, meant to ensure that only those who have suffered or are likely to suffer persecution (as well as meeting other necessary criteria) obtain asylum status.

By analyzing in detail the substantive issues regarding the law on asylum, this chapter provides a framework for understanding the factors necessary to compile a strong asylum application. We then explore the application procedure and the types of benefits available to those granted status. Next, we examine alternative forms of relief available for those who may not qualify for asylum but still need protection. After a brief review of temporary forms of protection, the chapter concludes with an investigation into the treatment of refugees seeking protection in the United States.

Convention or Protocol: An agreement between states and nations on the regulation of particular matters between them.

Refugee: Any person who is outside their country of nationality and is unwilling or unable to return because of fear of persecution because of that person's race, nationality, religion, membership in a particular social group, or political opinion and the government is unable or unwilling to provide protection.

Non-refoulement: A fundamental principle of international refugee law that prevents the return of a foreign national to a country where there is reason to believe s/he will be persecuted.

A. Overview and Sources of Law for Asylum

A.1. Sources of Law: INA § 101(a)(42); INA § 208; INA § 209; 8 C.F.R. § 208; 8 C.F.R. § 1208; 8 C.F.R. § 1209

The foundation of asylum law and other related humanitarian protections is international refugee law. The primary sources of law in this area are the 1951 United Nations Convention Relating to the Status of Refugees, or the *Convention*,[1] and the 1967 U.N. Protocol relating to the Status of Refugees, or the *Protocol*.[2]

Article 1 of the Convention defines a *refugee*, while Article 33 obligates signatories to the treaty not to return a refugee to a country where "his life or freedom would be threatened on account of his race, religion, nationality, membership of a particular social group, or political opinion." This is known as the *non-refoulement* obligation or principle.

---

[1] United Nations, Treaty Series, vol. 189, p. 137.
[2] United Nations, Treaty Series, vol. 606, p. 267.

The United States is a signatory to the Protocol but not the Convention. Since the Protocol incorporates all the articles within the Convention other than Article 1, which contains the definition of a refugee, the United States still has extensive obligations to refugees under international law. The **United Nations High Commissioner for Refugees**, or **UNHCR** (also known as the UN Refugee Agency) is a body created by the United Nations and given the responsibility to lead and coordinate international action for the worldwide protection of refugees, *internally displaced people,* and those who are *stateless.* The UNHCR also has a mandate to find resolutions to refugee problems.

At the request of governments, UNHCR created the *Handbook and Guidelines on Procedures and Criteria for Determining Refugee Status Under the 1951 Convention and 1967 Protocol Relating to the Status of Refugees.*[3] It was written for "government officials concerned with the determination of refugee status" and was "conceived as a practical guide and not as a treatise on refugee law."[4] Even though it is not legally binding, the Supreme Court has referred to it as an aid in interpreting asylum law in the United States. Written in simple language, it is an important document as it provides guidance and helps in the understanding of this complex area of law.

Prior to 1980, neither the Convention nor the Protocol was codified in U.S. law. Congress then passed the Refugee Act expressly to bring U.S. law into line with international refugee law, and it has now been incorporated into the Immigration and Nationality Act, or INA. The relevant sections of the statute are §§ 101(a)(42)(A), 207, 208, and 209.

In Chapter 1, we noted that regulations provide guidance to agencies charged with implementing a statute. They are particularly important in helping to interpret asylum law, so there is heavy reliance on them as a source of law. The relevant regulatory sections are found in Title 8 of the Code of Federal Regulations, or 8 C.F.R. §§ 207, 208, 209, 1207, 1208, and 1209.[5] While these regulations are lengthy, it is useful to review them.

> **Internally Displaced People:** People who, because of conflict or other disruption to their lives, have been forced to leave their homes and find refuge in another area of their country.
>
> **Stateless:** A person with no legal or formal nationality or citizenship who therefore cannot receive protection from any government.

A.2. Definitions

Section 101(a)(42)(A) of the INA defines a refugee as follows:

> Any person who is outside any country of such person's nationality or, in the case of a person having no nationality, is outside any country in which such person last habitually resided and who is unable or unwilling to return to, and is unable or unwilling to avail himself or herself of the protection of, that country because of persecution or a well-founded fear of persecution on account of race,

---

[3] HCR/IP/4/Eng/REV.1, January 1992, available at http://www.unhcr.org/4d93528a9.pdf.
[4] *Id.* at paragraph V.
[5] As mentioned in Section D.2.b of Chapter 1, Historical Background and Introduction to the U.S. Immigration System, Title 8 of the Code of Federal Regulations is divided into two parts, one for the Department of Homeland Security, or DHS, and one for the Executive Office for Immigration Review, or EOIR. In this chapter, all references to the regulations will be to the DHS section.

nationality, religion, membership in a particular social group, or political opinion.

Refugees are those foreign nationals granted protection before they are permitted to enter the United States. However, there are those who arrive in the country who need to request asylum. These foreign nationals are referred to as asylum seekers and those granted protection are known as asylees. Section I. later in this chapter discusses other differences between these two groups.

Essentially, in order to qualify for asylum, a foreign national must show that:

- S/he has experienced persecution in the past or has a fear it will occur in the future;
- The fear is "well-founded";
- The persecution is "on account of" one of the **enumerated grounds**, which are the person's race, nationality, religion, membership in a particular social group, or political opinion; and
- S/he is unable or unwilling to return to his or her country of nationality.

These factors were provided as guidance by the Board of Immigration Appeals, or BIA, in *Matter of Mogharrabi*, 19 I&N Dec. 211 (BIA 1987), a case where an Iranian student sought asylum based on a political opinion expressed for the first time in the United States. As each of these elements is important, we analyze them separately.

A.2.a. Persecution

Persecution is a central element in any application for asylum. However, despite its importance, there is no statutory or regulatory definition of the term. While the UN Convention may provide guidance as to what may or may not constitute persecution, it too fails to provide a precise definition. Interpreting the term in accordance with evolving standards rather than constraining it by a definition that, with the passage of time, may no longer be appropriate, is certainly beneficial. For example, a form of persecution more recently recognized is female circumcision, or *female genital mutilation,* a practice in some African, Arabic, and Asian countries that has drawn attention over the last few decades. Had there been a specific definition of persecution that did not include FGM, only a change in the law would enable the recognition of this practice as a form of mistreatment eligible for protection.

Female Genital Mutilation: The total or partial alteration of the external female genitalia for non-medical purposes.

Even though there is no statutory definition of persecution, case law does help to define the term. The BIA in *Matter of Acosta*, 19 I&N Dec. 211, 222 (BIA 1985), considered persecution to be "a threat to life or freedom of, or the infliction of suffering or harm upon, those who differ in a way regarded as offensive." The Supreme Court in *INS v. Stevic*, 467 U.S. 407 (1984), noted that persecution is broader than merely threats to life and freedom.

Cumulative and repeated actions may be enough to establish persecution and do not have to cause permanent or serious injuries. For example, in *Matter of O-Z- & I-Z-*, 22 I&N Dec. 23 (BIA 1998), the BIA found that the consistent discrimination and harassment of a Jewish father and son in the Ukraine, even though non-life threatening, could qualify them for asylum because the treatment they had suffered, taken together, rose to the level of persecution. Some types of harm that courts have found to rise to the level of persecution include:

- Threats of death
- Torture, whether physical or mental
- Emotional or psychological trauma
- Substantial economic deprivation amounting to threats to life or freedom
- Rape or sexual assault
- Female genital mutilation
- Prolonged detention without trial
- Forced sterilization or other forms of interference with private or family life

There are harmful acts that do not rise to the level of persecution. In fact, the United States Court of Appeal for the Third Circuit in *Lukwago v. Ashcroft*, 329 F.3d 157, 167-168 (3d Cir. 2003), noted that "persecution does not encompass all treatment that our society regards as unfair, unjust, or even unlawful or unconstitutional." Some acts that do not constitute persecution include the following:

- Discrimination
- Harassment
- Prosecution
- Conscription
- Civil war

● EXAMPLE

Tesfay was a major in the Eritrean army. He was dismissed from his position because he sought to expose corruption in the military. In this case, the treatment of Tesfay, while unjust, would not constitute persecution because losing his job would not rise to the level necessary for it to be considered persecution.

Whether these and other similar acts constitute persecution will depend on the facts of the individual case. For example, prosecution for breaking the law ordinarily would not be persecution. However, paragraphs 56 to 60 of the *U.N. Handbook* state that if the punishment for the crime is excessive, it may actually be an act of persecution. Similarly, while discrimination and harassment alone might not constitute persecution, multiple such acts, in some circumstances, might rise to the level of persecution.

> **Case for Discussion 5.1**
>
> Sharaf is an Iranian national. He is Baha'i, a minority religion in a country where Islam is dominant. Sharaf could not apply for any government jobs nor obtain a business license, all because of his religion. Private employers would not hire him, and as a result, he remained unemployed for long stretches of time. Sharaf's children could not attend the local public school because of their religion and his non-Baha'i neighbors often harassed his family. Because of the difficulty finding employment, the family was very poor and found it almost impossible to earn a living.
>
> - Is Sharaf merely a victim of discrimination and harassment or would his situation rise to the level of persecution?

Civil wars and general anarchy often create harsh conditions typically experienced by a country's entire population. Such situations alone would not give rise to a presumption of persecution. While the BIA has acknowledged that "persecution can and often does take place in the context of civil war," *see Matter of Villalta*, 20 I&N Dec. 142 (BIA 1990), each foreign national is still required to demonstrate that the treatment s/he received targeted him or her individually.

> **● EXAMPLE**
>
> **During the civil war in Liberia from 1999–2003, many citizens fled their country and now wish to apply for asylum in the United States. You have been asked by your employer to attend a community meeting organized by a local Liberian Church in order to give information about the asylum process and conduct initial screenings of the newly arrived to determine whether any would qualify for asylum because of the harm they may have suffered. Some of the questions you might ask would include: "Are you a member of a particular tribe or ethnic group? If so, which one? What, if anything, happened to you in Liberia? Do you know the identity and political or tribal affiliations of your attacker? Did the attacker say anything that would lead you to believe you were being specifically targeted because of your ethnic background or political beliefs?"**

Persecution can also occur indirectly. For instance, if a persecutor is unable to gain access to his primary target because s/he is in hiding or has already left the country, s/he may try to harm the target's family or friends instead. This type of targeting is known as constructive persecution and may be relevant evidence of the persecutor's continued desire to harm the primary target. It would be useful information to submit as evidence that persecution is still ongoing and likely to occur in the future.

A.2.b. Agents of Persecution

In every asylum application, the perpetrator of the persecution must be one of a few specific actors. The *U.N. Handbook* offers a helpful guide when referring to agents of persecution. It states, "[P]ersecution is normally related to action by the authorities in the country. It may also emanate from sections of the population that do not respect the standards established by the laws of the country concerned."[6]

Clearly, a government can be an agent of persecution since it has the power and usually the resources to persecute targeted individuals and groups among its people. On the other hand, an individual can also be an agent of persecution in two particular situations. Either the persecutor is acting as a government agent (for instance, as a police officer) or the government is unable or unwilling to control that person's actions.

Matter of O-Z- & I-Z- discussed the treatment of a Jewish father and his son in the Ukraine. The father was physically attacked on three occasions while his son endured beatings at school, requiring surgery to treat an injury. The son also suffered extreme humiliation when his classmates forced him to undress in front of them. The perpetrators were anti-Semites intent on harming the father and son simply because they were Jewish. Even though the father reported many of these incidents to the police, no significant action was taken to safeguard the family. The BIA decided that even though the persecutors were private actors, the government's failure to protect the father and his son demonstrated it was unable or unwilling to do so. The perpetrators of the attacks would therefore be considered agents of persecution.

Militia or paramilitary groups can also be agents of persecution because they may in fact be acting on behalf of the government. This is particularly true in civil war situations. People operating within such groups could be government agents, even though they may not have formal government roles.

A.2.c. Past Persecution

A foreign national seeking asylum must show that s/he has been persecuted either in the past, known as past persecution, or that harm is likely to occur in the future, known as a well-founded fear of future persecution.

Individuals who have been victims of past persecution may be eligible for asylum even if they cannot show a likelihood of persecution in the future. That is because when a foreign national is able to prove that s/he has experienced past persecution, by law there is a presumption that s/he will face persecution in the future. The U.S. government may challenge, or rebut, this presumption in one of two ways. First, it can show that there has been a fundamental change in circumstances such that the applicant no longer has a well-founded fear of persecution.[7] Once the government proves its case, the foreign national then has the burden to present additional evidence and/or facts that would counter the government's claim.

---

[6] *U.N. Handbook*, Rev. 3, para. 65.
[7] 8 C.F.R. § 208.13(b)(1)(i)(A).

> **Case for Discussion 5.2**
>
> Hamid was a prominent and outspoken University Professor in Afghanistan in 1986. He publically denounced the occupation of his country by and his government's alliance with the former Soviet Union. The government targeted Hamid and sought to silence him. He was arrested as a traitor but later released from detention after 18 months in prison, where he was beaten constantly. Hamid then fled to the United States and claimed asylum. While Hamid's case was pending, the Soviets withdrew, and the government that harmed him was overthrown. However, Hamid now claims he cannot return home because control of many regions in his country is in the hands of the Taliban, a group that opposes all things American and the moderate form of Islam Hamid practices. He claims if he returns, the Taliban will persecute him for having been to the "land of the infidel" and that they will force him to adhere to fundamentalist practices.
>
> - Has Hamid suffered past persecution?
> - Can he rebut an argument that circumstances in Afghanistan have changed substantially so that it is now safe for him to return?
> - What additional information would you like to know to inform your decision?

The other option would be for the government to show that it is reasonable to expect the foreign national to relocate to a safe place within the country. This may be possible if the persecution is limited to one area.[8] The foreign national has the burden to prove it would not be reasonable for him or her to relocate. However, if the persecutor is the government, then countywide persecution is assumed and **internal relocation** is presumed to be unreasonable.

Where a foreign national who is otherwise eligible for asylum has suffered such a severe level of harm in the past but is unlikely to suffer further harm in the future, s/he may nevertheless receive asylum for compelling humanitarian reasons. In *Matter of Chen*, 20 I&N Dec. 16 (BIA 1989), the BIA granted asylum to a Chinese Christian minister and his family who were persecuted during the Cultural Revolution. The family's home was ransacked many times. The father was dragged through the streets by the Red Guards on over 50 occasions and had to write a public "confession" of his "crime" that related to his faith. He even survived being pushed into a burning fire that had been set to burn bibles. Although he applied for asylum when conditions in China had changed significantly, the BIA found that, as an exercise of discretion, he should receive asylum because of the extreme level of persecution he suffered in the past. This type of grant is referred to as humanitarian asylum and is available where a foreign national can demonstrate compelling reasons for being unwilling or unable to return to the

---

[8] 8 C.F.R. § 208.13(b)(1)(i)(B).

country where the persecution occurred, or can demonstrate a reasonable possibility of suffering other serious harm there.[9]

A more recent decision of the BIA is *Matter of L-S-*, 25 I&N Dec. 705 (BIA 2012). Here, the BIA held that, in order to grant a foreign national asylum on a humanitarian basis, an adjudicator may look not only at the severity of persecution suffered in the past, but also at the reasonable possibility that s/he may suffer other serious harm when returned to his or her country. "Other serious harm" need not be afflicted on account of one of the five enumerated grounds, discussed later, but must relate to current country conditions and can include such things as extreme economic deprivation or psychological trauma.[10]

● **EXAMPLE**

Ndume is a preacher from Kivu, in the eastern side of the Democratic Republic of Congo, or DRC, an area that has been under armed conflict for many years. He frequently traveled between rebel and government held areas, advocating for a peaceful solution to the crisis. One Sunday, Ndume was abducted on his way home and taken to a government prison where he was held for two months, during which time he was brutally beaten and given very little to eat and drink. Finally, a guard helped him to escape. Ndume made his way to the United States and claimed asylum. During consideration of his case, government forces searching for him killed his wife and son. Peace talks have convened between the government and rebel forces and it is likely the war will be over soon. However, Ndume remains afraid to return home. He has been diagnosed with post-traumatic stress disorder or PTSD, because of his treatment in detention in the DRC, and, following the news of the killing of his wife and son, he is suffering from survivor's guilt for which he receives counseling. Ndume would be a candidate for humanitarian asylum because it is likely he would suffer psychological harm if he is forced to return to the place where his wife and son were killed. He may suffer additional harm if he could not work to support himself on his return or could not continue to access counseling services.

A.2.d. Well-Founded Fear of Future Persecution

In some cases, an applicant for asylum may not have suffered persecution prior to filing a claim for asylum. If the foreign national can demonstrate a fear that persecution will occur in the future *and* that the fear is both subjectively and objectively reasonable, s/he may still be able to qualify for protection. Evidence of the subjective fear requires a review of the foreign national's state of mind. A statement from the foreign national, voicing his or her concerns about what might happen if returned, or a comprehensive report from a psychologist detailing any anxiety the person may be experiencing and its effects on his or her ability to function, may help to demonstrate this.

In order to substantiate that the fear of persecution is objectively reasonable, the foreign national must show that s/he has a belief or characteristic to be

---

[9] 8 C.F.R. § 208.13(b)(1)(iii).
[10] *Matter of L-S-*, at 713-715.

overcome by the persecutor and that the persecutor is aware or has the ability to become aware of it and the ability and inclination to overcome the characteristic or belief.[11] In addition, the foreign national should provide objective evidence of the conditions in the country that would support a finding that it is reasonable for him or her to be afraid. Such evidence might be available in newspapers or other reputable articles or media sources reporting on what is going on in the country and how the government is responding to a particular activity. This requires researching and gathering material on the country conditions, in many instances particularly in relation to the human rights record. Once the information is collated and reviewed, a useful question to ask to help determine whether a fear is objectively reasonable might be "would a reasonable person in the same circumstances as the applicant fear persecution?"

Case for Discussion 5.3

Omar, an Egyptian, is on a J-1 visa as a visiting scholar of religion at a prominent U.S. university. While here, he decides to convert from Islam, the majority religion in his country, to Christianity, a minority. Omar is afraid to return to Egypt because he believes Christians are targeted because of their faith and because he will be further singled out as an apostate, or religious convert. He believes the government will not protect him. In order to support his claim, Omar must provide subjective evidence of his fear and objective evidence of the treatment of Christians and apostates in his country as well as evidence of how the government responds to attacks on them.

- What types of documents would you suggest Omar gather?

A.3. The Enumerated Grounds

Establishing that someone has suffered persecution is not enough for a grant of asylum. The evidence must show that the persecution was "*on account of*" one of the five grounds, also known as the enumerated or listed grounds. These grounds are race, religion, nationality, membership in a particular social group, or political opinion. The *on account of* element is also referred to as the *nexus* or connection.

What does *on account of* mean? In essence, a foreign national must show the persecution s/he has or will suffer results from or is connected to, one of the five grounds. A persecutor may have more than one reason for causing harm. In such a case, a foreign national must demonstrate that a *central reason* for the harm is

---

[11] *See Pitcherskaia v. INS,* 118 F.3d 641 (9th Cir. 1997).

related to one of the enumerated grounds. The REAL ID Act of 2005[12] introduced this as a requirement.[13] Analysis of each of the enumerated grounds follows, with some emphasis on membership of a particular social group, as it is the most complex and legally unsettled of the five grounds.

A.3.a. Race

A person's race is very different from his or her nationality. The population of Mauritania, for example, consists of two racial groups: people with African and Arabic ancestry, with the latter controlling the political system and the country.

The *U.N. Handbook* states at paragraph 68, "[D]iscrimination for reasons of race has found world-wide condemnation as one of the most striking violations of human rights. Racial discrimination, therefore, represents an important element in determining the existence of persecution." Paragraph 69 continues, "[D]iscrimination on racial grounds will frequently amount to persecution in the sense of the 1951 Convention."

● **EXAMPLE**

Thaba, a Black African student activist in South Africa during the 1960s, was arrested many times by the white government regime because he organized street protests against Apartheid. Thaba's family lives in a segregated township outside of Johannesburg. The government will not permit them to live in other areas. In addition, black children cannot attend "white" schools, which are better equipped than the segregated schools in the township. Thaba receives an invitation to come to the United States to speak about his work. After he arrives, he claims asylum. In this instance, Thaba has a strong claim that he faces persecution on account of his race.

A.3.b. Religion

Persecution of a foreign national may occur because of his or her *actual or perceived* religious views. The most obvious example of this would be members of a religious minority targeted by a majority group. The *U.N. Handbook* offers the following guidance:

> "Persecution for "reasons of religion" may assume various forms, e.g. prohibition of membership of a religious community, of worship in private or in public, of religious instruction, or serious measures of discrimination imposed on persons

---

[12] Pub. L. 109-13, div. B, 119 Stat. 231, 302-23 (2005).
[13] Recently, the BIA issued a precedential decision that expands the application of the "central reason" provision in asylum applications. In *Matter of M-A-F-*, 26 I&N Dec. 651 (BIA 2015), the BIA decided that (1) where an applicant has filed an asylum application before May 11, 2005 (the effective date of the REAL ID Act) and, on or after that date, submits a subsequent application that is properly viewed as a new application, the later filing date controls for purposes of determining the "central reason" requirement to credibility determinations; (2) a subsequent asylum application is a new application if it presents a new basis for relief or is predicated on a new or substantially different factual basis. This decision also changed the way to calculate the filing date of an application as it relates to the one-year deadline and a discussion of this follows in Section A.5.a.

because they practice their religion or belong to a particular religious community."[14]

A.3.c. Nationality

Many countries include within their borders people with different nationalities. For instance, prior to its collapse, the former Yugoslavia consisted of Serbians, Croatians, Bosnians, Slovenians, and Kosovans, among others. While they shared the same citizenship—Yugoslavian—they were of different nationality. During the civil war that took place in that country in the 1990s, many atrocities were perpetrated between these groups *on account* of nationality. The *U.N. Handbook* notes that nationality "refers also to membership of an ethnic or linguistic group and may occasionally overlap with the term 'race.'"[15]

● EXAMPLE

Danica, a Serbian, and Petar, a Croat, are married with two children. Their neighbors are Bosnians, Kosovans, and other nationals. Once the war in Yugoslavia began, tensions between the neighbors surfaced. The war required people to support their ethnic group. Danica and Petar are under pressure to separate because of their different nationalities. If they do not, Croats and Serbians alike will treat them as traitors. They have heard of the killing of other mixed nationality families simply because they refused to declare support for one or other nationality. Danica and Petar can raise a claim for asylum because they fear persecution because of their nationalities.

A.3.d. Membership in a Particular Social Group

As with the term persecution, "membership in a particular social group" has no statutory definition either in international or domestic law. The BIA articulated the standard for determining "membership in a particular social group" in *Matter of Acosta*, 19 I&N Dec. 211 (1985), where it interpreted the phrase to mean persecution directed toward a person who is a member of a group of persons who share a common, ***immutable characteristic***.

Immutable Characteristic: An unchangeable physical attribute.

The BIA held that, whatever the common characteristic, it must be one that its members either cannot change, or should not be required to change, because it is fundamental to their individual identities or consciences. The characteristic can be innate, such as a person's sex, color, or kinship ties, or it can relate to shared past experiences.

Acosta established a framework for deciding asylum cases in this category that courts used for many years. It led to the recognition of a number of social groups, such as: "young women who are members of the Tchamba-Kunsuntu Tribe of northern Togo who have not been subjected to female genital

---

[14] *U.N. Handbook*, paragraph 72.
[15] *U.N. Handbook*, paragraph 74.

mutilation or FGM, as practiced by that tribe, and who oppose the practice," *see Matter of Kasinga*, 21 I&N Dec. 357 (BIA 1996); "homosexuals forced to register as such in Cuba," *see Matter of Toboso-Alfonso*, 20 I&N Dec. 819 (BIA 1990); and "former members of the El Salvador national police," *see Matter of Fuentes*, 19 I&N Dec. 658 (BIA 1988). Other social groups recognized include clans, *see Matter of H-*, 21 I&N Dec. 337 (BIA 1996); and family, *see Gebremichael v. INS*, 10 F.3d 28, 36 (1st Cir. 1993).

Kasinga was one of the first cases to recognize that gender could define a social group, while *Toboso-Alfonso* was similarly groundbreaking in relation to claims based on sexual orientation. Applications on these grounds have been made ever since, although the law surrounding them is still evolving. The former Immigration and Naturalization Service, or INS,[16] issued guidelines to assist asylum officers in identifying forms of persecution that disproportionately affect women and could qualify them for asylum. They are available in the Memorandum from Phyllis Coven, Office of International Affairs, U.S. Department of Justice, *Considerations for Asylum Officers Adjudicating Asylum Claims from Women, to All INS Asylum Officers and HQASM Coordinators* (May 26, 1995) or *INS Gender Guidelines*. The INS Gender Guidelines are a useful tool to use in gender-based asylum claims. Although the USCIS has not issued similar guidance for sexual orientation cases, UNHCR has.[17]

Case for Discussion 5.4

Akinbola is a Nigerian national. He has been living in the United States undocumented since 2008. Akinbola has been struggling with his sexual identity for some time because he recognizes he is only attracted to men. After several visits with a therapist, Akinbola is finally able to come to terms with this. However, he does not know how to share this information with his family. Akinbola knows that if he were to reveal his sexual preference to them, his family would disown him. In the past, he has heard his father say he would rather arrange the death of any child in order to preserve the family's honor in the community than publicly admit s/he is homosexual. Yet, Akinbola also wants to be true to himself because he knows he will never be attracted to women.

- Is Akinbola a member of a particular social group?
- If so, how would you define it?

---

[16] Chapter 1, Historical Background and Introduction to the U.S. Immigration System, discusses this former agency.
[17] *See UNHCR Guidance Note on Refugee Claims Relating to Sexual Orientation and Gender Identity*, 21 November 2008, available at http://www.refworld.org/docid/48abd5660.html.

The BIA introduced changes to the *Acosta* definition and added two new factors for consideration before a social group claim can be established.[18] These were social visibility, which requires the social group to be visible to society at large and particularity, which requires the group to be defined in such a way that it can in fact be identified as a group.

The Circuit Courts have split on whether they agree with the BIA that additional requirements are needed for social group claims. All but the Third and Seventh Circuits have followed the BIA. The Third Circuit rejected these requirements in a case called *Valdiviezo-Galdamez v. Attorney General*, 663 F.3d 582 (3d Cir. 2011). The Seventh Circuit also rejected them in a case called *Gatimi v. Holder*, 578 F.3d 611 (2009). These two cases are worth reading.

Judge Posner in *Gatimi* noted, "[I]f you are a member of a group that has been targeted for assassination or torture or some other mode of persecution, you will take pains to avoid being socially visible; and to the extent that the members of the target group are successful in remaining invisible, they will not be 'seen' by other people in the society 'as a segment of the population.'"

Similarly, the Third Circuit in *Valdiviezo-Galdamez* agreed with Judge Posner and found no practical use for social visibility and particularity. However, the Court of Appeal noted that changing the requirements for establishing an asylum claim is possible if the BIA provides a principled reason for doing so. In this instance, the court found the BIA had not and therefore rejected these additions. The Court **remanded** the case back for further deliberation, resulting in two new decisions, which essentially reaffirm the BIA's position that additional factors should be considered with respect to social group claims. They are *Matter of M-E-V-G-*, 26 I&N Dec. 227 (BIA 2014), and *Matter of W-G-R-*, 26 I&N Dec. 208 (BIA 2014). Now, applicants for asylum based on their membership in a particular social group must establish that the group is (1) composed of members who share a common immutable characteristic, (2) defined with particularity, and which is (3) socially distinct within the society in question.

In *Matter of M-E-V-G-*, the BIA clarified that social visibility did not require literal or ocular visibility but rather evidence that society considered the group a socially distinct unit. Although the BIA's stated intent was to "provide guidance to courts and those seeking asylum" (*see Matter of M-E-V-G-, supra,* at 234), this is likely to remain an area of continued litigation.

At the time of writing, only the Seventh Circuit continues to apply the strict *Acosta* test, while other Circuits hold that applicants must also meet the newer requirements articulated in *Matter of M-E-V-G* and *Matter of W-G-R-*.[19] A recent groundbreaking precedential decision, *Matter of A-C-R-G-*, 26 I&N Dec. 388 (BIA 2014), has applied this new test, with the BIA recognizing domestic violence as a basis for asylum.

---

[18] *See Matter of C-A-*, 23 I&N Dec. 951 (BIA 2006); *Matter of S-E-G-*, 24 I&N Dec. 579 (BIA 2008); *Matter of E-A-G-*, 24 I&N Dec. 591 (BIA 2008).

[19] Because the Third Circuit has not yet ruled on the applicability of these cases, the decision of the BIA is binding on immigration judges in this jurisdiction.

A.3.e. Political Opinion

A claim for asylum based on political opinion requires a foreign national to demonstrate two things. First, that s/he holds an opinion unacceptable to the persecutor, and second, a reasonable possibility exists that the opinion will or has come to the attention of the persecutor. Involvement in political, union, or professional organizations may be a way others can know a foreign national's political opinion. Alternatively, s/he may have openly expressed a view to authorities or in a public setting, for instance at a political rally or demonstration.

In some instances, a foreign national may not have disclosed a political opinion before leaving the country of origin. Therefore, the persecutor could not have become aware of any political views. The *U.N. Handbook* at paragraph 82 states that, where a foreign national has strong convictions, "it may be reasonable to assume that his opinion will sooner or later find expression and that the foreign national will, as a result, come into conflict with the authorities." In such circumstances, it may still be possible to demonstrate a likelihood of persecution.

A persecutor may incorrectly assign an opinion to his or her target that the person in question does not in fact possess. The term for this is ***imputed or perceived political opinion***. This may still constitute a protectable ground.

Imputed or Perceived Political Opinion: A political view attributed to a person which he or she does not actually hold.

Case for Discussion 5.5

Youssouf is from a prominent political family in Cote d'Ivoire. In 2012, a coups d'etat, widely believed to have been financed by his uncle, was foiled. The government has accused Youssouf, his entire family, and prominent members of the opposition party of which they are members, of treason. At the time of the coups attempt, Youssouf was in the United States on an H1-B, skilled worker visa, and knew nothing about the coups. In fact, he had renounced his membership in the party before coming to the United States. Youssouf's employment contract is ending and he is afraid to return home because he believes his association with his family will result in his arrest, torture, and possible death.

- Can Youssouf claim asylum and remain here instead?

Congress has the authority to define by statute what constitutes a ground for asylum. A good example of this is the position it took with respect to China's policy on family planning, adopted as a way to control population growth. Under the original form of this policy, many of its citizens were permitted to have only one child, although the rules have now been relaxed so that they can have two. Chinese citizens who did not comply with the policy and tried to have a second child without permission were subject to a number of punishments, including forced abortions or sterilization by the authorities.

In *Matter of Chang,* 20 I&N Dec. 38 (BIA 1989), the BIA rejected an asylum application where the applicant claimed he would be persecuted because he was opposed to this policy. The BIA found that whatever punishment the applicant would suffer on return to China would not be *on account* of any of the enumerated grounds. Congress disagreed with the BIA, however, and included a provision in the Illegal Immigration Reform and Immigrant Responsibility Act, or IIRAIRA, that opposition to China's one child policy could constitute a political opinion and therefore a ground for asylum in certain cases.

It is common for a foreign national to fear harm because of more than one of the enumerated grounds. Competent representation requires complete analysis of an applicant's case in order to decide how many of the grounds might apply to his or her set of facts. For instance, recall Thaba from South Africa, in the earlier example. His activities against Apartheid might qualify as an expression of his political opinion, establishing another basis for his claim to asylum. A foreign national can file an application claiming more than one of the grounds for asylum, but evidence supporting each is required.

Case for Discussion 5.6

Denny is an ethnic Chinese citizen of Indonesia. He was raised as an Evangelical Christian. Denny discovered he was attracted to men when he was 15. He joined an informal group of gay activists who shared experiences and attended support groups. Their eventual goal was to work against discrimination and stigmatization of gays in Indonesia. While Denny was coming home from a support meeting with a friend, two members of the army attacked and badly beat him. They yelled at him, "filthy Cina woman." Cina is considered a derogatory racial term for the Chinese in Indonesia. Denny tried to report the incident to both the police and army and neither would accept the complaint. Instead, they told him to be careful. They openly declared that there would be no place in Indonesia for "unnatural" people like him who defied Islam. Denny's family disowned him once they learned of his sexual orientation because they consider homosexuality to be a sin against their religion.

- If Denny applies for asylum in the United States, which, if any, of the enumerated grounds would apply to his situation?

A.4. Standard of Proof and Credibility

In asylum cases, the foreign national has the **burden of proof** to show that s/he suffered past persecution and/or will suffer persecution in the future. The burden of proof refers to the type and amount of evidence needed to resolve a dispute. The U.S. Supreme Court has said an applicant need only show there is a

10 percent chance of harm to meet this burden.[20] In principle, this is a low standard, but in practice, a much higher one applies because of the amount of evidence an adjudicator may request to corroborate an applicant's story.

An applicant's testimony alone is enough to meet his or her burden to show past persecution or a well-founded fear of future persecution.[21] The Real ID Act further elaborated that the demeanor, candor, responsiveness, inherent plausibility of the claim, the consistency between any oral and written statements, and the internal consistency of such statements, may be considered in determining the credibility of the asylum seeker. An immigration judge may require other evidence to verify or corroborate testimony unless the applicant does not have the evidence or cannot reasonably obtain it. Any inaccuracy or falsehood in statements, whether they go to the heart of the claim or not, are also considered when determining an applicant's **credibility**.

The credibility or believability of the applicant is a key factor in determining whether the individual has been persecuted or faces a well-founded fear of future persecution. This is because often, asylum seekers are fleeing dangerous or violent situations and may not have time to collect any written evidence or even identity documents to bring with them. Therefore, their oral testimony is often the only evidence of what happened to them, placing an adjudicator in the position of having to decide whether to believe the story or not. International and U.S. law recognize the difficulty asylum seekers may have in securing documents or even passports. However, trying to decide if a foreign national is telling the truth or not when there is little or no supporting evidence can also be a challenge.

● **EXAMPLE**

Gilberto, a pastor in Angola, was in charge of an orphanage for boys. One day, the army arrived and demanded that all boys 13 and older leave with them to be conscripted. Gilberto refused to release the boys and managed to lock the doors, preventing the army from entering. The army came the next day and arrested Gilberto. They took him to prison, where they beat him so badly that upon release, he had to go to the hospital for treatment. After his recovery, he believed it was not safe for him to remain in Angola because the army would arrest him again. Gilberto made his way to the United States, where he claimed asylum. Because he received treatment at a hospital, it would appear reasonable for the immigration judge to request medical records to corroborate Gilberto's injury and treatment. However, hospitals in many countries do not keep records and so they are unavailable. If research showed this to be the case in Angola, Gilberto can demonstrate it would be unreasonable for him to produce the records.

A.5. Bars to Asylum Eligibility

Some factors would disqualify a foreign national from a grant of asylum, even if all other requirements are met. These are known as "bars to asylum eligibility".

---

[20] *Cardoza-Fonseca*, 480 U.S. 421 (1987) at 431.
[21] *Matter of Dass*, 20 I&N Dec. 120,124 (BIA 1989).

A.5.a. One-Year Deadline

The law requires all applicants for asylum to file their application within one year of arrival in the United States.[22] This is referred to as the **one-year deadline**. Congress introduced this limitation in IIRAIRA, believing a year was sufficient time for foreign nationals to submit genuine applications. The law allows an applicant to show **changed** or **extraordinary** circumstances to excuse the late filing of an application. Guidance on what these terms mean can be found in 8 C.F.R. § 208.4(a)(2).

Changed circumstances can include changes in the foreign national's country of origin. For instance, there may be a recent change in political leadership or government policy. Alternatively, there may be a change in a foreign national's personal circumstances that would materially affect his or her eligibility for asylum. Recall Akinbola from an earlier example who is only now ready to file an application for asylum eight years after he entered the United States. Unless he can explain why it took him so long to file, he may be ineligible for this relief. In his case, he has only recently come to terms with his homosexuality and that might constitute a change in personal circumstances that would excuse his late filing. Akinbola is still required to file an application within a reasonable period after this change and, although this term is not specifically defined, the general consensus is that it should be filed within six months.

Extraordinary circumstances refer to factual issues directly related to the foreign national's ability to file.[23] One example would be a foreign national with a serious mental or physical disability. A person who is suffering from PTSD because of his or her past experience may find it extremely difficult to talk about what happened to him or her. This fear may cause delay in seeking assistance to file the application. Other examples of extraordinary circumstances include the serious illness or death of an immediate family member or legal representative, or being given poor legal advice that leads to a delay in filing. Being in the United States in legal status may also be an extraordinary reason for a delay in filing an application. Minors are considered to be under a legal disability that would excuse a delay in filing.[24] Generally, the first day counted towards the one-year deadline starts after their 18th birthday. However, the situation is different for *unaccompanied minors*, also known as *unaccompanied children,* or **UACs**, defined as youth under the age of 18 who enter the United States without parents or a legal guardian. They retain their UAC designation throughout any legal proceedings to determine whether to grant asylum, even if their actual age is over 18.[25]

These are all just examples of situations that might explain why an applicant filed late. Even if it is not possible to argue changed or extraordinary

Unaccompanied Minors or Children: Any child under the age of 18 without legal immigration status in the United States who arrives without a parent or legal guardian.

---

[22] INA § 208(a)(2)(D).
[23] 8 C.F.R. § 208.4(a)(5).
[24] 8 C.F.R. § 208.4(a)(5)(ii). While the regulation refers specifically to unaccompanied minors, in practice minors who may arrive with parents or legal guardians are also generally given this protection.
[25] INA § 208(a)(2)(E); Trafficking Victims Protection Reauthorization Act (TVPRA), Pub. L. 110-457, 122 Stat. 5044, § 235(d)(7)(A), (2008).

circumstances exist to excuse the delay in filing, a foreign national may still qualify for other humanitarian relief, which is discussed in Sections E and F.

The BIA, recently issued a decision that affects how the one-year deadline might be calculated. In *Matter of M-A-F-, 26 I&N Dec. 651 (BIA 2015)*, the BIA held that, where a foreign national has filed more than one application for asylum and the subsequent one is deemed to be a new application, the filing date of the later application controls for purposes of determining whether the one-year statutory time bar applies under § 208(a)(2)(B) of the INA. A subsequent asylum application is a new application if it presents a new basis for relief or is predicated on a new or substantially different factual basis. Therefore, if a legal representative decides that it is necessary to file a new asylum application because the first one is missing substantial facts or is riddled with inaccuracies, it may have the effect of changing the date of filing so that the original application that was filed within one year of arrival is now considered out of time.

● EXAMPLE

Kormassa is from Liberia. The government brutally killed her husband, a prominent opponent of Charles Taylor, during the civil war. Within months of arriving in the United States, she sought assistance for a claim to asylum from an attorney who a friend recommended. The attorney's main area of practice was not immigration, but he wanted to help Kormassa as best he could because he was sympathetic to her story. The attorney filed her application about nine months after she arrived in the United States. After waiting two years for an interview date, Kormassa has finally been called. In order to prepare, she reads over the application for asylum and supporting documents that the attorney filed on her behalf and notes that there are many inaccuracies. She seeks out a new attorney who listens to her story and compares the information Kormassa is giving now with that in the asylum application already filed and advises that a new application should be submitted to correct and supplement the information already provided. However, he explains that, if she does this, Kormassa will lose the protections she has from filing within one year of her arrival in the United States because this new filling will require substantial changes that are likely to constitute a new application. This is especially true because the central reason for Kormassa's claim was never mentioned in the prior application and has no relationship to the claims already presented. If this is indeed the case, the date that the USCIS will assign to her application will be the date of receipt of this new filing and not that of the original one, unless the attorney can find a way to present the new information as merely an amendment to the original application.

A.5.b. Persecutors

Anyone found to have ordered, incited, assisted, or participated in any way in the persecution of others *on account of one of the enumerated grounds* is ineligible for an asylum grant. This is known as the **persecutor bar**. Following the U.S. Supreme Court decision in *Negusie v. Holder*, 555 U.S. 511 (2009), a person's motivation for acting *may* be relevant when deciding whether s/he should be barred from a grant of asylum. Therefore, it is important to present evidence that a foreign national acted under duress or coercion in order to show engagement in the persecution of others was not voluntary. It is also critical to explore whether the persecution in question was *on account* of one of the five enumerated grounds. If it was not, then a foreign national may still be eligible to receive asylum because the act committed, while possibly unlawful, would not meet the definition of persecution.

> **Case for Discussion 5.7**
>
> Emmanuel was an officer in the Cameroonian army who often acted as an interpreter because he spoke many different languages and dialects. He was stationed in Bakasi, a war zone in the south west, bordering Nigeria. It is disputed territory, made up mainly of Nigerian nationals. Following the arrest of two Nigerian community leaders, Emmanuel is asked to interpret while they are questioned. During the interrogation, the men are brutally beaten and tortured. Although Emmanuel did not participate in these acts, he was present the whole time and was diligent about providing accurate interpretation.
>
> - Is Emmanuel ineligible for asylum as a persecutor of others?
> - Is there additional information that you would like to have before responding to this question?

A.5.c. Convicted of an Aggravated Felony or Particularly Serious Crime

As discussed in Section C.2.a of Chapter 9, Grounds of Inadmissibility and Deportation, an **aggravated felony** is a term of art in immigration law, referring to several specific crimes or types of crimes. Anyone convicted of an aggravated felony crime is ineligible for asylum. In addition, anyone convicted of a **particularly serious crime** *and* found to be a danger to the community is also ineligible for asylum.[26] An experienced attorney should analyze whether a crime is an aggravated felony or a particularly serious crime as it requires examination and understanding of cases primarily focused on issues of criminal law.

A.5.d. Firm Resettlement

If a foreign national has lived in another country where s/he could be considered resettled, then the applicant would be barred from qualifying for asylum in this country.[27] **Firm resettlement** requires that the foreign national receive an offer

---

[26] INA § 208(b)(2)(A)(ii).
[27] 8 C.F.R. § 208.13(c)(2)(i)(B).

of permanent residency, citizenship, or other type of permanent resettlement in that other country.[28] Notwithstanding this grant, if the foreign national can show there were substantial restrictions on his or her enjoyment of this status, then s/he may be able to argue there was no effective resettlement.

> **Case for Discussion 5.8**
>
> Zulaika witnessed the massacre of her family during the civil war in Angola when she was only 12 years old. She has suffered from PTSD and severe depression ever since. Zulaika and a number of other orphaned children were airlifted to Cuba for safety, where they were required to live in special dormitories and provided with all their needs, including education and health care. Zulaika completed a PhD program. She wants to seek employment but has learned from Cuban government officials that refugees like her are not allowed to work. In addition, if she travels out of the country, she will be unable to return. Zulaika decides to come to the United States and tries to cross the border from Mexico into Texas, where officers from Customs and Border Protection, or CBP, apprehend and detain her. Zulaika has been told it may be difficult for her to be successful in a claim for asylum because she has lived in Cuba for so many years and would be considered firmly resettled there.
>
> - Is this correct?
> - What evidence could she present to counter this assertion?

A.5.e. Safe Third Country

A foreign national may also be denied asylum if it is possible to remove him or her to a safe third country with which the United States has entered a bilateral or multilateral agreement.[29] There must be assurances that the foreign national's life or freedom will not be threatened in that country *on account* of an enumerated ground. At present, the United States only has such an agreement with Canada. The parties have agreed to return to a partner country anyone who first travels through its territory in order to arrive at the border of the destination country. Even though return is generally required, there are some circumstances where exceptions to this rule may apply.[30] Unaccompanied minor children are not subject to this bar.[31]

---

[28] 8 C.F.R. § 208.15.
[29] INA § 208(a)(2)(A).
[30] *Safe Third Country Agreement regarding asylum claims made in transit and at land border ports of entry*, 69 Federal Register 69480.
[31] Trafficking Victims Protection and Reauthorization Act (TVPRA) 2008, 6 USC § 279.

> ● **EXAMPLE**
>
> Kadiatou arrives at JFK airport from Mali and receives permission to enter. However, the United States is not her final destination. She speaks French and has no English. She is anxious to apply for asylum in Canada because she has heard there are French speakers there. She also has distant relatives there who are willing to assist her. Kadiatou believes it will be easier for her to integrate in Canada rather than in the United States. She travels by Greyhound to the Canadian border and claims asylum. Under the terms of the United States—Canada Safe Third Country Agreement, Canada is obliged to return Kadiatou to the United States so that her claim to asylum can be considered there in the first instance as it was the first safe country in which she arrived.

A.5.f. Terrorism and Danger to U.S. Security

Anyone who has engaged in terrorist activity identified in INA §§ 212(a)(3)(B)(i)(I)-(IV) and (VI),[32] is ineligible for a grant of asylum. The REAL ID Act introduced this provision, which affects all cases filed after the date of the Act's implementation in 2005. Older applications only bar those who are inadmissible or removable as terrorists. The foreign national bears the burden to show by clear and convincing evidence that s/he has not engaged in any of the identified terrorist activities.

Where there are reasonable grounds for regarding a person as a danger to U.S. security, that person will be denied asylum.[33]

A.5.g. Multiple Asylum Applications

Anyone who has previously filed and been denied asylum may not file a new application unless s/he can demonstrate changed or extraordinary circumstances that materially affect his or her current eligibility for asylum and that have occurred since consideration of the prior application.[34]

A.6. Denial, Revocation, or Termination of Asylum

Asylum is a discretionary relief that requires an adjudicator (asylum officer or immigration judge) to exercise discretion in favor of the applicant. The judge could decide, in the exercise of discretion that, even though a foreign national meets all the statutory eligibility requirements and there are no grounds to bar him or her from a grant of asylum, s/he will deny the application because the foreign national is guilty of tax evasion or for other reasons that impugn the foreign national's character. This is an unlikely scenario, but if it did occur, the denial could be challenged if it can be shown it is arbitrary or an abuse of discretion.

---

[32] This is discussed further in Section B.3 of Chapter 9, Grounds of Inadmissibility and Deportation.
[33] INA § 208(b)(2)(A)(iv). The discussion in Chapter 9 on terrorist activities and organizations and danger to U.S. security is also applicable to the respective bars and is not duplicated here.
[34] INA § 208(a)(2)(C) and (D).

A grant of asylum can be revoked if it is later discovered that there was fraud in the application.[35] The USCIS fraud unit regularly reviews applications to check for duplicated claims. For instance, unrelated claims may present exactly the same facts, suggesting fabrication. Prior to revocation, the foreign national granted asylum must be given an interview with the opportunity to prove no fraud was involved in his or her claim. If unsuccessful, s/he will be placed into **removal proceedings** where there will be another chance to argue the case before a judge. However, if the foreign national has adjusted to a lawful permanent resident, or LPR,[36] and held that status for at least five years before removal proceedings are initiated to rescind his or her LPR status, then s/he may be protected by the statute of limitations provisions contained in INA § 246(a).[37]

Grants of asylum may be terminated when an asylee is no longer in need of protection, perhaps because there have been changed circumstances in the country of asylum. However, before this happens, the asylee has an opportunity to demonstrate that there is still reason for him or her to be afraid to return and therefore the protection status should remain in place. Asylees who travel back to the country where they claimed they would be persecuted before they acquire U.S. citizenship, may also be indicating they are no longer in need of protection. If the reason for return was for an emergency (possibly the serious illness of a family member) and during the time the asylee was in the country from which asylum was granted s/he was essentially in hiding, it may be enough to avert termination of status.

B. Asylum Procedure

A request for asylum is either made affirmatively through an administrative process conducted by an Asylum Office that is part of the USCIS, or defensively in U.S. Immigration Court that is part of the Executive Office for Immigration Review, or EOIR.[38] Immigration judges hold removal proceedings to determine whether a foreign national who has violated immigration laws should be allowed to remain or be deported. While the application materials for each type of application are very similar, the consideration process is not.

B.1. Building the Asylum Case

The necessary form to file an asylum application is Form I-589, Application for Asylum and for Withholding of Removal. It is necessary for both affirmative and defensive cases. The application asks for detailed information about the foreign national, his or her education, work history, and family. In addition, the form asks the foreign national to explain the basis for the asylum claim. A sample

---

[35] 8 C.F.R. § 208.24(a)(1).
[36] This is discussed further in Section D.
[37] *Garcia v. Attorney General of the United States*, 553 F.3d 724 (3d Cir. 2009).
[38] Court procedures are discussed in detail in Chapter 10, Immigration Court Practice and Relief from Removal.

completed Form I-589, Application for Asylum and for Withholding of Removal, appears in Figure 5.1

A well-prepared application should include a supplemental statement or affidavit from the foreign national explaining what happened and the reason for claiming asylum. Allowing the foreign national to tell the story in chronological

Figure 5.1

Sample Form I-589, Application for Asylum and for Withholding of Removal

---

Department of Homeland Security
U.S. Citizenship and Immigration Services

U.S. Department of Justice
Executive Office for Immigration Review

OMB No. 1615-0067; Expires 12/31/2016

I-589, Application for Asylum and for Withholding of Removal

START HERE - Type or print in black ink. See the instructions for information about eligibility and how to complete and file this application. There is NO filing fee for this application.

NOTE: Check this box if you also want to apply for withholding of removal under the Convention Against Torture. ☐

Part A.I. Information About You

1. Alien Registration Number(s) (A-Number) (if any)	2. U.S. Social Security Number (if any)
None	None

3. Complete Last Name	4. First Name	5. Middle Name
DOE	JOHN	NONAME

6. What other names have you used (include maiden name and aliases)?
NONE

7. Residence in the U.S. (where you physically reside)

Street Number and Name	Apt. Number
4582 Yellow Brick Road	#1

City	State	Zip Code	Telephone Number
Wichita	Kansas	67227	(316) 555 5555

8. Mailing Address in the U.S. (if different than the address in Item Number 7)

In Care Of (if applicable):	Telephone Number ( )

Street Number and Name	Apt. Number

City	State	Zip Code

9. Gender: ☒ Male ☐ Female   10. Marital Status: ☒ Single ☐ Married ☐ Divorced ☐ Widowed

11. Date of Birth (mm/dd/yyyy)	12. City and Country of Birth
02/25/1974	Kingston

13. Present Nationality (Citizenship)	14. Nationality at Birth	15. Race, Ethnic, or Tribal Group	16. Religion
Jamaican	JAMAICA	Black	Catholic

17. Check the box, a through c, that applies: a. ☒ I have never been in Immigration Court proceedings.
    b. ☐ I am now in Immigration Court proceedings.   c. ☐ I am **not** now in Immigration Court proceedings, but I have been in the past.

18. Complete 18 a through c.
    a. When did you last leave your country? (mm/dd/yyyy) 03/17/1999   b. What is your current I-94 Number, if any? None
    c. List each entry into the U.S. beginning with your most recent entry. List date (mm/dd/yyyy), place, and your status for each entry. (Attach additional sheets as needed.)

    Date 03/17/1999   Place Miami, Florida   Status Visitor   Date Status Expires 03/08/2016
    Date _____   Place _____   Status _____
    Date _____   Place _____   Status _____

19. What country issued your last passport or travel document?	20. Passport Number Not known	21. Expiration Date (mm/dd/yyyy)
Jamaica	Travel Document Number	

22. What is your native language (include dialect, if applicable)?	23. Are you fluent in English? ☒ Yes ☐ No	24. What other languages do you speak fluently?
English		None

For EOIR use only.	For USCIS use only.	Action: Interview Date: _____ Asylum Officer ID#: _____	Decision: Approval Date: _____ Denial Date: _____ Referral Date: _____

Form I-589 (Rev. 12/29/14) Y

B: Asylum Procedure

**Figure 5.1
(Continued)**

Part A.II. Information About Your Spouse and Children

Your spouse   [X] I am not married. (Skip to **Your Children** below.)

1. Alien Registration Number (A-Number) (if any)	2. Passport/ID Card Number (if any)	3. Date of Birth (mm/dd/yyyy)	4. U.S. Social Security Number (if any)
5. Complete Last Name	6. First Name	7. Middle Name	8. Maiden Name
9. Date of Marriage (mm/dd/yyyy)	10. Place of Marriage		11. City and Country of Birth
12. Nationality (Citizenship)	13. Race, Ethnic, or Tribal Group		14. Gender [ ] Male [ ] Female

15. Is this person in the U.S.?
[ ] Yes *(Complete Blocks 16 to 24.)*   [ ] No *(Specify location):*

16. Place of last entry into the U.S.	17. Date of last entry into the U.S. (mm/dd/yyyy)	18. I-94 Number (if any)	19. Status when last admitted (Visa type, if any)
20. What is your spouse's current status?	21. What is the expiration date of his/her authorized stay, if any? (mm/dd/yyyy)	22. Is your spouse in Immigration Court proceedings? [ ] Yes [ ] No	23. If previously in the U.S., date of previous arrival (mm/dd/yyyy)

24. If in the U.S., is your spouse to be included in this application? *(Check the appropriate box.)*
[ ] Yes *(Attach one photograph of your spouse in the upper right corner of Page 9 on the extra copy of the application submitted for this person.)*
[ ] No

Your Children. List **all** of your children, regardless of age, location, or marital status.

[ ] I do not have any children. *(Skip to Part A.III., **Information about your background**.)*
[X] I have children.   Total number of children: 3

(**NOTE:** *Use Form I-589 Supplement A or attach additional sheets of paper and documentation if you have more than four children.*)

1. Alien Registration Number (A-Number) (if any)	2. Passport/ID Card Number (if any)	3. Marital Status (Married, Single, Divorced, Widowed)	4. U.S. Social Security Number (if any)
Noen	None	Single	None
5. Complete Last Name	6. First Name	7. Middle Name	8. Date of Birth (mm/dd/yyyy)
Doe	John	Jim	02/25/1988
9. City and Country of Birth	10. Nationality (Citizenship)	11. Race, Ethnic, or Tribal Group	12. Gender
Kingston Jamaica	Jamaican	Black	[X] Male [ ] Female

13. Is this child in the U.S. ?   [ ] Yes *(Complete Blocks 14 to 21.)*   [X] No *(Specify location):* Kingston, Jamaica

14. Place of last entry into the U.S.	15. Date of last entry into the U.S. (mm/dd/yyyy)	16. I-94 Number (If any)	17. Status when last admitted (Visa type, if any)
18. What is your child's current status?	19. What is the expiration date of his/her authorized stay, if any? (mm/dd/yyyy)	20. Is your child in Immigration Court proceedings? [ ] Yes [ ] No	

21. If in the U.S., is this child to be included in this application? *(Check the appropriate box.)*
[ ] Yes *(Attach one photograph of your spouse in the upper right corner of Page 9 on the extra copy of the application submitted for this person.)*
[ ] No

Figure 5.1 (Continued)

Part A.II. Information About Your Spouse and Children (Continued)

1. Alien Registration Number (A-Number) (if any)	2. Passport/ID Card Number (if any)	3. Marital Status (Married, Single, Divorced, Widowed)	4. U.S. Social Security Number (if any)
None	None	Single	None

5. Complete Last Name	6. First Name	7. Middle Name	8. Date of Birth (mm/dd/yyyy)
Doe	Jona	Jim	02/25/1995

9. City and Country of Birth	10. Nationality (Citizenship)	11. Race, Ethnic, or Tribal Group	12. Gender
Kingston, Jamaica	Jamaican	Black	[X] Male [ ] Female

13. Is this child in the U.S.? [ ] Yes (Complete Blocks 14 to 21.) [X] No (Specify location): Kingston Jamaica

14. Place of last entry into the U.S.	15. Date of last entry into the U.S. (mm/dd/yyyy)	16. I-94 Number (If any)	17. Status when last admitted (Visa type, if any)

18. What is your child's current status?	19. What is the expiration date of his/her authorized stay, if any? (mm/dd/yyyy)	20. Is your child in Immigration Court proceedings? [ ] Yes [ ] No

21. If in the U.S., is this child to be included in this application? (Check the appropriate box.)
[ ] Yes (Attach one photograph of your spouse in the upper right corner of Page 9 on the extra copy of the application submitted for this person.)
[ ] No

1. Alien Registration Number (A-Number) (if any)	2. Passport/ID Card Number (if any)	3. Marital Status (Married, Single, Divorced, Widowed)	4. U.S. Social Security Number (if any)
None	None	Single	None

5. Complete Last Name	6. First Name	7. Middle Name	8. Date of Birth (mm/dd/yyyy)
Doe	Johanna	None	02/25/2003

9. City and Country of Birth	10. Nationality (Citizenship)	11. Race, Ethnic, or Tribal Group	12. Gender
New York, USA	USC	Black	[ ] Male [X] Female

13. Is this child in the U.S.? [ ] Yes (Complete Blocks 14 to 21.) [X] No (Specify location): Kingston, Jamaica

14. Place of last entry into the U.S.	15. Date of last entry into the U.S. (mm/dd/yyyy)	16. I-94 Number (If any)	17. Status when last admitted (Visa type, if any)

18. What is your child's current status?	19. What is the expiration date of his/her authorized stay, if any? (mm/dd/yyyy)	20. Is your child in Immigration Court proceedings? [ ] Yes [ ] No

21. If in the U.S., is this child to be included in this application? (Check the appropriate box.)
[ ] Yes (Attach one photograph of your spouse in the upper right corner of Page 9 on the extra copy of the application submitted for this person.)
[ ] No

1. Alien Registration Number (A-Number) (if any)	2. Passport/ID Card Number (if any)	3. Marital Status (Married, Single, Divorced, Widowed)	4. U.S. Social Security Number (if any)

5. Complete Last Name	6. First Name	7. Middle Name	8. Date of Birth (mm/dd/yyyy)

9. City and Country of Birth	10. Nationality (Citizenship)	11. Race, Ethnic, or Tribal Group	12. Gender
			[ ] Male [ ] Female

13. Is this child in the U.S.? [ ] Yes (Complete Blocks 14 to 21.) [ ] No (Specify location): _____

14. Place of last entry into the U.S.	15. Date of last entry into the U.S. (mm/dd/yyyy)	16. I-94 Number (If any)	17. Status when last admitted (Visa type, if any)

18. What is your child's current status?	19. What is the expiration date of his/her authorized stay, if any? (mm/dd/yyyy)	20. Is your child in Immigration Court proceedings? [ ] Yes [ ] No

21. If in the U.S., is this child to be included in this application? (Check the appropriate box.)
[ ] Yes (Attach one photograph of your spouse in the upper right corner of Page 9 on the extra copy of the application submitted for this person.)
[ ] No

Part A.III. Information About Your Background

1. List your last address where you lived before coming to the United States. If this is not the country where you fear persecution, also list the last address in the country where you fear persecution. *(List Address, City/Town, Department, Province, or State and Country.)*
   (NOTE: Use Form I-589 Supplement B, or additional sheets of paper, if necessary.)

Number and Street *(Provide if available)*	City/Town	Department, Province, or State	Country	Dates From *(Mo/Yr)*	To *(Mo/Yr)*
82 Gardenia Road	Kingston		Jamaica	01/64	07/99

2. Provide the following information about your residences during the past 5 years. List your present address first.
   (NOTE: Use Form I-589 Supplement B, or additional sheets of paper, if necessary.)

Number and Street	City/Town	Department, Province, or State	Country	Dates From *(Mo/Yr)*	To *(Mo/Yr)*
4582 Yellow Brick Rd #1	Wichita,	KS	USA	05/2010	Present
1129 Mes Avenue	New York,	NY	USA	12/2009	04/2010

3. Provide the following information about your education, beginning with the most recent.
   (NOTE: Use Form I-589 Supplement B, or additional sheets of paper, if necessary.)

Name of School	Type of School	Location *(Address)*	Attended From *(Mo/Yr)*	To *(Mo/Yr)*
Kingston Secondary School	Secondary School	Kingston, Jamaica	01/80	01/84
Kingston Primary School	Primary School	Kingston, Jamaica	01/72	01/80

4. Provide the following information about your employment during the past 5 years. List your present employment first.
   (NOTE: Use Form I-589 Supplement B, or additional sheets of paper, if necessary.)

Name and Address of Employer	Your Occupation	Dates From *(Mo/Yr)*	To *(Mo/Yr)*
Self Employed	Handyman	07/99	Present

5. Provide the following information about your parents and siblings (brothers and sisters). Check the box if the person is deceased.
   (NOTE: Use Form I-589 Supplement B, or additional sheets of paper, if necessary.)

Full Name	City/Town and Country of Birth	Current Location
Mother Austin, Jane	Spanish Town, Jamaica	☐ Deceased Kingston, Jamaica
Father Doe, James	West Moreland, Jamaica	☒ Deceased
Sibling Doe, Albert	Kingston, Jamaica	☐ Deceased Kingston, Jamaica
Sibling Doe, Carl	Kingston, Jamaica	☒ Deceased
Sibling Doe, Manuella	Kingston, Jamaica	☐ Deceased Kingston, Jamaica
Sibling Doe, Felicity	Kingston, Jamaica	☐ Deceased Kingston, Jamaica

Figure 5.1 (Continued)

Chapter 5: Asylum and Other Related Humanitarian Relief

Figure 5.1 (Continued)

Part B. Information About Your Application

(NOTE: Use Form I-589 Supplement B, or attach additional sheets of paper as needed to complete your responses to the questions contained in Part B.)

When answering the following questions about your asylum or other protection claim (withholding of removal under 241(b)(3) of the INA or withholding of removal under the Convention Against Torture), you must provide a detailed and specific account of the basis of your claim to asylum or other protection. To the best of your ability, provide specific dates, places, and descriptions about each event or action described. You must attach documents evidencing the general conditions in the country from which you are seeking asylum or other protection and the specific facts on which you are relying to support your claim. If this documentation is unavailable or you are not providing this documentation with your application, explain why in your responses to the following questions.

Refer to Instructions, Part 1: Filing Instructions, Section II, "Basis of Eligibility," Parts A - D, Section V, "Completing the Form," Part B, and Section VII, "Additional Evidence That You Should Submit," for more information on completing this section of the form.

1. Why are you applying for asylum or withholding of removal under section 241(b)(3) of the INA, or for withholding of removal under the Convention Against Torture? Check the appropriate box(es) below and then provide detailed answers to questions A and B below.

   I am seeking asylum or withholding of removal based on:

   ☐ Race   ☐ Political opinion
   ☐ Religion   ☒ Membership in a particular social group
   ☐ Nationality   ☒ Torture Convention

   A. Have you, your family, or close friends or colleagues ever experienced harm or mistreatment or threats in the past by anyone?

   ☐ No   ☒ Yes

   If "Yes," explain in detail:
   1. What happened;
   2. When the harm or mistreatment or threats occurred;
   3. Who caused the harm or mistreatment or threats; and
   4. Why you believe the harm or mistreatment or threats occurred.

   ```
   I witnessed the murder of the son of a friend of mine back in Jamaica before I came to the
   United States. The group that committed the murder began to threaten me because they were
   afraid I would tell the police. If I spoke out, they would kill me. The threats increased and I
   believed they would kill me, therefore I fled for my safety. Please see my attached statement
   for further details.
   ```

   B. Do you fear harm or mistreatment if you return to your home country?

   ☐ No   ☒ Yes

   If "Yes," explain in detail:
   1. What harm or mistreatment you fear;
   2. Who you believe would harm or mistreat you; and
   3. Why you believe you would or could be harmed or mistreated.

   ```
   I recently learned that I have been diagnosed with HIV. As a Jamaican male, I will be
   persecuted for this health status. There is a lot of stigma and discrimination in my country
   against those living with AIDs. In addition, it would be assumed that I am a homosexual, even
   though I am not. Jamaicans assume it is only through homosexual contact that a person can be
   infected with AIDs. Homophobia is pervasive to the point that those suspected of living a gay
   lifestyle are often injured and sometimes killed. Please see my attached statement for further
   details.
   ```

B: Asylum Procedure

Figure 5.1
(Continued)

Part B. Information About Your Application (Continued)

2. Have you or your family members ever been accused, charged, arrested, detained, interrogated, convicted and sentenced, or imprisoned in any country other than the United States?

    [X] No   [ ] Yes

    If "Yes," explain the circumstances and reasons for the action.

3.A. Have you or your family members ever belonged to or been associated with any organizations or groups in your home country, such as, but not limited to, a political party, student group, labor union, religious organization, military or paramilitary group, civil patrol, guerrilla organization, ethnic group, human rights group, or the press or media?

    [X] No   [ ] Yes

    If "Yes," describe for each person the level of participation, any leadership or other positions held, and the length of time you or your family members were involved in each organization or activity.

3.B. Do you or your family members continue to participate in any way in these organizations or groups?

    [X] No   [ ] Yes

    If "Yes," describe for each person your or your family members' current level of participation, any leadership or other positions currently held, and the length of time you or your family members have been involved in each organization or group.

4. Are you afraid of being subjected to torture in your home country or any other country to which you may be returned?

    [ ] No   [X] Yes

    If "Yes," explain why you are afraid and describe the nature of torture you fear, by whom, and why it would be inflicted.

    ```
    I am afraid because of my HIV status. The stigma and discrimination attached to this status
    would make it impossible for me to live freely and without harm. It is so pervasive, that even
    government police officers are known to physically abuse those who are diagnosed with HIV
    because they believe it was contracted through homosexual contact. Please see my attached
    statement for further details.
    ```

Chapter 5: Asylum and Other Related Humanitarian Relief

Figure 5.1 (Continued)

Part C. Additional Information About Your Application

(NOTE: Use Form I-589 Supplement B, or attach additional sheets of paper as needed to complete your responses to the questions contained in Part C.)

1. Have you, your spouse, your child(ren), your parents or your siblings ever applied to the U.S. Government for refugee status, asylum, or withholding of removal?

    [X] No   [ ] Yes

    If "Yes," explain the decision and what happened to any status you, your spouse, your child(ren), your parents, or your siblings received as a result of that decision. Indicate whether or not you were included in a parent or spouse's application. If so, include your parent or spouse's A-number in your response. If you have been denied asylum by an immigration judge or the Board of Immigration Appeals, describe any change(s) in conditions in your country or your own personal circumstances since the date of the denial that may affect your eligibility for asylum.

2.A. After leaving the country from which you are claiming asylum, did you or your spouse or child(ren) who are now in the United States travel through or reside in any other country before entering the United States?

    [X] No   [ ] Yes

2.B. Have you, your spouse, your child(ren), or other family members, such as your parents or siblings, ever applied for or received any lawful status in any country other than the one from which you are now claiming asylum?

    [X] No   [ ] Yes

    If "Yes" to either or both questions (2A and/or 2B), provide for each person the following: the name of each country and the length of stay, the person's status while there, the reasons for leaving, whether or not the person is entitled to return for lawful residence purposes, and whether the person applied for refugee status or for asylum while there, and if not, why he or she did not do so.

3. Have you, your spouse or your child(ren) ever ordered, incited, assisted or otherwise participated in causing harm or suffering to any person because of his or her race, religion, nationality, membership in a particular social group or belief in a particular political opinion?

    [X] No   [ ] Yes

    If "Yes," describe in detail each such incident and your own, your spouse's, or your child(ren)'s involvement.

Form I-589 (Rev. 12/29/14) Y Page 7

B: Asylum Procedure 211

Figure 5.1 (Continued)

Part C. Additional Information About Your Application (Continued)

4. After you left the country where you were harmed or fear harm, did you return to that country?

   [X] No [ ] Yes

   If "Yes," describe in detail the circumstances of your visit(s) (for example, the date(s) of the trip(s), the purpose(s) of the trip(s), and the length of time you remained in that country for the visit(s).)

5. Are you filing this application more than 1 year after your last arrival in the United States?

   [ ] No [X] Yes

   If "Yes," explain why you did not file within the first year after you arrived. You must be prepared to explain at your interview or hearing why you did not file your asylum application within the first year after you arrived. For guidance in answering this question, see Instructions, Part 1: Filing Instructions, Section V. "Completing the Form," Part C.

   ```
   I am filing this application now because of changed circumstances.  I was diagnosed with HIV six
   months ago.
   ```

6. Have you or any member of your family included in the application ever committed any crime and/or been arrested, charged, convicted, or sentenced for any crimes in the United States?

   [X] No [ ] Yes

   If "Yes," for each instance, specify in your response: what occurred and the circumstances, dates, length of sentence received, location, the duration of the detention or imprisonment, reason(s) for the detention or conviction, any formal charges that were lodged against you or your relatives included in your application, and the reason(s) for release. Attach documents referring to these incidents, if they are available, or an explanation of why documents are not available.

Form I-589 (Rev. 12/29/14) Y Page 8

Chapter 5: Asylum and Other Related Humanitarian Relief

Figure 5.1 (Continued)

Part D. Your Signature

I certify, under penalty of perjury under the laws of the United States of America, that this application and the evidence submitted with it are all true and correct. Title 18, United States Code, Section 1546(a), provides in part: Whoever knowingly makes under oath, or as permitted under penalty of perjury under Section 1746 of Title 28, United States Code, knowingly subscribes as true, any false statement with respect to a material fact in any application, affidavit, or other document required by the immigration laws or regulations prescribed thereunder, or knowingly presents any such application, affidavit, or other document containing any such false statement or which fails to contain any reasonable basis in law or fact - shall be fined in accordance with this title or imprisoned for up to 25 years. I authorize the release of any information from my immigration record that U.S. Citizenship and Immigration Services (USCIS) needs to determine eligibility for the benefit I am seeking.

Staple your photograph here or the photograph of the family member to be included on the extra copy of the application submitted for that person.

WARNING: Applicants who are in the United States illegally are subject to removal if their asylum or withholding claims are not granted by an asylum officer or an immigration judge. Any information provided in completing this application may be used as a basis for the institution of, or as evidence in, removal proceedings even if the application is later withdrawn. Applicants determined to have knowingly made a frivolous application for asylum will be permanently ineligible for any benefits under the Immigration and Nationality Act. You may not avoid a frivolous finding simply because someone advised you to provide false information in your asylum application. If filing with USCIS, unexcused failure to appear for an appointment to provide biometrics (such as fingerprints) and your biographical information within the time allowed may result in an asylum officer dismissing your asylum application or referring it to an immigration judge. Failure without good cause to provide DHS with biometrics or other biographical information while in removal proceedings may result in your application being found abandoned by the immigration judge. See sections 208(d)(5)(A) and 208(d)(6) of the INA and 8 CFR sections 208.10, 1208.10, 208.20, 1003.47(d) and 1208.20.

Print your complete name.	Write your name in your native alphabet.
JOHN DOE	

Did your spouse, parent, or child(ren) assist you in completing this application? [X] No   [ ] Yes *(If "Yes," list the name and relationship.)*

_____ _____ _____ _____
      (Name)   *(Relationship)*   *(Name)*   *(Relationship)*

Did someone other than your spouse, parent, or child(ren) prepare this application?   [ ] No   [X] Yes *(If "Yes," complete Part E.)*

Asylum applicants may be represented by counsel. Have you been provided with a list of persons who may be available to assist you, at little or no cost, with your asylum claim?   [ ] No   [X] Yes

Signature of Applicant *(The person in Part A.I.)*

[➡ _____]
      Sign your name so it all appears within the brackets   Date *(mm/dd/yyyy)*

Part E. Declaration of Person Preparing Form, if Other Than Applicant, Spouse, Parent, or Child

I declare that I have prepared this application at the request of the person named in Part D, that the responses provided are based on all information of which I have knowledge, or which was provided to me by the applicant, and that the completed application was read to the applicant in his or her native language or a language he or she understands for verification before he or she signed the application in my presence. I am aware that the knowing placement of false information on the Form I-589 may also subject me to civil penalties under 8 U.S.C. 1324c and/or criminal penalties under 18 U.S.C. 1546(a).

Signature of Preparer	Print Complete Name of Preparer
	A.T. Torney

Daytime Telephone Number	Address of Preparer: Street Number and Name		
(620) 555 5555	Non-profit Legal Services of Wichita, Kansas, 1, Oz Lane		
Apt. Number	City	State	Zip Code
3rd Floor	Wichita	Kansas	67228

order is probably the easiest format to follow and understand. A sample of a statement in support of an asylum application appears in Box 5.1.

Box 5.1 **Applicant Statement: In Support of Application for Asylum**

STATEMENT OF JOHN DOE I, JOHN DOE, of 4582 Yellow Brick Road, Wichita, Kansas, PA, WILL SAY AS FOLLOWS:

1. I am a citizen of Jamaica. In January or February of 1999, someone in the community murdered the son of my friend. He had been a member of a gang, which was in a dispute with another gang.
2. Jamaican youth often join gangs and get into a lot of trouble. The police do very little to stop the activities of the gangs even though they create a great deal of insecurity for the community.
3. The boy was not living with his father. However, one night, there seemed to be a lot of trouble and he ran to his father's home, thinking it would be safe for him there.
4. On that day, I had been talking to a friend nearby when I heard a gunshot. I looked around and saw my friend's son fall to the ground. I also saw the boys who had been chasing him carrying a gun and realized they were the ones who had shot him.
5. Within minutes, a crowd arrived to see what had happened. Later, the police came to investigate and take away the body. I did not admit to having witnessed the event. However, within a few days, the community knew that I had been around when the murder took place.
6. The gang members of the boy who was killed started to put pressure on me to go to the police to identify the killers. My friend also wanted me to go to the police so that there could be some justice for his son's murder.
7. Soon after, members of the gang who had carried out the murder approached me. They told me that they knew I was a witness to what had happened. They threatened me that, if I ever said anything, it would be a problem for my family and me.
8. I knew I had to take this threat seriously when I started noticing these gang members coming into the area more often and hanging around my house, to see what I was doing. I became concerned about the safety of my family and knew that I had to do something.
9. Another friend of mine who understood my dilemma suggested that I should leave the country as the only way I could keep my family safe. I thought this was a good idea and he said he could put me in touch with someone who could get me travel documents for the right price.
10. Two or three weeks later, I had purchased a passport to leave the country and made plans to come to the United States, believing that at least this way, there would be no more pressure on me to speak with

the police and no more concern on the part of the other gang that I would snitch on their members. My hope was that, with me gone, they would leave my family alone.

11. When I first arrived in the United States in the summer of 1999, I was not planning to stay because it was too hard for me to support myself. I did not think about applying for asylum at that time and did not know that I could have done that anyway.

12. About four years ago, I started dating a woman in New York who was also a Jamaican national. We were together for about three years and lived together for a very short period, probably a month or two.

13. We began living together because neither of us had any money and we thought this would be a good way to pool our resources. However, once we moved in, I noticed that she was having a number of doctor's visits. Then she found a nice apartment and she was getting help from an organization to pay for it. She wanted me to come with her but we were already having problems in our relationship, so I did not think it was a good idea.

14. I never took the time to ask my girlfriend how she was affording her place or what was going on. I thought she had just got lucky.

15. A friend of mine suggested that I move to Wichita, KS, so I moved there in May, 2014. By then, my girlfriend and I had been separated for about six months or so. When I arrived in Wichita, I managed to find somewhere to stay and found odd jobs in construction, nothing steady.

16. Soon after leaving New York, I began to hear a rumor that my ex-girlfriend was sick from AIDs. I decided to be tested for my own peace of mind. I went to a small medical office close to me and returned a week later for the results. When I was told I was positive, I did not fully understand what that meant.

17. When I finally realized, I was devastated and frightened because I did not know how I would manage my condition. I began to worry about my life moving forward, particularly what would happen to me if I were to return to Jamaica, given the prejudices that exist there around this disease.

18. It was recommended that I go to an organization set up to provide social Service support to those who are HIV positive. Through them, I have received a medical card, which I may use to pay for medicines when I eventually need them. I have not been able to access any other benefits because of my immigration status.

19. Now that I know my health status, I also understand that it is impossible for me to return to Jamaica. Even before I left, the country was extremely homophobic. I believe there has not been much change.

20. I am not a homosexual, but in Jamaica, there is a view that, if you are HIV+, there is an assumption, regardless, that you acquired this through homosexual contact. There is a widely held belief that homosexuals are the only ones in the community spreading the disease.

21. Homosexuality is frowned upon in Jamaica and people take it upon themselves to "punish" those who are believed to be gay. The brutality that is used against the homosexual community is frightening.

> 22. I believe that if I return to Jamaica, it will be like sending me to my death. People in the community would shun me or attack me for being gay—even though I am not. I would suffer substantial injuries from these attacks, and likely death. I would be discriminated against, as no one would be willing to treat me fairly.
> 23. I have not had the courage to tell any of my family members about my condition. I deliberately did not tell them because if I do, my status will gradually be known by the wider community and those who hate homosexuals will make my life hell.
> 24. There is no privacy in the medical community in Jamaica. Medical personnel disclose medical conditions to anyone, as they believe it is important for the community to know what is going on. The medical facilities for those who are HIV+ or living with AIDs are separate and so anyone seen entering or leaving them can easily be identified as HIV+.
> 25. I do not believe that the government is able or willing to protect me from my potential attackers. There is neither the resources to make protection available to an individual, nor the desire, since the police are also known to attack people believed to be gay. I know I will not be safe if I return to Jamaica.
>
> JOHN DOE

Since credibility is such an important element in asylum determinations, it is very important that statements and corroborating evidence be consistent and plausible. Therefore, it is essential to review each document carefully and to address any inconsistencies that may exist. This may be as simple as catching mistakes in understanding the information given or, in more complex cases, obtaining detailed explanations for identified differences.

As discussed earlier in Section A.2.d, a foreign national must prove s/he has both a subjective and objective basis for a claim. It may be necessary to speak with an expert on the particular country issues in question in order to get a better understanding of what is going on there or even to counter information that is in print that the foreign national may insist is untrue. It is all too easy to disbelieve an applicant simply because reputable sources are silent on a particular issue that may be relevant to his or her case. Speaking with an expert, where necessary, may provide a different perspective.

An important country conditions resource is the annual human rights reports compiled by the U.S. Bureau for Democracy, Human Rights, and Labor, within the Department of State, or DOS. The DOS posts these on its website.[39] In 1998, Congress passed the International Religious Freedom Act,

---

[39] The reports can be accessed at http://www.state.gov/j/drl/rls/hrrpt/humanrightsreport/#wrapperd.

or IRFA,[40] which required the monitoring and preparation of annual reports of religious persecution around the world. These reports are also produced under the auspices of the DOS and can offer important general information that may need supplementing with documents that are more recent.[41] Amnesty International, Human Rights Watch, and Asylum Law also publish reports considered to be sources of reliable information.[42]

In many law firms or nonprofit organizations, paralegals, or accredited representatives[43] play an active, if not primary, role in interviewing the foreign national and any witnesses or experts and preparing the first, if not several, drafts of statements. They will also work on gathering country conditions evidence and compiling the completed application for submission.

B.2. Compiling the Affirmative Asylum Request

A foreign national in the United States who is not in removal proceedings may submit an **affirmative asylum request** to the USCIS.

● EXAMPLE

Mohammed, from Darfur, is a student from Sudan who wishes to apply for asylum in the United States. He states that paramilitaries known as the Janjaweed, allies with the government, came to his village and burned it down. Mohammed explains that people from his tribe or ethnic group have had conflicts with the government for some time over land. During the attack, Mohammed's parents were killed and he was shot in the leg and has a large scar. After the attack, the paramilitary and the government routinely targeted young men of his background because they considered the men opponents. Before the attack on him, Mohammed had applied for and received a B-2 visa to visit his brother who lives in the United States. He decided to go ahead and make the trip, which is why he is here.

If Mohammed decides to apply for asylum, here is how a case handler might prepare and compile his application:

- Form I-589, Application for Asylum and for Withholding of Removal, for Mohammed
- Form G-28, Notice of Entry of Appearance of Attorney or Accredited Representative
- One passport photo attached to the application
- A table of contents
- A supplemental statement or affidavit from Mohammed in support of his application

---

[40] Pub. L. 105-292, 112 Stat. 2787 (1999).
[41] The reports are available at http://www.state.gov/j/drl/rls/irf.
[42] You can visit their websites at www.amnesty.org, www.hrw.org, and www.asylumlaw.org.
[43] Discussed in Section A.3 of Chapter 10, Immigration Court Practice and Relief from Removal.

- Statement or affidavit from Mohammed's brother explaining what he knows about what happened to Mohammed and his parents and how he knows this information; his statement will carry more weight if he learned the news independently of his brother
- Forensic evaluation from a medical doctor in the United States who has conducted an examination of Mohammed's entire body and is able to state whether scars on it are consistent with how Mohamed says he acquired them
- Psychological evaluation to explain Mohammed's subjective fear of return
- Death certificates of Mohammed's parents, if available, as proof they are dead, and possibly, how they died
- Birth certificate of Mohammed, if available, to establish his relationship to his parents and also to show that he is Sudanese
- Country conditions evidence concerning the Sudan generally and Darfur in particular, where available

Any documents that are not in English must be translated.

In this example, Mohammed is unmarried and without children. If the facts were different and these relationships did exist, he could include in his application his wife and any unmarried children under 21 years old who are with him in the United States. They would be his **qualifying derivative family members**.[44] In this case, Mohammed would need to include evidence of his relationship to each of them in his application, such as a marriage certificate for his spouse and birth certificates for his eligible children, where available.

If any of Mohammed's listed children becomes older than 21 years before a decision is made on his asylum application but after he has filed it, then the **Child Status Protection Act**, or **CSPA**, will allow them to continue to be treated as his derivatives as though they were under 21, so long as they remain unmarried.[45]

● EXAMPLE

Mohammed's wife and two children are still in Darfur. The children were 13 and 19 when he filed his application for asylum. It takes three years for the approval of his application, by which time the children are 16 and 22. Mohammed is still able to file applications for his wife and both children to join him. Even though the eldest child is now over 21, because he was under that age when the asylum application was filed, he is still eligible to come to the United States as Mohammed's child so long as he remains unmarried because the filing of the application froze the age of the child.

The CSPA can provide useful protections to those who timely file applications for immigration benefits that are dependent on them being minors at the time of adjudication but, because of the delays in processing applications, might otherwise age out and therefore be excluded from receiving the benefits.

---

[44] 8 C.F.R. 208.21(a).
[45] INA § 208(b)(3)(B).

Figure 5.2

Sample Asylum Application Receipt Notice

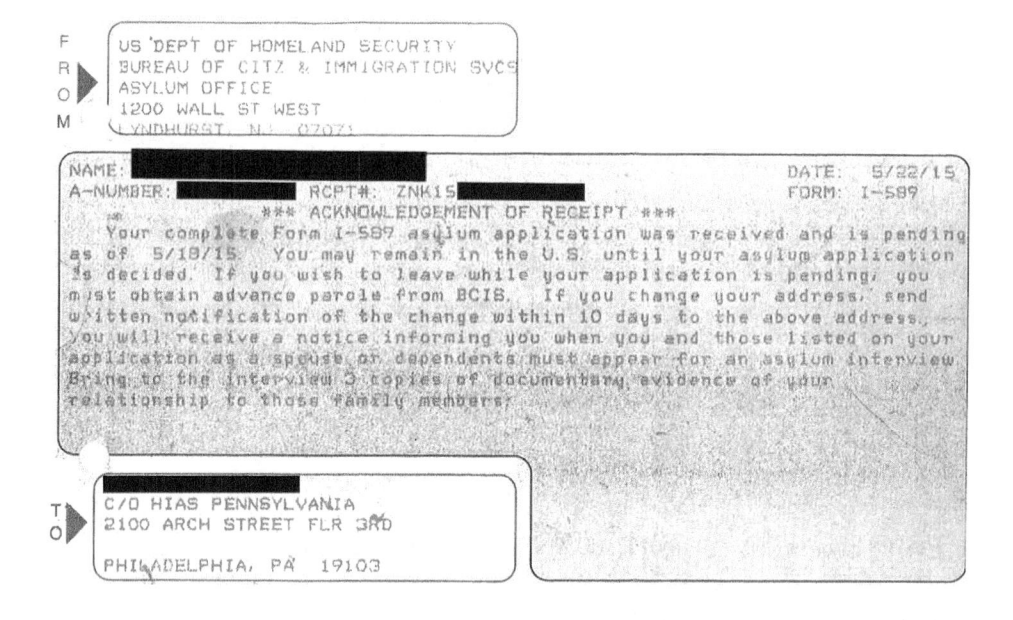

```
FROM:  US DEPT OF HOMELAND SECURITY
       BUREAU OF CITZ & IMMIGRATION SVCS
       ASYLUM OFFICE
       1200 WALL ST WEST
       LYNDHURST, NJ 07071

NAME: ▮▮▮▮▮▮▮▮                                    DATE: 5/22/15
A-NUMBER: ▮▮▮▮▮   RCPT#: ZNK15▮▮▮▮                FORM: I-589
          *** ACKNOWLEDGEMENT OF RECEIPT ***
   Your complete Form I-589 asylum application was received and is pending
   as of 5/18/15. You may remain in the U.S. until your asylum application
   is decided. If you wish to leave while your application is pending, you
   must obtain advance parole from BCIS. If you change your address, send
   written notification of the change within 10 days to the above address.
   You will receive a notice informing you when you and those listed on your
   application as a spouse or dependents must appear for an asylum interview.
   Bring to the interview 3 copies of documentary evidence of your
   relationship to those family members.

TO:  ▮▮▮▮▮▮▮▮▮▮▮▮
     C/O HIAS PENNSYLVANIA
     2100 ARCH STREET FLR 3RD
     PHILADELPHIA, PA  19103
```

The CSPA is discussed in greater detail in Section C.4 of Chapter 6, Family Sponsored Immigration and Permanent Resident Status.

There is no fee to file an asylum application. The form and accompanying instructions are on the USCIS website at www.uscis.gov. It is important to review the instructions on the website regularly as the USCIS often updates versions of the forms it is accepting. The website will also give the most current address for mailing the application package and what to include. An original plus two copies of the application are sent to a designated **USCIS Service Center** with jurisdiction over where the foreign national lives. It is then processed and sent to an Asylum Office that will interview the applicant and make the initial decision on the case. If there are any derivatives included in the application, an extra copy of Form I-589, Application for Asylum and for Withholding of Removal, should be included for each person, with a passport photograph of the family member to be included, stapled to the right hand corner of Part A.II.

Once received, the USCIS will issue a receipt for the application that will include the date it came into its office. This date is important because it will help to keep track of how long it is taking to process the application and also of when the asylum seeker will be entitled to apply for permission to work while the application remains pending. A sample of a receipt notice appears in Figure 5.2.

The law requires asylum applications to be expedited within the immigration system and to be adjudicated within a period of 180 days, even if they are referred to an immigration judge for consideration at a later stage.[46] Given this rather tight timeframe, the USCIS tries hard to complete adjudication of affirmative applications within a period of six weeks. However, currently many offices

---

[46] INA § 208(d)(5)(iii).

have considerable backlogs such that waiting up to two years for an interview alone is not uncommon. The one benefit to this is that an applicant should receive permission to work after waiting 180 days after filing an asylum application, so long as no negative decision has been issued within that time.[47] This is discussed in detail in Section B.5.

As with all other forms of immigration relief, asylum status cannot be granted unless a foreign national appears for a biometrics appointment, where digital fingerprints and photographs are captured and submitted for security clearance purposes. The application can only be approved if the results raise no security issues or concerns. A sample biometrics appointment notice is shown in Figure 5.3.

The next step in the application process is a non-adversarial interview conducted by an asylum officer who will have reviewed the entire application package. It generally involves only the foreign national, his or her legal representative, if any, and an interpreter provided by the applicant, if needed. Qualifying derivative family members who are in the United States are also called for the interview, but generally wait in the waiting area unless they have something to add to the principal applicant's story. Where the foreign national uses an interpreter, the asylum officer will often call in an independent interpreter over the telephone from a commercial company, to listen in and monitor the quality of interpretation. The purpose of the interview is to allow the foreign national to explain what happened to him or her in the past and why s/he is afraid to return home now.

Following the interview, a foreign national must return to the Asylum Office in 14 days in order to receive the decision on his or her case in person. Sometimes it may take longer than this because of staffing priorities within the office or because an application raises novel or complex issues, which must be reviewed by headquarters in Washington. In such cases, a foreign national will be advised when to return. The decision may also be mailed to the applicant instead, but this is less common for those whose applications have not been approved.

An asylum officer can decide to grant an application for asylum or refer it to an immigration judge. If the application is granted, then the decision is final unless it is later revoked for fraud in the application process. The foreign national now becomes an asylee and is given an Asylum Approval letter with an I-94 card or Arrival/Departure Record attached that includes the date of grant of status. Any derivatives included in the application will also be granted asylum and issued their own letters and I-94 cards. Sometimes, a foreign national may receive a letter advising that his or her application has been recommended for approval. This generally means that security and other background checks have not been completed and, so long as no concerns arise, the application will be approved at a later date. The benefit of receiving a recommendation for approval letter is that the foreign national can immediately apply for permission

---

[47] 8 C.F.R. § 208.7(a)(1).

Figure 5.3

Sample Form I-797C, Notice of Action for Biometrics Appointment

---

Department of Homeland Security
U.S. Citizenship and Immigration Services

Form I-797C, Notice of Action

THIS NOTICE DOES NOT GRANT ANY IMMIGRATION STATUS OR BENEFIT.

Fingerprint Notification

			NOTICE DATE
			May 22, 2015
CASE TYPE			USCIS A#
I589 Application For Asylum			A_____
RECEIPT NUMBER	RECEIVED DATE	PRIORITY DATE	PAGE
ZNK_____	May 18, 2015	May 18, 2015	1 of 1

APPLICANT NAME AND MAILING ADDRESS

HIAS PENNSYLVANIA
2100 ARCH STREET FLR 3RD
PHILADELPHIA PA 19103

You have been scheduled to appear at the below USCIS Application Support Center (ASC) to be fingerprinted and photographed (biometrics collection) during the 14-day period specified below. Completion of background identity and security checks is required in order to process your application.

Address	14-Day Period	Hours of Operation CLOSED ON FEDERAL HOLIDAYS
USCIS PHILADELPHIA 10300 DRUMMOND ROAD SUITE 100 PHILADELPHIA PA 191543804	05/25/2015 to 06/08/2015	Sat - Sun Closed Mon - Fri 8am-3pm

Failure to appear as scheduled for fingerprinting and biometrics collection during the 14-Day period may delay eligibility for work authorization and/or result in an asylum officer dismissing your asylum application, and/or referring it to an Immigration Judge.

When you appear for fingerprinting and biometrics collection, you MUST BRING THIS LETTER. Even if you are scheduled at the same time as your family members, each individual must bring his or her own notice. **If you do not bring this letter, you will not be able to have your fingerprints taken.** This may cause a delay in the processing of your application and your eligibility for work authorization. You should also bring photo identification such as a passport, valid driver's license, national ID, military ID, State-issued photo ID, or USCIS-issued photo ID. If you do not have any photo identification, please expect a minor delay, as you will need to be interviewed by a USCIS officer regarding your identity. Note: Asylum applicants are not required to present identification documents in order to have fingerprints and biometrics collected.

Please note that the staff at the ASC will not be able to answer any questions about the status of your application. We appreciate your patience during the process.

Pursuant to Section 265 of the Immigration and Nationality Act, you are required to notify the USCIS, in writing, of any address changes, within 10 days of such change. If you were placed in removal proceedings before an Immigration Judge, you are also required to notify the Immigration Court having jurisdiction over your case of any change of address within 5 days of such change, on Form EOIR-33. Include your name, signature, address, and USCIS A# on any written notice of change of address. The USCIS will use the last address you provided for all correspondence, and you are responsible for the contents of all USCIS correspondence sent to that address. Failure to provide your current address as required may result in dismissal or referral of your asylum application, institution of removal proceedings, the entry of a removal order in your absence if you fail to appear for a hearing before an immigration judge, and removal from the United States. If you have any questions or comments regarding the status of your application, please contact the office with jurisdiction over your application.

If you have any questions regarding this notice, please call 1-800-375-5283.   REPRESENTATIVE COPY

Form I-797C 07/11/14 Y

to work, although there will be no entitlement to other benefits available to those granted asylum until there is a final decision in the case.

If the foreign national is not granted asylum, what happens next will depend on his or her current immigration status. Where a foreign national who applies for asylum is out of status at the time of adjudication of the claim, the asylum officer has no authority to deny the case. Instead, it must be *referred* to an immigration judge for ***de novo*** review in removal proceedings.[48] Any derivative family members who are out of status will also be referred to an immigration judge.

Where the foreign national is in legal status at the time of adjudication, the application can be denied and the applicant and any derivative family members will retain the status they currently have, with no steps taken to refer them to an immigration judge.

De Novo: A review of a previously decided case as though it has not been considered before.

● EXAMPLE

Deena is from Syria. She entered the United States on an F-1 student visa and her stay is valid for as long as she remains a student because she has duration of status, or D/S.[49] She attends classes regularly and will not complete her studies for another year. Civil war broke out in Syria recently and conditions there have changed since she arrived in the U.S. Prior to leaving her country, Deena was a student leader in a group that has joined forces with those fighting against the government. She believes she will be targeted if she returns home. She files an affirmative asylum application. If Deena is ineligible for asylum, she will receive a denial of her application. However, she can legally remain in the United States on her student visa because it has not yet expired. She will not be placed into removal proceedings. This may not be the best option for Deena, particularly if she feels that the facts of her case are strong and wants an immigration judge to review her case. For now, she has no avenue for this to happen. However, once Deena's studies are complete and she is no longer in student status and is unable to change into a category that allows her to stay in the United States to work, she may decide to renew her application for asylum, including any changes that may have occurred in the interim. If Deena's application is not granted this second time, she will be referred to an immigration judge who will review her case de novo.

The flowchart in Figure 5.4 shows the typical route of an affirmative application for asylum.

B.3. Defensive Asylum Claims

Defensive asylum applications come before an immigration judge in one of three ways. First, as discussed earlier, where the asylum officer does not grant asylum in an affirmative case and the foreign national is out of status, his or her application must be referred to immigration court for *de novo* consideration, requiring the foreign national to be placed into removal proceedings.

---

[48] Detailed discussion of the removal process is in Chapter 10, Immigration Court Practice and Relief from Removal.
[49] *See* Section E.3.c of Chapter 2, Nonimmigrant Visas for Brief Stays, Studies, and Cultural Exchange.

Figure 5.4

Typical Route of an Affirmative Asylum Application

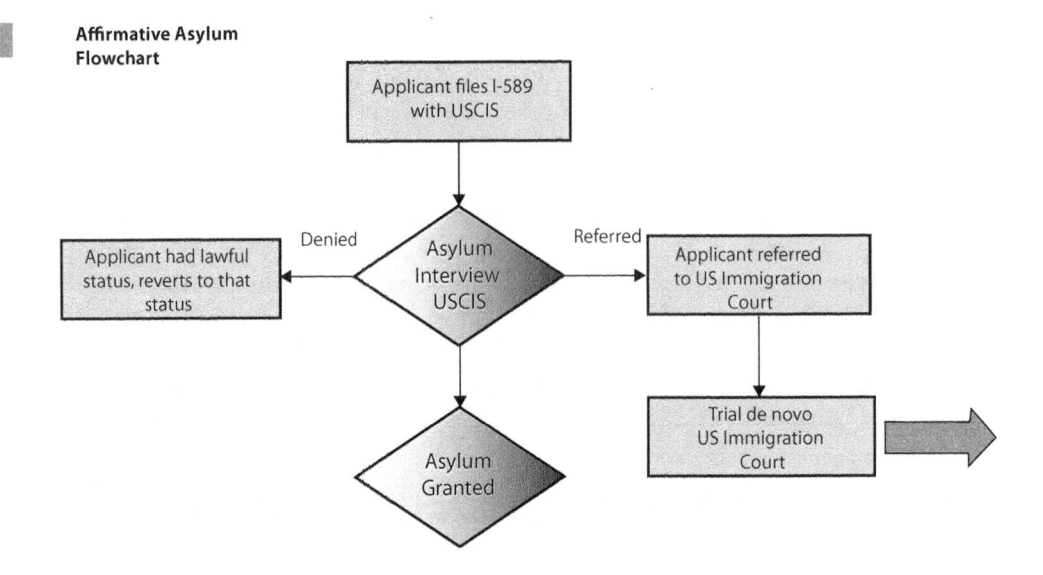

Affirmative Asylum Flowchart

```
                    Applicant files I-589
                        with USCIS
                             │
                             ▼
        Denied          Asylum          Referred
    ┌──────────────── Interview ────────────────┐
    ▼                   USCIS                   ▼
Applicant had lawful      │              Applicant referred
status, reverts to that   │              to US Immigration
      status              │                   Court
                          ▼                    │
                      Asylum                   ▼
                      Granted            Trial de novo
                                         US Immigration  ──▶
                                             Court
```

Arriving Alien: An applicant for admission who either arrives clandestinely and is apprehended at or near a border or within the United States or who presents him or herself to an official at a designated port of entry, and who has not yet been given permission to enter in the immigration status sought.

The second way a defensive claim is brought is when a foreign national is already in removal proceedings based on unrelated charges of immigration violations, at which point, the asylum claim is presented for the first time in order to prevent removal from the United States. For instance, a foreign national who entered without inspection, or EWI because s/he entered the country other than at a designated border and without seeing a CBP officer, may be in removal proceedings. Or the police may hand over an **overstayer** apprehended during a routine traffic stop to Immigration and Customs Enforcement, or ICE, because they learn that s/he has stayed in the country longer than the time allowed to remain. Once handed over to ICE, it becomes clear on questioning that s/he is without immigration status, at which point ICE may decide to process the foreign national for removal.

When the foreign national first appears before the immigration judge for a status hearing, known as a **master calendar hearing**, s/he may decide to concede the immigration violation while also making known that returning home is unsafe because of a likelihood of persecution. At this point, a defensive application for asylum can be filed in order to prevent his or her removal, if it is successful.

The third way a claim to asylum is brought defensively is when an *arriving alien*[50] is apprehended at the border and indicates a fear of returning home at that time.

The foreign national will be given a threshold interview, known as a credible or reasonable fear interview, depending on his or her past immigration history.

---

[50] This is a term of art for immigration purposes and is discussed further in Chapter 10, Immigration Court Practice and Relief from Removal.

Anyone deported from the United States previously and who is seeking to reenter illegally while that deportation order is still effective, will be held to the higher standard of reasonable fear of persecution as compared to someone who does not have this immigration history, who only has to prove s/he has a credible fear of persecution. If an asylum officer determines the arriving alien has demonstrated a credible or reasonable fear of persecution if returned to his or her country of origin, then the foreign national will be given an asylum-only hearing before an immigration judge who must give the case full consideration. No other immigration benefit can be claimed during these proceedings. The procedure for considering an asylum application filed by an arriving alien is different from the other two forms of defensive applications and is conducted in a process known as *expedited removal*, which is discussed in more detail in Section C.

Expedited Removal: A procedure used by DHS to remove foreign nationals who arrive at a U.S. border without proper documents or who have other problems causing them to be barred from entering or remaining in the United States, without the opportunity to see an immigration judge.

Unlike the interview in the affirmative asylum process, a case before an immigration judge is similar to an adversarial court proceeding. An attorney from ICE represents the government. The foreign national or applicant is the defendant, although actually referred to in immigration court as the respondent.

The immigration judge hears testimony and weighs all the evidence before making a decision. If the request is granted, then a spouse and any unmarried children under 21 at the time the application was filed, regardless of age now, and included in the original application, will also be granted asylum as derivatives. If the judge denies the asylum claim, the foreign national can appeal the decision to the BIA, which can either reverse the immigration judge's decision and grant the respondent asylum, or affirm the judge's denial and dismiss the appeal. A foreign national can then challenge the dismissal of his or her case by filing a Petition for Review before the United States Court of Appeals for the Circuit in which the case originated. Petitions for Review are complex and require representation by an attorney, although in some cases petitions are filed by an applicant *pro se*. Chapter 10, Immigration Court Practice and Relief from Removal, discusses removal procedures in detail.

In removal proceedings, an application package similar to the one filed with the USCIS is prepared, except that rather than including a Form G-28, Notice of Entry of Appearance of Attorney or Accredited Representative, it will include instead a Form EOIR-28, Notice of Entry of Appearance as Attorney or Representative before the Immigration Court. A copy of the first three pages of Form I-589, Application for Asylum and for Withholding of Removal, the entire Form EOIR-28, and a cover sheet called the Instructions for Submitting Certain Applications in Immigration Court, will then be sent to the Texas Service Center. A sample of the cover sheet is in Figure 5.5. A receipt is issued and an appointment set for the foreign national to appear for biometrics processing. The entire application package is then handed to the immigration judge, in court, with an identical copy given to the ICE attorney representing the government. If there is no receipt to show that the application was sent to the Service Center, the judge may not accept the application.

Figure 5.5

Instructions for Submitting Certain Applications in Immigration Court

INSTRUCTIONS FOR SUBMITTING CERTAIN APPLICATIONS IN IMMIGRATION COURT AND FOR PROVIDING BIOMETRIC AND BIOGRAPHIC INFORMATION TO U. S. CITIZENSHIP AND IMMIGRATION SERVICES

A. Instructions for Form I-589 (Asylum and for Withholding of Removal)*

In addition to filing your application and supporting documents with the Immigration Court and serving a complete copy of your application on the appropriate Immigration and Customs Enforcement (ICE) Office of Chief Counsel, you must also complete the following requirements before the Immigration Judge can grant relief or protection in your case:

SEND these 3 items to the address below:

(1) A clear copy of the **first three pages** of your completed Form I-589 (Application for Asylum and for Withholding of Removal) that you will be filing or have filed with the Immigration Court, which must include your **full name, your current mailing address, and your alien number (A-number)**. (Do Not submit any documents other than the first three pages of the completed I-589),

(2) A copy of Form G–28 (Notice of Entry of Appearance as Attorney or Accredited Representative) if you are represented, and

(3) A copy of these instructions.

       USCIS Nebraska Service Center
       Defensive Asylum Application With Immigration Court
       P.O. Box 87589
       Lincoln, NE 68501-7589

Please note that there is **no filing fee required** for your asylum application.

After the 3 items are received at the USCIS Nebraska Service Center, **you will receive**:

- A **USCIS receipt notice** in the mail indicating that USCIS has received your asylum application, and
- An **ASC notice** for you, and separate Application Support Center (ASC) notices for each dependent included in your application. Each ASC notice will indicate the individual's unique receipt number and **will provide instructions for each person to appear** for an appointment **at a nearby ASC for collection of biometrics** (such as your photograph, fingerprints, and signature). If you do not receive this notice in 3 weeks, call (800) 375-5283. If you also mail applications under Instructions B, you will receive 2 notices with different receipt numbers. You must wait for and take both scheduling notices to your ASC appointment.

You (and your dependents) must then:

- **Attend** the biometrics appointment at the ASC, and obtain a **biometrics confirmation** document before leaving the ASC, and
- **Retain** your **ASC biometrics confirmation** as proof that your biometrics were taken, and bring it to your future Immigration Court hearings.

* NOTE: IF YOU ARE FILING A FORM I-589 AND/OR ANOTHER APPLICATION, SEE THE REVERSE OF THIS FORM FOR ADDITIONAL INSTRUCTIONS.

Important: Failure to complete these actions and to follow any additional instructions that the Immigration Judge has given you could result in delay in deciding your application or in your application being deemed abandoned and dismissed by the court. Revised 9/5/13

B: Asylum Procedure

Figure 5.5 (Continued)

B. Instructions for Form(s) I-485, I-191, I-601, I-602, I-881, EOIR-40, EOIR-42A, or EOIR-42B

In addition to filing your application(s) with the Immigration Court and serving a complete copy of any such application(s) on the appropriate Immigration and Customs Enforcement (ICE) Office of Chief Counsel, you must also complete the following requirements before the Immigration Judge can grant relief in your case:

SEND these 5 items to the address below:

(1) A clear copy of the entire application form(s) that you will be filing or have filed with the Immigration Court. (Do not submit any documents such as attachments – send only the completed form itself),

(2) The appropriate application fee(s) or the Immigration Judge's order granting your fee waiver. (The fee can be found in the instructions with the application, the regulations, and at www.uscis.gov or for the EOIR forms, at www.usdoj.gov/eoir),

(3) The mandatory $85 USCIS biometrics fee,

(4) A copy of Form G–28 (Notice of Entry of Appearance as Attorney or Accredited Representative) if you are represented, and

(5) A copy of these instructions.

>   USCIS Texas Service Center
>   P.O. Box 852463
>   Mesquite, Texas 75185-2463

All fees must be submitted in the form of a check or a money order (or separate checks/money orders) and be made out to: "Department of Homeland Security."

After the 5 items are received at the USCIS Texas Service Center, **you will receive:**

• A **USCIS fee receipt notice** showing that you have paid the application fee (unless waived) and the mandatory biometrics fee. **Keep a copy for yourself.**

• A **USCIS notice with instructions to appear** for an appointment at a nearby **Application Support Center (ASC) for collection of your biometrics** (such as your photographs, fingerprints, and signature). This notice contains your important USCIS application receipt number which must be presented to the ASC. Your dependents will receive separate ASC notices if they are required to provide biometrics. If you do not receive this notice in 3 weeks, call (800) 375-5283. If you also apply for asylum, take both scheduling notices to your ASC appointment (*see* side A). **Keep copies of all ASC scheduling notices for your records.**

You (and your dependents) must then:

• **Attend** this ASC biometrics appointment and obtain a **biometrics confirmation** document from the ASC,

• **File** the following with the Immigration Court within the time period directed by the Immigration Judge: (1) the original **application Form**, (2) all **supporting documentation**, and (3) the **USCIS fee receipt notice** that serves as evidence that you paid the filing fees (unless the Immigration Judge granted you an application fee waiver), and

• **Retain** your **ASC biometrics confirmation** as proof that your biometrics were taken, and bring it to your future Immigration Court hearings.

DO NOT SUBMIT THE ORIGINAL APPLICATION TO USCIS. DO NOT SUBMIT ANY APPLICATIONS TO THIS POST OFFICE BOX OTHER THAN THOSE APPLICATIONS LISTED. ALL OTHER APPLICATIONS, INCLUDING APPLICATIONS FOR EMPLOYMENT AUTHORIZATION AND IMMIGRANT PETITIONS, WILL BE RETURNED TO YOU IF SENT TO THIS POST OFFICE BOX. FOR SUBMITTING APPLICATIONS NOT LISTED ON SIDE A OR SIDE B OF THIS PAPER, PLEASE FOLLOW THE INSTRUCTIONS THAT ACCOMPANY THE APPLICATION.

Important: Failure to complete these actions and to follow any additional instructions that the Immigration Judge has given you could result in delay in deciding your application or in your application being deemed abandoned and dismissed by the court. Revised 9/5/13

Figure 5.6

Typical Route of a Defensive Asylum Application

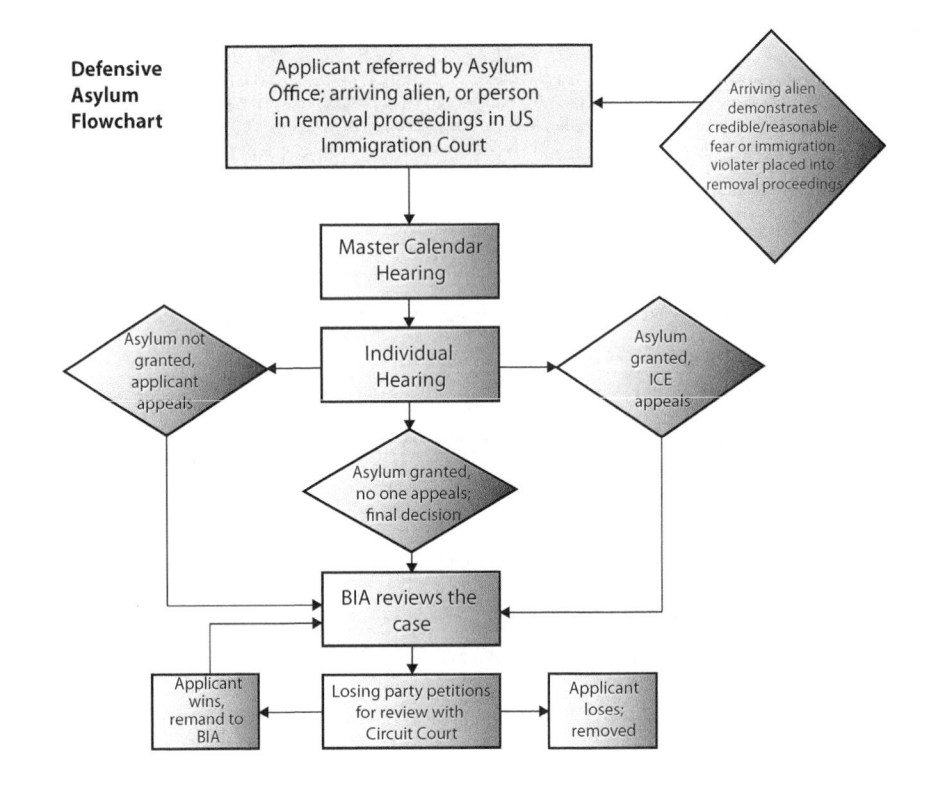

Defensive Asylum Flowchart

[Flowchart: Applicant referred by Asylum Office; arriving alien, or person in removal proceedings in US Immigration Court → Master Calendar Hearing → Individual Hearing. Arriving alien demonstrates credible/reasonable fear or immigration violater placed into removal proceedings feeds into the top. From Individual Hearing: Asylum not granted, applicant appeals; Asylum granted, ICE appeals; Asylum granted, no one appeals; final decision. Appeals go to BIA reviews the case → Losing party petitions for review with Circuit Court → Applicant wins, remand to BIA / Applicant loses; removed.]

At a master calendar hearing, the immigration judge will set a date and time for an **individual hearing**, when the entire case will be heard.[51] That date must be at least 45 days away, to allow enough time for case preparation.[52] Judges are also under pressure to hear a case and issue a decision before 180 days have elapsed from the time the USCIS accepted the application, if it is an affirmative one that has been referred by an asylum office. However, if the case is referred to immigration court after more than 75 days have already elapsed, it will no longer be subject to this stringent timeframe.[53]

In a defensive asylum case, it is more common to have witnesses to testify in person, including experts, although telephonic testimony may be taken at the judge's discretion, from someone who is unable to travel to the court. The flowchart in Figure 5.6 shows the typical route of a defensive application for asylum in court.

B.4. Frivolous Asylum Applications

The law treats those who abuse the asylum process harshly. Asylum applicants discovered to have deliberately lied on their applications or to have misrepresented

---

[51] *See* Section B of Chapter 10, Immigration Court Practice and Relief from Removal, for further details.
[52] *A.B.T., et al v. USCIS, et al*, No. CV11-2108-RAJ (W.D. Wash.).
[53] *See* Operating Policies and Procedures Memorandum 13-02: *The Asylum Clock*, From the Office of the Chief Immigration Judge, Dated December 2, 2013, available at http://www.justice.gov/sites/default/files/eoir/legacy/2013/12/03/13-02.pdf.

Figure 5.7

Sample Frivolous Application Warning

```
                    IMMIGRATION COURT
                 900 MARKET STREET, SUITE 504
                    PHILADELPHIA, PA  19107


    FILE:  ███████████████

    RE:    ██████████████████████████


             NOTICE OF PRIVILEGE OF COUNSEL AND CONSEQUENCES
           OF KNOWINGLY FILING A FRIVOLOUS APPLICATION FOR ASYLUM

    Before you file an asylum application (Form I-589) the law (section 208(d)(4)
    of the Immigration and Nationality Act) requires that you be advised
    specifically about the consequences of knowingly filing a frivolous application
    for asylum in the United States.

    If you knowingly file a frivolous application for asylum, YOU WILL BE BARRED
    FOREVER from receiving any benefits under the Immigration and Nationality Act.
    A frivolous application for asylum is one which contains statements or
    responses to questions that are deliberately fabricated.  Not being granted
    asylum does not mean that your application is frivolous.

    Please be advised you have the privilege of being represented by counsel of
    your choice, at no expense to the government.




                           CERTIFICATION OF SERVICE
    THIS DOCUMENT WAS SERVED BY:   MAIL (M)      PERSONAL SERVICE  (P)
    TO: [ ] ALIEN  [ ] ALIEN c/o Custodial Officer  [X] ALIEN's ATT/REP  [X] DHS
    DATE:   5/6/15            BY: COURT STAFF
          Attachments:  [ ] EOIR-33  [ ] EOIR-28  [ ] Legal Services List   [ ] Other

                                                                          U9
```

a material or key fact in their claims, can be charged with filing a **frivolous asylum application**.[54] If an immigration judge determines the application was frivolous and had earlier explained, whether orally or in writing, the consequences of filing such a claim, the foreign national will be permanently barred from receiving *any* immigration benefits in the future.[55] A sample of a frivolous application warning is shown in Figure 5.7.

---

[54] INA § 208(d)(6).
[55] *Id.*

B.5. Asylum Applicants and Employment Authorization

Foreign nationals applying for asylum must wait at least 150 days from the date the USCIS receives the application or it is filed with the immigration court before they are eligible to apply for an Employment Authorization Document, or EAD. This document allows lawful employment in the United States. This is why the date on the receipt notice from the USCIS is so important. The instrument that counts the days is known informally as the **asylum EAD clock,** which can be stopped, however, if the foreign national causes any delays in processing the asylum application. For instance, s/he may not be able to attend an interview appointment with the USCIS on the date given, in which case the clock will stop and will not restart until the foreign national appears at a rescheduled date. Applicants have 45 days to show good cause for having missed their interview, which may then prevent the stopping of the clock.[56]

Delays in the progress of cases referred to immigration court also stop the clock, although judges are required to provide a foreign national with a written notice about the impact of different codes allocated to delays and explain clearly on the record the reason for any adjournment.[57] The ability to stop and start the clock means most defensive asylum applicants who were not referred by an asylum office, rarely accumulate enough days to make them eligible to apply for an EAD card.

Following the decision in *A.B.T., et al v. USCIS, et al*, No. CV11-2108-RAJ (W.D. Wash.), however, a foreign national may now lodge an application for asylum with the court administrator at any time, even before filing it with an immigration judge in open court. Once lodged, the EAD clock will count the number of days that have elapsed since this date. After the 150 days have accumulated, the foreign national is eligible to file an application for work authorization. Filing a defensive application directly with the court administrator is particularly useful as it will begin accruing time towards the required 150 days to apply for employment authorization. The administrator will simply date stamp the application and then return it to the representative. Even though the application is lodged with the court administrator, it must still be physically filed with an immigration judge, in court, for it to be an application properly filed for consideration.

● EXAMPLE

Assume Mohammed from the earlier example waited nine months before his affirmative asylum application was adjudicated. He would have been eligible to apply for permission to work after 150 days and to receive his EAD card 30 days later, making a total of 180 days. If Mohammed's case is later referred to an immigration judge, he will already have an asylum application for consideration and will have received his permission to work, so would not need to lodge anything with the court clerk. Now assume that Mohammed did not file an affirmative application for asylum,

---

[56] *A.B.T., et al v. USCIS, et al, supra.*
[57] *Id.*

but instead was picked up in a traffic stop shortly after his arrival in the U.S. Following questioning, it was determined that he was in the United States undocumented and therefore placed in removal proceedings for an immigration judge to decide if he must leave the country. In order to avoid that, Mohammed decides to file for asylum because it is not safe for him to return home. His first master calendar hearing date will not be for another six months and he knows that, in order to file his application, he must hand it to an immigration judge, probably at that hearing, if it is ready. Because Mohammed wants to qualify to work as soon as possible, it will be advisable for him to lodge his asylum application with the court administrator as quickly as he can so that he can begin to accrue the 150 days that he needs to qualify to apply to work, even though he will not be in court to hand in the application for some time.

C. Credible and Reasonable Fear Interviews: INA § 235(b); 8 C.F.R. §§ 208.30-31; 8 C.F.R. §§ 1208.30-31

An arriving alien who is apprehended at a U.S. border and expresses a fear of returning home is typically held in a detention facility until an interview can be conducted to determine whether the fear is either credible or reasonable. The applicable standard depends on his or her past immigration history, if any. Those who are apprehended at a U.S. border and have never been issued a deportation order are given a **credible fear interview**, requiring the arriving alien to demonstrate that there is "a significant possibility ... that the alien could establish eligibility for asylum" under the statutory asylum provisions.[58] If this standard is met, then the foreign national will be allowed to present his or her claim before an immigration judge for full consideration and is generally released from detention to live with relatives or friends in the United States, either on bond or, less likely, on his or her own recognizance.

Arriving aliens who have previously been removed from the United States under a deportation order and who try to re-enter illegally, i.e., without presenting themselves to a border agent while that order is still in effect, will also be interviewed but held to a higher standard. It requires a showing of "a reasonable possibility that he or she would be persecuted on account of his or her race, religion, nationality, political opinion, or membership in a particular social group, or a reasonable possibility that he or she would be tortured in the country of removal."[59] These are known as **reasonable fear interviews**.

In both cases, an asylum officer conducts the interviews and decides whether the applicant's claim met the appropriate threshold standard. If it has, then the case is referred to an immigration judge who will hold expedited removal proceedings to consider the asylum claim only. No other immigration relief can be requested in this hearing. When the asylum officer finds that the claim did not

---

[58] INA § 235(b)(1)(B)(v), 8 C.F.R. § 208.30.
[59] 8 C.F.R. § 208.31(c).

meet the appropriate standard, the foreign national has the opportunity to have his or her case reviewed by an immigration judge who will only determine whether the asylum officer's decision was correct. If the judge agrees with the officer that the claim fell short of the required standard, there are limited rights to challenge that decision in judicial review proceedings. However, if the judge disagrees with the finding of the officer, then the arriving alien proceeds to have his or her full asylum only application heard.[60] Those who meet the reasonable fear standard are not eligible to receive asylum, only withholding of removal or protection under CAT,[61] forms of relief that are discussed in detail in Sections E and F.

D. Benefits of Asylum Grant

As a humanitarian immigrant, a foreign national granted asylum can access many immigration and social safety net benefits, including medical insurance, if needed. The asylee can also apply for an employment authorization document,[62] which is evidence of his or her right to work legally, and obtain a social security card and driving license, where appropriate. After one year as an asylee, s/he may apply for adjustment of status to that of an LPR.[63] This process is discussed in more detail in Section G.1 of Chapter 6, Family Sponsored Immigration and Permanent Resident Status. The foreign national files Form I-485, Application to Register Permanent Residence or Adjust Status. An asylee who cannot afford the application fee can apply to have it waived, using Form I-912, Request for Fee Waiver. Once the application is granted, the date on the I-551 Permanent Resident or green card, will be backdated one year from the date of approval of the application, essentially giving credit for the one year spent as an asylee. Those granted LPR status are eligible to apply to become U.S. citizens 90 days before the fifth anniversary of that date.[64]

Case for Discussion 5.9

Ashok is from India and was granted asylum on January 1, 2011. He applies to become an LPR at the earliest point and is granted that status on September 11, 2013.

- What will be the date on his Permanent Residency card?
- In what year can Ashok apply to become a citizen?

---

[60] For further discussion of the expedited removal process, see Section C. of Chapter 10, Immigration Court Practice and Relief from Removal.
[61] INA § 241(5).
[62] It should be noted that an asylee has permission to work incidental to this immigration status, see INA § 274.12(a)(5). However, many apply for a work authorization card, as this may be one of very few photo identity documents they may have and it is a document that employers readily recognize.
[63] INA § 209(b).
[64] Citizenship is discussed in Chapter 11, Citizenship and Naturalization.

Family members of asylees who are in the United States but were not included in the original asylum application,[65] or who live abroad,[66] are eligible to receive derivative asylum status through a separate petition. This includes spouses and unmarried children under the age of 21 years of age at the time the application for asylum was filed. The petition for both family members abroad and those in the United States is made using Form I-730, Refugee/Asylee Relative Petition, and must be filed within two years of the asylum grant. Once again, the CSPA[67] will allow a child who has aged out of an immigration benefit to continue to be treated as a derivative, so long as s/he remains unmarried.[68]

E. Withholding of Removal: INA § 241(b)(3); 8 C.F.R. § 208.16, 8 C.F.R. § 1208.16

As previously stated, a grant of asylum is discretionary. Therefore, even if someone meets all the eligibility requirements, an immigration judge, in the exercise of discretion, might still deny relief. Certain statutory bars to asylum have also been noted. In contrast, **withholding of removal** is a form of mandatory humanitarian relief and must be granted to anyone who can show it is more likely than not, or there is at least a 51 percent chance, of persecution if returned home. This higher standard was established by the Supreme Court in *INS v. Stevic*, 467 U.S. 407 (1984).

The INA § 241(b)(3) provides the statutory authority for withholding of removal, which requires a foreign national to show that his or her "life or freedom would be threatened" *on account of* one of the five enumerated grounds. Essentially, a claim for withholding is made in much the same way as an asylum application, using the same form and arguments. The relief is available to those who are barred from qualifying for asylum or in cases where an immigration judge declines to exercise discretion favorably. Even though this is a mandatory form of relief, however, there are still bars to eligibility. One major bar relates to those convicted of an aggravated felony or "particularly serious crime". Since the one-year deadline does not apply to withholding of removal, these applications can be filed at any time.

Only an immigration judge can grant withholding of removal; asylum officers do not have the authority to do so.[69] This is because, when a judge grants this relief, two things occur. First, an order of removal is issued against the foreign national because s/he has been found to be deportable from the United States. Second, because the judge accepts that it is more likely than not that harm will occur if the person is returned home, s/he is also ordering that

Withholding of Removal: An order by an immigration judge forestalling a foreign national's removal to a country where it has been shown it is more likely than not that harm will occur based on one of the enumerated grounds, yet allowing removal to a third country that provides assurances it will not return the person to the country where harm is feared.

---

[65] 8 C.F.R. § 208.21(c).
[66] 8 C.F.R. § 208.21(d).
[67] *See* Section B.2.
[68] INA § 208 (b)(3)(B).
[69] 8 C.F.R. § 208.16(a).

enforcement of the removal order be withheld or not effected so that the foreign national can remain in the United States. While this relief provides the foreign national the most important protection sought, *non-refoulement* and ultimately protection from persecution, it does not offer much more than this.

Unlike asylum, a grant of withholding of removal does not create a pathway to citizenship because the prerequisite, lawful permanent residency, can never be granted to a foreign national while a deportation order remains in place. S/he would have to qualify for this status through some other means only after revocation of the order. In addition, the relief provides no avenue for bringing family members to the United States or for granting derivative status to those already here. Withholding of removal is individual in nature, meaning each family member must apply and qualify for this protection in his or her own right.

Withholding of removal also means that, should the grantee leave the United States for any reason, it is unlikely s/he will be allowed to return. This is because, by leaving the country, the foreign national has triggered the deportation order issued by the judge, thereby authorizing CBP officers to deny permission to reenter. A foreign national granted withholding is essentially in limbo. While applications for permission to work should be granted and renewed without difficulty each year, s/he is ineligible to access many federal, state, or local benefits. This could be a serious problem if the foreign national is later injured and unable to work.

The other important difference is that withholding prevents removal to the foreign national's home country only. It does not prevent the immigration service from finding a third country that would be willing to receive him or her. However, this third country must abide by the obligation not to persecute or *refoule* the foreign national to the country where persecution is more likely than not to occur.

F. Convention Against Torture: 8 C.F.R. §§ 208.16-18, 8 C.F.R. §§ 1208.16-18

The final form of humanitarian relief directly related to international law emanates from the UN Convention Against Torture and Other Cruel, Inhuman, or Degrading Treatment or Punishment,[70] also known as the **Convention Against Torture,** or **CAT**. Article 3 contains an absolute prohibition against expelling, returning, or extraditing a foreign national to a country where there are "substantial grounds for believing that he would be in danger of being subjected to torture." The regulations at 8 C.F.R. § 208.18(a)(1) define torture as follows:

> any act by which severe pain or suffering, whether physical or mental, is intentionally inflicted on a person for such purposes as obtaining from him or

---

[70] GA res. 39/46, annex, 39 UN GAOR Supp. (No. 51) at 197, UN Doc. A/39/51 (1984), available at http://www.refworld.org/cgi-bin/texis/vtx/rwmain?page=search&docid=3b00f2224&skip=0&query=convention%20against%20torture.

her or a third person information or a confession, punishing him or her for an act s/he or a third person has committed or is suspected of having committed, or intimidating or coercing him or her or a third person, or for any reason based on discrimination of any kind, when such pain or suffering is inflicted by or at the instigation of or with the consent or acquiescence of a public official or other person acting in an official capacity.

Clearly, a number of the criteria for qualifying for protection under CAT differ from those for asylum and withholding of removal. Moreover, a significant difference between this relief and asylum or withholding of removal is that CAT does not require the harm to be inflicted based on any of the five enumerated grounds. The harm in question must be inflicted *intentionally*, by or with the acquiescence of the government, whether directly or through someone acting in an official capacity. Similar to withholding of removal, it is a mandatory form of relief.

While some foreign nationals might be ineligible for asylum or withholding of removal, anyone who can demonstrate that it is more likely than not that s/he will be tortured with the consent or acquiescence of a public official or someone acting in an official capacity, is entitled to protection. The status available under CAT can be either withholding of removal, where the mandatory bars to relief still apply, or deferral of removal, where they do not. Therefore, deferral is available to those who would otherwise be excluded from the other forms of relief because of their criminal record or because they persecuted others. Again, similar to withholding of removal, a foreign national granted this relief is not on a pathway to lawful permanent residency or citizenship. The relief simply prevents his or her removal to a country where it has been proven that torture is more likely than not to occur. While protection under CAT generally allows a foreign national to obtain permission to work, in some cases deferral of removal may mean that s/he remains in detention.[71] Table 5.1 compares some of the differences between asylum, withholding of removal, and CAT relief.

Table 5.1 Comparison of Asylum, Withholding, and Convention Against Torture Reliefs

Issue	Asylum	Withholding of Removal	Convention Against Torture
Legislative Provisions	INA § 101(a)(42); INA § 208; INA § 209; 8 C.F.R. § 208; 8 C.F.R. § 209 8 C.F.R. § 1208; 8 C.F.R. § 1209	INA § 241(b)(3); 8 C.F.R. § 208.16; 8 C.F.R. § 1208.16;	8 C.F.R. §§ 208.16-18; 8 C.F.R. §§ 1208.16-18
Type of Relief	Discretionary	Mandatory	Mandatory

---

[71] 8 C.F.R. §§ 208(17)(b)(1)(ii), (c).

Issue	Asylum	Withholding of Removal	Convention Against Torture
Applicability of Enumerated Grounds	Enumerated grounds apply	Enumerated grounds apply	Enumerated grounds irrelevant
Standard of Proof	Reasonable possibility or 10 percent chance that harm will occur	More likely than not or 51 percent chance of harm	More likely than not or 51 percent chance of torture
One-Year Deadline	Applies	File any time	File any time
Agent of Harm	Government or unwillingness to provide protection	Government or unwillingness to provide protection	Intentionally inflicted by or at instigation or acquiescence of government
Eligibility Bars	Apply	Apply	Irrelevant for deferral of removal only
Relief Granted	Asylum	Withholding of removal	Withholding of removal or deferral of removal
Possibility of Removal	Permission to remain in the United States indefinitely; qualifies to become an LPR and apply for citizenship	Deportation order entered. Protected from removal to country of persecution; can be removed to third country	Deportation order entered; protected from removal to country of persecution; can be removed to third country
Benefits for Qualifying Derivative Family Members	Derivative status and immediate grant of asylum for those already present in the United States; file Form I-730 petition within two years of grant for those present in the United States but not included in application or are abroad	Relief is individual; no benefits for relatives	Relief is individual; no benefits for relatives
Employment Authorization	Incidental to grant of status; EAD operates only as evidence of permission	Must apply for permission and renew documents annually	Must apply for permission and renew documents annually, for those who are not detained
Social Benefits	May be eligible	Limited access	Limited access
Travel Privileges	Can travel freely, using refugee travel document; should not return to country of persecution until becomes U.S. citizen	Cannot travel; if should leave the United States, unlikely to be allowed to return because will have effected deportation order	Cannot travel; if should leave the United States, unlikely to be allowed to return because will have effected deportation order
Lawful Permanent Residency	Apply after holding asylee status for one year; status backdated one year from date of grant	Ineligible	Ineligible

G. Temporary Protected Status and Deferred Enforced Departure: INA § 244; 8 C.F.R. § 244; 8 C.F.R. § 1244

There are times when conditions in a country or region change due to violent clashes, environmental disasters such as earthquakes, major health concerns, or other temporary emergency conditions that make it unsafe for individuals who reside in or are visiting the United States to return to their home country. In these circumstances, the secretary of the DHS can designate **Temporary Protected Status,** or **TPS**, for foreign nationals from the affected country. For example, Haiti was designated for TPS following the massive earthquake there in 2010; Guinea, Liberia, and Sierra Leone were designated following the Ebola epidemic in those countries and more recently, Syria was redesignated following the continued civil war conflict in that country.

When the secretary designates that citizens of a country are eligible for TPS, it is only for foreign nationals from that country present in the United States before a certain date and who are able to prove continuous physical presence from another given date. For example, citizens from the Ebola affected countries had to have arrived in the United States by November 20, 2014, and to be living here continuously, except for short absences, from November 21, 2014 straight through until the approval of their TPS applications.

Individuals seeking TPS with convictions for serious crimes are ineligible and all foreign nationals must submit for biometric data collection. Those ordered removed by an immigration judge but still physically in the United States are eligible to apply for and receive TPS. An individual granted TPS can legally work in the United States if permission to work is granted. The request can be made at the same time as the TPS application. As a result of the grant of TPS, the recipient is temporarily protected against removal.

Once granted TPS, the foreign national can apply to travel outside the United States and to return with the permission of the USCIS. Before leaving, s/he must request and receive ***advanced parole***, using Form I-131, Application for Travel Document.

Advanced Parole: Prior permission to leave and re-enter the United States before any travel outside of the country takes place.

Care should be taken to review the foreign national's prior immigration history because, even with advanced parole, a CBP officer is not obligated to grant permission to reenter, although, in most circumstances, it is likely that s/he will.

The BIA recently held that a foreign national who reenters the United States with advanced parole does not trigger the three- or ten-year unlawful presence bars and therefore is able to adjust status in the United States. *See Matter of Arrabally & Yerrabelly*, 25 I&N Dec. 771 (BIA 2012). A detailed discussion of these bars is in Section B.9.b of Chapter 9, Grounds of Inadmissibility and Deportation. Essentially, anyone and who has been present in the United States for more than 180 days but less than one year, and who voluntarily departs before the initiation of removal proceedings, is barred from reentry for a period of three years. Anyone present for a year or more without permission and who departs, regardless of whether removal proceedings have begun, is barred for ten years. A foreign national seeking to enter earlier than these periods of exclusion must request and receive a waiver first, unless s/he is reentering with advanced parole.

One of the benefits of the *Arrabally* decision is that a TPS recipient who might otherwise have the opportunity to adjust status to an LPR, perhaps through a family based petition,[72] but for an **inadmissibility** issue related to his or her current undocumented status, may now adjust in the United States. In order to do so, the foreign national must first apply for and receive advanced parole and then leave the country and return with this permission. In doing so, a CBP officer will have inspected and admitted the foreign national, bringing him or her into compliance with this requirement of INA § 245(a).

● EXAMPLE

Marie is from Haiti and entered the United States EWI by entering the country five years ago by boat into Florida. She is married to a U.S. citizen but cannot adjust her status to an LPR here because the law does not permit this for those who enter EWI. Marie was granted TPS following the earthquake and has been legally present ever since. She has applied for and received advanced parole so that she can visit her sick grandmother. Once she returns, Marie will have been inspected and paroled into the United States and therefore eligible to adjust her status to an LPR through her husband.

TPS is granted in 12 months or longer periods, typically 18 months, and can end when conditions in the affected country improve. A foreign national from a TPS designated country may have elected to apply for asylum, depending on the nature of the crisis in his or her country, or his or her personal circumstances and history. If the application is not successful, s/he can still apply for TPS as a means of preventing return to a dangerous situation, so long as the period for application submission has not expired. Unlike asylees, however, those in TPS status cannot petition for family members to join them here, apply for LPR status, or gain access to most government benefits.

Deferred Enforced Departure, or **DED**, is similar to TPS. It is granted by the President of the United States as part of his or her power to regulate foreign affairs. Like TPS, it is granted in incremental periods and is usually available to those who have already been granted TPS, at a point when conditions in the target country have improved significantly, but not enough to terminate all forms of protection. Table 5.2 indicates the USCIS forms associated with TPS and DED applications.

---

[72] This is discussed further in Chapter 6, Family Sponsored Immigration and Permanent Resident Status.

| Table 5.2 | Immigration Forms for TPS and DED |

TPS	DED
Form G-28, Notice of Entry of Appearance of Attorney or Accredited Representative	Same
Form I-821, Application for Temporary Protected Status	Not required
Form I-765 Application for Employment authorization	Same
Form I-912, Request for Fee Waiver, where required	Same

H. Refugees: INA § 101(a)(42); INA § 207; INA § 209; 8 C.F.R. § 201; 8 C.F.R. § 1207; 8 C.F.R. § 209; 8 C.F.R. § 1209

The Refugee Act 1980 established protocols for the admission and provision of services to refugees in the United States. Unlike asylees, a refugee receives his or her designation while outside the United States and generally outside his or her country of origin. Similar to asylees, however, refugees are given protection only if they can demonstrate they have been persecuted *on account* of one or more of the five enumerated grounds.

H.1. Determination of Refugees to the United States

The agency that oversees refugee admissions, the **United States Refugee Admissions Program,** or **USRAP**, is made up of three other government agencies: the Bureau of Population, Refugees, and Migration, or PRM, within the DOS; USCIS within the Department of Homeland Security; and the Office of Refugee Resettlement, or ORR, within the Department of Health and Human Services, or HHS. USRAP also contains representatives from *Non-Governmental Organizations,* or **NGO**s, who work with refugees.

Each year, government entities in USRAP consult with various cabinet offices and members of Congress to decide how many refugees to accept and from which regions they should come. They must create and approve the **admissions plan**. The agreed upon number is considered a maximum, which need not be reached. From 2010 to 2013, the ceiling on annual admission levels ranged from 70,000 to 80,000. The actual number of arrivals was below that. This can occur because of tightening of security screening procedures each refugee must undergo, causing delays in processing.

Non-Governmental Organization: An organization that operates independently from the government and, in some cases, may supplement it.

Working with UNHCR, the DOS, in conjunction with other governments, first attempts to develop plans so that refugees can return home safely. The return and re-integration of refugees is known as **repatriation**. A second alternative that is explored is **integration** into a foreign country where the refugee currently resides, often in a refugee camp. If repatriation and integration into that country is not feasible, especially in instances where refugees have lived in camps for many years or where there is continued instability and conflict in the home country, then UNHCR works with countries that do receive refugees to find a permanent, durable solution for them to enter and live in those countries.

Under INA § 207(a), the USRAP is mandated to establish refugee admission priorities based on "special humanitarian interest to the U.S." In 2015, the priorities included:

- **Priority 1 refugees**, abbreviated as P-1 refugees, which include individuals of any nationality who have a compelling need for protection. They can be referred to the DOS, PRM Regional Refugee Coordinators located in consulates abroad, or to certain **Refugee Support Centers,** or **RSC**, which are funded by PRM and run by a non-governmental organization with specially trained staff who prepare the case for consideration for resettlement. The RSC staff collects biographical and other information on the individual, required for security screening. Officers from the USCIS then review the case and interview the foreign national to determine eligibility for P-1 status.
- **Priority 2 refugees,** or P-2, are vulnerable groups of special humanitarian concern, identified by USRAP. These generally include refugees living in third countries who cannot return to their country of origin. For example, in 2013, minorities from Burma/Myanmar living in refugee camps in Thailand and other third countries were among those designated P-2 refugees and represented one of the largest groups of refugee admissions to the United States. In certain situations, an office within the country of the refugee may be established to process applications for refugee admission. This is known as "in-country" processing. In 2015, this was available in Iraq, Cuba, the former Soviet Union, and Baltic States, and in Honduras, El Salvador, and Guatemala, for certain minors.[73] As in P-1 processing, RSC staff generally prepare case files of P-2 individuals. All individuals in P-2 groups must undergo security screening and be interviewed by USCIS officers to determine eligibility for admission as a refugee.
- **Priority 3 refugees** or P-3, are those of designated nationalities outside of the United States whose family members have already been admitted as refugees, asylees, LPRs, or citizens who were previously refugees or asylees, in an

---

[73] This is a new program that allows certain lawfully present qualifying relatives in the United States to request that an unmarried child under 21 from one of these countries come to join him or her in the United States. More discussion of this is in Section U of Chapter 8, Immigration Relief for Vulnerable Populations.

attempt to achieve family reunification. Spouses, unmarried children under 21, and parents may be able to enter subsequently as refugees.[74]

In some circumstances, the identified family members who may enter as refugees may not include all those who lived in the household of the refugee when in his or her country of origin. The P-3 category allows for a broader interpretation of family members in certain circumstances. For an individual to be included, it must be established that s/he:

- Lived in the same household as the qualifying family member in the country of nationality or, if stateless, last habitual residence,
- Was part of the same economic unit as the qualifying family member in the country of nationality or, if stateless, last habitual residence, and
- Demonstrates exceptional and compelling humanitarian circumstances that justify inclusion on the qualifying family member's case.[75]

Because these individuals are not spouses, unmarried children under 21, or parents (in other words, the identified family members) they cannot derive refugee status from the P-3 refugee. Rather, they must establish that they qualify as refugees in their own right. However, this provision does allow for culturally appropriate family units that lived together abroad to remain intact in the United States.

In contrast to foreign nationals seeking asylum in the United States, individuals rejected for refugee status cannot appeal the decision. Nevertheless, those individuals can request a reconsideration of the claim, supplying additional facts or evidence to support that request. No specific form is required for this; a letter to the entity or person who rejected the claim will suffice. Where an attorney or accredited representative is sending the reconsideration letter on behalf of the foreign national, s/he must also submit a Form G-28, Notice of Entry of Appearance as Attorney or Accredited Representative, if s/he is to be acknowledged and sent any information about the case.

H.2. Family Reunification

Where a foreign national is a member of a designated P-3 nationality and is outside his or her country of origin, a family member in the United States can work with staff from a voluntary agency to complete an **Affidavit of Relationship,** or **AOR**. The family member filing the affidavit must be a refugee who has been in the United States for five years or less, be over 18 years old, and demonstrate s/he is the parent, spouse, or adult child of the intended beneficiary of the application. The refugee in the United States completing the form is

---

[74] A list of the designated countries can be found at http://www.state.gov/documents/organization/247982.pdf.
[75] Department of State Proposed Refugee Admissions for Fiscal Year 2016 Report to Congress, found at http://www.state.gov/documents/organization/247982.pdf.

known as the "anchor" relative. The affidavit is filed on State Department Form DS 7656, Affidavit of Relationship (AOR).

There are nine approved national voluntary agencies in the United States, known as national Volags, that the DOS recognizes as having authority to complete and submit the form. A caseworker, paralegal, or accredited representative staff member of the Volag can do this. They submit AORs to the Refugee Processing Center, operated by PRM. Following submission of the AOR, the USCIS will interview the intending beneficiary abroad to verify the relationship and eligibility. In order to combat fraud, stringent evidentiary requirements are in place to prove the familial relationship. In cases involving children, this can include DNA testing. Upon approval, the beneficiary is then able to travel to the United States and enter as a refugee.

Family members of refugees who are not eligible for P-3 family reunification may still be reunited within the United States. In these cases, the refugee here can file a Form I-730, Asylee/Refugee Relative Petition, instead, which must set forth facts and evidence establishing the relationship between the refugee and the family member who is the subject of the petition. Only the spouse and unmarried children under 21 years of age are eligible for family reunification using this process. The CSPA[76] will allow a child who becomes over 21 years old before approval of the application to continue to be treated as a derivative, so long as s/he remains unmarried.[77]

H.3. Adjustment of Status[78]

Unlike asylees who *may* be adjusted to lawful permanent residency one year after the grant of asylum status,[79] refugees *shall* apply to adjust one year after entry as a refugee.[80] The application is filed in the same way as asylee adjustment applications, except that refugees are not required to pay a fee for the Form I-485, Application to Register Permanent Residence or Adjust Status, application and so do not need to file fee waivers. Once granted, adjustment is backdated to the date of *entry* into the United States in refugee status, regardless of the date of application. Refugees are eligible to apply for citizenship 90 days before the fifth anniversary of the date of their entry into the United States so long as they are LPRs.[81]

---

[76] Discussed in detail in Section C.4 of Chapter 6, Family Sponsored Immigration and Permanent Resident Status.
[77] INA § 207(c)(2)(B).
[78] A detailed discussion of the process for applying for adjustment of status or lawful permanent residency is in Chapter 6, Family Sponsored Immigration and Permanent Resident Status.
[79] INA § 209(b).
[80] INA § 209(a).
[81] Discussed in detail in Chapter 11, Citizenship and Naturalization.

> ● **EXAMPLE**

Rashid had worked as an interpreter with the U.S. military in Iraq before he received refugee status. He and his family arrived in Philadelphia, PA in the summer of 2010. In 2013, he applied for permanent residency for himself and his wife and children, even though they could have applied in 2011. When their applications were granted, their I-551, Permanent Residency cards noted that they were granted permanent resident status in 2010 (the date of entry to the United States) and not 2013 when they applied or were granted LPR status. Because of this backdating, they will be eligible to apply for citizenship 90 days before the fifth anniversary of their entry, therefore sometime in 2015.

H.4. Refugee Resettlement Program

The U.S. government has recognized that refugees require special services after arrival. They usually arrive with few financial resources and may have experienced traumatic events that led to their need to claim refugee status. In addition, refugees may lack experience in living in complex industrialized environments because they have spent extended periods in refugee camps with rudimentary facilities or lived in underdeveloped countries and therefore experience culture shock on arrival, resulting from resettlement into a new and unfamiliar society. PRM has a cooperative agreement with the nine approved Volags. This is known as the Reception and Placement Program. PRM funds initial reception and core services to arriving refugees, which include the provision of housing, furnishings, clothing, and food, as well as assistance with access to medical, employment, educational, and social services.

National Volags have 350 affiliates in cities throughout the United States that provide Reception and Placement services to new refugees in the first 30 to 90 days after arrival. Supplemental social services and assistance, including eight months of medical coverage, are available through the ORR, within HHS.

I. Comparison of Refugee and Asylum Status

This survey of refugee and asylum law demonstrates that, while they are essentially the same form of relief in international law, the manner in which each is granted and resources provided to support a foreign national once given status differs considerably depending on the location of the grant of protection. Table 5.3 provides a helpful side-by-side comparison of these two forms of relief.

Table 5.3 Comparison Chart of Refugee and Asylum Status

Issue	Refugee	Asylee
Legislative Provisions	INA § 101(a)(42); INA § 207; INA § 209; 8 C.F.R. § 207; 8 C.F.R. § 1207; 8 C.F.R. § 1209 Uses 5 enumerated grounds	INA § 101(a)(42); INA § 208; INA § 209; 8 C.F.R. § 208; 8 C.F.R. § 1208; 8 C.F.R. § 1209 Uses 5 enumerated grounds
Where Is Status Conferred?	Abroad	In United States
Who Confers This Status?	The US Refugee Admissions Program working with UNHCR and USCIS officials abroad	USCIS asylum officer, immigration judge
Appeals Process	None; requests for reconsideration can be made	Trial de novo, BIA and judicial review only through appropriate Circuit Court of Appeals
Adjustment of Status	*Must* apply one year after admission, and date of adjustment is backdated to date of admission; there is no fee for this application and a modified examination is required from a civil surgeon	*Can* apply one year after grant of asylum and date of adjustment is backdated to one year from the date of approval of adjustment application; a fee waiver may be requested by those unable to pay the fee
Social Benefits	Refugees receive resettlement assistance and are eligible for means-tested public benefits in the same manner as citizens	Asylees may receive post asylum assistance and are treated the same as refugees for means tested public benefits
Eligible Beneficiaries for Family Reunification	Spouses, parents, unmarried children under 21 of designated nationalities	Spouses, unmarried children under 21 at time application is filed
Who Is Eligible to Apply/Petition?	Refugees over 18 in United States less than 5 years can file an AOR for family members from nationalities designated for P-3 resettlement or refugees in United States for 2 years or less if filing Form I-730, Refugee/Asylee Relative Petition for those of any nationality	Asylee within 2 years of the date of the grant of asylum, filing Form I-730, Refugee/Asylee Relative Petition
What Forms Are Used?	Form DS 7656, Affidavit of Relationship (AOR) for beneficiaries outside their country of origin or Form I-730, Refugee/Asylee Relative Petition, for spouses and children	Form I-730, Refugee/Asylee Relative Petition
Who Can Assist?	Only a staff member from a BIA recognized Volag can complete a Form DS 7656, Affidavit of Relationship (AOR)	An accredited staff member from a BIA recognized Volag, paralegal under the supervision of an attorney, or an attorney
Who Adjudicates/Decides?	Form DS 7656, Affidavit of Relationship (AOR), is sent to the DOS, Office of Refugee Processing, and then to DHS officers in the field who interview family member	Form I-730, Refugee/Asylee Relative Petition, sent to USCIS Service Center, which must first approve the petition; then sent to U.S. consulate, which interviews family member

J. Humanitarian Parole: INA § 212(d)(5)(A)

Individuals outside the United States who face an emergency situation but do not qualify for refugee status or other means of legal entry, may file an application for **humanitarian parole**. INA § 212(d)(5)(A) provides that the USCIS has the discretion to parole such an individual into the United States for urgent humanitarian reasons or significant public benefit on a case-by-case basis. Humanitarian parole is granted sparingly. Examples of individuals granted permission to enter in this category include parents abroad seeking to visit a terminally ill child in the United States or victims of the earthquake in Haiti in 2010, coming to the United States for medical treatment.

The foreign national requesting humanitarian parole must have a relative or other sponsor in the United States. The application is filed on Form I-131, Application for a Travel Document, and the relative or sponsor in the United States completes Form I-134, Affidavit of Support, to indicate the funds available to support the foreign national while here. These documents, with the fee for the application or request for fee waiver, are sent to the designated USCIS Service Center for consideration. The foreign national granted humanitarian parole can enter for a temporary period, renewable if the situation requires it.

K. Conclusion

Ultimately, U.S. asylum and refugee law is an attempt to bring the United States in line with its international obligations to those in need of protection. It provides important safeguards to individuals who meet eligibility requirements while also ensuring asylees and refugees have the opportunity to reunite with immediate family members and to become U.S. citizens. However, until they do, refugees and asylees who violate aspects of their status could find themselves in removal proceedings where they may be ordered deported.

For now, we review in detail the process for applying for and receiving LPR status, both for relatives in Chapter 6, Family Sponsored Immigration and Permanent Resident Status, and through employment in Chapter 7, Employment-Based and Self-Sponsored Immigration.

6

Family Sponsored Immigration and Permanent Resident Status

Key Terms and Acronyms

Adjustment of Status Application
Affidavit of Support
Beneficiary
Bona Fide Relationships
Child
Child Status Protection Act (CSPA)
Conditional Residency
Consular Processing

Family Sponsored Immigrant Visa
Fiancé(e) Petitions
INA § 245(i)
National Visa Center (NVC)
Petitioner
Visa Bulletin
Visa Petition

Chapter Objectives

- Understand the basics of family sponsored immigrant visa petitions
- Analyze and assess requirements to demonstrate a good faith marriage
- Understand the basics of family sponsored adjustment of status applications
- Understand adjustment of status applications and the differences with consular processing of immigrant visa applications
- Review procedures for change of conditional residency status to indefinite lawful permanent resident status

People seek to live in the United States permanently. Family sponsorship is the most common route to lawful permanent resident, or LPR, status. For example, in 2013, 649,763 foreign nationals became or entered the United States as LPRs through family sponsored petitions, representing more than 65 percent of the total number of individuals granted LPR status.[1] In most cases, permanently immigrating to the United States requires an application that is anchored either to a U.S. citizen, an LPR family member, or attached to an employment opportunity. It is also possible for a person to apply for LPR status on his or her own, although these are in the minority.

Most applications for LPR status involve a two-step process; first, to approve the petition that forms the basis on which an application will be filed, whether family, employment, or self-petition, and then to apply for the permanent resident status itself. In order for a foreign national to be granted LPR status under family sponsorship, s/he must have a qualifying relative who will petition and sponsor him or her. The U.S. citizen or LPR relative is known as the petitioner, while the person who will benefit from the approved petition is the beneficiary.

Additionally, applications for permanent residency or immigrant processing can only be filed either in the United States or through processing an application with a consular office abroad. Which method is applicable will generally depend on the foreign national's location at the time of his or her application. However, an important difference between the two methods is that denials of immigrant visas at the consular office have no avenue for review by the judiciary,[2] whereas an immigration judge has authority to review denials of adjustment of status applications in the United States.

This chapter focuses on how foreign nationals can become permanent residents based on certain family relationships only. Chapter 7, Employment-Based and Self-Sponsored Immigration, discusses immigration through employment. This chapter explores the two-step process, including the difference between adjustment of status and consular processing. It also touches on applications filed for family sponsored adjustment of status while the foreign national is in removal or deportation proceedings.

A. Part I: Family Relationships and the Petitioning Process

A.1. Sources of Law and Quotas: INA §§ 201-4; 8 C.F.R. § 204

Congress limits the number of people coming into the country in any one fiscal year. Statutory authority for this is found in the Immigration and Nationality Act, or INA § 201, which provides 226,000 annual visas for those seeking LPR status as family-sponsored immigrants, 140,000 for employment-based immigrants, and 50,000 for diversity lottery winners. INA § 202 allows a maximum of seven percent of the total annual family-sponsored and

---

[1] Department of Homeland Security, *2013 Yearbook of Immigration Statistics*, https://www.dhs.gov/sites/default/files/publications/ois_yb_2013_0.pdf.
[2] *Kerry v. Din*, 576 U.S. ___, 135 S. Ct. 2128 (2015).

employment-based immigrants to be allocated to any one foreign state, or two percent to a dependent area or colony of that state. This means that nationals from some countries, like Mexico or the Philippines, who have large numbers of foreign nationals seeking to apply for LPR status here, must wait longer than nationals from other countries. There are also different waiting times, depending on whether the petitioner is a U.S. citizen or LPR, and the relationship between the petitioner and beneficiary. The INA § 203 sets out **preference categories** that allocate visas and priority numbers, which determine how long a person has to wait before s/he can come to the United States.

A.2. Family Preference Categories

Family applications are divided into four preference categories:[3]

- F-1, First Preference, or family first: Unmarried sons and daughters of U.S. citizens who are over 21 years of age
- F-2, Second Preference, or family second: This is divided into
    - ☐ F2A, Spouses and unmarried children under 21 of LPRs
    - ☐ F-2B, Unmarried sons and daughters of LPRs who are over 21
- F-3, Third Preference, or family third: Married sons and daughters of U.S. citizens
- F-4, Fourth Preference, or family fourth: Brothers and sisters of U.S. citizens

Within each of these preference categories, more applications are filed than there are available visas allocated to each group. In order to determine who will be processed first, the United States Citizenship and Immigration Service, or USCIS, assigns a **priority date** or visa number to each application on the date it is received. This means that whenever the USCIS receives a *relative petition*, it notes the date the petition came in, which then becomes the priority date, determining where the application is in relation to other applications filed before, after, or at the same time. In other words, it registers its place on the waiting list. For example, a fourth preference or sibling application filed for a Mexican national in 2016 will likely wait over 19 years for a visa number to become current, because presently, the USCIS is processing applications for beneficiaries in that category who filed in 1997.

Each month, the U.S. Department of State, or DOS, prepares a **visa bulletin** that provides information on the number of immigrant visas available for distribution in any one month, taking into account the number processed both abroad and in the United States. Based on visa numbers available, both the USCIS and the DOS can determine when they will be able to allocate new visas to a particular group. Using the bulletin allows the public to also have a sense of the waiting time because each category will list the priority dates of visas that are available that month. Another agency, the National Visa Center, or NVC, will keep track of

Relative Petition: A petition filed by a parent, spouse, or adult child (petitioner) for the benefit of a foreign national (beneficiary) who can demonstrate a legal family relationship that then forms the basis of an application by the beneficiary to either apply for an immigrant visa abroad or adjust status to become an LPR in the United States once a visa number is available.

---

[3] There are preference categories that are applicable in the employment-based immigration context also. These are addressed in Chapter 7, Employment-Based and Self-Sponsored Immigration.

Table 6.1 State Department Visa Bulletin, July 2015

Family—Sponsored	All Chargeability Areas Except Those Listed	China—Mainland Born	India	Mexico	Phillippines
F1	01OCT07	01OCT07	01OCT07	15NOV94	15MAR00
F2A	08NOV13	08NOV13	08NOV13	15SEP13	08NOV13
F2B	15OCT08	15OCT08	15OCT08	08APR95	15MAY04
F3	15MAR04	15MAR04	15MAR04	22APR94	22AUG93
F4	22OCT02	22OCT02	22OCT02	01MAR97	08DEC91

Source: U.S. Department of State, available at https://travel.state.gov/content/visas/en/law-and-policy/bulletin/2015/visa-bulletin-for-july-2015.html.

priority dates for an applicant. A sample bulletin for July 2015 is in Table 6.1, listing the different family sponsored preference categories and the priority or processing dates the USCIS and DOS have reached for applications received.

Case for Discussion 6.1

Diego, a naturalized U.S. citizen, filed a relative petition for his married sister, Magdalena, in March, 2015. She is a citizen of Mexico.

- Based on the visa numbers available in July 2015 for a fourth preference relative from Mexico, how long can Magdalena expect to wait before a visa number becomes available?
- What if the family was from China instead?

It is important to note that the priority dates in the visa bulletin provide only an approximate idea of which applications are being processed at the current time. This is because, depending on the number of visas available, the cutoff dates may progress, regress, or remain stagnant from month to month. Some categories may remain stagnant for many years. For instance, the sibling or family fourth preference is one of the slowest moving because there are so few visas available for this category. In order to have a sense of when a visa number may be available, it is important to check the visa bulletin each month to see how things are moving since the waiting times may not progress as quickly as the calendar year. Therefore, it is difficult to give an accurate prediction of waiting times by merely looking at the current visa bulletin.

As previously mentioned, a maximum of seven percent of available visa numbers can be allocated to a particular country in any one year. This is referred

Table 6.2 State Department Visa Bulletin May 2016: Application Final Action Dates for Family-Sponsored Preference Cases

Family-Sponsored	All Chargeability Areas Except Those Listed	China—Mainland Born	India	Mexico	Philippines
F1	22NOV08	22NOV08	22NOV08	08FEB95	01OCT04
F2A	01NOV14	01NOV14	01NOV14	15AUG14	01NOV14
F2B	01SEP09	01SEP09	01SEP09	08SEP95	01MAY05
F3	01DEC04	01DEC04	01DEC04	08OCT94	22JAN94
F4	22JUL03	22JUL03	22JUL03	08APR97	01OCT92

Source: U.S. Department of State, available at https://travel.state.gov/content/visas/en/law-and-policy/bulletin/2016/visa-bulletin-for-november-2015.html.

to as the country quotas. The column that is headed "Chargeability Areas" refers to the country against which the number is charged with respect to the country quota. Currently, China, India, Mexico, and the Philippines are considered to be over represented in the population and therefore nationals from these countries must wait longer to be issued a visa. The bulletin separates applications for these countries since different cutoff dates will apply to them. As a result, citizens from some of these countries can wait over 20 years to be issued a visa.

In September 2015, the USCIS and DOS made significant changes to how they will determine the availability of visas for the future. Now there will be two charts for each visa preference category posted in the visa bulletin prepared by the DOS. The first will indicate the application final action date, which will indicate the date when visas can actually be issued because they are available. A sample of the new final action date chart is in Table 6.2.

The second is the earliest date for filing applications, even though a visa may not be issued for several months. A sample of the new dates for filing appears in Table 6.3. In order to use this second chart, USCIS must determine that there are more immigrant visas available for a fiscal year than there are known applicants for such visas. This will be indicated on the USCIS website.[4]

The benefit of filing an application to adjust status to a permanent resident, months before a visa number is actually available, when possible, is that the beneficiary may apply for advanced parole to travel out of and return to the United States and to apply for permission to work.

---

[4] The website can be accessed here: https://www.uscis.gov/visabulletininfo and will state that the Dates for Filing Visa Applications chart may be used. Otherwise, the page will indicate that only the Application Final Action Dates chart may be used to determine when a foreign national may file an adjustment of status application.

Table 6.3 State Department Visa Bulletin May 2016: Dates for Filing Family-Sponsored Visa Applications

Family-Sponsored	All Chargeability Areas Except Those Listed	China—Mainland Born	India	Mexico	Philippines
F1	01OCT09	01OCT09	01OCT09	01APR95	01SEP05
F2A	15JUN15	15JUN15	15JUN15	15JUN15	15JUN15
F2B	15DEC10	15DEC10	15DEC10	01APR96	01MAY05
F3	01AUG05	01AUG05	01AUG05	01MAY95	01AUG95
F4	01MAY04	01MAY04	01MAY04	01JUN98	01JAN93

Source: U.S. Department of State, available at https://travel.state.gov/content/visas/en/law-and-policy/bulletin/2016/visa-bulletin-for-november-2015.html.

● **EXAMPLE**

Aldo is a lawful permanent resident and has filed a visa petition for the benefit of his wife, Dorkas. They are both from Indonesia but met in the United States. Dorkas is currently here as a student in F-1 status and has permission to work on campus only. Aldo filed a relative petition for the benefit of Dorkas in February 2015. That petition is a family 2A category. A visa number will not become available for some time as the USCIS is currently processing applications filed in November 2014, as indicated in the chart in Table 6.2. However, according to the chart in Table 6.3, Dorkas may be able to file her application to adjust status and become an LPR as early as June of 2015, even though no visa number is ready for her at this time. A review of the USCIS website in May 2016 seeking instruction on whether this chart is actually available shows that Dorkas must wait to use the chart in Figure 6.3 and so cannot file her adjustment application yet. Had she been able to file now, Dorkas could then obtain the benefits of someone who has filed to become an LPR (permission to work and travel with advanced parole) that is currently not available to her in her student status.

A.3. Chargeability Issues

As previously discussed, country quota limits play an important role in determining how long a foreign national must wait for a visa number to be available. Typically, a person is chargeable to the country of his or her birth, regardless of any subsequent changes in citizenship.[5] However, in certain circumstances, a foreign national can benefit from the ability to be charged to the country of citizenship of another family member, whether or not that person is the principal beneficiary. This is known as cross-chargeability and may apply where:

---

[5] 22 C.F.R. § 42.12(a).

- A child is accompanying or following to join a parent[6]
- A spouse is accompanying or following to join a spouse[7]
- An immigrant is born in the United States but charged to the foreign state of which he or she is a citizen or subject, or the place of last residence[8]
- A foreign national born in a foreign state where neither parent was born or resided, may be charged to the country of either parent[9]

● EXAMPLE

Katarina is from the Philippines. Her sister, a U.S. citizen, has filed a fourth preference family-sponsored immigrant visa petition for her benefit that will hopefully allow her, her Russian-born husband, and minor children to come here. In reviewing the visa bulletin, Katarina sees that she is classified as an F-4, Fourth Preference relative and, according to the current visa bulletin, must wait over 20 years until a visa number becomes available. Katarina is concerned that her children will age out[10] and not be able to immigrate with her, as they are likely to be over 21 by then. However, Katarina's husband is a Russian citizen. Katarina can ask that her petition be cross-charged to Russia and not the Philippines. While the wait is still approximately 13 years, it is shorter than the wait for an F-4 relative from the Philippines and there is some possibility that her priority date will become current before her children age out.

B. Family Relationships Under Immigration Law

Both U.S. citizens and LPRs are able to sponsor relatives. However, U.S. citizens can bring the broadest category of relatives because they can sponsor their spouses, minor unmarried children under 21, parents, sons and daughters over 21(whether married or single), and their siblings, to come to immigrate. In contrast, LPRs can only sponsor spouses and unmarried children of any age.

In many instances, the application to become an LPR is a two-step process; the first requires filing of a relative petition to establish the *bona fides* or validity of the claimed relationship and the second is to apply to become a permanent resident. Whether these two steps will be completed one after the other or simultaneously will depend on the immigration status of the petitioner and his or her relationship with the beneficiary. Immigration law differentiates

---

[6] 22 C.F.R. § 42.12(b).
[7] 22 C.F.R. § 42.12(c).
[8] 22 C.F.R. § 42.12(d). The Foreign Affairs Manual, or FAM, clarifies that this provision refers to those born in the U.S. but who are not automatically citizens because they are not subject to U.S. jurisdiction at the time of birth (such as children of diplomats) or because they have since lost their status as U.S. citizens on acquiring citizenship of another country. *See* 9 FAM 503.2-4(B).
[9] 22 C.F.R. § 42.12(e).
[10] Discussed in Section B.2 of Chapter 5, Asylum and Other Humanitarian Related Relief.

between those filing who are U.S. citizens and those who are LPRs. This difference will also determine the length of time it will take for the beneficiary of the petition to move to the next stage.

B.1. Preferential Treatment of Immediate Relatives

When a petitioner files an application on behalf of a beneficiary, how long that person must wait to apply to become an LPR will depend on whether or not s/he is considered an immediate or preference relative. Beneficiaries who are classified as immediate relatives are not counted towards visa quotas and so never have to wait for a visa number to become available for them to use. Therefore, their wait time is dependent only on the time it takes to complete the two-step process necessary to achieve LPR status through family sponsorship.

For immigration purposes, an immediate relative is

- A spouse,
- A parent, or
- An unmarried child under 21 of a United States citizen.

Whereas LPRs may also file for spouses and unmarried children, they cannot file for parents. Another major difference between applications filed by U.S. citizens and LPRs is that immediate relatives who may have violated certain immigration laws can still adjust to LPRs without leaving the United States, in most circumstances.[11] For example, a foreign national who enters the United States on a tourist B-2 visa who remains beyond the permitted period of stay and later marries a United States citizen can adjust status to that of an LPR in the United States. Those who have not maintained legal status and are married to LPRs, however, cannot adjust status here and must do so at a consular office abroad. Finally, only U.S. citizens may simultaneously file the relative petition and the application to become an LPR. This is because generally there is no visa number immediately available for those in the second preference category, requiring them to wait until their priority dates become current. We now explore the first step needed by a foreign national to become an LPR in the family sponsored context, the relative petition.

C. The Relative Petition

Filing Form I-130, Petition for an Alien Relative, initiates the family sponsorship process. The purpose of this petition is to determine the *bona fides* of the relationship for the conferring of immigration benefits. Evidentiary requirements will differ depending on the nature of the relationship. Because the spousal relationship generates the most scrutiny in order to combat fraud, our discussion

---

[11] But see the discussion on INA § 245(i) in Section G.3.b for situations when this may not be possible.

focuses on this relationship in particular, while referencing others where specific issues may arise.

C.1. Petitions for Spouses

In order for the relationship of spouse to exist for immigration purposes, the marriage must be valid according to the laws where it was celebrated. As a result, marriages that are legal in foreign countries but may not be in the United States are generally recognized for immigration purposes. This includes polygamous marriages, so long as the petitioner is seeking to bring only the first wife, since this will be the only marriage that would be considered valid; customary marriages that follow all of the necessary formalities; and common law marriages where recognized in certain states. The one exception to this rule is in relation to *proxy marriages,* which will only be recognized once the marriage is consummated.[12]

A U.S. citizen or LPR petitioner filing for the benefit of a spouse has the highest burden of all petitioners. Whereas married parents petitioning for a child[13] and U.S. citizens petitioning for a sibling need only demonstrate their relationship through the production of a contemporaneously issued birth certificate indicating their connection, spouses must not only prove that the marriage is valid, but also that the marriage was not entered into purely to confer an immigration benefit. While this may be one of the reasons for a couple to marry, the primary reason must be the intent to establish a life together.[14] Therefore, the USCIS is required to ascertain whether or not a ***bona fide* relationship** exists between the couple.

Proxy Marriage: A marriage conducted when one of the contracting parties is not physically present.

***Bona Fide* Relationship**: A familial relationship between spouses that is authentic and not simply entered into in order to obtain immigration benefits.

Case for Discussion 6.2

Edward, a U.S. citizen, and his girlfriend, Ana, from El Salvador, have been dating for nine months. They love each other and have decided they will marry one day. Ana obtains a visa to visit the United States so that she can meet Edward's family and friends. She realizes that life here is easier than she is used to in her country and decides she does not wish to return, mainly because she has a tendency to be jealous and has become suspicious about some of Edward's female friends that he has known since childhood. She persuades Edward that they should marry while she is visiting so that she will not have to return home. She wants to be certain that Edward's eye will not stray.

- Will the couple violate immigration rules if they marry and apply for Ana to remain in the United States?
- Explain your answer.

---

[12] INA § 101(a)(35).
[13] The situation is different where the parents are unmarried, with a greater burden also being placed on fathers to demonstrate a father child relationship exists with their relative. This is discussed in Section C.2.
[14] *Matter of Laureano,* 19 I&N Dec. 1 (BIA 1983).

To determine whether a bona fide relationship exists, the USCIS will review a number of factors during the couple's adjustment interview. For instance, it may examine their conduct prior to and after their marriage. How have they held themselves out to the community? What facts do they know about each other's daily or working lives and family members? Has the couple made an effort to comingle its finances? Has either of the couple added the other to his or her health, car, or medical insurance plans? How has the couple filed tax returns, as married or single? These and many others are the types of questions that may be asked in an interview and the couple will be expected to explain any apparent anomalies.

At times, the USCIS may become suspicious about whether in fact the petitioner and beneficiary are in a genuine marriage. In such cases, it may conduct a *Stokes*[15] interview to assist in its determination. For this, the couple is separated and placed into different rooms, with one being interviewed and all responses recorded, before the other spouse will be invited in and asked the same questions. For example, the interviewing officer might ask each spouse how they met and inquire about one spouse's knowledge of the other's family. The expectation is that fairly similar responses will be given. Sometimes responses are not similar, but that does not mean the couple is involved in any deception. The individuals could simply perceive the same facts differently or one could be more attentive to his or her surroundings than the other. However, any significant inconsistencies that cannot reasonably be explained could lead to a denial of the petition. Notwithstanding this deeper query into the couple's life, the investigation must still be a reasonable one.[16]

Marriage petitions can give rise to some special situations. For instance, what if the parties are no longer living together at the time of the interview or adjudication of the petition? This alone should not be the reason for denial.[17] Since the USCIS is required to determine the intent of the couple at the time they entered into the marriage, lack of intent cannot be established simply because the couple no longer lives together.[18] If the couple is neither legally separated nor divorced, the marriage is still viable for immigration purposes, so long as the intent at the time of the marriage was genuine.[19] Sleeping in separate bedrooms, in and of itself, will not invalidate a marriage,[20] and neither will lack of consummation unless it is a proxy marriage.

With the growth of the use of social media, the Fraud Detection and National Security, or FDNS, unit advises immigration officers to check if either the petitioner or beneficiary has a Facebook or other media presence on the internet that might provide inconsistent information from that submitted in

---

[15] *See Stokes v. INS*, 393 F. Supp. 24 (S.D.N.Y. 1975).
[16] Id. at 30.
[17] *Matter of Mckee*, 17 I&N Dec. 332 (BIA 1980).
[18] *Bark v. INS*, 511 F.2d 1200 (9th Cir. 1975).
[19] *Matter of Boromand*, 17 I&N Dec. 450 (BIA 1980).
[20] *See Matter of Peterson*, 12 I&N Dec. 663 (BIA 1968), where, an elderly couple married because the husband was in need of a housekeeper and the wife was willing to take care of him. The Board of Immigration Appeals, or BIA, determined that the "reasons for the marriage appear to be far sounder than exist for most marriages." *Id.* at 665.

support of a marriage application. FDNS provides a number of other possible social networking sites for the purpose of information gathering.[21] The USCIS has also produced a fraud referral sheet, providing indicators of fraudulent behavior in the context of a number of different immigration applications.[22]

● **EXAMPLE**

Monika is from Poland and came to the United States on a B-2 visa. She has remained in the U.S. beyond her authorized stay. Her husband is a U.S. citizen. They appear together for an interview so that the USCIS can approve her application to adjust status to an LPR. In the waiting room, the couple's body language suggests that there may be some tension between them. During the interview, Monika's husband appears very nervous, with beads of sweat on his face. When the officer asks if he is feeling ok, he simply nods his head, with his eyes to the ground. Monika eagerly answers the officer's questions, even those directed at her husband. The few questions he does answer lead the officer to wonder what basic facts he knows about his wife since they often contradict what she has said or are evasive. In this situation, it would not be a surprise if the officer decided to call the couple back for re-interview, during which time the officer could do further research based on the FDNS fraud guidance to see if there is information available that may help him or her make a decision on their application.

In some cases, a couple may seek immigration advice before getting married. This may be a good time to explain the law and what will be required in order to demonstrate that the marriage is genuine. One of the factors that the USCIS considers is the timing of the marriage, particularly in relation to the date the foreign national enters the country. When applying for a temporary visa, such as a B-2 visitor's visa, the foreign national must demonstrate s/he intends to return to the home country at the end of the visit. This is also known as demonstrating non immigrant or temporary intent. As previously discussed in Section D of Chapter 2, Nonimmigrant Visas for Brief Stays, Studies, and Cultural Exchange, any attempt to change immigration status within 30 or 60 days of entering the United States raises questions about whether the foreign national misrepresented the real reason why s/he applied for a particular visa classification at the consular office abroad, or requested permission to enter in a particular category at a port of entry.[23]

This is particularly true for marriages that take place shortly after entry, since it is reasonable to assume that few people will have formulated a genuine intent to marry in such a short period of time. Therefore, a couple that chooses to marry before the 60-day period has expired could find itself dealing with an allegation of misrepresentation in the act of one of the parties obtaining a visitor's visa, because a material fact (the intent to marry and remain in the United

---

[21] *See* https://www.eff.org/files/filenode/social_network/dhs_customsimmigration_socialnetworking.pdf.
[22] The fraud referral sheet can be found at http://www.latinamericanstudies.org/immigration/USCIS_Fraud_Referral_Sheet.pdf.
[23] 9 FAM 302.9-4(B)(3)(g).

States indefinitely) was withheld from the consular officer during the visa application process. If the couple is unable to rebut the presumption, then the only way the beneficiary will be granted permission to remain as an LPR is if a hardship waiver—known as an INA § 212(i) waiver—is filed and approved to waive the fraud in obtaining the visa. This is discussed in Section B.6.c of Chapter 9, Grounds of Inadmissibility and Deportation. Approval of the waiver application may be difficult, since it requires establishing that the U.S. citizen spouse will experience extreme hardship[24] if the beneficiary is denied permission to remain in the United States as an LPR. This may not be easy to demonstrate where the marriage is relatively recent and the necessary equities to support a waiver application have not yet been established.

A marriage that takes place when one party is already in removal proceedings gives rise to a presumption that it was entered into for immigration purposes. Section 5 of the Immigration Marriage Fraud Amendments Act of 1986[25] added INA § 204(g), which requires a foreign national who marries while in removal proceedings to leave the United States for a period of two years after the marriage before an immediate relative or preference category visa can be made available to him or her. However, a waiver of this requirement is available under INA § 245(e)(3). Applying for the waiver does not require a particular form, but must still be formally referenced at the time the family-sponsored immigrant visa petition is filed. Such waivers will be approved if the petitioner can prove by the higher standard of clear and convincing evidence that the marriage was entered into in good faith and not for immigration purposes.[26]

Another difference with petitions filed for the benefit of a spouse is that both the petitioner and the beneficiary are required to provide a passport style photograph and also complete Form G-325A, Biographic Information, which provides biographical information about each of them that will include any prior marriages, residences, and employment in the last five years. It will also include the last place of employment or residence abroad prior to entry to the United States. The photos allow the interviewing officer to identify accurately the parties to the marriage. The photos and this form are not required for relative petitions filed for any other categories.

A previous marriage of either the petitioner or the beneficiary must be properly terminated if s/he is to be free to enter into a valid marriage. This can be by either death, divorce, or annulment, so long as it meets all the criteria of the country where the termination took place. Evidence of the death, divorce, or annulment must be submitted with the relative petition application and, where either party was married more than once, documents to show the termination of each prior marriage will be required.

---

[24] A further discussion of extreme hardship is in Section B.2.b of Chapter 9, Grounds of Inadmissibility and Deportation.
[25] Immigration Marriage Fraud Amendments Act of 1986, Pub. L. 99-639, 100 Stat. 3541 (1986).
[26] INA § 245(e)(3).

C.2. Petitions for Children and Siblings

For immigration purposes, a child is defined in INA § 101(b) as an unmarried person under 21 who is either:

- A child born in wedlock
- A stepchild who was under the age of 18 at the time of the marriage creating the relationship of stepchild
- A legitimated child, so long as legitimation took place prior to the child reaching 18 years of age and the child was in the legal custody of the parent(s) at the time such legitimation took place
- A child born out of wedlock and the person filing a benefit on his or her behalf is either the natural mother or father, where the father is able to demonstrate a *bona fide* parent-child relationship to the child before the child reached the age of 21
- An adopted child, where the relationship of adoption was entered into before the child's 16 birthday and s/he was in the legal custody of and residing with the adoptive parent for at least two years; any siblings of such child can be adopted up to the age of 18 years; adopted children who have been battered or subjected to extreme cruelty by the adopting parent or his or her family member residing in the same household, do not have the two year residence requirement
- An orphan child who has either been adopted or is coming to the United States to be adopted by a citizen, along with certain other factors

No child may file a petition for a parent before reaching 21 years of age,[27] but can petition for a spouse or child from the age of 18. Petitions filed for the benefit of children are fairly straightforward, if the parents were married before the child's birth. Where a child was born out of wedlock but was legitimated by the father prior to reaching the age of 18 following the legitimation rules of the child's country of citizenship, proof of legitimation must be submitted. The situation is different, however, where legitimation never took place.

Petitions filed by or for the benefit of fathers who were never married to the mother of the child, involve additional evidentiary burdens to prove a *bona fide* father/child relationship existed between the two prior to the child reaching the age of 21. This may include proof of any financial support provided to the child, proof of parental interest in the child's development through acknowledgment in school or other records, or evidence that the father and child lived together at some stage.

---

[27] INA § 201(b)(2)(A)(i).

> **Case for Discussion 6.3**
>
> Alexis is from Costa Rica. When he was just 17, he became a father. He never married Esther, the mother of his son Jaime, and they never lived together. His name is not on his son's birth certificate. At 20, Alexis acknowledged to his family that he is the father of Jaime. Alexis' parents were elated because this is their first grandchild. They established a relationship with Esther and began to take Jaime into their home for weeks at a time to take care of him so that Esther could work to support herself and her son. Alexis maintained little contact with his son and traveled to the United States three years later, where he met his wife, a U.S. citizen. After Alexis became an LPR, he began to think about his son in Costa Rica, who is now living exclusively with his parents because Esther abandoned him to them when she found a new partner. Alexis has occasionally sent money to his parents to help them take care of Jaime. Alexis and his wife learn that they cannot have children and decide they would one day like to apply for Jaime to come to the United States to live with them.
>
> - Based on the nature of the relationship between Alexis and Jaime currently, is it likely that a family-sponsored immigrant visa petition would be approved?
> - If not, what could Alexis do now to improve the chances of an approval?

A stepparent may file a petition for a child so long as the relationship between them began prior to the child reaching the age of 18. An application may still be filed if there is a subsequent divorce from the biological parent, so long as the stepparent and child continue to maintain a relationship. As for an adopted child, once an immigration benefit is obtained as a result of the relationship created by the adoption, a relative petition can never be filed by the adopted child for the benefit of his or her biological parent.[28]

U.S. citizens can file petitions for their children at any age, even if the children are married. The age or marital status of that child will determine if s/he is an immediate relative or belongs to the family first or third preference category. The preference category s/he is in will determine the length of time it will take before a visa number becomes available. If a child was unmarried at the time the initial petition was filed and then later marries, the USCIS should be notified by sending a copy of the marriage certificate. Once received, the petition will be downgraded from a family first to a family third preference category. Likewise, if the beneficiary was married at the time of filing the application and subsequently

---

[28] INA § 101(b).

divorces, s/he can then send a copy of the divorce decree to the USCIS at which time the application will be upgraded from a family third to a family first petition.

U.S. citizen siblings are able to file for each other, so long as they have at least one parent in common, whether or not they were born in wedlock. The birth certificate is the best evidence of the relationship to their parents.

C.3. Adam Walsh Child Protection and Safety Act

In 2006, President Bush signed into law the Adam Walsh Child Protection and Safety Act of 2006, or AWA,[29] which triggered sweeping reforms to sex offender laws throughout the United States. It amended the immigration laws in an effort to protect children from sexual exploitation and violent crime among other things, by preventing sex offenders from petitioning for beneficiaries who might face harm due to the petitioner's criminal record. A U.S. citizen or LPR convicted of "specified offenses against a minor" is prohibited from filing an immigrant visa petition for a beneficiary in any of the preference categories or their qualifying derivative family members, unless the USCIS determines that s/he poses "no risk" to the beneficiary.[30] The USCIS, in its own internal training memorandum, has indicated that it will not approve a petition under the AWA unless the petitioner proves that s/he poses "no risk" at the "beyond a reasonable doubt" standard.[31] By statute, the specified offenses are:

- An offense (unless committed by a parent or guardian) involving kidnapping,
- An offense (unless committed by a parent or guardian) involving false imprisonment,
- Solicitation to engage in sexual conduct,
- Use in a sexual performance,
- Solicitation to practice prostitution,
- Video voyeurism,
- Possession, production, or distribution of child pornography,
- Criminal sexual conduct involving a minor, or the use of the Internet to facilitate or attempt such conduct, or
- Any conduct that by its nature is a sex offense against a minor.[32]

Although it continues to be the subject of federal litigation throughout the country, the statute declares that the "no risk" determination is not subject to judicial review. The Board of Immigration Appeals, or BIA, has held that it will not review the USCIS' risk assessments under the AWA.[33]

---

[29] Pub. L. 109-248, 120 Stat. 587 (2006).
[30] INA § 204(a)(1)(A)(viii)(I). This provision also applies to petitions filed for fiancé(e)s, discussed in Section J.
[31] See Aytes memo dated February 8, 2007, Guidance for Adjudication of Family-Based Petitions and I-129F Petition for Alien Fiancé(e) under the Adam Walsh Child Protection and Safety Act of 2006.
[32] See 42 U.S. C. § 16911(7).
[33] Matter of Aceijas-Quiroz, 26 I&N Dec. 294 (BIA 2014).

C.4. Documenting the Relationship

In all relative petitions, primary evidence of relationship (marriage or contemporaneously issued birth certificates) is always preferred. However, in some countries, such documents may not be available for a number of reasons. The DOS maintains a catalogue of which documents are available in various countries. This is listed in the Reciprocity Schedule contained in Volume 9, part IV, Appendix C of the FAM, which also provides guidance on how to obtain available documents and from which local government departments.[34]

When the FAM indicates that primary evidence or documents are not available, an applicant can provide secondary evidence of relationship, which can include baptismal records, where applicable, school or medical records, or affidavits from contemporaneous witnesses of the event to be established, such as guests at a wedding or witnesses at the birth of a child.

In order to combat fraud, the USCIS is moving towards requiring DNA testing to prove the relationship of parent and child for nationals from certain countries, even when primary evidence may be available, but was not contemporaneously issued. For example, birth certificates from Liberia have been reissued in recent years because many government records were destroyed during the decade's long civil war that ravaged the country. Because the recent issuance of birth certificates was not contemporaneous to the actual date of the individual's birth, families are asked to submit DNA test results as the clearest way to prove parentage.

The DNA tests are conducted under exacting standards, following a request from either the USCIS or the DOS. Tests are initiated in the United States with the petitioner. Then the foreign national abroad who needs to be tested is instructed to appear at the consular office with appropriate identification documents so specimens gathered through cheek or mouth swabs or drawn blood can be sent to specific testing companies in the United States, which are required to maintain strict control of all samples. Results are then sent directly to the requesting government agency for review as part of the final decision on whether an appropriate relationship exists to support the issuance of an immigrant visa. A request for DNA testing may occur at the time the relative petition is adjudicated or during the immigrant visa interview at the consular office, a process discussed in Section H.

Any family-sponsored immigrant visa petition that is denied by the USCIS can be appealed directly to the Board of Immigration Appeals, or BIA, which will make a final determination. If the denial is upheld, the petitioner can file a petition for review with the United States Court of Appeals for the circuit with jurisdiction over the case, if appropriate arguments exist. Denial of the petition does not preclude the foreign national from qualifying to remain in the United States in another family-sponsored immigrant basis unless the reason for the denial was that the marriage on which the application for a visa was based is

---

[34] The Reciprocity Schedule can be accessed electronically at http://travel.state.gov/content/visas/english/fees/reciprocity-by-country.html.

a sham. In these cases, no waiver of the fraud is available and the foreign national is precluded from ever immigrating through any other petition.[35]

> ● **EXAMPLE**
>
> Fatoumata was denied a visa back in 1998 because the USCIS alleged the marriage that her application for an immigrant visa was based on was fraudulent. Her son, a U.S. citizen, recently turned 21 years old and wants to file a relative petition for her benefit. Fatoumata cannot benefit from a family-sponsored relative petition filed by her son because the finding of a fraudulent marriage in 1998 bars her from benefiting from any family based petitions, despite the fact that her biological U.S. citizen son is otherwise eligible to petition for her. If Fatoumata was denied a visa because she divorced the original petitioner and no fraud was found, her U.S. citizen son could file a petition for her benefit.

Although relative petitions are filed for the benefit of an individual, in some cases qualifying family members of that person may also be included as **derivative relatives**. Qualifying derivative relatives are treated as either accompanying or following to join the principal or main beneficiary, so long as the qualifying relationship existed before the principal beneficiary entered the United States. A derivative beneficiary who enters at the same time or within six months of the principal's entry or adjustment of status is referred to as an **accompanying relative**.[36] Those traveling more than six months after are **following to join**.[37] A new relative petition must be filed for any qualifying relative acquired after the principal beneficiary entered the United States.

Derivative Relatives: The spouse or unmarried children under 21 years old of preference relatives.

> ● **EXAMPLE**
>
> Hans, a German national and LPR, recently visited Germany and met Hilda who has a three-year old daughter, Angela, from a previous relationship. Hans and Hilda marry in Germany. Hans wants to petition for Hilda and her child Angela to come to the United States. Hilda, as the spouse of an LPR, is in the 2A family preference category. Hans files the petition and after three years, a visa becomes available. Hilda can emigrate as an LPR, and her daughter, Angela, now six years old, will be a derivative beneficiary and can accompany Hilda and both will receive LPR status upon entry.

Unfortunately, children of immediate relative parents or spouses of U.S. citizens do not derive status through their foreign national principal parent and so cannot accompany or follow to join in the same way that other relatives might. The only redress for this anomaly is to file a separate relative petition for the child, who will then have to qualify for entry in his or her own right. There are some exceptions to this, discussed in the following sections.

---

[35] INA § 204(c).
[36] 22 C.F.R. § 40.1(a)(1).
[37] *Id.*

EXAMPLE

If Hans from the previous example naturalized, Hilda would now be the spouse of a United States citizen and therefore an immediate relative. In this case, while Hilda would not have to wait for a visa so that she could come to the United States, her daughter, Angela, could not emigrate as a qualifying derivative family member as there are no provisions for immediate relatives to bring family members. Hans would have to file a separate petition for Angela so that she could come as his stepchild.

Case for Discussion 6.4

Violet, a Jamaican citizen, is the mother of two children, ages 8 and 12. She and her childhood sweetheart, Cedric, marry during one of his visits to Jamaica to visit his family. The couple has agreed that they will live in the United Sates where Cedric lives and works. Currently, he is an LPR but qualifies to apply to become a U.S. citizen. He comes to you for help on which would be the best way to file an application for Violet and her children.

- What factors would he need to bear in mind before deciding whether to apply for Violet as a U.S. citizen or an LPR?

C.5. Benefits of the Child Status Protection Act

Because the waiting time for visas to become available can be very long, sometimes a child for whom an application was filed may turn 21 or age out before s/he can process for a visa or apply to adjust his or her immigration status. This can have a devastating effect as it prolongs the separation of families. For instance, if a U.S. citizen files an application for a minor child when that child is 20 years and 8 months, but it is taking the USCIS 9 months to process and approve the underlying relative petition, that child will be 21 years and 5 months old, and therefore will no longer be considered a minor child and be ineligible to process as an immediate relative.

C.5.a. CSPA Benefits for Children of U.S. Citizens

Previously, that child would then be moved to the family first category and have to wait several years before being eligible to obtain a visa for immigration purposes. However, since August 6, 2002, the Child Status Protection Act, or CSPA, has operated to protect such children from losing their status as minors. They are no longer penalized for the time it takes the USCIS to adjudicate petitions filed for their benefit. In effect, the CSPA freezes the age of an eligible child on the date the petition is filed so that the child will, for immigration purposes, continue to be considered a child under the age of 21 even though in reality the child may be older. This protection exists for children of U.S. citizens and for those children who would derive immigration status from a parent who has filed an application for asylum or for protection under the Violence Against Women Act.[38]

● **EXAMPLE**

Svetlana has become a citizen of the United States. She wants to file for her son Uri, who lives with her mother, in Russia. Uri will be 21 years old in 6 months. It is currently taking the USCIS at least 10 months to process relative petitions. Once Svetlana files the relative petition for Uri, his age will "freeze" so that he will be considered 20 years and 6 months old, even if he is really 21 and 4 months old when the petition is approved. Since Uri's age is frozen at 20 years and 6 months, he can still be considered a minor child of a United States citizen and enter in that classification.

C.5.b. CSPA Benefits for Children of Lawful Permanent Residents

The situation for children of LPRs is not as comprehensive and involves a rather complicated calculation. The CSPA provides more limited protection based on the length of time a relative petition has been pending for consideration. That time may be subtracted from the beneficiary's biological age at the time a visa number becomes current or available. For example, Denise, the minor child of an LPR, is 19 years and 8 months at the time the relative petition for her benefit is filed and therefore is in the Family 2A preference category. It takes the USCIS 10 months to approve her petition. However, the priority date that determines when Denise can process for her immigrant visa is backdated two years, so that when a visa number is available, Denise is now 21 years and 8 months old and therefore should be relegated to the Family 2B category with its attendant longer wait times.

Utilizing the CSPA, Denise will be able to subtract the 10 months it took the service to approve her relative petition from her current age so that Denise is now effectively 20 years and 10 months old and therefore under 21 for immigration purposes. As a result of the CSPA, she is still eligible to adjust status as a Family 2A beneficiary. Without the CSPA, Denise would have been re-classified into the Family 2B category as an unmarried son or daughter of an LPR, with its longer waiting times. Had Denise been 21 years and 11 months when her priority date became current, the CSPA would not have given her sufficient time credit to reduce her age so that she could claim to be under 21. In such cases, the child would be allowed to retain the original priority date from when the petition was

---

[38] VAWA relief is discussed in Chapter 8, Immigration Relief for Vulnerable Populations.

first filed but would automatically be converted to the appropriate applicable family preference category, in this case Family 2B[39]

Even when a child is found to have preserved his or her age for immigration purposes, in order to benefit from the provisions of the CSPA, s/he must have "sought to acquire" LPR status within one year of the visa number becoming available.[40] This is so whether the application for permanent residency is filed with the DOS at one of the consular offices abroad, or through an application to adjust status filed with the USCIS in the U.S. To satisfy the "sought to acquire" requirement, a beneficiary must take active steps towards becoming an LPR by filing or attempting to file a substantially complete application or by showing that there were other extraordinary circumstances in the case, particularly those where the failure to timely file was due to circumstances beyond the foreign national's control.[41]

D. Termination and Revocation of Immigrant Visas: INA § 205; 8 C.F.R. § 205

An approved visa petition can be revoked or terminated in two ways: automatically or upon notice by the USCIS, which is authorized to revoke an immediate or family-sponsored petition for any reason other than those already covered by automatic revocation in the INA. The petitioner must receive a **Notice of Intent to Revoke** with an explanation of the issues and be given enough time to respond. An ultimate decision to revoke must also have a detailed explanation. The petitioner may then appeal that decision to the USCIS Administrative Appeals Office.[42]

Title 8 of the Code of Federal Regulations at § 205.1(a)(1)—(3)(i) governs the automatic revocation of petitions in immediate relative and family-sponsored immigrant visa applications. The reasons for revocation include:

- Failure to apply for a visa within one year of the Department of State notifying an applicant that a visa is available;
- Filing fee and any associated service charge is not paid within 14 days of any returned check or financial instrument;
- Petitioner withdraws his or her petition in writing, addressed to a USCIS officer authorized to grant or deny the petition;
- Beneficiary or self-petitioner dies, thereby terminating any benefits for derivatives;

---

[39] INA § 203(h)(3).
[40] INA § 203(h)(1)(A).
[41] *See Matter of O. Vazquez*, 25 I&N Dec. 817 (BIA 2012).
[42] 8 C.F.R. § 205.2(d).

D: Termination and Revocation of Immigrant Visas: INA § 205; 8 C.F.R. § 205

- Petitioner dies, unless the relative is approved to immigrate as a widow(er),[43] or USCIS decides, for humanitarian reasons, not to revoke the petition; for this to happen, the beneficiary must make a specific request for the reinstatement of the petition and establish that a substitute person is available to complete the required affidavit of support;
- Legal termination of a qualifying marriage through divorce or annulment;
- Unmarried child of an LPR in preference category Family 2A who reaches 21 years of age before a visa number is available; in such cases, the child moves down to preference category Family 2B, unmarried son or daughter of an LPR;
- Marriage of a minor child of a U.S. citizen; however, such petition can instead convert to a Family third preference category, married children of a U.S. citizen;
- Marriage of an unmarried son or daughter of a U.S. citizen after filing a petition; however, such petition can instead convert to a Family third preference category, married children of a U.S. citizen;
- Marriage of an unmarried son or daughter of an LPR after filing a petition; as there is no preference category available for this class, the petition will be revoked retroactive to the date of approval; or
- Legal termination of the petitioner's LPR status, unless this is because s/he became a citizen.

When a petitioner notifies the USCIS that s/he wishes to withdraw his or her petition, the USCIS may not continue to adjudicate it, but must treat it as withdrawn. *See Matter of Cintron*, 16 I&N Dec. 9 (BIA 1976), where a District Director proceeded to deny an immigrant relative petition even though the petitioner had written to notify that he wished to withdraw it and that letter had been acknowledged as received. The BIA found that the denial of the petition was improper because the petitioner had already withdrawn it.

Death of a petitioner is a significant event affecting the viability of the immigrant visa application, leading to automatic revocation. Where the petitioner dies *after* approval of the petition, it may be possible for the beneficiary to revive the petition and still adjust status.[44] A specific request must be made to the USCIS to reinstate the petition. In doing so, the beneficiary should provide information on any equities for the USCIS to consider when deciding whether to reinstate. Factors can include length of stay in the United States, conditions in the home country if the foreign national were to be returned, health issues, and community and family ties.[45]

As part of the adjustment application (the second stage of the immigrant application process), an **affidavit of support**[46] is required to be submitted by the petitioner to demonstrate that the intending immigrant will not become a public

---

[43] Discussed in Section E.1.
[44] INA § 204(l).
[45] USCIS Policy Memorandum, *Approval of Petitions and Applications after the Death of the Qualifying Relative under New Section 204(l) of the Immigration and Nationality Act*, dated December 16, 2010.
[46] This is an important part of the adjustment application or immigrant visa package. A detailed discussion is in Section G.2.f.

charge because there is sufficient income to support him or her. When a petitioner dies, the required submission of the affidavit of support cannot be fulfilled unless another person is substituted for this purpose, which the statute allows. The list of family members who are eligible for substitution for the petitioner is broad and can include spouse, parent, mother-, father-, son-, daughter-, brother-, or sister-in-law of the beneficiary, as well as siblings, minor or over-aged children, grandparents, grandchildren, or a legal guardian.[47] Any person acting as a substitute must be a U.S. citizen or LPR and be at least 18 years old.

Case for Discussion 6.5

Marie-Pierre is a Haitian citizen. His mother, Josephine, filed a Family First preference category relative petition for him in 2008 when she became a U.S. citizen. It was approved in 2010. Josephine is very sick and is not expected to live much longer. She is very worried that the relative petition she filed for her son will no longer be valid after her death and he will have no other way of leaving Haiti in the near future.

- What options are available that may still allow her son to immigrate to the United States?

E. Immigration Benefits Available When a Petitioner Dies: 8 C.F.R. § 204.2

In some cases, a petitioner may die *before* a relative petition can be filed, ostensibly leaving the foreign national who wants to remain in the United States without an avenue to do so. Changes in the law now make it possible for him or her to self-petition for immigration benefits in two situations, which are discussed in the following sections.

E.1. Immigration Benefits Available to Widow(er)s When Spouse Dies Before Petition Filed

Previously, there was provision in the law for widow(er)s to be granted an immigrant visa, but only if they had been married to a U.S. citizen for at least two years prior to his or her death. Much litigation surrounded this provision as

---

[47] INA § 213(f)(5)(B).

it was considered unfair that the length of the marriage should be the determining factor for whether a widow(er) could retain the status of an immediate relative and gain immigration benefits. The issue has now been resolved.

On October 28, 2009, President Obama signed the FY2010 DHS Appropriations Act[48] into law, which removed what had become known as the "widow's penalty" provision. Section 568(c) of the Act amended INA § 201(b)(2)(A)(i) so that it now reads,

> In the case of an alien who was the spouse of a citizen of the United States and was not legally separated from the citizen at the time of the citizen's death, the alien (and each child of the alien) shall be considered, for purposes of this subsection, to remain an immediate relative after the date of the citizen's death but only if the spouse files a petition . . . within 2 years after such date and only until the date the spouse remarries.[49]

Now, where the death of the U.S. citizen spouse takes place before the filing of a relative petition, the surviving spouse may file a petition on his or her own. The classification of immediate relative will be retained if the widow(er) can establish that:

- S/he was the citizen's legal spouse at the time of the U.S. citizen's death, regardless of the length of the marriage,
- The marriage was *bona fide* and not an arrangement solely to confer immigration benefits on the beneficiary,
- S/he has not remarried nor was legally separated from the deceased U.S. citizen spouse,
- S/he is admissible as an immigrant, and
- S/he meets all other adjustment eligibility requirements and merits a favorable exercise of discretion.

An application for these benefits must be filed within two years of the spouse's death.

Qualifying widow(er)s may file a self-petition using Form I-360, Petition for Amerasian, Widow(er), or Special Immigrant. Any children of the widow(er), whether or not they were children of the deceased spouse, will also be considered immediate relatives and therefore able to derive an immigrant visa.[50] This extension of benefits is not available to children of immediate relatives of *living* U.S. citizens, as previously discussed in section C.3.

---

[48] Pub. L. 111-83, 123 Stat. 2142, 2187-88 (2009).
[49] A similar provision applies for lawful permanent residents. *Id.* at, § 568(d).
[50] 8 C.F.R. § 204.2(b)(4).

> **Case for Discussion 6.6**
>
> Anand is a Pakistani citizen who arrived on a B-2 visa and has overstayed his permission to remain in the United States. He married Begum two years after his arrival in the country. This is his first marriage and her second. She has two young children from her prior marriage. She is a U.S. citizen. Before the couple could file a relative petition for the benefit of Anand, Begum died suddenly.
>
> - Can Anand still adjust to become a permanent resident despite the fact that he is now a widower?
> - If so, in what category and what does he have to show in order to have his application approved?

E.2. Immigration Benefits Available When Petitioner Dies After Petition Filed

The prior section addressed options available to a beneficiary spouse when a petitioner dies *before* the petition is filed. In this section, we discuss what happens if the petitioner dies *after* filing the relative petition but *before* it is adjudicated.[51] INA § 204(l)(1) allows the visa petition and any adjustment or related application to be approved if the applicant seeking the benefit:

- Resided in the United States when the qualifying relative died;
- Continues to reside in the United States on the date of the decision on the pending petition or application; and
- Is at least one of the following:
    - ☐ The beneficiary of a pending or approved immediate relative visa petition;
    - ☐ The beneficiary of a pending or approved family-based visa petition, including both the principal beneficiary and any derivative beneficiaries;
    - ☐ Any derivative beneficiary of a pending or approved employment-based visa petition;[52]
    - ☐ The beneficiary of a pending or approved Form I-730, Refugee/Asylee relative petition;[53]

---

[51] Information on this can be obtained from Policy Memo PM-602-126, Approval of a Spousal Immediate Relative Visa Petition under Section 204(l) of the Immigration and Nationality Act after the Death of a U.S. Citizen Petitioner, dated November 15, 2015, accessible at http://www.uscis.gov/sites/default/files/USCIS/Laws/Memoranda/2015/2015-1118_Approval_of_a_Spousal_Immediate_Relative_Visa_Petition.pdf.
[52] Discussed in Chapter 7, Employment Based and Self-Sponsored Immigration.
[53] Discussed in Chapter 5, Asylum and Other Related Humanitarian Relief.

- ☐ A [foreign national] admitted as a derivative "T" or "U" nonimmigrant;[54] or
- ☐ A derivative asylee under section 208(b)(3)[55] of the [Immigration and Nationality] Act.

While the section does not expressly define the "qualifying relative," the USCIS infers it to refer to an individual who, immediately before death, was:

- The petitioner in a family-based immigrant visa petition under sections 201(b)(2)(A)(i) or 203(a) of the INA;
- The principal beneficiary in an employment-based visa petition case under section 203(b) of the INA;
- The petitioner in a refugee/asylee relative petition under sections 207 or 208 of the INA;
- The principal [foreign national] admitted as a T or U nonimmigrant; or
- The principal asylee granted asylum under section 208 of the INA.[56]

F. Compiling the Application Package for a Relative Petition

A complete application package for a relative petition should include the following documents:

- Form I-130, Petition for Alien Relative
- Form G-28, Notice of Entry of Appearance of Attorney or Accredited Representative, if the applicant has legal representation
- Form G-325A, Biographic Information, to be completed by both the petitioner and the beneficiary when filing for a spouse only; it gathers biographical information about both of them
- Evidence of petitioner's status as a U.S. citizen or LPR, such as a birth certificate, U.S. passport, Certificate of Naturalization, or green card
- Evidence of relationship to petitioner such as marriage or birth certificate or, in some cases, results of DNA tests
- For petitions based on marriage, evidence of the *bona fides* of the relationship, such as joint bank accounts, leases, utility or medical bills, and other documents tending to show a comingling of assets
- Evidence of the termination of any prior marriages of the petitioner or beneficiary

---

[54] Discussed in Chapter 8, Immigration Relief for Vulnerable Populations.
[55] Discussed in Chapter 5, Asylum and Other Related Humanitarian Relief.
[56] INA § 204(l)(2).

- For petitions where a child was born out of wedlock, evidence of a relationship between the father and child, such as payment of child support or other remittances for the child's upkeep and school or medical records that might support a father/child relationship
- For petitions based on marriage, one passport photograph of the petitioner and the beneficiary
- USCIS fees

All documents issued in a language other than English must be accompanied by a notarized translation.

After the petition package is compiled, it should be sent to the USCIS lockbox with jurisdiction over the location of the petitioner's address. Once received, a receipt notice will be sent, confirming that the appropriate fee for the petition has been paid. There is no fee waiver available for relative petitions in any category. Those filed based on marriage where the beneficiary is in the United States will be sent to the local USCIS Field Office and an interview date arranged for the couple. All other relative petitions will be adjudicated by the assigned USCIS Service Center based on the documents filed.

If the petition is approved, the petitioner and beneficiary will receive Form I-797, Notice of Action Approval Notice, which is the form on which the USCIS notifies applicants of approval of any applications filed. A copy of this form is available at Figure 1.14 in Chapter 1, Historical Background and Introduction to the U.S. Immigration System. This form must be included as part of the package for the second stage of the process, which will either be applying for adjustment of status here or consular processing abroad, depending on the location and immigration status of the beneficiary.

G. Part II: Becoming a Lawful Permanent Resident Through Adjustment of Status in the United States or Consular Processing Abroad: INA § 245; 8 C.F.R. § 245

Once a visa number is available, an applicant with an approved relative petition can move to the next stage of applying either to adjust status in the United States to become an LPR, or consular process at a consular office abroad for an immigrant visa. Which path to follow will depend on the physical location of the beneficiary at the time of the application or, in some cases, his or her current immigration status. In the case of immediate relatives in the United States, Form I-130, Petition for Alien Relative, and Form I-485, Application to Register Permanent Residence or Adjust Status, can be filed concurrently and adjudicated simultaneously, following an interview with an immigration officer at a local immigration Field Office. All concurrent Forms I-130/I-485 applications filed for the benefit of a spouse must be scheduled for interview, while other family categories may sometimes be adjudicated without an interview.

Anyone seeking to enter the United States must be admissible or have no impediment to receiving permission to come in to the country. However, there are times when a foreign national is inadmissible, perhaps because s/he entered at a place other than a designated border entry point, or simply walked across the border. These types of entries are referred to as entries without inspection, or EWI. In other cases, a foreign national may have misrepresented material facts when applying for a visa to enter the country, making him or her inadmissible. Foreign nationals who are inadmissible cannot apply to adjust status in the United States unless there is a waiver available to overcome the inadmissibility issue. Further discussion of these situations is in Chapter 9, Grounds of Inadmissibility and Deportation.

Recall Anand from Pakistan in Case for Discussion 6.6. If he lied to get a visa to enter the United States by saying he was married with children when in fact he was not, then he misrepresented a material fact, i.e. his marital status. It does not matter that Anand did this because he knew that visitor's visas are very hard for single young men in Pakistan to obtain, since it is difficult for them to persuade a consular officer that they will return to their country after the visit is over. Even though he is now married to a U.S. citizen, he would be inadmissible under INA § 212(a)(6)(C) because he had previously misrepresented a material fact by saying that he was married with children because he thought it was the only way to obtain his visitor's visa. If Begum did not die and the couple decides to file an application for Anand to be given permission to remain in the United States as the spouse of a U.S. citizen, he would need to apply for and be granted a waiver under INA § 212(i). It is available to those who are the spouse, son, or daughter of a U.S. citizen or LPR and, if granted, would excuse Anand for the misrepresentations he made when applying for his visa. However, to qualify for the waiver, Anand must show that refusing him permission to remain in the United States would cause extreme hardship to a qualifying relative, in this case Begum, his wife.[57] Where there is no waiver available, a foreign national has no option but to leave the United States and instead apply for an immigrant visa at the consular office abroad that is responsible for his or her country of origin. We review both of these procedures, but first we examine lawful permanent residency applications filed by those eligible to do so who are already in the United States.

G.1. Adjustment of Status in the United States

Applications to adjust status or to request LPR status are governed by INA § 245, which states that:

> (a) The status of a [foreign national] who was inspected and admitted or paroled into the United States or the status of any other [foreign national] having an approved petition ... may be adjusted by the Attorney General, in his discretion and under such regulations as he may prescribe, to that of a [foreign national] lawfully admitted for permanent residence if

---

[57] INA § 212(i). This is discussed further in Section B.6.c of Chapter 9, Grounds of Inadmissibility and Deportation.

(1) the [foreign national] makes an application for such adjustment,

(2) the [foreign national] is eligible to receive an immigrant visa and is admissible to the United States for permanent residence, and

(3) an immigrant visa is immediately available to him at the time his application is filed.

Therefore, in order for a foreign national to apply to become an LPR while in the United States, s/he must prove a Customs and Border Protection, or CBP, officer inspected and admitted or paroled him or her on the most recent entry to the United States from abroad. Without evidence of this, the foreign national cannot adjust status here and must process at a consular office abroad. The statute specifically excludes the following from adjusting in the United States:

- Those who arrived as crewmen,
- Those who have accepted or continue in unauthorized employment prior to filing an application for adjustment of status,
- Those who have failed to maintain continuously a lawful status since entry into the United States, other than through no fault of their own or for technical reasons,
- Those admitted in transit without visa under section 212(d)(4)(C),
- Those admitted as nonimmigrant visitors without a visa under section 212(l) for health related reasons or the visa waiver program under section 217, unless they are immediate relatives,
- Those admitted as S visa nonimmigrants described in section 101(a)(15)(S), because special adjustment provisions in 8 C.F.R. § 245.11 apply to them,
- Those deportable under section 237(a)(4)(B) for engagement in terrorist activities,
- Those not in a lawful nonimmigrant status at the time of filing the application, other than immediate relatives, and
- Those employed without authorization or who have otherwise violated the terms of a nonimmigrant visa.[58]

It should be noted that none of these exclusions, other than those who arrived as crewmen, apply to immediate relatives, certain graduates of medical schools or those licensed to practice medicine,[59] certain abused spouses,[60] certain family members of those who worked for international organizations,[61] special immigrant juveniles,[62] or those who have served in the military on active duty.[63] The typical route of an adjustment of status application is illustrated in Figure 6.1.

---

[58] INA § 245(c).
[59] INA § 101(a)(27)(H).
[60] INA § 245(c).
[61] INA § 101(a)(27)(I).
[62] INA § 101(a)(27)(J). Detailed discussion of this category is in Section Q of Chapter 8, Immigration Relief for Vulnerable Populations.
[63] INA § 101(a)(27)(K).

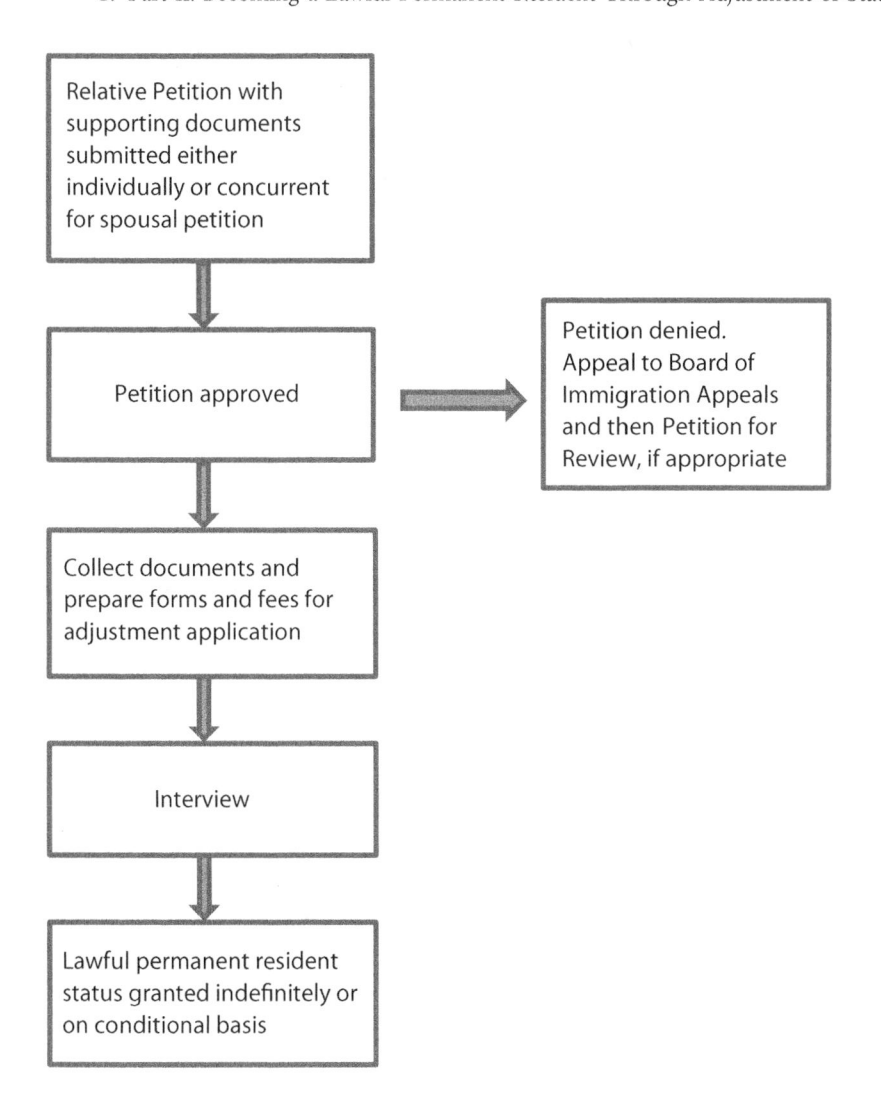

Figure 6.1

Typical Route of an Adjustment Application

```
┌─────────────────────────┐
│ Relative Petition with  │
│ supporting documents    │
│ submitted either        │
│ individually or concurrent│
│ for spousal petition    │
└───────────┬─────────────┘
            ↓
┌─────────────────────────┐      ┌─────────────────────────┐
│                         │      │ Petition denied.        │
│   Petition approved     │ ───→ │ Appeal to Board of      │
│                         │      │ Immigration Appeals     │
│                         │      │ and then Petition for   │
│                         │      │ Review, if appropriate  │
└───────────┬─────────────┘      └─────────────────────────┘
            ↓
┌─────────────────────────┐
│ Collect documents and   │
│ prepare forms and fees for│
│ adjustment application  │
└───────────┬─────────────┘
            ↓
┌─────────────────────────┐
│       Interview         │
└───────────┬─────────────┘
            ↓
┌─────────────────────────┐
│ Lawful permanent resident│
│ status granted indefinitely or│
│ on conditional basis    │
└─────────────────────────┘
```

G.2. Compiling the Adjustment Application

A complete adjustment package should include the following:

- Form I-485, Application to Register Permanent Residence or Adjust Status
- Form G-28, Notice of Entry of Appearance of Attorney or Accredited Representative, if the applicant has legal representation; this should indicate all the applications for which representation is being provided
- Form G-325A, Biographic Information, which gathers biographical information about the applicant only
- Evidence of lawful entry into the United States, either through a Form I-94 Arrival/Departure Record[64] or passport stamp

---

[64] Customs and Border Protection stopped issuing I-94 records on April 30, 2013. Instead, the information on each foreign national is retained electronically and can be retrieved at https://i94.cbp.dhs.gov/I94/consent.html.

- Birth certificate of applicant, with notarized translation, if applicable
- Results of medical examination, which is prepared by the civil surgeon and placed into a sealed envelope that must remain unopened
- Form I-864, Affidavit of Support, with supporting documents
- Certified dispositions of any arrests, where applicable
- Form I-765, Application for Employment Authorization, if needed
- Form I-131, Application for Travel Document, if needed
- Form I-797, Approval notice for previously approved Form I-130 petition, or, if the beneficiary is an immediate relative filing concurrently, the petitioner's Form I-130 application with supporting documentation
- Immigration fees
- 2 passport pictures

We review the need for each of these forms and documents individually.

G.2.a. Form I-485, Application to Register Permanent Residence or Adjust Status

The application process begins by completing Form I-485, Application to Register Permanent Residence or Adjust Status. It is used whenever a person is seeking to change to LPR status, from whatever immigration category that s/he may be in currently. For instance, this is the same form that a refugee or asylee would use when s/he is ready to become a permanent resident.

The adjustment form asks many background questions along with a series of questions about a person's criminal history, likelihood to engage in subversive activities, or past involvement in acts of torture and genocide or paramilitary groups, to name just some. Although each question is in a "yes" or "no" format, where there is any affirmative response, additional information or an explanation must be provided in an addendum. If an applicant has ever been arrested for anything other than a traffic offense, s/he is required to produce a court- or police-*certified disposition* of the outcome, which will then help to determine a person's admissibility or eligibility for LPR status. The form requires any person who has assisted in completing it to be identified and for interpreters to also indicate their identities and competency in English and the foreign language used.

The fee for the application includes the cost of applications for permission to work and also for advanced parole if requested. A review of the USCIS website should always be made to ensure that both the correct form is being used and fee paid, and the application sent to the correct USCIS office, as these change often.

G.2.b. Form G-28, Notice of Entry of Appearance as Attorney or Accredited Representative

As previously discussed, Form G-28 notifies the USCIS that an applicant has an attorney or accredited representative authorized to act on his or her behalf

Certified Dispositions: A certified document issued by a court that adjudicated a case, bearing its seal or stamp, providing an official explanation of the case outcome.

in the specific matter before them, which may relate to more than one application at a time. Filing this form should mean that copies of all correspondence sent to the beneficiary or petitioner will also be sent to the legal practitioner, but this is not always the case. Best practice would be for the parties to agree to notify the other whenever correspondence is received from the USCIS.

In immediate relative cases, a legal representative may often represent both the petitioner *and* beneficiary, since the relative petition and the application to adjust status to an LPR can be filed simultaneously, unless there are strategic reasons for filing them separately. The legal representative will represent the petitioner in his or her petition for the benefit of the beneficiary *and* represent the beneficiary in his or her application for LPR status, requiring each to sign a separate Form G-28. Therefore, the idea of dual representation must be clearly explained to the clients.

Typically, dual representation is rarely a problem where there is no conflict between the represented parties. However, if a problem later arises, then the legal representative is likely to be obliged to withdraw from representing both parties because s/he will be privy to information that could be detrimental to either simply from the initial relationship of representing both.[65]

Case for Discussion 6.7

Karen and Michael come to see you for help in filing an application for her to become an LPR based on their marriage. She is from England and Michael is a U.S. citizen. You discuss with them the process for filing a marriage-based application and provide them with a list of documents they will need to gather in support of their application. Before the next scheduled appointment when you plan to review what they have and to complete forms, Karen arrives at your office in tears. She informs you that she does not wish to go ahead with the application as Michael is abusing her, physically and mentally. She believes that their marriage cannot work and she wants to leave him. She has heard there may be a way for her to get her immigration status on her own and wants you to help her through the process.

- Is there any way your law firm/organization can do that, given its earlier representation of Karen and Michael as a couple?

---

[65] Section J in Chapter 12, Managing an Immigration Practice, discusses this further and provides strategies on how to manage dual representation.

G.2.c. Form G-325A, Biographic Information

Form G-325A gathers biographic information on the foreign national who is seeking to adjust status. It requests information on any current or prior spouses; full names and places of birth of parents and whether or not they are living or deceased; and address and work history in the United States for the last five years and for the last year abroad. It also asks the applicant to write his or her name in the native alphabet. This form is then used as part of the process of conducting background security checks and will be sent to the consular post abroad governing the foreign national's citizenship, where more information may be gathered, particularly with respect to any discrepancies with the nonimmigrant application.

In most cases, the foreign national applying for an immigration benefit completes the form. However, in family-sponsored immigrant petitions based on marriage, both spouses must complete and submit Form G-325A, Biographic Information when the relative petition is filed.

G.2.d. Form I-94 Arrival/Departure Record

As part of the application process, the foreign national must show how s/he entered the country. If entry occurred at a designated port of entry before April 30, 2013, a Form I-94 Arrival/Departure Record card will have been issued. After that date, CBP stopped issuing them on entry and instead, information is maintained in an electronic database, which can be accessed as needed. Individuals who arrived in the United States before the electronic database system was implemented may still have been issued the white I-94 card on entry, a sample of which is in Figure 1.5 of Chapter 1, Historical Background and Introduction to the U.S. Immigration System. If the foreign national still has this card, then a copy can be submitted as evidence of entry. However, many people lose it. In this case, it may be possible to use a passport that has an entry stamp as evidence of lawful entry.

Where no passport or I-94 card is available but the foreign national entered the country lawfully, an application can be filed with the USCIS for a replacement I-94 card. This is submitted on Form I-102, Application for Replacement/Initial Nonimmigrant Arrival-Departure Document, with applicable fee. The USCIS is not always able to find evidence of a prior I-94 card, but an application may yield something helpful. In the event that nothing comes up, the foreign national may be treated as a person who entered without inspection, since there is no evidence of him or her making a lawful entry. This can raise a number of inadmissibility issues, discussed in Chapter 9, Grounds of Inadmissibility and Deportation.

G.2.e. Birth Certificates and Immigration Medical Examination

Including a birth certificate for the applicant is an important part of the application package as this is proof of a person's nationality. Even if the birth certificate was provided when the relative petition was filed, it still must be submitted as part of the adjustment application. A person (not the petitioner or beneficiary) who is competent in both English and the foreign language must translate any document that is not in English. The person does not need to be a professional.

All applicants for LPR status are required to undergo a medical examination, which a special doctor, known as a ***civil surgeon***, conducts.

The examination determines whether there are any health reasons, such as the presence of a contagious disease, that would make the foreign national inadmissible.[66] The examination will test for the presence of certain diseases and will ensure that required vaccinations have been administered. A foreign national who has received some or all of the required immunizations at some point previously may prove this by providing a vaccination record at the time of the exam so that vaccinations will not be administered again. However, a waiver is available when a foreign national is unable to document that vaccinations have already been received, where it would not be medically appropriate to readminister them given the condition of the foreign national or where the vaccinations, by regulation, can be refused on religious or moral grounds.[67]

Civil Surgeons are available through a list provided by the USCIS. An electronic locator for a surgeon can be found at https://my.uscis.gov/findadoctor. There is a separate fee for this exam, which must be paid directly to the doctor. Foreign nationals submitting to a medical examination should bring the following to the exam:

Civil Surgeon: A physician selected by the immigration service to conduct medical examinations of foreign nationals seeking LPR status in the United States.

- Form I-693, Report of Medical Examination and Vaccination Record, although often the doctor will have a supply of these already
- Government-issued photo identification, such as a valid passport or driver's license Children 14 years old or younger should bring identification that shows their name, date and place of birth, and parent's full name
- Vaccination or immunization records, where available. This will help the civil surgeon to know what vaccinations the foreign national already has and will avoid any unnecessary duplication
- Payment of the civil surgeon's fee, as most will not accept health insurance. It is also a good idea to call a few civil surgeons to find out how much they charge for the exam, because prices can vary by a few hundred dollars

During the exam, the civil surgeon will test for communicable diseases such as tuberculosis and syphilis. The tuberculosis test is done in two parts, requiring the foreign national to return to the civil surgeon's office within two to three days to have the results read to see whether or not there has been a reaction suggesting the presence of tuberculosis antibodies. For those who have been inoculated against this disease, the test will most likely result in a positive reaction. Where this occurs, the civil surgeon will then take a chest x-ray to ensure no reactive tuberculosis is currently present. In the event that it is, then the foreign national

---

[66] *See* Section B.1, Chapter 9, Grounds of Inadmissibility and Deportation.
[67] INA § 212(g)(2).

will be referred to the public health department for treatment and will have to wait until clearances are given that the person is not contagious.

The foreign national will also submit to a blood test for the presence of syphilis and to see if s/he is HIV positive. While this will not make a person inadmissible, it is an issue that must be referred to the public health department. The civil surgeon will also check the foreign national's health records to see if s/he needs any vaccinations.

After the exam, the civil surgeon will complete Form I-693, Report of Medical Examination and Vaccination Record, and seal the results in an envelope for submission to USCIS. Because it must remain sealed, the foreign national should request a separate copy of the report for his or her records. Currently, medical exam results are only valid for one year from the date of preparation. Therefore, if the USCIS has not completed adjudication of the application within that time frame, an updated report will be required which can generally be obtained from the same civil surgeon for substantially less money than the original cost of the examination.

G.2.f. Form I-864, Affidavit of Support

Foreign nationals seeking to adjust their status while in the United States or to enter the country in a family-sponsored immigrant category must submit an affidavit of support that is legally enforceable against the sponsor by the foreign national and any entity that provides a means tested public benefit. This can include federal, state, and local governments.[68] The Form I-864, Affidavit of Support[69] must be completed by the petitioner, that is, the person who filed the relative petition for the **intending** or **sponsored immigrant**, i.e., the beneficiary. The sponsor must be domiciled in the United States,[70] preventing any person living abroad from sponsoring the intending immigrant. This can be problematic for those petitioners living abroad at the time that an affidavit of support is to be submitted. However, this can be overcome if s/he demonstrates an intent to reestablish residency in the United States by providing evidence of employment or a place to live that have already been secured prior to the application.[71]

The affidavit of support must show that the annual income available to support such immigrant is at least 125 percent of the annual federal poverty guidelines for the size of the family that comprises the household into which the intending immigrant will be based. The household size is determined by counting the sponsor, any spouse and person claimed as dependents on the sponsor's tax return, the intending immigrant and, if relevant, the immigrant's family members, and any prior immigrants sponsored by the petitioner for whom an obligation remains.

---

[68] INA § 213A.
[69] For immigration purposes, there are in fact two types of affidavits of support. In addition to the Form I-864, Form I-134, Affidavit of Support can be used in some applications. It is generally used for nonimmigrants who may wish to show they have sufficient income to support their stay in the United States.
[70] INA § 213A(f)(1)(C).
[71] Department of State Cable, DOS, 98-State-042068 (Mar. 12, 1998), Interpreter Releases Vol. 75, No. 13, 468-70 (April 6, 1998).

● EXAMPLE

Liam is a U.S. citizen who has four dependent children from a prior marriage. He meets Nellie, an Irish national, in a café in Boston. They fall in love, marry, and begin to live together. He plans to file a family petition for her. Liam's household size is six, counting himself, his four children, and Nellie. Liam must demonstrate he has sufficient income to support six people at 125 percent of the Department of Health and Human Services poverty level calculated at the time Nellie applies for LPR status.

Any sponsor signing an affidavit of support must be a U.S. citizen or LPR[72] who is over 18 years of age.[73] S/he is required to submit evidence of his or her immigration status, if not already submitted as part of the relative petition process, and of income. Typically, the signer is required to provide the last tax return filed and the total income declared on returns in the two years before that. The returns must be accompanied by any W-2s issued. The sponsor is also required to provide evidence of current earnings, which can be in the form of a letter from his or her employer or paystubs for the last six months. In the event that the income is insufficient to meet the levels required, the sponsor could seek to use assets to offset any short fall. With this option, the sponsor can apply 20 percent of any assets to the annual income to make up the shortfall.

● EXAMPLE

Liam from the previous example works as a roofer, but hurt his back in an accident a year before he met Nellie. At the time of filing in February, 2016, he receives Workers' Compensation, totaling an annual income of $38,000. This income is less than the $40,725 needed for the Affidavit of Support for Nellie based on the household size of six. However, Liam has investments worth $50,000. By applying 20 percent of the value of these investments, or $10,000, to his annual income, Liam can show that he meets the $40,725 required by the Affidavit of Support for his household size.

If the family member sponsoring the immigrant has insufficient income and assets to meet the requirements of the affidavit of support based on the family size, it may be possible to meet the income levels by adding income from any other adult **household member** who is willing to make available his or her income for the benefit of the intending immigrant. In such cases, Form I-864A, Contract Between Sponsor and Household Member, should be completed, as it creates a contract between the affidavit sponsor and the household member. If this is still not enough to meet the required level, then an additional person who does earn enough will need to sign a separate affidavit of support as a **joint sponsor**. It may also be possible to include the income of the intending immigrant if s/he is in the United States and working with permission. As the intended beneficiary of the affidavit of support, the intending immigrant or

---

[72] INA § 213A(f)(1)(A).
[73] INA § 213A(f)(1)(B).

household family member is not required to sign an affidavit of support since s/he cannot enter into the same contractual obligation that the affidavit creates.

● EXAMPLE

Liam is still receiving Workers' Compensation but has depleted his savings before he could complete the application process for Nellie who is not working because she does not have employment authorization. Liam needs a joint sponsor so that he can show he satisfies the requirement of income of 125 percent of the poverty level. He approaches his sister, Maura, who is married with six children. Her family size is eight and her income alone is over $70,000. If Maura agrees to be a joint sponsor, her household size will now be calculated as nine because Nellie, the intending immigrant, will be added as an additional person. The 2016 federal poverty level for a family of that size is $56,312. Therefore, Maura will have to show that she earns at least that much if she is to qualify as a joint sponsor. With her current income, she is well over this limit. If Maura's income alone was insufficient and therefore she needed to add that of her spouse to meet the requirement, he would need to sign Form I-864A together with Maura.

● EXAMPLE

Sam, a Liberian national, has Temporary Protected Status, or TPS,[74] which allows him to work legally in the United States. He meets Myra, a U.S. citizen and they marry. Myra is sponsoring Sam's LPR application; Sam is the intending immigrant. Myra is a widow, and has two children from her previous marriage. There are four people in this household size for the purposes of the affidavit of support, which include Myra, her two children, and Sam. Myra works as a home health aide and earns $25,000 a year, below the $30,375 needed in 2016 for a family of four to reach 125 percent of the poverty level. However, since Sam has work authorization, his income can be included in determining household income and may bring the couple over the limit required. Since he is the intending immigrant, he would not have to sign the affidavit of support.

Case for Discussion 6.8

Sunshine, a U.S. citizen, has been living in Egypt with her husband, Syed, and his family for the last three years. They have one daughter who is five years old. The couple decides that they would like their daughter, a U.S. citizen, to be educated in the United States and so begin the process of applying for an immigrant visa for Syed. Sunshine has already made arrangements for their daughter to be registered in a school close to her mother's house, where the

---

[74]Discussed in Section G of Chapter 5, Asylum and Other Related Humanitarian Relief.

family will live until they are on their feet. She has also arranged to work in a local coffee shop once she returns. Because Sunshine has not worked in the United States recently, she is unable to show that she has sufficient income to support a family of three (herself, her husband, and her daughter) in accordance with the requirements of the affidavit of support. A family friend with a wife and two children has agreed to assist the couple by filing as a joint sponsor.

- As a resident abroad, can Sunshine file the affidavit of support for her husband?
- Is there a way that Sunshine might file the affidavit of support on her own?
- If not, how many additional people will be added to the potential joint sponsor's family size for the purposes of the affidavit of support?

By signing the affidavit of support, the sponsor (and joint sponsor, where appropriate) contract to repay any means-tested public benefits[75] received by the sponsored immigrant to which s/he is not entitled. This obligation remains in place for a period of 40 qualifying quarters of Social Security contributions[76] (typically considered to be about ten years of consistent work history) or until the sponsored immigrant becomes a citizen of the United States, whichever comes first. Responsibility to maintain the sponsored immigrant has been held to continue to exist even after a divorce.[77]

In some circumstances, an affidavit of support may not be needed for the benefit of an intending immigrant. For instance, any person who on entering the United States will immediately become a U.S. citizen[78] or who has already accumulated the 40 quarters of social security contributions will not need an affidavit of support and therefore can complete Form I-864W, Intending Immigrant's Affidavit of Support Exemption, instead.

● EXAMPLE

Sam, the Liberian national who is married to Myra, has been in the United States on TPS since 2001. He has a solid work history. Because he can demonstrate that he has accrued 40 qualifying quarters of social security contributions, Sam, as the intending immigrant, can complete the I-864W, exempting him from the Affidavit of Support requirements.

---

[75] These include Supplemental Security Income (SSI); Medicaid; Temporary Assistance to Needy Families (TANF), and State or local cash assistance programs for income maintenance, also known as "General Assistance" programs. 62 Fed. Reg. 45256, 45258 (Aug. 26, 1997); 8 C.F.R. § 213a.4 (b). Emergency medical assistance is exempt because it is available to anyone in the United States, regardless of immigration status. Therefore, a sponsored immigrant who needs to claim this benefit would not have to repay it.
[76] A sponsored immigrant can be credited with any quarters earned by a spouse during their marriage, so long as they remain married. See Title II of the Social Security Act, 42 U.S.C.A. § 401 et seq.
[77] See *Stump v. Stump*, 2005 WL 2757329 (N.D. Ind. Oct. 25, 2005).
[78] See Section E of Chapter 11, Citizenship and Naturalization, for discussion.

As discussed previously,[79] a petitioner can be substituted as the sponsor of the affidavit of support from a broad list of family members, in the event that a petitioner dies before the intending immigrant is approved for LPR status. There is no fee for an affidavit of support when it is completed in conjunction with an application to adjust status only. The situation is different when the affidavit is used in consular processing. This is discussed in Section H.

G.2.g. Certified Dispositions

If a foreign national has ever been arrested for any reason other than for a non-criminal traffic stop, s/he must provide a certified disposition from the appropriate court, or police department if the case never proceeded to court. It provides information on the nature of the arrest, charges, and the final disposition of the case. This information will then be used to determine whether there are any applicable criminal grounds that would make the applicant inadmissible and therefore require a waiver, where available.[80]

Sometimes, a foreign national's criminal case may have been resolved through an alternate resolution disposition that does not require an admission of guilt. The punishment for the offense may be a suspended sentence, a fine, community service, probation, or a combination of any of these. So long as the assigned penalty is completed without problems, the foreign national's arrest record will then be expunged and treated as though it never occurred, allowing the person to honestly state, in most other contexts, that s/he has never been arrested. However, the criminal record is still relevant and continues to exist for immigration purposes. Therefore, even though in all other spheres the foreign national may state that s/he has never been arrested, it *must* be declared when seeking immigration relief, and a certified disposition of the arrest should be produced. There can be practical problems with obtaining a record that has been expunged because the criminal justice system no longer has any evidence of its existence. This may require some liaising with the attorney who represented the foreign national in the criminal proceedings, who may be able to access some records needed to demonstrate the criminal matter was resolved. If this fails, however, then a letter from the court certifying that no record exists will suffice.

G.2.h. Form I-765, Application for Employment Authorization

As part of the adjustment package, a foreign national may apply for permission to work, using Form I-765, Application for Employment Authorization. S/he is entitled to receive permission while the adjustment application remains pending. The authorization is granted for a period of one year and should take no more than 90 days for processing by the USCIS. In some areas around the country, however, the wait time for adjustment of status interviews can be within that time frame. If so, the card may not be issued in time, which may impact any

---

[79] *See* Section D.
[80] *See* Section B.2 of Chapter 9, Grounds of Inadmissibility and Deportation.

plans the couple might have to include income from the beneficiary in order to meet any affidavit of support requirements. The fee for applying for permission to work is included in the overall adjustment of status fee and entitles an applicant to renew the work authorization as many times as necessary before a decision is made on his or her adjustment application.

G.2.i. Form I-131, Application for a Travel Document

Once a foreign national files an application to adjust status, s/he is expected to remain in the country until it is adjudicated. However, if there is a need to travel abroad before that time, advanced parole must be obtained first or else the foreign national will be treated as having abandoned his or her application. The form used for this is Form I-131, Application for a Travel Document.

Previously, before advising a foreign national that s/he could travel out of the country on advanced parole while his or her application to adjust status was pending, a determination had to be made about whether any period of unlawful presence[81] had accrued that might trigger one of the bars to reentry after the foreign national departed the United States. This is no longer necessary, since the BIA has held that a person "who leaves the United States temporarily pursuant to a grant of advance parole does not thereby make a 'departure... from the United States'" for the purposes of triggering the unlawful presence bar.[82] A detailed discussion of these bars is in Section B.9.b of Chapter 9, Grounds of Inadmissibility and Deportation.

One of the benefits of the *Arrabally* decision is that an adjustment applicant who might need to travel while the application is pending but who has accrued unlawful presence, may do so without triggering the bars, so long as advanced parole has been requested and received first.

● EXAMPLE

Maanda is from Zimbabwe and originally entered the United States on a B-2 visitor visa. She has filed a marriage adjustment application with her new wife, Mary, who is a U.S. citizen. While waiting for her interview, Maanda learns that her elderly grandmother is seriously ill. She wants to travel to see her as quickly as possible. However, she has overstayed her original stay by some two years and therefore will be subject to the ten-year unlawful presence bar unless she applies for advanced parole on Form I-131 and it is approved before she leaves. This will allow her to return to the United States after her visit and resume her adjustment application. If Maanda leaves before her advanced parole application is approved, she abandons both the advanced parole and adjustment of status applications.

---

[81] *See* Section B.9.b of Chapter 9, Grounds of Inadmissibility and Deportation.
[82] *See Matter of Arrabally, Yerrabelly,* 25 I&N Dec. 771 (BIA 2012).

G.2.j. Photographs and Fees

The immigration fee must be submitted with the application, as either a personal check or a money order, along with two passport photographs of the adjustment applicant. Therefore, in marriage based cases where Forms I-130, Petition for Alien Relative, and I-485, Application to Register Permanent Residence and Adjust Status, are filed concurrently, there will be three photographs of the foreign national in the package, one to support the relative petition and two for the adjustment application, and a separate photo of the petitioning spouse.

G.3. Inadmissibility Issues and Waivers

In order to enter the United States in any capacity, a foreign national must not be inadmissible. Inadmissibility is a legal concept, and does not necessarily describe the physical location of the foreign national. For example, an individual who entered without inspection, or EWI, may have physically lived in the United States for many years, but legally may be considered "inadmissible" because of the manner of entry. A complete discussion of the grounds of inadmissibility is in Chapter 9, Grounds of Inadmissibility and Deportation.

For the purposes of family sponsored immigration, those who enter EWI typically cannot adjust in the United States because they have not entered after having been inspected and admitted, or paroled, as required by Section 245(a) of the INA. Instead, they are required to apply for immigrant visas at a consular office abroad. Anyone accruing unlawful presence in the United States who later departs is subject to a bar to re-entry. However, there are some exceptions to this, discussed in the Section G.3.b.

G.3.a. Unlawful Presence and Provisional Waiver[83]

The general rule is that those who have accrued unlawful presence for more than 180 days but less than one year and who leave voluntarily before the initiation of removal proceedings will be barred from re-entering the United States for three years, while those unlawfully present for one year or more and who leave, are barred for ten years. These are known as the unlawful presence bars. Those foreign nationals who are ineligible to process in the United States and therefore must leave to complete their applications at a consular office abroad, and who therefore trigger the unlawful presence bar, must apply for a waiver in order to re-enter the country if they do not wish to wait out the required period.

The three and ten year bars may be waived for an intending immigrant who is a spouse, son, or daughter of a U.S. citizen or permanent resident, if the foreign national can prove that excluding him or her would cause extreme hardship to the citizen or LPR spouse or parent.[84] It is important to note that a waiver is not

---

[83] As this is discussed in greater detail in Section B.9.b of Chapter 9, Grounds of Inadmissibility and Deportation, it is only summarized here.
[84] INA § 212(a)(9)(B)(v).

available if there is extreme hardship to a U.S. citizen or LPR minor child of an intending immigrant because a child is not considered a qualifying relative for these purposes. However, any hardship that child may face can be introduced if it will affect the qualifying relative parent or spouse.

> ● **EXAMPLE**
>
> Kemi is an unmarried Nigerian citizen. She came to the United States as a visitor but never left because the rest of her family is here. She has lived here for over ten years, during which time she gave birth to a U.S. citizen son, who is autistic and has a rare heart condition. Kemi's family help her to take care of her son as they all live together. Her father, who is an LPR, filed a relative petition for her as a Family 2B, son or daughter, many years ago. Her visa number is now current. Kemi cannot apply to adjust her status here, however, because she does not meet the requirements of INA § 245(a) as she is an overstayer and is not classified as an immediate relative of a U.S. citizen because she is not a minor child. She must travel back to Nigeria to consular process. Once she leaves, she will trigger the unlawful presence bar and must stay out of the country for a period of ten years. Kemi does not want to take her son with her because she believes he will not get the medical treatment that he needs in Nigeria. At the same time, she does not want to be separated from him for ten years. While she is processing for her visa at the consular office abroad, Kemi can apply for a waiver of the unlawful presence bar. Her qualifying relative will be her father. To demonstrate that refusing her a waiver will cause extreme hardship to him, Kemi can introduce evidence to show that he will now have greater responsibility for taking care of her son because Kemi cannot take him with her. Because of this, her father will need to take her son to his many medical and therapy appointments, which will cause him to be absent from work a great deal and could lead to him losing his job. There will also be additional expenses that he will have to absorb for his grandchild since Kemi will not be here to cover them. In this way, Kemi is able to use her son's condition to support a finding that denying her the opportunity to return to the United States earlier than ten years will cause extreme hardship to her father.

The waiver request is filed on Form I-601, Application for Waiver of Ground of Inadmissibility along with the appropriate fee, and with evidence to support a finding of extreme hardship, and is part of a consular processing package. This is because, in order to trigger the unlawful presence bar, the foreign national must have already left the United States and be seeking reentry. A detailed discussion of these waivers is in Section B.9.b of Chapter 9, Grounds of Inadmissibility and Deportation.

An application for a provisional waiver may be filed while a foreign national is still in the United States, but this is available only for immediate relatives of U.S. citizens who meet the following criteria:

- Physically present in the United States
- At least 17 years of age at the time of filing
- The beneficiary of an approved Form I-130, Petition for Alien Relative, or Form I-360, Petition for Amerasian, Widow(er), or Special Immigrant, that classifies him or her as the immediate relative of a U.S. citizen

- Have a pending immigrant visa case classifying him or her as an immediate relative with DOS
- Believe s/he is or will be inadmissible only for a period of unlawful presence in the United States that was:
  - ☐ More than 180 days, but less than 1 year, during a single stay (INA section 212(a)(9)(B)(i)(I)); or
  - ☐ One year or more during a single stay (INA section 212(a)(9)(B)(i)(II))

This request is filed on Form I-601A, Application for Provisional Unlawful Presence Waiver. Again, the waiver would be submitted along with evidence to document the extreme hardship that the qualifying relative will suffer if the waiver is not granted, along with the appropriate immigration fee. Once granted, the foreign national can then travel abroad to consular process without the unlawful presence bar preventing him or her from returning to the United States within the proscribed period. However, the provisional waiver relates only to the unlawful presence bar. Its grant does not mean the consular officer cannot investigate any other ground of inadmissibility that may apply and ultimately deny the application for a visa because of that other ground.

● EXAMPLE

Maria, from the Dominican Republic, entered the United States through Puerto Rico eight years ago, without being inspected and admitted, or paroled. She meets and marries Harry, a U.S. citizen. Because Maria entered EWI, she cannot adjust her status in the United States and therefore must return to the Dominican Republic to apply for an immigrant visa. Once Maria leaves the country, she will be subject to the ten-year bar because she was unlawfully present here for eight years. Therefore, Maria must also apply for a provisional waiver and demonstrate that if she is not allowed to return to the United States before the ten-year waiting period is over, Harry will experience extreme hardship. If Maria had entered on a tourist visa, and then married Harry, she would be considered an immediate relative who was inspected and admitted. Even if she lived in the United States for eight years without permission after that type of entry, she would not require a waiver and could adjust status without leaving the country.

● EXAMPLE

Maria entered the United States without inspection eight years ago, forms a relationship with Harry, and they have a child, Luis, who is a U.S. citizen by birth. Harry does not marry Maria; in fact, Harry is married to another woman. Maria meets and marries Tom who is also undocumented, but very caring and attentive to her son. Luis becomes very ill with childhood diabetes. Maria realizes she must remain in the United States to care for Luis. She inquires about whether there is any basis for her to adjust her status or whether she must return to the Dominican Republic and apply for an immigrant visa there. Under current law, there is no way for Maria to adjust status in the United States because she has no one to petition

for her and because she is also inadmissible. Moreover, if she leaves, she faces a ten-year bar and no waiver is available to her because her child is not a qualifying relative for the purposes of filing a waiver and establishing the requisite hardship.

G.3.b. Section 245(i) of the Immigration and Nationality Act

Another alternative for a person who entered without inspection or is present here but without lawful immigration status, perhaps because s/he stayed longer than the period allowed without seeking an extension, is to seek to adjust under former INA § 245(i). This section permitted ineligible foreign nationals to become LPRs under INA § 245(a) without leaving the United States, so long as they paid a $1,000 fine in addition to the fees for the adjustment application. Statute sets the amount of this fine. Minor children under the age of 17 and certain beneficiaries under the Immigration Reform and Control Act of 1986 were not required to pay the fine.[85] The statutory provision is lengthy, but it is worth including most of it here. It reads:

> (1) Notwithstanding the provisions of subsections (a) and (c) of this section [which prevent certain foreign nationals from adjusting in country], a [foreign national] physically present in the United States—
> (A) who—
> (i) entered the United States without inspection; or
> (ii) is within one of the classes enumerated in subsection (c) of this section;
> (B) who is the beneficiary (including a spouse or child of the principal [foreign national], if eligible to receive a visa under section 203(d)) of—
> (i) a petition for classification under section 204 that was filed with the Attorney General on or before April 30, 2001; or
> (ii) an application for a labor certification under section 212(a)(5)(A) that was filed pursuant to the regulations of the Secretary of Labor on or before such date; and
> (C) who, in the case of a beneficiary of a petition for classification, or an application for labor certification, described in subparagraph (B) that was filed after January 14, 1998, is physically present in the United States on the date of the enactment of the LIFE Act Amendments of 2000; may apply to the Attorney General for the adjustment of his or her status to that of a [foreign national] lawfully admitted for permanent residence. The Attorney General may accept such application only if the [foreign national] remits with such application a sum equaling $1,000 as of the date of receipt of the application, but such sum shall not be required from a child under the age of 17.

---

[85] INA § 245(i)(1)(C).

The main categories of people who benefit from INA § 245(i), are those who:

- Entered without inspection,
- Entered as crewmen,
- Had violated their immigration status in some way, or
- Entered as transit passengers without a visa.

INA § 245(i) originally expired on January 14, 1998 but was later extended until April 30, 2001. Although it is no longer available for new filings, it is still important to review as it continues to affect and benefit those who were grandfathered. In order to be grandfathered, a foreign national must be the beneficiary of either a visa petition[86] (adjudicated by the USCIS) or an application for labor certification (adjudicated by the Department of Labor) filed after January 14, 1998 and on or before April 30, 2001. In addition, the beneficiary must demonstrate physical presence in the United States on the date of enactment of the statute that extended the availability of INA § 245(i) to April 2001. This was the LIFE Act Amendments of 2000 and it came into force on December 21, 2000.

For the relative petition or labor certificate application to confer a benefit, it had to meet certain criteria. 8 C.F.R. § 245.10 required the petition or application be postmarked no later than April 30, 2001 and that it had to be "approvable when filed." This did not mean that it had to be approved at some later date. In fact, denial would not in and of itself mean that it did not meet the approvable when filed requirement. Rather, it simply had to be a meritorious or non-frivolous application at the time of filing.

It is important to note that INA § 245(i) only sought to cure the issue of unlawful presence where certain foreign nationals are permitted to file their application to adjust status in the United States. It did not waive any other grounds of inadmissibility that might apply which would still require any applicable waivers to be granted.

While INA § 245(i) is an individual benefit, it attaches to the person and not to the petition or labor certification in question. Therefore, a foreign national who benefits from the provision may still apply it to a different petition or labor certificate that may become available, even today, because the benefit is grandfathered with that person until he or she successfully adjusts status to an LPR. Congress allowed spouses and children who could demonstrate that a relationship with the principal beneficiary of a visa petition or labor certification application existed on or before April 30, 2001 to also be grandfathered as INA § 245(i) recipients. This is so, even if subsequently, the relationship conferring the benefit should later change, perhaps through divorce.[87]

---

[86] The visa petition includes applications filed on Forms I-130, Petition for Alien Relative, I-140, Immigrant Petition for Alien Worker, I-360, Self Petition for Amerasian, Widow(er), or Special Immigrant, and I-526, Immigrant Petition by Alien Entrepreneur.

[87] *See* Yates Memo dated March 9, 2005, *Clarification of Certain Eligibility Requirements Pertaining to an Application to Adjust Status Under Section 245(i) of the Immigration and Nationality Act*.

● **EXAMPLE**

Adolfo last entered the United States without inspection in April 1998 from Mexico along with his wife Yessica and their five-year old son, Manuel. The family has never left. On April 29, 2001, Adolfo's employer filed a labor certification for his benefit so that Adolfo could work as a horse trainer for his stables. The certificate was approved two years later but the employer died soon after so that Adolfo could not complete his application. If a new employer decides to apply for Adolfo and that new labor certification application is approved, Adolfo can adjust in the United States because his initial labor certification was 'approvable when filed,' allowing him to be grandfathered under INA § 245(i). Yessica and Manuel are also grandfathered and can also file applications to become LPRs in the United States because a qualifying relationship, spouse and child, existed at the time the labor certification was filed.

● **EXAMPLE**

Assume the same facts, with all family members grandfathered. However, before the new employer files a labor certification, the couple's relationship deteriorates and they finally decide to divorce. All of the family members will continue to be grandfathered because the qualifying relationship existed at the time the labor certification was filed. However, Yessica will need to find an alternative basis on which to adjust her status, since she is no longer married to Adolfo and so cannot process through the new labor certification filed for his benefit. If Yessica re-marries a U.S. citizen who now petitions for her, she will be able to adjust her status to that of LPR in the United States because she was independently grandfathered by Adolfo's previous labor certification.

● **EXAMPLE**

Adolfo last entered the United States without inspection in April 1998 from Mexico. He is unmarried and has never left the country. In April 2001, his employer filed a labor certification for his benefit, so that Adolfo could work as a horse trainer for his stables. The certificate was approved two years later but the employer died soon after so that Adolfo could not complete his application. In 2005, he met and married Yessica, who also entered the United States from Mexico without inspection in 2004. If a new employer decides to apply for Adolfo and that labor certification is approved, Adolfo can adjust in the United States because his initial labor certification was 'approvable when filed,' allowing him to be grandfathered under INA § 245(i). Yessica may adjust status only as Adolfo's dependent because she was not married to him prior to April 30, 2001. If Yessica divorces Adolfo before she adjusts her status to an LPR and marries a U.S. citizen, she cannot adjust status in the United States through him because she has no independent benefit of INA § 245(i).

● **EXAMPLE**

Assume the same facts, with Adolfo unmarried. In 2005, a new employer files a labor certification that is approved in 2006. Adolfo applies to adjust his status to an LPR, which is granted in 2007. That same year, he meets and marries Yessica. She cannot adjust in any capacity and is not grandfathered because the qualifying relationship came into existence only after Adolfo had adjusted status.

G.4. Submitting the Application

Once the finalized application package is sent to the address specified by the USCIS based on the beneficiary's residence, a receipt will be issued after which an appointment for biometrics (digital capturing of fingerprints and picture) will be set up. The application will then be sent on to the appropriate USCIS Service Center for further processing and forwarded to the local USCIS Field Office, which will schedule an interview, after all background security checks have been completed and returned without cause for concern.

Legal representatives and an interpreter, if needed, may accompany applicants to their interview. In most cases, an adjudications officer will notify an applicant at the end of the interview of the outcome of the application. Where further information is required before a decision can be made, however, the applicant will be notified of a request for evidence, or RFE, and given a time frame in which to present it.[88] If the adjustment application is denied by the USCIS, the foreign national will be referred to immigration court for an immigration judge to decide whether s/he should be deported.[89] This will only occur if the foreign national is not in valid nonimmigrant status at the time the application is reviewed. Otherwise, s/he will remain in his or her lawful nonimmigrant status.

H. Consular Processing

Foreign nationals who are not physically present in the United States or who, for one reason or another, cannot apply to adjust their status while in the country must apply for an immigrant visa with a consular office abroad.[90] In many ways, the process is very similar to that for applying to adjust status in the United States. Unlike the adjustment application, however, which if denied, can be appealed to an immigration judge, there is no avenue to legally challenge the denial of an immigrant visa.[91]

---

[88] A sample RFE is available in Figure 1.13 in Chapter 1, Historical Background and Introduction to the U.S. Immigration System.
[89] Further discussion of this process is in Chapter 10, Immigration Court Practice and Relief from Removal.
[90] The procedure for consular processing for immigrant visas is similar to that discussed in Chapter 2, Nonimmigrant Visas for Brief Stays, Studies, and Cultural Exchange, for nonimmigrant visas.
[91] *Kerry V. Din*, 576 U.S. ___, 135 S. Ct. 2128 (2015).

The application is still a two-part process, requiring a family-sponsored relative petition to be filed and approved before an application for an immigrant visa can be made. Generally, the relative petition is filed with the USCIS either in the United States or in one of the countries abroad where it has overseas offices.[92] In very limited cases, it may be possible to file the relative petition request directly with the consular office, which has authority to accept and adjudicate applications that are "clearly approvable".[93] All others must be referred to the USCIS in the United States for approval. Where a consular officer later uncovers information that calls into question the validity of information submitted to support approval of the petition, however, s/he has no authority to revoke it. Instead, the petition must be sent back to the USCIS for further investigation and possible revocation.

● **EXAMPLE**

Anna, a national of Italy, is being sponsored for immigration to the United States by her U.S. citizen husband, who lives here. She is a devout catholic. During the interviewing process at the consular office, Anna reveals she was briefly married for one month, but the marriage was annulled. This information was not disclosed on the Form I-130, Petition for Alien Relative, because in Anna's eyes, an annulled marriage should not be considered a real marriage. Anna states she does not have any documents showing the marriage or annulment. Given this omission, the consular officer must return the approved relative petition to the USCIS in the United States for further action, because there has been no opportunity to assess whether Anna's annulment is valid and therefore whether she was actually free to marry her U.S. citizen husband.

Once the immigrant visa petition has been approved, it is sent to the National Visa Center, or NVC. Part of the DOS, the NVC then takes over processing of the application until the package is ready to be sent to the consular office for scheduling of the interview.

As discussed in Section A.2, a new visa bulletin is issued each month, indicating which priority date is current for family-sponsored, employment-based, and diversity immigrant visa petitions. Shortly before a priority date becomes current, NVC will notify the petitioner that the next stage of the process will begin soon. At this time, the petitioner is asked to use Form DS-261, Online Choice of Address and Agent, to provide an address and elect an agent who will receive any correspondence pertaining to the application and will also be sent instructions on how to pay the processing fees for the immigrant visa and required Form I-864, Affidavit of Support. The agent can be any legal representative who may have submitted a Form G-28, Notice of Entry of Appearance of Attorney or Accredited Representative, at the time of filing the relative petition, or anyone else the petitioner selects. If Form G-28 has already been filed with the relative petition, there

---

[92] 9 FAM 504.2-3(B).
[93] 9 FAM 504.2-4.

is no need to complete Form DS-261. The fees must be paid electronically, with a receipt and reference number generated immediately on payment.

Once all fees are paid, NVC will send the designated agent a bar-coded cover letter along with instructions on how to download forms to be completed as part of the application package, including the electronic Form DS-260, Immigrant Visa and Alien Registration, which must be completed online. The use of this form has been required for all applications filed after September 1, 2013. The letter from NVC also contains the beneficiary's full name, address, visa number, and visa status code. The supplied cover sheet must be included with any documents sent to NVC so that they can be appropriately tracked. A copy of this letter will also be sent to the beneficiary, advising that s/he should begin the application process within one year of receipt. If the beneficiary is not able to complete processing within that time, s/he can notify NVC of this fact and make a request that the application remain open. NVC will then hold the application in abeyance for a year, at which time another reminder is sent. This can continue indefinitely.

The foreign national must gather a number of documents in preparation for the immigrant visa interview. The particular requirements are listed on the country specific information page on the DOS' website. Generally the applicant is required to produce the following:

- Birth certificate or other secondary evidence of birth where permitted by the FAM
- Marriage certificate, where applicable
- Evidence of termination of all prior marriages, where applicable; this can be a divorce decree, annulment agreement, or death certificate
- Police certificate, indicating the foreign national's record since the age of 16 and providing information on the entire period of the applicant's residence of more than six months in a particular area; the certificate must be issued by the appropriate police authority and include information on all arrests, the reason for the arrests, and the disposition of each recorded case
- Military records for those who served
- Court or prison records where a foreign national has a conviction for a crime; the applicant must provide a certified copy of each court and prison record, regardless of whether amnesty, a pardon, or other act of clemency was later granted and the records should include complete information about the circumstances of the crime and the disposition of the case, including sentence, fines, or other penalties imposed
- Biographical page of passport which must be valid for travel for at least six months
- Two passport photographs

All of these documents should be submitted as copies, other than the passport photographs. Originals of each should be brought to the interview at the consular office for inspection. A properly completed affidavit of support, where needed, will also be sent to NVC for review, along with supporting documents. There is a fee paid for the affidavit when it is used for consular processing. This is different from the adjustment of status application, where no fee is paid.

Once all documents are obtained, they are then sent to NVC, where they will be reviewed to ensure that they meet all requirements and then sent on to the consular office, which will schedule an interview for the intending immigrant. Some U.S. Embassies require the documents to be scanned and emailed to the NVC, rather than submitted by regular mail. A list of these countries is available on the DOS website, which may be accessed at https://travel.state.gov/content/visas/en/immigrate/immigrant-process/approved/contact.html. A copy of everything sent should be kept so that it can be taken along to the interview with the original documents. Unlike in adjustment of status cases processed in the United States, documents in the language of the adjudicating consular office do not need to be translated into English as there will be native language speakers on staff who can translate the documents.

As with adjustment cases, the foreign national will need to arrange a medical examination in his or her home country with a designated doctor approved by the United States Consulate or Embassy in the particular country. Depending on the practice there, the exam results may be given to the applicant in a sealed envelope, or sent directly to the consulate or embassy office. As in the procedure for adjustment of status in the United States, the examination is in two parts because of the tuberculosis test.

Immigrant visa interviews are scheduled at the consular office. A letter advising of the date and time is sent to the beneficiary, the petitioner, and the legal representative or agent. The beneficiary should take along his or her passport, which must be valid for at least six months. As with adjustment of status applications, a legal representative may accompany the foreign national to the interview. It is unlikely that s/he will need to bring an interpreter, however, since the consular posts have many native language speakers working for them who will be available to interpret.

If the application for an immigrant visa is approved, the foreign national will be notified and given information on how and when his or her passport and visa will be returned. The visa will be valid for a period of only six months, so travel plans need to be made relatively quickly. If the application is denied, the consular office will provide a letter explaining the reason.

Along with the visa, the intending immigrant will be given further instructions on how to pay to the USCIS the Immigrant Fee that covers the cost of processing and maintaining his or her immigrant visa packet and to produce and deliver the permanent resident card following arrival in the United States. The fee can be paid online using the USCIS Electronic Immigration System, or ELIS. If the fee is paid before the immigrant leaves his or her country, the green card will be sent within a few weeks of arrival. If the fee is paid after the foreign national leaves, the wait to receive the green card will be longer. In either case, upon arrival in the United States, the immigrant will receive a temporary I-551 stamp in his or her passport as indication of the LPR status granted.[94] The typical route of consular office immigrant processing is shown in Figure 6.2.

---

[94] A sample of the stamp is in Figure 1.7 of Chapter 1, Historical Background and Introduction to the U.S. Immigration System.

Figure 6.2

Typical Route of Immigrant Visa Consular Processing
Source: Adapted from the DOS.

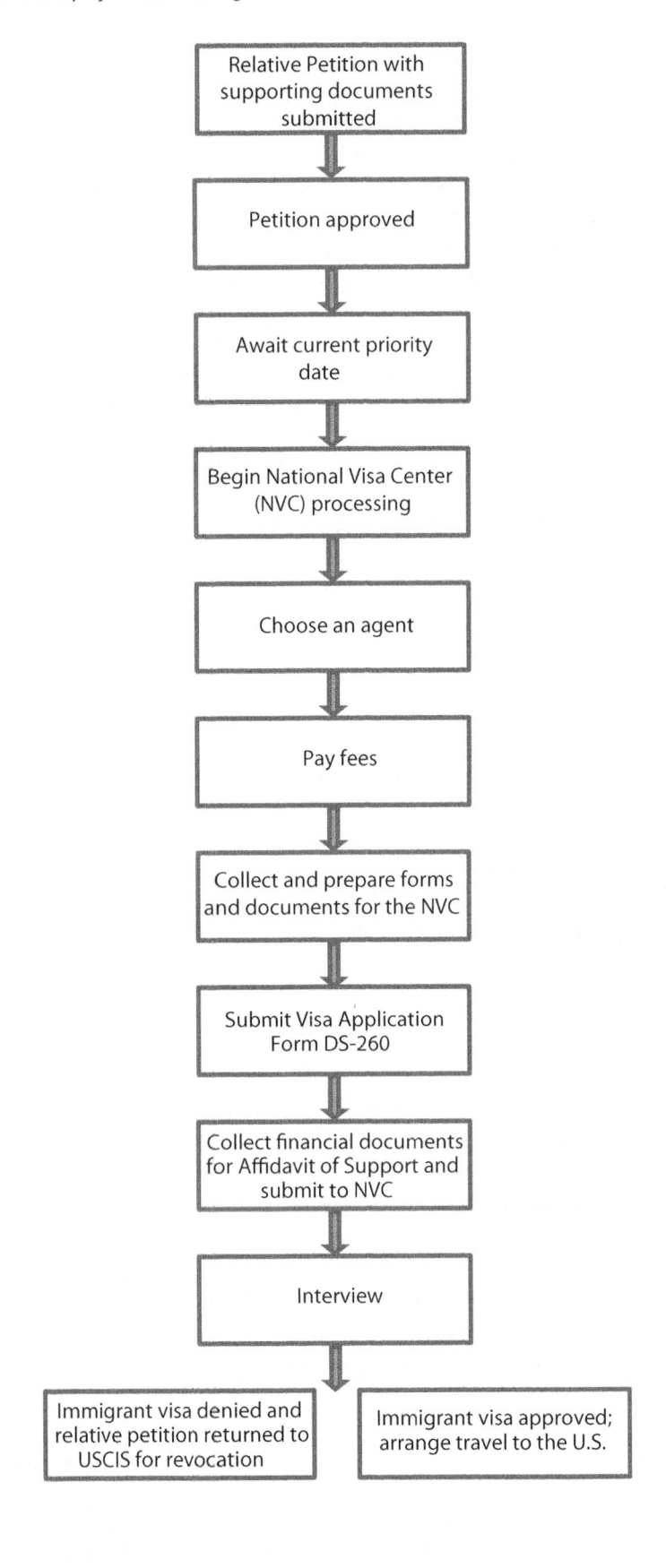

```
┌─────────────────────────────┐
│ Relative Petition with      │
│ supporting documents        │
│ submitted                   │
└──────────────┬──────────────┘
               ▼
┌─────────────────────────────┐
│ Petition approved           │
└──────────────┬──────────────┘
               ▼
┌─────────────────────────────┐
│ Await current priority date │
└──────────────┬──────────────┘
               ▼
┌─────────────────────────────┐
│ Begin National Visa Center  │
│ (NVC) processing            │
└──────────────┬──────────────┘
               ▼
┌─────────────────────────────┐
│ Choose an agent             │
└──────────────┬──────────────┘
               ▼
┌─────────────────────────────┐
│ Pay fees                    │
└──────────────┬──────────────┘
               ▼
┌─────────────────────────────┐
│ Collect and prepare forms   │
│ and documents for the NVC   │
└──────────────┬──────────────┘
               ▼
┌─────────────────────────────┐
│ Submit Visa Application     │
│ Form DS-260                 │
└──────────────┬──────────────┘
               ▼
┌─────────────────────────────┐
│ Collect financial documents │
│ for Affidavit of Support    │
│ and submit to NVC           │
└──────────────┬──────────────┘
               ▼
┌─────────────────────────────┐
│ Interview                   │
└──────────────┬──────────────┘
         ┌─────┴─────┐
         ▼           ▼
┌──────────────────┐ ┌──────────────────┐
│ Immigrant visa   │ │ Immigrant visa   │
│ denied and       │ │ approved;        │
│ relative petition│ │ arrange travel   │
│ returned to USCIS│ │ to the U.S.      │
│ for revocation   │ │                  │
└──────────────────┘ └──────────────────┘
```

I. Post Interview

Once the application for adjustment of status or for an immigrant visa is approved, the status granted to the foreign national will be that of an LPR, issued at the end of an adjustment interview or on entering the United States for the first time following consular processing. The status allows the holder to work and travel freely in and out of the country, so long as the United States is the recipient's main country of domicile. If it appears that the foreign national does not actually live here but is merely traveling here in order to maintain his or her LPR status, s/he could be referred to immigration court so that an immigration judge can decide whether or not the status should be revoked. Length of continuous residence and physical presence in the United States can also affect eligibility to naturalize as a U.S. citizen.[95]

I.1. Conditional Residency: INA § 216; 8 C.F.R. § 216

The grant of LPR status is indefinite in all cases except for those who obtain status through a marriage that is less than two years old at the time of adjudication of the application or entry into the United States with the immigrant visa. In those cases, the foreign national will be issued **conditional lawful permanent resident status**[96] for a period of two years, with all the rights and privileges of an unrestricted LPR. This is also the category that is granted to any children who may have derived status from the foreign national who is a conditional LPR. As previously mentioned, children of immediate relatives must enter with a relative petition filed for their individual benefit rather than as a dependent of the immigrating parent. It is very rare for spouses or children of LPRs to be classified as conditional LPRs because of the lengthy wait times for a visa number to become available for them, which often is longer than two years.

Conditional LPR status was introduced in the Immigration Marriage Fraud Amendment Act of 1986, which sought to deter marriage fraud, believed by Congress to be rampant. A grant of conditional LPR status created a period during which the marriage would be tested to see whether or not it was genuine. If it lasted, then 90 days before the second anniversary of the grant of conditional status, the couple could jointly apply to have the conditions removed and LPR status would be granted indefinitely.

The petition to remove conditions is filed on Form I-751, Petition to Remove Conditions on Residency. The couple should submit as many documents as possible to demonstrate that they have lived together and comingled their lives as spouses over the two-year period. The types of documents for submission are similar to those gathered for the initial relative petition to prove the *bona fides* of

---

[95] Discussion of this is in Section C.3 of Chapter 11, Citizenship and Naturalization.
[96] INA § 216(a)(1).

the relationship.[97] This can include evidence of joint finances and property, such as joint leases, a mortgage, bank accounts, joint insurance coverage, or the birth of a child to the couple. Again, submitting as many different documents covering as much of the relevant time span as possible will tend to indicate a strong application. If the couple fails to file the application within the 90-day period allowed, the USCIS may terminate the conditional residency status and refer the foreign national to an immigration judge for removal proceedings.

Once the petition to remove conditions is filed, the USCIS will issue a receipt that extends the conditional LPR status for a year, allowing the foreign national to continue working and travelling. Requests for renewals of the automatic extension will be granted if adjudication of the application takes longer than a year, which often happens. The petition to remove conditions may be approved without the need for an interview, unless there are issues that the USCIS wishes to explore with the couple. There are also a number of nonproblematic petitions that are randomly called for interview simply for quality control purposes. Once it is approved, the foreign national will be granted indefinite LPR status, preserving the date of the initial conditional lawful permanent residence grant so that any accrued time is not lost.

● EXAMPLE

Rodrigo from Brazil became a conditional permanent resident on July 3, 2012. In mid April 2014, he and his wife, Paola, applied to have the conditions removed. This was approved in December, 2015. His new I-551, Permanent Resident, or green card, shows that he has been an LPR since July 3, 2012.

If the Form I-751, Petition to Remove Conditions on Residency, is denied, the foreign national will have the opportunity to have the case reviewed by an immigration judge who will make an independent decision on the *bona fides* of the marriage. Discussion of the immigration removal process is in Chapter 10, Immigration Court Practice and Relief from Removal.

A joint petition to remove conditions is possible only if the couple remains together during the two-year test period. However, in some cases the marriage may have been a genuine one but just did not work out. Even if the couple is separated, with no final decision regarding the viability of the marriage, they can still go ahead and file a joint petition for removal of conditions. But if this is not possible, then INA § 216(c)(4) permits the foreign national to apply, on his or her own, for a waiver that will allow a petition to remove the conditions, for one of three reasons:

- A good faith marriage has ended through divorce or annulment,
- The foreign national will experience extreme hardship if not allowed to remain in the United States, or
- The foreign national was battered or subjected to extreme cruelty by the U.S. or LPR spouse.

---

[97] *See* discussion in Section C.1.

To succeed in a petition based on termination of a good faith marriage, the foreign national must show that the marriage was entered into in good faith, that it has ended other than through death of the U.S. citizen spouse, and that the foreign national was not at fault for failing to timely file a petition before the expiration of the conditional residency period, if applicable.[98] To demonstrate the *bona fides*, as many documents as possible should be produced that suggest the couple intended to comingle their lives, focusing on evidence acquired after the grant of conditional residency. A divorce decree or annulment agreement will be required to demonstrate that the marriage has been terminated. As for demonstrating that the foreign national was not at fault if the petition was filed late, it may be possible to provide evidence of how long completion took for the legal procedures to end the marriage, as these can take a long time and may be the reason for the delayed filing.

Alternatively, the foreign national may seek a waiver based on extreme hardship if not allowed to remain in the United States.[99] Interestingly, the regulation does not make clear who must experience the hardship, therefore it should be construed as widely as possible, to include other family members, both here and abroad, who may suffer hardship if the foreign national is not allowed to remain. For instance, perhaps s/he is sending remittances to family members abroad and may not have the opportunity to continue to support them because of poor employment prospects back home. Extreme hardship factors considered were articulated by the BIA in *Matter of Anderson*, 16 I&N Dec. 596 (BIA 1978) and include:

- Length of stay in the United States,
- Relatives present here and abroad,
- Conditions in the country where the foreign national would return,
- Medical or health issues for him or her and any relatives,
- Community ties,
- Educational opportunities that may be lost or interrupted if removal occurs, and
- Any other factors that may be relevant to a particular case.[100]

Finally, the foreign national may self-petition to have the conditions removed on his or her LPR status by showing that the U.S. citizen or LPR spouse subjected him or her to battery or extreme cruelty. Detailed discussion of this is in Chapter 8, Immigration Relief for Vulnerable Populations.

The I-551, Permanent Residency, or green card, issued after the conditions are removed is valid for a period of ten years, at which time it will need to be

---

[98] 8 C.F.R. 216.5(a)(1)(ii).
[99] 8 C.F.R. 216.5(a)(1)(i).
[100] Further discussion of extreme hardship is in Section B.3 of Chapter 8, Immigration Relief for Vulnerable Populations.

renewed, unless the foreign national has become a citizen.[101] Even though the card may expire, LPR status remains indefinite unless terminated by an immigration judge or forfeited by a foreign national who remains outside of the country for protracted periods and is unable to show that the United States is his or her primary domicile. The green card operates only as evidence of the foreign national's immigration status and not of how long the status is held.

> **Case for Discussion 6.9**
>
> Adia, from Kenya, met her U.S. citizen husband, Abasi, when he traveled to visit his family there. They were married on December 12, 2011. The couple had known each other for some time and had decided to wait until Adia's mourning period was over after the death of her first husband. Abasi finally applied for her to come and join him in the United States. After a number of delays in processing her application, Adia was issued an immigrant visa on December 1, 2013. She entered the United States on December 13, 2013 and was issued a conditional LPR status stamp. Within a year of her entry, the marriage broke down and the couple separated. They did not file to remove her conditions within the 90 days prior to her second anniversary. On December 23, 2015, Adia received a letter from the USCIS, telling her that, because she had not filed her petition in time, she was to be placed into removal proceedings so that an immigration judge could decide whether she should be allowed to remain in the United States.
>
> - Does Adia have any defenses to this action, since her husband has made it clear he no longer wishes to be with her?

J. FIANCÉ(E)S: INA § 101(a)(15)(K)

In some cases, a couple may not have made a decision about whether or not to marry, may need time to decide where to live after marriage or may want to marry in the United States rather than abroad. Immigration law does not allow couples in this situation to file family sponsored relative petitions because the qualifying family relationship does not yet exist. For those *intending* to marry, the law allows fiancé(e)s to enter on a K-1 nonimmigrant visa and any unmarried children under 21 of that foreign national to enter on K-2 visas. Only U.S. citizens can file this petition; the fiancé(e) petition process is not available to LPRs.

---

[101] Renewal of an I-551 Permanent Resident card is done by using Form I-90, Application to Replace Permanent Resident Card. Discussion of the process to become a citizen is in Chapter 11, Citizenship and Naturalization.

Using this allows time for a couple to marry here, if they choose to do so.[102] The fiancé(e) visa is filed on Form I-129F, Petition for Alien Fiancé(e).

To be eligible for a K visa, a petitioner must show that s/he has met his or her fiancé(e) in person within two years of the date of filing the petition. The USCIS can waive this requirement, however, if compliance would cause extreme hardship to the petitioner or would violate long-established cultural norms for either of the parties to the marriage. The petitioner must also show that s/he and the beneficiary have a genuine intent to marry, have the capacity to marry, and are willing to enter into a valid marriage within 90 days of the beneficiary's admission to the United States.

● EXAMPLE

The families of Sahar and Ijaz agreed many years ago in Pakistan that their children should marry once they complete their college education. Sahar, the prospective wife, has lived with her family in the United States for over a decade since this agreement and they are now all U.S. citizens. Sahar and Ijaz have not seen each other since her family's last visit to Pakistan six years ago. Both have graduated and plans are being made for their marriage. Their families are very traditional and do not believe that the couple should meet before the marriage contract is complete. If the wedding ceremony is to take place in the United States, Sahar can file an application for Ijaz to come as a fiancé, explaining that arranged marriages are a part of Pakistani culture where the couple is expected to see each other for the first time on their wedding day.

There are now additional K-type visas available to spouses and unmarried minor children of U.S. citizens. Sometimes, for those already married, the waiting time for approval of a family sponsored immigrant visa petition as well as the requirement to complete consular processing can be considerable. Rather than keeping families apart, there is a provision that allows U.S. citizens who have received a receipt for filing Form I-130, Petition for Alien Relative for a spouse and any unmarried children under 21 to also file a Form I-129F Petition for Alien Fiancé(e), even though the marriage has already taken place. This will then allow the qualifying family members to come to the United States with K-3 and K-4 nonimmigrant visas respectively, in order to await approval of the relative petition and then file an application for adjustment of status so that they can become LPRs. Although this is a more expensive route to gaining LPR status because fees will be paid for both the relative and fiancé(e) petitions, it does limit the time that families spend separated.

---

[102] INA § 214(d).

> **Case for Discussion 6.10**
>
> Kristin, a U.S. citizen, has returned from South Africa leaving her husband David behind. She wants to file a relative petition for him but is anxious about how long it will take for David to join her because she is pregnant with their first child and she has no family support. You inform her that the relative petition is taking approximately ten months to process, after which you will need about a month to send necessary documents to the National Visa Center that will then send David's application to the consular office in Johannesburg so that an appointment for an interview can be arranged in three months' time. Kristin is visibly upset and asks if there is any other way for David to come here sooner.
>
> - What can you tell her?
> - If it is possible for David to join her sooner, what will she need to do?

Once USCIS approves the fiancé(e) or K visa, the principal beneficiary of the petition and any derivative family members may enter the United States in K-1 and K-2 categories respectively. The marriage must take place within 90 days of entry. The foreign national is eligible to immediately apply for employment authorization and, once granted, it will be valid for the initial 90-day period only. Following the marriage, the couple may then file an application for adjustment of status in the usual way.[103] The Form I-130, Petition for Alien Relative, is not required because the Form I-129F, Petition for Alien Fiancé(e) stands in its stead, unless the marriage takes place outside of the 90 days, after which the petition is no longer valid. In this case, the couple must file a full adjustment application, including a Form I-130 relative petition. In either adjustment scenario, USCIS waives the medical report requirement because the beneficiary would have already submitted one as part of the non immigrant K visa processing abroad. If the marriage is less than two years old at the time of adjudication of the adjustment application, USCIS will grant the foreign spouse LPR status on a conditional basis, as discussed in Section I.1.

There are two legislative provisions that seek to protect fiancé(e)s and K-3 spouses of U.S. citizens from possible abusive situations. The first is the Adam Walsh Act, discussed in Section C.5. INA 204.(a)(viii)(A)(I) prevents any U.S. citizen who has been convicted of a "specified offense against a minor" from filing either a K-1 or K-3 petition unless a determination has been made that s/he poses no risk to the beneficiary.[104]

---

[103] *See* Section 6.G.1.
[104] *See* INA § 101(a)(15)(K).

The second legislation is the International Marriage Broker Regulation Act of 2005,[105] or IMBRA, which requires that, as part of the application process, the petitioner must provide certified dispositions for any past convictions for "specified crimes" s/he may have. The crimes include, among others:

- Murder or manslaughter
- Rape
- Incest
- Child abuse
- Domestic violence
- Sexual assault
- Kidnapping
- False imprisonment
- Three convictions involving controlled substances

The information will then be shared with the beneficiary at the time of his or her consular interview.

IMBRA also requires that a consular officer may not approve a fiancé(e) petition where a petitioner has filed at least two fiancé(e) petitions in the past or is now filing a petition within two years of the last one approved.[106] This requirement may be waived unless the petitioner has "a record of violent criminal offenses against a person or persons"[107] This too may be waived for those who have been battered or subjected to extreme cruelty, so long as s/he was not the primary perpetrator of violence in the relationship and who acted in self-defense or was in violation of a protection from abuse order that was issued to protect him or her.[108] Factors for consideration when deciding whether to grant the waiver include:

- Whether unusual circumstances exist, such as death or incapacity of prior beneficiary(ies),
- Whether the petitioner appears to have a history of domestic violence,
- Whether it appears the petitioner has a pattern of filing multiple petitions for different beneficiaries at the same time, of filing and withdrawing petitions, or obtaining approvals of petitions every few years.[109]

---

[105] Pub. L. 109-162, 119 Stat. 2960 (2006), Title VIII, Subtitle D. *See* Aytes memo dated July 21, 2006 on International Marriage Broker Regulation Act Implementation Guidance, HQOPRD 70/6.2.11, which can be found at http://www.uscis.gov/sites/default/files/USCIS/Laws/Memoranda/Static_Files_Memoranda/Archives%201998-2008/2006/imbra072106.pdf.
[106] 105 INA §§ 214(d)(1) and (3)(B).
[107] 106 INA § 214(d)(2)(B).
[108] INA § 214(d)(2)(C).
[109] Aytes memo dated July 21, 2006 on International Marriage Broker Regulation Act Implementation Guidance, HQOPRD 70/6.2.11.

> ● **EXAMPLE**
>
> **Duke, a U.S. citizen with a penchant for Eastern European women, has previously filed fiancée petitions on at least three occasions. One of them was approved 18 months ago but the relationship broke down soon after his fiancée arrived from Russia. He now wants to file a new petition for a Ukrainian model, Eleanor, he met during Paris fashion week as they have decided to marry. Duke is likely to have this petition denied for one of two reasons. First, he has already filed fiancée petitions on more than two occasions. Second, he is now filing a fiancée petition within two years of the approval of a prior petition. Duke can seek a waiver to overcome this impediment so that his petition for Eleanor can be granted, but he must provide evidence to show that none of the factors to be considered apply to him.**

IMBRA further requires the Department of Homeland Security, or DHS, to maintain a database of U.S. citizens who have filed multiple petitions for fiancé(e)s or K-3 spouses. Once a second petition for either of these categories has been approved, DHS must notify the petitioner that a record is being maintained in the database tracker.[110] Any additional petitions filed by the same petitioner will be entered into the database. Also, filing a third petition within ten years of the approval of two prior petitions will result in the notification of both petitioner and beneficiary of the number of previous petitions approved.[111] In addition, the USCIS will mail a copy of a pamphlet on domestic violence information and resources to the beneficiary.[112]

It is important to note that a foreign national who enters the United States in K-1 or K-2 status can only adjust status through marriage to the U.S. citizen petitioner who filed for his or her benefit. S/he cannot be granted status to remain in any other capacity, other than asylum[113] or cancellation of removal. Should the marriage break down and the foreign national seek to obtain immigration benefits through a different U. S. citizen, s/he must first return home and consular process for a different visa.

The BIA has held that a fiancé(e) who enters into a *bona fide* marriage within 90 days of entry to the United States but later separates from or divorces the U.S. citizen petitioner before adjusting status may still be granted LPR status.[114] By marrying the fiancé(e) petitioner within the required time frame and demonstrating that it was a *bona fide* marriage, the beneficiary has complied with all of the requirements of the K visa. Thus, despite the fact that the couple were unable to stay together, the beneficiary may be able to adjust status based on that marriage.

---

[110] INA § 214 (r)(4)(A).
[111] INA § 214(r)(4)(B)(i).
[112] INA § 214(r)(4)(B)(ii). For information on this pamphlet, *see* https://www.uscis.gov/sites/default/files/USCIS/Humanitarian/Battered%20Spouse%2C%20Children%20%26%20Parents/IMBRA%20Pamphlet%20Final%2001-07-2011%20for%20Web%20Posting.pdf.
[113] *See* Chapter 5, Asylum and Other Related Humanitarian Relief.
[114] *See Matter of Sesay*, 25 I&N Dec. 431 (BIA 2011).

Although this appears to benefit those who separate or divorce, there is a major hurdle preventing many from utilizing the BIA's decision. This is because both the USCIS and some immigration judges appear to require that the *original petitioner* complete an affidavit of support, as required under the law for sponsored immigrants. Consequently, only a small number of people may benefit from this decision, namely those who filed adjustment applications, including a qualifying affidavit of support filed by the petitioning U.S. citizen spouse, before the separation of the couple or the U.S. citizen withdrew the approved fiancé(e) petition. Yet this too is unsatisfactory since it would be unfair to hold a petitioner to the contractual obligations of the affidavit of support when s/he clearly no longer wishes to be married to and presumptively responsible for the beneficiary. Resolution of this issue will likely require further guidance from the USCIS or the courts.

K. Conclusion

The process of adjusting status in the United States or of applying for immigrant visas at consular posts abroad cut across many types of immigration benefits, whether based on a relationship to a family member or through employment. As we move through some of the other categories of immigration status, it will be helpful to review the procedures explained here, since the basic principles on how to complete consular processing abroad or file adjustment applications in the United States are substantially the same. They will be particularly useful as we now move on to applications for LPR status based on employment.

Employment-Based and Self-Sponsored Immigration

Key Terms and Acronyms

Academic Field
Actual Wage
Advanced Degree
Affiliate
BALCA
Commercial Enterprise
Department of Labor
EB-1, EB-2, EB-3, EB-4, EB-5
Extraordinary Ability
New Enterprise
PERM
Permanent Research Position
Prevailing Wage
Regional Center
Skilled Worker Subsidiary
Targeted Employment Area
Troubled Business
U.S. Worker

Chapter Objectives

- Review sources of law for employment-based and other lawful permanent resident status processes
- Understand the various employment-based and other lawful permanent resident status processes
- Analyze the criteria and/or standards for the various employment-based and other lawful permanent resident status processes
- Review the procedure for obtaining lawful permanent resident status

Employment-based immigration law is essentially divided into two categories: nonimmigrant and immigrant visas. The latter is also referred to as lawful permanent resident status, or LPR, or colloquially as "having a green card." Non-immigrant visas, discussed in Chapters 2 to 4, are for those who wish to come to the United States for only a temporary period to visit, study, or work, although that might be for several years at a time. Immigrant visas allow foreign nationals to remain in the United States on a permanent basis and to make it their home.

Similar to family sponsored immigration, employment-based immigrant visas delineate preference categories[1] available for those who are of extraordinary ability or outstanding professors or researchers; are highly skilled workers or professionals; specific types of immigrants; or those who decide to take risks by investing in or creating jobs for the American workforce. Established by the Immigration and Nationality Act of 1990, the employment based preference system recognizes the achievements of the many foreign nationals who contribute to the rich tapestry that is the American economy.

This chapter focuses primarily on employment-based pathways to obtain LPR status where an employer must be the sponsor, but will also discuss other types of LPR status applications where the foreign national can self-sponsor. It will also discuss obtaining LPR status through investment in the U.S. or through qualified work in a religious occupation.

A. Overview and Sources of Law

As discussed in Chapter 1, Historical Background and Introduction to the U.S. Immigration System, the foundation of immigration law is the Immigration and Nationality Act, or INA. The relevant sections of the statute for this chapter include §§ 201-206, with § 203 specifically dealing with the "Allocation of Immigrant Visas," including those for employment purposes.

Various agencies of the federal government, including the United States Citizenship and Immigration Service, or USCIS, the Department of State, or DOS, and the Department of Labor, or DOL, all of which are involved in the implementation of immigration law, issue federal regulations that help to interpret and implement the INA. These regulations, found in the Code of Federal Regulations, or C.F.R., are extremely important to help interpret the employment-based and other immigrant visa options discussed in this chapter. Because there are often multiple agencies involved throughout the immigrant visa or LPR status process, it is essential to consult the various agencies' regulations, which are sometimes in conflict. The relevant regulations include:

- The Department of Homeland Security's, or DHS's, Immigration and Naturalization regulations. Section 204 of Title 8 C.F.R. refers to "Immigrant Visa Petitions," with §§ 204.5-204.13 dealing with employment-based LPR status and other options to be discussed in this chapter. Carefully reading and

---

[1] *See* Section A.2 of Chapter 6, Family Sponsored Immigration and Permanent Resident Status.

regularly consulting these regulations when preparing immigrant petitions is essential.
- The DOS's Foreign Relations regulations. Section 42 of Title 22 C.F.R. includes helpful information regarding consular processing for employment-based immigrants,[2] while 22 C.F.R. § 42.33 deals with Diversity Immigrants, discussed in Section I.1 of this chapter.
- The DOL's Employment and Training Administration's Labor Certification for Permanent Employment of Aliens in the United States regulations. Section 656 of Title 20 C.F.R. contains the Program Electronic Review Management process, commonly referred to as the labor certification, or **PERM,** regulations, includes the DOL regulations related to the recruitment-based PERM labor certification application process. As described in Section D, this process is, in many cases, the first step of the employment-based LPR status procedure. It requires the U.S. employer to obtain labor certification from the DOL before it can submit an immigrant petition to the USCIS on behalf of its intended foreign employee.

Case law also plays a very important role in interpreting and applying the INA as well as the C.F.R. especially when dealing with employment-based immigrant visas. In addition to opinions from U.S. Federal Courts, careful attention should be given to case law stemming from administrative and appellate courts, including:

- The Board of Immigration Appeals, or BIA. Under the U.S. Department of Justice, the BIA is the highest administrative body for interpreting and applying immigration laws. It has nationwide jurisdiction to hear appeals from certain decisions issued by immigration judges and by district directors of the USCIS in a wide variety of proceedings in which the Government of the United States is one party and the other party is a foreign national, a citizen, or a business.[3]
- The Administrative Appeals Office, or AAO. Under the DHS, the AAO is the appellate body that reviews most appeals from the USCIS petition or application denials.
- The Board of Alien Labor Certification Appeals, or BALCA. Under the DOL, BALCA is the appellate body that reviews appeals for PERM labor certification application denials.

In addition to the statutes, regulations, and case law, there are other very helpful sources relied on by both the USCIS and the DOL when interpreting and applying immigration law. These include the USCIS' Policy Manual and Memoranda, and the DOL's Employment and Training Administration's Foreign Labor Certification Frequently Asked Questions.

---

[2] 22 C.F.R. § 42.32.
[3] Chapter 10, Immigration Court Practice and Relief from Removal, discusses the role of this agency in detail.

Employment-based, or EB, LPR status is divided essentially into five groups:

- Employment-Based First Preference Category, or EB-1, for "Priority Workers," which includes foreign nationals with extraordinary ability in the sciences, arts education, business, or athletics; outstanding professors and researchers; and certain multinational executives and managers
- Employment-Based Second Preference Category, or EB-2, for foreign nationals who are members of the professions holding advanced degrees or of exceptional ability
- Employment-Based Third Preference Category, or EB-3, for skilled workers, professionals, and "other workers"
- Employment-Based Fourth Preference Category, or EB-4, for certain special immigrants, including, among many others, religious workers
- Employment-Based Fifth Preference Category, or EB-5, for employment creation available to wealthy business investors who are willing to place their capital at risk and create full-time jobs in the United States for at least ten U.S. citizens or LPRs

As with the family sponsored preference categories discussed in Section A.2 of Chapter 6, Family Sponsored Immigration and Permanent Resident Status, each of the employment-based preference categories are subject to extremely strict, annual limitations or quotas in addition to the per-country limits. Based on country of birth and not country of citizenship, these per-country limits cap the percentage of visa numbers that can be given to individuals from each country annually. This means that every country, no matter how large or small, is given the exact same maximum percentage allocation of the worldwide quota.

As a result of these limitations, individuals in certain highly sought after employment-based preference categories and/or from countries with high rates of employment-based U.S. immigration, such as India and China, are subject to long waiting times.[4] A sample bulletin for July 2015 is shown in Table 7.1, listing the different employment-based preference categories and the priority or processing dates the USCIS and DOS have reached for applications received.

In recognition of the need for these highly skilled professionals to become permanent members of the U.S. workforce, on November 20, 2014, President Barack Obama announced an Executive Order directing the DOS and the USCIS to work together to review the manner in which these limited visa numbers are allocated and to take steps to ensure that none of them are wasted in the future.[5]

---

[4] This is discussed in detail in Section A.2 of Chapter 6, Family Sponsored Immigration and Permanent Resident Status, which references the Visa Bulletin for July 2015. The Department of State's monthly-issued Visa Bulletin is available at https://travel.state.gov/content/visas/en/law-and-policy/bulletin.html.
[5] *See* U.S. Department of Homeland Security November 20, 2014 Memorandum entitled "Policies Supporting U.S. High-Skilled Businesses and Workers."

Table 7.1 State Department Visa Bulletin, July 2015

Employment-Based	All Chargeability Areas Except Those Listed	China—Mainland Born	India	Mexico	Philippines
1st	C	C	C	C	C
2nd	C	01OCT13	01OCT08	C	C
3rd	01APR15	01SEP11	01FEB04	01APR15	U
Other Workers	01APR15	01JAN06	01FEB04	01APR15	U
4th	C	C	C	C	C
Certain Religious Workers	C	C	C	C	C
5th Targeted Employment Areas/Regional Centers and Pilot Programs	C	01SEP13	C	C	C

Source: U.S. Department of State.

In September 2015, in response to this directive and a subsequent White House Report,[6] the USCIS and the DOS revised the Visa Bulletin to include two charts per visa preference category. Now, one chart indicates application "final action" dates (i.e., dates when visas may be issued) and the other dates for filing applications (i.e., the earliest dates that applicants may apply for permanent residency).[7] This revised two-tiered system is designed to more accurately predict visa demand and determine the cut-off dates for visa issuance as published in the bulletin. It will also maximize visa issuance by ensuring that the highest number of immigrant visas allowed by Congress is used while minimizing the monthly fluctuations in the final adjudication of these applications for permanent residency. A sample of the new final action date chart is shown in Table 7.2.

The second is the earliest date for filing applications, even though a visa may not be issued for several months. As mentioned in Chapter 6, Family Sponsored Immigration and Lawful Permanent Resident Status, in order to use this second chart, USCIS must determine that there are more immigrant visas available for a fiscal year than there are known applicants for such visas, as indicated on its website.[8] A sample of the new dates for filing appears in Table 7.3.

---

[6] *See* July 2015 White House Report, "Modernizing & Streamlining Our Legal Immigration System for the 21t Century," available at https://www.whitehouse.gov/sites/default/files/docs/final_visa_modernization_report1.pdf.
[7] This is discussed in detail in Section A.2 of Chapter 6, Family Sponsored Immigration and Permanent Resident Status.
[8] The website can be accessed at https://www.uscis.gov/visabulletininfo and will state that the Dates for Filing Visa Applications chart may be used. Otherwise, the page will indicate that only the Application Final Action Dates chart may be used to determine when a foreign national may file an adjustment of status application.

Table 7.2 State Department Visa Bulletin May 2016: Application Final Action Dates for Employment-Based Preference Cases

Employment-Based	All Chargeability Areas Except Those Listed	China—Mainland Born	El Salvador Guatemala Honduras	India	Mexico	Philippines
1st	C	C	C	C	C	C
2nd	C	01SEP12	C	22NOV08	C	C
3rd	15FEB16	15AUG13	15FEB16	01SEP04	15FEB16	08AUG08
Other Workers	15FEB16	22APR07	15FEB16	01SEP04	15FEB16	08AUG08
4th	C	C	01JAN10	C	C	C
Certain Religious Workers	C	C	01JAN10	C	C	C
5th Non-Regional Center (C5 and T5)	C	08FEB14	C	C	C	C
5th Regional Center (I5 and R5)	C	08FEB14	C	C	C	C

Source: U.S. Department of State.

In most cases, a job offer from a qualifying employer, acting as a petitioner, is required to commence an employment-based immigrant case. In some cases, however, the foreign national can self-petition based on the importance, benefit, or need for his or her work to the U.S. economy. However, s/he must still show income-producing work is available in the United States in the field where permission to enter is sought. Fortunately, the requirements for some of these immigrant categories often somewhat mirror their nonimmigrant counterparts. For example, the nonimmigrant O-1 Extraordinary Ability, compared to the immigrant EB-1 Extraordinary Ability, and the nonimmigrant L-1A Multinational Executives and Managers, compared to the immigrant EB-1 Multinational Executives and Managers, have similar criteria, though there are some critical distinctions. This allows the individual preparing the immigrant petition to draw and expand upon work previously done and submitted to the USCIS for the earlier temporary visa classification. It also underscores the importance of the best practice of always referring to prior petitions to ensure consistency between nonimmigrant and immigrant processes.

Table 7.3 State Department Visa Bulletin May 2016: Dates for Filing Employment-Based Visa Applications

Employment-Based	All Chargeability Areas Except Those Listed	China— Mainland Born	India	Mexico	Philippines
1st	C	C	C	C	C
2nd	C	01JUN13	01JUL09	C	C
3rd	C	01MAY15	01JUL05	C	01JAN10
Other Workers	C	01APR08	01JUL05	C	01JAN10
4th	C	C	C	C	C
Certain Religious Workers	C	C	C	C	C
5th Non-Regional Center (C5 and T5)	C	01MAY15	C	C	C
5th Regional Center (I5 and R5)	C	01MAY15	C	C	C

Employment-based applications, when successful, lead to the ultimate end goal for many foreign nationals, a green card or LPR status for him or her, as well as for qualifying derivative family members such as a spouse and any unmarried children under the age of 21 years.

B. Shared Requirements for Permanent Residency Categories

Each section of this chapter discusses the applicable procedure for obtaining LPR status within the classification discussed. However, it is important to understand the big picture of the employment-based immigration process, which is similar to family sponsored applications. Typically, the employment-based immigration process is either a two- or three-step process.

As mentioned earlier, most of the employment-based categories require the foreign national to have an existing job offer from a U.S. employer, who will serve as the petitioner.[9] Moreover, for some of these categories, before the U.S. employer can submit an immigrant petition to the USCIS, it must first obtain

---

[9] The categories requiring an employer-petitioner are: Outstanding professors and researchers, INA § 203(b)(1)(B)(iii); professionals holding advanced degrees, INA § 203(b)(2), except those applying for a National Interest Waiver, *see* INA § 203(b)(2)(B); skilled workers, professionals and other workers, INA § 203(b)(3).

labor certification approval from the DOL.[10] The certification, commonly referred to by its acronym, PERM[11] will verify that: 1) there are insufficient available, qualified, and willing U.S. workers to fill the position being offered at the prevailing wage;[12] and 2) hiring a foreign worker will not adversely affect the wages and working conditions of similarly employed U.S. workers.[13]

Once an employer obtains the approved labor certification if required, the entity can then file a Form I-140, Immigrant Petition for Alien Worker, with the USCIS for the appropriate employment-based preference category.

If no labor certification is required for the employment-based category sought, the employer commences the process with the filing of Form I-140, Immigrant Petition for Alien Worker. This petition is the equivalent of the relative based petition, or Form I-130, Petition for Alien Relative, required in family adjustment cases, as discussed in Section C of Chapter 6, Family Sponsored Immigration and Permanent Resident Status.

Whenever there is a petitioning employer, the entity must submit evidence of the ability to pay the proffered wage[14] with Form I-140, Immigrant Petition for Alien Worker, or Form I-360, Petition for Amerasian, Widow(er), or Special Immigrant (but in this context used for Special Immigrants only, as discussed in Section G). Evidence of this must be in the form of copies of annual financial reports, federal tax returns, or audited financial statements. If the employer employs 100 or more workers, a statement from a financial officer attesting to the employer's ability to pay is generally sufficient.[15]

If an immigrant visa is immediately available for the foreign national in his or her employment-based preference category, meaning there are no backlogs and the person is in the United States, then s/he and any qualifying derivative family members who are also here can apply to adjust status to an LPR using Form I-485, Application to Register Permanent Residence or Adjust Status, at the same time. If the foreign national is in the United States but his or her qualifying derivative family members are abroad, s/he can apply to adjust status and, once granted, the family members can apply at a consular office abroad for immigrant visas through following-to-join. If, however, the foreign national is outside the country or does not wish to apply for adjustment of status from within the United States, then s/he and any qualifying family members will be eligible to apply for an immigrant visa at the consulate once the Form I-140, Immigrant Petition for Alien Worker, is approved.[16] It is important to note, however, that if an immigrant visa is not available due to the quota and/or per country annual limit, the foreign national and any qualifying derivatives

---

[10] INA § 212(a)(5)(A).
[11] This is discussed in detail in Section 7.D.
[12] 20 C.F.R. § 656.1(a)(1).
[13] *Id.* at § 656.1(a)(2).
[14] 8 C.F.R. § 204.5(g)(2).
[15] *Id. See also* USCIS May 4, 2004 Policy Memorandum entitled "Determination of Ability to Pay Under 8 CFR 204.5(g)(2)," HQOPRD 90/16.45.
[16] Detailed discussion of adjustment of status and consular processing are discussed in greater detail in Chapter 6, Family Sponsored Immigration and Permanent Resident Status.

must wait until the foreign national's priority date is reached, which will be reflected on the DOS's online monthly Visa Bulletin. If the foreign national is in the United States, s/he and any qualifying family members *must* maintain valid nonimmigrant status until his or her priority date becomes current and the adjustment application is filed or else they will be ineligible to file here and must do so from abroad.[17] Certain beneficiaries of employment-based petitions may apply for permanent resident status in the United States even if they failed to maintain nonimmigrant status, engaged in unauthorized employment, or otherwise violated the terms of their admission, so long as they have not done so for an aggregate period of more than 180 days.[18] This benefit is not available to those nonimmigrants who are not immediate relatives.[19]

In the employment-based immigration context, the foreign national's priority date is either the filing date of the labor certification application or, for categories that do not require labor certification, the filing date of the immigrant petition.[20] In some heavily impacted employment-based categories, the waiting period is more than ten years. Because of these long waiting times, many foreign nationals, especially those who are dependent upon an employer's sponsorship for their LPR status, may choose to simultaneously file employment-based petitions in several different categories *and* family sponsored petitions where there are qualifying family relatives able to file for them. These strategies are permissible and sometimes advisable, so long as all submissions to the USCIS and DOL are carefully prepared and examined to ensure consistency.

C. Priority Workers, Aliens with Extraordinary Ability, Outstanding Professors and Researchers, and Certain Multinational Executives and Managers (EB-1): INA § 203(b)(1)(A), 8 C.F.R. § 204.5(h); 8 C.F.R. § 204.5(i); 8 C.F.R. § 204.5(j)

The EB-1 category includes three sub categories: 1) aliens with extraordinary ability, 2) outstanding professors and researchers, and 3) certain multinational executives and managers.

---

[17] As discussed in Section B.1 of Chapter 6, Family Sponsored Immigration and Permanent Resident Status, those seeking to adjust status here must be in lawful nonimmigrant status unless, in limited circumstances, they are the immediate relatives of U.S. citizens. This will not apply in the employment-based context. In addition, those who have accrued unlawful presence but need to consular process abroad for an immigrant visa may find that they have run afoul of the three- and ten-year bar, thereby requiring an unlawful presence waiver to be approved. Section G.3.a of Chapter 6 discusses this in further detail.
[18] INA § 245(k). *See also* USCIS July 14, 2008 Policy Memorandum entitled "Applicability of Section 245(k) to Certain Employment-Based Adjustment of Status Applications filed under Section 245(a) of the Immigration and Nationality Act" HQDOMO 70/23.1-PA06-07.
[19] *See* Section G.1. of Chapter 6, Family Sponsored Immigration and Permanent Resident Status.
[20] 8 C.F.R. § 204.5(d).

C.1. EB-1A Aliens with Extraordinary Ability in the Sciences, Arts, Education, Business, or Athletics

Foreign nationals who possess an extraordinary ability in the sciences, arts, education, business, or athletics can obtain permanent resident status if they will be working in the area of extraordinary ability and such work will substantially benefit prospectively the United States.[21] This classification is known as the employment-based first preference category for those with extraordinary ability, or EB-1A. It is reserved for those foreign nationals who are truly the best and brightest in their field. In fact, the USCIS regulations specifically define the term "extraordinary ability" as "a level of expertise indicating that the individual is one of that small percentage who have risen to the very top of the field of endeavor."[22] This definition establishes a very high standard for EB-1A classification for which a job offer is not required.[23] Therefore, the foreign national can either self-petition or have an employer petition on his or her behalf. It is important to note however, that if a self-petition is submitted, the foreign national must still prove that s/he intends to be employed in his or her specialty field.[24]

To meet the high standard for EB-1A Extraordinary Ability classification, the foreign national must be able to demonstrate an extraordinary ability in the sciences, arts, education, business, or athletics through sustained national or international acclaim demonstrated through extensive documentation. The USCIS has clarified in its *Adjudicator's Field Manual*, or AFM, that the word "sustained" does not imply an age limit or career limit on the foreign national. Therefore, even a young foreign national may be able to establish sustained national or international acclaim, so long as the person can show that s/he has maintained such acclaim, even if for a relatively short period.

Foreign nationals can substantiate their extraordinary ability and sustained national or international recognition in two ways. First, evidence of a one-time achievement, defined in the regulations as receipt of a major, internationally recognized award, will in and of itself qualify a foreign national for EB-1A classification.[25] Examples of such awards would include a Nobel or Pulitzer Prize, an Olympic Medal, an Emmy, a Grammy, etc. If the foreign national has not won an award of such caliber, then s/he will need to satisfy a two-part test, sometimes referred to as the *Kazarian* test. *See Kazarian v. USCIS*, 596 F.3d 1115 (9th Cir. 2010). In this case, the U.S. Court of Appeals for the Ninth Circuit established a two-step process for analyzing and adjudicating EB-1A petitions that was subsequently adopted by the USCIS in its December 22, 2010 Policy

> **Adjudicator's Field Manual:** A USCIS publication that details its policies and procedures for adjudicating applications and petitions.

---

[21] INA § 203(b)(1)(A), 8 C.F.R. § 204.5(h).
[22] 8 C.F.R. § 204.5(h)(2).
[23] 8 C.F.R. § 204.5(h)(5).
[24] *Id.*
[25] 8 C.F.R. § 204.5(h)(3).

Memorandum entitled "Evaluation of Evidence Submitted with Certain Form I-140 Petitions,"[26] and incorporated into the USCIS' AFM at Chapter 22.2.

Step one of the *Kazarian* test requires that the foreign national provide evidence showing that s/he meets at least three of ten criteria listed in the regulations. The ten criteria are:

- Evidence of receipt of lesser nationally or internationally recognized prizes or awards for excellence;
- Evidence of membership in associations in the field that demand outstanding achievement of their members;
- Evidence of published material about the foreign national in professional or major trade publications or other major media;
- Evidence that the foreign national has been asked to judge the work of others, either individually or on a panel;
- Evidence of the foreign national's original scientific, scholarly, artistic, athletic, or business-related contributions of major significance to the field, typically attested to by experts in the field via expert testimonial letters;
- Evidence of the foreign national's authorship of scholarly articles in professional or major trade publications or other major media;
- Evidence that the foreign national's work has been displayed at artistic exhibitions or showcases;
- Evidence of the foreign national's performance of a leading or critical role in distinguished organizations;
- Evidence that the foreign national commands a high salary or other significantly high remuneration in relation to others in the field; and/or
- Evidence of the foreign national's commercial successes in the performing arts.[27]

Interestingly, the USCIS regulations provide that, if the ten listed criteria do not readily apply to the foreign national's area of extraordinary ability, the foreign national can submit "comparable evidence" to establish his or her eligibility for EB-1A classification.[28] Because the USCIS does not define this term, individuals preparing the EB-1A petition have a considerable amount of flexibility in the type of documentation they can submit. For example, depending on the particular field, comparable evidence may include prestigious fellowships, expertise with advanced technology, patents, or a rare combination of skills. The type of comparable evidence used will depend largely on the foreign national's area of expertise and the factors relied on in the field to judge and evaluate the best of the best.

Objectively meeting the regulatory criteria, however, will not establish alone that the foreign national meets the requirements for EB-1A classification. The foreign national must still satisfy the second step of the *Kazarian* test: the final merits decision. This step involves a more subjective evaluation of the quality of

---

[26] Available here: https://www.uscis.gov/sites/default/files/USCIS/Laws/Memoranda/i-140-evidence-pm-6002-005-1.pdf.
[27] *Id. See also* 8 C.F.R. § 204.5(h)(3).
[28] 8 C.F.R. § 204.5(h)(4).

the submitted evidence in its entirety by the USCIS adjudicator. In essence, s/he must decide, after considering all the evidence together, whether the foreign national has truly demonstrated a level of sustained national or international acclaim in the field of expertise that indicates that s/he is one of that small percentage who has risen to the very top of his or her field of endeavor.

Therefore, in addition to providing evidence of each of the criteria satisfied, the foreign national must also explain or show how his or her satisfaction of each criterion sets him or her apart, distinguishing him or her from others in the field. It is not sufficient to provide the USCIS with only copies of the foreign national's scholarly articles. Instead, it might also be shown that the article was published in a prestigious and top-ranked journal in the field and that other scholars in his or her field from around the country or the world have cited the article numerous times since publication. Similarly, it is not sufficient merely to provide evidence that major trade publications or other media outlets have reported on the foreign national's work. Instead, s/he might also show that the particular trade publication is the most widely read in the industry, or that those media outlets that reported on the work are reputable and highly respected.

Case for Discussion 7.1

Craig, from New Zealand, is the Principal French Horn player with the Chicago Symphony Orchestra, or CSO, listed among the world's top ten orchestras. Craig has previously played as both part of the orchestra and as a soloist with the New Zealand Symphony Orchestra as well as the Berlin Philharmonic, which is listed among the top ten orchestras in the world. In addition, the renowned Colorado Music Festival has repeatedly invited him to perform as a soloist. His performances have received rave reviews in major media outlets, including an article in the Chicago Tribune that described his performance with the CSO as "flawless." He is interested in pursuing an EB-1A petition. The conductor of the CSO, recognized internationally as one of the best conductor's in the world, is eager to support his petition.

- Which criteria would Craig satisfy under step one of the *Kazarian* test?
- What types of documents would Craig need to provide the USCIS to satisfy both step one and two of the *Kazarian* test?

Of course, the type of documentation used to establish a high level of sustained national or international acclaim will vary significantly depending on the foreign national's area of extraordinary ability. An athlete will certainly provide different documentation and arguments to that offered by a scientist, artist, or businessperson. Also, it is important to note that the "extraordinary ability" standard an artist must meet to obtain temporary O-1 nonimmigrant classification—i.e., "distinction" in the field[29]—is much lower than that required for EB-1A classification for purposes of permanent residency—i.e., "one of that small percentage who have risen to the very top of the field of endeavor."[30] Thus, O-1 artists who were previously deemed "extraordinary" by USCIS may have a harder time convincing the agency that they meet the higher "extraordinary" standard, thus meriting EB-1A classification. It is up to the person preparing the extraordinary ability petition to work closely with the foreign national to determine which criteria the foreign national satisfies and what type of documentation can be included to highlight the foreign national's high level of sustained national or international acclaim so that s/he can meet this higher standard.

Finally, in addition to satisfying the *Kazarian* test, the foreign national must establish s/he intends to continue working in the area of extraordinary ability upon entry to or adjustment of status in the United States and must demonstrate that his or her entry or change of status will substantially benefit the country prospectively.[31] In other words, the foreign national must want to continue working in his or her field and the work must in some way benefit or help the United States.

Case for Discussion 7.2

Craig, the French Horn player introduced earlier, is feeling burnt out after 15 years of constant performing and frequent travel. Through his performances, he has collected a considerably large nest egg and is hoping that, once he obtains LPR status in the United States, he can retire and pursue full time his other passion and hobby, composing music.

- Can Craig still pursue an EB-1A Petition?
- What if he plans to compose music for french horns?

C.2. EB-1B for Outstanding Researchers and Professors

Professors and researchers at institutions of higher education and at certain companies, who are internationally recognized as outstanding within their *academic field*,[32] can obtain LPR status based on their employment and stature in that field.[33]

Academic Field: A body of specialized knowledge offered for study at an accredited U.S. university or institution of higher education.

---

[29] 8 C.F.R. § 214.2(o)(3)(ii). This category is discussed in Section A of Chapter 4, Nonimmigrant Visas for Extraordinary Ability, Religious Workers, and Ancillary Activities.
[30] 8 C.F.R. § 204.5(h)(2).
[31] 8 C.F.R. § 204.5(h)(5).
[32] 8 C.F.R. § 204.5(i)(2).
[33] INA § 203(b)(1)(B), 8 C.F.R. § 204.5(i).

This classification is known as the employment-based first preference category for outstanding professors and researchers, or EB-1B. Professors, researchers, and scientists employed by higher education institutions, nonprofit research organizations, for-profit companies with research departments, or divisions such as pharmaceutical companies or biotechnology companies commonly use this category.

There are three threshold requirements for the EB-1B classification. The first requirement is that the foreign national must have an offer of employment from a prospective U.S. employer.[34] Therefore, unlike the EB-1A Extraordinary Ability Category, the foreign national cannot self-petition. Instead, the employer files the petition, as petitioner, on behalf of the foreign national who is the beneficiary. The offer of employment must come from a qualifying employer, which, per the regulations and as suggested earlier, include only:

- U.S. universities or institutions of higher learning, or
- A department, division, or institute of a private employer that employs at least three persons full-time in research positions.[35]

In addition, only certain types of positions qualify for EB-1B classification:

- A tenured or tenure-track position at a U.S. university or institution of higher learning,
- A **permanent research position** at a U.S. university or institution of higher learning, or
- A permanent research position with a private employer, within the department, division, or institute that employs at least three full-time researchers.[36]

For researcher positions, the immigration regulations define the term permanent as either tenured, tenure-track, or for a term of unlimited duration, and in which the employee will ordinarily have an expectation of continued employment.[37] A signed employment contract or offer letter that specifies the title and nature of the position will typically suffice as evidence of a qualifying offer of permanent employment. Most assistant professors at U.S. universities receive offer letters defining the position as tenure-track. Some employment contracts, however, may not be as clear. For example, many research positions at institutions of higher education, and even at private companies, are funded by grant money that is issued for a project of a specific duration or that is issued on a yearly or bi-annual basis.

The USCIS clarified in its June 6, 2006 Policy Memorandum, entitled "Guidance on the Requirement of a 'Permanent Offer of Employment' for

---

[34] 8 C.F.R. § 204.5(i)(3)(iv).
[35] 8 C.F.R. § 204.5(i)(3)(iv)(C).
[36] Id.
[37] 8 C.F.R. § 204.5(i)(2).

Outstanding Professors and Researchers,"[38] that even positions funded by grants of a limited duration will be considered permanent, so long as the petitioning employer demonstrates both the intent to continue to seek funding and a reasonable expectation that funding will continue. The employer can provide the USCIS with evidence of prior approvals of grant renewal applications and a statement confirming that it will seek a renewal of the current grant to satisfy the requirement of a permanent offer of employment. Other evidence that would show that a position is permanent might include the benefits attached to the position, such as health insurance benefits, which are typically only offered to these employees.

The second threshold requirement for EB-1B classification is that the foreign national must have at least three years of experience in teaching and/or research in his or her academic field.[39] The USCIS makes an important distinction, however, between experience gained after receiving an advanced degree versus experience gained while pursuing an advanced degree. The regulations state that experience in teaching while working on an advanced degree will only be acceptable if the teaching duties were such that the foreign national had full responsibility for the class taught.[40] Therefore, a graduate student teaching assistant position that involved providing classroom support to a full-time professor would not count toward satisfying the three-year experience requirement. Similarly, research conducted toward the advanced degree will only be acceptable if it has been recognized within the academic field as outstanding.[41] Essentially, the USCIS understands that most graduate students are required to conduct research, publish, and engage in scholarly activities such as presentations, etc. This will only count as graduate research experience, however, if it is unusually significant within the field and has received a high level of international recognition.

● **EXAMPLE**

After six years of studies, Dr. Chaudry received her Ph.D. in Bioengineering last month. During her doctoral studies, Dr. Chaudry developed a new drug delivery system for diabetes medication. The number one ranked journal in her field published her research and more than ten leading bioengineering conferences around the world have invited her to present her findings. Scientists have widely praised her research as outstanding and she received multiple job offers from leading pharmaceutical companies. She has just accepted an offer from a major pharmaceutical company in the United States. Even though Dr. Chaudry just received her Ph.D. degree, the USCIS will accept her graduate research experience as qualifying research experience because it has been recognized within the field as outstanding. Moreover, she has a qualifying job offer from a U.S. private employer that employs hundreds of full time researchers.

---

[38] Available at https://www.uscis.gov/sites/default/files/USCIS/Laws/Memoranda/Static_Files_Memoranda/Archives%201998-2008/2006/eb1visa060606.pdf.
[39] 8 C.F.R. § 204.5(i)(3)(iii).
[40] *Id.*
[41] *Id.*

The last threshold requirement for EB-1B classification is that the foreign professor or researcher must demonstrate that s/he is internationally recognized as outstanding within the academic field.[42] Similar to the EB-1A extraordinary ability process, this requires satisfying the two-part *Kazarian* test. In its December 22, 2010 Policy Memorandum, entitled "Evaluation of Evidence Submitted with Certain Form I-140 Petitions," the USCIS clarified that it would apply the *Kazarian* two-part analysis to both EB-1A, extraordinary ability petitions, and EB-1B, outstanding professor and researcher petitions.

For EB-1B, outstanding researcher petitions, step one of the *Kazarian* test requires that the foreign national provide evidence showing that s/he meets at least two of six criteria listed in the regulations. The six criteria include:

- Evidence of receipt of major prizes or awards for outstanding achievement;
- Evidence of membership in associations that require their members to demonstrate outstanding achievement;
- Evidence of published material in professional publications written by others about the foreign national's work in the academic field;
- Evidence of participation, either on a panel or individually, as a judge of the work of others in the same or an allied academic field;
- Evidence of original scientific or scholarly research contributions in the field, typically attested to by experts in the field via expert testimonial letters; and
- Evidence of authorship of scholarly books or articles in scholarly journals with international circulation in the field.[43]

As with the EB-1A extraordinary ability classification, the EB-1B regulations allow the production of comparable evidence if the listed criteria do not readily apply to the foreign national's academic field.[44]

Case for Discussion 7.3

Dr. Romanov received her Ph.D. in Computer Science last year. Since then, she has been working in a non-tenure track, temporary instructor position at a top university. She accepted the position because the university has the best computer security program in the country, which is her research focus. Over the past year, in addition to teaching she has been busy researching and has developed a new program for enhancing security and privacy in cloud systems. She is thrilled because a top computer science journal just accepted for

---

[42] 8 C.F.R. § 204.5(i)(3)(i).
[43] *Id.*
[44] 8 C.F.R. § 204.5(i)(3)(ii).

publication her article discussing her research. In addition, she has already presented her article and research at three international computer security conferences and is receiving great feedback. A tenure-track assistant professor position just opened up at the university and she is in the process of applying for the position. She is anxious to become a permanent resident so that she can apply for more grants.

- What are the strengths and weaknesses of her case vis-à-vis the EB-1B outstanding professor requirements?

In addition to satisfying step one of the *Kazarian* test, demonstrating at least two of the six regulatory criteria listed, the foreign national professor and/or researcher must also satisfy step two of the *Kazarian* test, which is the final merits determination. As with the EB-1A extraordinary ability standard, the USCIS adjudicator is required to evaluate the quality of all the evidence in its totality to determine if the foreign national professor or researcher has demonstrated a degree of expertise and international recognition within his or her field that is "significantly above that ordinarily encountered" within the field.[45] In other words, the foreign national needs to demonstrate that s/he is "above others in the field."[46] Again, this might be established by including testimonial letters from international experts, attesting to the foreign national's international reputation and recognition and/or by showing not only that the foreign researcher has published articles in internationally circulated journals, but also that the journals are the best in the field and the articles have been heavily cited by scholars from around the world.

Case for Discussion 7.4

Dr. Yang, from China, is a Senior Robotics Researcher at Massachusetts Institute of Technology, or MIT. He has developed a prototype for the world's first four-legged robot capable of traveling across rugged terrain and equipped with sensors that can detect both human life and human remains. The robot is expected to be a critical tool in search and rescue and recovery efforts in the aftermath of natural disasters such as tornadoes, hurricanes, and earthquakes. Over the past ten years, Dr. Yang has published 15 articles about this and related robotics projects, all in the highest ranked journals in his field, and his

---

[45] USCIS December 22, 2010 Policy Memorandum, entitled "Evaluation of Evidence Submitted with Certain Form I-140 Petitions," PM-602-005.1.
[46] *Id.*

articles have resulted in over 500 citations by scientists from around the world. National Public Radio also interviewed him and reported on the robot. He was just appointed as an editor for a top journal in the field but is still working at MIT. Dr. Yang would like to pursue an EB-1B Petition.

- What types of documents would he need to provide to satisfy step one of the *Kazarian* test?
- What types of documents could he provide or arguments could he make to satisfy step two of the *Kazarian* test?
- Who will be the petitioner?

C.3. EB-1C for Certain Multinational Executives and Managers

Foreign nationals employed for at least one of the three preceding years by an overseas affiliate, parent, subsidiary, or branch of a U.S. employer and who are working in either an executive or managerial capacity can obtain LPR status based on their employment with the U.S. employer.[47]

Corporate relationships are often very complex and, sometimes, companies can be very secretive about them. Therefore, it is important to always identify the exact nature of the corporate relationship when preparing an EB-1C, Multinational Executive and Manager petition.[48]

● EXAMPLE

Kelly's Koffee, Inc. is a U.S. based company, founded by Kelly Krinkles and headquartered in Seattle, Washington, that has been in existence since 2007. Kelly Krinkles owns 100 percent of the U.S. based company and owns 100 percent of Madrid Coffee Beans, S.A. Kelly's Koffee, Inc. and Madrid Coffee Beans, S.A. are qualifying affiliate corporations because they are owned and controlled by the same individual, Kelly Krinkles.

● EXAMPLE

Kelly's Koffee recently purchased its own roasting company in Buenos Aires, Argentina, Kelly's Koffee, S.A. Kelly's Koffee, Inc. owns 100 percent of the Argentinian Company. Therefore, Kelly's Koffee, S.A. is a wholly owned subsidiary of Kelly's Koffee, Inc.

---

[47] INA § 203(b)(1)(C); 8 C.F.R. § 204.5(j).
[48] For a detailed discussion regarding the various corporate relationships, see Section B.2.a of Chapter 3, Nonimmigrant Visas for Intracompany Transferees, Trade and Investment, and Professional Employment.

When submitting a petition for a multinational executive or manager, the U.S. employer must prove and explain in a statement from an authorized official of the company the following:

- If the [foreign national] is outside the United States, in the three years immediately preceding the filing of the petition the foreign national was employed abroad for at least one year in a managerial or executive capacity by a firm, corporation, or other legal entity, or by an affiliate or subsidiary of such a firm, corporation or other legal entity, which is a "qualifying organization," or
- If the [foreign national] is already in the United States working for the same employer or a subsidiary or affiliate of the firm or corporation, or other legal entity by which the [foreign national] was employed abroad, in the three years preceding entry as a nonimmigrant, s/he was employed by the entity abroad for at least one year in a managerial or executive capacity
- The qualifying relationship between the prospective employer in the United States and the [foreign national's] employer overseas including whether such firms, corporations, or legal entities have a parent-subsidiary relationship, affiliate relationship, or are branch offices of the same firm, corporation, or legal entity, and
- The prospective United States employer has been doing business for at least one year[49]

The USCIS strictly defines what types of executives and managers qualify,[50] and the U. S. employer must include in its petition documentation as well as evidence of the foreign national's "work product" to establish that the foreign national has been and will continue to work in an executive or managerial capacity, defined by the regulations as follows:[51]

- Executive capacity means an assignment within an organization in which the employee primarily:
  - ☐ Directs the management of the organization or a major component or function of the organization;
  - ☐ Establishes the goals and policies of the organization, component, or function;
  - ☐ Exercises wide latitude in discretionary decision- making; and
  - ☐ Receives only general supervision or direction from higher level executives, the board of directors, or stockholders of the organization.

---

[49] 8 C.F.R. § 204.5(j)(3)(i).
[50] It should be noted that unlike the L-1 nonimmigrant visa classification which allows a foreign national who worked abroad in a "specialized knowledge" capacity to qualify for L-1A classification as an executive or manager upon his/her transfer to the United States, a foreign national *must* have worked in an executive or managerial capacity abroad in order to qualify for the EB-1C Multinational Executive or Manager classification for LPR purposes. 8 C.F.R. § 204.5(j)(3). The L-1 nonimmigrant visa classification is discussed in Section B, of Chapter 3, Nonimmigrant Visas for Intracompany Transferees, Trade and Investment, and Professional Employment.
[51] 8 C.F.R. § 204.5(j)(2).

- Managerial capacity means an assignment within an organization in which the employee primarily:
  - ☐ Manages the organization or a department, subdivision, function, or component of the organization;
  - ☐ Supervises and controls the work of other supervisory, professional, or managerial employees, or manages an essential function within the organization, or a department or subdivision of the organization;
  - ☐ If another employee or other employees are directly supervised, has the authority to hire and fire or recommend those as well as other personnel actions, such as promotion and leave authorization, or, if no other employee is directly supervised, functions at a senior level within the organizational hierarchy or with respect to the function managed; and
  - ☐ Exercises direction over the day-to-day operations of the activity or function for which the employee has authority.

The type of documentation that the U.S. employer can include to show that the foreign national was and will continue to work in an executive or managerial capacity includes organizational charts demonstrating the foreign national's position within the company, emails, or letters supporting executive or managerial functions.

Case for Discussion 7.5

Susan, a Canadian citizen, has worked for Yummy Treats Ltd. in Canada for over 16 years as an assistant to the President, where her job duties have mostly included answering the telephones, scheduling appointments for him, and researching international marketing outlets for the company's yummy products. She has an MBA in finance, with a minor in marketing, from Stanford University and speaks four languages fluently. Yummy Treats Ltd has recently established a wholly owned subsidiary in the United States, Yummy Treats, Inc., in Philadelphia. Because of Susan's long-standing relationship with the company and her knowledge of its inner workings, it has decided to transfer her to the United States to set up the new office and hire staff. Her new title will be U.S. Office Manager.

- What problems might Yummy Treats Ltd. encounter in attempting to achieve Susan's transfer to the U.S.?

C.4. Compiling the EB-1 Priority Worker Petition

As with adjustments for family sponsored immigrants,[52] the LPR status application for EB-1 priority workers is a two-step process. First, the qualifying U.S. employer or self-petitioning foreign national must submit to the USCIS Form I-140, Immigrant Petition for Alien Worker, requesting the specific EB-1 sub-classification that it is seeking. The filing packet should include the following:

- Form I-140, Immigrant Petition for Alien Worker
- Form G-28, Notice of Entry of Appearance of Attorney or Accredited Representative, if the applicant has legal representation
- USCIS Filing Fee
- If there is a petitioning employer, evidence of its ability to pay the proffered wage
- Evidence of the employer's and the foreign national's eligibility for the classification sought, unless the foreign national is self-petitioning
- Visa type-specific supporting material:
  - ☐ EB-1
    - Evidence of the foreign national's satisfaction of the two-part *Kazarian* test, including:
      - ☐ Evidence of a one-time achievement, or evidence that s/he satisfies at least three of the ten listed regulatory criteria; or, if the criterion does not readily apply to the foreign national's occupation, any comparable evidence to establish his or her extraordinary ability, and
      - ☐ A demonstration that, collectively, the evidence indicates that the foreign national has sustained national or international acclaim and that his or her achievements have been recognized in the field of expertise
    - Evidence that the foreign national is coming to the United States to continue work in his or her area of expertise, such as letters from prospective employers, evidence of prearranged commitments such as contracts, or a statement from the foreign national detailing plans on how s/he will continue his or her work in the United States
  - ☐ EB-1B
    - Evidence of a qualifying job offer, such as a signed employment contract
    - Evidence of a qualifying employer, such as proof of status as institution of higher education, nonprofit organization, or, if a private company, evidence that such company employs at least three full-time researchers
    - Evidence of a qualifying position, such as a signed employment contract or a letter or statement from the employer
    - Evidence of the foreign national's qualifying three years of research experience, such as employment confirmation letters

---

[52] *See* Section B of Chapter 6, Family Sponsored Immigration and Permanent Resident Status.

- Evidence of the foreign national's satisfaction of the two-part *Kazarian* test including:
    - ☐ Evidence that the foreign national satisfies at least two of the six listed regulatory criteria, and
    - ☐ A demonstration that, collectively, the evidence shows a high level of international recognition for his or her work
- ☐ EB-1C
    - Evidence that the U.S. employer and the foreign national's employer overseas have a qualifying relationship including documents that demonstrate the ownership of the entities such as audited financials that list ownership information, stock certificates, tax returns, and corporate organizational charts
    - Evidence that the foreign national has the requisite one year of experience abroad in an executive or managerial capacity such as an employment confirmation letter and pay stubs or records and
    - Evidence of the foreign national's qualifying executive or managerial position, such as an organizational chart showing the foreign national's subordinates, work product, correspondence between the foreign national and his or her subordinates, and contracts signed by the foreign national on behalf of the company

Although possible, the immigrant visa quota is almost never met in the EB-1 category. Therefore, the foreign national, if in the United States, can typically concurrently file with the employer's Form I-140, Immigrant Petition for Alien Worker, his or her Form I-485, Application to Register for Permanent Residence or Adjust Status, as well as adjustment applications for his or her qualifying derivative family members who are in legal status in the United States. If abroad when the petition is approved, or if the foreign national does not wish to adjust status here, s/he can commence the process of applying for an immigrant visa through consular processing at a consular office abroad.

Detailed discussion of adjustment of status, including how to compile an adjustment of status packet, and consular processing are in Chapter 6, Family Sponsored Immigration and Permanent Resident Status. However, adjustment applications filed in the employment-based context do differ in that the foreign national is not required to submit Form I-864, Affidavit of Support. Instead, evidence of his or her offer of prospective or current employment, including salary demonstrated by paystubs or a letter from the employer, is sufficient to prove that s/he will not become a public charge.[53]

---

[53] *See* Section G.2.f of Chapter 6, Family Sponsored Immigration and Permanent Resident Status, and Section B.4 of Chapter 9, Grounds of Inadmissibility and Deportation, for further discussion of public charge.

D. Advanced Degree Professionals (EB-2) and Skilled Workers, Professionals, and Other Workers (EB-3), and the Perm Labor Certification Application Process: INA § 203(b)(2); INA § 203(b)(3); 8 C.F.R. § 204.5(k); 8 C.F.R. § 204.5(l); 20 C.F.R. § 656

D.1. EB-2 for Advanced Degree Professionals

Foreign nationals who hold an advanced degree and are employed by a U.S. employer in a profession or position that requires such degree, can obtain LPR status in the employment-based second preference category, or EB-2, for professionals with advanced degrees or exceptional ability.[54] In most cases, the foreign national cannot self-petition, with the exception of National Interest waivers,[55] which is addressed in Section F.1. Instead, the U.S. employer must file Form I-140, Immigrant Petition for Alien Worker, on behalf of the foreign national after obtaining an approved Labor Certification from the DOL. Section D.3 discusses this process. No Labor Certification is required for those with exceptional ability in the sciences and the arts (excluding the performing arts) who can show that they have received widespread and international acclaim and meet other regulatory criteria.[56]

An advanced degree is defined in the regulations as any U.S. academic or professional degree or a foreign equivalent degree above that of baccalaureate.[57] In addition, the USCIS will consider any U.S. baccalaureate degree or a foreign equivalent degree followed by at least five years of post-degree, progressively responsible experience in the foreign national's specialty as equivalent to a master's degree.[58]

● **EXAMPLE**

Raul came to the United States as a student and received a baccalaureate degree in environmental engineering. Immediately after graduating, he accepted an entry-level position as a Junior Environmental Engineer with an environmental consulting company. After two years in that position, he was promoted to a higher-level position as a Senior Environmental Engineer, a post he held for three years. He just accepted a Manager of Environmental Engineering position with another environmental consulting company, which typically requires a Master's degree for these positions, but will also accept a Bachelor's degree plus at least five years of experience. The company can pursue LPR status for Raul in the EB-2 category because it requires either a Master's degree or, in the alternative, a Bachelor's degree plus five years of experience for the position, and because Raul holds the equivalent of a U.S. Master's degree, since he has a bachelor's degree plus five years of progressive experience in environmental engineering.

---

[54] INA § 203(b)(2).
[55] INA § 203(b)(2)(B)(i).
[56] 8 C.F.R § 204.5(k)(3)(ii), 20 C.F.R. § 656.15(d).
[57] 8 C.F.R § 204.5(k)(2).
[58] *Id.*

The EB-2 petition must be accompanied by either: 1) an official academic record, such as a degree and/or transcript, showing that the foreign national possesses a U.S. advanced degree, and 2) an official academic record, such as a degree and/or transcript, showing that the foreign national possesses a U.S. baccalaureate degree or a foreign equivalent, as well as letters from current or former employers confirming that the foreign national has at least five years of progressive post-baccalaureate experience.[59] If the foreign national holds a foreign degree, it is critical for him or her to obtain a professional educational evaluation confirming that the foreign degree is equivalent to a U.S. degree.

The USCIS will, in most cases, only accept single four-year foreign baccalaureate degrees as equivalent to U.S. baccalaureate degrees. In other words, and unlike degree equivalencies in the H-1B context,[60] the USCIS will not accept a combination of a lesser degree plus experience, or a combination of two or more lesser degrees as equivalent to a U.S. baccalaureate degree.

Some foreign countries, including India, issue three-year baccalaureate degrees for certain fields of study. An Indian national with a three-year Indian baccalaureate degree will not be able to file in the EB-2 category, even if s/he has more than five years of progressive experience after completing the degree. This is because the USCIS recognizes neither the Indian three-year degree nor a combination of the Indian degree plus progressive experience as equivalent to a U.S. four-year baccalaureate degree.[61] However, there are some three-year degrees, such as certain three-year degrees from the United Kingdom, which require students to first pass the A-level examination. This reflects advanced standing credit that USCIS considers to be equivalent to a four-year U.S. baccalaureate degree, since the passing of the A-level examination is viewed as equivalent to one additional year, totaling four altogether. Many other tricky situations can arise when evaluating foreign degrees. Therefore, the importance of a strong and reliable educational evaluation that relies upon EDGE, the credentials evaluation service that the USCIS uses, cannot be overestimated.

D.2. EB-3 for Skilled Workers, Professionals, and Other Workers

The employment-based third preference category, or EB-3,[62] which also requires a job offer as well as an approved labor certification,[63] is for the following three sub-groups of foreign nationals:

---

[59] 8 C.F.R § 204.5(k)(3)(i).
[60] This is discussed in Section C.1. of Chapter 3, Nonimmigrant Visas for Intracompany Transferees, Trade and Investment, and Professional Employment.
[61] See Ronald Y. Wada, AILA's Focus on EB2 & EB3 Degree Equivalency, American Immigration Lawyers Association (2007).
[62] INA § 203(b)(3); 8 C.F.R. § 204.5(l).
[63] See PERM labor certification application in Section D.3.

- Professionals: members of the professions whose jobs require at least a baccalaureate degree from a U.S. university or college or its foreign equivalent degree,[64]
- **Skilled workers**: persons whose jobs require a minimum of two years of training or work experience that are not temporary or seasonal,[65] and
- **Unskilled or other workers**: persons capable of filling positions that require less than two years training or experience that is not temporary or seasonal.[66]

Again, if the foreign national holds a foreign baccalaureate degree, it is critical to obtain a professional educational evaluation confirming that the foreign degree is equivalent to a U.S. baccalaureate degree. As noted in the EB-2 section, the USCIS will only accept a single-source foreign degree, meaning that it will not accept a combination of some education that is less than a baccalaureate degree plus experience to attain equivalency with a U.S. baccalaureate degree.

Case for Discussion 7.6

Rami, from India, obtained a three-year bachelor's degree in computer science from a university in India. Afterwards, an information technology consulting company offered him a position in the United States. Since joining five years ago, he has risen through the ranks and is now a manager. The company typically requires managers to hold at least a master's degree or a bachelor's degree plus five years of experience. Rami's company really values him and would like to sponsor him for LPR status.

- Based on the Employer's job requirements, what is the appropriate employment-based preference category for this position?
- What issues will the employer and Rami face?

D.3. Labor Certification Application: The PERM process

Before an employer can file an immigrant petition for an employee in the EB-2 or EB-3 category, the employer must first obtain an approved labor certification from the DOL,[67] which implemented the PERM labor certification application process in March 2005 to protect the U.S. job market. Section 212(a)(5)(A) of the INA specifically provides that, with limited exceptions, before an immigrant petition can be filed, the Secretary of Labor must determine and certify to the Secretary of State and the Attorney General that:

---

[64] INA § 203(b)(3)(A)(ii).
[65] *Id.* § 203(b)(3)(A)(i).
[66] *Id.* § 203(b)(3)(A)(iii).
[67] INA § 203(b)(3)(C).

- There are not sufficient workers who are able, willing, qualified (or equally qualified in the case of an alien described in the clause II), and available at the time of application for a visa and admission to the United States and at the place where the alien is to perform such skilled or unskilled labor; and
- The employment of such foreign national will not adversely affect the wages and working conditions of workers in the United States similarly employed.

In essence, the PERM labor certification application process requires the employer to test the labor market and prove, via extensive recruitment, that during the six months prior to filing the PERM labor certification application, it was unable to hire a U.S. worker[68] with the *minimum* required education, skills, and/or experience, despite the fact that the employer was offering to pay the higher of either the actual wage or the DOL determined prevailing wage for the position.

Only if, after its extensive recruitment effort, the employer is not able to identify a minimally qualified, available, and willing U.S. worker, can the employer file the PERM labor certification application, using Form ETA 9089, Application for Permanent Employment Certification, on behalf of its foreign national employee. An employer may only submit a PERM labor certification application for a permanent full-time position (at least 35 hours per week) and the employee holding such position cannot be self-employed.[69]

It is important to note that the employer is responsible for all costs, including attorney fees and advertising costs, associated with the requisite recruitment and preparation and filing of the PERM labor certification application.[70] There are very limited exceptions that would permit a third-party person or entity to pay if the work to be performed by the foreign national would benefit or accrue to that third party. However, it cannot be emphasized strongly enough that an employer who fails to pay such costs opens itself up to huge governmental liabilities, fines, and even criminal prosecution from several U.S. agencies, including, but not limited to, the DOL, the USCIS, and the DOS.

The PERM labor certification application process is a complicated and time sensitive procedure that requires tremendous attention to detail, exhaustive timeline and deadline management, and extensive documentation and record keeping. Those legal practitioners tasked with assisting with PERM labor certification applications typically receive extensive training and constant guidance from attorneys. The following outline provides an introductory overview of the basic steps of the process.

D.3.a. Step 1: Identify Minimum Requirements and Draft the Job Description

The employer's minimum job requirements, reflected in its job description, are the most critical elements of the PERM labor certification application process, as

---

[68] 20 C.F.R § 656.3.
[69] 20 C.F.R § 656.3.
[70] 20 C.F.R. § 656.12(b).

they dictate what employment-based, or EB, preference category the foreign national will be eligible for, whether EB-2 for advanced degreed professionals or EB-3 for professional or skilled workers, for example. They will also form the basis of the prevailing wage request (*see Step 3*), the advertisement's text (*see Step 4*), the criteria for reviewing applicants (*see Step 5*), and the criteria that the foreign national ultimately must satisfy in order to receive the requested immigrant visa status.

In addition to describing the duties of the position, the job description must include the *minimum* educational, experience, and training requirements for the position, as well as any essential specialized or hard-to-find skills needed to perform the duties of the position.[71] The job description must also include any other special job requirements, such as travel obligations, licensure or certification requirements, etc. The job description cannot include any preferences that the employer may have for the position, such as a preferred higher degree or a preferred level of experience. The job description and requirements information obtained from the employer will be used to draft the PERM labor certification job description.

When drafting the job description, the DOL's Occupational Information Network, or O*NET, which is a free online database that contains hundreds of occupational definitions, must also be consulted to identify the appropriate DOL O*NET occupational classification for the position[72] that will provide several key pieces of information, including:

- What the DOL considers to be the normal educational and experience requirements for positions within the O*Net classification
- The position's **Job Zone** classification, which identifies the amount of education, experience, and on-the-job training the DOL believes is necessary to perform the work, and
- What the **specific vocational preparation,** or **SVP**, is for the position. SVP is the amount of time required by a typical worker to learn the techniques, acquire the information, and develop the abilities needed for average performance in a specific work situation. Each Job Zone is assigned a specific SVP range.

Included in Figure 7.1 is information from the DOL introducing and defining the five Job Zones as well as explaining SVP. In an ideal scenario, the employer's job requirements will closely match the DOL's O*Net classification requirements. Unfortunately, O*Net classifications and the assigned Job Zone and SVP often do not reflect employers' real world job descriptions and requirements. Nevertheless, they are very important to the PERM labor certification process.

If the employer's requirements for the position exceed the requirements listed in the O*Net classification, the employer must be prepared to establish,

---

[71] 20 C.F.R. §§ 656.17(h) and (i).
[72] 20 C.F.R. § 656.17(h)(1). O*NET occupational codes and other pertinent information can be found at www.onetcenter.org.

Figure 7.1

Department of Labor's Five Job Zones: Information and Specific Vocational Preparation

O*Net™ Job Zones
http://www.flcdatacenter.com/JobZone.aspx#4

Job Zone One: Little or No Preparation Needed

Experience: Little or no previous work-related skill, knowledge, or experience is needed for these occupations. For example, a person can become a waiter or waitress even if he/she has never worked before.

Education: Some of these occupations may require a high school diploma or GED certificate.

Job Training: Employees in these occupations need anywhere from a few days to a few months of training. Usually, an experienced worker could show you how to do the job.

Examples: These occupations involve following instructions and helping others. Examples include taxi drivers, amusement and recreation attendants, counter and rental clerks, nonfarm animal caretakers, continuous mining machine operators, and waiters/waitresses.

SVP Range: Below 4.0

Job Zone Two: Some Preparation Needed

Experience: Some previous work-related skill, knowledge, or experience is usually needed. For example, a teller would benefit from experience working directly with the public.

Education: These occupations usually require a high school diploma.

Job Training: Employees in these occupations need anywhere from a few months to one year of working with experienced employees. A recognized apprenticeship program may be associated with these occupations.

Examples: These occupations often involve using your knowledge and skills to help others. Examples include sheet metal workers, forest fire fighters, customer service representatives, physical therapist aides, salespersons (retail), and tellers.

SVP Range: 4.0 to < 6.0

Job Zone Three: Medium Preparation Needed

Experience: Previous work-related skill, knowledge, or experience is required for these occupations. For example, an electrician must have completed three or four years of apprenticeship or several years of vocational training, and often must have passed a licensing exam in order to perform the job.

Education: Most occupations in this zone require training in vocational schools, related on-the-job experience, or an associate's degree.

Job Training: Employees in these occupations usually need one or two years of training involving both on-the-job experience and informal training with experienced workers. A recognized apprenticeship program may be associated with these occupations.

Examples: These occupations usually involve using communication and organizational skills to coordinate, supervise, manage, or train others to accomplish goals. Examples include food service managers, electricians, agricultural technicians, legal secretaries, occupational therapy assistants, and medical assistants.

SVP Range: 6.0 < 7.0

Figure 7.1 (Continued)

Job Zone Four: Considerable Preparation Needed

Experience: A considerable amount of work-related skill, knowledge, or experience is needed for these occupations. For example, an accountant must complete four years of college and work for several years in accounting to be considered qualified.

Education: Most of these occupations require a four-year bachelor's degree, but some do not.

Job Training: Employees in these occupations usually need several years of work-related experience, on-the-job training, and/or vocational training.

Examples: Many of these occupations involve coordinating, supervising, managing, or training others. Examples include accountants, sales managers, database administrators, teachers, chemists, art directors, and cost estimators.

SVP Range: 7.0 < 8.0

Job Zone Five: Extensive Preparation Needed

Experience: Extensive skill, knowledge, and experience are needed for these occupations. Many require more than five years of experience. For example, surgeons must complete four years of college and an additional five to seven years of specialized medical training to be able to do their job.

Education: Most of these occupations require graduate school. However, many also require graduate school. For example, they may require a master's degree, and some require a Ph.D., M.D., or J.D. (law degree).

Job Training: Employees may need some on-the-job training, but most of these occupations assume that the person will already have the required skills, knowledge, work-related experience, and/or training.

Examples: These occupations often involve coordinating, training, supervising, or managing the activities of others to accomplish goals. Very advanced communication and organizational skills are required. Examples include librarians, lawyers, sports medicine physicians, wildlife biologists, school psychologists, surgeons, treasurers, and controllers.

SVP Range: 8.0 and above

Job Zone Not Available

Some occupations do not have a Job Zone designation. The most common reason for this is that the occupation is a broad occupation that O*Net™ has broken out into more detailed occupations. Another reason may be that the duties and requirements of the occupation are too broad or detailed to fit in one primary Job Zone.

through documentation, that there is a **business necessity**[73] for such requirements. Several factors that may trigger a business necessity justification are:

- Educational and experience requirements that exceed those of the O*Net classification. The "employer must demonstrate the job duties and requirements bear a reasonable relationship to the occupation in the context of the employer's business and are essential to perform the job in a reasonable manner."[74]
- Foreign language requirements. The employer must establish that either the nature of the occupation requires fluency in a foreign language, such as an

---

[73] *Id.*
[74] 20 C.F.R. § 656.17(h)(1); *J.P. Morgan Chase & Co.*, 2011-PER-01000 (BALCA 2012) (certifying officer impermissibly substituted judgment for employers with respect to requirements). *Matter of LA Cantina Toscana*, 2009-PER-00237 (BALCA 2010) (did not establish business necessity for two years' experience as a cook).

Figure 7.1 (Continued)

An Explanation of SVP
http://www.flcdatacenter.com/svp.aspx

Specific Vocational Preparation is defined as the amount of lapsed time required by a typical worker to learn the techniques, acquire the information, and develop the facility needed for average performance in a specific job-worker situation.

This training may be acquired in a school, work, military, instructional, or vocational environment. It does not include the orientation time required of fully qualified worker to become accustomed to the special conditions of any new job. Specific vocational training includes: vocational education, apprenticeship training, in-plant training, on-the-job training, and essential experience in other jobs.

Specific vocational training includes training given in any of the following circumstances:

a. Vocational education (high school; commercial or shop training; technical school; art school; and that part of college training which is organized around a specific vocational objective):
b. Apprenticeship training (for apprenticeable jobs only);
c. In- plant training (organized classroom study provided by an employer);
d. On-the-job training (serving as learner or trainee on the job under the instruction of a qualified worker);
e. Essential experience in other jobs (serving in less responsible jobs which lead to the higher grade job or serving in other jobs which qualify).

The following is an explanation of the various level of specific vocational preparation:

SVP 1 - Short demonstration only
SVP 2 - Anything beyond short demonstration up to and including 1 month
SVP 3 - Over 1 month up to and including 3 months
SVP 4 - Over 3 months up to and including 6 months
SVP 5 - Over 6 months up to and including 1 year
SVP 6 - Over 1 year up to and including 2 years
SVP 7 - Over 2 years up to and including 4 years
SVP 8 - Over 4 years up to and including 10 years
SVP 9 - Over 10 years

Note: The levels of this scale are mutually exclusive and do not overlap.

interpreter or foreign language teacher, or fluency in a foreign language is needed to communicate with a large majority of the employer's customers, contractors, or employees who cannot effectively communicate in English. The employer must furnish the number and proportion of its clients, contractors, or employees who cannot communicate in English and/or a detailed plan to market products for services in the foreign country, requiring frequent contact and communication with those who cannot communicate in English.[75] Unless it is truly an absolute requirement for the position, a foreign language requirement should not be included, as this often leads to an audit of the PERM application, lengthy adjudication delays, and subsequent denials.

- Requirements or duties that indicate a combination of occupations.[76] If the position involves what the DOL perceives to be a combination of occupations

---

[75] 20 C.F.R. § 656.17(h)(2).
[76] 20 C.F.R. § 656.17(h)(3).

or duties that fall under two different O*Net occupational classifications, the employer must document that it normally employs persons with that combination of occupations, workers customarily perform the combination of occupations in the area of intended employment, and/or a combination of job opportunities is based on a business necessity. For example, if a small company employs an "accountant" to perform both human resources and accounting functions, the employer would need to explain why such a combination of duties or occupations is a business necessity.

In addition, there are some limitations as to what the employer can require. For example, the employer cannot generally require experience or skills that the foreign national did not have when hired for the position that are the subject of the labor certification.[77] In other words, any experience the foreign national gained in the job will not count as qualifying experience. There are two limited exceptions, however, that allow the employer to require and use experience the foreign worker gained with the employer:

- The foreign national gained the experience while working for the employer in a position "not substantially comparable," i.e., a job or position requiring performance of the same job duties more than 50 percent of the time to the position for which certification is sought,[78] or
- The employer can demonstrate that it is no longer feasible to train a U.S. worker to qualify for the job.[79]

● **EXAMPLE**

A software development company hired Shan, a Software Developer, four years ago and would now like to pursue PERM labor certification for him. Over that time, Shan developed a new computer software program called GRADE A for university and college registrar offices to use in developing transcripts. For each university or college client, special modifications must be made to GRADE A to suit the client's specifications and needs. At present, Shan is the only person at the company who knows how to write the codes for GRADE A and its various modifications. GRADE A is now the company's highest selling product. To maintain its clientele and good standing in the market, the company must turn out the modified GRADE A within eight weeks of order from a university or college. Because of the complexities of the program and the coding required, the company estimates that it would take at least six months to train a new worker to perform the job of Software Developer. Such a long training period would result in a tremendous financial loss to the company, which can be documented. Because it is not feasible to train a U.S. worker on GRADE A without significant and catastrophic impact to its business operations, should Shan be unable to remain with the company, it can require experience with GRADE A for

---

[77] 20 C.F.R. § 656.17(i)(3).
[78] 20 C.F.R. § 656.17(i)(3)(i) and 20 C.F.R. § 656.17(i)(5)(ii).
[79] 20 C.F.R. § 656.17(i)(3)(ii).

the PERM labor certification application even though Shan did not have experience with GRADE A prior to joining the company. Note that such "infeasible to train" arguments are not always successful, and generally result in an audit. In anticipation of such audit, the employer must carefully document and demonstrate that it is no longer feasible to train a worker to qualify for the position.[80]

D.3.b. Step 2: Confirm that the Foreign National Satisfies the Employer's Minimum Requirements

The DOL must assess whether the foreign national possesses all the qualifications for the employer's job opportunity at the time of the filing of the PERM application. As described in Section E, the foreign national will additionally need to provide the USCIS with documentary evidence of his or her qualifications for the job opportunity by furnishing copies of degrees, employment experience or skill confirmation letters, certificates, licenses, etc. at the time the EB-2 or EB-3 immigrant petition is submitted.

It is critical to verify and obtain documentation of the foreign national's qualifications at the outset of the PERM labor certification process. Special attention should be paid to the foreign national's education and experience qualifications in order to establish that the degrees are equivalent to U.S. degrees and meet the requirements of the job being offered. With regards to education, and as discussed in Section D, if the foreign national has a foreign baccalaureate or master's degree, a professional educational evaluation must be obtained confirming the U.S. equivalency. In addition, if the employer requires a Bachelor's degree and five years of progressive experience and is seeking to pursue EB-2 advanced degree classification for the foreign national, the educational evaluation must confirm that the foreign degree is a four-year degree. Otherwise, the foreign national will not qualify for the EB-2 category because the USCIS will accept only four-year foreign baccalaureate degrees as equivalent to U.S. degrees. Moreover, it is important to be mindful of the USCIS' different interpretations of degree equivalencies within the H-1B nonimmigrant and the EB-2/EB-3 immigrant contexts. As noted earlier, while the USCIS will accept a combination of experience and education as being equivalent to a U.S. baccalaureate degree for purposes of obtaining an H-1B nonimmigrant visa, it will not accept such a combination of education and experience as equivalent to a U.S. baccalaureate or advanced degree within the EB-2 and EB-3 classifications.

With regards to experience, the foreign national must be able to obtain confirmation letters from former employers verifying his or her period of employment, job title, and job duties, including specific skills used. In most cases only experience gained with different employer(s) can be relied on as qualifying experience, unless business necessity can be established. However, if the foreign national has held position(s) with the petitioning employer and the duties of such position(s) are substantially different from the sponsored position, i.e., the duties of the prior position(s) are at least 50 percent different than the duties of the

---

[80] *Id.*

position that is the subject of the PERM labor certification application process, then the DOL will accept such prior positions as qualifying experience.

> ● **EXAMPLE**
>
> Délicieux, a five star French cuisine restaurant, would like to file a PERM labor certification application for its new Head Chef, Pierre. The restaurant requires him to have at least two years of experience as a Head Chef or in a related position such as Sous Chef, including experience costing and ordering ingredients, supervising the cooking and plating operations in the kitchen, and cooking complex dishes. The Head Chef spends 50 percent of his time planning menus and developing new recipes, 30 percent of his time managing the kitchen operations, such as hiring, firing, developing a budget, etc., and 20 percent of his time supervising the cooking and plating operations. Chef Pierre joined Délicieux three years ago as Sous Chef and just accepted the position of Head Chef. As Sous Chef and under the supervision of the previous Head Chef, Pierre spent 25 percent of his time costing and ordering ingredients, 60 percent of his time supervising the cooking and plating operations in the kitchen, and 15 percent of his time cooking complex dishes. Chef Pierre's experience as a Sous Chef at Délicieux will count as qualifying experience for the Head Chef position because the duties of the Sous Chef positions are at least 50 percent different from the duties of the Head Chef position.

In addition to documenting the foreign national's qualifying education and experience, the PERM Form ETA 9089, Application for Permanent Employment Certification also must clearly reflect that the foreign national meets all the job requirements at the time that the application is submitted. The form functions as an attestation made by the employer and foreign national and is submitted electronically without supporting documentation. Sections J and K of the form specifically elicit information about the foreign national's education, training, and experience. The DOL has clarified in an FAQ indicating that the employer must use Section K to indicate that the foreign national possesses specific skills or other requirements for the job, such as certificates, licenses, professional coursework, or other required credentials.[81] If any required experience, skills, or other requirements are omitted from Sections J and/or K of the PERM application, the DOL will deny the application.

D.3.c. Step 3: Prevailing Wage Determination

The employer must agree to offer and pay a salary for the position that is at least the higher of either the *actual wage* offered by the employer for the position or the *prevailing wage*, as determined by the DOL,[82] whose regulations pertaining to prevailing wage determinations are found at 20 C.F.R. § 656.40. In addition, the DOL has informally issued information pertaining to prevailing wage determinations in FAQs and other material.[83]

---

[81] Available at https://www.foreignlaborcert.doleta.gov/faqsanswers.cfm#q!222.
[82] INA § 212(p).
[83] These are available on the DOL's Employment and Training Administration's Foreign Labor Certification website at www.foreignlaborcert.doleta.gov/pwscreens.cfm.

To request a prevailing wage determination, the employer must submit Form ETA 9141, Application for Prevailing Wage Determination, to the DOL's National Prevailing Wage Center, or NPWC. The application normally is filed electronically by going on the DOL's iCERT Visa Portal System website.[84] The NPWC will evaluate the form and return it via email with a Prevailing Wage Determination. The prevailing wage depends on a variety of factors including the O*NET classification, the job location, and the job requirements. Included in Figure 7.2 is a sample Form ETA 9141, Application for Prevailing Wage Determination.

When determining the prevailing wage, the DOL typically relies on its Occupational Employment Statistics, or OES, wage survey.[85] There are four OES wage levels assigned to each O*Net occupational classification. Which wage level the NPWC assigns to a given position depends on what the employer's requirements are for the position as compared to what the O*NET classification determines are the minimum and normal requirements. Factors that might increase the wage level include educational and/or experience requirements that exceed the minimum for the specific O*Net classification, foreign language requirements for positions that do not typically require a foreign language skill, travel requirements, supervisory duties for positions that typically do not require supervision of others, and atypical licensing or certification requirements.

In cases where there is uncertainty regarding the appropriate O*Net classification or appropriate wage level, an addendum should be included with ETA Form 9141, Application for Prevailing Wage Determination, explaining or arguing which O*Net classification and wage level should be assigned to the position.

● EXAMPLE

Employer A, a luxury hotel management company, would like to pursue the PERM labor certification application process for Julio, a Senior Project Manager for the company's South America Division. The job duties include frequent travel to South America to coordinate and oversee the opening of new hotels and the maintenance of existing hotel clients. At least 75 percent of all spoken and written communication with the contacts at the hotels in South America is in Spanish. The employer requires a minimum of a Master's degree and two years of related experience for the position, as well as fluency in Spanish and frequent travel to the client hotels in South America. The O*Net classification indicates the normal requirements for this type of position are a bachelor's and two years of experience. Fluency in a foreign language and travel are not listed as normal requirements. In this situation, the educational requirement of a Master's degree, the language requirement, and the travel requirement would each increase the wage level. In other words, these requirements would bump the prevailing wage up by three levels. The language requirement will also require a "business necessity" argument explaining why fluency in Spanish is needed to perform the job.

---

[84] Available at http://icert.doleta.gov.
[85] Available at www.flcdatacenter.com.

D: Advanced Degree Professionals (EB-2) and Skilled Workers

Figure 7.2
Sample Prevailing Wage Determination

OMB Approval: 1205-0466
Expiration Date: 03/31/2016

**Application for Prevailing Wage Determination
ETA Form 9141
U.S. Department of Labor**

Please read and review the instructions carefully before completing this form and print legibly. A copy of the instructions can be found at http://www.foreignlaborcert.doleta.gov/.

A. Employment-Based Visa Information

1. Indicate the type of visa classification supported by this application *(Write classification symbol)*: * | PERM

B. Requestor Point-of-Contact Information

1. Contact's last (family) name *	2. First (given) name *	3. Middle name(s) *
MARIA	PEREZ	C.

4. Contact's job title *
PEREZ & COOPER, PC

5. Address 1 *
1234 STENTON AVENUE

6. Address 2
N/A

7. City *	8. State *	9. Postal code *
PHILADELPHIA	PA	19141

10. Country *	11. Province (if applicable)
UNITED STATES OF AMERICA	N/A

12. Telephone number *	13. Extension	14. Fax Number
215-555-1234	N/A	215-555-1235

15. E-Mail Address
MARIA@PEREZCOOPER.COM

C. Employer Information

1. Legal business name *
Panda Gifts Inc.

2. Trade name/Doing Business As (DBA), if applicable §
N/A

3. Address 1 *
3434 Poplar Street

4. Address 2
N/A

5. City *	6. State *	7. Postal code *
Philadelphia	PA	19101

8. Country *	9. Province (if applicable)
UNITED STATES OF AMERICA	N/A

10. Telephone number *	11. Extension
215-555-4321	N/A

12. Federal Employer Identification Number (FEIN from IRS) *	13. NAICS code (must be at least 4-digits) *
234567888	454111

D. Wage Processing Information

1. Is the employer covered by ACWIA? * ☐ Yes ☑ No	
2. Is the position covered by a Collective Bargaining Agreement (CBA)? *	☐ Yes ☑ No
3. Is the employer requesting consideration of Davis-Bacon (DBA) or McNamara Service Contract (SCA) Acts? *	☐ Yes ☑ No ☐ DBA ☐ SCA

ETA Form 9141   FOR DEPARTMENT OF LABOR USE ONLY   Page 1 of 4

Case Number: PW-000-16050-42695!   Case Status: INITIATED   Validity Period: N/A   to N/A

Figure 7.2 (Continued)

OMB Approval: 1205-0466
Expiration Date: 03/31/2016

Application for Prevailing Wage Determination
ETA Form 9141
U.S. Department of Labor

D. Wage Processing Information (cont.)

4. Is the employer requesting consideration of a survey in determining the prevailing wage? *	☐ Yes ☑ No
4a. Survey Name: §	
4b. Survey date of publication: §	

E. Job Offer Information

a. Job Description:

1. Job Title * Senior Java Developer	
2. *Suggested* SOC (ONET/OES) code * 15-1132	2a. *Suggested* SOC (ONET/OES) occupation title * Software Developers, Applications
3. Job Title of Supervisor for this Position (if applicable) § President	
4. Does this position supervise the work of other employees? * ☐ Yes ☑ No	4a. If "Yes", number of employees worker § will supervise: N/A
4b. If "Yes", please indicate the level of the employees to be supervised:	☐ Subordinate ☐ Peer

5. Job duties – Please provide a description of the duties to be performed with as much specificity as possible, including details regarding the areas/fields and/or products/industries involved. A description of the job duties to be performed **MUST** begin in this space. *

Working independently, design, develop and modify software applications for an online order management system using experience with Java, JavaScript, JQuery, AngularJS, HTML5, CSS3, and SQL. Analyze user needs to develop new application features using experience with Java Server Pages (JSP) and Tomcat application servers. Modify existing software to correct errors and ensure application integration using experience with REST and SOAP web services. Develop software system testing for all applications using experience with CVS version control systems. Port applications to iOS and Android mobile device platforms using experience with Objective-C, Swift and Linux.

6. Will travel be required in order to perform the job duties? * ☐ Yes ☑ No	6a. If "Yes", please provide details of the travel required, such as the area(s), frequency and nature of the travel. § N/A

ETA Form 9141   FOR DEPARTMENT OF LABOR USE ONLY

Case Number: PW-000-16050-426955   Case Status: INITIATED   Validity Period: N/A   to N/A

D: Advanced Degree Professionals (EB-2) and Skilled Workers 341

Figure 7.2
(Continued)

OMB Approval: 1205-0466
Expiration Date: 03/31/2016

Application for Prevailing Wage Determination
ETA Form 9141
U.S. Department of Labor

E. Job Offer Information (cont.)

b. Minimum Job Requirements:

1. Education: minimum U.S. diploma/degree required *

☐ None ☐ High School/GED ☐ Associate's ☑ Bachelor's ☐ Master's ☐ Doctorate (PhD) ☐ Other degree (JD, MD, etc.)

1a. If "Other degree" in question 1, specify the diploma/degree required §	1b. Indicate the major(s) and/or field(s) of study required § (May list more than one related major and more than one field)
N/A	Computer Science/Engineering or rel'd

2. Does the employer require a second U.S. diploma/degree? *	☐ Yes ☑ No

2a. If "Yes" in question 2, indicate the second U.S. diploma/degree and the major(s) and/or field(s) of study required §
N/A

3. Is training for the job opportunity required? *		☐ Yes ☑ No
3a. If "Yes" in question 3, specify the number of months of training required §	3b. Indicate the field(s)/name(s) of training required § (May list more than one related field and more than one type)	
N/A	N/A	

4. Is employment experience required? *		☑ Yes ☐ No
4a. If "Yes" in question 4, specify the number of months of experience required §	4b. Indicate the occupation required §	
36	Java Developer or related occ.	

5. Special Requirements - List specific skills, licenses/certificates/certifications, and requirements of the job opportunity. *

No special requirements.

c. Place of Employment Information:

1. Worksite address 1 *	3434 Poplar Street
2. Address 2	N/A

3. City * Philadelphia	4. County * PHILADELPHIA
5. State/District/Territory * PA	6. Postal code * 19101

7. Will work be performed in multiple worksites within an area of intended employment or a location(s) other than the address listed above? *	☐ Yes ☑ No

7a. If "Yes", identify the geographic place(s) of employment indicating each metropolitan statistical area (MSA) or the independent city(ies)/township(s)/county(ies) (borough(s)/parish(es)) and the corresponding state(s) where work will be performed. If necessary, submit a second completed ETA Form 9141 with a listing of the additional anticipated worksites. Please note that wages cannot be provided for unspecified/unanticipated locations. §

N/A

ETA Form 9141   FOR DEPARTMENT OF LABOR USE ONLY   Page 3 of 4

Case Number: PW-000-16050-426955 Case Status: INITIATED   Validity Period: N/A to N/A

Figure 7.2 (Continued)

OMB Approval: 1205-0466
Expiration Date: 03/31/2016

Application for Prevailing Wage Determination
ETA Form 9141
U.S. Department of Labor

F. Prevailing Wage Determination

FOR OFFICIAL GOVERNMENT USE ONLY

1. PW tracking number	2. Date PW request received

3. SOC (ONET/OES) code	3a. SOC (ONET/OES) occupation title

4. Prevailing wage $	4a. OES Wage level ☐ I ☐ II ☐ III ☐ IV ☐ N/A

5. Per: (Choose only one) ☐ Hour ☐ Week ☐ Bi-Weekly ☐ Month ☐ Year ☐ Piece Rate

5a. If Piece Rate is indicated in question 5, specify the wage offer requirements :*

6. Prevailing wage source (Choose only one)
☐ OES (All Industries) ☐ OES (ACWIA – Higher Education) ☐ CBA ☐ DBA ☐ SCA ☐ Other/Alternate Survey

6a. If "Other/Alternate Survey" in question 6, specify

7. Additional Notes Regarding Wage Determination

8. Determination date	9. Expiration date

F. OMB Paperwork Reduction Act *(1205-0466)*
Persons are not required to respond to this collection of information unless it displays a currently valid OMB control number. Respondent's reply to these reporting requirements is mandatory to obtain the benefits of temporary employment certification (Immigration and Nationality Act, Section 101). Public reporting burden for this collection of information is estimated to average 55 minutes per response, including the time for reviewing instructions, searching existing data sources, gathering and maintaining the data needed, and completing and reviewing the collection of information. Send comments regarding this burden estimate to the Office of Foreign Labor Certification * U.S. Department of Labor * Room C4312 * 200 Constitution Ave., NW, * Washington, DC * 20210. **Do NOT send the completed application to this address.**

ETA Form 9141   FOR DEPARTMENT OF LABOR USE ONLY

Case Number: PW-000-16050-426955 Case Status: INITIATED   Validity Period: N/A to N/A

Under the following circumstances, the NPWC will rely on wage data other than its OES surveys if:

- A position is covered by a collective bargaining agreement negotiated at arm's length between the union and the employer (the wage rate set forth in that agreement will always determine the prevailing wage);[86]
- The position is for a professional athlete covered by professional sports league rules or regulations (the wage established by those rules and regulations will constitute the prevailing wage);[87]
- The employer is an institution of higher education or an affiliated or related nonprofit entity, a nonprofit research education, or a governmental research organization (the prevailing wage determination will only take into account employees with such employers as reflected in the DOL's American Competitiveness and Workforce Improvement Act, or ACWIA, wage data);[88]
- If the employer wishes, and as long as the position is not governed by a collective bargaining agreement or professional sports rules or regulations, it can submit an alternative wage survey to the NPWC.[89] The survey must be recent (i.e., published within 24 months of the date that the prevailing wage determination request is submitted) and based on data collected within 24 months of the publication date of the survey.[90] In addition, the survey must reflect the arithmetic mean of wages of similarly employed workers in the area of intended employment collected across industries.[91]

Timelines and deadline management are critical throughout the PERM labor certification process. Because the NPWC processing times have varied significantly over the years, ranging from two to nine weeks, the prevailing wage determination request should be submitted early in the process, especially if a case is time-sensitive, for example, because a foreign national's nonimmigrant status will be expiring soon. In some cases, where there is uncertainty regarding the applicable O*Net code or wage level, it is advisable for the employer to wait to commence recruiting until the prevailing wage is obtained and the employer can confirm that it is able to offer and pay a salary that is at least equal to the prevailing wage.[92]

---

[86] 20 C.F.R. § 656.40(b)(1).
[87] 20 C.F.R. § 656.40(f).
[88] 8 C.F.R. § 656.40(e). The ACWIA wage date is available at www.flcdatacenter.com.
[89] 20 C.F.R. § 656.40(b).
[90] 20 C.F.R. § 656.40(g).
[91] *See* Department of Labor Employment and Training Administration, "Prevailing Wage Determination Policy Guidance" (November 2009), available at http://www.flcdatacenter.com/download/NPWHC_Guidance_Revised_11_2009.pdf.
[92] In some cases, the DOL issues prevailing wage determinations that are not consistent with the job description (using an inconsistent O*Net code) and minimum requirements, thus resulting in a very high wage. If the legal practitioner disagrees with the determination, a request for redetermination can be submitted to the DOL. Unfortunately, in practice, such requests typically result in the DOL upholding its original determination in about the same amount of time as an initial request. Therefore, in lieu of a redetermination, it may be prudent to consider resubmitting a new prevailing wage request after revising the job description.

Once the Prevailing Wage Determination, or PWD, is issued, its validity period must be closely monitored. The DOL will issue a prevailing wage with a validity period of no less than 90 days and no more than one year from the PWD date.[93] This validity period is critical, because either recruitment must commence, or the PERM labor certification application must be filed during that time. If recruitment commences before the prevailing wage validity period *and* the PERM application is filed after it, the DOL will deny the PERM labor certification application.[94]

D.3.d. Step 4: Recruitment

The DOL requires employers to conduct an extensive recruitment effort to test the labor market and confirm that no minimally qualified U.S. workers are available for, and interested in, the available position. The regulations set forth the specific advertisement sources and steps that employers must use and follow as well as the content of the ads, which must:

- Name the employer;
- Direct applicants to report and send resumes, as appropriate, for the occupation to the employer;
- Provide a description of the vacancy specific enough to apprise the U.S. workers of the job opportunity for which certification is sought;
- Indicate the geographic area of employment with enough specificity to apprise applicants of any travel requirements and where applicants would likely have to reside;
- Not contain a wage lower than the prevailing wage, although the wage does not have to be advertised;
- Not contain any job requirements or duties not listed on the PERM labor certification application; and
- Not contain wages or terms and conditions of employment that are less than those offered to the person who is sponsored.[95]

Documentation of each recruitment step must be kept in a "compliance file" (*see Step 5*).

Mandatory Recruitment or Notices

All PERM labor certification applications, except for those filed for faculty members and other teachers at institutions of higher education, must include the following mandatory recruitment steps:

---

[93] 20 C.F.R. § 656.40(c).
[94] *Matter of Karl Storz Endoscopy-America*, 2011-PER-0040, (BALCA Dec. 1, 2011)(en banc).
[95] 20 C.F.R. § 656.17(f). *See Matter of Pixar*, 2011-PER-00627 (BALCA 2012), ads cannot contain matters not contained in, or different from, contents of labor certification application. *But see Matter of Symantec Corp.*, 2011-PER-01856 (BALCA 2014), advertising content requirements of 20 C.F.R. § 656.17(f) do not apply to the additional recruitment steps for professional positions found in § 656.17(e)(1)(ii).

- Two advertisements in a Sunday newspaper of general circulation in the area most appropriate to the occupation.[96] However, if the job opportunity is located in an area that does not have a newspaper that publishes a Sunday edition, the employer may use a newspaper edition with the widest circulation in the area of intended employment.[97] Also, if an employer is filing a PERM labor certification application for a professional position where advertising in a professional journal is appropriate, the employer can place an advertisement with the professional journal in lieu of one of the Sunday newspaper ads.[98] The employer must keep either certified tear sheets, certified copies of the newspaper page with the advertisement, or photocopies of the entire newspaper page showing the ad, the name of the newspaper, and the date of publication, as proof that the ads were placed.
- Job Order with the State Workforce Agency.[99] The employer must place a Job Order with the State Workforce Agency for at least 30 days. The regulations indicate that merely listing the start and end date of the Job Order posting in the PERM Form ETA 9089 Application for Permanent Employment Certification, is sufficient documentation of this recruitment step, and BALCA has confirmed this.[100] However, employers should keep a printout of the Job Order on the first and last day of posting as a precaution
- Mandatory recruitment in the event of layoffs. If there has been a layoff by the employer in the occupation and at the location that is the subject of the labor certification application within the six months prior to filing the application, the employer must document that it has notified and considered all potentially qualified laid off U.S. workers of the job opportunity and must be prepared to provide the results of the notification and consideration.[101]
- Notice of Filing.[102] If this is a union position, the employer must give notice of filing to the appropriate bargaining representative. This is documented by retaining a copy of the letter, notice, or email that includes a read receipt, with a copy of the PERM labor certification application provided to the bargaining representative.[103] If one does not exist, then there must be a notice of filing posted for at least ten consecutive business days at the place of employment where such notices are commonly posted.[104] The DOL defines business days as only Monday through Friday. However, the DOL does indicate in its FAQs that, if in fact the business is open during weekends or holidays, such as a hospital, then those days can be counted. The posted notice of filing can be documented by retaining a signed copy, indicating the dates it was posted. Also, if the employer normally would post or recruit for

---

[96] 20 C.F.R. § 656.17(e)(1)(i)(B)(1). *Matter of Discovery Networks Latin America–Iberia*, 2011-PER-00035 (BALCA 2012) (Wall Street Journal a newspaper of general circulation).
[97] 20 C.F.R. § 656.17(e)(1)(i)(B)(2).
[98] 20 C.F.R. § 656.17(e)(1)(i)(B)(4).
[99] 20 C.F.R. § 656.17(e)(1)(i)(A).
[100] *A Cut Above Ceramic Tile*, 2010-PER-224 (BALCA Mar. 8, 2012) (*en banc*).
[101] 20 C.F.R. § 656.17(k).
[102] 20 C.F.R. § 656.10(d).
[103] 20 C.F.R. § 656.10(d)(1)(i).
[104] 20 C.F.R. § 656.10(d)(1)(ii).

Figure 7.3
Sample Notice of Filing

POSTING NOTICE

This notice is being provided as a result of the filing of an application with the U.S. Department of Labor for permanent labor certification for the relevant job opportunity indicated below. This Notice of Filing will be posted for 10 consecutive business days, ending between 30 and 180 days before filing the application.

Position Title: Senior Java Developer

Position Duties/Responsibilities: Working independently, design, develop and modify software applications for an online order management system using experience with Java, JavaScript, JQuery, AngularJS, HTML5, CSS3 and SQL. Analyze user needs to develop new application features using experience with Java Server Pages (JSP) and Tomcat application servers. Modify existing software to correct errors and ensure application integration using experience with REST and SOAP web services. Develop software system testing for all applications using experience with CVS version control systems. Port applications to iOS and Android mobile device platforms using experience with Objective-C, Swift and Linux. Requires a Bachelor's degree in Computer Science, Computer Engineering or a related field plus 3 years of experience as a Java Developer or a related occupation.

No. of Openings: 1

Rate of Pay: $81,619 to $90,000 per year
The employer will pay or exceed the prevailing wage, as determined by the U.S. Department of Labor.

Location of Employment: Panda Gifts, Inc.
3434 Poplar Street
Philadelphia, PA 19101

Hours: 40 hours/week

Contact: Ang Lee
Tel - 215-555-1234

This notice is provided in compliance with 20 CFR 656.10(d). Any person may provide documentary evidence bearing on the application to the Certifying Officer of the U.S. Department of Labor holding jurisdiction over the location of the proposed employment, listed below:

United States Department of Labor
Employment and Training Administration
Atlanta National Processing Center
Harris Tower, 233 Peachtree St. Ste. 410
Atlanta, GA 30303
Tel: (404) 893-0101 / Fax: (404) 893-4642

This notice is being provided to workers in the place of intended employment by the following means:

____ Posting a clearly visible and unobstructed notice, for at least ten (10) consecutive business days, in conspicuous location(s) in the workplace, where the employer's U.S. workers can readily read the posted notice, including but not limited to locations in the immediate vicinity of the wage and hour notices.

AND

____ Publishing the notice in any and all in-house media, whether electronic or printed, in accordance with the normal procedures used for the recruitment of similar positions in the employer's organization.

Date Posted: _____
Date Removed: _____
Location(s) where the Notice was posted: _____
Means of In-House Notice, if applicable: _____
Explanation of any lack of in-house notice: _____

I attest, under penalty of perjury, that the above notice was provided as shown.

_____   _____
Ang Lee   Date

Figure 7.3 (Continued)

similar positions on its in-house media, whether electronic or in print, then the notice of filing must also be published there.[105] Copies of the Notice of Filing must be retained for the compliance file.

Included in Figure 7.3 is a sample Notice of Filing.

The regulations also provide specific instructions regarding the content of the notice of filing, which must state that it is being provided in connection with the filing of a labor certification application, that any person may provide documentary evidence bearing on the application to the certifying officer of the DOL, and the address of the appropriate certifying officer.[106] In addition, it must include the name of the company, the location of the position, the wage rate, and a description of the duties and minimum job requirements.[107]

Timeline and deadline management is critical for the notice of filing. It must be provided to the bargaining representative or posted for the full ten business day period, between 30 and 180 days before the filing of the application.[108] In other words, the PERM labor certification application cannot be filed within the 30-day period following the completion of the notice of filing period, but

---

[105] Id.
[106] 20 C.F.R. § 656.10(d)(3).
[107] 20 C.F.R. § 656.17(f).
[108] 20 C.F.R. § 656.10(d)(3)(iv).

must be filed within 180 days from the beginning of the posting. Failure to do so will result in a denial of the PERM application.

Additional Recruitment Requirements for Professional Cases

If the position is one for which a bachelor's degree or higher is a normal condition, there are additional recruitment requirements.[109] The employer must place a further three ads selected from a list of ten specified recruitment options in the regulations.[110] These are:

- Job fairs—documented by brochures advertising the fair, newspaper advertisements naming the employer as a participant in the job fair, or other evidence of the employer's participation
- Employer's website—documented by providing dated copies of printouts of the online ad on the first and last day it appeared on the website
- Job search website other than employer's—documented by providing dated copies of printouts of the online ad on the first and last day it appeared on the website
- On-campus recruiting—documented by providing copies of the notification issued or posted by the college's or university's placement office naming the employer and, if applicable, the date it conducted interviews for the position. However, this is generally not appropriate for positions that require experience
- Trade or professional organization—documented by providing copies of pages of newsletters or trade journals containing the ad for the position or printouts of professional organization online job boards
- Private employment firms—documented by providing documentation sufficient to demonstrate that recruitment has been conducted by a private firm for the position, such as copies of contracts between the employer and the private employment firm and copies of ads placed by the private employment firm for the position
- Employee referral program—documented by providing dated copies of employer notices or memoranda advertising the established referral program and specifying the incentive offered, as well as a copy of the company notice to employees of the specific job opportunity
- Campus placement office—documented by providing a copy of the notice of the job opportunity provided to the campus placement office
- Local and ethnic newspapers—documented by providing a dated copy of the page in the newspaper that contains the ad or a certified tear sheet

---

[109] 20 C.F.R. § 656.17(e)(1).
[110] There are companies that provide recruitment/advertising services that are specifically designed to ensure compliance with the PERM regulatory requirements.

- Radio and television advertisements—documented by providing a copy of the text of the ad along with a written confirmation from the radio or television station stating when the ad was aired[111]

Case for Discussion 7.7

Environment Pros is an environmental consulting company that provides consulting services to oil companies regarding how to comply with environmental regulations. Environment Pros currently employs Kimani, a Kenyan national, as an Environmental Engineer in H-1B nonimmigrant status. He is a very dedicated and hard worker and the company wants to retain him as a permanent employee, especially since they have tremendous difficulty recruiting and hiring qualified Environmental Engineers in their area. Environment Pros requires that their Environmental Engineers hold at least a Bachelor's degree in Environmental Engineering plus two years of related experience.

- What recruitment steps would Environment Pros need to conduct to support a PERM application?
- What timing concerns would the Company need to bear in mind?

Results of Recruiting: Applicant Review, Timing, and Filing

Timeline and deadline management is critical with the recruitment process. The PERM labor certification application must be filed within 180 days of the date the first recruitment step was initiated.[112] In addition, the application cannot be filed until 30 days after the mandatory recruitment steps, including the job order, have been completed.[113] There is one exception to this rule, for professional positions. One of the three additional recruitment steps discussed can occur during the 30-day period prior to filing the PERM labor certification application.[114] If the application is filed even one day too soon or too late, it will be denied. For example, if an employer posts a Notice of Filing on Monday, April 19th, the notice must remain posted for 10 business days (including April 19th), or until Friday, April 30th. Once the 10-business-day posting is completed, the employer must wait 30 calendar days (referred to as a "quiet period") before it can file the PERM labor certification application. In this example, May 30th would be the 30th day and would be the earliest date the employer could file the PERM labor certification application. The "deadline" for filing the PERM labor

---

[111] 20 C.F.R. § 656.17(e)(1)(ii).
[112] 20 C.F.R. §§ 656.17(e)(1)(i) and (e)(2).
[113] *Id. See also Matter of Industrial Steel Products, LLC*, 2012-PER-00542 (BALCA 2012), 180-day period vis-à-vis job order begins to run from beginning of job order, not from end.
[114] 20 C.F.R. § 656.17(e)(1)(ii).

certification application would be October 16, 2016, the 180th day since the posting of the notice.[115]

Prior to filing the PERM application, all submitted resumes or other contacts with the company must be reviewed to determine whether or not there is a U.S. worker who is potentially qualified, willing, able, and available to perform the duties sought by the employer. Where a potentially qualified applicant is a U.S. worker, the employer must contact him or her immediately, either by phone or email to conduct first-round screening and/or scheduling an in-person interview.[116] If the employer is unable to reach such applicant by these means, the DOL has advised that the employer must send him or her a letter by certified mail, return receipt requested, to prove the attempt to contact the person.[117]

A recruitment report signed by the employer describing the steps undertaken and the results achieved, including the number of hires, if any, and, if applicable, the number of U.S. workers rejected, categorized by the lawful job-related reasons for such rejections, must be prepared and maintained in the compliance file.[118]

Special Recruitment or Handling for Faculty Members and Other Teachers at Institutions of Higher Education

There are different standards and recruitment requirements with respect to showing unavailability of U.S. workers for members of the post-secondary teaching professions.[119] Special Handling, also referred to as Special Recruitment, can be pursued for positions at institutions of higher education that require "some actual classroom teaching."[120] For such cases, the institution of higher education must be able to prove that, after conducting a competitive recruitment effort, it was unable to identify a willing and available U.S. worker who was equally or more qualified than the foreign national. In other words, the foreign national must be *more* qualified than all U.S. workers who applied for the position.

For such cases, there must have been a competitive recruitment process consisting of a Notice of Filing as well as at least one ad in a national professional journal, appearing either in print or online for a 30-day period.[121] The process must also include a statement by an official who has actual hiring authority

---

[115] The DOL has prepared a FAQ that gives further guidance on filing timelines during the PERM process. It is available at *https://www.foreignlaborcert.doleta.gov/pdf/faq_timelines_timeperiods_8_26_2011.pdf*

[116] *See Matter of Loma Lind Foods Inc.,* 1989-INA-410 (BALCA Nov. 26 1991). *See also Matter of Yaron Development Co.,* 1989-INA-178 (BALCA Apr. 19, 1991).

[117] *See Matter of Yaron Development Co.,* 1989-INA-178 (BALCA Apr. 19, 1991).

[118] 20 C.F.R. § 656.17(g).

[119] 20 C.F.R. § 656.18.

[120] DOL, Technical Assistance Guide, 656.21a—Application for Labor Certification for Occupations Requiring Special Handling (1981), reproduced in *8 Immigration Law Service 2d PSD,* Technical Assistance Guide I. D. (2008). The TAG is not readily found on the internet but can be found through a detailed Lexis/Westlaw search. *See also Matter of Mercer University,* 2011-PER-00162 (March 6, 2012), sufficient teaching responsibilities for special handling.

[121] 20 C.F.R. § 656.18(b).

outlining in detail the complete recruitment procedures, including, among other things, the specific lawful job-related reasons why the foreign national is more qualified than each U.S. worker who applied for the job.[122]

Alternatively, the DOL regulations permit colleges and universities to choose to go through the basic PERM recruitment process for professional positions, rather than the competitive recruitment process. However, even if the institution recruits utilizing the basic PERM recruitment steps, it may still use the Special Recruitment standard and pursue labor certification for the foreign national on the basis that s/he is more qualified than any willing and available U.S. worker that applied for the position.[123]

For Special Handling cases, the PERM labor certification application must be filed within 18 months of the date the foreign national was selected for the position.[124] However, the notice of filing must still be provided to the bargaining representative or posted for the full 10 business day period between 30 and 180 days before the filing of the application. In addition, the institution of higher education must obtain a PWD and, as noted, either must submit the PERM labor certification application during the validity period of the PWD or must have started the recruitment during that time.

D.3.e. Step 5: PERM Filing Procedure and Document Retention Requirements

Filing of the application takes place following the conclusion of all recruitment and the vetting of resumes. Prior to filing the PERM labor certification application, the employer must compile and maintain a compliance or audit file for each application that includes:

- A copy of the draft PERM labor certification application, to be replaced by a printout of the one electronically submitted, which should be a mirror copy, signed by the employer, the foreign national, and, if applicable, the person preparing the form;
- A copy of the PWD;
- Documentation of all advertisements, including the job order;
- A copy of the signed notice of filing;
- A copy of the signed recruitment report; and
- Copies of all resumes received as well as evidence of all communications with potentially qualified applicants.[125]

The vast majority of applications are filed electronically through the DOL's Foreign Labor Certification Permanent Online System.[126] Almost immediately

---

[122] 20 C.F.R. § 656.18(b)(1).
[123] 20 C.F.R. § 656.18(d). *See Matter of East Tennessee State University*, 2010-PER-00038 (BALCA 2011) (en banc).
[124] 20 C.F.R. § 656.18(b)(1).
[125] 20 C.F.R. § 656.10(f).
[126] Available at www.plc.doleta.gov.

upon filing, the DOL will send an e-mail confirming receipt of the application and very shortly thereafter will send another to the employer with several questions regarding the position. The response is due within a specified period of time or else the PERM application will be denied.

Retaining a signed printout of the electronically filed PERM labor certification application is best practice because, in the event of an audit, described in Section D.4, a signed copy will be required.[127] Therefore, having one already on file will ensure a timely response to an audit. If, however, the PERM application is submitted by mail, the form must also be signed by the employer, foreign national, and the person preparing the form prior to submitting it to the DOL.[128] The employer is required to retain copies of the filed PERM labor certification application and all supporting documentation in the recommended compliance file for five years from the date of filing.[129] Included in Figure 7.4 is a sample completed PERM labor certification application.

D.4. Determinations

After consideration of the application, the DOL will take one of three actions:

- Certification.[130] Upon certification, the DOL will provide a hardcopy of the certified PERM labor certification application. The employer and the sponsored individual, as well as the person who prepared the application, must then sign and submit it in support of the employer's immigrant visa petition on Form I-140, Immigrant Petition for Alien Worker, within 180 days of certification by the DOL.
- Audit.[131] No documents are submitted with the initial application, only the application itself. However, the DOL can request an audit, asking for such things as proof of recruitment, the PWD, and the recruitment report. All matters must be submitted within 30 days, although a 30-day extension may be granted at the DOL's discretion. After the audit response is submitted, the DOL will either approve or deny the PERM application.
- Denial. The DOL's notice must state the reason for the denial. An appeal can be made to BALCA and must be filed within 30 days of the date of the determination. A new PERM labor certification application in the same occupation for the same person cannot be filed while an appeal to BALCA is pending. Alternatively, the employer may also request reconsideration by the certifying officer within 30 days of the denial.[132] The regulations set forth the procedures for the appeal to BALCA.[133]

---

[127] 20 C.F.R. § 656.17(a)(1).
[128] Id.
[129] 20 C.F.R. § 656.10(f).
[130] 20 C.F.R. § 656.24(d).
[131] 20 C.F.R. § 656.20.
[132] 20 C.F.R. §§ 656.24(e)-(g).
[133] 20 C.F.R. § 656.26.

D: Advanced Degree Professionals (EB-2) and Skilled Workers 353

Figure 7.4
Sample PERM Application

OMB Approval: 1205-0451
Expiration Date: 06/30/2011

Application for Permanent Employment Certification
ETA Form 9089
U.S. Department of Labor

Please read and review the filing instructions before completing this form. A copy of the instructions can be found at http://www.foreignlaborcert.doleta.gov/pdf/9089inst.pdf

Employing or continuing to employ an alien unauthorized to work in the United States is illegal and may subject the employer to criminal prosecution, civil money penalties, or both.

A. Refiling Instructions

1. Are you seeking to utilize the filing date from a previously submitted Application for Alien Employment Certification (ETA 750)? ☐ Yes ☒ No

1-A. If Yes, enter the previous filing date

1-B. Indicate the previous SWA or local office case number OR if not available, specify state where case was originally filed:

B. Schedule A or Sheepherder Information

1. Is this application in support of a Schedule A or Sheepherder Occupation? ☐ Yes ☒ No

If Yes, do NOT send this application to the Department of Labor. All applications in support of Schedule A or Sheepherder Occupations must be sent directly to the appropriate Department of Homeland Security office.

C. Employer Information (Headquarters or Main Office)

1. Employer's name: Panda Gifts, Inc.
2. Address 1: 3434 Poplar Street
   Address 2:
3. City: Philadelphia State/Province: PA Country: United States Postal code: 19101
4. Phone number: 215-555-1234 Extension:
5. Number of employees: 20 6. Year commenced business: 2010
7. FEIN (Federal Employer Identification Number): 23-8974021 8. NAICS code: 454111
9. Is the employer a closely held corporation, partnership, or sole proprietorship in which the alien has an ownership interest, or is there a familial relationship between the owners, stockholders, partners, corporate officers, incorporators, and the alien? ☐ Yes ☒ No

D. Employer Contact Information (This section must be filled out. This information must be different from the agent or attorney information listed in Section E).

1. Contact's last name: Lee First name: Ang Middle initial:
2. Address 1: 3434 Poplar Street
   Address 2:
3. City: Philadelphia State/Province: PA Country: United States Postal code: 19101
4. Phone number: 215-555-4321 Extension:
5. E-mail address: Ang.Lee@pandagifts.com

ETA Form 9089

Figure 7.4 (Continued)

OMB Approval: 1205-0451
Expiration Date: 06/30/2011

Application for Permanent Employment Certification
ETA Form 9089
U.S. Department of Labor

E. Agent or Attorney Information (If applicable)

1. Agent or attorney's last name	First name	Middle initial
Perez	Maria	C.

2. Firm name
Perez & Cooper, PC

3. Firm EIN	4. Phone number	Extension
12-3456777	215-555-1234	

5. Address 1
1234 Stenton Avenue

Address 2

6. City	State/Province	Country	Postal code
Philadelphia	PA	USA	19141

7. E-mail address
maria@perezcooper.com

F. Prevailing Wage Information (as provided by the State Workforce Agency)

1. Prevailing wage tracking number (if applicable)	2. SOC/O*NET(OES) code
P10016050426955	15-1132

3. Occupation Title	4. Skill Level
Software Developer, Applications	2

5. Prevailing wage: $ 81619.00 Per: (Choose only one) ☐ Hour ☐ Week ☐ Bi-Weekly ☐ Month ☒ Year

6. Prevailing wage source (Choose only one)
☒ OES ☐ CBA ☐ Employer Conducted Survey ☐ DBA ☐ SCA ☐ Other

6-A. If Other is indicated in question 6, specify:

7. Determination date	8. Expiration date
12/18/2015	06/30/2016

G. Wage Offer Information

1. Offered wage
From: $ 81619.00 To: (Optional) $ 90000.00
Per: (Choose only one) ☐ Hour ☐ Week ☐ Bi-Weekly ☐ Month ☒ Year

H. Job Opportunity Information (Where work will be performed)

1. Primary worksite (where work is to be performed) address 1
3434 Poplar Street

Address 2

2. City	State	Postal code
Philadelphia	PA	19101

3. Job title
Senior Java Developer

4. Education: minimum level required:
☐ None ☐ High School ☐ Associate's ☒ Bachelor's ☐ Master's ☐ Doctorate ☐ Other

4-A. If Other is indicated in question 4, specify the education required:

4-B. Major field of study
Computer Science

5. Is training required in the job opportunity? ☐ Yes ☒ No
5-A. If Yes, number of months of training required:

ETA Form 9089

D: Advanced Degree Professionals (EB-2) and Skilled Workers

Figure 7.4 (Continued)

OMB Approval: 1205-0451
Expiration Date: 06/30/2011

Application for Permanent Employment Certification
ETA Form 9089
U.S. Department of Labor

H. Job Opportunity Information Continued

5-B. Indicate the field of training:

6. Is experience in the job offered required for the job? [x] Yes [ ] No
6-A. If Yes, number of months experience required: 36

7. Is there an alternate field of study that is acceptable? [x] Yes [ ] No

7-A. If Yes, specify the major field of study: Computer Engineering or a related field

8. Is there an alternate combination of education and experience that is acceptable? [ ] Yes [x] No

8-A. If Yes, specify the alternate level of education required:
[ ] None [ ] High School [ ] Associate's [ ] Bachelor's [ ] Master's [ ] Doctorate [ ] Other

8-B. If Other is indicated in question 8-A, indicate the alternate level of education required:

8-C. If applicable, indicate the number of years experience acceptable in question 8:

9. Is a foreign educational equivalent acceptable? [ ] Yes [x] No

10. Is experience in an alternate occupation acceptable? [x] Yes [ ] No
10-A. If Yes, number of months experience in alternate occupation required: 36

10-B. Identify the job title of the acceptable alternate occupation:
Java Developer or a related occupation

11. Job duties – If submitting by mail, add attachment if necessary. Job duties description must begin in this space.

Working independently, design, develop and modify software applications for an online order management system using experience with Java, JavaScript, JQuery, AngularJS, HTML5, CSS3, and SQL. Analyze user needs to develop new application features using experience with Java Server Pages (JSP) and Tomcat application servers. Modify existing software to correct errors and ensure application integration using experience with REST and SOAP web services. Develop software system testing for all applications using experience with CVS version control systems. Port applications to iOS and Android mobile device platforms using experience with Objective-C, Swift and Linux.

12. Are the job opportunity's requirements normal for the occupation? [x] Yes [ ] No

If the answer to this question is No, the employer must be prepared to provide documentation demonstrating that the job requirements are supported by business necessity.

13. Is knowledge of a foreign language required to perform the job duties? [ ] Yes [x] No

If the answer to this question is Yes, the employer must be prepared to provide documentation demonstrating that the language requirements are supported by business necessity.

14. Specific skills or other requirements – If submitting by mail, add attachment if necessary. Skills description must begin in this space.

Any suitable combination of education, training or experience is acceptable.

Figure 7.4 (Continued)

OMB Approval: 1205-0451　　Application for Permanent Employment Certification
Expiration Date: 06/30/2011　　　　　　　ETA Form 9089
　　　　　　　　　　　　　　　　　　U.S. Department of Labor

H. Job Opportunity Information Continued

15. Does this application involve a job opportunity that includes a combination of occupations?	☐ Yes ☒ No
16. Is the position identified in this application being offered to the alien identified in Section J?	☒ Yes ☐ No
17. Does the job require the alien to live on the employer's premises?	☐ Yes ☒ No
18. Is the application for a live-in household domestic service worker?	☐ Yes ☒ No
18-A. If Yes, have the employer and the alien executed the required employment contract and has the employer provided a copy of the contract to the alien?	☐ Yes ☐ No ☒ NA

I. Recruitment Information

a. Occupation Type – All must complete this section.

1. Is this application for a **professional occupation**, other than a college or university teacher? Professional occupations are those for which a bachelor's degree (or equivalent) is normally required.	☒ Yes ☐ No
2. Is this application for a college or university teacher? **If Yes, complete questions 2-A and 2-B below.**	☐ Yes ☒ No
2-A. Did you select the candidate using a competitive recruitment and selection process?	☐ Yes ☐ No
2-B. Did you use the basic recruitment process for professional occupations?	☐ Yes ☐ No

b. Special Recruitment and Documentation Procedures for College and University Teachers – Complete only if the answer to question I.a.2-A is Yes.

3. Date alien selected:
4. Name and date of national professional journal in which advertisement was placed:
5. Specify additional recruitment information in this space. Add an attachment if necessary.

c. Professional/Non-Professional Information – Complete this section unless your answer to question B.1 or I.a.2-A is YES.

6. Start date for the SWA job order　01/11/2016	7. End date for the SWA job order　02/11/2016
8. Is there a Sunday edition of the newspaper in the area of intended employment?	☒ Yes ☐ No
9. Name of newspaper (of general circulation) in which the first advertisement was placed: Philadelphia Inquirer	
10. Date of first advertisement identified in question 9: 01/17/2016	
11. Name of newspaper or professional journal (if applicable) in which second advertisement was placed: Philadelphia Inquirer	☒ Newspaper ☐ Journal

D: Advanced Degree Professionals (EB-2) and Skilled Workers

Figure 7.4
(Continued)

OMB Approval: 1205-0451
Expiration Date: 06/30/2011

Application for Permanent Employment Certification
ETA Form 9089
U.S. Department of Labor

I. Recruitment Information Continued

12. Date of second newspaper advertisement or date of publication of journal identified in question 11:	01/24/2016

d. Professional Recruitment Information – Complete if the answer to question I.a.1 is YES or if the answer to I.a.2-B is YES. Complete at least 3 of the items.

13. Dates advertised at job fair From: To:	14. Dates of on-campus recruiting From: To:
15. Dates posted on employer web site From: 01/11/20■ To: 02/11/2016	16. Dates advertised with trade or professional organization From: To:
17. Dates listed with job search web site From: 01/11/20■ To: 02/11/2016	18. Dates listed with private employment firm From: To:
19. Dates advertised with employee referral program From: To:	20. Dates advertised with campus placement office From: To:
21. Dates advertised with local or ethnic newspaper From: 01/18/20■ To: 01/18/2016	22. Dates advertised with radio or TV ads From: To:

e. General Information – All must complete this section.

23. Has the employer received payment of any kind for the submission of this application?	☐ Yes ☒ No
23-A. If Yes, describe details of the payment including the amount, date and purpose of the payment:	
24. Has the bargaining representative for workers in the occupation in which the alien will be employed been provided with notice of this filing at least 30 days but not more than 180 days before the date the application is filed?	☐ Yes ☐ No ☒ NA
25. If there is no bargaining representative, has a notice of this filing been posted for 10 business days in a conspicuous location at the place of employment, ending at least 30 days before but not more than 180 days before the date the application is filed?	☒ Yes ☐ No ☐ NA
26. Has the employer had a layoff in the area of intended employment in the occupation involved in this application or in a related occupation within the six months immediately preceding the filing of this application?	☐ Yes ☒ No
26-A. If Yes, were the laid off U.S. workers notified and considered for the job opportunity for which certification is sought?	☐ Yes ☐ No ☐ NA

J. Alien Information (This section must be filled out. This information must be different from the agent or attorney information listed in Section E).

1. Alien's last name Park	First name Thomas	Full middle name
2. Current address 1 2003 Spring Garden Street		
Address 2 Apt. 4		

3. City Philadelphia	State/Province PA	Country United States	Postal code 19130
4. Phone number of current residence 215-555-2369			
5. Country of citizenship South Korea		6. Country of birth South Korea	
7. Alien's date of birth 05/25/1988		8. Class of admission H-1B	
9. Alien registration number (A#)		10. Alien admission number (I-94) 30352901877	

11. Education: highest level achieved relevant to the requested occupation:

☐ None ☐ High School ☐ Associate's ☒ Bachelor's ☐ Master's ☐ Doctorate ☐ Other

Chapter 7: Employment-Based and Self-Sponsored Immigration

Figure 7.4 (Continued)

OMB Approval: 1205-0451
Expiration Date: 06/30/2011

Application for Permanent Employment Certification
ETA Form 9089
U.S. Department of Labor

J. Alien Information Continued

11-A. If Other indicated in question 11, specify	
12. Specify major field(s) of study	Computer Science
13. Year relevant education completed	2010
14. Institution where relevant education specified in question 11 was received	Drexel University
15. Address 1 of conferring institution	3141 Chestnut Street
Address 2	

16. City	State/Province	Country	Postal code
Philadelphia	PA	United States	19104

17. Did the alien complete the training required for the requested job opportunity, as indicated in question H.5?	☐ Yes ☐ No	☒ NA
18. Does the alien have the experience as required for the requested job opportunity indicated in question H.6?	☒ Yes ☐ No	☐ NA
19. Does the alien possess the alternate combination of education and experience as indicated in question H.8?	☐ Yes ☐ No	☒ NA
20. Does the alien have the experience in an alternate occupation specified in question H.10?	☒ Yes ☐ No	☐ NA
21. Did the alien gain any of the qualifying experience with the employer in a position substantially comparable to the job opportunity requested?	☐ Yes ☒ No	☐ NA
22. Did the employer pay for any of the alien's education or training necessary to satisfy any of the employer's job requirements for this position?	☐ Yes ☒ No	
23. Is the alien currently employed by the petitioning employer?	☒ Yes ☐ No	

K. Alien Work Experience

List all jobs the alien has held during the past 3 years. Also list any other experience that qualifies the alien for the job opportunity for which the employer is seeking certification.

a. Job 1

1. Employer name	Panda Gifts, Inc.
2. Address 1	3434 Poplar Street
Address 2	

3. City	State/Province	Country	Postal code
Philadelphia	PA	United States	19101

4. Type of business	5. Job title
Online Retailer	Sr. Java Developer

6. Start date	7. End date	8. Number of hours worked per week
08/05/2015		40

ETA Form 9089

D: Advanced Degree Professionals (EB-2) and Skilled Workers

Figure 7.4 (Continued)

OMB Approval: 1205-0451
Expiration Date: 06/30/2011

Application for Permanent Employment Certification
ETA Form 9089
U.S. Department of Labor

K. Alien Work Experience Continued

9. Job details (duties performed, use of tools, machines, equipment, skills, qualifications, certifications, licenses, etc. Include the phone number of the employer and the name of the alien's supervisor.)

Working independently, design, develop and modify software applications for an online order management system using experience with Java, JavaScript, JQuery, AngularJS, HTML5, CSS3, and SQL. Analyze user needs to develop new application features using experience with Java Server Pages (JSP) and Tomcat application servers. Modify existing software to correct errors and ensure application integration using experience with REST and SOAP web services. Develop software system testing for all applications using experience with CVS version control systems. Port applications to iOS and Android mobile device platforms using experience with Objective-C, Swift and Linux.
Supervisor: Ang Lee / Telephone: 215-555-1234

b. Job 2

1. Employer name			
AutoParts Online			
2. Address 1			
1890 North Broad Street			
Address 2			
3. City: Philadelphia	State/Province: PA	Country: United States	Postal code: 19122
4. Type of business: Online Auto Parts		5. Job title: Java Developer	
6. Start date: 03/01/2012	7. End date: 08/01/2015	8. Number of hours worked per week: 40	

9. Job details (duties performed, use of tools, machines, equipment, skills, qualifications, certifications, licenses, etc. Include the phone number of the employer and the name of the alien's supervisor.)

Developed applications for an online order management system for an auto parts warehouse company using Java, JavaScript, JQuery, AngularJS, HTML5, CSS3, and SQL. Designed and deployed new features and modules using Java Server Pages (JSP), Java Server Faces (JSF), and Enterprise JavaBeans (EJB) on Tomcat application servers. Integrated applications using Microsoft SharePoint, REST and SOAP web services, and SQL Server. Performed testing for all applications using Git and CVS version control systems. Ported applications to iOS and Android mobile device platforms using Objective-C, Swift and Linux.
Supervisor: Joseph Miller / Telephone: 215-555-3600

c. Job 3

1. Employer name			
Super Consulting			
2. Address 1			
2424 Market Street			
Address 2: Suite 203			
3. City: Philadelphia	State/Province: PA	Country: United States	Postal code: 19103
4. Type of business: Software Consulting		5. Job title: Java Developer Intern	
6. Start date: 08/01/2010	7. End date: 02/28/2012	8. Number of hours worked per week: 40	

Figure 7.4 (Continued)

OMB Approval: 1205-0451
Expiration Date: 06/30/2011

Application for Permanent Employment Certification
ETA Form 9089
U.S. Department of Labor

K. Alien Work Experience Continued

9. Job details (duties performed, use of tools, machines, equipment, skills, qualifications, certifications, licenses, etc. Include the phone number of the employer and the name of the alien's supervisor.)

In this entry-level position, assisted the Senior Java Developer in developing online applications using programs including Java, JavaScript, JQuery, Java Server Pages (JSP), Java Server Faces (JSF), Enterprise JavaBeans (EJB), AngularJS, HTML5, CSS3, and SQL. Assisted in integrating applications using Microsoft SharePoint, REST and SOAP web services, and SQL Server. Assisted in testing all applications using Git and CVS version control systems. Assisted in developing applications for mobile devices using Objective-C, Swift and Linux.
Supervisor: Steve Smith / Telephone: 215-555-8520

L. Alien Declaration

I declare under penalty of perjury that Sections J and K are true and correct. I understand that to knowingly furnish false information in the preparation of this form and any supplement thereto or to aid, abet, or counsel another to do so is a federal offense punishable by a fine or imprisonment up to five years or both under 18 U.S.C. §§ 2 and 1001. Other penalties apply as well to fraud or misuse of ETA immigration documents and to perjury with respect to such documents under 18 U.S.C. §§ 1546 and 1621.

*In addition, I **further declare** under penalty of perjury that I intend to accept the position offered in Section H of this application if a labor certification is approved and I am granted a visa or an adjustment of status based on this application.*

1. Alien's last name	First name	Full middle name
Park	Thomas	
2. Signature	Date signed	

Note – The signature and date signed do not have to be filled out when electronically submitting to the Department of Labor for processing, but must be complete when submitting by mail. If the application is submitted electronically, any resulting certification MUST be signed *immediately upon receipt* from DOL before it can be submitted to USCIS for final processing.

M. Declaration of Preparer

1. Was the application completed by the employer? If No, you must complete this section.	☐ Yes	☒ No

I hereby certify that I have prepared this application at the direct request of the employer listed in Section C and that to the best of my knowledge the information contained herein is true and correct. I understand that to knowingly furnish false information in the preparation of this form and any supplement thereto or to aid, abet, or counsel another to do so is a federal offense punishable by a fine, imprisonment up to five years or both under 18 U.S.C. §§ 2 and 1001. Other penalties apply as well to fraud or misuse of ETA immigration documents and to perjury with respect to such documents under 18 U.S.C. §§ 1546 and 1621.

2. Preparer's last name	First name	Middle initial
Perez	Maria	C
3. Title		
Attorney		
4. E-mail address		
maria@perezcooper.com		
5. Signature	Date signed	

Note – The signature and date signed do not have to be filled out when electronically submitting to the Department of Labor for processing, but must be complete when submitting by mail. If the application is submitted electronically, any resulting certification MUST be signed *immediately upon receipt* from DOL before it can be submitted to USCIS for final processing.

D: Advanced Degree Professionals (EB-2) and Skilled Workers

Figure 7.4 (Continued)

OMB Approval: 1205-0451
Expiration Date: 06/30/2011

Application for Permanent Employment Certification
ETA Form 9089
U.S. Department of Labor

N. Employer Declaration

By virtue of my signature below, I HEREBY CERTIFY the following conditions of employment:

1. The offered wage equals or exceeds the prevailing wage and I will pay at least the prevailing wage.
2. The wage is not based on commissions, bonuses or other incentives, unless I guarantees a wage paid on a weekly, bi-weekly, or monthly basis that equals or exceeds the prevailing wage.
3. I have enough funds available to pay the wage or salary offered the alien.
4. I will be able to place the alien on the payroll on or before the date of the alien's proposed entrance into the United States.
5. The job opportunity does not involve unlawful discrimination by race, creed, color, national origin, age, sex, religion, handicap, or citizenship.
6. The job opportunity is not:
    a. Vacant because the former occupant is on strike or is being locked out in the course of a labor dispute involving a work stoppage; or
    b. At issue in a labor dispute involving a work stoppage.
7. The job opportunity's terms, conditions, and occupational environment are not contrary to Federal, state or local law.
8. The job opportunity has been and is clearly open to any U.S. worker.
9. The U.S. workers who applied for the job opportunity were rejected for lawful job-related reasons.
10. The job opportunity is for full-time, permanent employment for an employer other than the alien.

I hereby designate the agent or attorney identified in section E (if any) to represent me for the purpose of labor certification and, by virtue of my signature in Block 3 below, **I take full responsibility** for the accuracy of any representations made by my agent or attorney.

I declare under penalty of perjury that I have read and reviewed this application and that to the best of my knowledge the information contained herein is true and accurate. *I understand that to knowingly furnish false information in the preparation of this form and any supplement thereto or to aid, abet, or counsel another to do so is a federal offense punishable by a fine or imprisonment up to five years or both under 18 U.S.C. §§ 2 and 1001. Other penalties apply as well to fraud or misuse of ETA immigration documents and to perjury with respect to such documents under 18 U.S.C. §§ 1546 and 1621.*

1. Last name	First name	Middle initial
Lee	Ang	
2. Title		
President		
3. Signature	Date signed	

Note – The signature and date signed do not have to be filled out when electronically submitting to the Department of Labor for processing, but must be complete when submitting by mail. If the application is submitted electronically, any resulting certification MUST be signed *immediately upon receipt* from DOL before it can be submitted to USCIS for final processing.

O. U.S. Government Agency Use Only

Pursuant to the provisions of Section 212 (a)(5)(A) of the Immigration and Nationality Act, as amended, I hereby certify that there are not sufficient U.S. workers available and the employment of the above will not adversely affect the wages and working conditions of workers in the U.S. similarly employed.

Signature of Certifying Officer   Date Signed

Case Number   Filing Date

Figure 7.4 (Continued)

OMB Approval: 1205-0451
Expiration Date: 06/30/2011

Application for Permanent Employment Certification
ETA Form 9089
U.S. Department of Labor

P. OMB Information *Paperwork Reduction Act Information Control Number 1205-0451*

Persons are not required to respond to this collection of information unless it displays a currently valid OMB control number.

Respondent's reply to these reporting requirements is required to obtain the benefits of permanent employment certification (Immigration and Nationality Act, Section 212(a)(5)). Public reporting burden for this collection of information is estimated to average 1¼ hours per response, including the time for reviewing instructions, searching existing data sources, gathering and maintaining the data needed, and completing and reviewing the collection of information. Send comments regarding this burden estimate to the Division of Foreign Labor Certification * U.S. Department of Labor * Room C4312 * 200 Constitution Ave., NW * Washington, DC * 20210.
Do NOT send the completed application to this address.

Q. Privacy Statement Information

In accordance with the Privacy Act of 1974, as amended (5 U.S.C. 552a), you are hereby notified that the information provided herein is protected under the Privacy Act. The Department of Labor (Department or DOL) maintains a System of Records titled Employer Application and Attestation File for Permanent and Temporary Alien Workers (DOL/ETA-7) that includes this record.

Under routine uses for this system of records, case files developed in processing labor certification applications, labor condition applications, or labor attestations may be released as follows: in connection with appeals of denials before the DOL Office of Administrative Law Judges and Federal courts, records may be released to the employers that filed such applications, their representatives, to named alien beneficiaries or their representatives, and to the DOL Office of Administrative Law Judges and Federal courts; and in connection with administering and enforcing immigration laws and regulations, records may be released to such agencies as the DOL Office of Inspector General, Employment Standards Administration, the Department of Homeland Security, and the Department of State.

Further relevant disclosures may be made in accordance with the Privacy Act and under the following circumstances: in connection with federal litigation; for law enforcement purposes; to authorized parent locator persons under Pub. L. 93-647; to an information source or public authority in connection with personnel, security clearance, procurement, or benefit-related matters; to a contractor or their employees, grantees or their employees, consultants, or volunteers who have been engaged to assist the agency in the performance of Federal activities; for Federal debt collection purposes; to the Office of Management and Budget in connection with its legislative review, coordination, and clearance activities; to a Member of Congress or their staff in response to an inquiry of the Congressional office made at the written request of the subject of the record; in connection with records management; and to the news media and the public when a matter under investigation becomes public knowledge, the Solicitor of Labor determines the disclosure is necessary to preserve confidence in the integrity of the Department, or the Solicitor of Labor determines that a legitimate public interest exists in the disclosure of information, unless the Solicitor of Labor determines that disclosure would constitute an unwarranted invasion of personal privacy.

E. Procedure for EB-2 and EB-3 Labor Certification Cases

The LPR status process for EB-2 and EB-3 labor certification cases is a three-step process. First, after conducting its recruitment effort, the U.S. employer must submit the PERM labor certification application to the DOL. Once the PERM application is certified, the employer can submit step two, the Form I-140, Immigrant Petition for Alien Worker. The approved or certified PERM application is only valid for 180 days from the date of certification. The certified Form ETA 9089, Application for Permanent Employment Certification, will indicate at the bottom of each page the 180-day validity period of the certification. The Form I-140, Immigrant Petition for Alien Worker, must be submitted with a valid, unexpired, certified PERM labor certification application signed by the employer, the sponsored employee, and the legal representative. If the Form I-140 is submitted even one day after the PERM labor certification expires, the petition will be denied and the employer will need to start the entire PERM process over again.

If an immigrant visa number is immediately available, a foreign national who is in the United States can concurrently file Form I-485, Application to Register Permanent Residency or Adjust Status, to become an LPR. Any qualifying derivative family members may also adjust, with the original petition filed by the employer. If abroad, the foreign national can then apply for immigrant visa consular processing through the National Visa Center, or NVC. Again, discussion of adjustment of status and consular processing is in Chapter 6, Family Sponsored Immigration and Permanent Resident Status.

However, if an immigrant visa is not immediately available due to quota limits (typical in the EB-2 category for Indian and Chinese Nationals and in the EB-3 category for all foreign nationals), s/he and any qualifying derivatives must wait until the foreign national's priority date is reached, which will be reflected on the DOS' online monthly Visa Bulletin. As discussed in Section A.2 of Chapter 6, Family Sponsored Immigration and Permanent Resident Status, those foreign nationals who cannot adjust immediately, but who are present in the United States in lawful status, can now use the Visa Bulletin Dates (after cross referencing with the chart on the USCIS website) for Filing of Employment-Based Visa Applications chart to determine the date when they can file their adjustment application, even though it may not be adjudicated for several months or years into the future.[134]

The benefit of filing an application to adjust status to a permanent resident months before a visa number is available means that the beneficiary may apply for advanced permission to travel out of and return to the United States, as well as apply for permission to work. Once granted, the foreign national may be able

---

[134] This follows the Sept. 9, 2015 announcement made by the USCIS and the DOS regarding revisions to their procedures for determining visa availability for applicants waiting to file for employment-based or family-sponsored preference adjustment of status applications.

to transfer employment without ties to the employer who filed the Form I-140, Immigrant Petition for Alien Worker. Specifically, the American Competitiveness in the 21st Century Act of 2000, or AC21,[135] permits a foreign national to change employers without the new employer needing to file a new petition, if the following conditions are met: (1) the new employment is in the "same or similar" occupational classification; (2) Form I-140 has been approved, or is approvable when filed concurrently with Form I-485, Application to Register Permanent Residence or Adjust Status; and (3) Form I-485 has been pending for at least 180 days.[136] This is referred to as "I-485 portability" and gives foreign nationals who are stuck waiting for a visa number to become available per the visa bulletin, a certain degree of flexibility to change jobs without negatively impacting their eligibility for LPR status.

E.1. Compiling an EB-2 and EB-3 Petition Based on Labor Certification

The Form I-140, Immigrant Petition for Alien Worker, must attach evidence proving that both the employer and the foreign national qualify for the category sought as well as evidence that the worker qualifies for the job opportunity. The petition packet must include:

- Form I-140, Immigrant Petition for Alien Worker;
- Form G-28, Notice of Entry of Appearance of Attorney or Accredited Representative, if the applicant has legal representation;
- USCIS Filing Fee;
- A signed copy of the ETA Form 9089, Application for Permanent Employment Certification;
- Evidence of the employer's ability to pay the proffered wage;
- A letter from the employer confirming its job offer and intent to employ the foreign national in the offered and certified position; and
- Evidence that the foreign national satisfies all the job requirements listed in the employer's PERM application, including the education, experience, training, and/or any other specified requirements. Such evidence must include, as applicable, official academic records indicating the foreign national's degree or diploma, with foreign equivalency evaluation, if applicable, letters from former employers attesting to prior qualifying experience and to the foreign national's possession of any required skills or expertise, copies of certificates or licenses, etc.

---

[135] Pub. L. 106-313, 114 Stat. 1251 (2000).
[136] *Id.* at § 106(c). *See also* USCIS December 27, 2005 Interoffice Memorandum, entitled "Interim guidance for processing I-140 employment-based immigrant petitions and I-485 and H-1B petitions affected by the American Competitiveness in the Twenty-first Century Act of 2000" (AC21) (Public Law 106-313),HQPRD 71/6.2.8, *and* USCIS March 18, 2016 Policy Memorandum entitled "Determining Whether a New Job is in 'the Same or a Similar Occupational Classification' for Purposes of Section 204(j) Job Portability," PM-602-0122.1.

F. Exceptions to the Perm Labor Certification Application Process, National Interest Waivers (EB-2), and EB-2 or EB-3 Schedule A Labor Certification: INA § 203(b)(2)(A); 8 C.F.R. § 204.5(k); 8 C.F.R. § 204.12

F.1. EB-2 National Interest Waiver for Advanced Degree Professionals, Those with Exceptional Abilities, and for Physicians Working in Shortage Areas or Veterans Facilities

The National Interest Waiver, or NIW, provisions of the INA grant a waiver of the labor certification requirement in the EB-2 preference category to individuals in business, the sciences, or the arts with advanced degrees or exceptional ability who will "substantially benefit prospectively the national economy, cultural or educational interest, or welfare of the United application States."[137] Essentially, the foreign national can skip the PERM labor certification application step and file his or her own Form I-140, Immigrant Petition for Alien Worker, with a NIW request establishing eligibility for the NIW. A job offer is not required for NIW eligibility so foreign nationals can actually self-petition.[138]

"National interest" is not defined by any statute or regulation. Instead, the USCIS relies on a three-part test established in a 1998 Administrative Appeals Office, or AAO, case, *Matter of New York State Department of Transportation (NYSDOT)*, as the legal standard for adjudicating NIW Petitions.[139] To qualify for a NIW, the foreign national must show that:

- His or her work is in an area of "substantial intrinsic merit"—the importance of the foreign national's proposed work must be readily apparent based on the documentation submitted;
- His or her work is national in scope—the foreign national must show through documentation that the benefit of his or her work goes beyond a particular region of the country; and
- Requiring the labor certification process would be contrary to the national interest.

As a reminder, the purpose of the labor certification process is to protect the national interests of the United States by protecting the U.S. workforce. Therefore, when waiving the labor certification requirement based on the national interest, the DOL must evaluate all the evidence to determine if the benefits offered by the foreign national outweigh the national interests inherent in

---

[137] INA § 203(b)(2)(A).
[138] 8 C.F.R. § 204.5(k)(1).
[139] 22 I&N Dec. 206 (AAO 1998).

recruiting and hiring minimally qualified U.S. workers. Typically, this is demonstrated by showing a past record of specific prior achievements that indicate future benefits to the national interest of the United States. This prong can be further satisfied by providing evidence that the foreign national possesses a specific unique skill set or esoteric experience or expertise that cannot be replicated by any person in the U.S. workforce.

> **Case for Discussion 7.8**
>
> Dr. Roth is a physicist from France. Her expertise is in studying and improving the fluid dynamics of airflow and ventilation in subway and high-speed train tunnels. She has a consulting business in France and has already designed airflow and ventilation improvements for train systems in numerous cities, including in major cities, such as Lyon, France; Barcelona, Spain; and Milan, Italy. Numerous news articles across Europe have featured reports about her work on these train systems. The Department of Transportation of a major U.S. city recently contacted her to help design and upgrade the ventilation and airflow system in their subway tunnels. Of particular concern is the safety of such tunnels in the event of an emergency, such as a fire or explosion. The city is, unfortunately, the recipient of repeated terrorist threats. Dr. Roth is excited by the opportunities in the United States, as many of its train systems are outdated and numerous high-speed train proposals will require new and safe tunnels. Although she only has one contract lined up, she is in negotiation with several other cities in the United States as well.
>
> - Would Dr. Roth qualify for an NIW?
> - How might she satisfy each prong of the NIW test?

The INA also establishes that physicians working in shortage areas or Veteran's Affairs, or VA, hospitals may qualify for an NIW.[140] The USCIS does provide specific regulatory requirements for such waivers. Specifically, the physician must establish the following:

- S/he agrees to work full-time for at least 40 hours per week, in a clinical practice for an aggregate of five years, not including time served in J-1 nonimmigrant status;
- S/he must be providing service at a healthcare facility under the jurisdiction of the secretary of Veterans Affairs, or in a geographical area or areas designated by the secretary of Health and Human Services, or HHS, as a Medically Underserved Area, a Primary Medical Health Professional Shortage

---

[140] INA § 203(b)(2)(B)(ii).

Area, or a Mental Health Professional Shortage Area, and in a medical specialty that is within the scope of the secretary's designation for the geographic area; and

- S/he must have received a determination by a Federal agency or the department of public health of a State, territory of the United States, or the District of Columbia, confirming that the physician's work in the area or facility is in the public interest.[141]

The USCIS recently adopted a decision of the AAO clarifying that medical specialists who agree to practice in any area designated by the Secretary of HHS as having a shortage of health care professionals may be eligible for the physician national interest waiver under INA § 203(b)(2)(B)(ii).[142] It has issued policy guidance that applies to and binds all USCIS employees who are now directed to follow the decision in similar cases.[143]

F.2. Schedule A Occupations

Schedule A, found in 20 C.F.R. § 656.5, is comprised of certain occupations that the DOL has pre-certified as having insufficient U.S. workers who are able, willing, qualified, and available, such as registered nurses and physical therapists.[144] Therefore, the employment of foreign nationals in these occupations will not adversely affect the wages and working conditions of similarly employed U.S. workers, making the PERM labor certification application recruitment process unnecessary.

Rather than submitting the labor certification application to the DOL, the employer must submit a completed and signed application, using the paper version of Form ETA 9089, Application for Permanent Employment Certification, to the USCIS along with its Form I-140, Immigrant Petition for Alien Worker. Although a recruitment effort is not required, the employer must obtain a PWD and must provide the required Notice of Filing prior to filing, and include evidence of it with its submission to the USCIS.

There are two Groups of Schedule A occupations. Group I consists of physical therapists and registered nurses.[145] Group II consists of foreign nationals of exceptional ability in the sciences or arts, excluding those in the performing arts.[146] For these individuals, the employer must file documentary evidence showing: 1) the foreign national's widespread acclaim and international recognition by recognized experts in his or her field; 2) the foreign national's work in his or her field during the year prior to filing required his or exceptional

---

[141] 8 C.F.R. § 204.12(a)(3).
[142] *Matter of H-V-P-*, ID# 16270 (AAO Feb. 9, 2016).
[143] Department of Homeland Security Policy Memorandum, *Matter of H-V-P-*, Adopted Decision 2016-01 (AAO Feb. 9, 2016).
[144] Although not a part of Schedule A, sheepherders also do not require the submission of a labor certification application to the DOL. *See* 20 C.F.R. § 656.16.
[145] 20 C.F.R. § 656.5(a).
[146] 20 C.F.R. § 656.5(b).

ability; 3) the foreign national's intended work in the United States also will require his or her exceptional ability; and 4) the foreign national satisfies at least two of seven regulatory criteria,[147] which include:

- Documentation of the [foreign national's] receipt of internationally recognized prizes or awards for excellence in the field of endeavor
- Documentation of the [foreign national's] membership in international associations in the field for which classification is sought, which require outstanding achievements of their members, as judged by recognized international experts
- Material published in professional publications about the [foreign national] and relating to the [foreign national's] work in the field for which classification is sought, including the title, date, and author of the published material, and any necessary translation
- Evidence of the [foreign national's] participation on a panel, or individually, as a judge of the work of others in the same or an allied field of specification for which classification is sought
- Evidence of the [foreign national's] original scientific, scholarly research contributions of major significance in the field for which certification is sought
- Evidence of the [foreign national's] authorship of published scientific or scholarly articles in the field that have been published in international professional journals or professional journals with an international circulation
- Evidence of the display of the [foreign national's] work in the field at artistic exhibitions in more than one country

G. Certain Special Immigrants, Including Religious Workers (EB-4): INA § 101(a)(27)(C); 8 C.F.R. § 204.5(m)

The employment-based, fourth preference, or EB-4, category is reserved for certain "Special Immigrants," including, but not limited to, foreign employees of the U.S. government,[148] broadcasters,[149] Iraqi or Afghan translators or interpreters who worked with the U.S. Armed Forces or under Chief of Mission authority,[150] employees of international organizations,[151] religious workers,[152] certain members of the armed forces,[153] and retired NATO-6 employees.[154]

---

[147] 20 C.F.R. § 656.15(d).
[148] INA § 101(a)(27)(D).
[149] INA § 101(a)(27)(M).
[150] National Defense Authorization Act for Fiscal Year 2006, Pub. L. 109–163, 119 Stat. 3137 (2006).
[151] INA § 101(a)(27)(I).
[152] INA § 101(a)(27)(C).
[153] INA § 101(a)(27)(K).
[154] INA § 101(a)(27)(L).

This preference category also includes immigrants in categories unrelated to employment, including children declared dependent in a juvenile court who are placed in long-term foster care or in the care of appointed guardians and may be eligible for Special Immigrant Juvenile status.[155] Discussion of these applications is in Section Q of Chapter 8, Immigration Relief for Vulnerable Populations. Although there are a number of discreet groups who qualify for LPR status in the EB-4 category, the focus of this section will be on religious workers, who make up the majority of foreign nationals in this preference category.

Often, LPR status is a logical extension of the immigration status of those who entered in the religious worker nonimmigrant category, as discussed in Section C. of Chapter 4, Nonimmigrant Visas for Extraordinary Ability, Religious Workers, and Ancillary Activities. There are many similarities between the non- and immigrant classifications, so it may be useful to review that section again. As previously mentioned, if a religious worker wishes to remain in the United States on a permanent basis, s/he can seek LPR status through adjustment of status specifically available for religious workers without it negatively impacting his or her nonimmigrant status as a religious worker.[156]

Religious workers include ministers and those working in a religious vocation or religious occupation who have received job offers from legitimate, nonprofit religious organizations in the United States.

According to 8 C.F.R. § 204.5(m)(5), a minister is defined as an individual who:

- Is fully authorized by a religious denomination, and fully trained according to the denomination's standards, to conduct such religious worship and perform other duties usually performed by authorized members of the clergy of that denomination;
- Is not a lay preacher or a person not authorized to perform duties usually performed by clergy;
- Performs activities with a rational relationship to the religious calling of the minister; and
- Works solely as a minister in the United States, which may include administrative duties incidental to the duties of a minister.

Christian priests and pastors, Jewish rabbis, Islamic imams, and Buddhist monks are all examples of leaders of religious organizations who would qualify for LPR status as ministers. Petitioners must submit a copy of the foreign national's certificate of ordination or similar documents to establish that the religious denomination accepts the beneficiary's qualifications as a minister.[157]

---

[155] INA § 101(a)(27)(J).
[156] 8 C.F.R. § 214.2(r)(15).
[157] 8 C.F.R. § 204.5(m)(5).

Non-ministers may qualify if they are working in a religious occupation or a religious vocation.[158] This category does not include workers for religious organizations that are performing purely secular or nonreligious functions, such as receptionists, fundraisers, or singers.

> **Case for Discussion 7.9**
>
> Prama is a religious worker from Indonesia. He initially came to the United States to pursue a Master of Divinity degree at an accredited theological seminary. After completing his theological studies four years ago, he began working for a church in the United States for three years in the religious occupation of Acting Pastor of the Indonesian congregation, pursuant to valid R-1 nonimmigrant status. However, he is only eligible to remain in this status for five years. Although his Church desperately wants to retain him as a permanent Pastor and Prama does not want to abandon his Indonesian congregation here, he has not completed the ordination process and is not expected to be fully ordained for at least another year.
>
> - Can the Church nevertheless pursue the LPR status process on his behalf?

Religious worker immigrant petitions must establish that the religious organization meets certain requirements. To begin, it must be a *bona fide*, nonprofit religious organization.[159] Proof of this may include a letter from the U.S. Internal Revenue Service, or IRS, demonstrating that the organization is exempt from federal income tax as a nonprofit organization, described in § 501(c)(3) of the Internal Revenue Code. Other documentation that may suffice could include:

- Articles of incorporation and by-laws
- Proof of state tax exemption
- Website excerpts
- Redacted lists of members of the religious organization
- Photographs of the church or other religious worksite, both inside and outside
- Deeds to the congregation's buildings
- Service bulletins
- Calendar of holidays and special religious events
- Annual reports of congregation and parent organizations
- Statement of faith, etc.

---

[158] 8 C.F.R. § 204.5(m)(2).
[159] 8 C.F.R. § 204.5(m)(3).

It should be noted that, because the USCIS scrutinizes these petitions very closely, even petitions filed on behalf of large denominations must include extensive documentation.

In addition, the religious organization typically includes an attestation letter attesting that:

- The prospective employer is a bona fide nonprofit religious organization or a bona fide organization which is affiliated with the religious denomination and is exempt from taxation;
- The number of members of the prospective employer's organization;
- The number of employees who work at the same location where the beneficiary will be employed and a summary of the type of responsibilities of those employees. USCIS may request a list of all employees, their titles, and a brief description of their duties at its discretion;
- The number of [foreign nationals] holding special immigrant or nonimmigrant religious worker status currently employed or employed within the past five years by the prospective employer's organization;
- The number of special immigrant religious worker and nonimmigrant religious worker petitions and applications filed by or on behalf of any [foreign nationals] for employment by the prospective employer in the past five years;
- The title of the position offered to the [foreign national], the complete package of salaried or non-salaried compensation being offered, and a detailed description of the [foreign national]'s proposed daily duties;
- The [foreign national] will be employed at least 35 hours per week;
- The specific location(s) of the proposed employment;
- The [foreign national] has worked as a religious worker for the two years immediately preceding the filing of the application and is otherwise qualified for the position offered;
- The [foreign national] has been a member of the denomination for at least two years immediately preceding the filing of the application;
- The [foreign national] will not be engaged in secular employment, and any salaried or non-salaried compensation for the work will be paid to the [foreign national] by the attesting employer; and
- The prospective employer has the ability and intention to compensate the [foreign national] at a level at which the [foreign national] and accompanying family members will not become public charges, and that funds to pay the [foreign national]'s compensation do not include any monies obtained from the [foreign national], excluding reasonable donations or tithing to the religious organization[160]

The immigrant petition should also include verifiable primary documentary evidence of how the organization intends to pay the religious worker and of its

---

[160] 8 C.F.R. § 204.5(m)(7).

ability to compensate him or her, e.g. pay stubs or Forms W-2, showing actual payment of wages in the past, audited budgets, etc.[161]

The foreign national beneficiary must meet the regulatory criteria for Special Immigrant classification. To begin, the petition must establish that s/he was a member of the denomination of the religious organization, working in a qualifying position, for at least two years immediately preceding the filing.[162] Finally, it must be demonstrated that the foreign national beneficiary will be working in a full-time capacity as a minister or in a religious vocation or occupation, and that s/he is qualified for the position.[163]

While the description of the position can be chronicled in the attestation letter the religious organization submits with the petition, it is important to also provide primary documentary evidence of the worker's qualifications. For example, a petition for a minister must include not only an ordination certificate,[164] but also proof that the foreign national beneficiary has the appropriate theological education to qualify as a minister, perhaps through copies of theological degrees and transcripts.[165] For non-ministers, it is critical to include documentary evidence of the religious nature of the position. For example, to distinguish a religious teacher from a worker who only cares for children, it would be important to include evidence of the religious nature of the instruction, such as work product that establishes that s/he is incorporating religious doctrine and teaching into the instruction, as well as proof that the teacher is qualified to work in such capacity based on his or her religious training, experience, and/or education.

G.1. Compiling the EB-4 Religious Worker Petition

The religious worker immigrant petition should include:

- Form I-360, Petition for American, Widow(er), or Special Immigrant
- Form G-28, Notice of Entry of Appearance of Attorney or Accredited Representative, if the applicant has legal representation
- USCIS Filing Fee

For the Petitioner:

- Evidence of petitioner's tax-exempt organization status through IRS documentation
- Attestation letter
- Verifiable evidence of salaried or non-salaried compensation through

---

[161] 8 C.F.R. § 204.5(m)(10).
[162] 8 C.F.R. § 204.5(m)(1).
[163] 8 C.F.R. § 204.5(m)(2).
[164] 8 C.F.R. § 204.5(m)(9)(i).
[165] 8 C.F.R. § 204.5(m)(9)(ii).

☐ W-2 for beneficiary as evidence of prior payments
☐ Copy of a tax return for beneficiary, if applicable
☐ Copy of cancelled checks paid for lodging and utilities, etc.

For the Beneficiary:

- Evidence of membership in a religious denomination having a *bona fide* nonprofit religious organization in the United States for at least two years immediately preceding the filing of the petition
- If the beneficiary is a minister, provide:
  ☐ Copy of the beneficiary's certificate of ordination or similar documents
  ☐ Documents reflecting acceptance of the beneficiary's qualifications as a minister in the religious denomination
  ☐ Evidence that the beneficiary has completed any course of prescribed theological education at an accredited theological institution normally required or recognized by that religious denomination (e.g., transcripts, curriculum, and documentation that establishes that the theological institution is accredited by the denomination)
- If the denominations do not require a prescribed theological education, provide:
  ☐ Denomination's requirements for ordination to minister
  ☐ Duties allowed to be performed by virtue of ordination
  ☐ Denomination's levels of ordination, if any, and
  ☐ Beneficiary's completion of the denomination's requirements for ordination
- Evidence of beneficiary's past employment with petitioner in the form of prior approval notices issued by the USCIS
- Once the Form I-360 is approved, the beneficiary may then file a Form I-485, Application to Register Permanent Residence or Adjust Status, adjustment package, which will include the documents in Section G.2 of Chapter 6, Family Sponsored Immigration and Permanent Resident Status, without Form I-864, Affidavit of Support, for the principal applicant, but may be necessary for any qualifying derivative family members

To begin the application process, the employer generally files Form I-360, Petition for Amerasian, Widow(er), or Special Immigrant. However, there are circumstances in which the foreign national may self-petition. No labor certification or PERM application is required. The Form I-360 petition contains an employer attestation detailing information about the religious organization, who it employs, the position being offered to the foreign national, the proposed daily duties of such position, and the beneficiary's qualifications. It also includes a religious denomination certificate, in which the religious organization attests under penalty of perjury that it is a qualifying nonprofit religious organization.[166] The petition is then filed with the USCIS in accordance with the most up-to-date instructions on its website.

---

[166] 8 C.F.R. § 204.5(m)(8)(iii)(D).

The USCIS believes there is a high level of fraud in religious worker cases and, consequently, will conduct an unannounced, on-site inspection of the religious organization to verify that the petition is genuine, unless it has already conducted a site visit within the last few years. An inspector will verify the existence of the organization and speak with the signatory or other organizational representatives to verify details of the petition. If the USCIS deems a site inspection necessary, the petition cannot and will not be adjudicated until it is complete.

Once the Form I-360, Petition for Amerasian, Widow(er), or Special Immigrant, is approved, the foreign national may submit Form I-485, Application to Register Permanent Residency or Adjust Status, to change from a nonimmigrant to an LPR if s/he is in the United States and has maintained valid nonimmigrant status. Unlike other employment-based categories, it is important to understand that the Form I-485 adjustment application cannot, under any circumstances, be filed concurrently with the Form I-360 petition filed for a religious worker. The latter must be approved first before moving on to the adjustment application stage, once a visa number is available. This category is typically current for all country classifications. However, in the May 2016 DOS online visa bulletin, there was retrogression so that only applications filed on January 1, 2010 by nationals from El Salvador, Guatemala, and Honduras are being accepted, indicating that there are no visas available at the present time because nationals from these countries have met their seven percent per country limits.[167] Therefore, even though a religious worker may have an approved Form I-360 petition, s/he cannot file an adjustment application until a visa number is available for him or her.

If the period of stay in R-1 nonimmigrant status will expire before the foreign national religious worker is able to adjust to an LPR here, then s/he will have to leave the country in order to avoid being undocumented. This is because only those foreign nationals who are in lawful status can adjust to LPRs in the United States. Another option would be to change to a different nonimmigrant status, such as an H-1B, if qualified. According to the May 2016 visa bulletin, religious worker petitions for foreign nationals from countries other than El Salvador, Guatemala, and Honduras are current and so they do not have to wait to file their applications to adjust status to an LPR once their Form I-360, Petition for Ameriasion, Widow(er), or Special Immigrant, petition is approved. If the foreign national is not in the United States or is not eligible for adjustment of status, s/he can apply for an immigrant visa by consular processing at a consulate office abroad, following approval of the Form I-360 petition, again, when a visa number is available.

---

[167] See Section A.1 of Chapter 6, Family Sponsored Immigration and Permanent Resident Status.

> **Case for Discussion 7.10**
>
> Chinwe is a religious worker from Nigeria who came to the United States three months ago in R-1 nonimmigrant status to work for a church affiliated with the religious denomination that she has been a member of for more than 15 years. In her current position as Director of Youth and Children's Ministry, Chinwe is responsible for developing the religious curriculum for her parish's teachers. This includes imparting the values of the church, working directly with the parish's children to study and discuss the Bible and its teachings, counseling the parish's children to use the teachings of the Bible to surmount the peer pressures they face, and developing and implementing age-appropriate children's programs. The church selected her for the position based on the religious training and experience she obtained in Nigeria. Specifically, she completed two intensive training programs related to Bible studies and abstinence. Moreover, the church ordained her as a deacon and she served as a part-time volunteer for the children's ministry of her church in Nigeria for one year before coming to the United States.
>
> - Can the church pursue LPR status on Chinwe's behalf at this time?
> - If the church does submit a Form I-360, Petition for Amerasian, Widow(er), or Special Immigrant, for Chinwe, what type of evidence can it submit to establish the religious nature of her position?

H. Investor Visa (EB-5): INA § 203(b)(5); 8 C.F.R. § 204.6

The fifth preference category for employment-based immigration is the petition for employment creation foreign nationals,[168] or more commonly referred to as the EB-5 investor visa. Specifically, 10,000 of these immigrant visas are available each year to foreign nationals who invest or are in the process of actively investing capital in a commercial enterprise in the United States that meets certain requirements. As reflected by the requirements discussed later, this preference category was created in an effort to create U.S. jobs and increase U.S. investment in order to stimulate the U.S. economy.

Generally, a foreign national may meet the requirements for this preference category by making a direct investment in a business or by investing in a project through a **Regional Center** pursuant to the Immigrant Investor Pilot Program.[169] Defined as a geographical area, a Regional Center is also a business

---

[168] 8 C.F.R. § 204.6.
[169] 8 C.F.R. § 204.6(m). The Immigrant Investor Pilot Program was created by the Judiciary Appropriations Act of 1993, Pub. L. 102-395, 106 Stat. 1828 (1992), § 610, and has since been reauthorized several times. As of the time of writing, the program was last extended on December 18, 2015, when President Obama signed into law the Omnibus Appropriations Act. This law extended the program until the end of the fiscal year, September 30, 2016.

entity that coordinates investment, which can include both foreign and domestic financing, within the defined geographical area in compliance with the EB-5 preference category requirements.[170] Regardless of the path the foreign national pursues, whether through a direct investment or investing through a Regional Center, the foreign national must meet the basic requirements.

First, the foreign national must invest $1 million in a commercial enterprise.[171] If the enterprise is located in a **targeted employment area,** or TEA,[172] however, then the required investment is reduced to $500,000.[173]

Second, the foreign national must invest in a **new enterprise**,[174] defined as a commercial enterprise established after November 29, 1990.[175] However, the foreign national may invest in a commercial enterprise that was established *before* this date and still satisfy the requirement, so long as the commercial enterprise is restructured or reorganized at the time the enterprise was purchased or soon after such investment so that, ultimately, a new commercial enterprise is created.[176]

In the alternative, the foreign national may invest in a **troubled business** to meet the requirement. A troubled business means "a business that has been in existence for a least two years, has incurred a net loss for accounting purposes . . . during the twelve or twenty-four month period prior [to the date the foreign national's Petition for Alien Entrepreneur is accepted by the USCIS] and the loss for such period is at least equal to twenty percent of the troubled business's (sic) net worth prior to such loss."[177] Furthermore, if the foreign national invests in an existing commercial enterprise, but it is not restructured or reorganized as a new enterprise, the foreign national may still meet this requirement if it is expanded by utilizing the required investment that results in a 40 percent increase in the enterprise's net worth or number of employees.[178] Note that a passive investment, such as owning and operating a personal residence, is insufficient to meet this requirement.[179]

Third, the ***capital*** that the foreign national invests must be placed at risk.[180] The mere intent to invest, or prospective investment arrangements without current commitment, is insufficient and such capital generally cannot be

Capital: Cash, equipment, inventory, other tangible property, cash equivalents, and indebtedness secured by assets owned by the foreign national entrepreneur, provided that s/he is personally and primarily liable and that the assets of the new commercial enterprise upon which the petition is based are not used to secure any of the indebtedness.

---

[170] As of December 3, 2014, the USCIS approved approximately 601 regional centers. The current list can be found at http://www.uscis.gov/working-united-states/permanent-workers/employment-based-immigration-fifth-preference-eb-5/immigrant-investor-regional-centers.
[171] 8 C.F.R. § 204.6(f)(3).
[172] A targeted employment area is defined as "an area which, at the time of investment, is a rural area or an area which has experienced unemployment of at least 150 per cent of the national average rate." 8 C.F.R. § 204.6(e). In addition, a "rural area" is defined as "any area not within either a metropolitan statistical area (as designated by the Office of Management and Budget) or the outer boundary of any city or town having a population of 20,000 or more." 8 C.F.R. § 204.6(e).
[173] 8 C.F.R. § 204.6(f)(2).
[174] 8 C.F.R. § 204.6(h)(1).
[175] 8 C.F.R. § 204.6(e).
[176] 8 C.F.R. § 204.6(h)(2).
[177] 8 C.F.R. § 204.6(e).
[178] 8 C.F.R. § 204.6(h)(3).
[179] 8 C.F.R. § 204.6(e).
[180] 8 C.F.R. § 204.6(j)(2).

borrowed.[181] However, the capital may be gifted to the foreign national as long as it is free and clear. Therefore, in order to satisfy this requirement, the foreign national must provide documentary evidence that actual capital has been committed to the enterprise. This can include business bank account statements that show the amount transferred into the business account, as well as invoices, receipts, and purchase contracts demonstrating that assets and services have been purchased for the use of the business. Note that an escrow account may be utilized when investing, but the terms of the account must clearly reflect that the capital is at risk and irrevocable.

Fourth, the source of the capital invested must be lawful.[182] Specifically, any funds obtained through unlawful means, whether directly or indirectly, cannot be counted toward the minimum amount of capital that must be invested in order to meet the requirements for this preference category. The USCIS imposes a strict requirement that such funds must be traced back to their actual source to establish that they were obtained by the foreign national investor through only lawful means.

Fifth, the foreign national must be actively involved in the management of the commercial enterprise or in making policy decisions regarding it.[183] Interestingly, this requirement may also be satisfied if the foreign national is a limited partner and the limited partnership agreement provides the foreign national "with certain rights, powers, and duties normally granted to limited partners under the Uniform Limited Partnership Act."[184]

Sixth, the commercial enterprise must create at least ten full-time positions for qualifying employees in the United States.[185] The USCIS defines "qualifying employees" to be U.S. citizens, LPRs, asylees, and refugees, and any other person present with permission to work.[186] It should be noted that family members of the foreign national as well as anyone in the United States in nonimmigrant status are not included in this definition.

The foreign national must meet all the requirements enumerated earlier regardless of whether the investment is a direct investment or through a Regional Center. However, in determining the best path to follow for the individual foreign national, many factors have to be considered.[187] For example, if a direct investment is made, the foreign national must be directly and actively involved in the management of the business or in making policy decisions regarding it. In addition, the foreign national may only count jobs that were *directly* created by the business in which the investment was made. By contrast,

---

[181] *Id.*
[182] 8 C.F.R. § 204.6(j)(3).
[183] 8 C.F.R. § 204.6(j)(5).
[184] 8 C.F.R. § 204.6(j)(5)(iii).
[185] 8 C.F.R. § 204.6(j)(4).
[186] 8 C.F.R. § 204.6(e).
[187] *See* E. Peng & C. Weber, "Practical Planning Strategies Using EB-5 and Other Options for Immigrant Investors and Entrepreneurs," Immigration Options for Investors & Entrepreneurs, 3d Ed. (AILA 2014); E. Peng, T. Lee, & C. Weber, "Insiders' Guide to EB-5 Immigrant Investor Law and Practice," Immigration Options for Investors & Entrepreneurs, 3rd Ed. (AILA 2014).

if s/he made the investment through a Regional Center approved by the USCIS, the foreign national may, and most likely will, be a limited partner in a limited liability partnership, thus restricting the level of direct management and involvement in the business the foreign national will have.

Unlike with the direct investment where only those jobs directly created by the business are counted toward the ten-job creation requirement, in a Regional Center, direct, indirect and induced jobs are counted toward this required total.[188] The words "direct jobs," "indirect jobs," and "induced jobs" are economic terms. Federal agencies such as the Bureau of Economic Analysis, or BEA, apply these economic concepts to develop tables that indicate how many jobs will be created based upon each dollar invested in a particular industry sector in a particular location. These concepts are applied when analyzing job creation at an EB-5 Regional Center.

● **EXAMPLE**

EB-5 funds are used by Happy Construction, Inc. to build a Convention Center that will employ 100 U.S. workers on a full-time basis. These are considered "direct jobs" as they are required to operate the facility. Happy Construction Inc. must purchase goods, like steel and lumber, and services, such as engineering, architectural, and even legal, in order to build the Convention Center. The jobs created for those workers who manufacture the goods and provide such services are "indirect jobs." Now armed with a bountiful and consistent paycheck, 20 Happy Construction, Inc. workers rent new apartments, buy clothing and food for their family members, and purchase "Disney on Ice" tickets as a special treat. The jobs created by this spending are "induced jobs."

Furthermore, if the foreign national invests through a Regional Center, the jobs created can be pooled so that jobs created by both foreign national and non-foreign national investors will be counted together with the jobs created by non-foreign investors being credited towards the foreign national's ten-job creation requirement. Note, however, if numerous foreign nationals are investing in the same project in order to submit EB-5 petitions and insufficient jobs are created, those jobs that are created will be attributed to those who apply first, i.e. first investor in, first investor out. Therefore, if the project, despite projections, only creates 100 jobs that can be counted for EB-5 purposes, then only the ten foreign nationals who submit EB-5 petitions first using this project will be able to utilize those jobs to meet their job creation requirement, since each must be responsible for at least ten. The remaining foreign national investors will be unable to satisfy the USCIS criteria for an EB-5 Investor Visa, therefore losing their chance at receiving a "green card" from this particular EB5 investment. For this reason, a foreign national is generally advised to be careful to vet rigorously any Regional Center through which s/he decides to invest, as well as the specific project,

---

[188] 8 C.F.R. § 204.6(m)(7).

paying particular attention to the ultimate goal: the creation of ten jobs that will be attributed to that individual investor.

Engaging in such vetting and due diligence is of paramount importance for when a foreign national obtains LPR status in the EB-5 preference category, the foreign national and all qualifying derivative family members are initially approved for a two-year *conditional* period.[189] Therefore, before it expires, the foreign national must have his or her conditions removed by re-submitting evidence regarding the continued viability of the business or the Regional Center and project, as well as documentary evidence that ten full-time positions for qualified U.S. workers were indeed created.[190] If the Regional Center ceases to operate or the specific project fails to generate sufficient jobs during the two years the foreign national is a conditional LPR, the foreign national will not be able to remove the conditions and will no longer be an LPR. Thus, there is a strong incentive to scrutinize properly Regional Centers and/or projects before any investments are made. The process for removing the conditions is discussed in the next section.

H.1. Compiling the EB-5 Petition

The foreign national investor seeking immigrant status should file the following documents in support of his or her petition for LPR status:

- Form I-526, Immigrant Petition by Alien Entrepreneur
- Form G-28, Notice of Entry of Appearance of Attorney or Accredited Representative, if the applicant has legal representation
- USCIS Filing Fee
- Evidence of investment in a new commercial enterprise to the required $500,000 or $1 million amount
- Evidence that the enterprise is either new, restructured, or expanded
- Evidence of certificate giving authority to do business in a particular state or statement that none is required
- Evidence that the money invested has been placed at risk through bank statements, assets purchased, property or money transfers, or evidence of borrowing secured by stocks or assets
- Evidence that the enterprise will create ten full time positions for qualifying employees
- Evidence that the foreign national will be actively engaged in the management of the enterprise

---

[189] 8 C.F.R. § 204.6(l). This is similar to the conditional LPR status granted to those married for less than two years on the date of adjudication of an adjustment of status application or issuance of a family sponsored immigrant visa and is discussed in Section I.1. of Chapter 6, Family Sponsored Immigration and Permanent Resident Status.
[190] 8 C.F.R. § 216.6.

Once the Form I-526, Immigrant Petition by Alien Entrepreneur, is approved, the beneficiary may then file Form I-485, Application to Register Permanent Residence or Adjust Status, adjustment package, which will include the documents in Section G.2 of Chapter 6, Family Sponsored Immigration and Permanent Resident Status. There is no need to file Form I-864, Affidavit of Support, for the principal applicant, but it may be necessary for any qualifying derivative family members.

Similar to the Religious Worker immigrant petition, a foreign national seeking LPR status based on employment creation must file his or her application in two stages. First, s/he submits the Form I-526, Immigrant Petition by Alien Entrepreneur. Only after its approval can the foreign national submit Form I-485, Application to Register Permanent Residence or Adjust Status, if the foreign national is in the United States in lawful status. In addition, if the qualifying derivative family members of the foreign national investor are also in the United States in lawful status, they can submit their own adjustment applications. If the foreign national is not here, then s/he and any qualifying derivative family members can request consular processing at a consular office abroad.

LPR status is granted to foreign nationals in the EB-5 preference category and any qualifying derivative family members for a conditional two-year period. Therefore, much like the foreign national who obtains conditional LPR status pursuant to marriage to a U.S. citizen, discussed in Section I.1 of Chapter 6, Family Sponsored Immigration and Permanent Resident Status, the foreign national investor and his or her qualifying derivative family members must apply to have the conditions removed before the two-year anniversary of the date the LPR status was granted. To do so, the foreign national must timely submit Form I-829, Petition by Entrepreneur to Remove Conditions, at least 90 days before the second anniversary of the grant of conditional residency, and provide evidence that the foreign national's investment did indeed create ten full-time jobs for U.S. workers.[191]

I. Other Categories: INA § 203(c); 22 C.F.R. § 42.33

I.1. Diversity Visa Lottery

The Diversity Immigrant Visa Program,[192] or DV Program, administered by the DOS, provides up to 50,000 immigrant visas annually to foreign nationals from designated countries with historically low rates of immigration to the United States. The DVs are distributed among six geographic regions and no single country may receive more than 7 percent of the available DVs in any one

---

[191] 8 C.F.R. § 216.6.
[192] INA § 203(c).

year. The DV instructions provide the list of countries or areas by region whose natives are eligible for the program.

To qualify, the principal DV applicant must possess at least a ***high school education***[193] or its equivalent, or, within the five years preceding the date of his or her application for a diversity visa, have two years of work experience in an occupation requiring at least two years of training or experience.[194]

> **High School Education:** The successful completion of a formal course of elementary and secondary education comparable to completion of a 12-year course in the United States.

I.1.a. Procedure for DV Immigrants

Entries for the DV Program must be submitted electronically at www.dvlottery.state.gov during a brief annual application period. Upon submitting a complete entry, the foreign national will be provided a unique confirmation number, which s/he must use to check the status of the entry on the website at *Entrant Status Check*. This is the only way DOS informs applicants who have been selected for the program. It also provides instructions on further processing as well as notification of the interview date for the immigrant visa. Many unscrupulous individuals and organizations consistently target and scam DV applicants by informing them that they have won the lottery and instruct them to forward large payments to them directly so that they can assist in processing the supposed winner's application. Therefore, DV applicants should be warned to always check with a legal representative prior to submitting payment to any entity.

Once selected in the DV Lottery, the principal applicant and his or her qualified derivative family members can file Form I-485, Application to Register Permanent Resident and Adjust Status, if lawfully in the United States, or follow instructions for immigrant visa consular processing, if abroad. Chapter 6, Family Sponsored Immigration and Permanent Resident Status discusses these two methods. However, all selected and eligible applicants *must* obtain their visa or adjust status by the end of the fiscal year in which they are selected, which is September 30th. There is no carry-over of DV benefits into the next year for those selected but who do not obtain visas by this date. Therefore, those whose processing is not completed in time lose all rights to attain LPR status through this benefit. This also applies to any derivatives such as spouses and unmarried children under 21 years, who must also obtain their immigrant visas or adjust status within this timeframe.

J. Conclusion

The acquisition of LPR status through employment is a multi-faceted area of immigration practice that offers a wide range of options to a select few. It is dependent upon the foreign national's level of education, experience, field of endeavor, the need for his or her education and/or skill set in the United States,

---

[193] 22 C.F.R. § 42.33(a)(2).
[194] 22 C.F.R. § 42.33(a)(1).

and/or his or her ability to invest sufficient funds in a qualifying U.S. investment, or alternatively, luck in winning the DV lottery.

Those who do meet the statutory criteria for any of the employment-based categories are not precluded from filing immigrant petitions in as many categories in which they qualify, provided that the filing of such additional petitions does not contradict any statements made in prior petitions and is always truthful. For example, nothing precludes an Indian national, a computer programmer, who is the beneficiary of a third preference employment based Form I-140, Immigrant Petition for Alien Worker, who has been waiting for an immigrant visa to become available for four years, with many more years to go, from simultaneously submitting an EB-5 Investor Visa petition. Similarly, a foreign national who is the beneficiary of a family sponsored immigrant petition, described in Chapter 6, Family Sponsored Immigration and Permanent Resident Status, is not precluded from being the beneficiary of a parallel filed employment-based immigrant petition. The ultimate goal is the foreign national's receipt of the prize: LPR status in the United States, pursuant to any and all legally permitted and ethical options.

Having explored the ways to pathways to LPR status, we now look to the immigration relief available to those who are vulnerable in the United States, either as victims of abusive crimes committed here or as victims of several forms of human trafficking. We also review protections available to unaccompanied children.

Immigration Relief for Vulnerable Populations

Key Terms and Acronyms

Central American Minors Program
Continued Presence
Deferred Action for Childhood Arrivals (DACA)
Dependent Child
Law Enforcement Certification
Predicate Order
Principal Applicant
Self-Petition
Severe Form of Human Trafficking
Special Immigrant Juvenile (SIJ)
T Nonimmigrant Status
U Nonimmigrant Status
William Wilberforce Trafficking Victim's Protection Reauthorization Act of 2008 (TVPRA)
Violence Against Women Act (VAWA)

Chapter Objectives

- Review immigration options for immigrant survivors of domestic violence, victims of crime, and victims of severe forms of human trafficking
- Discuss special protections in immigration law for neglected, abused, and abandoned juveniles
- Review sources of law for the various forms of available immigration relief
- Analyze eligibility criteria for each form of available immigration relief
- Understand application process for each form of immigration relief

Immigrant populations are not immune from experiencing harm, whether in domestic relations or because they are victims of criminal activity. In some instances, immigration status can be used as a means of control to keep the foreign national tied to the United States citizen or lawful permanent resident, or LPR, who may be the perpetrator of the harm. When undocumented immigrants are victims of crime, they may be reluctant to come forward to report for fear of arrest because they lack lawful immigration status. This can result in the vulnerable remaining in environments that may seriously compromise their safety.

Recognizing this dilemma, Congress chose to eliminate immigration status as a weapon of control. In 1994, it introduced important protections for those who are abused by passing the **Violence Against Women Act,** or **VAWA**. As a result, certain foreign nationals were free to leave their abusers without worrying that this would affect their ability to gain legal immigration status because they could self-petition for status. The VAWA 2000 reauthorization provision expanded protections for married victims and included those who were victims of certain types of crimes or who have been **trafficked** in the United States. These victims were permitted to seek immigration benefits through U and T Nonimmigrant Status petitions or applications. VAWA 2000 also introduced waivers for domestic violence survivors who might otherwise be inadmissible for immigration relief because of actions taken in self-defense.

VAWA was reauthorized again in 2005 and expanded the availability of self-petitions to survivors of child abuse and incest up to the age of 25; elders who experience abuse from sons or daughters who are U.S. citizens; and in the case of adopted children who have been abused, they no longer need to have lived in the custody of the abusive adoptive parent for two years before qualifying for immigration relief.

The Illegal Immigration Reform and Immigrant Responsibility Act of 1996, or IIRAIRA, provides protections by guaranteeing confidentiality in the petition process. Section 384 of IIRAIRA prohibits all Department of Homeland Security, or DHS, employees from providing information about self-petitions to a third party, at the risk of disciplinary action or fines. In addition, information provided by an abuser cannot be the sole basis for any adverse determination of admissibility or deportability unless an unrelated party independently verifies it.

Relief is also available for abused children, including those who enter the United States unaccompanied by an adult. Under federal law, children can self-petition and adjust their status as **Special Immigrant Juveniles**, or **SIJ**. In June, 2012, the President of the United States used his executive authority to grant temporary benefits through the **Deferred Action for Childhood Arrivals,** or **DACA,** program. Under DACA, certain foreign nationals who were brought here or entered before the age of 16 and lived in the United States since June, 2007 can receive employment authorization and protection against deportation. More recent executive action allows parents lawfully in the United States to apply for children from certain Central American countries to enter as refugees.

All these provisions seek to ensure that the vulnerable may gain lawful immigration status, which, in many cases, may be the first step to removing themselves from a dangerous environment. This chapter explores each of these forms of immigration relief in detail. While it is true that both men and women experience domestic abuse, statistically women are more often the victims, with men the perpetrator. For this reason, discussions in this chapter will focus on the experience of women but reference men where appropriate.

A. Overview and Sources of Law Protecting Immigrant Victims of Domestic Abuse and Crimes: INA § 204; 8 C.F.R. § 204.2

VAWA permits abused women and men to petition on their own for LPR status, as long as they meet certain criteria. The Immigration and Nationality Act, or INA, § 204 incorporates the VAWA enactments, authorizing those who are abused or subjected to extreme cruelty to self-petition for immigration benefits. 8 C.F.R. § 204.2(c)(1)(i) requires that the petitioner:

- Be the spouse of a citizen or LPR of the United States;
- Be eligible for immigrant classification under § 201(b)(2)(A)(i) or § 203(a)(2)(A) of the Act based on that relationship;
- Be residing in the United States;
- Have resided in the United States with the citizen or LPR spouse at some point;
- Have been battered by, or been the subject of extreme cruelty perpetrated by, the citizen or LPR during the marriage; or is that parent of a child who has been battered by, or has been the subject of extreme cruelty perpetrated by, the citizen or LPR during the marriage;
- Be a person of good moral character;
- Be a person whose deportation would result in extreme hardship to himself, herself, or his or her child;[1] and
- Entered into the marriage to the citizen or LPR in good faith.

A.1. Petitions Based on Marriage

A.1.a. Validity of the Marriage and Residency Requirements

To qualify for immigration relief as a battered person, a foreign national must establish that a familial relationship exists between her and the abuser who is either a U.S. citizen or LPR, spouse, parent, son, or daughter. When the relationship is that of spouses, proving the marital relationship may involve many factors to establish that a marriage exists. For instance, is the couple living together in a spousal relationship? Have they comingled bank accounts? Do

---

[1] VAWA petitions can be filed either affirmatively or defensively, as discussed in Section D.4. Extreme hardship, while a listed eligibility factor in the regulations, is only applicable to defensive VAWA petitions filed in immigration court.

they jointly own property, such as houses, cars, or other assets? Does the couple have children in common? These are all factors that may tend to suggest that the marriage is genuine or *bono fide*.[2] In addition to this, VAWA applicants must also show that they established a joint residence in the United States with the abuser. There is no minimum time during which the couple must have lived together, so long as it was during the marriage.

● EXAMPLE

Kalpna and her husband Amit are both citizens of India. They have two children. Throughout the duration of the relationship in India, Amit and his family have abused Kalpna, physically and mentally, often leaving her with broken ribs and bruises. Kalpna told only her family about this but there was nothing they could do to help her. Amit receives an offer of a great job in technology from a small startup company in California and obtains an H1-B visa. Eventually he sends for Kalpna and their children to join him as H-1B dependents. Amit wants to decide whether to stay married to Kalpna. One week after Kaplna arrives, Amit receives his LPR status, but he did not include Kalpna or the children in his application. Soon after Kalpna's arrival, Amit resumes the abuse and Kalpna leaves with the children to go to a shelter. Because Amit is an LPR and Kalpna lived with Amit in the United States, even for a short duration, she is able to file a petition for VAWA relief.

To demonstrate that the foreign national has lived with the abuser, any credible evidence[3] is acceptable. Therefore, an abused spouse could present lease or rental agreements that list both husband and wife as residing at a particular address; utility, insurance, or other bills addressed to them both or separately, but using the same address; and bank statements, although this may be problematic. Many banks will now only allow accounts to be opened for those with social security numbers and these are only issued if a foreign national can demonstrate an immigration status that would entitle him or her to one. Alternatively, affidavits or statements from friends willing to attest to the fact that the couple lived together could also be presented.

In some circumstances, the validity of a marriage may be questioned, perhaps because the husband was previously married but did not obtain a valid divorce prior to marrying the foreign national, or because he had engaged in a **polygamous marriage**. The statute acknowledges these problems and will still recognize the validity of the following marriages for the purpose of applying for relief under VAWA:

- A *bona fide* marriage that is in fact bigamous
- A marriage that ended in the death of the abuser within the last two years, but only for those married to U.S. citizens and not LPRs

---

[2] It may be helpful to review Section C of Chapter 6, Family Sponsored Immigration and Permanent Resident Status, to understand factors to be considered when demonstrating a valid marriage, particularly as it relates to the *bona fides* of the relationship.
[3] INA § 204(a)(1)(J); 8 C.F.R. § 204.2(c)(2)(i).

- A marriage where the abuser either renounced or lost his citizenship or LPR status within the last two years due to an incident of domestic violence
- A marriage that ended in divorce within the last two years but where the termination is connected to battery or extreme cruelty[4]

Case for Discussion 8.1

Aminata is a citizen of Mali. She arrived on a visitor's visa to visit her sister, and met and married Moussa, another native of Mali. Moussa obtained his U.S. citizenship many years ago following a successful application for asylum. Moussa has abused Aminata continuously throughout their marriage and she has told no one. The couple has a disabled child who receives early childhood intervention services from a social worker who suspects there are issues of domestic violence. She advises Aminata to seek legal help but Aminata is afraid to do so because she lacks legal immigration status. The social worker brings Aminata to see you so that you can explain what legal remedies may be available to her. During the conversation with Aminata, you learn that Moussa may not have been free to marry her because his first wife is alive and well in Mali.

- Is there a way for Aminata to apply for VAWA benefits despite this?
- What more would you need to know before you can determine whether she qualifies?

While the foreign national is required to demonstrate that she was married to the abuser at the time of the abuse, she is not required to remain with the abuser during consideration of the self-petition.[5] At the same time, there is no penalty for those who decide to remain in the relationship. This approach recognizes the myriad decisions women in violent relationships make on a daily basis. Some may not have the resources to leave and support themselves or perhaps they are so emotionally entwined with their abuser that leaving is something that cannot be contemplated. Even those who divorce their abuser may still qualify for relief, so long as the divorce occurred after the filing of the petition.[6] However, remarriage *prior* to a decision would void it, whereas marriage *after* approval of the self-petition will not.[7] For example, if Aminata decided to divorce Moussa, doing so after she has filed the VAWA self-petition will have no impact on her petition

---

[4] INA § 204(a)(1)(A)(iii)(II)(aa) and § 204(a)(1)(B)(ii)(II)(aa).
[5] 8 C.F.R. § 204.2(c)(1)(v).
[6] INA § 204(a)(1)(A)(vi); INA § 204(a)(1)(B)(v)(I).
[7] INA § 204(h).

whatsoever. If she decided to remarry, she must wait until after approval of her petition or else the USCIS can deny it simply because of the remarriage.[8]

A.1.b. Proof of Immigration Status of the Abuser

The applicant for relief has the burden to prove that her spouse is either a U.S. citizen or an LPR. Copies of any immigration documents or a birth certificate may be helpful if they can be accessed. However, it is just as likely that the foreign national has no documentation of her husband's nationality or immigration status. The standard of proof applicable to VAWA self-petitions generously permits the submission of any credible evidence to substantiate any element of the petition. Some creative thinking in order to obtain the documentation needed may be necessary.

For instance, if a relative based immigrant petition has already been filed for the benefit of the foreign national but the petitioner subsequently withdraws that petition, documentation previously submitted to the USCIS, to prove immigration status at that time can be referenced as proof of status for the self-petition, even if copies of the petition were not retained by the foreign national. The USCIS can review that prior petition to retrieve the necessary documentation. Similarly, if the foreign national knows that the petitioner naturalized as a U.S. citizen, that information can be referenced in the petition, with information from the self-petitioner on how she came to know this, with an approximate date of when the suspected naturalization took place. A request to the USCIS can then be made for a review of the relative's file for the appropriate documentation. Another way to obtain evidence of an abuser's immigration status is to consider requesting that he submit relevant documents as part of protection from abuse proceedings, where appropriate.

● EXAMPLE

Mai, who is from Cambodia, is in the United States as a B-2 overstay. Recently, she called the police because her husband, a U.S. citizen, held a knife to her throat and threatened to kill her because his dinner was not ready when he returned home from a long day at work. The police advised her to apply for a protection from abuse order, or PFA. Mai sought advice on this from a women's rights organization. One of the lawyers there has agreed to accompany Mai to the court hearing where a decision on whether or not to issue a final PFA order will be determined. The lawyer knows that Mai has no immigration status, and so has sought advice from an immigration attorney on the best way to assist Mai in legalizing her status. Because she knows any future immigration application Mai applies for must prove her husband has U.S. citizenship, the lawyer can consider asking the family court judge to include ordering him to produce evidence of his citizenship as part of the overall PFA order.

---

[8] 8 C.F.R. § 204.2(c)(1)(ii).

A.2. Petitions by Children[9]

Children who have been abused by a parent may file self-petitions.[10] In Section C.2 of Chapter 6, Family Sponsored Immigration and Permanent Resident Status, we review who is a child for immigration purposes. The term includes unmarried minor children under the age of 21. While that definition is also applicable to VAWA petitions, there is one significant difference in that the definition of child for VAWA relief purposes is broader so that it may be possible for foreign nationals to file self-petitions who are older than 21 but less than 25-years old. This special circumstance applies to those children who *could* have filed a self-petition before they reached the age of 21 but did not do so *and* can demonstrate that at least one central reason for that failure connects to the abuse suffered.[11] The child must be unmarried at the time of filing the petition. Marriage after approval, however, will not revoke the approved petition.[12] In addition, the child need not be in the legal custody of the parent at the time of filing, nor does termination of the parental rights of the abuser affect the child's eligibility to self-petition.[13]

● EXAMPLE

Svetlana is from Russia. She and her mother came to the United States as visitors when she was 12 years old and overstayed their visas. Her mother married Stanley, a U.S. citizen, when Svetlana was 14 years old. He promised to file for them both to become LPRs, but did not do so. Stanley began sexually abusing Svetlana soon after her arrival here and warned her that if she told anyone, he would kill her mother. Because Svetlana believed these threats, she told no one what was happening for many years. At the age of 22, she became pregnant with Stanley's child. Initially, she tried to hide it from her mother, but finally told her the truth about what had been happening all these years. Her mother called the police and they arrested Stanley. Even though Svetlana is now over 21 years old, she can still file for immigration benefits based on the abuse she suffered. She can demonstrate that a central reason why she did not file for relief sooner was that she believed Stanley's threats to harm her mother if she told anyone.

Adopted children may also qualify for VAWA benefits. Those adopted by U.S. citizen parents prior to the issuance of an immigrant visa will automatically become citizens themselves once they receive LPR status.[14] However, those that do not, may self-petition to regularize their immigration status if they have been abused. The adoption of the child must take place before his or her

---

[9] While children may file self-petitions in their own right, a U.S. citizen or LPR parent may also file for an abused child who may not have derived immigration benefits directly through him or her. *See* 8 C.F.R. § 204.2(d).
[10] 8 C.F.R. § 204.2(e).
[11] INA § 204(a)(1)(D)(v).
[12] 8 C.F.R. § 204.2(e)(1)(ii).
[13] *Id.*
[14] Cable, DOS, 01-State-105804 (June 16, 2001), reprinted in 78 No. 25 Interpreter Releases 1077-78 (July 2, 2001). *See* Section E of Chapter 11, Citizenship and Naturalization, for further details.

16th birthday, unless s/he is the sibling of another child adopted in the same family, in which case adoption can take place prior to the child turning 18 years of age.[15] INA § 101(b) has a special rule for adopted children who have been abused, since any period of residence with the abusive parent will qualify him or her for VAWA benefits and no longer requires the child to live with that parent for a period of two years.

It is possible that a child will turn 21 before a decision is made on his or her self-petition for VAWA benefits. This is important because the definition of child for immigration purposes only includes those below this age.[16] However, it is quite possible that a child could age out before a decision is made on his or her petition simply because of the time it takes for the USCIS to process the volume of petitions it gets. If this were to happen, then so long as the child filed the self-petition prior to his or her 21st birthday and is the child of a U.S. citizen who did not derive[17] or acquire[18] citizenship through a parent, s/he will not age-out and will remain eligible for benefits even if the petition is approved after that age. This is because the Child Status Protection Act of 2002, or CSPA, allows the age to freeze as of the date the petition was filed.[19] Children of LPRs who filed before 21 but subsequently aged out are automatically moved to the preference category applicable to their situation, retaining the same priority date from the initial filing of the petition.[20] For example, if the 20-year-old son of an LPR filed a self-petition that was not approved before he turned 21 years old, he would automatically be transferred from the preference category for unmarried minor children of LPRs that he was in when he first filed his petition, to the preference category for sons and daughters over 21 of an LPR. This means that he will still be able to derive a benefit from the self-petition he filed, even though he is no longer classified as a child for immigration purposes and may have to wait a little longer to obtain his status.

Children of a self-petitioner who are under 21 may derive VAWA benefits from their parents without a separate petition. The child does not need to be in the United States in order to derive this benefit. For example, in Kalpna's case, discussed earlier, her two children are eligible to derive benefits from Kalpna's petition, if approved. If the children had remained in India, they could also enter the United States as derivatives once Kalpna's self-petition is approved. Where the child qualifies for benefits as the derivative of a qualifying parent and turns 21 before a decision is made on the petition of the principal, s/he will automatically be transferred to the appropriate preference category applicable for his or her age. The child will then wait until a visa number is available for him or her to adjust status to LPR. S/he will be allocated the same priority date as the principal VAWA self-petitioning parent.[21]

---

[15] INA § 101(b)(1)(E)(ii).
[16] INA § 101(b) for a definition of a child.
[17] See Section E. of Chapter 11, Citizenship and Naturalization.
[18] See Section F. of Chapter 11, Citizenship and Naturalization.
[19] See Section C.4.a of Chapter 6, Family Sponsored Immigration and Permanent Resident Status, for a discussion of the CSPA.
[20] INA § 204(a)(1)(D)(i)(I).
[21] INA § 204(a)(1)(D)(i)(III).

> **Case for Discussion 8.2**
>
> Violet is a citizen of Jamaica. She came to the United States on a B2 visa, leaving her four-year old son in the care of her mother. Even though she overstayed her leave, she was recently granted status as an LPR because she had been severely abused by her U.S. citizen husband, Cedric. Violet wants desperately to reunite with her son, who she has not seen for over ten years. Friends have told her that she cannot file for her son because he is still in Jamaica.
>
> - Is this true?

A.3. Parents

Parents abused by their U.S. citizen sons and daughters may file self-petitions to allow them to adjust to LPRs so long as the relationship of parent and child continues to exist.[22] There is no equivalent benefit available to parents of LPRs. Unlike other potential self-petitioners, while parents must show they have resided or continue to reside with the abuser, the statute does not require this to have taken place in the United States.[23]

B. Qualifying Criteria for Relief

The criteria for a foreign national to establish eligibility for VAWA benefits as an abused spouse are set out in 8 C.F.R. § 204.2(c)(1)(i). Some are straightforward, such as the requirement that the couple must have lived together in the United States at some time. Other criteria for this immigration benefit can be more complicated. We explore some of the factors.

B.1. Battery or Extreme Cruelty

Domestic abuse can encompass many different forms. The language of the statute references "extreme cruelty," which can include psychological or economic abuse and many forms of control, including threats of harm, possessive and restricting behavior, verbal abuse, or deliberate isolation from friends and family. Section 204.2(c)(1)(vi) of Title 8 of the Code of Federal Regulations defines battery and extreme cruelty broadly. It includes "being the victim of any act or

---

[22] INA § 204(a)(1)(A)(vii).
[23] INA § 204(a)(1)(A)(vii)(IV).

threatened act of violence, including any forceful detention, which results or threatens to result in physical or mental injury."[24]

Whatever the form of abuse, it must have taken place both during the relationship that gives rise to the qualification for benefits, *and* in the United States. Acts of abuse that take place prior to a marriage or outside the country may still be relevant to document as they may help to demonstrate a pattern of harm and deliberate control. In certain limited circumstances, abuse that takes place exclusively outside the United States including abuse perpetrated by military members stationed abroad, the foreign national victim may still qualify for immigration benefits.[25]

> ● **EXAMPLE**
>
> **John is a U.S. citizen enlisted in the army, stationed at a base in Germany. He is married to Gretchen, a citizen of Germany. She has never left her country. In the beginning of their relationship, John was attentive and kind. However, over time, he has become physically and mentally abusive towards her. She has called the military police on several occasions, therefore documenting the abuse. Even though Gretchen has never entered the United States, she can file a petition as an abused spouse that will allow her to immigrate here.**

In many domestic violence cases, survivors are reluctant to file a complaint about their abuser with the police, perhaps fearful that they will not get the support they need, that a report may escalate the situation with the abusive spouse, or that the police may alert the USCIS of the undocumented status of the person reporting. The foreign national may also have avoided making requests for PFA orders or medical treatment for the same reasons. Therefore, there may be no independent evidence of the abuse. Applying the "any credible evidence" standard, an applicant could obtain statements from friends and relatives with firsthand knowledge of what happened or who were informed of the situation by the foreign national either at the time of or shortly after an incident. Other evidence may include statements from the applicant herself, any photographs taken of bruising on the body, counseling records, evidence that the foreign national spent some time in a domestic violence shelter, or 911 transcripts in lieu of a formal filed police report.

B.2. Good Moral Character

An applicant for VAWA relief must also show that she has been a person of **good moral character**, or **GMC**,[26] for a period of at least three years prior to

---

[24] There is interesting discussion by the U.S. Court of Appeals for the Ninth Circuit on what constitutes extreme cruelty in *Hernandez v. Ashcroft*, 345 F.3d 824, 835-842 (9th Cir. 2003).
[25] INA § 204(a)(1)(A)(v) and § 204(a)(1)(B)(iv) permit applications from a foreign national whose abuser is a U.S. citizen or LPR government employee or member of the armed forces, wherever s/he may be working or stationed.
[26] It may be helpful to review the section on good moral character in Section I.4 of Chapter 10, Immigration Court Practice and Relief from Removal, as the information there is relevant to this discussion.

filing the petition, although activity outside this time frame may also be considered as relevant. This does not mean that the foreign national can have no criminal history, since misdemeanor convictions may not be a bar to demonstrating the requisite GMC. Where a conviction is connected to the abuse, a waiver may be available.[27]

Case for Discussion 8.3

Nicolette comes to see you because she wants to legalize her immigration status. She tells you that her husband has been abusing her. He is an LPR and regularly beats her. On one occasion, he smashed a bottle over her head, creating a huge gash that needed several stitches. She tells you that his violence terrorized her so much that she was too afraid to disobey any of his orders. At one point, Nicolette explains, her husband became a pimp to several women and forced her to engage in prostitution along with them. She did not want to do this, but believed her husband when he said that he would kill her if she did not comply. Nicolette has several arrests for prostitution and served time in prison for this offense. She tells you that she was only able to break free from her husband after he was also imprisoned, which is where he still is.

- Are there any impediments to Nicolette demonstrating that she is a person of good moral character?
- If so, is there anything she can do to overcome them?

Before filing a VAWA petition, it may be prudent to file a criminal background check request with the Federal Bureau of Investigations, or FBI, in order to obtain information on a foreign national's criminal history in any state she may have lived. The local state criminal background check may suffice for those who have only ever lived in one state. This way, any adverse information will be disclosed before a petition is filed and a plan set in place for how to deal with it. A report that shows no arrest record can also be presented as evidence of GMC.

Where a foreign national does in fact have a criminal record for an offense that is not connected to the abuse and is not listed as one of the statutory bars, she will have the opportunity to balance GMC factors against the bad and hopefully demonstrate that the totality of the circumstances tends to support a favorable finding. Documents proving her involvement in the community, perhaps through her church, local community groups or shelters, or in her children's school, would be useful evidence to counter bad facts. Any evidence of

---

[27] INA § 204(a)(C).

rehabilitation would also be helpful, along with information on a stable work history, or letters of support from friends, co-workers, or employers.

A sample statement in support of a VAWA self-petition might look like the one in Box 8.1.

Box 8.1   Sample Statement in Support of a VAWA Self-Petition

I K.Z., of 123 Survivor Street, St. Paul, Minnesota WILL SAY AS FOLLOWS:

1. I am a citizen of the Democratic Republic of Congo (DRC). I first entered the United States in December 2000. I was seeking asylum because of what had happened to me in my country. I entered using someone else's passport as it was not possible for me to get my own.
2. I was detained on my arrival and taken to York County Prison where I remained until 2004, when I was released following a grant of Withholding of Removal by an Immigration Judge. I remain in this status today and am required to report to the USCIS twice a year.
3. I married my husband on February 25, 1999 in Tanzania. When I was released from detention, I traveled with my husband to his home in Minnesota.
4. When we arrived, I learned my husband did not have his own living space but shared a one-bedroom apartment with his cousin. My husband had no intention of finding somewhere separate for us to live. All three of us lived together for about six or seven months after which time I began to insist that we find our own place so that we could have some privacy and more space.
5. This upset my husband and we began to argue because he knew, for us to have our own place, it would require us to earn enough money to cover the additional expense. He did not want to work. One morning, we had been having one of our many arguments about when we were going to move. Later, when there was no resolution, I thought that we had finished the discussion and went back to bed because I was upset. Next thing I knew, my husband had thrown a bucket of cold water on me. I was so shocked. I didn't say anything to him or anyone else about what he had done.
6. I began to work at the end of 2004 or the beginning of 2005, but would hand over my check to my husband. However, if I needed transportation money to get to work, my husband would not give it to me. This continued for a long time until I learned that I could open a bank account in my name and cash my own check. When my husband found out that I had done this, he was very angry and began beating me. But I did not close the account as I realized this was the only way for me to control the money I was making.

7. The first time my husband hit me was with a belt. This was in early 2005. We were arguing about something or other and he was telling me that I did not know how to talk to him. Most of the time, we would argue about my cooking. He would tell me that my food did not taste good. This time, after I thought we had finished arguing, I went to take a shower and then went to bed.

8. Next thing I knew, my husband was hitting me with a belt, complaining about my cooking and the way I had talked to him. I began screaming with pain and fear. My husband's cousin came into the bedroom to see what was happening. Immediately he stopped my husband from hitting me further. The belt left many marks on my body.

9. One of the neighbors who had heard the noise called the police. They came to the apartment and asked me questions, to see if I was ok, but I did not tell them that my husband had hit me because I was afraid.

10. My husband had always told me that my immigration status meant that I could be deported if I was involved in a crime and that he would report me to immigration so that I could be returned to my country. I was afraid that I might be deported because of the horrors I had experienced when I was there, so I said nothing to the police about what had really happened and why I had been screaming. I truly believed they would arrest me. My body was covered so they could not see the marks on me in any event. The police said they would return in another 24 hours to check on us but they didn't come back.

11. In 2009, I was working double shifts in order to save money. The checks from my second shift I set aside in a drawer in the house so that I would not spend it. Close to Thanksgiving, I went to the drawer to add another check but didn't see any of the ones that I had already placed there. My husband told me that he had already deposited them into our joint savings account. This totaled about $6000. There was no reason for me not to believe him so I did not think anymore about it.

12. On Black Friday, I wanted to shop for a new television. I called the bank to find out what the balance was in our joint account and was told that it was only about $1000. I was shocked. When I asked my husband about this, he started to fight with me, asking why I needed the money anyway. He finally told me that he had taken the checks, forged my signature, and placed the money into an account in only his name. He told me that he no longer had the money as he had spent it. I was so angry and felt helpless, because I did not know what to do. I did not report the fact that he had forged my signature to the police.

13. In January 2010, my husband and I were leaving a funeral gathering together. The wife of one of his cousins had given me some food to help her prepare for the next day's events. I sat in the back of the car with the food.

14. My husband told me to move to the other side because I was fat and therefore unbalancing it. So I moved to the middle. Again he complained and told me to move to the other side of the car in a very

aggressive way, calling me names. I asked him why he was talking to me like that because this was the first time he had told me that I was unbalancing the car.

15. My husband then said that when I was ready to sit on the other side of the car, he would be ready to drive. He then got out of the car. I asked him for the key to the car because he had switched off the engine and it was getting cold. It was about ten o'clock at night at this time. In any event, this was my car and I should have been able to drive it if he decided he wouldn't.

16. When my husband heard me ask for the key, he got upset and came to the back of the car, asking me what I had said. I tried to explain that I was getting cold and wanted to go home. He then took his jacket off and he began punching me and pulling out the extensions in my hair. I was screaming, "Help me! Help me!" Some people came by and called my husband's cousin and other people from the house because we had not left the funeral gathering yet.

17. They tried to stop my husband from hitting me. I managed to lock the door, thinking I would be safe. But my husband had the remote control and opened it again so that he could continue hitting me. Anyone who was trying to stop him from hurting me was pushed away. Finally, people managed to hold my husband down.

18. For a long time, I had been trying to tell my husband's relatives about how he had been treating me and now they were able to see with their own eyes. This was the worst he had ever done. I ended up staying at his cousin's house that night because everyone agreed it would not be safe for me to return to my house. I could not sleep. In the morning, the entire community knew what had happened to me and I was embarrassed that my husband had treated me this way in public.

19. My husband's nephew took me home the next day so that I could retrieve some things and think through where I should go. When we arrived, all of my husband's things were in our living room. He said he was going to leave the apartment. I took a few of my things, took the car and went to a friend's house for about a week and a half. I also went to the hospital because the bruises on my body were so bad. They gave me some sleeping pills to help me to sleep. I was told to stay out of work for about a week. I did not make a police report.

20. A week later, my husband was calling me, begging me to come back home, that everything was going to be fine. Again, I believed him and decided to return. Four or five months later, he was at it again.

21. I had been invited to a bridal shower. I told my husband a week before that I was going to go. He then called my friend without telling me, to say that he would only let me go if he came too. My friend explained the shower was for women only and my husband argued that this was not true. He said that if my friend came to pick me up to take me, then I could not come back to the house again.

22. I found all this out when my friend called me to tell me what my husband had said to her. I agreed that I would not go to the bridal shower with her because I did not want to start problems with him. However, I said I would visit with my friend for a little while before she went to the shower.
23. When my friend dropped me back home later that night, I found I could not enter the apartment because my husband had put a chair against the door so that it would not open. I did not understand what was going on. I called him but he did not respond to me. I called my friend to come and pick me up again because there was nowhere for me to sleep.
24. When I was finally allowed back in the house some days later, my husband and I began to argue and then he picked up a flower vase on the table and he threw it at me. This frightened my friend who had come to make sure I was safe. My friend then told me it was not safe for me to stay at the house and I should leave with her. My husband threatened that if I left, he would destroy my life. I decided to leave.
25. I heard later from his cousin that my husband called the police to tell them that I had left and had taken the car in an attempt to have me arrested. They said they could not help him with a domestic dispute. The car was in my name and I had made all payments on it so it wasn't his anyhow.
26. Throughout our marriage, I have had gynecological problems, which prevented me from conceiving a child. Despite several tests and examinations, the doctors have been unable to find out what is wrong with me. My husband would often use this as a way to be cruel to me, telling me that I have no womb and would remain childless all my life. This has been very painful since I believe that part of our problems stemmed from the fact that I could not conceive.
27. However, shortly after I left my husband for the last time, I had terrible abdominal pains and had to be rushed to the hospital. It turned out that I was suffering a miscarriage from the stress of the treatment I had suffered from my husband. This has left me devastated and has helped me make the decision not to return to him.

C. Compiling the VAWA Petition

A request for VAWA immigration benefits should include the following:

- Form I-360, Petition for Amerasian, Widow(er), or Special Immigrant
- Form G-28, Notice of Entry of Appearance as Attorney or Accredited Representative
- Statement from the self-petitioner in support of the petition

- Corroborative statements from others regarding the *bona fides* of the qualifying relationship, or the abuse suffered, where that information is known
- Documentation of the abuser's status as a U.S. citizen or LPR
- Police reports, 911 transcripts, or medical records to corroborate the abuse, where available
- Psychological Evaluation to substantiate extreme cruelty suffered by applicant
- Counseling or shelter records or statements from friends who either directly or indirectly were aware of the abuse
- Police or FBI criminal record checks to corroborate GMC of applicant
- Certified dispositions of any arrests of applicant
- Form I-485, Application to Register Permanent Residence or Adjust Status, where self-petitioner's priority date is current and therefore eligible to adjust status to LPR immediately
- Form I-765, Application for Employment Authorization
- Passport photographs of the self-petitioner

Once compiled, the petition is sent to the USCIS Vermont Service Center VAWA Unit, which has exclusive jurisdiction over the consideration of abused spouse petition. The officers there receive special training to deal with these petitions, ensuring an appropriate level of sensitivity and expertise. The address of the unit is and the petition package should be addressed to:

> Vermont Service Center
> ATTN: VAWA/U/T UNIT
> 75 Lower Welden St.
> St. Albans, VT 05479-0001

Form I-360, Petition for Amerasian, Widow(er), or Special Immigrant, is used for a number of different petitions. Here, it is the form that must be completed by those who wish to self-petition for benefits under VAWA. The self-petitioner must complete the relevant sections of the form seeking information on her, the abuser, and any qualifying derivative family members. As with all forms, no question should be left blank as that may be interpreted as an omission.[28]

As previously discussed, a foreign national must show how s/he meets each of the eligibility criteria for benefits. This can either be done by producing primary documentation,[29] or, where this is not possible, then by secondary

---

[28] Interestingly, the Form I-360, Petition for Amerasian, Widow(er), or Special Immigrant, collects no designated information on those seeking VAWA benefits as parents abused by U.S. citizen sons or daughters. This oversight may be addressed in future versions of the form, but until then, this is the form to use and responses should be adapted accordingly.

[29] A useful guide to document gathering is "Document Gathering for Self-Petitioning Under Violence Against Women Act, a Step-by-Step Guide" published by the Immigrant Legal Resource Center and available at http://www.ilrc.org/files/document_gathering_for_self-petitioning_under_the_violence_against_women_act.pdf.

information that meets the "any credible evidence" standard. A detailed statement or affidavit from the petitioner is always useful as it helps to provide a full picture of the relationship with the abuser, from the time when there were no or few problems in the relationship, to the point when the foreign national decided to apply for immigration benefits. It can also address each of the criteria that need to be met and explain in the applicant's own words how she believes they have been satisfied.

Where an abuser is no longer a U.S. citizen, an LPR, or is deceased, the petition should include whatever information the foreign national has regarding any immigration or criminal proceedings that may have led to the divesting of such status, together with evidence to prove that there was a connection between the loss of status and the domestic violence. Additionally, it should provide evidence of filing the self-petition within two years of that incident.

● EXAMPLE

Recall Nicolette, whose husband was convicted and sent to prison for his role as a pimp in a prostitution ring. He was sentenced to five years in prison and is placed into removal proceedings where an immigration judge orders him deported. Even though Nicolette's husband is no longer an LPR, she will still be able to obtain VAWA benefits because there is a link between his deportation and loss of status and the domestic violence that she suffered.

For those self-petitioners who have a visa number immediately available, either because they are the spouse, child, or parent of a U.S. citizen, or an earlier priority date has become current, an application to adjust status to an LPR can be filed at the same time as the Form I-360, Petition for Amerasian, Widow(er), or Special Immigrant. Once the VAWA Unit approves the petition, then the application to adjust to LPR status can be forwarded to the local USCIS Field office for an interview to be arranged and a decision made on the adjustment application. Discussion on the procedure for those who are not able to file an adjustment package concurrently is in Section D.

In some cases, a foreign national who is married to a U.S. citizen or who has a current priority date for a relative petition previously filed may have already submitted an adjustment package with her husband in accordance with the procedures laid out in Section G of Chapter 6, Family Sponsored Immigration and Permanent Resident Status, because they were filing as a married couple. However, subsequent to the filing but prior to the interview, the U.S. citizen or LPR spouse may decide that he no longer wishes to continue with the application, either because of a breakdown in the relationship or as a way to further control or abuse the foreign national. Where an adjustment application is still pending, a letter should be sent to the local USCIS Field office as soon as possible, asking for the application to be held in abeyance so that a VAWA self-petition can be filed with the Vermont Service Center and adjudicated there first.

Once notified that a VAWA self-petition is to be filed, the policy of the USCIS is to wait until a decision has been made at the Vermont Service Center before adjudicating the prior filed adjustment application. This then allows a foreign national with an approved petition the opportunity to adjust status based on the original adjustment application, which has now converted to a self-petition. This may be financially helpful to the foreign national, since that initial adjustment application could only have been filed after payment of all applicable fees. While a fee waiver is available for those seeking to adjust because of abuse, the self-petitioner must still demonstrate qualification for the waiver, which may be difficult if the foreign national is working and is just outside the financial limits.

● **EXAMPLE**

Janeth entered the United States as a visitor from Zimbabwe. She married her long time sweetheart Joseph, now a U.S. citizen. Six months after the marriage, Joseph is still dragging his feet about filing an application for Janeth to become an LPR. He finally files for her and they learn that the waiting time for an interview is approximately nine months long. During this time, the marriage breaks down and Joseph begins to physically abuse Janeth, who leaves the home because she is afraid for her safety. Joseph tells her that he will no longer support her application with the USCIS unless she returns home. If Janeth decides to file a self-petition based on the abuse she has suffered, she could write to the USCIS to notify them that she will be filing a Form I-360, Petition for Amerasian, Widow(er), or Special Immigrant, and that she would like them to delay making a decision on the adjustment application she filed with her husband until the petition is adjudicated. This will then save her the expense of paying for a new adjustment application in the event that she does not qualify for a fee waiver.

Because the adjustment application is filed in conjunction with Form I-360, Petition for Amerasian, Widow(er), or Special Immigrant, the foreign national is not required to include an affidavit of support, since this is not required in self-petition cases. In fact, this would be inappropriate because the applicant is her own petitioner. She also does not need to show that she is unlikely to be a public charge as this provision does not apply to her.[30]

A foreign national who has a visa number immediately available may decide not to file the adjustment package at the same time as the self-petition as a strategic matter. She may decide to wait until approval of the self-petition before paying the high fee for adjustment, particularly if she is uncertain of the outcome of the petition for VAWA relief. While this may delay the ultimate adjudication of the adjustment package, it may provide peace of mind to those foreign nationals with limited income.

---

[30] INA § 212(a)(4)(E)(i).

D. Processing the VAWA Self-Petition

D.1. Prima Facie Finding

Shortly after receipt, the petition will be reviewed by a specially trained USCIS adjudications officer. This is done to ensure that, at least on its face, all eligibility requirements have been addressed so that, if the stated facts are true and properly substantiated, the petition will be approved. If this is the case, then a foreign national will receive a ***prima facie* eligibility** notice from the USCIS. This can be an important document because it allows the self-petitioner access to certain public benefits. The notice is valid for 100 days and can be renewed prior to expiry by writing to the Vermont Service Center to request an extension.

Following issuance of the *prima facie* eligibility notice, the next step will be for the USCIS to issue a request for further evidence, or RFE, if it determines that more information is needed before it can make a final decision on the self-petition. Any response must be sent within the time allowed, or else a decision can be made based on the information already available. The USCIS can then either approve the self-petition or send a **notice of intent to deny**, or **NOID**, which will document the reasons for deficiency in the self-petition. The foreign national will then have the opportunity to respond to the NOID with additional information that may support an approval of the petition.

In the event of denial of the VAWA petition, there is no appeal. Instead, a self-petitioner can challenge the decision by filing a Motion to Reopen or Reconsider with to the Administrative Appeals Office, or AAO, for a final decision. The other alternative is to file a new self-petition, possibly addressing the problematic areas that caused the prior one to be denied. The advantage of this approach is that the foreign national is guaranteed to benefit from the special expertise of officers in the VAWA unit, compared to when AAO officers, who are not specially trained to deal with these cases, consider the matter.

D.2. Deferred Action Status

Approved self-petitions confer a number of benefits. For instance, those who have visas immediately available to them can adjust their status to LPRs. Those who must wait for a priority date to become current because their abuser is an LPR and there is no visa number immediately available, receive ***deferred action status*** instead. This allows the foreign national the opportunity to apply for an employment authorization document, or EAD. Those who filed adjustment applications concurrently with the self-petition are eligible for the EAD after deferred action has been granted, and so are able to work while waiting for a decision on the self-petition, which can take some time. This is another tactical issue for consideration when deciding a time to file the adjustment application. Any deferred action status granted to the principal applicant will also be available for qualifying derivative children, along with adjustment of status, if that is also available to the principal.

Deferred Action Status: A discretionary decision taken by the USCIS not to prosecute a foreign national known to be present in the United States without legal status, formally acknowledging that the recipient is of lower priority for removal proceedings.

Deferred action is granted for an initial period of 15 months but can be renewed until the approved self-petitioner's priority date becomes current and she is able to file an adjustment application. While deferred action status acknowledges that the recipient is of a lower priority for removal purposes, however, it does not make the foreign national immune to deportation. Therefore, if a person is placed subsequently into removal proceedings, the immigration judge should be made aware of the approved VAWA self-petition and asked to administratively close the court case until a visa number becomes available. This means that the case will be temporarily removed from the judge's docket so that it has a lower priority on the judge's list for hearing. Where proceedings commence before the self-petition is approved, most judges are willing to grant continuances of the case to allow a decision on the petition to be made.

● EXAMPLE

Maria is from Costa Rica. Her LPR husband has abused her for some time. She filed Form I-360, Petition for Amerasian, Widow(er) or Special Immigrant, some months ago and has just learned that the USCIS has approved it. However, because her husband is an LPR, Maria is not able to adjust status immediately because no visa number is available for her. She is in the Family 2A preference category and must wait two years until her priority date is reached. In the meantime, Maria can receive deferred action while she waits, along with similar status conferred on any qualifying derivative children applying with her who are under 21 years of age. She and her children can apply for and receive employment authorization while they are in deferred action status. If Maria's husband was a U.S. citizen, she could have filed her application to adjust status to LPR on Form I-485, Application to Register Permanent Residence or Adjust Status, concurrently with her Form I-360 self-petition. However, if she decided to delay filing her adjustment application due to cost considerations because she is not eligible for a fee waiver, she may prefer to wait to file her adjustment of status application until she can afford it. In this case, even though she is an immediate relative, she will receive deferred action status until she is ready to file for her green card.

D.3. Inadmissibility Issues

Guidance from USCIS for interpreting INA § 245(a) as it pertains to VAWA beneficiaries provides that foreign nationals with an approved Form I-360, Petition for Amerasian, Widow(er), or Special Immigrant, are able to adjust status in the United States even if they entered without inspection.[31] Under the 2013 reauthorization, VAWA beneficiaries are not subject to being inadmissible due to public charge issues, but may be subject to other inadmissibility grounds, as discussed in Chapter 9, Inadmissibility and Deportability.

---

[31] Michael Aytes Memorandum, *Adjustment of Status for VAWA Self-Petitioner Who is Present Without Inspection* dated April 11, 2008, HQDOMO 70/23.1.

Any person who obtained immigration status as a result of an approved self-petition, whether directly or as a derivative, can never file a nonimmigrant application or immigrant petition for the benefit of the abuser.[32] This protects the integrity of the process and is the same as the prohibitions that apply to adopted children or special immigrant juveniles who are also prohibited from filing for biological parents.[33]

D.4. Affirmative Petitions vs. Defensive Applications

Individuals who have suffered physical abuse or extreme mental cruelty are eligible to apply for benefits under VAWA even if they are in removal proceedings. Those not in removal file affirmative petitions with the USCIS as discussed earlier. Those in removal proceedings can file for relief in the form of cancellation of removal because of the abuse. This is known as a defensive application. Section I.5 of Chapter 10, Immigration Court Practice and Relief from Removal, discusses VAWA-based cancellation of removal in greater detail.

D.5. Confidentiality

As previously noted, IIRAIRA § 384 prohibits all DHS employees from providing information about self-petitions to a third party, at the risk of disciplinary action or fines. In addition, any adverse determination of admissibility or deportability cannot be based solely on information provided by an abuser unless an unrelated party independently verifies it. Denied petitions for these immigration benefits rarely result in the initiation of removal or deportation proceedings based on information supplied through the self-petition alone. Rather, information from other sources must be obtained for this purpose. This attempt to ensure confidentiality recognizes the complicated relationships that many abused foreign nationals experience, the sensitive nature of the self-petitions, and seeks to remove concerns about immigration from the picture.

E. Removal of Conditions for Abused Conditional Lawful Permanent Residents: INA § 216; 8 C.F.R. § 216

Immigration relief is available for those who are married to U.S. citizens and who have been granted conditional LPR status based on that marriage. As discussed in Section I.1 of Chapter 6, Family Sponsored Immigration, the couple is

---

[32] INA § 204(a)(1)(L).
[33] *See* Sections C.2. of Chapter 6, Family Sponsored Immigration and Permanent Resident Status and Q.1, respectively.

expected to jointly apply to remove the conditions at least 90 days before the expiry of the conditional status. However, where the foreign national is in an abusive relationship, she may apply to have the conditions removed at any time, even before the 90-day deadline. The foreign national may apply on her own, by seeking a waiver of the requirement to file jointly with the abusive spouse.

As with VAWA self-petitions, the foreign national must demonstrate that the marriage forming the basis of the petition was entered into in good faith, that she resided with the abuser, and that she suffered physical abuse or extreme cruelty during the marriage. Any credible evidence may be produced to substantiate the abuse suffered.[34]

E.1. Compiling the Removal of Conditions Petition

Unlike the VAWA self-petition, the petition to remove conditions is filed on Form I-751, Petition to Remove Conditions on Residence. A petition package should contain:

- Form I-751, Petition to Remove Conditions on Residence
- Form G-28, Notice of Entry of Appearance as Attorney or Accredited Representative
- Statement from the foreign national in support of the petition
- Evidence of the *bona fides* of the marriage
- Corroborative statements from others regarding the *bona fides* of the marriage, or the abuse suffered, where that information is known
- Evidence of the abuse or extreme cruelty which can include Police reports, 911 transcripts, or medical records to corroborate, where available
- Psychological Evaluation to substantiate extreme cruelty suffered by applicant
- Counseling or shelter records
- Copy of foreign nationals I-551 Permanent Residency stamp or LPR card
- Copy of passport to show that any travel outside of the United States did not exceed limits that may have terminated the conditional residency status and
- Immigration fee or
- Form I-912, Request for Fee Waiver, where appropriate, together with evidence to support financial eligibility

If the petition is approved, the foreign national's conditional status will be converted to LPR status for an indefinite period.

---

[34] INA § 216(c)(4).

F. U Nonimmigrant Status, Victims of Enumerated Crimes: INA § 101(a)(15)(U); 8 C.F.R. § 214.14

U Nonimmigrant visas are a special type of immigration status available to victims of specific criminal activity occurring in the United States.[35] It was introduced in the Victims of Trafficking and Violence Protection Act of 2000, or VTVPA,[36] recognizing the need to offer protection to crime victims who agree to cooperate with law enforcement. The USCIS has stated that:

> The legislation was intended to strengthen the ability of law enforcement agencies to investigate and prosecute cases of domestic violence, sexual assault, trafficking of aliens, and other crimes, while also protecting victims of crimes who have suffered substantial mental or physical abuse due to the crime and are willing to help law enforcement authorities in the investigation or prosecution of the criminal activity. The legislation also helps law enforcement agencies to better serve victims of crimes.[37]

F.1. Eligibility for the U Nonimmigrant Status

The Immigration and Nationality Act § 101(a)(15)(U) defines eligibility requirements for a U visa which include:

- The foreign national has suffered substantial physical or mental abuse as a result of having been a victim of criminal activity involving an enumerated crime
- The foreign national or parent, guardian, or next friend of a child under 16 possesses information concerning the criminal activity
- The foreign national or parent, guardian, or next friend of a child under the age of 16
  - ☐ has been helpful,
  - ☐ is being helpful, or
  - ☐ is likely to be helpful to a Federal, State, or local law enforcement official, to a Federal, State, or local prosecutor, to a Federal or State judge, to the Service [USCIS], or to other Federal, State, or local authorities investigating or prosecuting criminal activity

The criminal activity must have violated the laws of the United States or occurred in the United States, including in Indian country and military

---

[35] INA § 101(a)(15)(U), 8 C.F.R. § 214.14.
[36] Pub. L. 106-386, 114 Stat. 1464 (2000).
[37] See USCIS website entry, Victims of Criminal Activity: U Nonimmigrant Status, found here: http://www.uscis.gov/humanitarian/victims-human-trafficking-other-crimes/victims-criminal-activity-u-nonimmigrant-status/victims-criminal-activity-u-nonimmigrant-status.

installations, or the territories and possessions of the United States.[38] No familial relationship needs to exist between the foreign national and the perpetrator of the crime. This provision is often used in domestic violence situations where neither the abuser nor the abused have lawful immigration status.

F.2. Certification for Qualifying or Enumerated Crimes

The INA § 101(a)(15)(U)(iii) lists the types of crimes that are eligible for consideration under this relief, as shown in Box 8.2.

Box 8.2 — U Visa Enumerated Crimes

Abduction	Murder
Abusive Sexual Contact	Obstruction of Justice
Blackmail	Peonage
Domestic Violence	Perjury
Extortion	Prostitution
False Imprisonment	Rape
Female Genital Mutilation	Sexual Assault
Felonious Assault	Sexual Exploitation
Fraud in Foreign Labor Contracting	Slave Trade
Hostage	Stalking
Incest	Torture
Involuntary Servitude	Trafficking
Kidnapping	Witness Tampering
Manslaughter	Unlawful Criminal Restraint

Other related crimes, which includes any similar activity where the elements of the crime is substantially similar. It also includes attempt, conspiracy, or solicitation to commit any of the above and other related crimes.

A central requirement for eligibility is that the applicant must be willing to assist in an investigation or prosecution of a crime.[39] However, U nonimmigrant status protection will still be available to a foreign national where:

- An investigation does not result in a prosecution, since this decision remains in the sole discretion of the investigating agency
- The helpful victim ultimately does not testify at trial. While the victim cannot *refuse* to testify if requested, sometimes the investigating agency may decide

---

[38] INA § 101(a)(15)(U)(i)(IV).
[39] INA § 101(a)(15)(U)(i)(III).

that oral testimony from the victim is not required. Only in this circumstance will a failure to testify not be held against the foreign national
- The abuser eludes arrest
- The investigating agency decides to dismiss any criminal charges (again, this is within the prerogative of the agency and therefore cannot be held against the reporting victim)
- The foreign national comes forward to make a report but the police or District Attorney decide not to prosecute
- A prosecution ensues but no conviction results
- The foreign national is a victim of one of the enumerated crimes, but the law enforcement agency decides to prosecute the perpetrator for a different crime that may not be within one of the required specific criminal activities
- Prosecution cannot take place because the perpetrator enjoys diplomatic immunity or his or her extradition cannot be affected.[40]

Many of these overrides seek to protect the integrity of the decision making process of the investigating law enforcement agency and therefore should not negatively impact the foreign national's ability to seek immigration relief.

Case for Discussion 8.4

Mario, an undocumented Peruvian national, was the victim of a robbery at gunpoint and is now suffering from post-traumatic stress disorder, or PTSD. He cannot get out of bed and is afraid to leave his home. The police have caught the perpetrator and have subpoenaed Mario to appear in court to testify. He is afraid to do so because he does not want to come face-to-face with his attacker again. However, he is willing to give a written statement.

- Has Mario been a victim of an enumerated crime and if so, which?
- Assume that the crime does qualify him for relief. Can he demonstrate his willingness to assist in the investigation of a crime by providing a written statement instead of testifying in court as he has been asked to do?

As part of the petition process, the foreign national must obtain a certificate of helpfulness from a law enforcement agency or similar investigative body authorized to issue such a certificate. This can include any of the following:

- Police officer
- Judge

---

[40] 72 Fed. Reg. 53,014, 53,020 (Sept. 17, 2007).

- Prosecutor
- Immigration officer
- Other authority with responsibility for investigation or prosecution of criminal activity
- Agencies with criminal investigative jurisdiction in a particular area of expertise, which can include:
  - ☐ Child Protective Services Worker
  - ☐ Equal Employment Opportunities Commission
  - ☐ Department of Labor[41]

An investigation into criminal activity can consist of detection, investigation, prosecution, conviction, or sentencing for one of the enumerated crimes.[42] This broad definition encompasses most activities involved in a criminal activity probe.

The head of the designated law enforcement agency, or a person or persons the head delegates, or a federal, state, or local judge,[43] may complete the certificate, which is on a special immigration form known as Form I-918, Supplement B, Law Enforcement Certification Form. The designated person decides only the issue of whether the person requesting the certificate has been helpful in the investigation or prosecution of a crime. There is no authority for such a person to determine whether immigration benefits should or should not be conferred as a result of that cooperation, since the USCIS has the exclusive power to grant the U visa immigration benefit.

F.3. Substantial Physical or Emotional Abuse

A foreign national must demonstrate that s/he has suffered substantial physical or emotional abuse from the criminal activity.[44] This can encompass injury or harm to the victim's physical person or impairment of his or her mental soundness.[45] In deciding whether or not a person has suffered substantial harm, the following factors should be considered:

- The nature of the injury inflicted or suffered,
- The severity of the perpetrator's conduct,
- The severity of the harm suffered,
- The duration of the infliction of the harm, and
- The extent to which there is permanent or serious harm to the appearance, health, or physical or mental soundness of the victim.[46]

---

[41] 8 C.F.R. § 214.14(a)(2).
[42] 8 C.F.R. § 214.14(a)(5).
[43] 8 C.F.R. § 214.14(a)(3).
[44] INA § 101(a)(15)(U)(i)(I).
[45] 8 C.F.R. § 214.14(b)(1).
[46] *Id.*

It is important to note that the substantial harm determination is made on a case-by-case basis, with no one particular factor required as a prerequisite to meeting the standard. A pattern of criminal conduct towards the foreign national victim may be considered, as may behaviors that exacerbate any pre-existing conditions or injuries.

F.4. Identifying the Victim

Applicants for relief will be ineligible if it is determined that they have some culpability for any of the enumerated crimes that will form the basis for the U Nonimmigrant Status petition.[47] However, this exclusion does not apply to a foreign national who committed a different crime from the one under investigation or prosecution, even if the crimes are related.[48]

● EXAMPLE

Isabella is from Italy. She is without legal immigration status. She is seeking U Nonimmigrant Status because she has been forced to work as a prostitute for a boyfriend. If Isabella worked as the supervisor of the establishment, it is likely that she was part of the prostitution ring and therefore culpable in the crime from which she seeks immigration benefits. If, however, she is arrested for a theft offense, she will still be eligible to apply for U Nonimmigrant Status benefits.

A person seeking U Nonimmigrant Status can either be a direct or **indirect victim** of one of the enumerated criminal activities.[49] A **direct victim** is someone who has suffered direct and ***proximate harm*** resulting from the crime. Bystanders can also qualify as direct victims, if they suffer direct injuries as a result of the crime. For instance, a pregnant woman who witnesses a murder might be so paralyzed by fear that she suffers a heart attack or a miscarriage.[50]

Indirect victims may also qualify and are classified as those family members of a direct victim who has died as a result of murder or manslaughter or is incapacitated or incompetent and therefore cannot be helpful in the investigation or prosecution of the crime.[51] The indirect victim of an adult direct victim must be either the spouse or minor child under the age of 21 years. Where the direct victim is a child, then indirect victims include the child's spouse and any children, parents, and unmarried siblings under the age of 18.[52]

Proximate Harm: Harm suffered immediately as a direct result of the actions of another.

---

[47] 8 C.F.R. § 214.14(a)(14)(iii).
[48] 72 Federal Register 53014-53042, September 17, 2007, 53018.
[49] 8 C.F.R. § 214.14(a)(14).
[50] 72 Federal Register 53014-53042, September 17, 2007, at 53017.
[51] *Id.*
[52] 8 C.F.R. § 214.14(a)(10). It may also be possible for an undocumented parent of a U.S. citizen child victim of a qualifying crime to qualify for U nonimmigrant status relief as an indirect victim.

> **Case for Discussion 8.5**
>
> Laila's husband was murdered during a burglary in his store that went horribly wrong. She is devastated because he was the only one working while she stayed home to take care of their two young children. She does not want to return to her family in Iran because there are fewer freedoms for women there.
>
> - Can she qualify for a U nonimmigrant visa based on these facts?

Qualifying derivative family members may also be granted U Nonimmigrant Status once the principal applicant's petition is approved.[53] For adult victims, the qualifying family members are their spouse and any children under 21 years of age. For victims under 21 at the time of the criminal activity, the qualifying family members are their spouse, children, parents, and any unmarried siblings under the age of 18 at the time of filing the petition but not necessarily at the time of adjudication.[54] Except in the case of qualifying derivative children born after the U visa petition has been filed,[55] the qualifying relationship must exist at the time of filing the U visa petition and continue through adjudication and entry to the United States for those qualifying family members living abroad.[56] Derivative family members cannot include the perpetrator of a family violence or trafficking qualifying crime.[57] The family members need only show that the qualifying relationship exists and that they are admissible to the United States.[58] They do not need to file a separate certification as to their helpfulness in investigating the crime.

G. Compiling the U Nonimmigrant Status Petition

A complete U Nonimmigrant Status petition package should contain the following:

- Cover letter that explains why the foreign national is eligible for a U Nonimmigrant Status and a "roadmap" to the evidence submitted with the petition
- Form I-918, Petition for U Nonimmigrant Status

---

[53] INA § 101(a)(15)(U)(ii).
[54] 8 C.F.R. § 214.14(f)(4)(ii).
[55] 8 C.F.R. § 214.14(f)(4)(i).
[56] 8 C.F.R. § 214.14(f)(4).
[57] 8 C.F.R. § 214.14(f)(1).
[58] *Id.*

- Form G-28, Notice of Entry of Appearance as an Attorney or Accredited Representative
- Form I-918, Supplement B, U Nonimmigrant Status Certification
- Evidence of the criminal activity, including police records or newspaper articles about the event
- Victim's statement describing facts of the victimization, including
    - ☐ The nature of the enumerated criminal activity
    - ☐ When it occurred
    - ☐ Who was responsible for the crime, if known
    - ☐ Details about the events surrounding the crime
    - ☐ Details about any investigation, prosecution, or court or other appearances as a witness to the crime, including any subpoenas issued to the victim
    - ☐ What substantial physical and/or mental abuse was suffered as a result of the crime, and
    - ☐ Any other information that might support other aspects of the eligibility requirements
- Documentation of substantial physical and/or mental abuse, including:
    - ☐ Medical records of any physical injury
    - ☐ Records of any counseling received
    - ☐ Evaluation of a psychologist or other mental health professional
    - ☐ Statements of witnesses to the crime, and
    - ☐ Photographs of any physical injuries sustained
- Birth certificate
- Two passport-style photos (if applying from outside the United States)
- Form I-192, Application for Advance Permission to Enter as Nonimmigrant, if relevant where inadmissibility grounds apply, and
- Valid, unexpired passport or
- Form I-193, Application for Waiver of Passport and/or Visa

Once compiled, the petition is sent to the same special unit in the Vermont Service Center that adjudicates the VAWA petitions discussed above and should be addressed to:

Vermont Service Center
ATTN: VAWA/U/T UNIT
75 Lower Welden St.
St. Albans, VT 05479-0001

A sample petition cover letter might look like the one in Box 8.3.

> **Box 8.3** **Sample Cover Letter Requesting U Nonimmigrant Status**
>
> Vermont Service Center
> ATTN: VAWA/U/T UNIT 75
> Lower Welden St.
> St. Albans, VT 05479-0001
>
> Date
>
> RE: U NONIMMIGRANT VISA PETITION FOR J.L., DOB 01/01/1967, INDONESIA
>
> Dear Sir/Madam:
>
> Please find enclosed a petition for U Nonimmigrant Status for my above-named client. The following documents in support are attached:
>
> 1. Form G-28
> 2. Form I-918
> 3. Statement of petitioner describing victimization
> 4. Newspaper report of criminal incident
> 5. Police U visa certification, together with police report
> 6. Evidence of substantial physical injury to applicant in the form of medical records from Mercy Hospital
> 7. Evidence of mental injury to petitioner in the form of psychological evaluation and report from Dr. Zhivago
> 8. Letter from Victims/Witness Services of South Philadelphia, Inc. confirming services provided
> 9. Copy of petitioner's current passport
> 10. Petitioner's birth certificate with translation
> 11. Petitioner's certificate of name change, with translation
> 12. 2 passport pictures of petitioner
>
> My client entered the United States from Indonesia on January 1, 2014 in B1/B2 status and has never left or applied to extend her status. On November 25, 2015, she was the victim of a robbery within her own home, in the middle of the night. She was held at gunpoint while two masked men ransacked her home looking for valuables. At one point, she tried to escape from them and fell down a flight of steps, breaking her ankle. The men carried her back to her bedroom where they tied her to her bed and threatened her with the gun, demanding money and other valuables from her. She sustained shattered bones in her leg and ankle. The men who attacked Ms. L. stole approximately $1500 and a cell phone from her while also stealing valuables from others living in the home she occupied. Further details regarding the attack are contained in her supporting statement, which is submitted as item 3 of the petition package.
>
> Once her attackers had left, Ms. L. was able to break free and call the police. She was taken to the hospital for treatment for her leg injury. The incident attracted some publicity as media organizations were present after the fact and reported on

what happened. These articles are submitted as item 4 of the petition package. There is also a police report of the incident, submitted as item 5.

I believe that Ms. L. is eligible for U Nonimmigrant Status as a person who has suffered substantial physical and psychological injury as a result of having been a victim of a qualifying criminal activity, namely false imprisonment and/or felonious assault. When I met with Ms. L., it was immediately clear that she suffers from both physical and psychological problems. Her psychological anguish is detailed more fully in the enclosed psychological evaluation conducted by Dr. Zhivago, who notes that my client is suffering from Post Traumatic Stress Disorder. His report is submitted as item 7 of the petition package. Recounting with me what happened to her was extremely painful for my client, as she would often cry inconsolably. I refer you specifically to paragraphs 22-26 of her statement, where Ms. L. explains how the robbery continues to affect her emotionally and physically. She details vividly the constant nightmares and sleepless nights that she suffers on a regular basis along with her inherent distrust of people she does not know.

In addition to the ongoing psychological trauma that Ms. L. suffers, she continues to experience ongoing difficulties with walking as a result of the injury to her leg. It is evident that every step is excruciating for her. Evidence of her physical injury is substantiated by copies of her medical records from Mercy Hospital, submitted as item 6 of the petition package.

I am working with the Victims/Witness Services of South Philadelphia, Inc., an organization that provides support to victims of crimes, including assistance with making claims to the Pennsylvania Victims Compensation Assistance Program, to ensure that adequate arrangements are made for Ms. L. to receive appropriate medical and counseling services. A letter from the organization is also enclosed as item 8 of the petition package, confirming that Ms. L. is receiving services from them.

In addition, please find copies of Ms. L's passport as item 9, which is current through 2022 and includes her entry stamp; her birth certificate with certified translation as item 10; her name change certificate with certified translation as item 11; and two passport photographs.

I look forward to hearing from you in due course and trust you will agree that this is a case deserving of a grant of U Nonimmigrant Status. Should you require any further information, please do not hesitate to call me.
Sincerely,

A. T. Torney, Esq.
Encs.
cc. Ms. L.

Form I-918, Petition for U Nonimmigrant Status, collects biographical information on the foreign national seeking immigration relief. There is no fee for filing this petition. Form I-918 Supplement B, U Nonimmigrant Status Certification, which confirms the helpfulness of the victim in the investigation or prosecution of a qualifying crime, must accompany the petition. It is helpful to complete the form before sending it for certification, listing the statutory criminal or other code provisions that have been breached. Where there is other independent evidence of the commission of the crime, such as police reports or newspaper articles, it should be included as it may help the designated person signing the certificate to reach a favorable decision. The USCIS must receive the certificate within six months of issuance or it will become invalid and will need to be requested again.[59]

The statement from the foreign national explaining what happened to him or her is crucial, mainly because none of the forms for submission allow for a coherent account of what happened. The statement should be in the foreign national's own words, expressing any concerns regarding the medical treatment received, effects of the substantial mental or physical harm on his or her life, and ability to function after the criminal activity.

A sample statement in support of a petition might look like the one in Box 8.4.

Box 8.4   **Statement in Support of U Nonimmigrant Status Petition**

STATEMENT OF J.L.

1. I am a citizen of Indonesia. I first came to the United States in 2014 as a visitor. I was given permission to remain here for six months, but never left or applied to extend my status.

2. I stayed in the United States beyond the time given to me because I needed to work to support my family. I have two teenage children. My husband died two years ago and it was getting difficult for me to support my children on the money I earned in my country. I could not rely on relatives because they too were just surviving.

3. On Sunday, November 24, 2015, my handbag was stolen. I was walking by myself towards my church. All was quiet. Two guys approached very close behind me. I was praying because I was afraid. Before I could finish, one of them took my handbag and ran. I had $50, a bible, some personal letters, and an umbrella in it. My cell phone and keys were in my jacket. I did not report this to the police but told my Pastor and congregation once I arrived at Church. I was very shaken up by this.

4. A few days later, on Wednesday November 25, I was home in my house, which I was sharing with four friends. They were all out at work and I was by myself, lying awake on my bed. It was about 2:30 in the afternoon.

5. The door to my room opened and I thought it was one of my roommates who had returned home early and was trying to collect

---

[59] 8 C.F.R. § 214.14(c)(2)(i).

something from my room. The person then left to go to another bedroom and I was wondering why my roommate would have left my door open without speaking to me.
6. I got up and went out of my room to travel down to the first floor where the living room is. Something was not right but I was not sure what it was.
7. I then noticed that the door of my roommate's bedroom was open, which was strange because she always keeps it closed. I went to check what was happening. When I looked in, I saw two big guys with hoodies and masks, holding guns.
8. I tried to run back to my room but this alerted them to the fact that there was someone in the house. They had not noticed me when they came into my room because there are two beds there, one higher than the other, which, from a certain angle from the door, is hidden. I was resting on the lower bed and so they had not seen me.
9. I tried to close the door to my room but before I could do so, one of the men pushed it open. I fell down and they put me on the bed and held the gun to my neck, asking for money. I was crying and trying to communicate that I don't have money. My English is limited.
10. The men began to search the whole room. I was trying to see if there was a chance for me to run away. I made every effort to run to the front door. One of the men began to chase after me and I tripped and fell down the stairs.
11. I was told to go back to my room but I could not move because my leg was broken. One of the men picked me up and carried me back to my bed. I was crying and they told me to be quiet.
12. Finally, they found money in my room. It was about $1500. This was my savings, which I had planned to send to my children in Indonesia. I do not have a bank account.
13. One of the men stayed in my room to continue searching. The other went to a different room to look. He found other things of value there. My roommate later told me that $300, an i-Pod, watch, PlayStation, and camera had been taken from her room.
14. I was afraid because I did not expect any of my roommates to be back until nighttime. I thought the men would rape me if they stayed much longer, so I told the man in my room, as best as I could, that they should leave soon as my roommate would be back.
15. When his accomplice came back into my room, the men had a short conversation that I did not understand. The next thing I knew, they had taken my cell phone from me. I was crying, begging them not to take my phone but they did not listen.
16. The men tied my hands behind my back, tied my feet at the ankles, tied me to the bed, and put duct tape around my mouth. Then they left the house.
17. I waited a long time to hear if the men were still in the house. I managed

to untie my hands so that I could break free. I found an old cell phone that I had and called my pastor for help. In a short while, he came to my house and then we called the police.

18. The police asked me lots of questions about what happened. I was able to give them a description of the men but not their faces because of their hoodies and mask. To date, the police have not contacted me again because they have not been able to find the men who robbed me.

19. I remember seeing a television crew that had come to report on the crime. My pastor was able to talk with them and explain what had happened.

20. Paramedics were called because I could not move. I was taken to the Emergency Department of Mercy Hospital where I stayed for four days while they treated me. Since then, I have been assigned health insurance through Victim/Witness of South Philadelphia, an organization set up by the City of Philadelphia to provide support services to the victims of crimes.

21. The injury to my leg was severe and I had to have surgery to reconstruct it and to wear a caste for a long time. However, this caused problems with my right knee because it had to support my body. I now need to receive medical treatment and physical therapy for that as collateral damage from the robbery.

22. Mentally, I continue to suffer. I am afraid to open the door when someone knocks or when I see people in hoodies. I am afraid to be around people I do not know as I am afraid that I will be attacked.

23. I suffer from nightmares that take me back to what happened to me. When this happens, I always wake up in a cold sweat and have trouble going back to sleep. I am afraid to be in the dark and now sleep with the light on by my bed.

24. I could not stay in the house where the incident took place because it caused so many bad memories for me. I also have trouble walking up stairs so I had to find somewhere to live that does not have them.

25. Because the thieves stole my savings and I have not been able to work since the robbery, I was unable to send money to my children and so they have been without many essentials that I usually provide for them. As a result, they have had to rely on other family members, which has caused me a lot of emotional pain because I know my relatives do not have much to take care of others, let alone themselves. I had been sending them money too, so I know how difficult it is for them.

26. My hope is that one day, I will recover from this incident but because it is always in my head, I do not know how I will do this.

U Nonimmigrant Status petitioners are required to show that they are not inadmissible to the United States. However, if a foreign national is in breach of an admissibility ground, then a waiver on Form I-192, Application for Advance

Permission to Enter as Nonimmigrant must also be filed. All possible inadmissibility grounds that may relate to the applicant should be raised in the waiver request, as it is a onetime application. The USCIS has broad discretion to decide whether the waiver should be granted or not. There is a fee waiver available for those who cannot afford to pay the immigration fee for this form.

● **EXAMPLE**

Hilaria is from Guatemala and is seeking U Nonimmigrant Status. She entered the United States many years ago by crossing over the border with an old boyfriend who has since returned home. Because Hilaria entered the United States without inspection when she walked across the border, she is inadmissible and therefore must apply for a waiver of this ground of inadmissibility on Form I-192, Application for Advance Permission to Enter as Nonimmigrant, as part of her U Nonimmigrant Status petition.

Petitioners are required to have a valid passport at the time they apply for U Nonimmigrant status and throughout the period they hold the status, if granted. Those who do not must either apply for one, or file an application for a waiver of this requirement on Form I-193, Application for Waiver of Passport and/or Visa, explaining why a passport cannot be obtained. There is no fee waiver available for this form.

G.1. Petitions for Qualifying Derivative Family Members

Petitions for qualifying derivative family members included in the principal's petition will be filed on Form I-918, Supplement A, Petition for Qualifying Family Member of U-1 Recipient, and will include:

- Evidence of relationship to principal applicant
- Copy of either the principal applicant's Form I-918, if Supplement A is filed concurrently, or Notice of Approval, if filed subsequent to the principal's grant of status
- Birth certificate
- Valid, unexpired passport
- Birth certificate
- Two passport-style photos (if applying from outside the United States), and
- Form I-192, Application for Advance Permission to Enter as Nonimmigrant, where inadmissibility grounds apply

H. U Nonimmigrant Status Benefits

A foreign national whose petition for U Nonimmigrant Status is approved is granted permission to remain in the United States for a period of four years,

Chapter 8: Immigration Relief for Vulnerable Populations

with authorization to work throughout this time for those who requested such permission during the petition process. A sample Notice of Action granting U Nonimmigrant Status is at Figure 1.15 in Chapter 1, Historical Background and Introduction to the U.S. Immigration System. Only 10,000 U Nonimmigrant Status petitions can be approved in any one fiscal year, counting only principal applicants against this number. In recent years, there have been many more approvable petitions than there are U Nonimmigrant Status numbers. Therefore, once the quota is reached, others must remain on a waiting list until the new fiscal year begins on October 1, when approvals will again be issued. Those who are on the list receive Deferred Action status and are allowed to apply for permission to work in the interim.

Once U Nonimmigrant Status has been granted, it is useful to advise the foreign national of the next step in the immigration process, particularly with respect to what will be required if LPR status is desired. By advising ahead of time, the foreign national can begin to gather documents that will support the application to adjust to an LPR at a later date. A sample closing letter providing such information is available in Box 8.5.

Box 8.5   Sample Closing Letter to Client

Dear Client

RE: YOUR PETITION FOR U NONIMMIGRANT STATUS

Congratulations, your petition for U Nonimmigrant Status has been approved! I enclose your original approval notice with your I-94 card and your new employment authorization document. Please guard these documents carefully. You may use them to apply for a social security number and state identification or driver's license or to show that you are authorized to work in the United States.

This letter is to advise you of a few important rules that apply to you as a person with U nonimmigrant status. You may obtain further information about your new status if you look at the immigration web site at http://www.uscis.gov. I encourage you to do this.

The U Nonimmigrant Status remains valid for a period of four years. However, you can apply to become a lawful permanent resident, or LPR, or receive a green card after the third year of being in this status. In order to do this, you will have to show that you have been in the United States for a continuous period, with no absences of more than 90 days in any one trip or more than 180 days during the three-year period. Because this is very difficult to maintain, I advise you not to travel outside the United States for any reason. If you do travel, you will not be able to return to the United States without a visa allowing you to enter as a U Nonimmigrant Status holder. To get this visa, the application has to be made with the U.S. Citizenship and Immigration Service (USCIS) here in the United States. The consular office abroad cannot decide this application. Because the USCIS has to decide your application for a visa, it will take a very long time and most likely more than the maximum period of 90 days that you are allowed out of the country during any one trip. If you are out longer than this period, you will lose the ability to apply for your green card and will have to apply for an extension of your U Nonimmigrant Status, which will mean it will take an even longer time for you to get your green card. To avoid this, it is better not to travel out of the country at all. If there is an emergency and you feel you must travel, you must not make any firm plans without consulting with me or another qualified immigration practitioner first. There are complicated rules that apply to you and I want to be sure that you obtain appropriate advice in order to avoid any problems in the future.

Other actions can also put your U Nonimmigrant Status in danger. These include not filing tax returns each year or failing to pay taxes at any time, certain criminal convictions, or lying to immigration officials. Please note that you have a continuing duty to cooperate with requests from law enforcement related to the crime that was reported when you applied for the U visa. You also have an obligation to notify the USCIS within ten days if your address changes. You must do this using Form AR-11, Change of Address, which you can do online at www.uscis.gov. I have also enclosed a blank copy of the form, in case you prefer to do this by mail. If you do it this way, please be sure to keep a copy of the completed form and to send it to the USCIS by certified mail so that you have a record that you sent it to them.

Your U Nonimmigrant Status will expire on [DATE (four-year anniversary of grant of status)]. It cannot be extended except in special circumstances. You will be eligible to apply for LPR (green card) status in the United States after you have had "continuous physical presence" here as a U visa holder for three years. This simply means that you must have lived in the United States for much of those three years before you will be able to apply for permanent residency. Although you are allowed to be absent for no more than 90 days in any one trip or more than 180 days for all of the trips you make during the three-year period, because of the difficulties with getting a visa to return to the United States, I repeat that it is better that you do not leave the country at all unless there is an emergency and you have spoken with a legal advisor about your situation first. You should be eligible to apply for permanent residency on [DATE (three-year anniversary of grant of status)]. I recommend that you consult with me or another qualified immigration practitioner about four to five months before you are eligible to apply for your permanent residency so that you can begin to gather documents and be ready to apply promptly once your date of eligibility arrives.

Please keep as many documents as possible to demonstrate your continuous physical presence in the United States since [DATE of grant of status]. I have attached a list of examples of appropriate documents that you may wish to consider gathering over the next three years. The USCIS will require at least one document with your name, address, and the date for every three months (at least four documents per year) during this three-year period.

You are required to have a valid passport throughout the period of your grant of U Nonimmigrant Status. If you do not have one, please make arrangements to apply for one now. If your passport is about to expire, please be sure to apply for a new one as soon as possible. Failure to have a current passport could cause your application for LPR status to be denied. If you are having difficulty with getting a new passport, please let me know as soon as possible.

Please bear in mind that a grant of LPR status is not automatic. You will still have to show that it should be granted to you because of your contributions to the community. In order to do this, you will need to gather documents that would show your community involvement. If you are not already, it is a good idea to get involved with positive activities such as volunteering for a school, charity, or religious organization in order to demonstrate why the United States would benefit if you are allowed to stay here permanently. You should save documents related to any counseling, medical treatment, or other important services you receive in the United States that relate to any treatment you need to recover from the crime that was the basis of your U Nonimmigrant Status petition, especially if you anticipate a continuing need to access these services. All of these documents will be used to show that you should be granted LPR status.

Please find enclosed a copy of your file, which includes all correspondence regarding the U Nonimmigrant Status Petition that my office filed on your behalf. You should keep this in a safe place in case you decide to use another legal representative when filing your application to become an LPR. My office will also keep your file in this matter for X years, after which time we will destroy it. You have the right at any time within that period to request a copy of your file. However, we reserve the right to charge you for any reasonable file recovery and copying charges applicable at the time of your request.

On behalf of One Firm, LLC, thank you for giving us the opportunity to help you.

Sincerely Yours,
A. T. Torney, Esq.

Sample documents to prove continuous presence for application to apply for lawful permanent residency:

1. Government documents
2. Other official documents
3. Immigration documents
4. School transcripts and records
5. Employment records incl. pay stubs, letter from employer(s) confirming place, hours, and dates of employment
6. Rent receipts, leases
7. Tax records
8. Utility bills and records of payments for phone or credit cards
9. Bank account statements
10. Car or health insurance documents

> Travel: NOT ADVISED UNTIL AFTER ADJUSTMENT TO LAWFUL PERMANENT RESIDENT STATUS
> * If you feel you must travel for an emergency please consult with your legal representative before making firm plans
> Cooperation with law enforcement
> * Cannot refuse any reasonable request for assistance

If the petition for U Nonimmigrant Status is denied, an appeal can be filed with the AAO for a final decision.[60] The other alternative is for a new petition to be filed, possibly addressing the problematic areas that caused the prior petition to be denied. The advantage of this approach is that the foreign national is guaranteed to benefit from the special expertise of officers in the VAWA unit of the USCIS Vermont Service Center, which has responsibility for considering the petition, compared to when AAO officers who are not specially trained to deal with these cases consider the matter.

I. U Nonimmigrant Petitioners in Removal Proceedings

Only the USCIS can adjudicate a U Nonimmigrant Status petition. However, foreign nationals who are victims of one of the enumerated crimes and who have been placed in removal proceedings may still apply for this benefit with the agency. They should ask the immigration judge to administratively close the case, which means to temporarily take it off the judge's docket so that it has a lower priority on the judge's list for hearing, or to continue the hearing to another day to allow the petitioner time to gather evidence and apply for the U Nonimmigrant relief. Once approved, the foreign national can then request that the judge terminate his or her removal proceedings. However, if the petition is unsuccessful, the removal case will be placed back onto the docket and the judge will determine whether or not the foreign national should be deported. If there is an alternative form of immigration relief available, it should be filed at the same time as a defense against deportation. This is discussed further in Chapter 10, Immigration Court Practice and Relief from Removal. Those for whom a deportation order has already been issued may still petition for U Nonimmigrant Status and if granted, can file a motion with the immigration court to reopen the earlier removal proceedings in order to have the deportation order terminated.

---

[60] 8 C.F.R. § 214.14(c)(5)(ii).

J. Adjustment of Status for U Nonimmigrant Status Recipients: INA § 245(m); 8 C.F.R. § 245.24

After remaining in U Nonimmigrant Status for just three of the four years granted, the recipient can apply to become an LPR. The criteria for qualification for adjustment of status are set out in 8 C.F.R. § 245.24, and applies to an applicant who:

- Applies for such adjustment;
- [Demonstrates that s/he]
  - ☐ was lawfully admitted to the United States as either a U-1, U-2, U-3, U-4, or U-5 nonimmigrant, as defined in 8 C.F.R. 214.1(a)(2), and
  - ☐ continues to hold such status at the time of application;
- Has continuous physical presence [in the United States] for 3 years;
- Is not inadmissible under § 212(a)(3)(E) of the [Immigration and Nationality] Act;
- Has not unreasonably refused to provide assistance to an official or law enforcement agency that had responsibility in an investigation or prosecution of persons in connection with the qualifying criminal activity after the alien was granted U nonimmigrant status, as determined by the Attorney General, based on affirmative evidence; and
- Establishes to the satisfaction of the Secretary that the alien's presence in the United States is justified on humanitarian grounds, to ensure family unity, or is in the public interest.

In order to ensure that the application for adjustment will not fall foul of the continuous physical presence requirement, the U Nonimmigrant Status recipient should limit any travel outside of the country after the status has been granted. This is because, in order to qualify for permanent residency, U Nonimmigrant Status recipients cannot be absent from the United States for longer than 90 days at any one time or more than 180 days in total, if they are to maintain the continuous physical presence required to qualify for adjustment of status.[61] However, once a U Nonimmigrant Status holder leaves the United States, s/he cannot return without applying for advanced permission to enter the country using Form I-192, Application for Advance Permission to Enter as Nonimmigrant. These applications are filed with the Vermont Service Center only and generally take longer than 90 days to be adjudicated. A grant is then relayed to the consular office responsible for issuing the visa that will allow the nonimmigrant to return.

In the event that the 90-day limit for absences has expired before all of this is complete, those who break the continuous physical presence period will have no option but to begin to count their three-year period again, from the date of reentry to the United States. This may require an application to extend the U Nonimmigrant Status, which is filed on Form I-539, Application to Extend/

---

[61] 8 C.F.R. § 245.24(a).

Change Nonimmigrant Status, along with a complete U nonimmigrant visa petition, accompanied by a new law enforcement certificate and an explanation as to why the petitioner remained outside the United States for an extended period of time.

U Nonimmigrant Status recipients filing for lawful permanent residency should also begin to gather as many documents as possible to demonstrate continuous presence in the United States for the requisite period. Typically, at least one document with the U Nonimmigrant Status recipient's name, address, and date should be kept for every three months of the three years. Because the USCIS is fairly strict about receiving documentation, clients should be advised of this requirement immediately after the initial grant of their status so that they can begin to gather the documents they will need early on in the process. Those who do not have a valid passport should be advised to obtain one, as this will be strong evidence of any travel outside the country during the three-year period.

Adjustment of status is not automatic. Applicants must show that they continue to be helpful in an investigation, which can require obtaining a new certificate from the law enforcement agency that issued the first one. However, where a case has been closed following a prosecution or because the law enforcement agency declined to investigate further, evidence of this will show that, even though the applicant was willing to assist, his or her services were no longer needed. As with the Nonimmigrant Status petition, a statement from the foreign national is helpful to explain to the adjudicator how s/he meets all of the eligibility criteria for adjustment. A sample statement is available in Box 8.6.

J.1. Compiling the Application for U Nonimmigrant Adjustment of Status

A typical application package for adjustment of status for a U Nonimmigrant Status holder should look like this:

- Form I-485, Application to Register Permanent Residence or Adjust Status
- Form G-28, Notice of Entry of Appearance as Attorney or Accredited Representative
- Form G-325, Biographic Information
- Medical Report completed by a civil surgeon
- Statement of applicant in support of application for permanent residency; a sample of such a statement is at Box 8.6
- Birth certificate, with translation if necessary
- Original passport with entry stamp or U Nonimmigrant Status approval notice
- Evidence of the criminal activity
- Form I-918 Supplement B, U Nonimmigrant Status Certification, or evidence that investigation or prosecution is complete
- Evidence of continued substantial harm or physical injury suffered, if appropriate, as evidence of humanitarian grounds to support a grant

- Copy of applicant's current passport showing that s/he has never left
- Two passport pictures of applicant
- Evidence of physical presence in the United States in the form of letters, utility bills, insurance, employment information, bank statements, medical bills, or appointment letters, etc.
- Form I-912, Request for Fee Waiver, where appropriate, together with evidence to support financial eligibility

---

Box 8.6 — Sample Statement in Support of U Nonimmigrant Adjustment Application

STATEMENT IN SUPPORT OF ADJUSTMENT APPLICATION

1. I am a citizen of Ecuador and entered the United States without inspection in September 2000. I have never left.
2. I was granted U Nonimmigrant Status in July 2011 because I was attacked when some boys stole my bike as I was trying to park it in the garage behind my house.
3. Following the attack, I was taken to the emergency room at Mercy Hospital where I was treated for my injuries. I suffered posttraumatic or concussion headaches, a nasal bone fracture, and cuts to my face that required five stitches.
4. Despite this, I appeared in court whenever I was asked and assisted in the prosecution of two of the boys who attacked me. I went to court about four times to testify, but I never saw either of them in court. Eventually the judge decided that, because they were both juveniles, he would give them community service and issue an order to make sure they were attending school. He did not call me to testify. The court proceedings have been complete for some time.
5. After the attack, I remained anxious about my surroundings, particularly around groups of young men, because I was never really sure if I would be attacked again. I would say that I have been hyper-vigilant for a long time. However, I could not do anything about this because I did not have health insurance and therefore could not afford to pay for treatment out of my own pocket.
6. Finally, in December 2013, I was able to purchase insurance through Obamacare. I was so happy about this because it was the first time since I have been in the United States that I have been covered. It meant that I could finally find someone to treat me. However, it took some time for me to find someone because many places would not take my insurance.
7. In September, 2014, I was able to see a therapist so that I could try to deal with my anxiety. I have been diagnosed as suffering from Posttraumatic Stress Disorder.

8. In the beginning, I was seeing my therapist once a week for about three months. I told her that after my attack, I was afraid to go out and having nightmares where I was reliving what had happened to me. I preferred being at home on my own because it was safe for me. Outside of going to work and essential errands, I would stay home.

9. It took some time before my therapy sessions had any effect on relieving my anxiety. The therapist gave me some good strategies on what to do when I am most stressed and how to avoid situations that would cause me the most anxiety. I wish I could have started to see her much sooner than this. At the present time, I am seeing my therapist once a week, as I have ongoing anxiety and stress issues, ultimately related to my attack.

10. In Ecuador, we have two systems of healthcare that are run by the government. One that is free, but does not offer much in the way of services, and one where you volunteer to buy healthcare insurance. I do not know how much that is at the present time, but I am sure it will be at a cost that I cannot afford.

11. If I were to return to Ecuador, I would not have work and so few resources to support me or to cover the cost of my continued treatment. My father still lives in Ecuador, along with four of my siblings. One brother works, but is supported by me and my siblings in the United States. My sisters do not work and two of them are back in school because they did not finish when they were younger. We pay for them.

12. If I return to Ecuador, it will create greater strain on my family here and in Ecuador because they will have to support me because I do not have any skills that will help me to find work. At least here I am able to work and support myself and to help contribute to the support of other family members abroad. We are a large family and so anything each of us can do to help the others is needed and appreciated.

13. I have lived in the United States for nearly 15 years now, a significant part of my life. I am used to being here; I feel very disconnected from Ecuador. My mother and two older brothers are here also, with their families.

14. I live with my mother and we are very close. It would be very devastating for me if I had to leave her here because she cannot return to Ecuador as she is a survivor of domestic violence. She does not work and I am the main person supporting her because my brothers have young children to maintain.

15. My mother has been really helpful to me in dealing with the trauma I experience as a result of my attack. I think I would not cope very well without her.

16. I am hoping to return to school to get my degree. This will be easier for me once I am a permanent resident because then I can apply for loans to cover the cost of my education. Right now my income is too low for me to afford school. Once I have my degree, I can have better employment opportunities and improve myself and the life of my family.

Chapter 8: Immigration Relief for Vulnerable Populations

Once compiled, the application is sent to the USCIS Vermont Service Center for further processing. A receipt notice will be generated and an appointment date set for the capturing of biometrics information. Also, the foreign national will be sent a notice extending the U Nonimmigrant Status until such time as the application for adjustment is adjudicated. A sample of that notice is in Figure 8.1. The adjustment application is usually approved without calling the foreign national to an interview.

Figure 8.1

Sample Notice of Extension of Status

Department of Homeland Security
U.S. Citizenship and Immigration Services

APR 0 6 2015

Form I-797C, Notice of Action

THIS NOTICE DOES NOT GRANT ANY IMMIGRATION STATUS OR BENEFIT.

RECEIPT NUMBER: EAC		CASE TYPE: Application to Register Permanent Residence or Adjust Status (Form I-485)
RECEIPT DATE: 3/27/2015	PRIORITY DATE: 3/27/2015	Applicant:
NOTICE DATE: March 30, 2015	PAGE: 1 of 1	Applicant A#: A

Notice Type: Extension of T or U Nonimmigrant Status

HIAS PENNSYLVANIA
2100 ARCH STREET
PHILADELPHIA, PA 19103

EXTENSION GRANTED BASED ON PENDING APPLICATION TO REGISTER PERMANENT RESIDENCE OR ADJUST STATUS (FORM I-485)

If you were still in valid U or T nonimmigrant status on the date your Application to Register Permanent Residence or Adjust Status (Form I-485) was received, that status is extended until a decision is reached on your Form I-485. If your status was no longer valid by the date your Form I-485 was received, you will need to file the Application to Extend/Change Nonimmigrant Status (Form I-539) with this office to request an extension of your nonimmigrant status.

EMPLOYMENT AUTHORIZATION:

You are authorized to work in the United States while your Application to Register Permanent Residence or Adjust Status (Form I-485) is pending. You may apply for work authorization by submitting an Application for Employment Authorization (Form I-765), pursuant to 8 Code of Federal Regulations section 274a.12(c)(9), to this office. If you have already filed this application, the decision on your application will be sent under separate cover.

DEPARTING FROM THE UNITED STATES:

If you plan to depart the United States you must obtain permission to return to the United States by requesting advance parole before you leave. If you do not obtain advance parole before your departure, you will be considered to have abandoned your application for adjustment of status and the application will be denied. Please see 8 CFR section 245.23(j), for T adjustment of status applications, and 245.24(j), for U adjustment of status applications.

In addition, you may be unable to re-enter the United States, or you may be placed in removal proceedings before an Immigration Judge. You may apply for advance parole by submitting an Application for Travel Document (Form I-131) to this office. If you have already filed this application, the decision on your application will be sent under separate cover.

Please see attached additional information on the back. You will be notified separately about other cases you filed.

United States Citizenship and Immigration Services
Vermont Service Center
75 Lower Welden Street
St. Albans, VT 05479

Form I-797 (rev. 6/8/2012)

K. T Nonimmigrant Status, Severe Forms of Human Trafficking: INA § 101(a)(15)(T); 8 C.F.R. § 214.11

T Nonimmigrant Status is another special type of immigration classification available to victims of severe forms of human trafficking, described by the Department of Homeland Security as "a form of modern-day slavery in which the traffickers often lure individuals with false promises of employment and a better life."[62] The Victims of Trafficking and Violence Protection Act of 2000, or VTVPA,[63] as amended by the William Wilberforce Trafficking Victims Protection Reauthorization Act of 2008 or TVPRA 2008[64] and reauthorized by the Trafficking Victims Protection Reauthorization Act of 2013, or TVPRA 2013,[65] sets out two forms of trafficking as follows:

- Sex trafficking, in which a commercial sex act is induced by force, fraud, or coercion, or in which the person induced to perform such act has not attained 18 years of age,[66] or
- The recruitment, harboring, transportation, provision, or obtaining of a person for labor or service, through the use of force, fraud, or coercion for the purpose of subjection to involuntary servitude, peonage, debt bondage, or slavery.[67]

Traffickers isolate and control their victims, threating to have them deported and/or harm them if they leave the sex trade or their employment. Many victims do not identify as being trafficked, as they are in complex relationships with the person who has trafficked them. For example, a woman who provides sex for money at the insistence of a "boyfriend," who also controls her movements, may feel it is both disloyal and dangerous to flee. Others are ashamed they are involved in the commercial sex trade and this prevents them from seeking help. Those who are in an involuntary servitude situation may fear loss of income and deportation if they report on their working conditions. Trafficking victims who have relatives in the home country are especially vulnerable, as traffickers have global networks and may threaten to hurt any family members left behind.

In order to combat human trafficking and deal with the unique danger faced by victims, Congress created the T Nonimmigrant Status, which allows a foreign national to remain in the United States and, in a similar way to U Nonimmigrant Status beneficiaries, eventually apply for LPR status. Victims can also apply for a spouse, unmarried children under 21, and siblings, if under 21 and unmarried, to enter the country as qualifying derivative family members. Similar to the U Nonimmigrant Status, the number of T Nonimmigrant Status applications

---

[62] Information for Law Enforcement Officials, Department of Homeland Security Blue Campaign, available at http://www.dhs.gov/xlibrary/assets/blue-campaign/ht-information-for-law-enforcement-officials-immigration-relief-for-victims-of-human-trafficking.pdf.
[63] Pub. Law 106-386, 114 Stat. 1464 (2000).
[64] Pub. L. 110-457, 49 Stat. 651.
[65] Pub. L. 113-4, 127 Stat. 54 (2013).
[66] 22 U.S.C. § 7102(9)(A).
[67] 22 U.S.C. § 7102(9)(B).

that can be approved each year is capped. While the U Nonimmigrant Status number is 10,000, only 5,000 T Nonimmigrant Status grants can be issued per fiscal year.[68] However, unlike the U Nonimmigrant Status category, the T Nonimmigrant Status limit has not been reached since the passage of the VTVPA.

K.1. Eligibility for T Nonimmigrant Status

INA § 101(a)(15)(T) defines eligibility requirements for a T Nonimmigrant Status that include:

- The foreign national must be a victim of a severe form of human trafficking as described above
- The foreign national is either physically present in the United States, American Samoa, or the Commonwealth of Northern Mariana Islands, or at a port of entry, on account of trafficking
- The foreign national has complied with reasonable requests for assistance in Federal, State, or local investigations or prosecution of acts of trafficking unless:
  - ☐ The individual is unable to cooperate due to trauma
  - ☐ The individual is under 18 years old
- The foreign national would suffer extreme hardship involving unusual and severe harm if removed

Case for Discussion 8.6

An Nguyen, from Vietnam, signed a contract with the owner of a garment company and the Vietnamese government to travel to American Samoa and work in a clothing factory. She borrowed money and paid the Vietnamese government $8,000 American dollars for the position. She planned to repay her lenders through her wages. When she arrived at her destination, she was sent to live in crowded barracks with other workers. The living area and factory were surrounded by razor wire and there were guards at the factory with plastic pipes. An and other workers were subject to strict curfews and worked 12- to 16-hour days, six days a week. There were inadequate sanitary facilities shared by male and female workers. The foreman engaged in sexually inappropriate behavior with many of the women, and in An's case often groped her while she worked. He told her she would be fired if she complained. An had to pay rent and buy food from the employer and this money was deducted from her wages each week. Her supervisor told her that if she complained, she would be sent home to Vietnam, would have to pay a fine, and would be out of favor with the Vietnamese government because she broke the contract.

- Is An a victim of human trafficking?

---

[68] INA § 214(o)(2).

As with the U Nonimmigrant Status process, foreign nationals who are victims of trafficking may provide "any credible evidence" of what happened to them in support of their applications for the T Nonimmigrant Status.[69] This is particularly useful as there is often little documentary evidence of the treatment that constitutes trafficking.

K.2. Protection for Victims in the United States

Trafficking victims seeking escape often fear deportation, may face immediate danger from their trafficker, and lack means to support themselves. In order to encourage them to step forward, procedural safeguards have been put in place so that immediate action can be taken to protect the victim by granting him or her temporary immigration relief.

K.2.a. Continued Presence and Eligibility for Public Benefits

The first step in the process of applying for T Nonimmigrant Status is for an application for **Continued Presence** to be filed and granted for the benefit of the trafficking victim in the United States by an authorized agency.[70] The Immigration and Customs Enforcement's, or ICE's, office of Homeland Security Investigations, or HSI, which is also under the auspices of the DHS, and the FBI, along with federal prosecutors from the U.S. Attorney's Office, are all authorized to submit Continued Presence applications, which are primarily adjudicated by HSI's Law Enforcement Parole Unit, or LEPU. Local or state law enforcement officials who identify victims of trafficking must contact federal enforcement officials who will submit an application on behalf of a victim.[71]

Continued Presence provides temporary immigration relief to individuals identified by Federal, State, local, tribal, or territorial law enforcement as victims of human trafficking. An adult victim over 18 years old can be granted Continued Presence status, which permits the foreign national to remain in the United States while the investigation into trafficking and application for T Nonimmigrant Status is pending. During this period, s/he can also receive employment authorization. Those approved for Continued Presence and who are cooperating with law enforcement can be referred to the Department of Health and Human Services, or HHS, for additional benefits,[72] such as health care and case management, in a similar way to that afforded to refugees.[73] HHS will then issue an eligibility letter that enables the victim to seek help from a refugee resettlement agency and to access federal and state public benefits. It is issued in renewable one-year increments.

---

[69] 8 C.F.R. § 214.11(d)(3).
[70] Section 107(c) of the VTVPA of 2000, codified at 22 U.S.C. § 7105(c)(3); 28 C.F.R. § 1100.35.
[71] Information on the Continued Presence procedure is available on the website of Immigration and Customs Enforcement (ICE) at http://www.ice.gov/doclib/human-trafficking/pdf/continued-presence.pdf.
[72] 22 U.S.C. § 7105 (b)(1)(A).
[73] See Section H.4 of Chapter 5, Asylum and Other Related Humanitarian Relief, for further details.

While Continued Presence can be awarded to individuals who are not currently assisting with an investigation, they will not be eligible for social service benefits. If it is ultimately determined that an individual is not a victim of human trafficking, then the Continued Presence status can be revoked, even before the one-year period of validity ends, which then places the applicant at risk of removal.[74]

Minors under 18 who are identified as potential victims of human trafficking do not need a grant of Continued Presence to become eligible for federal or state public benefits. Instead, TVPRA 2008 authorizes the Secretary of HHS, after receipt of credible evidence that the minor is a victim of a severe form of human trafficking, to determine promptly if the child is eligible for 90 days of interim social service benefits.[75] After consulting with the Department of Justice, or DOJ, and Department of Homeland Security, or DHS, HHS can issue an Interim Assistance Letter. Requests for interim assistance can be made through a form developed by HHS.[76] Once interim assistance expires, the minor can receive an eligibility letter for longer-term benefits, provided there remains credible evidence that s/he is a victim of a severe form of human trafficking.

L. Applying for T Nonimmigrant Status

Individuals who are victims of trafficking apply for T Nonimmigrant Status as individuals only. The victim is known as the principal applicant and, if under 21, can file for the following qualifying family members as derivatives while filing his or her own application:

- Spouse
- Unmarried children under 21
- Parents
- Unmarried Siblings under 21

T Nonimmigrant Status applicants who are over 21 can only file for their spouse and unmarried children under 21. Additionally, derivative family members must demonstrate that they will suffer extreme hardship if not allowed to join the principal applicant here.[77]

A very important, though not essential, part of the T Nonimmigrant Status application is the requirement for a declaration completed by a law enforcement official working in an authorized agency, in a similar way to the law enforcement agency certificate required in a U Nonimmigrant Status application. However, in the T Nonimmigrant Status application process, the declaration is optional.[78]

---

[74] 8 C.F.R. § 214.11(f)(2).
[75] 22 U.S.C. § 7105 (b)(1)(G).
[76] The form is available at www.acf.hhs.gov/trafficking.
[77] 8 C.F.R. § 214.11(o)(1)(ii).
[78] 8 C.F.R. § 214.11(f)(1).

A wide range of agencies are authorized to complete the form, including federal, state, or local law enforcement agencies that have authority to investigate or prosecute human trafficking offenses, including but not limited to the DHS, HSI, DOJ, the FBI, and the federal or state Department of Labor. The declaration is provided on a special form known as Form I-914, Supplement B, Declaration of Law Enforcement Officer for Victim of Trafficking in Persons, and must be signed by a supervising official responsible for the investigation or prosecution of the trafficking offense. Since this form is an optional part of the application, an applicant who does not include it, but can demonstrate reasonable efforts to obtain one, will not be penalized. Because juveniles under the age of 18 do not need to comply with requests to assist in an investigation, the declaration plays no role in consideration of their case. However, there is nothing to prevent an official from completing the form for a juvenile if it would be helpful.

● **EXAMPLE**

Practitioner Marisol has interviewed Rosalba from Mexico who was placed in removal proceedings when police raided a massage parlor and found it was a front for commercial sex activity. Rosalba has one child in Mexico, age seven. After interviewing her, Marisol discovers that she was recruited to come to the United States by the parlor's operator, to work as an escort for high-end businessmen and was assured she did not have to engage in sex with them. When Rosalba arrived, things were much different. Rosalba lived in the massage parlor with several other women. The doors were locked from the outside. The operator confiscated her passport and Rosalba was forbidden to leave the premises without someone accompanying her. She was denied access to a phone. Rosalba was terrified of returning home to Mexico, not just because of the shame, but also because the operator is a distant relative who knows where her family lives and had threatened to harm them if she left the parlor. Rosalba is cooperating with the police and FBI to prosecute the operator. Despite repeated attempts, Marisol has been unable to get an official from the FBI to endorse the requested declaration providing details of her trafficking. Rosalba wants to resolve her immigration status as soon as possible. She can still submit her application without the declaration because she has complied with reasonable requests to cooperate, but should be sure to enclose other evidence of cooperation and her efforts to obtain the declaration.

L.1. Compiling the T Nonimmigrant Status Application Package

A T Nonimmigrant Status application package should contain the following items:

- Cover letter, which explains why the foreign national is eligible for T Nonimmigrant Status, and a "roadmap" to the evidence submitted with the application; a sample statement is available in Box 8.7
- Form I-914, Application for T Nonimmigrant Status

- Form G-28, Notice of Entry of Appearance as Attorney or Accredited Representative
- Form I-914 Supplement B, if available
- Personal statement or affidavit describing how the foreign national was treated
- Current passport, if available, or other document to establish identity
- Evidence that the foreign national has complied with any reasonable request for assistance in the investigation or prosecution of acts of severe forms of trafficking in persons
- Evidence that the foreign national would suffer extreme hardship involving unusual and severe harm if removed from the United States
- If helpful, country condition reports to demonstrate why return to that country would constitute extreme hardship
- Form I-192, Application for Advance Permission to Enter as a Nonimmigrant, depending on the foreign national's manner of entry
- Form I-912 Fee Waiver request, where appropriate, together with evidence to support financial eligibility
- Three passport photos
- Form I-914 Supplement A, Application for Immediate Family Member of T-1 Recipient, for any qualifying relatives
- Evidence of the relationship to the qualifying relative

A sample application cover letter might look like the one in Box 8.7.

Box 8.7 — **Sample Letter in Support of T Adjustment Application**

USCIS

Vermont Service Center
75 Lower Welden Street
St. Albans, VT 05479-0001
Attn: T Visa Unit

Date

Re: X Y, M J – A000-000-000
      I-914, Application for T Nonimmigrant Status
      I-192, Application for Advance Permission to Enter as Nonimmigrant

Dear Sir or Madam:

We represent Ms. M X Y(M), a juvenile, in the above applications. A signed G-28 is attached. M seeks adjudication of her T visa application for having been trafficked into the United States.

Statement of Relevant Facts

M is 16 years old and a native of Guatemala. In February 2013, at the age of 14, she traveled to the United States from Guatemala. An adult man named R Doe paid for M's trip. He met her after she had crossed the border and transported her to a house in California. Before her trip, M had spoken with Mr. Doe over the phone from Guatemala. He had told her that he was 18-years old and that he would have a place for her to live and a job for her. When Mr. Doe came to get M, M saw that he was really much older. She was afraid of him, but having no other choice, she got into his car and travelled with him to San Diego.

Once in San Diego, Mr. Doe took M to a house where he left her alone, locked inside a room overnight. He told her he wanted to have sex with her and that he wanted her to be his wife. He told her that if she agreed to be his wife, she would not have to pay back the money she owed him for her travel to the United States. M was afraid and uncomfortable. She told him she would "think about it" in order to buy some time, hoping to find a way to escape before Mr. Doe could force her to have sex with him or to become his "wife."

The following day, M confessed her fear to Ms. A, the owner of the house where Mr. Doe had brought her. Ms. A called the police who arrived as Mr. Doe was trying to reenter the house. M hid inside a bathroom while Ms. A locked all of the doors and refused to let Mr. Doe inside. At the time of his arrest, Mr. Doe referred to M as his "wife" in the presence of the police and admitted that he wanted to have a marital relationship with her even though he knew she was only 14 years old.

M was taken into Department of Homeland Security (DHS) and, later, Office of Refugee Resettlement (ORR) custody. She was sent to live at the children's shelter in the state of Pennsylvania. While living at the children's shelter, M gave an interview to DHS investigators and was issued letters by DHS and ORR confirming her status as a victim of human trafficking. Based on her status as a trafficking victim, M was admitted to the Unaccompanied Refugee Minors (URM) foster care program and in October 2009 went to live with a foster family in Reading, PA, through Family Services. M remains in foster care at this time and is in ninth grade.

T Visa Eligibility

1. M is a victim of a severe form of trafficking in persons.

"The term 'severe forms of trafficking in persons' means sex trafficking in which a commercial sex act is induced by force, fraud, or coercion, or in which the person induced to perform such act has not attained 18 years of age; or the recruitment, harboring, transportation, provision, or obtaining of a person for labor or services, through the use of force, fraud, or coercion for the purpose of subjection to involuntary servitude, peonage, debt bondage, or slavery." 8 C.F.R. 214.11(a).

The term "sex trafficking" is in turn defined as "the recruitment, harboring, transportation, provision, or obtaining of a person for the purpose of a commercial sex act." *Id.* "Commercial sex act" means "any sex act on account of which anything of value is given to or received by any person." *Id.*

M qualifies for a T visa as the victim of sex trafficking. Mr. Doe helped transport M to the United States, and then received and harbored her, for the purpose of engaging in a commercial sex act with her. The sex she was expected to engage in was commercial because in exchange, Mr. Doe offered her food, shelter, and the forgiveness of debt she was told she owed him. While M was able to escape before any sex act actually took place, it is clear that Mr. Doe's intention was to induce her to engage in commercial sex and that he transported, received, and harbored her for this purpose. The fact that no sex act actually took place is therefore immaterial.

Mr. Doe also intended to subject M to peonage in that in addition to expecting M to marry him, he planned to require her to provide domestic services or work in an unspecified job in order to repay her debt. He used fraud or coercion to do this in that he lied to M before she agreed to come to the United States, telling her that he was only 18-years old and thus making her feel safer and more comfortable than she would have had she known his true age. He also used force when he isolated her at a house in San Diego and attempted to limit her movement from that house.

2. M is physically present in the United States on account of trafficking.

M is present in the United States precisely because Mr. Doe paid for her trip and told her that he would house and employ her. Once she arrived in the United States and Mr. Doe came for her, she had virtually no choice but to do as he said and accompany him to San Diego. M's and Ms. A's call to the police led to M being placed in ORR care where she remains to this day. She is now in a foster care program open only to child refugees and certain other vulnerable children including trafficking victims.

3. M has complied with reasonable requests from a law enforcement agency for assistance in the investigation or prosecution of traffickers *or* has not attained 18 years of age.

M is sixteen years old at this time and as such is not required to show that she has complied with requests from law enforcement for assistance. Nonetheless, she did assist law enforcement by participating in two interviews with Superior County Detective Wise and U.S. Dept. of Homeland Security Agent Savvy on March 17, 2009 and April 1, 2009. Following these interviews, she was assessed to be a victim of human trafficking.

4. M will suffer extreme hardship involving unusual and severe harm upon removal.

To be eligible for T-1 nonimmigrant status under § 101(a)(15)(T)(i) of the Act, an applicant must demonstrate that removal from the United States would subject the applicant to extreme hardship involving unusual and severe harm. 8

C.F.R. 214.11(i). Factors that may be considered in evaluating whether removal would result in extreme hardship involving unusual and severe harm should take into account both traditional extreme hardship factors and those factors associated with having been a victim of a severe form of trafficking in persons. 8 C.F.R. § 214.11(i)(1).

Those factors may include: "the age and personal circumstances of the applicant . . .; the nature and extent of the physical and psychological consequences of severe forms of trafficking in persons; the impact of the loss of access to the United States courts and the criminal justice system for purposes relating to the incident of severe forms of trafficking in persons or other crimes perpetrated against the applicant . . .; the reasonable expectation that the existence of laws, social practices, or customs in the foreign country to which the applicant would be returned would penalize the applicant severely for having been the victim of a severe form of trafficking in persons; the likelihood of re-victimization and the need, ability, or willingness of foreign authorities to protect the applicant; the likelihood that the trafficker in persons or others acting on behalf of the trafficker in the foreign country would severely harm the applicant; and the likelihood that the applicant's individual safety would be seriously threatened by the existence of civil unrest or armed conflict as demonstrated by the designation of Temporary Protected Status, under § 244 of the Act, or the granting of other relevant protections." 8 C.F.R. § 214.11(i)(1)(i)-(viii).

M is a 16-year old survivor of human trafficking. In her statement, she explains how she became responsible for supporting her younger siblings at age ten, when her mother moved out of the house, leaving M and her siblings to fend for themselves. From that point forward, M stopped attending school and instead worked sewing and selling blouses, making very little money and, as a result, having to go without food some days. This history of childhood neglect is what led M to be trafficked into the United States in the first place. If returned to Guatemala, M's responsibilities for caring for herself and her siblings would resume. Moreover, as M also describes in her statement, her trafficker is currently in Guatemala and has approached M's mother asking when M will repay her debt. This history of childhood neglect, past trafficking, and the demands from her trafficker would make M particularly vulnerable to being re-victimized.

Additionally, M continues to suffer the mental consequences of being trafficked. She remains very afraid of her trafficker and continues to spend nights crying while remembering what happened to her. She currently receives mental health services in the United States that would not be available to her if she were forced to return to Guatemala.

If removed, M would also lose access to the U.S. criminal justice system for the purposes of protection. In the United States, M's traffickers do not know her location and are consequently unable to retaliate against her for escaping, reporting the trafficking to police, or failing to repay the debt owed to her traffickers. Even if they did learn of M's location and seek to harm her, M would be able to seek and receive protection from U.S. law enforcement.

Conversely, if M were returned to Guatemala, she would be in danger of being located and retaliated against by her traffickers. Country condition documents for Guatemala indicate that the Guatemalan government would not be able to protect M from such retaliation nor to provide her services or ensure she is not forced into trafficking again. Violent crime is extremely high and at a rate considered "critical" by the U.S. State Department. Criminals are rarely caught or punished. Although the Guatemalan government has recently made efforts toward prosecuting traffickers and assisting victims, it still does not fully comply with the minimum standards for the elimination of trafficking. As a result, trafficking remains a problem throughout the country, particularly for women and girls, in addition to homicide and other violent crime, which remains widespread.

For these reasons, M would face extreme hardship involving unusual and severe harm if removed to Guatemala. In contrast, if granted a T visa, M would be able to remain in foster care, access the services she needs, finish high school, and pursue her dreams.

The following documents are enclosed in support of this application:

1. Forms G-28, I-912, I-914, and I-192
2. Two passport-style photographs (attached to form I-914)
3. Birth certificate of applicant with certified English translation
4. Declaration of M X Y
5. Copy of Eligibility Letter issued by the ORR stating M is eligible for benefits as a victim of human trafficking
6. ORR Division of Anti-Trafficking in Persons (ATIP) Summary and Recommendation (m/d/y)
7. Letter from the DHS dated (m/d/y) stating M was encountered as a potential victim of human trafficking
8. Law Enforcement Assessment of Potential Minor Trafficking Victim stating M is a victim of human trafficking per the TVPRA
9. Records from District Court of DDDD for X County (Disposition, Statement of Charges, and Statement of Probable Cause) concerning arrest and prosecution of R Doe for human trafficking and related charges
10. U.S. Dept. of State 2014 Trafficking in Persons Report for Guatemala
11. U.S. Dept. of State 2014 Guatemala Crime and Safety Report
12. Court order showing M is currently in foster care with Family Service, is in ninth grade, and received individual counseling

Thank you for your attention to this matter. Please do not hesitate to contact me at 000-000-0000 with any questions.

Sincerely,

A. T. Torney, Esq.

The principal applicant must complete Form I-914, Application for T Nonimmigrant Status, for him or herself, and Form I-914 Supplement A, Application for Immediate Family Member of T-1 Recipient, for each eligible family member, because these are individual applications. No fee is charged for these forms.

Many T Nonimmigrant Status applicants are inadmissible because of their manner of entry and are therefore required to complete Form I-192, Application for Advance Permission to Enter as a Nonimmigrant, in order to waive any inadmissibility grounds that may apply. The USCIS will waive the fee for this application only if the T Nonimmigrant Status applicant files and qualifies for the waiver.

Once compiled, the application is mailed to:

> Vermont Service Center
> ATTN: VAWA/U/T UNIT
> 75 Lower Welden St.
> St. Albans, VT 05479-0001

If the application for T Nonimmigrant Status is denied, an appeal can be filed with the AAO, for a final decision.[79] The other alternative is for a new petition to be filed, possibly addressing the problematic areas that caused the prior petition to be denied. The advantage of this approach is that the foreign national is guaranteed to benefit from the special expertise of officers in the VAWA unit of the USCIS Vermont Service Center, which has responsibility for considering the petition, compared to when AAO officers who are not specially trained to deal with these cases consider the matter.

L.2. Applications for Qualifying Derivative Family Members

As mentioned previously, a principal applicant can file for qualifying derivatives who live in the United States or in the home country, using Form I-914, Supplement A, Application for Immediate Family Member of T-1 Recipient. The application can be filed concurrently with the principal's application or subsequently after the foreign national has been granted status. If it is not filed concurrently, then a copy of the application for T Nonimmigrant Status must be submitted with Form I-914, Supplement A, Application for Immediate Family Member of T-1 Recipient.

Once the application is granted, an approval notice will be sent to the consular office abroad in the country where the qualifying relative resides so that a visa can be issued for him or her to travel to join the principal applicant here. As part of that process, family members abroad are required to complete the nonimmigrant visa application, Form, DS-160, Online Nonimmigrant Visa Application, electronically. S/he will then have an interview to ensure there are no issues

---

[79] 8 C.F.R. § 214.11(r).

that might render him or her inadmissible. Minor children of T Nonimmigrant Status holders must undergo DNA testing for definitive proof of relationship to the principal applicant. Initial costs of the test are borne by the family, but subsequently reimbursed if the DNA results confirm the parent-child relationship.

M. T Nonimmigrant Status Benefits

Those whose application for T Nonimmigrant Status is approved are granted permission to remain in the United States for four years, with authorization to work throughout this period for those who requested it at the time of their application. As previously discussed, there is a cap on the number of grants of T Nonimmigrant Status applications in any one year, but this has never been reached at the time of writing. If this changes in the future, then T Nonimmigrant Status applicants who apply after the quota has been reached will be placed on a waiting list and granted deferred action in much the same way as those seeking U Nonimmigrant Status when it is oversubscribed.[80]

N. T Nonimmigrant Applicants in Removal Proceedings

Only the USCIS can adjudicate a T Nonimmigrant Status application. However, trafficking victims who are placed in removal proceedings may still apply for this benefit with the agency. The victim should ask the immigration judge to either administratively close the case and temporarily remove it from the judge's docket, or continue the hearing to another day to allow the applicant time to gather evidence and apply for T Nonimmigrant Status relief. If an applicant is granted Continued Presence status, the legal practitioner should notify the government trial attorney so that either a continuance, administrative closure, or termination of removal proceedings can be granted while the trafficking investigation proceeds. If the T Nonimmigrant Status is approved and the case was previously administratively closed or continued, the applicant can now request that his or her removal proceedings be terminated. However, if the application is unsuccessful, the case will be placed back onto the judge's docket and s/he will determine whether or not the foreign national should be deported. Requests for any alternative form of immigration relief should be made at this time as a defense against deportation. These options are discussed further in Chapter 10, Immigration Court Practice and Relief from Removal. Those for whom a deportation order has already been issued can still apply for T Nonimmigrant Status

---

[80] *See* Section H.

and if granted, can file a motion with the immigration court to reopen the earlier removal proceedings in order to have the deportation order terminated.

O. Adjustment of Status for T Nonimmigrant Status Recipients: INA § 245(l); 8 C.F.R. § 245.23

After remaining in T nonimmigrant status for just three of the four years granted, the recipient can apply to become an LPR. The criteria for qualification for adjustment of status for a T Nonimmigrant Status recipient are set out in 8 C.F.R. § 245.23 and applies to an applicant who:

- Applies for such adjustment;
- [Demonstrates that s/he]
    - ☐ was lawfully admitted to the United States as a T-1 nonimmigrant as defined in 8 CFR 214.11(a)(2), and
    - ☐ continues to hold such status at the time of application;
- Has continuous presence for three years since grant of status. Any time spent with a Continued Presence grant counts toward the three year continuous period requirement;[81]
- Is admissible to the United States, or otherwise has been granted a waiver by USCIS of any applicable ground of inadmissibility, at the time of examination for adjustment;
- Has been in the United States for a continuous period during the investigation or prosecution of acts of trafficking, and the Attorney General has determined the investigation or prosecution is complete, whichever period of time is less;
- Is a person of good moral character since first being admitted as a T nonimmigrant and until the decision on Form I-485, Application to Register Permanent Residence and Adjust Status;
- Has complied with any reasonable request for assistance in the investigation or prosecution of acts of trafficking since being admitted to T nonimmigrant status and until a decision on Form I-485, Application to Register Permanent Residence and Adjust Status, is made; or
- Demonstrates that s/he would suffer extreme hardship involving unusual and severe harm upon removal from the United States.

After three years as a T Nonimmigrant Status recipient, the applicant and any derivatives can apply to adjust status to that of an LPR.[82] Most applicable grounds of inadmissibility should have already been disclosed and waived when the applicant applied for the T Nonimmigrant Status, which is why it is important to disclose all inadmissibility issues at that stage. However, INA § 245(l)(2) gives

---

[81] INA § 245(l)(1)(A).
[82] *Id.*

the USCIS authority to waive most grounds of inadmissibility during the adjustment process, if not previously waived and it is in the national interest to do so.

T Nonimmigrant Status recipients are subject to the same continuous presence requirements as U Nonimmigrant Status recipients and so should also be wary to avoid absences from the United States of 90 days at one time or more than 180 days in total.[83] There is also the requirement to file Form I-192, Application for Advance Permission to Enter as Nonimmigrant, in order to return to the United States in the event there is any travel outside the country.

Adjustment of status is not automatic. Applicants must show that they continue to be helpful in an investigation, which can require a new certificate to be obtained from the law enforcement agency that issued the first one. However, where a case has been closed following a prosecution or because the law enforcement agency declined to investigate the case further, evidence of this will show that, even though the applicant was willing to assist, his or her services were no longer needed. The applicant must also show that s/he would experience extreme hardship involving unusual and severe harm upon removal from the United States. This will depend on the facts of the case, but can relate to:

- The age and personal circumstances of the applicant,
- Serious physical or mental illness of the applicant that necessitates medical or psychological attention not reasonably available in the foreign country,
- The nature and extent of the physical and psychological consequences of severe forms of trafficking in persons,
- The impact of the loss of access to the United States courts and the criminal justice system for purposes relating to the incident of severe forms of trafficking in persons or other crimes perpetrated against the applicant, including criminal and civil redress for acts of trafficking in persons, criminal prosecution, restitution, and protection,
- The reasonable expectation that the existence of laws, social practices, or customs in the foreign country to which the applicant would be returned would penalize the applicant severely for having been the victim of a severe form of trafficking in persons,
- The likelihood of re-victimization and the need, ability, or willingness of foreign authorities to protect the applicant,
- The likelihood that the trafficker in persons or others acting on behalf of the trafficker in the foreign country would severely harm the applicant, and
- The likelihood that the applicant's individual safety would be seriously threatened by the existence of civil unrest or armed conflict as demonstrated by the designation of Temporary Protected Status, under § 244 of the [Immigration and Nationality] Act, or the granting of other relevant protections.[84]

---

[83] *See* Section J.
[84] 8 C.F.R. § 214.11(i)(1).

O.1. Compiling the Application for T Nonimmigrant Adjustment of Status

A typical application package for T Nonimmigrant adjustment of status should look like this:

- Form I-485, Application to Register Permanent Residence or Adjust Status
- Form G-28, Notice of Entry of Appearance as Attorney or Accredited Representative
- Form G-325, Biographic Information
- Medical Report completed by a Civil Surgeon
- Statement of applicant in support of application for permanent residency
- Birth certificate with translation, if applicable
- T Nonimmigrant Status approval notice
- Evidence of good moral character since grant of T Nonimmigrant Status, perhaps in the form of an FBI criminal records check
- Evidence of compliance with any reasonable request for assistance in the investigation or prosecution of acts of trafficking, if relevant
- Evidence of extreme hardship involving unusual and severe harm to the applicant upon removal from the United States, perhaps in the form of medical records or country conditions information
- Copy of applicant's current passport showing that s/he has never left
- Two passport pictures of applicant
- Evidence of physical presence in the United States in the form of letters, utility bills, insurance, employment information, bank statements, medical bills, or appointment letters, etc.
- Form I-912, Request for Fee Waiver, where appropriate, together with evidence to support financial eligibility

Once compiled, the application is sent to the USCIS Vermont Service Center for further processing. A receipt notice will be generated along with a notice extending the T Nonimmigrant Status until adjudication of the adjustment application. A sample of this notice is at Figure 8.1. An appointment date for capturing biometrics information is also issued. The adjustment application is usually approved without calling the foreign national to an interview.

P. Differences and Similarities Between U and T Nonimmigrant Adjustment of Status Applications

There are some significant differences between the adjustment criteria for U and T Nonimmigrant Status holders, as shown in Table 8.1. For instance, waivers for

Table 8.1. Comparison Between U and T Nonimmigrants Applying for Adjustment of Status

Issue	U Nonimmigrant Status	T Nonimmigrant Status
Inadmissibility	Only applicable inadmissibility grounds are participation in Nazi persecution or genocide, commission of acts of torture or extrajudicial killing	Apply for waiver during adjustment process
Eligibility criteria	Has not unreasonably refused to assist law enforcement; presence is justified on humanitarian grounds, to ensure family unity, or is in the public interest	Good moral character; complied with reasonable request for assistance from law enforcement or would suffer extreme hardship involving unusual and severe harm upon removal

residual inadmissibility issues for T nonimmigrant recipients may be requested during the adjustment application process,[85] whereas U Nonimmigrant Status holders are only inadmissible to adjust if they participated in Nazi persecution, genocide, or the commission of acts of torture or extrajudicial killing.[86] In addition, U Nonimmigrant Status holders need only show that their continued presence in the United States is justified on humanitarian grounds, to ensure family unity or because it is in the public interest.[87] In contrast, a T Nonimmigrant Status recipient must show that s/he is a person of GMC[88] and has complied with all reasonable requests to assist in an investigation[89] or would suffer extreme hardship that would cause unusual and severe harm if s/he were not allowed to remain in the United States.[90] T nonimmigrant minors under 18 do not have to meet these additional requirements.[91]

As previously noted, IIRAIRA § 384 prohibits all Department of Homeland Security employees from providing information about self-petitions to a third party, at the risk of disciplinary action or fines. This extends to U and T Nonimmigrant Status petitioners and applicants. Denied applications for these immigration benefits rarely result in the initiation of removal or deportation proceedings based on information supplied through a petition or application alone. Rather, information from other sources must be obtained for this purpose. The attempt to ensure confidentiality in the process recognizes the sensitive nature of the disclosures foreign national victims of particular crimes and severe forms of human trafficking must make, while seeking to encourage them to cooperate with law enforcement.

---

[85] 8 C.F.R.§ 245.23(a)(4).
[86] 8 C.F.R. § 245.24(b)(4).
[87] INA § 245(m)(B).
[88] INA § 245(l)(B).
[89] INA § 245(l)(C)(i).
[90] INA § 245(l)(C)(ii).
[91] INA § 245(l)(C)(iii).

Q. Special Immigrant Juvenile Status: INA § 101(a)(27)(J); 8 C.F.R. § 204.11

Congress created a means by which youth who are abused or abandoned in the United States can self-petition for immigration benefits and adjust their status by filing a Special Immigrant Juvenile, or SIJ, petition. The definition of a special immigrant juvenile is contained in INA § 101(a)(27)(j). To be eligible for SIJ status, the child must be

> declared dependent in a juvenile court in the United States and legally committed or placed under the custody of an agency or an individual appointed by the State and whose reunification with one or both parents is not viable due to abuse, neglect, or abandonment, or a similar basis found under the State law.

There must also be a determination that it is not in the child's best interest to return to his or her home country.

Special Immigrant Juvenile petitions involve a two-step process. The first step is to obtain a court order from a **juvenile court,** which is a state court that has jurisdiction to rule on the custody and care of children. This can include family, orphans', dependency, guardianship, probate, and delinquency courts. Many practitioners use the term "predicate order" to describe the juvenile or state court order that contains the language declaring the child dependent. Once granted, the child can move to the second step of applying for SIJ status with the USCIS.

Q.1. Obtaining a Dependency Order

Under the Immigration and Nationality Act, a child, for the purposes of SIJ, must be under 21 and unmarried at the time of adjudication of the application.[92] The child must also have the predicate **dependency order** finding him or her dependent because of abuse, neglect, or abandonment, by his or her natural parents.[93] This specific language need not be used so long as a state court issued a dependency order under circumstances that are functionally on "a similar basis" or equivalent to abuse, neglect, or abandonment. The determination of whether a child is dependent varies from state to state. For example, Pennsylvania law defines a dependent child as one who is under the age of 18 years and is "without proper parental care or control, subsistence, education as required by law, or other care or control necessary for his physical, mental, or emotional health, or morals."[94] In such a case, a dependency order must be obtained before the child's 18th birthday. However, in New York, if a non-abusive parent or other guardian can obtain a custody or guardianship order before the child is 21, the

---

[92] 8. C.F.R. § 204.11(c).
[93] *Id.*
[94] 42 Pa. C.S. § 6302.

minor will still be eligible to apply for SIJ status because the requisite predicate dependency order has been properly obtained in that state.[95]

A significant development in the protection for youth occurred with the enactment of the TVPRA 2008, which expanded the qualifying group of applicants for SIJ status by allowing a child who was abused, neglected, or abandoned by one parent to be still eligible for relief, even if living with the non-abusive other parent. The procedure in these cases is known as "one parent SIJ." This is now codified in INA § 101(a)(27)(j)(i). Under the old rules, the juvenile had to show that it was impossible to reunite with *both* parents and that s/he was eligible for long-term foster care. Now, a youth residing with the non-abusive guardian or parent can apply for special immigrant juvenile status, regardless of the immigration status of the parent.

Because SIJ status requires a predicate state court order of dependency, immigration practitioners must coordinate their representation with child welfare or family law attorneys. It is important that the predicate order contain the precise language that supports an SIJ application. The order must state:

- That the child is dependent on the court, or that the court commits or places the child under the custody of either a state agency or department, such as a child welfare department, or provides that placement is with an individual or entity appointed by a juvenile court,
- That reunification with one or both parents is not viable because of abuse, neglect, abandonment or on a similar basis found under State law; the abuse can occur either in the United States or abroad, and
- That it is not in the child's best interest to return home.[96]

Trial courts are required to limit their jurisdiction to determining the child's eligibility regarding these issues only and not with respect to eligibility for SIJ status.[97]

R. Filing the SIJ Application After the State Court Order Is Issued

Once the predicate dependency order has been obtained from a juvenile court, the foreign national minor may proceed to apply for SIJ status by filing an application with the USCIS and, in some cases, concurrently filing to adjust status to a lawful permanent resident. The stage at which the foreign national is seeking SIJ status will determine which procedure is followed. The application can be filed

---

[95] Safe Passages Project at http://www.safepassageproject.org/what-is-sij-status/.
[96] INA § 101(a)(27)(j).
[97] *See H.S.P. v. J.K.* (A-114-13) (074241) *K.G. v. M.S.* (Deceased) (A-117-13) (074527), decided by the New Jersey Supreme Court, August 26, 2015.

either affirmatively or, for those already in removal proceedings, to determine whether they can stay in the United States or must leave, defensively.

R.1. Affirmative Applications

SIJ applications can be submitted affirmatively for children who have been identified as dependent on account of abuse, neglect, abandonment, or similar basis, by filing Form I-360, Petition for Amerasian, Widow(er), or Special Immigrant, with USCIS. If a visa is available, the Form I-360 can be filed concurrently with Form I-485, Application to Register Permanent Residence or Adjust Status. Unlike predicate orders, which can be obtained before the age of 18 and in some states before the age of 21, in all states the approval of the SIJ application *must* occur before the child is 21. Federal law governs this.

The Form I-360, Petition for Amerasian, Widow(er), or Special Immigrant, has many uses, including supporting an immigrant visa for religious workers. Because of its use in the employment context, it is assigned to the EB-4 priority classification in the Department of State's, or DOS' Visa Bulletin, as listed in Table 7.2, Chapter 7, Employment-Based and Self-Sponsored Immigration. This category is typically current for all country classifications. However, in the May 2016 DOS online Visa Bulletin, there was retrogression so that only applications filed on or before January 1, 2010 by nationals from El Salvador, Guatemala, and Honduras are being accepted, indicating that there are no visas available at the present time because nationals from these countries have met their seven percent per-country limits.[98] Therefore, even though an SIJ may have an approved Form I-360 petition or may wish to file it concurrently with the application to obtain LPR status, s/he cannot do so until a visa number is available for him or her. At the time of writing, children from these three countries can still file Form I-360, Petition for Amerasian, Widow(er), or Special Immigrant, on its own, with supporting evidence. Once approved, it can be submitted with an adjustment of status application, but only when an immigrant visa becomes available. Visa numbers for juveniles from countries other than El Salvador, Guatemala, and Honduras are current and so they do not have to wait to file their applications to adjust status to an LPR once their Form I-360, Petition for Ameriasian, Widow(er), or Special Immigrant is approved.

Since SIJ status is meant to protect vulnerable children from one or both parents, a juvenile granted SIJ status ceases to have a relationship with his or her biological or adoptive parents under immigration law, even if only one parent has been abusive and the child is in the custody of the non-abusive parent. Therefore, it should be borne in mind that the child can never petition for either parent to gain immigration benefits.

A concurrently filed affirmative SIJ package should include:

- Form I-360, Petition for Amerasian, Widow(er), or Special Immigrant
- Form G-28, Notice of Entry of Appearance as Attorney or Accredited Representative

---

[98] See Section A.1 of Chapter 6, Family Sponsored Immigration and Permanent Resident Status.

- Requisite state court dependency order
- Form I-485, Application to Register Permanent Residence or Adjust Status
- Form G-325, Biographical Information
- Child's birth certificate with translation or, if unavailable, secondary evidence proving age
- Proof of child's identity
- Medical examination by a Civil Surgeon
- Two passport photographs
- Form I-765, Application for Employment Authorization
- Form I-601, Waiver of Inadmissibility, if applicable
- Fees, or
- Form I-912 Request for Fee Waiver, where appropriate, together with evidence to support financial eligibility

Since this procedure involves an adjustment of status application, care should be taken if the juvenile has a criminal history, including problems with drugs that have been dealt with in criminal rather than juvenile court proceedings. This is because these will be considered to be convictions, raising issues of inadmissibility, rather than civil adjudications, which will not.[99] Where this is the case, an application for a waiver will need to be included, together with additional documentation to demonstrate that the juvenile is not considered inadmissible because of this history. A review of Chapter 9, Grounds of Inadmissibility and Deportation, may be helpful on this issue.

Most grounds of inadmissibility either do not apply to or are waivable for SIJ applicants. Those that cannot be waived relate to:

- Conviction of certain crimes[100]
- Multiple criminal convictions[101]
- Controlled substance traffickers[102]
- Entrance to engage solely, principally, or incidentally in unlawful activity, particularly espionage[103]
- Terrorist activities[104]
- Serious adverse foreign policy consequences[105]
- Participants in Nazi persecutions, genocide, or the commission of any act of torture or extrajudicial killing[106]

---

[99] Juvenile court proceedings are civil in nature and result in an adjudication of juvenile delinquency. Therefore, any judgements in these courts will not raise issues of inadmissibility for a minor foreign national as they do not constitute a conviction in a criminal matter. *See Matter of Devision*, 22 I&N Dec. 1362 (BIA 2000). In many cases, the records are sealed without access to them, even for immigration purposes.
[100] INA § 212(a)(2)(A).
[101] INA § 212(a)(2)(B).
[102] INA § 212(a)(2)(C).
[103] INA § 212(a)(3)(A).
[104] INA § 212(a)(3)(B).
[105] INA § 212(a)(3)(C).
[106] INA § 212(a)(3)(E).

As these are serious crimes that can forestall the ability to obtain immigration relief, consideration should be given to consulting with a criminal law practitioner, where possible, who is well versed in the immigration consequences of these crimes before a plea is taken or trial begins.

Where a fee waiver request is made, demonstrating an inability to pay the immigration fee is a prerequisite to approval. However, the USCIS takes a more lenient approach to requests filed by juveniles who are not of working age. Where a child is still at school, it may be possible to provide evidence of this. In such cases, the child's lack of income is then assumed and the waiver request approved. There is no assumption that the adult supporting the child should be responsible for paying applicable immigration fees.

Case for Discussion 8.7

Claudette is from Haiti and was brought to the United States at age five on a tourist visa by her mother, who formed a relationship with a man who sexually abused the child. She was placed in foster care when she was 14 years old.

- Is Claudette eligible for a SIJ status?
- On what basis?

Assume Claudette receives SIJ status and eventually gains citizenship. In 2010, there is a terrible earthquake in Haiti and Claudette seeks to petition for her biological father who remained in Haiti.

- Is this possible?

In most cases, SIJ applicants interview at the local USCIS Field office, but sometimes the application is approved administratively without an interview. The USCIS adjudications officer should not revisit the basis of the grant of the dependency order, because a judge issues it. However, the officer can probe to determine if the juvenile is eligible to adjust status because there are criminal issues or other impediments present.

R.2. Defensive Applications

Juveniles in removal proceedings can still file an SIJ application but the procedure for this differs. If the legal representative for the child plans to file an SIJ application, s/he should ask the court for a continuance to allow time to seek the predicate order from a state juvenile court. In some jurisdictions, the immigration judge, or IJ, and counsel for ICE will usually agree to administratively close the removal proceedings while the state court proceedings are ongoing.

Following issuance of the predicate order, the Form I-360, Petition for Amerasian, Widow(er), or Special Immigrant, can then be filed for adjudication with the USCIS, together with additional supporting documents. If the petition is granted, a request can be made to re-schedule the removal hearing before the court. However, it may also be prudent at this stage to ask the judge to terminate removal proceedings so that the adjustment of status application can be filed directly with the USCIS, which is otherwise without jurisdiction to consider the request once removal proceedings have begun. This is only possible if a visa number is immediately available. In the event that it is not, consideration should be given to pursuing any other immigration status the foreign national may qualify for or to seeking administrative closure of proceedings until such time as a visa number is available. If termination is denied, then the IJ and not the USCIS will have to determine if the juvenile is eligible to adjust status and become an LPR, if an immigrant visa is available.

● EXAMPLE

Lydia, age 12, from El Salvador, was abandoned by her father when she was six months old and lived with a maternal uncle. Lydia's mother, Maria, is in the United States, working to send money home. Maria entered the country without inspection six years ago and is undocumented. Lydia's uncle began beating her with a belt and would not let Lydia out of the house. She had scars from the beating. Lydia fled with a cousin to the United States to find her mother and now lives with her. Although Lydia has one caring parent, she is still eligible for SIJ status because of the history of abuse she suffered and because it would not be in her best interest for her to return to El Salvador to live in an abusive home. However, even if Lydia receives SIJ status and later becomes a U.S. citizen, she would not be able to petition for her mother, Maria.

S. Children in the Custody of the Department of Health and Human Services, Office of Refugee Resettlement

Under TVPRA 2008, unaccompanied children who enter the United States without inspection from non-contiguous countries (namely those who enter who are not from Mexico or Canada) are allowed to enter for screening for trafficking issues. Children apprehended by Customs and Border Protection, or CBP, must be transferred to the HHS or ORR, within 72 hours of arrival. ORR is obliged by law to provide food, shelter, and medical care for the children until it is able to release them to safe settings with sponsors, usually family members, while they await immigration removal proceedings, which begin while they are in ORR custody. Children in this situation are eligible to apply defensively for SIJ. A state court can make dependency findings for a predicate dependency order, but changes in custody of the child requires consent from HHS, provided by staff at ORR, because s/he is in their custody. ORR routinely gives consent for this change to occur.

● **EXAMPLE**

Angel is 14 years old. He is from Honduras. He crossed the border on his own and turned himself in to CBP officers stating his grandfather had mistreated him. Angel was sent to an ORR shelter in Pennsylvania and was placed in removal proceedings. Angel's mother is dead and he does not know the whereabouts of his father. Angel has an aunt in Philadelphia who offered to take him in and care for him. The Humanitarian Immigrant Aid Society interviewed Angel and agreed to provide him with free legal representation. His immigration attorney worked with a child advocate to schedule a hearing in Juvenile Court in order to obtain a predicate dependency order. Before going to court, the immigration attorney requested ORR provide specific consent for the Juvenile Court to determine if Angel's aunt could be a custodian if the state court juvenile judge issued a dependency order. ORR gave consent. If it did not, an order could still be issued finding Angel dependent on account of abuse, neglect, abandonment, or a similar basis and that it would not be in Angel's best interest to return to Honduras. In that case, Angel would remain in the ORR shelter while his removal case is decided. Since Angel is in removal proceedings, once a dependency order is issued, the legal practitioner can file a Form I-360, Petition for Amerasian, Widow(er), or Special Immigrant, defensively as described earlier.

T. Deferred Action for Childhood Arrivals, or DACA

As we have seen, youth who are abused, neglected, or abandoned may receive protection and LPR status through an application for SIJ status. In contrast, there are few immigration options for youth from intact or supportive families who arrive in the United States while undocumented and young. Legislation to address this has been in discussion for a number of years. First introduced in 2001, the **Development, Relief, and Education for Alien Minors**, or **DREAM**, Act, would have allowed young people who arrived in the United States before the age of 15 to eventually adjust their status to LPR, if they:

- Arrived in the United States at least five years before enactment of the legislation,
- Graduated high school or a General Educational Development, or GED, program,
- Attended college for two years, or
- Served in the military.

However, it did not become law, despite the mobilization of young immigrants to urge Congress to pass it. By 2010, a bi-partisan version passed the House of Representatives and received 55 votes in the Senate. Under Senate rules, 60 votes were required to move the bill forward, so the DREAM Act did not progress to the next stage.

Following the demise of the legislation, President Obama faced increasing pressure from young activists and their supporters to provide some immigration relief to undocumented youth who would have benefited from the DREAM Act. In June 2012, the president used his executive authority to create a temporary program known as Deferred Action for Childhood Arrivals, or DACA, which became operational on August 15, 2012. Under DACA, applicants are required to show that they:

- Were at least 15 years old and under 31-years old as of June 15, 2012,
- Arrived in the United States before the age of 16,
- Lived in the United States continuously for a period of five years from June 15, 2007 to the present,
- Are in or completed high school or a GED program, or have been honorably discharged from the military,
- Had no lawful immigration status on June 15, 2012,
- Were physically present in the United States on June 15, 2012, and
- Have no significant criminal history.

The program, which mirrored many of the eligibility requirements of the DREAM Act, grants employment authorization to DACA recipients in two-year increments.

Applicants for DACA apply using Form I-821D, Consideration of Deferred Action for Childhood Arrivals, Form I-765, Application for Employment Authorization and Form I-765WS, a worksheet to provide information on income and expenses in order to show why the employment authorization document should be issued. The fee for the DACA application can be waived only in very limited circumstances, such as for homeless youth or youth in foster care.

Once granted DACA, the foreign national can apply to travel outside the United States and to return with the permission of the USCIS. Before leaving, s/he must request and receive advanced parole, using Form I-131, Application for Travel Document. However, permission will be granted only if travel is for humanitarian, educational, or employment purposes. Any documentation to substantiate this need should be provided with the application. Care should be taken to review the foreign national's prior immigration history because, even with advanced parole, a CBP officer is not obligated to grant permission to reenter, although, in most circumstances, it is likely that s/he will.

The BIA recently held in *Matter of Arrabally, Yerrabelly* that a foreign national who reenters the United States with advanced parole does not trigger the three- or ten-year unlawful presence bars and therefore is able to adjust status in the United States.[107] Section B.9.b of Chapter 9, Grounds of Inadmissibility and Deportation discusses these bars in detail. Essentially, anyone who has been present in the United States for more than 180 days but less than one year, who voluntarily departs before removal proceedings have been initiated, is

---

[107] See *Matter of Arrabally, Yerrabelly*, 25 I&N Dec. 771 (BIA 2012).

barred from reentry for a period of three years. Anyone present for a year or more without permission, who then departs, regardless of whether removal proceedings have begun, is barred for ten years. A foreign national seeking to enter earlier than these periods must request and receive a waiver first, unless s/he is reentering with advanced parole.

One of the benefits of the *Arrabally* decision is that a DACA recipient who might otherwise have the opportunity to adjust status but for an inadmissibility issue related to his or her initial EWI entry, may now adjust in the United States once the foreign national returns with advanced parole. This is because s/he will have been inspected and admitted in compliance with the requirements of INA § 245(a).

● **EXAMPLE**

Gabriela is from Costa Rica and entered the United States without inspection with her parents when she was five years old. She is married to a U.S. citizen but cannot adjust her status to an LPR because the law does not permit this for those who entered EWI. Gabriela recently applied for and was granted DACA so that she could work legally and feel relatively secure that she will not be deported at any time. She has applied for and received advanced parole so that she can visit her grandmother, who is very sick. Once she returns, Gabriela will have been inspected and paroled into the United States because of her grant of advanced parole and therefore will be eligible to adjust her status to an LPR through her husband.

Case for Discussion   8.8

Ben was born in 1995. He came to the United States on a visitor's visa from Argentina with his parents in 2001 when he was six years old. He has been in the country ever since. On June 15, 2012, he was 17 and in high school. Ben and his parents visit the Humanitarian Law firm because they heard about DACA relief and want Ben to apply.

- What documents would you recommend that Ben and his family bring in to show he is eligible for the program?

U. Central American Minors Refugee/Parole Program, or CAM

In July 2014, there was a dramatic increase in the number of unaccompanied minor children, mainly from Honduras, El Salvador, and Guatemala, who sought to enter the United States to escape violence in their home countries. In an effort to provide a legal pathway for those who had parents already living here in some lawful status, the DHS created the **Central American Minors Refugee/Parole Program,** or **CAM**, which will allow up to 4,000 children to enter and reunite with their families.[108] To be eligible, the child must:

- Be a national of El Salvador, Guatemala, or Honduras, even if the parent is not,
- Be residing in his or her country of nationality,
- Be a biological, adopted, or stepchild of a qualifying parent, and
- Be unmarried and under 21 years of age.

As a humanitarian program created to promote family reunification, unmarried children of the qualifying child may also be given permission to enter as derivatives. Additionally, the parent of the minor child who is part of the same household and economic unit and is legally married to the qualifying parent in the United States may also be included.

● EXAMPLE

Byron is a citizen of El Salvador who has been living in the United States in Temporary Protected Status, or TPS, following the devastating earthquake in his country in 2001. When he left El Salvador, he left behind his wife Maria and their young son, Luis, who was just a few months old. Maria has been living with and caring for Luis on her own with money she receives from Byron. If Byron decides to file for Luis to come and join him under the CAM program, Maria can come too, since she is the parent of Luis, lives in the same household and economic unit as him, and is legally married to Byron.

A qualifying parent is an individual 18 years of age or older and lawfully present in the United States in one of the following categories:

- LPR,
- Temporary protected status,
- Parolee, if granted that benefit for at least one year,
- Deferred action status, if granted that benefit for at least one year,
- Deferred enforced departure, if granted that benefit for at least one year, or
- Withholding of removal.

The application process for these minor children is closer to refugee processing than applying for an immigrant visa. The qualifying parent completes a form known as Form DS-7699, Affidavit of Relationship, to prove the qualifying relationship and nationality of the child. The form can only be submitted to a local refugee resettlement agency, which then submits it to their national

---

[108] Information on the program is available at https://www.uscis.gov/CAM.

organization, which then sends it to the Office of Population, Refugees, and Migrants, or PRM for processing.[109] There is no application fee associated with the Form DS-7699.

The nearest consular office abroad will then call the qualifying child or relative for an interview to see if s/he will qualify as a refugee. For this, the child must establish that s/he has a well-founded fear of persecution on account of nationality, race, religion, political opinion, or membership in a social group. All qualifying biological children must undergo DNA testing to prove the relationship to the parent. Initial costs of the test are borne by the family, but subsequently reimbursed if the DNA results confirm the parent-child relationship.

If the child is granted refugee status, s/he can travel to the United States as a refugee and receive assistance and benefits through a resettlement agency on arrival. The child can then apply for adjustment of status one year after entry to the United States as a CAM refugee. If a child does not meet the legal standard for refugee classification, s/he might still be granted parole status, allowing the child to travel to the United States and, once here, obtain employment authorization. Children granted parole under the CAM program are required to obtain medical clearance and secure a sponsor in the United States who must complete Form I-134, Affidavit of Support. Unlike those granted humanitarian parole,[110] children and relatives granted parole under the CAM program are not eligible for federal, state, or local benefits or social services after they arrive. They are granted status for a period of two years, which can be renewed for a further two years. The status does not confer the ability to apply for lawful permanent residency.

V. Conclusion

From our survey of these different benefits, it is clear that efforts to understand and address the precarious position of immigrants are being made, ranging from the various immigration benefits available to provide protection to foreign nationals in different situations, to the specially trained USCIS staff available to adjudicate complex and sensitive applications. Some in the advocate community believe that more needs to be done to provide protection to vulnerable populations while others, who favor a more restrictionist approach to the undocumented, believe relief already available operates as incentives to encourage foreign nationals to continue to arrive here outside of legal channels. The fact that many immigrants have come forward to seek safety and cooperate with law enforcement indicates the scope of the need for protection in immigrant communities.

---

[109] *See* Section H.1 of Chapter 5, Asylum and Other Related Humanitarian Relief, for more details on this process.
[110] *See* Section J of Chapter 5, Asylum and Other Related Humanitarian Relief.

Grounds of Inadmissibility and Deportation

Key Terms and Acronyms

Admitted
Arriving Alien
Beneficiary
Deportation (Removal)
Illegal Immigration Reform and Immigrant Responsibility Act (IIRAIRA)

Inadmissible
Misrepresentation
Petitioner
Unlawful Presence
Waivers

Chapter Objectives

- Understand the concepts of inadmissibility and deportation and the distinction between the two
- Analyze the various grounds of inadmissibility and deportation
- Review who decides whether a foreign national is admissible or deportable
- Review possible waivers available to a foreign national

Every country has procedures to decide who may enter its borders and who must stay out. A country may also decide that those who have broken its laws are no longer welcome and must leave. Decisions are made about whether a foreign national should be **admitted** and allowed to enter the country, declared inadmissible and therefore must stay out, or, for those already in the country, should be **deported** and made to leave because they have violated certain laws.

As we discussed in Chapter 1, Historical Background and Introduction to the U.S. Immigration System there are five different groups of people in the United States at any one time: U.S. citizens; lawful permanent residents, or LPRs;

nonimmigrants; refugees/asylees; and the undocumented. In addition to these very specific categories, there are those who are present in the United States, with permission, but with no formal immigration status. These include those present as parolees,[1] those with temporary protected status,[2] and those with withholding of removal relief,[3] all terms discussed in earlier chapters. While citizens are fully protected and therefore can never be asked to leave the United States, unless they lose their status as citizens first,[4] this does not apply to any of the other groups. Decisions regarding who can enter, stay, or leave are made by different agencies and only after full consideration of whether a foreign national is admissible or deportable for some reason.

Significant changes to the law relating to inadmissibility and deportation were introduced by the Illegal Immigration Reform and Immigrant Responsibility Act of 1996,[5] or IIRAIRA. This resulted in an expansion of the grounds that determined whether a foreign national could enter or remain in the United States and a change in some terminology. In particular, entry of a person to the United States is now referred to as admission, while deportation is now **removal**. Despite these changes, the term deportation still remains firmly entrenched in practical usage. We use the terms removal, deportation, and deportability interchangeably.

We refer to IIRAIRA as necessary, while we analyze what admissibility and deportation mean and what factors determine who can be restricted from entering the United States or be required to leave it. We consider each of the grounds of admissibility or deportation in turn, while also reviewing the decision makers. Foreign nationals declared inadmissible or deportable can apply, in certain circumstances, for a *waiver* to allow admission to or permission to remain in the United States.

> **Waiver:** Permits an otherwise ineligible foreign national, i.e., one who is inadmissible or removable, to enter or remain in the United States because of special circumstances that apply to his or her case.

This chapter reviews what waivers may be available to a foreign national who would otherwise be prevented from entering or required to leave the country. However, any proper understanding of inadmissibility and deportation must first begin with a discussion of what these terms mean.

A. The Concepts of Admission and Deportation

Before we begin analyzing what factors would make a foreign national inadmissible or deportable, it may be useful to first define these two terms as they are used in immigration law. It is important to bear in mind the distinction between the two. Admission deals with those who are considered to be at the border, literally and figuratively, asking to be granted permission to enter the

---

[1] *See* Chapter 5, Asylum and Other Related Humanitarian Relief, and Chapter 10, Immigration Court Practice and Relief from Removal.
[2] *See* Chapter 5, Asylum and Other Related Humanitarian Relief.
[3] *See* Chapter 5, Asylum and Other Related Humanitarian Relief.
[4] The concept of denaturalization is discussed in detail in Chapter 11 and only refers to those who are naturalized citizens and not those who were either born as citizens or acquired citizenship through a parent.
[5] Pub. L. 104-208, div. C, 110 Stat. 3009 (1996).

United States or to remain in a temporary or indefinite status. Deportation or removal refers to those who may have violated a condition of their stay or entered illegally and a decision must now be made as to whether they should remain here or leave.

A.1. Admission and Admitted

The terms "admitted" and "**admission**" are defined as "the lawful entry of the [foreign national] into the United States, after inspection and authorization by an immigration officer."[6] Admission into the United States requires a foreign national to present him or herself to a designated officer and request permission to *enter* the country or, for someone who is already here, *remain* in a particular immigration status. The concept of admission, therefore, can arise in a number of different ways.

For many, the first opportunity to seek admission to the United States will be when an application is made at an embassy or consular office in the home country for a visa to enter, since having this document is often a prerequisite to even getting on a plane to travel here. The application process for receiving a visa provides a consular officer with the opportunity to assess whether there are any negative factors that would require denial of permission to enter the United States to the foreign national. A decision to deny issuance of a visa and therefore admission to the country is not subject to review, i.e., there is no formal process to appeal a consular officer's decision not to grant a visa.[7] If granted, the visa will specify the particular immigration status in which a foreign national is seeking to enter the country. For example, if a foreign national wants to come to the United States in order to study, the visa issued will indicate permission to enter as a student, or in F-1 category, also indicating the specific school where s/he is expected to study.

Being assessed for and issued a visa does not guarantee that the holder will automatically be given permission to enter the country on arrival at a port of entry. Rather, it simply provides the ability to seek admission at the border where a Customs and Border Protection, or CBP, officer will again assess whether or not the foreign national should be admitted. If permission to enter is given, then a decision will also be made as to how long the person can stay.

● **EXAMPLE**

Edgar, from the United Kingdom, wishes to enter the United States. He has heard that, as a Visa Waiver National, he should be allowed to remain in the country for 90 days. However, when questioned by the CBP officer about his purpose for entering the country, he explains that he is here to attend a conference that will last for one week. The CBP officer would be quite within his authority to refer Edgar to a supervisor to decide if Edgar should be granted less than the 90 days he expects, and instead a period closer to the actual time he needs to allow him to attend the conference.

---

[6] INA § 101(a)(13).
[7] *See Kerry v. Din*, 576 U.S. _, 135 S. Ct. 2128 (2015).

Another opportunity to seek admission to the United States is when a foreign national applies for adjustment of status with the United States Citizenship and Immigration Service, or USCIS, under the Immigration and Nationality Act, or INA, § 245(a). In this situation, the foreign national is physically within the country and is applying to change from a nonimmigrant and temporary status to become an immigrant in an indefinite status. In order for this application to be approved, an assessment will be made about whether or not all criteria have been met to warrant a grant of adjustment with no impediments to admission to the United States on a permanent basis.

● EXAMPLE

Anashe, a citizen of Zimbabwe, gains admission to the United States as a nonimmigrant visitor. During her visit, she meets, falls in love with, and marries a U.S. citizen, Nancy, who decides to file an application with the USCIS so that she can remain indefinitely with her wife. That application would change her status from a temporary purpose to one where Anashe is admitted to lawful permanent resident, or LPR status, giving permission for her to remain here indefinitely, even though she is already physically within the United States. This change of status is also known as an admission.

Finally, a foreign national may seek admission to the United States in proceedings before an immigration judge who will decide whether or not s/he can remain in the country. Typically, this will apply to someone who has never been a permanent resident before. However, in some limited circumstances, which are covered in Section B.1 of Chapter 10, Immigration Court Practice and Relief from Removal, a permanent resident may seek to apply in removal proceedings to retain his or her LPR status through proceedings for cancellation of removal.

So far, we have focused on nonimmigrants and situations when they might seek to be admitted into the United States. What if the applicant for entry is an LPR who is entitled to remain here indefinitely? Are there any circumstances when s/he might be considered to be an applicant for admission? An example may be helpful.

● EXAMPLE

Umberto, who has been an LPR for the last 25 years, takes a two-week vacation to Canada with his family because he has been told the view of Niagara Falls is beautiful from Ontario. On his return to the United States, he would not be considered to be seeking admission because his stay outside the country was brief and casual, and therefore he should have no problems with re-entering.

While the general rule is that LPRs who leave and return to the United States are not seeking admission, following IIRAIRA, there are now certain circumstances when an LPR in fact can be considered to be applying for a new admission. Under INA § 101(a)(13)(C)(i-vi), such situations would include when the LPR:

- Has abandoned or relinquished his or her status as an LPR,
- Has been absent for a continuous period of more than 180 days,

A: The Concepts of Admission and Deportation

- Has engaged in illegal activity outside of the country since departure,
- Left the United States while removal or extradition proceedings were ongoing,
- Has previously committed any offense listed in the inadmissibility grounds in INA § 212(a)(2) relating to criminal offenses without being granted a waiver under INA § 212(h)[8] or granted relief in the form of cancellation of removal under INA § 240A(a),[9] or
- Is not seeking to reenter the United States at a designated entry point, and has not been allowed to reenter after inspection and authorization by an immigration officer.

● EXAMPLE

Wen Bi is a Chinese national living in the United States as an LPR. On her return from her most recent trip to visit with her elderly parents, a CBP officer questions her because she has a conviction for assault arising from an altercation with someone in her workplace three years ago. This is the first time Wen Bi has left the country since that conviction, so she is now considered to be seeking admission to the United States, even though she is an LPR and has only been gone from the country for six weeks. Her conviction means that an immigration judge must decide whether Wen should be granted admission or must leave the United States.

Case for Discussion 9.1

Baraka, a citizen of Yemen, lives in the United States as an LPR. He has a conviction in New Jersey for possessing small amounts of marijuana. This was back in 1998, when he was a student. His brother, who also lives here, has arranged to get married in a destination wedding in the Dominican Republic. Baraka decides to attend to help him celebrate and is out of the country a total of four days. On his return to the United States, he presents his green card as evidence that he is an LPR, expecting to pass quickly through immigration control. Instead, security checks indicate his prior conviction for drug possession. He is detained and processed to see an immigration judge, who will decide whether he should be admitted to the United States.

- Why is Baraka, an LPR, subject to the grounds of "inadmissibility?"

---

[8] Discussed further in Section B.2.b.
[9] See Section B.1 Chapter 10, Immigration Court Practice and Relief from Removal.

A.2. Deportation

The administrative hearings where decisions are made about whether a foreign national can remain in the United States or must leave are referred to as removal proceedings. The agencies authorized to place a person into removal proceedings are Immigration and Customs Enforcement, or ICE, and USCIS. CBP only has authority to decide whether a person is inadmissible or not. If a determination is made that the foreign national is not admissible, then s/he will be placed into removal proceedings for an immigration judge to ultimately decide. In some circumstances, a CBP officer can remove a person without a judge hearing the case. This is known as expedited removal, which is discussed in Section C, of Chapter 10, Immigration Court Practice and Relief from Removal.

In exercising their authority, ICE and USCIS must decide whether a foreign national has violated a condition of his or her stay or has committed acts, including crimes, which make removal a possibility. If an immigration violation has occurred, then proceedings will be initiated to remove the foreign national from the country by serving the violator with a document known as a **Notice to Appear**, or **NTA**. This is discussed further in Chapter 10, Immigration Court Practice and Relief from Removal.

> **Case for Discussion 9.2**
>
> Cala, a citizen of Western Sahara, entered the United States as a student in F-1 status to study English. Three months after her entry, she learned that her father's business collapsed following his illness. She is no longer able to receive the financial support she needs to cover her study and living expenses. Her friend tells her of a vacancy in a local meat-packing factory. Cala begins work the next week while continuing with her studies. She did not request or receive permission to work from the USCIS before she started. Unfortunately, on her first day of employment, officers from ICE raid the factory because they have received a tip that there are undocumented workers present. Cala is detained and questioned.
>
> - What concerns should Cala have about this and how might this affect her immigration status?

Now that we have an understanding of what these important terms mean and how they are used, we can discuss what grounds would make a foreign national either inadmissible or deportable. As an aid to understanding, Tables 9.2 and 9.3 in Section D., respectively, provide a comparison of and the waivers to ameliorate the inadmissibility and deportation grounds. It may be useful to refer to them while reading through the different sections of this chapter.

B. Grounds of Inadmissibility

Section 212 of the INA lists ten grounds of inadmissibility, each of which contains sub-categories. Therefore, altogether there are close to 50 ways a foreign national can be refused admission into the United States. We analyze each of the ten grounds individually. Throughout our discussion, we also look to any waivers that may be available to alleviate the effects of the apparent inadmissibility.

B.1. Health-Related Grounds: INA § 212(a)(1)

The health-related grounds generally encompass communicable diseases or mental health disorders that may create a danger to the general public. INA § 212(a)(1) states that any foreign national who has any of the following health issues is inadmissible:

- A communicable disease of public health significance, as determined by the Secretary of Health and Human Services, or HHS. Such diseases include leprosy or active tuberculosis. The type of communicable diseases that can render a foreign national inadmissible may change over time.[10] For example, HIV infection had been included until 2008, when it was removed from the list.
- Without vaccinations required for those seeking to be LPRs.[11] There is a list of vaccine-preventable diseases for which inoculations are recommended.
- A physical or mental disorder and behavior that may pose or has posed a threat to property, safety, or welfare of the foreign national or others.[12]
- Is or has been a drug abuser or drug addict.[13]

For a foreign national to be inadmissible because of a physical or mental disorder, there must be evidence that behaviors that may pose or have posed a threat to the property, safety, or welfare of the applicant or others have been demonstrated, or that any such past behavior is likely to recur or lead to other harmful behavior.[14]

The presence of a physical or mental illness alone would not determine whether a foreign national poses a significant risk to the community. However, other factors such as a history of institutionalization for a mental disorder, DUI, and other criminal arrests suggesting mental disorder may be considered to determine whether a mental status examination is required before a decision on admissibility can be made.

---

[10] INA § 212(a)(1)(A)(i).
[11] INA § 212(a)(1)(A)(ii).
[12] INA § 212(a)(1)(A)(iii)(I).
[13] INA § 212(a)(1)(A)(iv).
[14] INA § 212(a)(1)(A)(iii), 42 C.F.R. §§ 34.2(d)(2), (n), and (p).

Chapter 9: Grounds of Inadmissibility and Deportation

> **Case for Discussion 9.3**
>
> Eddie, 23 years old, is from the United Kingdom and suffers from schizophrenia, of the paranoid type. He was diagnosed with this condition about five years ago and placed on appropriate medication that effectively helps him to manage his mental health. Eddie now seeks to enter the United States in order to join his parents who have filed a petition for him.
>
> - Is Eddie inadmissible?

Immigration law recognizes that separation can cause extreme hardship to family members, and even more so when a foreign national has mental health issues that need to be monitored or treated. Even if a foreign national does not meet the criteria for permission to enter because of a mental condition, s/he may apply for a waiver to overcome this ineligibility.

Waivers of inadmissibility are available for most health-related grounds of inadmissibility. For those with communicable diseases, INA § 212(g)(1) permits those who are otherwise inadmissible to enter if they:

- Are the spouse, unmarried son or daughter, or minor unmarried lawfully adopted child of a United States citizen, LPR, or foreign national issued an immigrant visa;
- Have a son or daughter who is a United States citizen, LPR, or foreign national issued an immigrant visa; or
- Are a VAWA self-petitioner

and meet whatever terms and conditions are imposed by the Attorney General, after consultation with the Secretary of Health and Human Services, or HHS for the setting of appropriate conditions or giving of an appropriate bond. Those without required vaccinations may still enter the United States if:

- They have been vaccinated but are without documentary proof of it;
- Vaccination would be medically inappropriate; or
- They are not required to submit to vaccinations because of their religious beliefs.[15]

Waivers are also available for those with physical or mental disorders and do not require a family relationship to exist before they are issued.[16] Again, the Attorney General, after consultation with the Secretary of HHS, could decide

---
[15] INA § 212(g)(2).
[16] INA § 212(g)(3).

to impose certain conditions or even request an appropriate bond to ensure that the foreign national's condition is controlled such that s/he does not pose a danger to others.

> ● **EXAMPLE**
>
> **Refer back to Eddie in Case for Discussion 9.3. Even though he has been prescribed medication, it becomes clear that Eddie has stopped taking them, leading to some arrests for arson, which he says he was driven to by the voices he hears talking to him. The consular officer reviewing Eddie's case has determined that he poses a threat to the safety and welfare of himself and others, even though the criminal charges against him were all dropped because of his mental condition. Eddie could request a waiver to allow him to enter the United States despite the concerns of the officer. If there were sufficient assurances that medical treatment that could stabilize Eddie's condition (the cost of which would be covered privately) would be available to him on entry to the United States, then the waiver might be granted. Without these assurances, however, it is unlikely.**

The situation for those who are drug addicts or abusers is different. The terms "drug abuse" and "addict" are defined as the non-medical use of a substance listed in § 202 of the Controlled Substances Act. Examples of such drugs include heroin, marijuana, methadone, and cocaine. While abuse of a drug need not result in physical or psychological dependence, dependency is necessary for a finding of addiction.[17] There is no waiver of this ground of inadmissibility for those seeking admission as immigrants. However, those coming to the United States temporarily may request a general waiver under INA § 212(d)(3).[18]

Any person accompanying a foreign national deemed inadmissible on health grounds, and requiring the protection or guardianship of the inadmissible foreign national because they are certified to be helpless as a result of infancy, sickness, or physical or mental disability, will also be denied admission.[19] This is because no one would be available to provide the care that person needs while s/he is in the United States. Where a waiver is available for the health related grounds, it is applied for using Form I-601, Application for Waiver of Grounds of Inadmissibility.

> ● **EXAMPLE**
>
> **Ivan is a 12-year old boy from Russia, traveling with his uncle on a visit to the United States for the first time. He will be cared for by his uncle while he is here. During questioning, his uncle discloses that he is addicted to heroin and has been trying to get clean for the last 18 months. Because his uncle has been determined to be inadmissible as a result of his drug use, Ivan is also inadmissible because he is dependent on his uncle for his care.**

---

[17] 42 C.F.R. §§ 34.2(d), (g), and (h).
[18] *See* Section B.11 for further discussion.
[19] INA § 212(a)(10)(B), 22 C.F.R. § 40.102.

B.2. Criminal Grounds: INA § 212(a)(2)

Determining whether a foreign national is inadmissible as a result of criminal activity is extremely complex. Where there are criminal issues for consideration, referral to or discussions with an attorney with experience in both criminal and immigration law should be considered as early as possible in the criminal proceedings. In criminal cases, considering the immigration consequences of a possible conviction or sentence imposed is now part of effective representation. The Supreme Court decision in *Padilla v. Kentucky*, 559 U.S. 356 (2010), held that defense counsel must advise on the risk of deportation arising from a particular plea in criminal proceedings.[20] Where it is suspected a foreign national was not provided with the appropriate legal warnings by the attorney representing him or her in the criminal case, an ineffective assistance of counsel claim may be appropriate under the Sixth Amendment.[21] This is because it could be argued that, had the information been provided, the foreign national may have opted for a different legal strategy, with an outcome that might not impact the immigration case in such a way as to leave very few avenues available for immigration relief. Convictions for crimes deemed aggravated felonies[22] in immigration law are always very worrisome as there is often very little that can be done to ensure a person remains in the United States. Claiming ineffective assistance of counsel may allow the foreign national to challenge the propriety of the conviction itself and, if successful, allow greater access to immigration options.

Criminal activity can either prevent a foreign national from being admitted to the United States or cause that same person to be deported. While we analyze the criminal activities separately in both the inadmissibility and deportation context, where there is overlap of information, we reference it at appropriate times. First, we analyze what types of convictions would make a person inadmissible.

B.2.a. Definition of Conviction

For immigration purposes, the term "conviction" is defined in INA § 101(a)(48)(A) as follows:

> a formal judgment of guilt of the [foreign national] entered by a court or, if adjudication of guilt has been withheld, where:
> (i) a judge or jury has found the [foreign national] guilty or the [foreign national] has entered a plea of guilty or **nolo contendere** or has admitted sufficient facts to warrant a finding of guilt, and
> (ii) the judge has ordered some form of punishment, penalty, or restraint on the [foreign national's] liberty to be imposed.

Nolo Contedere: Latin term meaning "no contest", allowing a defendant in criminal proceedings to neither admit nor deny levied charges even though s/he will be sentenced as though a guilty plea was entered.

---

[20] *Padilla v. Kentucky*, 559 U.S. 356, 371 (2010).
[21] *Id.* at 374.
[22] *See* discussion in Section C.2.a.

Courts have held that a sentence to house arrest is a conviction, since it is a form of restraint on liberty and therefore confinement.[23]

Some states or municipalities may dispose of criminal proceedings without requiring a plea, admission of facts, or finding of guilt. For example, in Philadelphia, PA, such cases are managed under a program known as Accelerated Rehabilitative Disposition, or ARD, meant to punish first time offenders who commit relatively minor crimes. The individual in a program like ARD will be subject to a fine, probation, or a period of community service. Such penalties would not be considered convictions for immigration purposes because no plea or finding of guilt occurred. After any penalties have been fulfilled, expungement of the criminal record may be requested and, once granted, the individual can answer honestly that s/he does not have a criminal record. However, immigration law is an anomaly since the arrest and disposition of the case must still be disclosed in any immigration application that requests information on a person's criminal history.

● EXAMPLE

Recall Baraka from Yemen in Case for Discussion 9.1. When he was arrested for possession of marijuana, the judge in the criminal proceedings decided to process his case under the ARD program because this was his first offense and the amount of marijuana involved was very little. Because Baraka agreed to this, he was not required to enter a plea of any kind. The judge gave him probation for 6 months, 20 hours of community service, and ordered to pay court costs. Once Baraka successfully completes all of these requirements, he will be able to petition the court to expunge his record. The fact that he was processed under the ARD program means that, for immigration purposes, he will be able to declare that he has no convictions, but must still disclose this arrest and provide information on its disposition.

An order in juvenile delinquency proceedings is not a conviction because these are considered to be civil rather than criminal in nature.[24] Therefore, there should be no detrimental immigration consequences as a result of such an adjudication. In many cases, the records are sealed in any event, without access to them, even for immigration proceedings.

For a conviction to sustain a finding of inadmissibility, it must be the result of a final judgment following a state or federal court proceeding.[25] However, vacating or setting aside a conviction solely to avoid the resulting immigration consequences will not change the fact that it is still a conviction that would render a foreign national inadmissible or deportable.[26] Generally, for post-conviction relief to be given full faith and credit by the immigration court, and thereby ameliorate immigration consequences, it must relate to a procedural or

---

[23] *See Ilchuk v. Attorney General of the U.S.*, 434 F.3d 618 (3d. Cir. 2006); *Herrera v. U.S. Attorney General*, _ F.3d_ (11th Cir. 2016).
[24] *Matter of Devision*, 22 I&N Dec. 1362 (BIA 2000).
[25] *Pino v. Landon*, 349 U.S. 901 (1955).
[26] *Matter of Pickering*, 23 I&N Dec. 621 (BIA 2003).

substantive defect in the underlying criminal proceedings.[27] This might include, for example, vacating a conviction because the foreign national did not knowingly enter a guilty plea. In contrast, post-conviction relief that modifies a sentence imposed for any reason will be recognized in immigration proceedings.[28]

A sentence, for immigration purposes, is defined as "the period of incarceration or confinement ordered by a court of law, regardless of any suspension of the imposition or execution of that imprisonment or sentence in whole or in part."[29] In other words, if a person is ordered to serve a period of 11 to 23 months in prison but only serves 11, s/he is considered to have been sentenced to the full 23 months for immigration purposes. This is an important concept, since many deportable offenses require that a minimum sentence of one year be imposed. In some cases, it may be prudent to seek post-conviction relief to reduce sentences imposed in order to avoid any harsh immigration consequences as a result, particularly since such sentence reductions, regardless of the reason for them, are given full faith and credit in immigration court.[30] Probation, because it does not involve confinement, is not considered a sentence.[31] Therefore, if it is the only punishment given for an offense, it would not be deemed a conviction for immigration purposes.

Case for Discussion 9.4

Florence is from Denmark and is here as a visitor. She was convicted of receiving stolen goods. She was advised by her criminal attorney to plead guilty so she would not be sent to jail. Florence pled guilty and was placed on probation.

- Does Florence have a conviction for the purposes of the INA?

B.2.b. Inadmissibility Based on Specific Criminal Offenses

We now briefly survey the list of criminal offenses that would render a person inadmissible. We review the most common types of crimes to allow identification when a more in-depth analysis by an attorney experienced in such matters may be necessary.

---

[27] *Id.*
[28] *See Matter of Song*, 23 I&N Dec. 173 (BIA 2001).
[29] INA § 101(a)(48)(B).
[30] *Matter of Song, supra.*
[31] *Matter of Martin*, 18 I&N Dec. 226, 227 (BIA 1982).

Crimes of moral turpitude: INA § 212(a)(2)(A)(i)(I)

Any person

- Convicted of,
- Who commits,
- Admits the commission of, or
- Admits the essential elements of

a crime of moral turpitude, or CIMT, is inadmissible. These requirements make clear that a conviction is not a prerequisite to finding someone inadmissible. Merely *committing* or *admitting* to facts that would constitute a moral turpitude crime is enough to find a foreign national inadmissible. By contrast, a person who has already been admitted to the United States can be removed or deported for the same offense *only* if s/he has been convicted.[32] Therefore, in this context, a foreign national who is seeking admission to the United States has fewer protections than a person who has already been admitted.

The term "moral turpitude" has no statutory definition. Courts generally agree that crimes of moral turpitude include crimes of violence, crimes that shock the public conscience, and crimes "commonly thought of as involving baseness, vileness, or depravity," and are defined, at least in part, by reference to current moral standards.[33] The following have been determined to be moral turpitude crimes: any crime involving fraud or deceit;[34] murder and manslaughter;[35] robbery;[36] and arson.[37] The general categories of CIMTs and their respective elements or determining factors are in Table 9.1.

Table 9.1 General Categories of Crimes Involving Moral Turpitude (CIMTs)

CIMT Category	Elements of Crime
Crimes Against a Person	Criminal intent or recklessness, or is defined as morally reprehensible by state (may include statutory rape)
Crimes Against Property	Involving fraud against the government or an individual (may include theft, forgery, robbery)
Sexual and Family Crimes	No one set of principles or elements; see further explanation (may include spousal or child abuse)
Crimes Against Authority of the Government	Presence of fraud is the main determining factor (may include offering a bribe, counterfeiting)
Source: USCIS	

---

[32] This is discussed further in Section C.2.
[33] See *Jordan v. De George*, 341 U.S. 223 (1951).
[34] *Id.*
[35] *Carter v. INS*, 90 F.3d 14 (1st Cir. 1996).
[36] *Matter of Martin*, 18 I&N Dec. 226 (BIA 1982).
[37] *Vuksanovic v. U.S. Attorney General*, 439 F.3d 1308 (11th Cir. 2006).

Since the elements of a crime can vary from state to state, a crime in one state may have immigration consequences, but the same crime committed in another may have a different result. For example, bad check writing in Pennsylvania is not considered a crime of moral turpitude, while the same crime in Georgia would be. Certain DUI crimes may not be crimes of moral turpitude.[38]

● EXAMPLE

Recall Florence in Case for Discussion 9.4. In the fact pattern presented, she would be both inadmissible to and removable from the United States because she has been convicted of a theft offense, which is a CIMT. If she had been entered into a program that did not require her to enter a plea, such as an ARD program, she would not be removable because there is no conviction. However, whether she is inadmissible will depend on the information she provides to an immigration official at her interview who must decide if she has admitted to facts that constitute the essential elements of a CIMT and therefore must be denied admission.

Exceptions to this ground of inadmissibility exist for a foreign national convicted of or who admits committing acts that constitute the essential elements of a CIMT, who can demonstrate that the crime in question was committed before the age of 18 *and* it happened more than five years before s/he applies for a visa and admission to the United States.[39] Alternatively, the foreign national may qualify for a **petty offense exception** if s/he can show that the maximum possible penalty for the crime involved is less than one year's imprisonment *and the actual sentence imposed* was a term of six months or less.[40] This exception is not available if more than one CIMT offense has been committed or admitted.[41]

Case for Discussion 9.5

Ivan, from Russia, is in the United States on a tourist visa. He meets Svetlana and they marry. Svetlana will petition for Ivan so he can adjust his status from that of a visitor to LPR. Before the interview takes place, Ivan is convicted of shoplifting because he took a cell phone from a store. He was charged with the summary offense of retail theft, punishable by 90 days in jail.

■ Will this crime make Ivan inadmissible?

---

[38] *Matter of Torres-Varela*, 23 I&N Dec. 78 (BIA 2001).
[39] INA § 212(a)(2)(A)(ii)(I).
[40] INA § 212(a)(2)(A)(ii)(II).
[41] *Matter of Jurado*, 24 I&N Dec. 29 (BIA 2009).

Drug related offenses: INA § 212(a)(2)(A)(i)(II) and INA § 212(a)(2)(C)

There are harsh consequences in immigration law for offenses that relate to controlled substances. Once again, conviction, or admission of either having committed or of engaging in acts constituting the essential elements of a crime relating to controlled substances under the laws of a state, the federal government, or a foreign country, including attempts or conspiracies to commit such a crime, renders a foreign national inadmissible.[42] A foreign national who a consular officer or the Attorney General knows or has reason to believe has been involved in the illegal trafficking of a controlled substance or listed chemical is also inadmissible.[43] The drug in question for either of these provisions must be a controlled substance as defined in Title 21 United States Code § 802. Under this provision, the lower standard of having a "reason to believe" is enough to support a finding that a person is inadmissible. Also, aiding, abetting, assisting, conspiring, or colluding with others in the illegal activity or attempting to do so, would also render a foreign national inadmissible.

While there is a waiver available for drug related offenses under INA § 212(h), it pertains only to a single offense involving simple possession of 30 grams or less of marijuana for personal use. Any other drug offenses would leave a foreign national with no avenue for permanent admission to the United States. Such a foreign national could apply for an INA 212(d)(3) waiver to permit temporary admission as a nonimmigrant.

● EXAMPLE

Recall Baraka from Yemen, in Section B.2.a., who has a conviction for possession of a small amount of marijuana. So long as the quantity is less than 30 grams, while Baraka is still inadmissible, he remains eligible for a waiver to ameliorate the effects of his conviction.

Multiple criminal convictions: INA § 212(a)(2)(B)

A foreign national convicted of two or more crimes with an aggregate sentence in prison of at least five years is inadmissible, even if the crimes in question are not CIMTs or if they arise out of a single scheme of criminal misconduct. Under this ground, a mere admission of the crimes is sufficient.

---

[42] INA § 212(a)(2)(A)(i)(II).
[43] INA § 212(a)(2)(C)(i). *See also* 9 FAM 302.4-3(B). Recent Board of Immigration Appeals, or BIA, case law held that a foreign national was inadmissible where an appropriate immigration official knew or had "reason to believe" that a person had trafficked in a controlled substance. *See Matter of Jose Casillas-Topete*, 25 I&N Dec. 317 (BIA 2010), where the BIA held that the foreign national was a trafficker in controlled substances at the time of admission to the United States.

> ● **EXAMPLE**
>
> **Volodymyr entered the United States as a student three years ago. However, he stopped going to school soon after his arrival when his country of citizenship, Ukraine, entered into political disputes with Russia that severely affected the economy. His parents could no longer send him the money he needed to survive. He is married to a U.S. citizen and they are planning to file his immigration papers so that he can become an LPR. The only thing holding them back is that they do not have the money to pay for the application. Persuaded by a friend, Volodymyr agrees to participate in a burglary of a jewelry store by driving the getaway car. In the middle of the night, his friends break down the door to the store, grab as much merchandise as they can, and speed off before the police arrive. Volodymyr is paid for his services with a few diamond necklaces. He is later arrested, following a tip off, and is charged with aiding and abetting and receiving stolen goods, among other offenses. Even though this was one event, a single scheme of criminal misconduct to steal from the jewelry store, more than one offense is involved here: aiding and abetting and receiving stolen goods. Volodymyr will be inadmissible if the judge deciding his criminal case sentences him to a combined sentence of five years or more in total for the charges against him. As a result, Volodymyr will be unable to adjust his status to an LPR because he will be deemed inadmissible because of his convictions.**

As demonstrated in this example, the concept of admission comes up in many different contexts. Volodymyr would have had to demonstrate that he was admissible when he arrived at a port of entry and asked for permission to enter as a student. Even though he is now physically in the United States, if he sought permission to adjust his status to that of an LPR based on his marriage, his admissibility will again be assessed by the immigration officer adjudicating that application. In this instance, his criminal conviction may make him inadmissible and therefore subject to removal or deportation proceedings.[44]

The criminal offenses of prostitution and commercialized vice, serious criminal activity with a claim of immunity from prosecution, severe religious freedom violations by government officials, significant traffickers in persons, and money laundering are also grounds of inadmissibility.[45]

A waiver of all of the criminal grounds, except those related to controlled substances other than possession of 30 grams or less of marijuana, is available under INA § 212(h). To qualify, a foreign national must demonstrate that either:

- S/he is inadmissible under the prostitution and commercialized vice provisions or that the offense took place more than 15 years ago,[46]
- His or her admission to the United States would not be contrary to the welfare, security, or safety of the country,[47]

---

[44] Further discussion of removal proceedings is in Chapter 10, Immigration Court Practice and Relief from Removal.
[45] INA § 212(a)(2)(D)-(I).
[46] INA § 212(h)(1)(A)(i).
[47] INA § 212(h)(1)(A)(i).

- Denying admission would cause extreme hardship to a U.S. citizen or LPR spouse, parent, son, or daughter of the foreign national,[48] or
- The foreign national is a VAWA self-petitioner.[49]

The term "hardship" has been used in immigration law for many years, applying different evidentiary standards. For instance, the most stringent form of hardship is reserved for those seeking a type of relief known as cancellation of removal for non-LPRs. Applicants are required to demonstrate that if they are not granted relief, qualifying family members will suffer "exceptional and extremely unusual hardship."[50] This is discussed in detail in Section I.2 of Chapter 10, Immigration Court Practice and Relief from Removal. Some applicants for immigration relief need only show that qualifying family members will suffer extreme hardship. The term is without statutory or regulatory definition, in similar fashion to the word persecution used in the asylum context, which allows for a more flexible interpretation.[51]

In Matter of Anderson, 16 I&N Dec. 596 (BIA 1978), the Board of Immigration Appeals, or BIA, provided guidance on factors to be considered when determining whether a likelihood of extreme hardship can be established. While *Matter of Anderson* was decided when immigration law provided more generous relief from deportation, the standard of extreme hardship described in that case is still used for waiver cases today. The BIA articulated the following as relevant:

- Length of stay in the United States,
- Relatives present here and abroad,
- Conditions in the country where the foreign national would return,
- Medical or health issues for the foreign national and any relatives,
- Community ties,
- Educational opportunities that may be lost or interrupted if removal occurs, and
- Any other relevant factor.

In this case extreme hardship to the foreign national himself was taken into account as it related to a particular immigration relief he was seeking that permitted this.[52] This relief is no longer available and there are now few forms of immigration benefits that allow consideration of hardship directly to the applicant rather than only qualifying relatives. There is also a waiver available for beneficiaries of self-petitions under VAWA.[53] Crimes involving murder, torture, or attempts to commit such crimes may not be waived.

---

[48] INA § 212(h)(1)(B).
[49] INA § 212(h)(1)(C).
[50] *See* INA § 240A(ab)(1)(c)(i)(D).
[51] *See* Section A.2.a of Chapter 5, Asylum and Other Related Humanitarian Relief.
[52] *See* former § 244 of INA, suspension of deportation, which has been replaced with INA § 240(A), cancelation of removal.
[53] INA § 212(h)(1)(C).

The waiver is applied for using Form I-601, Application for Waiver of Grounds of Inadmissibility, and must be granted before the foreign national applies for a visa or adjustment of status.[54]

B.3. Security and Related Grounds: INA § 212(a)(3)

Historically, national security concerns have been reflected in immigration laws and have played a part in the determination of who should be refused permission to enter the United States. The list of those inadmissible on this ground has most recently been expanded as a result of the USA Patriot Act of 2001,[55] which broadened the definition of terrorist activity and included representatives of terrorist groups and certain members of their family to the list of those who are inadmissible. The Act provides immigration officials with the authority to detain foreign nationals suspected of providing material support to or involvement in terrorist activity until such time as there is a final determination on whether they should be removed.[56]

The Secretary of the Department of Homeland Security, or DHS, has exempted those who have provided material support under duress to terrorist organizations from the inadmissibility provisions.[57] Before a favorable decision can be made however, consideration must be given to whether provision of material support could have been avoided, the severity and type of harm inflicted or threatened on the foreign national, the likelihood of harm arising from those threats, and to whom the threat of harm was directed. The totality of the circumstances should be considered when deciding whether to grant a duress exemption, taking into account the amount, type, and frequency of material support provided, the nature of the activities engaged in by the terrorist organization, the waiver applicant's awareness of those activities, the passage of time since material support was provided, and the foreign national's conduct subsequent to the provision of support.

● EXAMPLE

Hélène is from Rwanda. She is an ethnic Tutsi. During the war in her country in 1994, she was captured by Hutus and forced to cook and clean for them as they moved throughout the country. She was told that if she did not do as they said, she would be killed. One day, she managed to escape from her captors and, after trekking through the forest, reached the safety of a refugee camp and sought protection. She now wants to be admitted to the United States. Even though Hélène provided material support to the rebels, if she can show that it was under duress, she may be admitted.

---

[54] INA § 212(h)(2).
[55] USA Patriot Act of 2001, Pub. L. 107-56, 115 Stat. 272 (2001).
[56] INA § 236A.
[57] Chertoff Memo, Exercise of Authority Under § 212(d)(3)(B)(i) of the Immigration and Nationality Act, April 27, 2007.

Any foreign national whose entry into the United States would pose serious adverse foreign policy consequences,[58] who is or has been affiliated with the Communist or any other totalitarian party,[59] or participated in Nazi persecution,[60] genocide,[61] or the commission of acts of torture or extrajudicial killings,[62] is inadmissible. With the demise of the Cold War, the government excuses past membership in the Communist party as a ground of inadmissibility, if the foreign national was forced to join in order to obtain employment or other essentials of daily living.[63] An application for this waiver is made using Form I-601, Application for Waiver of Grounds of Inadmissibility.

The USA Patriot Act mandated that an integrated entry and exit data system be implemented at all ports of entry. It is known as **National Security Entry-Exit System**, or **NSEERS**, and was first discussed in IIRAIRA. As a first step to implementing NSEERS, non-LPR nationals from 26 predominately-Muslim countries had to register at local immigration offices from September 2002, in response to the bombing of the World Trade Center Towers on September 11, 2001. Most of those required to register were males over the age of 16. In addition, when leaving the country, these nationals had to report to particular ports of departure and register their exit from the United States. Although the in-country registration requirement has now been suspended, foreign nationals subject to NSEERS must still prove they initially registered or left at the designated ports before they re-enter or seek to adjust their status to LPRs. Those that fail to do so may be considered inadmissible or deportable and subject to removal.[64]

Case for Discussion 9.6

Gamal is from Syria and is here on a student visa. While in school, he met and married a U.S. citizen and fellow student. Gamal did not report for NSEERS registration when required to do so because he was ill. He never did anything about it later because he heard that he no longer had to register. His wife is sponsoring him to remain here. The couple is told to report to the USCIS for a joint interview, which will decide if Gamal can change his status to an LPR based on his marriage.

- What effect, if any, will Gamal's failure to register for NSEERS have on his current application for permanent residency?

---

[58] INA § 212(a)(3)(C).
[59] INA § 212(a)(3)(D).
[60] INA § 212(a)(3)(E)(i).
[61] INA § 212(a)(3)(E)(ii).
[62] INA § 212(a)(3)(E)(iii).
[63] INA § 212(a)(3)(D)(iii).
[64] Department of Homeland Security Memorandum dated April 16, 2012, *Department of Homeland Security Guidance on Treatment of Individuals Previously Subject to the Reporting and Registration Requirements of the National Security Entry-Exit Registration System.*

B.4. Public Charge: INA § 212(a)(4)

Any foreign national who is likely to become a public charge or is unable to support him or herself financially without needing certain federal, state, or local benefits, is inadmissible. These benefits are generally known as means-tested public benefits. Factors for consideration to decide if there is a public charge issue includes the foreign national's age, health, family status, financial status, assets and resources, education, and skills.

Foreign nationals seeking to enter the United States in a family sponsored immigrant category[65] must submit an affidavit of support[66] that is contractually binding with federal and state authorities. Those seeking to immigrate on the basis of an employment visa filed by a relative or an entity in which the relative has significant ownership interest, are also required to submit a similar affidavit. The person who filed the relative petition for the intending immigrant must complete the affidavit and show that the annual income available to support the foreign national is at least 125 percent of the annual federal poverty guidelines.[67]

If the family member sponsoring the immigrant has insufficient income to meet the requirements of the affidavit of support on his or her own, it may be necessary to look for a joint sponsor. Before this though, other individuals in the household who can act as co-sponsors can be considered, (including the beneficiary, if s/he is working legally or has substantial assets that will allow the required sums to be met, by combining any income s/he may have to reach the total amount required). If this is insufficient, then a joint sponsor or additional person who does earn enough on his or her own or with household income, will need to sign an affidavit of support also as a joint sponsor. By signing, the sponsor, and joint sponsor, where appropriate, contract to repay any means-tested public benefits received by the foreign national (also known as the sponsored immigrant) to which s/he is not entitled. This obligation remains in place for a period of 40 qualifying quarters of Social Security contributions (typically considered to be about ten years) or until the sponsored immigrant becomes a United States citizen, whichever comes first.[68]

● EXAMPLE

Jeremiah is sponsoring his husband, Joshua, a citizen of Israel, to join him here as an immigrant. They had married in the United States while Joshua was here as a student before returning home to his family. As part of the application process, Jeremiah must show that the income he has available to support his husband is at least at 125 percent of the poverty level. However, he is a recent graduate and has not been able

---

[65] See Chapter 6, Family Sponsored Immigration and Permanent Resident Status.
[66] INA § 213A.
[67] This is a requirement for those seeking to become permanent residents based on their family relationship and is discussed further in Chapter 6, Family Sponsored Immigration and Permanent Resident Status.
[68] This is a very complex area of law, so care should be taken not to concede inadmissibility without a careful review of the circumstances. For instance, there may be some federal or state benefits programs that sponsored immigrants qualify for despite the existence of an affidavit of support. Also, some sponsored immigrants may be credited with qualifying quarters earned by family members and therefore may be able to claim public benefits without waiting the full ten-year period. See Section G.2.f. of Chapter 6, Family Sponsored Immigration and Permanent Resident Status.

to find work. As the petitioner for Joshua, Jeremiah will have to complete an affidavit of support, even though he has no income. Jeremiah currently lives with his parents, both of whom are working. If he can persuade them to act as co-sponsors, since they live in the same household, it is likely that the required income level can be met and Joshua will not be inadmissible because of the public charge ground of inadmissibility.

Case for Discussion 9.7

Iqbal, a citizen of Qatar, entered as a visitor and has since married a U.S. citizen. Neither he nor his wife have any children. He wants to adjust his status so that he can become an LPR. However, Iqbal is not working and his wife is only able to find work as a waitress at a local restaurant while she completes her degree. Her monthly earnings are not enough for her to show that she is able to support herself and her husband at the rate of 125 percent of the poverty level.

- Is there anything the couple can do to ensure that Iqbal will not be found to be a public charge?

B.5. Labor Certification and Qualifications for Certain Immigrants: INA § 212(a)(5)

Most individuals seeking to immigrate to the United States to perform skilled or unskilled labor are required to have a labor certification issued by the Secretary of Labor. That certificate will confirm that insufficient workers are:

- Able,
- Willing,
- Qualified,
- Available at the time and place the foreign national seeks to perform such work, and
- That employment of a foreign national will not adversely affect wages and working conditions of similarly situated employees in the United States.

Without such a certificate, the foreign national will be found inadmissible. These requirements affect those who are members of the teaching profession and individuals with exceptional ability in the arts or sciences.[69] Additional requirements apply to professional athletes[70], physicians,[71] and other health workers[72] seeking to work in the United States. A waiver may be available for

---

[69] INA § 212(a)(5)(A)(ii).
[70] INA § 212(a)(5)(A)(iii).
[71] INA § 212(a)(5)(B).
[72] INA § 212(a)(5)(C).

those who possess a valid immigrant visa but did not know nor could have reasonably ascertained their inadmissibility before embarking on their journey to the United States[73]

B.6. Illegal Entrants and Other Immigration Violators: INA § 212(a)(6)

Individuals who cross into the United States without permission or visas, or who otherwise violate immigration law, are inadmissible. Following are some specific immigration violations addressed in the INA.

B.6.a. Aliens Present Without Permission or Parole: INA § 212(a)(6)(A)

People sometimes arrive in the United States surreptitiously, without presenting themselves to an immigration officer for inspection. Perhaps they arrive by walking across a land border with Texas, Arizona, California, or Canada, or find other ways to evade immigration border officers. Arriving in this way is problematic because it can ultimately limit the types of immigration relief available to a foreign national seeking to regularize his or her status. Under § 212(a)(6)(A)(i) of the INA, any foreign national present in the United States without being admitted or *paroled*, or who arrives in the United States at any time or place other than at a designated port of entry, is inadmissible.

We refer to this sort of entry as "entered without inspection," or EWI. With some exceptions, individuals who EWI must return to their home country to apply to be admitted to the United States. An exception to this requirement permits certain immigration violators to pursue adjustment to permanent residency while in the United States on payment of a fine of $1000. Formerly known as INA § 245(i), this provision has now been repealed but its retroactive applicability is discussed in detail in Section G.3.b of Chapter 6, Family Sponsored Immigration and Permanent Resident Status. INA § 245(i) is only available to those seeking to adjust in the United States and not to those applying for admission from overseas.[74]

> **Paroled:** Grant of permission to enter the United States to an ineligible foreign national under the legal fiction that s/he is standing at the border waiting for a decision to be made as to whether s/he will be authorized to enter in a particular immigration category.

● EXAMPLE

Juana from Peru entered the United States back in 1999, crossing from Mexico into Texas with a group of other migrants. They were not inspected by an immigration officer. Juana has never left the country since her initial entry. About a month after Juana's arrival, she reconnected with a long lost sister who is now a U.S. citizen. The sister filed a relative petition for Juana in December 2000. If approved, it would allow Juana to adjust her status here and remain in the United States. Because of the backlog in sibling petitions, it will take at least 10-15 years for approval of the petition filed by Juana's sister. Meanwhile, Juana marries a U.S. citizen and he

---

[73] INA § 212(k).
[74] Virtue Memo, HQIRT 50/5.12, 96 Act 026 Mar. 31, 1997.

decides he wants to file for her to adjust her status to a permanent resident so that they will not be separated. Since Juana entered the United States without inspection, or EWI, she would ordinarily be required to leave the country and process her application at a consular office abroad. However, because of the relative petition submitted by her sister that was "approvable when filed," Juana is grandfathered under INA § 245(i). This allows Juana to file her adjustment application through her husband without leaving the country, but does require her to pay a fine of $1000.

As this example demonstrates, in assessing a case, it is important to ask questions not only about the person's date of arrival here, but also about the existence and date of filing of any previous petitions that may have been filed for his or her benefit. In this way, it may be possible to discover forms of relief not readily apparent.

B.6.b. Failure to Attend a Removal Proceeding: INA § 212(a)(6)(B)

Individuals who fail or refuse without reasonable cause to attend or remain in attendance at a removal proceeding are inadmissible for five years after their departure or removal.

B.6.c. Misrepresentation: INA § 212(a)(6)(C)

Anyone who by fraud or willfully misrepresenting a material fact in order to obtain a visa, documentation, entry into the country, or other benefit provided under the INA is inadmissible.[75] A material fact has to be something that is important for an adjudicator to know when deciding whether an immigration benefit should be granted. It has been defined as a fact that would make a foreign national excludable or that would shut off a line of inquiry.[76] Silence or failure to volunteer information alone is not enough to sustain an allegation of misrepresentation.[77] Also, timely retractions of untrue statements "will serve to purge a misrepresentation and remove it from further consideration."[78]

Another important consideration in the process of seeking to change status in the United States is timing. When a foreign national either applies for a visa or enters on the VWP, there is an assumption that s/he is being truthful with respect to all aspects of that application. However, if once in the United States s/he requests to change status to another category, whether a non- or immigrant classification, the timing of that application may raise a presumption about his or her true intent, which may or may not be rebutted. The DOS applies a 30/60-Day Rule[79] to those who enter as visitors but violate the conditions of their stay, either by:

---

[75] INA § 212(a)(6)(C)(i).
[76] *Matter of S- and B-C-*, 9 I&N Dec. 436 (BIA 1960).
[77] 9 FAM 302.9-4(B)(3)(b).
[78] 9 FAM 302.9-4(B)(3)(f).
[79] 9 FAM 302.9-4(B)(3)(g).

- Actively seeking unauthorized employment and, subsequently, becoming engaged in such employment,
- Enrolling in a full course of academic study without the benefit of the appropriate change of status,
- Marrying and taking up permanent residence, or
- Undertaking any other activity for which a change of status or an adjustment of status would be required, without the benefit of such a change or adjustment.

A foreign national engaging in any of these activities within 30 days of arrival are presumed to have misrepresented their intent when applying for a visa.[80] This would then lead to him or her being placed into removal proceedings for an immigration judge to decide whether s/he is inadmissible under INA § 212(a)(6)(C)(i) for misrepresentation. Those who do so within 30 but less than 60 days of entering the United States will trigger a rebuttable presumption, which may be overcome, based on the facts of the case.[81] No such presumption arises after 60 days.[82]

A waiver of this ground of inadmissibility may be available under INA § 212(i) for immigrants whose inadmissibility would result in extreme hardship to a U.S. citizen or permanent resident spouse or parent. While the waiver does not specifically allow consideration of hardship to children, this may still be introduced if it affects the parent or spouse of the foreign national.

Case for Discussion 9.8

Kayode is from Nigeria. He is single and currently unemployed with few assets. He wants to travel to the United States to attend the wedding of a childhood friend who now lives here. Before applying, he seeks advice from a friend, who advises him he will never get a visa if he tells the truth about his situation, because he will not be able to persuade the consular officer that he will return to Nigeria after his visit. Kayode is advised to say that he is married with children and that these are the reasons why he will return home. He does and is granted a visa. Once here, he meets and falls in love with Bola, a U.S. citizen with Nigerian parents.

- Will Kayode experience any difficulties with his application to become an LPR so that he can remain here with his wife?
- If he does, what remedies might be available to him?
- What if Kayode had never lied to get his visa, knew Bola before he came to the United States, and the couple gets married 45 days after he entered the country?

---

[80] 9 FAM 302.9-4(B)(3)(g)(3).
[81] 9 FAM 302.9-4(B)(3)(g)(4).
[82] 9 FAM 302.9-4(B)(3)(g)(5).

B: Grounds of Inadmissibility

● **EXAMPLE**

Assume Bola and Kayode decide to wait to apply for Kayode to adjust his status to an LPR because he understands that the lies he told to get his visa in the first place will adversely affect him and he will require a waiver. They want to wait until they have built up some equities that might persuade an adjudicator that they qualify for an extreme hardship waiver. Soon after they marry, Bola becomes pregnant, but there are complications with the pregnancy. Their daughter, Damilola, is born with a congenital heart defect and will require intense medical attention. If Kayode files an application for permanent residency with a waiver application, he could refer to the extreme hardship his wife Bola would suffer if he were not permitted to remain in the United States. This would be based on the fact that she would have to care for their sick daughter on her own, while also having to cope with the emotional and physical stress that doing so would cause her.

Another inadmissibility provision relates to those falsely claiming U.S. citizenship after September 30, 1996 in order to obtain immigration or other government benefits.[83] An exception applies for biological or adopted children of U.S. citizens who were LPRs before their 16th birthdays and who *reasonably* believed they were citizens.[84]

● **EXAMPLE**

Jose is from Guatemala. He entered the United States at the age of six as an LPR, following a petition filed for him by his mother who later filed to become a U.S. citizen. At the time of approval of her application, Jose was 18 years and 3 days old and so just missed the cut off for deriving citizenship from her, which required him to be under 18 years old.[85] However, because all of Jose's younger siblings are U.S. citizens, he has always believed that he was too and so has held himself out to be so in job applications and whenever anyone has asked him questions about his citizenship. Even though he has falsely claimed to be a citizen, most likely he is covered by the exception because, given his family situation, he reasonably believed that he was a citizen.

Finally, INA § 212(a)(6)(D) renders inadmissible foreign nationals who:

- Are stowaways;
- Have encouraged, induced, assisted, abetted, or aided the illegal entry of other non-citizens (also referred to as alien smuggling) other than a spouse, parent, son, or daughter;[86]
- Are the subject of civil penalties for document fraud under INA § 274C; or
- Who have violated the terms of their F-1 student visa status.

---

[83] INA § 212(a)(6)(C)(ii)(I).
[84] INA § 212(a)(6)(C)(ii)(II).
[85] *See* Section E in Chapter 11, Citizenship and Naturalization.
[86] A waiver available under INA § 212(d)(11).

Student visa abusers are required to remain outside the United States for a continuous period of five years after the date of their violation before they can seek to reenter. Where a waiver is available for the misrepresentation related grounds, it is applied for using Form I-601, Application for Waiver of Grounds of Inadmissibility.

B.7. Documentation Requirements: INA § 212(a)(7)

A foreign national seeking to enter the United States who is without required and valid documentation such as a passport, identity card, or other valid entry document that supports the category in which s/he is seeking entry at the time of admission, is inadmissible. Foreign nationals are required to possess passports valid for at least six months beyond the date they are given permission to stay and a valid nonimmigrant visa.[87] Nationals of several countries, many of whom are also eligible to enter the United States through the visa waiver program, are exempted from the six month passport requirement.[88] A waiver of this ground in emergency or other situations, such as unexpected illness that prevents travel, may be available under INA § 212(d).

B.8. Ineligible for Citizenship: INA § 212(a)(8)

Any foreign national who is permanently ineligible for citizenship or who has evaded the draft is inadmissible. The BIA has interpreted this provision as relating to those barred from naturalization due to evasion of military service only.[89]

B.9. Aliens Previously Removed: INA § 212(a)(9)

As previously mentioned, IIRAIRA introduced many legislative changes in immigration law, some of which are reflected in this section. An important change is the introduction of the expedited removal process[90] under INA § 235(b)(1). This allows a CBP officer to remove a foreign national who arrives at a designated port of entry and attempts to enter the United States through fraud, misrepresentation, or without proper documents without a hearing before an immigration judge, but rather through the decision of the immigration officer. Now, any foreign national previously removed from the United States under this process after April 1, 1997 *and* who seeks to reenter the country within 5 years of that removal or 20 years following any subsequent attempt at reentry, is inadmissible.[91]

---

[87] INA § 212(a)(7)(B)(i).
[88] A list of nationals from countries referred to as the "Six Month Club" is available at https://www.cbp.gov/sites/default/files/documents/Six%20Month%20Club%20Update_0.pdf.
[89] *Matter of Kanga*, 22 I&N Dec. 1206 (BIA 2000).
[90] *See* Section C., Chapter 10, Immigration Court Practice and Relief from Removal for further discussion.
[91] INA § 212(a)(9)(A)(i).

Those convicted of *aggravated felony crimes* who seek to reenter the United States at any time after their deportations are inadmissible. A fuller discussion of what constitutes an aggravated felony appears in Section C.2.a.

Any foreign national subject to a deportation order following removal proceedings,[92] or who departed the United States while an order of deportation was outstanding, and who seeks to reenter the country within 10 years of his or her departure, 20 years for subsequent attempts, is inadmissible.[93] Foreign nationals removed under the expedited removal period or who are subject to deportation orders may enter the United States before the applicable time period has passed if s/he has sought and obtained permission from the Attorney General first.[94] The application is filed on Form I-212, Application for Permission to Reapply for Admission into the United States After Deportation or Removal and should include a statement of the equities in the case so that discretion can be exercised favorably.

Aggravated Felony Crimes: A term used to describe certain offenses that severely limit immigration relief available to those convicted of such crimes.

● EXAMPLE

Said is from Egypt. He had previously been in the United States as a student but was deported because he did not maintain his status and in fact was discovered by immigration authorities to be working without permission in a pizzeria. His longtime girlfriend, Sabina, traveled to Egypt so that they could be married. She has tried to live there but suffers from depression, for which she cannot obtain adequate treatment and therefore has returned back to the United States. Sabina wants to apply for Said to come and join her here as she recognizes that he is a great stabilizing influence for her. However, even if the relative petition that she files for Said is approved, he will not be able to apply for an immigrant visa to enter unless it has been more than ten years since he was deported. The other option is to request permission to enter sooner so that Said does not have to wait for the full ten year period to pass. If Sabina is able to demonstrate the extreme hardship she will suffer if Said is not able to join her here, it is possible that the application for the waiver will be granted.

B.9.a. Departing the United States After Being Unlawfully Present: INA § 212(a)(9)(B)

An important concept in immigration law is that of **unlawful presence,** which is defined as presence in the United States after the expiration of a period of authorized stay. It also includes periods in the country when a foreign national entered without inspection and therefore never had permission to be here. The length of exclusion from the United States for unlawful presence will depend on how much time was spent here without permission.

---

[92] These proceedings are discussed in detail in Chapter 10, Immigration Court Practice and Relief from Removal.
[93] INA § 212(a)(9)(A)(ii).
[94] INA § 212(a)(9)(A)(iii).

Any person,

- who has been unlawfully present in the United States for a period of more than one 180 days but less than one year, and
- who *voluntarily* leaves before removal proceedings are initiated

is inadmissible for a period of three years.[95] Interestingly, if the foreign national was placed into removal proceedings and then decided to leave,[96] or accepted an order of **voluntary departure**[97] that would allow him or her to leave at his or her own expense within a given time frame, then s/he would not be subject to the three-year bar.

There are harsher consequences for a foreign national who has been unlawfully present for one year or more. After departure, s/he may not reenter the United States for a period of ten years,[98] whether or not removal proceedings have been initiated.

● **EXAMPLE**

Laila is from Oman. She entered as a visitor for medical treatment and was given permission to stay for six months. If she does not apply to extend her stay, then once her leave ends, she will begin to accrue unlawful presence. If Laila stays 180 days but less than one year after her leave expires and then decides to depart from the country before removal proceedings have begun, she will be unable to return for a period of three years. If Laila is placed into removal proceedings and decides to leave on an order of voluntary departure, she will not trigger the three-year bar. If she stays in the United States for a year or more beyond the six months she was given to stay and then leaves, whether or not she has been placed into removal proceedings, she will not be able to return for a period of ten years.

There has been much discussion about whether the requisite period of the bar can be spent inside the United States. One Administrative Appeals Office, or AAO, decision suggests that it can, *see In re Salles-Vaz* (AAO, Feb. 22, 2005). USCIS Field offices are adjusting those who have legally entered the United States after triggering the three or ten year bar and have waited out the requisite period in the United States before filing their adjustment applications.

---

[95] INA § 212(a)(9)(B)(i)(I).
[96] While this type of departure may not trigger the three-year bar for unlawful presence, leaving the United States while removal proceedings are in progress may result in a deportation order being entered for failing to appear in court or create other inadmissibility issues. *See* INA § 212(a)(6)(b).
[97] Further discussion of this form of relief is in Section B of Chapter 10, Immigration Court Practice and Relief from Removal.
[98] INA § 212(a)(9)(B)(i)(II).

● **EXAMPLE**

Assume Laila had a multiple entry visa that was valid for five years. When she leaves the United States, she triggers the three-year bar. Eight months later, she decides to return to the United States, using the visa that she already has. At the border, the CBP officer asks Laila no questions about her prior entry and stamps her passport, giving her permission to stay for six months as a visitor. While here this time, she resumes her relationship with a prior partner who is a U.S. citizen and they subsequently marry. If Laila applies to adjust her status to an LPR with the USCIS three years after her entry, she will be eligible to do so because she has waited the prerequisite three-year period in order to satisfy the unlawful presence bar. The fact that she has done so in the United States should not bar her adjustment application.

Following the introduction of the unlawful presence provision, guidance on when it would apply was promised through the promulgation of regulations. However, they have yet to be produced. In the absence of regulations, there are several helpful government memos on the subject.[99]

In certain situations, unlawful presence only begins to accrue when immigration authorities commence removal proceedings or when an immigration judge determines that an individual has violated the terms of the nonimmigrant status granted. This is particularly true for students, who are permitted to remain in the United States for duration of status, or D/S. Without a determination, a violation of status will not trigger unlawful presence.

● **EXAMPLE**

Recall Said from Egypt, who was deported for violating his student visa because he was not attending school. Since students are typically granted permission to remain in the United States for the duration of their student status, or D/S, on the surface it would appear that once Said stopped attending school, his visa would have terminated and he would begin to accrue unlawful status. However, under immigration law, that is not the case. He does not begin to accrue unlawful presence until an immigration judge or the USCIS determines that he has violated the conditions of his stay and is no longer a student. Without a determination, a violation of status will not trigger unlawful presence. This may be several years after Said has stopped attending school. Therefore, he may or may not accrue the relevant period of unlawful presence that will trigger a bar to his reentry once he leaves the country.

Foreign nationals in removal proceedings continue to accumulate unlawful presence unless they ultimately prevail in those proceedings. Some exceptions and waivers may be available to ameliorate this ground of inadmissibility. The following categories will not accumulate unlawful presence in certain circumstances:

---

[99] In 2009, USCIS produced the *Consolidation of Guidance Concerning Unlawful Presence for Purposes of Sections 212(a)(9)(B)(i) and 212(a)(9)(C)(i)(I) of the Act*, May 6, 2009, and it is available at http://www.uscis.gov/sites/default/files/USCIS/Laws/Memoranda/Static_Files_Memoranda/2009/revision_redesign_AFM.PDF.

- Minors while they remain under the age of 18 years;
- Applicants for asylum once their applications have been filed, although they may have accrued unlawful presence prior to filing the application; also, working without permission while awaiting a decision on the application will render this protection no longer available;
- Persons protected by family-unity legislation;[100]
- Certain battered women and children;[101] and
- Those designated as unaccompanied minor children who retain that designation throughout their immigration proceedings.[102]

The three- and ten-year bars may be waived for an intending immigrant who is a spouse, son, or daughter of a U.S. citizen or LPR, if excluding the foreign national would cause extreme hardship to the qualifying relative.[103] Therefore, in the case of Said, in order for him to reenter the United States before the requisite period of the bar has expired, he must file a waiver to show that refusing him permission to enter will cause extreme hardship to Sabina, possibly because of her depression and therefore her need for his support. In effect, he will be applying for two waivers, one for the deportation order that requires him to remain outside the country for ten years, and one for the unlawful presence waiver that may bar his reentry for up to ten years, depending on how long he was unlawfully present in the United States before his departure. As discussed in Section G.3.a. of Chapter 6, Family Sponsored Immigration and Permanent Resident Status, the waiver may not be available if there is extreme hardship to a U.S. citizen or LPR child only, but that hardship can be introduced through the effect it has on the qualifying relative.

Case for Discussion 9.9

Moctar is a single father from Mali with two U.S. citizen children, one aged four, and the other six. His six year old has juvenile diabetes and Moctar would not be able to afford medicine for this in Mali. The children's mother is deceased. Moctar entered on a tourist visa nine years ago and overstayed his leave. Moctar took an emergency trip home to visit his ill mother and left the children with a cousin, expecting to be back within a few weeks.

- Will Moctar experience any problems when he arrives at the border?
- If so, is there any relief available to him so that he can reenter to join his children here?

---

[100] For instance, under the Immigration Act of 1990, § 301, or the Legal Immigration Family Equity Act of 2000, § 1504.
[101] INA § 212(a)(9)(B)(iii).
[102] INA § 208(a)(2)(E); Trafficking Victims Protection Reauthorization Act (TVPRA) of 2008, Pub. L. 110-457, 122 Stat. 5044 (2008), § 235(d)(7)(A).
[103] INA § 212(a)(9)(B)(v).

Previously, an application for the extreme hardship waiver could only be made once the intended beneficiary had left the United States and therefore triggered the unlawful presence bar. However, since March 3, 2013, those immediate relatives who would be subject to the bar should they leave the country can apply with the USCIS for a provisional waiver before they leave to process their applications for immigrant visas at the consular office abroad. The stated goal of this change "is to reduce the time that U.S. citizens are separated from their immediate relatives while those family members go through the consular process overseas to obtain an immigrant visa."[104] This means foreign nationals will know whether they meet the criteria to be issued a waiver before they have to leave the country.

According to the posting on the USCIS website, "[A]n individual may seek a provisional unlawful presence waiver if he or she:

- Is physically present in the United States;
- Is at least 17 years of age;
- Is the beneficiary of an approved immigrant visa petition (I-130) classifying him or her as an immediate relative of a U.S. citizen;
- Is actively pursuing the immigrant visa process and has already paid the Department of State immigrant visa processing fee;
- Is not subject to any other grounds of inadmissibility other than unlawful presence; and
- Can demonstrate that the refusal of admission would result in extreme hardship to a U.S. citizen spouse or parent."[105]

An immediate relative would not be eligible for the proposed process if s/he:

- Has an application already pending with USCIS for adjustment of status to LPR;
- Is subject to a final order of removal or reinstatement of a prior removal order;
- May be found inadmissible at the time of the consular interview for reasons other than unlawful presence; or
- Has already been scheduled for an immigrant visa interview at a U.S. Embassy or Consulate abroad.[106]

Application for the waiver is made using Form I-601A, Application for Provisional Unlawful Presence Waiver. Once the waiver is granted, the beneficiary is still required to leave the country in order to process for a visa to return from the consular office that governs his or her country of citizenship. So long as there are no other grounds of inadmissibility that might apply, since

---

[104] USCIS website information on Provisional Unlawful Presence Waiver is available at https://www.uscis.gov/family/family-us-citizens/provisional-waiver/provisional-unlawful-presence-waivers.
[105] An example of the application of the provisional waiver is in Section G.3.a. of Chapter 6, Family Sponsored Immigration and Permanent Resident Status.
[106] Id.

the provisional waiver only deals with the unlawful presence bars, there should be no difficulty with receiving a visa to return to the United States.

> ● **EXAMPLE**
>
> **Wilfredo is from Honduras and entered the United States five years ago by crossing the border through Texas. He recently married a U.S. citizen who has filed a relative petition for his benefit. Wilfredo cannot apply to adjust to an LPR while he remains here because he entered EWI and is not grandfathered under INA § 245(i). He is required to apply for the appropriate visa at the consular office in Honduras. However, once he leaves the country, the unlawful presence bar will prevent Wilfredo from reentering for a period of ten years because he accrued more than one year of unlawful presence here. Once the relative petition for Wilfredo's benefit is approved, he can apply for a provisional waiver in the United States. If it is approved, Wilfredo will have to leave the country and return to Honduras. Once there, he can apply to reenter the United States without having to wait ten years before returning because of the waiver.**

There is a permanent bar against individuals who have either been unlawfully present in the United States for an aggregate period of more than a year or who have been ordered removed, *and* who return or attempt to do so illegally.[107] In other words, those with prior immigration violations who attempt to enter EWI are permanently barred from obtaining LPR status. However, this provision will no longer apply once the foreign national has lived outside of the U.S. for a period of ten years and, prior to reentering, has obtained permission to do so through an approved Form I-212, Application for Permission to Reapply for Admission into the United States After Deportation or Removal.[108]

The permanent bar may be waived for battered women and children if there is a connection between the prior deportation, illegal reentry, or attempted reentry and the abuse.[109] The bar would not preclude a foreign national from seeking immigration relief in the form of cancellation of removal.[110]

The BIA has held that a foreign national who departs the United States with advanced parole does not trigger the three- and ten-year unlawful presence bars.[111] One of the benefits of this decision is that a foreign national who might otherwise have the opportunity to adjust status in the United States but for an inadmissibility issue related to his or her initial EWI entry, for example, may now adjust here once the foreign national returns with advanced parole. This is because, on this arrival, s/he will have been inspected and admitted in compliance with the requirements of INA § 245(a). This decision may not

---

[107] INA § 212(a)(9)(C). This may not be true for some in the jurisdiction of the Ninth Circuit Court of Appeals; see *Duran Gonzalez v. DHS*, 712 F.3d 1271 (9th Cir. 2013). An entry or attempted entry after being removed can also trigger criminal penalties under INA § 276.
[108] *See* INA § 212(a)(9)(C)(ii).
[109] INA § 212(a)(9)(C)(iii).
[110] Detailed discussion of this relief is in Section B.1 of Chapter 10, Immigration Court Practice and Relief from Removal.
[111] *See Matter of Arrabally, Yerrabelly*, 25 I&N Dec. 771 (BIA 2012).

benefit those in a preference category who can only adjust if they are currently in a lawful nonimmigrant status or who may have worked without permission, as they will fall foul of INA § 245(c). This is discussed further in Section G.1, Chapter 6, Family Sponsored Immigration and Permanent Resident Status.

● **EXAMPLE**

Esther is from El Salvador. She applied for and received Temporary Protected Status, or TPS, soon after she entered EWI back in the summer of 2001, following the earthquake in her country and its designation for TPS in March of that year. She is married to Jose, who is a U.S. citizen from Puerto Rico. However, Esther has been unable to adjust her status here because of her EWI entry. Now that she is on TPS, Esther is able to apply for advanced parole to visit with her family back in her country. She has not seen them for a long time. Once she returns, she will be able to file an adjustment application in this country, because she will have been inspected and paroled as required by INA § 245(a).

B.10. Miscellaneous Grounds: INA § 212(a)(10)

Rounding out the inadmissibility provisions are miscellaneous grounds that reflect current public policy concerns. The following are inadmissible:

- Polygamists coming to the United States to practice polygamy
- Guardians required to accompany helpless inadmissible foreign nationals
- Those retaining children outside the United States in violation of a court order or who assist others in such activity
- Those who have voted in any Federal, State, or local election when ineligible to do so
- U.S. citizens who have renounced their citizenship to avoid taxation

An exception is available for voters who are the biological or adopted children of U.S. citizens who were LPRs before their 16th birthday and reasonably believed they were citizens at the time they voted,[112] and for child abductors in limited circumstances.[113]

B.11. Waiver to Facilitate Temporary Admission of Nonimmigrants: INA § 212(d)(3)

As we have seen, most waivers are tied to a specific inadmissibility provision. However, INA § 212(d)(3) offers a general waiver for those seeking to enter the United States for a temporary, nonimmigrant purpose. It is known as a general waiver that, in the discretion of the attorney general, will forgive all

---

[112] INA § 212(a)(10)(D)(ii).
[113] INA § 212(a)(10)(C)(iii).

inadmissibility grounds other than for those whose activities relate to espionage and sabotage,[114] other unlawful activity,[115] attempts to overthrow the government,[116] potentially serious adverse foreign policy consequences,[117] and participation in Nazi[118] or genocide activities.[119]

In order to determine if the waiver should be granted, the USCIS will consider the following factors and balance the facts of the case:

- The risk of harm to society if the applicant is admitted,
- The seriousness of the applicant's immigration or criminal law violation, if any, and
- The nature of the applicant's reasons for wishing to enter the United States.[120]

The reasons for entry do not need to be compelling.[121] Both DHS and the consular officer must agree to grant the waiver.[122] Applications for these waivers are made on Form I-192, Application for Advance Permission to Enter as Nonimmigrant.

Having completed our survey of the grounds of inadmissibility, we now review deportation, which refers to a different section of the statute. As we go through, keep in mind that inadmissibility grounds are typically broader than their deportation counterpart.

C. Grounds of Deportation: INA § 237

Any foreign national physically within the United States generally may only be removed or deported if there is a deportation order authorizing the removal.[123] The order will only be issued after a hearing which allows a foreign national to apply for relief from removal and ensures that s/he receives due process of the law before such an important decision is made.[124] This hearing is known as a removal proceeding and is conducted before an immigration judge who is the decision maker for all grounds of deportation.[125] In this section we only address

---

[114] INA § 212(a)(3)(A)(i)(I).
[115] INA § 212(a)(3)(A)(ii).
[116] INA § 212(a)(3)(A)(iii).
[117] INA § 212(a)(3)(C).
[118] INA § 212(a)(3)(E)(i).
[119] INA § 212(a)(3)(E)(ii).
[120] *Matter of Hranka*, 16 I&N Dec. 491, 492 (BIA 1978).
[121] *Id.*
[122] INA § 212(a)(3)(B).
[123] INA § 237(a).
[124] In limited circumstances, a decision regarding removal is made by an ICE Field Director in administrative or expedited removal proceedings. Further discussion is in Section C.2.a.
[125] Information regarding these hearings is discussed in detail in Chapter 10, Immigration Court Practice and Relief from Removal.

in detail those deportation grounds that are in some way different from similar inadmissibility grounds or do not exist as an inadmissibility ground at all, in order to avoid duplication of information.

C.1. Inadmissible at Time of Entry or Adjustment of Status or Violates Status: INA § 237(a)(1)

Sometimes, foreign nationals may have obtained permission to enter or remain in the United States even though, at the time of the grant, they were not entitled to that status for one reason or another. For instance, the foreign national may have engaged in a fraudulent marriage in order to be granted lawful permanent residency. This ground, inadmissible at the time of entry or adjustment of status, allows the USCIS, once it becomes aware of the illegality, to request the foreign national be divested of the status improperly granted and to be deported. It applies to any foreign national who:

- Was inadmissible at the time of his or her entry into the country or adjustment of status to a permanent resident;
- Is present in the United States in violation of the law;
- Fails to maintain the status in which s/he was admitted;
- Has had terminated any conditional permanent resident status that may have been granted under the INA § 216 or § 216A;
- Knowingly encouraged induced, assisted, abetted, or aided any other [foreign national] to enter or attempt to enter the United States other than an immediate relative of a person eligible for benefits under the Immigration Act 1990 § 301(a), the [foreign national] smuggling provision; and
- Has procured a visa or other documentation through marriage fraud.[126]

Although misrepresentation at time of entry is a serious offense, a waiver may be available under INA § 237(a)(1)(H) for those who have engaged in misrepresentation and who are the spouse, parent, son, or daughter of a U.S. citizen or LPR. The foreign national must be in possession of an immigrant visa or other document and be otherwise admissible, but for the failure to have the appropriate documentation because of the fraud. These are the only requirements necessary to demonstrate eligibility for the waiver, since extreme hardship is not a factor. However, it may be wise to present evidence of hardship in any event, since an immigration judge must exercise his or her discretion in deciding whether to grant the waiver. One caveat to eligibility for this waiver is that the family relationship that provides the ability to obtain relief cannot emanate from the fraudulent marriage.

---

[126] INA § 237(a)(1).

> **● EXAMPLE**
>
> Nyonontee, a citizen of Liberia, wants to come to the United States to live. Her efforts to obtain a visitor's visa have not been successful. A friend tells her that he can arrange for her to marry a U.S. citizen for a few thousand dollars so that she can get an immigrant visa to come here permanently. If Nyonontee agrees to enter into a marriage that is not genuine, she will be engaging in marriage fraud and, if caught, will be subject to deportation for this violation of immigration law because she entered into the United States by fraudulent means. However, if that fraudulent marriage later ends and Nyonontee subsequently enters into a *bona fide* marriage with a U.S. citizen or an LPR, she may be eligible to receive a waiver from this ground of deportation if she is caught and placed into removal proceedings because of the earlier fraudulent marriage.

C.2. Criminal Offenses: INA § 237(a)(2)(A)

While deportation for criminal offenses is similar to the provisions that would make a person inadmissible, there is an important distinction; for a foreign national to be deportable, there has to be a *conviction* for certain crimes. Recall that for a foreign national to be inadmissible, s/he need only have *admitted* to the commission of certain acts or essential elements of a crime, allowing for a broader interpretation of what would make a foreign national inadmissible, as opposed to the factors that would make the same person removable or deportable. It may be useful to refer back to Section B.2.a for an explanation of the definition of conviction for the purposes of immigration law as it applies to the grounds of inadmissibility.

C.2.a. General Crimes: INA § 237(a)(2)(A)

Under INA § 237(a)(2)(A), any person is deportable who has been *convicted* of certain crimes after admission to the United States. These crimes are:

- One crime involving moral turpitude, or CIMT, committed within five years after admission to the United States; the crime in question must have the potential to have imposed a sentence of confinement of one year or more, even if the judge ultimately decides to issue a shorter sentence;
- Two CIMTs, not arising out of a single scheme of criminal misconduct, committed at any time; whether or not crimes arise out of a single scheme will depend on whether they "were performed in furtherance of a single criminal episode... or where two crimes flow from and are the natural consequences of a single act of criminal misconduct;"[127]
- An aggravated felony crime;
- High speed flight from law enforcement/immigration officials; and
- Failure to register as a sex offender.

---

[127] *Matter of Adetiba*, 20 I&N Dec. 506 (BIA 1992).

However, a convicted person, other than a sex offender, who is ultimately granted a full and unconditional pardon by the President or a governor of a state, would not be deportable.[128]

An important concept in immigration law is that of an "aggravated felony" crime, which has a specific meaning in immigration law. The INA § 101(a)(43) delineates certain specific crimes as aggravated felonies, such as murder, rape, sexual abuse of a minor, and drug trafficking. Others require a sentence of imprisonment of one year or more to be imposed before they will meet the definition of an aggravated felony crime, while still other offenses based on fraud require monetary loss exceeding $10,000. These offenses must also meet the definition of a crime of violence, as defined under Title 18 U.S.C. § 16. It should be noted that, at the time of writing, there are serious challenges to subsection (b) of this provision, following the U.S. Supreme Court's decision in *Johnson v. United States*, 135 S. Ct. 939 (2015). In that case, the Court struck down a provision in the Armed Career Criminal Act of 1984, or ACCA, finding it was unconstitutionally vague. Because the language and judicial application of the ACCA is similar to that of a crime of violence in the INA, it is likely to also be found to be void for vagueness. In fact to date, the 5th, 7th, and 9th Circuit Courts of Appeals have so held and other courts are considering the issue.

There are many factors that need to be considered in order to determine what is and what is not an aggravated felony crime. One important factor is the different treatment that similar crimes may receive under state law or even in immigration law. For instance, a misdemeanor crime in one state may in fact be an aggravated felony crime for immigration purposes.

● EXAMPLE

Mary Jane, a 14-year old minor, is dating Vlod, a 17-year old refugee from Ukraine. They agree to have sex. Under Pennsylvania law, this would not be a criminal offense, since minors between the ages of 13 to 15 can consent to sexual activity with peers within a four-year age range. However, in Ohio, a similar activity would be punishable with a fine of $1,000, because Vlod is less than four years older than Mary Jane. This would be considered a misdemeanor offense. However, for immigration purposes, it is possible that the Ohio conviction meets the definition of sexual abuse of a minor.[129]

Because of the discrepancies in treatment of various crimes by the states, deciding which are aggravated felonies is one of the most litigated areas in immigration law and requires constant review of case law at both the level of the BIA and the various Circuit Courts, leading to a very confusing picture, since what may be an aggravated felony in one Circuit may not be in another. The reason why it is important to determine whether a foreign national has been convicted of an aggravated felony crime is because, typically, there will be limited immigration

---

[128] INA § 237(a)(2)(A)(vi).
[129] *Matter of Small*, 23 I&N Dec. 448 (BIA 2002).

relief, if any, available to him or her. For instance, a foreign national convicted of an aggravated felony crime is ineligible for asylum because such convictions are considered to be particularly serious crimes and therefore exclude this form of relief.[130] The foreign national may also be disqualified from withholding of removal if the sentence imposed for the aggravated felony crime was a term of imprisonment of at least five years. If this is the case, then the foreign national may only qualify for the more limited relief of either withholding or deferral of removal under the Convention Against Torture.[131] Other forms of immigration relief that are unavailable include cancellation of removal[132] and voluntary departure.[133]

Although aggravated felony crimes are not specifically enumerated as a ground of inadmissibility, many of the offenses constitute a CIMT and would therefore render the person inadmissible under that ground. However, there may be the possibility of qualifying for a waiver of inadmissibility under INA § 212(h).[134]

In addition, those convicted of aggravated felony crimes who have not been lawfully admitted to the United States or have been granted lawful permanent residency on a conditional basis are subject to administrative or expedited removal proceedings under INA § 238.[135] This means that an immigration judge does not have jurisdiction to decide whether or not the foreign national should be deported. Instead, that decision is made by a designated official, typically a Field Director with ICE. Those subject to expedited removal proceedings are entitled to reasonable notice of the charges, to inspect any evidence presented, rebut any charges, and apply for any relief that does not require the exercise of discretion. Removal of the foreign national could take place 14 days after this type of order of removal has been issued.[136]

Because classifying a foreign national as an aggravated felon can lead to particularly harsh consequences that all but forestall any immigration relief, it is important that advice be sought from an immigration lawyer who is also versed in criminal law, or for an immigration lawyer to work closely with the criminal lawyer representing the foreign national in the criminal proceedings, so that this type of conviction can be avoided, where possible. Consideration should also be given to obtaining post-conviction relief, where necessary and available, especially where the designation of aggravated felon is sentence-driven. In such cases, it may be prudent to seek sentence reduction since it will be given full faith and credit in immigration court, regardless of the reason for the request.[137]

---

[130] *See* Section A.5.c of Chapter 5, Asylum and Other Humanitarian Relief.
[131] *See* Section F of Chapter 5, Asylum and Other Humanitarian Relief.
[132] *See* Section I.2 of Chapter 10, Immigration Court Practice and Relief from Removal.
[133] *See* Section B.1 of Chapter 10, Immigration Court Practice and Relief from Removal.
[134] *See* Immigrant Legal Resource Center, *Update on INA § 212(h) Defense Strategies: Many Permanent Residents Are Not Subject to the § 212(h) Permanent Resident Bar; The Eleventh Circuit Reaffirms § 212(h) as a Direct Waiver of Deportability; Additional Minor Drug Offenses are Waivable Under § 212(h); Using § 212(h) When LPR Cancellation Is Not an Option.*
[135] Further discussion is in Section C of Chapter 10, Immigration Court Practice and Relief from Removal.
[136] INA § 238(b)(3).
[137] *Matter of Song*, 23 I&N Dec. 173 (BIA 2001).

Other forms of modifying or vacating a conviction will only be recognized for immigration purposes if they relate to a procedural or substantive defect in the underlying criminal proceedings.[138]

A foreign national convicted of a crime prior to the enactment of IIRAIRA may be eligible to apply for relief under the provisions of the now repealed INA § 212(c).[139]

C.2.b. Controlled Substances: INA § 237(a)(2)(B)

A foreign national convicted of any offense relating to a controlled substance, except possession of 30 grams or less of marijuana for personal use, is subject to deportation. While similar to the comparable inadmissibility provision, this ground requires a conviction and not just an admission to elements of the offense.[140] A foreign national who is a drug abuser or addict is also deportable.[141]

C.2.c. Firearms Offenses: INA § 237(a)(2)(C)

The provision relating to firearms offenses does not have a comparable inadmissibility ground and creates a separate basis for deportation. Essentially, any foreign national convicted of certain firearms offenses, including the purchase, sale, or possession of a weapon defined as a firearm or destructive weapon under Title 18 United States Code § 921(a), is deportable. Because there is no equivalent inadmissibility ground for a firearms offense, however, in certain circumstances a foreign national with this type of conviction may still be able to adjust. This is because the foreign national, even though deportable for the firearms offense, would not be inadmissible for the same offense because no comparable ground of inadmissibility exists.[142] Similarly, this is also true for a ground of inadmissibility where there is no counterpart ground of deportation.[143]

● EXAMPLE

Ronald, a Jamaican national, has been an LPR for many years, having entered the United States following a relative petition filed for his benefit by his mother. He was recently convicted of possession of a firearm without a license and is therefore deportable. However, he is married to a U.S. citizen. If his wife files a relative petition for him that is approved while he is in removal proceedings, he can apply to the immigration judge to be admitted as an LPR, despite the firearms conviction, and thereby avoid deportation.

---

[138] *Matter of Pickering*, 23 I&N Dec. 621 (BIA 2003).
[139] *INS v. St. Cyr*, 533 U.S. 289 (2001). This is discussed in Section I.3. of Chapter 10, Immigration Court Practice and Relief from Removal.
[140] INA § 237(a)(2)(B)(i).
[141] INA § 237(a)(2)(B)(ii).
[142] *Matter of Gabryelsky*, 20 I&N Dec. 750 (BIA 1993).
[143] *Matter of Rainford*, 20 I&N Dec. 598 (BIA 1992).

C.2.d. Miscellaneous Crimes: INA § 237(a)(2)(D)

Any foreign national convicted of miscellaneous crimes, including treason, sedition, and failure to register for Selective Service, is deportable. There are no comparable inadmissibility grounds.

C.2.e. Domestic Violence Crimes: INA § 237(a)(2)(E)

IIRAIRA added domestic violence related crimes entered after September 30, 1996 as grounds for deportation. Under this provision, a foreign national who at any time after admission is convicted of a domestic violence crime, stalking, child abuse, child neglect, or child abandonment is deportable.[144] A crime of domestic violence is defined by referring to the definition of a **crime of violence** under 18 U.S.C. § 16 and includes acts by:

- Current or former spouses,
- A person similarly situated to a spouse, such as a long-time partner or common law spouse,
- A person who shares a child in common, and
- A current or former cohabitee.

There is no waiver available for this ground of deportation. However, there is an exception permitting the Attorney General to waive its application with respect to an abused foreign national who was not the main perpetrator of the violence in the relationship. The abused foreign national must have been acting in self defense; violated a protection from abuse order intended to protect her; either pled guilty to, committed, was arrested, or was convicted of a crime that did not cause serious bodily injury; and was connected to the abuse suffered.

While a foreign national enjoined under a protection from abuse order would not be deportable because the order originates from civil proceedings, a conviction for violating that order would be a deportable offense.[145]

Case for Discussion　9.10

Bashir, a refugee from Sudan, settled here with his family a few years ago and is now an LPR. Following an altercation with Aisha, Bashir's wife, in the couple's home, the police were called and he was arrested. He is to be charged with aggravated assault.

- What immigration consequences might flow if Bashir is convicted of this offense?

---

[144] INA § 237(a)(2)(E)(i).
[145] INA § 237(a)(2)(E)(ii).

C.3. Failure to Register and Falsification of Documents: INA § 237(a)(3)

With the exception of foreign diplomats and representatives, INA § 261 requires the government to register anyone applying for a visa to enter the country. Once here, the location of the foreign national must still be reported until s/he becomes a U.S. citizen. There are specific reporting requirements, which, if violated, are grounds for deportation.

C.3.a. Change of Address: INA § 237(a)(3)(A)

Certain foreign nationals present in the United States are required to report a change of address to the DHS within ten days of the change.[146] This includes nonimmigrants who will be present for more than 30 days and LPRs.[147] Form AR-11, Change of Address, is used to note the change and can be submitted electronically. While rarely if ever enforced, failure to provide this updated information will render the foreign national deportable unless there is evidence to support a finding that the omission was not willful or was reasonably excusable.[148]

C.3.b. False Documents: INA § 237(a)(3)(B)

Any foreign national convicted of failing to register, or of certain federal laws relating to fraud and misuse of a visa, is deportable. The grounds of document fraud and falsely claiming citizenship also contained in this provision are identical to the inadmissibility grounds discussed in Section B.6.c.

C.4. Security Related Grounds: INA § 237(a)(4)

This ground is identical to the inadmissibility ground and is discussed in Section B.3.

C.5. Public Charge: INA § 237(a)(5)

Foreign nationals who, within five years of admission or adjustment of status, become a public charge for reasons that have not arisen since entry into the United States, are deportable. IIRAIRA restricts the availability of means-tested benefits to most immigrants during the first five years after admission to the country. Refugees and asylees are exempt from this requirement. This provision is rarely if ever used to support removal proceedings.

---

[146] INA § 265.
[147] INA § 262.
[148] INA § 237(a)(3)(A).

> **● EXAMPLE**
>
> Boris entered the United States from Russia following an approved relative petition filed for his benefit by his daughter, Irina. At the time of the application, Irina completed an affidavit of support, confirming her ability to support her father at the appropriate financial limits. Subsequent to his entry, Irina had an accident and is no longer able to work. Boris visits his local public welfare office to claim benefits to live on. Since the situation causing him to need financial assistance occurred after his entry to the United States, he is unlikely to be deemed a public charge if any benefits are granted to him.[149]

C.6. Unlawful Voters: INA § 237(a)(6)

This ground is identical to the inadmissibility ground in Section B.10.

D. Inadmissibility vs. Deportation

The individual grounds of inadmissibility and deportation have some overlap. It may be helpful to view these in Table 9.2.

Table 9.2 Comparison of Inadmissibility and Deportation Statutory Provisions

Grounds	Inadmissibility: INA § 212	Deportation: INA § 237
Health	Health, INA § 212(a)(1)	No Equivalent Ground
Criminal Offenses	Crimes Involving Moral Turpitude, INA § 212(a)(2)(A)(i)(I)	Crimes Involving Moral Turpitude, INA § 237(a)(2)(A)(i)
	Controlled Substances, INA § 212(a)(2)(A)(i)(II) and INA § 212(a)(2)(C)	Controlled Substances, INA § 237(a)(2)(B)(i)
	Multiple Criminal Offenses, INA § 212(a)(2)(B)	Multiple Criminal Convictions, INA § 237(a)(2)(A)(ii)
	No Equivalent Ground	Aggravated Felonies, INA § 237(a)(2)(A)(iii)

---

[149] Because Irina completed an affidavit of support for Boris, she could be liable to repay any benefits Boris receives, although given her health situation, it is extremely unlikely she will be pursued for them. The relationship between eligibility for public benefits and immigration status is complex. *See* https://www.nilc.org/issues/economic-support/table_ovrw_fedprogs/ for further details.

Grounds	Inadmissibility: INA § 212	Deportation: INA § 237
	No Equivalent Ground	Firearms and Explosive Devices, INA § 237(a)(2)(C)
	No Equivalent Ground	Domestic Violence, INA § 237(a)(2)(E)
Security and Related Grounds	Security and Related Grounds, INA § 212(a)(3)	Security and Related Grounds, INA § 237(a)(4)
Public Charge	Public Charge INA § 212(a)(4)	Public Charge, INA § 237(a)(5)
Labor Certification and Qualification of Certain Immigrants	Labor Certification and Qualification of Certain Immigrants, INA § 212(a)(5)	No Equivalent Ground
Illegal Entrants and Other Immigration Violators	Illegal Entrants and other Immigration Violators, INA § 212(a)(6)(C)	No Equivalent Ground
	No Equivalent Ground	Inadmissible at Time of Entry or Adjustment of Status or Violates Status, INA § 237(a)(1)
	Falsely Claiming Citizenship, INA § 212(a)(6)(C)(ii)	Falsely Claiming Citizenship, INA § 237(a)(3)(D)(i)
Documentation Requirements	Documentation Requirements, INA § 212(a)(7)	No Equivalent Ground
	No Equivalent Ground	Failure to Register and Falsification of Documents, INA § 237(a)(3)(B) and (C)
Ineligible for Citizenship	Ineligible for Citizenship, INA § 212(a)(8)	No Equivalent Ground
Unlawful Presence Bars	Unlawful Presence Bars, INA § 212(a)(9)(B)	No Equivalent Ground
	Foreign Nationals Previously Removed, INA § 212(a)(9)(C)	No Equivalent Ground
Miscellaneous Grounds	Practicing Polygamists, INA § 212(a)(10)(A)	No Equivalent Ground
	Guardian Required to Accompany Helpless Foreign National, INA § 212(a)(10)(B)	No Equivalent Ground
	International Child Abduction, INA § 212(a)(10)(C)	No Equivalent Ground
	Unlawful Voters, INA § 212(a)(10)(D)(i)	Unlawful Voters, INA § 237(a)(6)(A)
	Renouncing Citizenship to Avoid Taxation, INA § 212(a)(10)(E)	No Equivalent Ground

It may also be helpful to see the waivers available for various inadmissibility and deportation grounds as shown in Table 9.3.

Table 9.3 Waivers to Ameliorate Inadmissibility or Deportation

Grounds	Inadmissibility: INA § 212	Deportation: INA § 237	Waiver Available
Health	Health, INA § 212(a)(1)	No Equivalent Ground	INA § 212(g), Except Drug Addicts or Abusers
Criminal Offenses	Crimes Involving Moral Turpitude, INA § 212(a)(2)(A)(i)(I)	Crimes Involving Moral Turpitude, INA § 237(a)(2)(A)(i)	INA § 212(h), Extreme Hardship to U.S. Citizen or LPR Spouse, Parent, Son, or Daughter; INA § 237(a)(2)(iv), Pardon Required from the President or Governor
	Controlled Substances, INA § 212(a)(2)(A)(i)(II) and INA § 212(a)(2)(C)	Controlled Substances, INA § 237(2)(a)(B)(i)	INA § 212(h) and INA § 237(a)(2)(B)(i), Excludes 30 Grams or Less of Marijuana Only
	Multiple Criminal Offenses, INA § 212(a)(2)(B)	Multiple Criminal Offenses, INA § 237(a)(2)(A)(ii)	INA § 212(h), Extreme Hardship to U.S. Citizen or LPR Spouse, Parent, Son, or Daughter; INA § 237(a)(2)(A)(vi), Pardon Required from the President or Governor
	No Equivalent Ground	Aggravated Felonies, INA § 237(a)(2)(A)(iii)	INA § 237(a)(2)(iv), Pardon Required from the President or Governor
	No Equivalent Ground	Firearms and Explosive Devices, INA § 237(a)(2)(C)	No Waiver Available
	No Equivalent Ground	Domestic Violence, INA § 237(a)(2)(E)	No Waiver Available
Security and Related Grounds	Security and Related Grounds, INA § 212(a)(3)	Security and Related Grounds, INA § 237(a)(4)	INA § 212(a)(3)(B)(ii), Exceptions Available for Inadmissible Spouse or Child Who Did Not or Could Not Reasonably Have Known of the Terrorist Activities of Principal or Have Renounced Such Activity; INA § 212(a)(3)(C), Those Inadmissible or Deportable for Potentially Serious Adverse Foreign Policy Consequences for the United

Grounds	Inadmissibility: INA § 212	Deportation: INA § 237	Waiver Available
			States; INA § 212(a)(3)(D), Waiver for Those Involved in Totalitarian or Communist Activities
Public Charge	Public Charge, INA § 212(a)(4)	Public Charge, INA § 237(a)(5)	No Waiver Available
Labor Certification and Qualification of Certain Immigrants	Labor Certification and Qualification of Certain Immigrants, INA § 212(a)(5)	No Equivalent Ground	INA § 212(k), Inadmissibility Was Not Known to and Could Not Be Ascertained by the Exercise of Reasonable Diligence
Illegal Entrants and other Immigration Violators	Illegal Entrants and Other Immigration Violators, INA § 212(a)(6)(C)	No Equivalent Ground	INA § 212(i), Extreme Hardship to U.S. Citizen or LPR Spouse or Parent
	No Equivalent Ground	Inadmissible at Time of Entry or Adjustment of Status or Violates Status, INA § 237(a)(1)	INA § 237(a)(1)(H), Is the Spouse, Parent, Son, or Daughter of a U.S. Citizen or LPR Now in Possession of an Immigrant Visa and Was Otherwise Admissible at the Time of Earlier Admission, but for the Misrepresentation or Fraud That Facilitated It
	Falsely Claiming Citizenship, INA § 212(a)(6)(C)(ii)	Falsely Claiming Citizenship, INA § 237(a)(3)(D)(i)	INA § 212(a)(6)(C)(ii)(II) and INA § 237(a)(3)(D)(ii), Exception for Inadmissibility and Deportation for Those Who Permanently Resided in the United States Before Their 16th Birthday and Reasonably Believed S/he Was a U.S. Citizen
Documentation Requirements	Documentation Requirements, INA § 212(a)(7)	No Equivalent Ground	INA § 212(k), Inadmissibility Was Not Known to a Foreign National and Could Not be Ascertained by the Exercise of Reasonable Diligence
	No Equivalent Ground	Failure to Register and Falsification of Documents, INA § 237(a)(3)(B) and (C)(i)	INA § 237(a)(3)(B) None; INA § 237(a)(3)(C)(ii), LPRs for Whom This Is a First Offense and Penalty Incurred Solely as a Result of Assisting Spouse or Child Only
Ineligible for Citizenship	Ineligible for Citizenship, INA § 212(a)(8)	No Equivalent Ground	No Waiver Available

continued

Chapter 9: Grounds of Inadmissibility and Deportation

Grounds	Inadmissibility: INA § 212	Deportation: INA § 237	Waiver Available
Unlawful Presence Bars	Unlawful Presence Bars, INA § 212(a)(9)(B)	No Equivalent Ground	INA § 212(a)(9)(B)(v), Extreme Hardship to U.S. Citizen or LPR Spouse or Parent
	Foreign Nationals Previously Removed, INA § 212(a)(9)(C)	No Equivalent Ground	INA § 212(a)(9)(C)(iii), Waiver for VAWA Self-Petitioner If There Is a Connection Between the Battery or Extreme Cruelty and the Foreign National's Departure from the United States
Miscellaneous Grounds	Practicing Polygamists, INA § 212(a)(10)(A)	No Equivalent Ground	No Waiver Available
	Guardian Required to Accompany Helpless Foreign National, INA § 212(a)(10)(B)	No Equivalent Ground	No Waiver Available
	International Child Abduction, INA § 212(a)(10)(C)	No Equivalent Ground	INA § 212(a)(10)(C)(iii), Exception for Government Officials Acting in Scope of Authority, Designated by Secretary of State or the Child Is in a Hague Convention Country
	Unlawful Voters, INA § 212(a)(10)(D)(i)	Unlawful Voters, INA § 237(a)(6)(A)	INA § 212(a)(10)(D)(ii) and INA § 237(a)(6)(B), Exception for Inadmissibility and Deportation for Those Who Permanently Resided in the United States Before Their 16th Birthday and Reasonably Believed S/he Was a Citizen
	Renouncing Citizenship to Avoid Taxation, INA § 212(a)(10)(E)	No Equivalent Ground	No Waiver Available

E. Agencies Involved in Inadmissibility and Deportation Decision Making

Now that we have analyzed the various grounds of inadmissibility and deportation, we can begin to review which agencies make the decisions about which ground will apply in a particular case.

Whether a foreign national is charged with inadmissibility or deportation will be clear from the Notice to Appear,[150] or NTA, that s/he has received, notifying that proceedings to remove him or her from the United States have begun. This is essentially the charging document that initiates legal proceedings in immigration court against any foreign national who the government seeks to remove from the United States. While removal proceedings are discussed in depth in Chapter 10, Immigration Court Practice and Relief from Removal, it is important to note the ways in which those proceedings have a bearing on inadmissibility and deportation. For instance, different standards and burdens of proof apply to each. A charge of inadmissibility requires a foreign national to prove that s/he is entitled to be admitted clearly and beyond a doubt,[151] whereas a deportation charge places the onus on the government to establish that the person is removable by the higher standard of clear and convincing evidence.[152] Since major legal consequences can result from the classification of a foreign national as either inadmissible or deportable, it is important to assess carefully each case and all documentation to determine which category actually applies to the foreign national rather than simply accepting the government's classification.

E.1. The Decision Makers

The structure of the immigration system was briefly covered in Chapter 1. We now review the role of some of these agencies in determining whether a foreign national is admissible or deportable.

E.1.a. U.S. Consulates

In many cases, the first opportunity to determine a foreign national's admissibility will be at the U.S. consular office abroad, conducted by State Department officials who will assess eligibility for a particular visa. A consular officer can either grant or deny an application for entry to the United States. However, unlike an application for admission that is made in country, applications filed abroad are not subject to any form of judicial review by a court.[153] Therefore there is no formal process to challenge a denial of an application. Where a foreign national is inadmissible but eligible for a waiver to forgive the inadmissibility ground, the application must be filed with the USCIS at one of its designated posts abroad and not with the consular office.

E.1.b. Enforcement Agencies

All agencies within the DHS have authority to determine whether a foreign national should be admitted or placed into removal proceedings and to issue

---

[150] Prior to IIRAIRA, the charging document was called an Order to Show Cause.
[151] INA § 240(c)(2)(A).
[152] INA § 240(c)(3)(A).
[153] *Kerry v. Din*, 576 U.S. ___, 135 S. Ct. 2128 (2015).

the NTA, if necessary.[154] For example, a CBP officer would determine the admissibility of Baraka from Yemen, in Case for Discussion 9.1, because Baraka is seeking to re-enter the country. The officer would then place him into removal proceedings by issuing him the appropriate papers. Similarly, following the raid on Cala's work place by ICE officers, they would most likely ask her a number of questions to establish that she is not a U.S. citizen or national and therefore can be referred to an immigration judge, who will decide whether she should be deported. The USCIS has authority to admit a foreign national seeking to adjust status to that of a permanent resident or to refer such a person to an immigration judge if s/he did not meet the criteria for a grant and had violated a condition of stay in the United States.

E.1.c. Executive Office for Immigration Review

As discussed in Chapter 1, the Executive Office for Immigration Review, or EOIR, is a branch of the Department of Justice and has the authority to determine the admissibility or deportability and eligibility for waivers of those placed under its jurisdiction in removal proceedings. It consists of immigration judges and the BIA. The role of the EOIR is discussed in greater detail in Chapter 10, Immigration Court Practice and Relief from Removal.

E.2. Comparison of the Grounds

As our survey of the grounds of inadmissibility and deportation show, there are many differences between the two. The main distinguishing factors are contained in Table 9.4.

Table 9.4. General Comparison of Inadmissibility and Deportation

INADMISSIBILITY	DEPORTATION
Broader: ten grounds of inadmissibility with numerous subsections	Narrower: only six grounds of deportation and few subsections
Burden on the foreign national to prove entitled to be admitted clearly and beyond a doubt	Burden on the government to establish deportability by clear and convincing evidence
Most inadmissibility decisions are made by consular officers or at the border by CBP officers, without administrative review	An immigration judge decides a foreign national's deportability in legal proceedings where legal representation is available, so long as it is at no cost to the government

---

[154] 8 C.F.R. § 239.1(a).

F. Conclusion

The concepts of inadmissibility and deportation can be complex but are essential to determining who can stay and who must leave the United States. While there is considerable overlap between the two categories, they serve different functions, depending on the immigration status of the foreign national. Now that we have a basic understanding of who is permitted to enter or remain in the United States, we will review the role of the immigration courts in determining who is able to be admitted and who is to be removed or deported.

Immigration Court Practice and Relief from Removal

Key Terms and Acronyms

Accredited Representatives
Administrative Closure
Appeals Practice
Board of Immigration Appeals
Cancellation of Removal
Expedited Removal
Federal Court Practice
Immigration Judge
Individual Hearing
Mandatory Detention
Master Calendar
Motions Practice
Notice of Hearing
Notice to Appear
Prosecutorial Discretion
Removal Order
Respondent
Voluntary Departure

Chapter Objectives

- Understand the basics of immigration court practice
- Analyze Notice to Appear and Notice of Hearing
- Understand prosecutorial discretion and its uses
- Review cancellation of removal in its many forms

Removal or deportation is the means by which the U.S. government sends a foreign national back to his or her country or to a third country because s/he is present in the U.S. in violation of the law. A person can become entangled in the removal process for many different reasons. However, the general rule is that each person is entitled to due process of the law and therefore must see an immigration judge who will decide whether the foreign national is entitled to remain or must leave. There are several circumstances when this rule would not apply and they are discussed later.

As we stated in Chapter 9, Grounds of Inadmissibility and Deportation, Congress passes legislation that contains rules regarding which foreign nationals can stay in the United States and which must leave. It may be useful to review that chapter before continuing because many of the concepts raised there are also applicable here. Citizens of the United States have the greatest protection against deportation because they cannot be removed unless they undergo a process of **denaturalization**. Every other category of person in the United States can be placed into removal proceedings if s/he has violated the immigration laws in some way.

> **Denaturalization:** A process by which a person who became a U.S. citizen by application can be stripped of that status, typically because citizenship was acquired fraudulently or through some withholding of critical relevant information.

During removal proceedings, the foreign national has the opportunity to apply for different types of relief from removal, some of which have already been discussed. In this chapter, we analyze other forms of relief that are available only in the removal context. We review the role of immigration judges in the removal process and discuss who is permitted to provide representation in proceedings. We also discuss the appeals process for those who might be dissatisfied with the judge's ruling and briefly discuss the possibility of judicial review in the circuit courts.

Immigration removal proceedings involve dealing with the Executive Office for Immigration Review, or EOIR. It is an administrative body within the Department of Justice and controls the immigration courts where cases are heard. Judges within the EOIR are administrative law judges and are generally referred to as immigration judges, or IJs. A typical removal case will begin in immigration court, presided over by an immigration judge who will decide whether or not a person should be ordered removed. From there, either party to the proceeding can appeal the decision to the Board of Immigration Appeals, also referred to as the BIA or the Board. This is the highest appellate body within EOIR.

Any decision made by the BIA is considered final and cannot be further contested administratively as there is no higher administrative court. Any additional challenges to decisions of the BIA must be made to the United States Court of Appeals for the circuit in which the case originated. In rare cases, the U.S. Supreme Court may decide legal issues presented to it in the event there are cases that pose novel statutory or constitutional issues or where there are conflicting decisions from different circuit courts.

A. Overview of the Removal Process

> **Respondent:** A foreign national placed into removal proceedings because of a violation of immigration laws.

A foreign national may become the subject of or **respondent** in removal proceedings when s/he:

- Arrives at an airport or port of entry without appropriate documentation to permit entry in the immigration category sought,

- Applies for an immigration benefit and an authorized official determines that the foreign national is ineligible,
- Has contact with the police or criminal justice system in such a way that it makes the foreign national subject to removal proceedings, or
- Violates his or her immigration status by staying too long or failing to comply with the terms of that status.

In some cases, individuals placed in removal proceedings because of contact with the police may have only committed minor offenses. For instance, a routine traffic stop for a broken brake light on a person's car could result in the police notifying the immigration service of the driver's undocumented status if this comes to light during questioning.[1] Immigration and Customs Enforcement, or ICE, charged with enforcing our immigration laws internally, may then place the individual in to removal proceedings.

A.1. Notice to Appear

Removal proceedings begin with the issuance of a charging document known as a notice to appear, or NTA, on Form I-862.[2] A sample is available in Figure 10.1 and may be useful to refer to as you read this section. The NTA may be issued by designated officers of any of the three agencies (ICE; United States Citizenship and Immigration Service, or USCIS; or Customs and Border Protection, or CBP) within the Department of Homeland Security, or DHS. For example, recall Case for Discussion 9.6 in Chapter 9, Grounds of Inadmissibility and Deportation, where Gamal had failed to register for National Security Entry-Exit System, or NSEERS, reporting and now wonders what the impact of that failure might be. Once the USCIS uncovers that Gamal failed to register, it can serve him with an NTA, alleging either that he is inadmissible and/or deportable for failing to report. Generally, ICE officials will issue NTAs. This is the first step in the process of beginning removal proceedings.

The NTA must be served on the foreign national to be placed into removal proceedings. Typically, service is achieved in person, and the recipient is required to sign to confirm receipt. For instance, an affirmative asylum applicant[3] is usually required to appear at the Asylum Office in person to receive the written decision on his or her case. Only in special circumstances will the asylum decision be sent by mail. However, if the case is to be referred to an immigration judge, every effort is made to serve the foreign national in person, as this will then provide strong evidence of proof of service.

---

[1] Some local and state governments have policies in place that prohibit police and local law enforcement officials from contacting ICE except in limited circumstances. For a list of some jurisdictions that limit cooperation with ICE, see https://cliniclegal.org/resources/newsletter/states-cities-and-counties-across-us-limit-cooperation-ice.
[2] INA § 239(a).
[3] *See* Section B.2 of Chapter 5, Asylum and Other Related Humanitarian Relief, for more details.

Figure 10.1

Notice to Appear

Source: Immigration and Customs Enforcement.

U.S. Department of Homeland Security   Notice to Appear

In removal proceedings under section 240 of the Immigration and Nationality Act:

Subject ID : ▒▒▒▒▒▒▒▒   File No: A▒▒▒▒▒▒▒▒
                         DOB: 03/17/1954   Event No: ESC11▒▒▒▒

In the Matter of: ▒▒▒▒▒▒▒▒▒▒▒▒▒▒▒▒▒▒▒▒

Respondent: _____ currently residing at:
                   ▒▒▒▒▒▒▒▒▒▒ PHILADELPHIA PENNSYLVANIA 19142
_____
                         (Number, street, city and ZIP code)   (Area code and phone number)

☐ 1. You are an arriving alien.
☐ 2. You are an alien present in the United States who has not been admitted or paroled.
☒ 3. You have been admitted to the United States, but are removable for the reasons stated below.

The Department of Homeland Security alleges that you:
1. You are not a citizen and national of the United States.
2. You are a citizen of Liberia and national of Liberia.
3. You were admitted to the United States at New York City, NY on or about December 23, 1979 as a nonimmigrant student (F1) for duration of status;
4. You violated the terms of your student status by failing to file the proper forms to continue/extend your student status, and by failing to attend an accredited institution and to maintain the required course load;

On the basis of the foregoing, it is charged that you are subject to removal from the United States pursuant to the following provision(s) of law:
Section 237(a)(1)(C)(i) of the Immigration and Nationality Act (Act), as amended, in that after admission as a nonimmigrant under Section 101(a)(15) of the Act, you failed to maintain or comply with the conditions of the nonimmigrant status under which you were admitted.

☐ This notice is being issued after an asylum officer has found that the respondent has demonstrated a credible fear of persecution or torture.
☐ Section 235(b)(1) order was vacated pursuant to: ☐ 8CFR 208.30(f)(2) ☐ 8CFR 235.3(b)(5)(iv)

YOU ARE ORDERED to appear before an immigration judge of the United States Department of Justice at:
900 Market Street Suite 504 Philadelphia PENNSYLVANIA US 19107
_____
                    (Complete Address of Immigration Court, including Room Number, if any)

on a date to be set   at a time to be set   to show why you should not be removed from the United States based on the
        (Date)   (Time)
charge(s) set forth above.   ▒▒▒▒▒▒▒▒▒▒▒▒▒▒▒▒   SUPERVISORY ADJUICATIONS OFFICER
                                                         (Signature and Title of Issuing Officer)
Date: SEP 1 6 2011   VSC St. Albans, Vermont
                                                         (City and State)

See reverse for important information   Form I-862 (Rev. 08/01/07)

A: Overview of the Removal Process

Figure 10.1

(Continued)

Notice to Respondent

Warning: Any statement you make may be used against you in removal proceedings.

Alien Registration: This copy of the Notice to Appear served upon you is evidence of your alien registration while you are under removal proceedings. You are required to carry it with you at all times.

Representation: If you so choose, you may be represented in this proceeding, at no expense to the Government, by an attorney or other individual authorized and qualified to represent persons before the Executive Office for Immigration Review, pursuant to 8 CFR 3.16. Unless you so request, no hearing will be scheduled earlier than ten days from the date of this notice, to allow you sufficient time to secure counsel. A list of qualified attorneys and organizations who may be available to represent you at no cost will be provided with this notice.

Conduct of the hearing: At the time of your hearing, you should bring with you any affidavits or other documents, which you desire to have considered in connection with your case. If you wish to have the testimony of any witnesses considered, you should arrange to have such witnesses present at the hearing.

At your hearing you will be given the opportunity to admit or deny any or all of the allegations in the Notice to Appear and that you are inadmissible or removable on the charges contained in the Notice to Appear. You will have an opportunity to present evidence on your own behalf, to examine any evidence presented by the Government, to object, on proper legal grounds, to the receipt of evidence and to cross examine any witnesses presented by the Government. At the conclusion of your hearing, you have a right to appeal an adverse decision by the immigration judge.

You will be advised by the immigration judge before whom you appear of any relief from removal for which you may appear eligible including the privilege of departure voluntarily. You will be given a reasonable opportunity to make any such application to the immigration judge.

Failure to appear: You are required to provide the DHS, in writing, with your full mailing address and telephone number. You must notify the Immigration Court immediately by using Form EOIR-33 whenever you change your address or telephone number during the course of this preceeding. You will be provided with a copy of this form. Notices of hearing will be mailed to this address. If you do not submit Form EOIR-33 and do not otherwise provide an address at which you may be reached during proceedings, then the Government shall not be required to provide you with written notice of your hearing. If you fail to attend the hearing at the time and place designated on this notice, or any date and time later directed by the Immigration Court, a removal order may be made by the immigration judge in your absence, and you may be arrested and detained by the DHS.

Mandatory Duty to Surrender for Removal: If you become subject to a final order of removal, you must surrender for removal to one of the offices listed in 8 CFR 241.16(a). Specific addresses on locations for surrender can be obtained from your local DHS office or over the internet at http://www.ice.gov/about/dro/contact.htm. You must surrender within 30 days from the date the order becomes administratively final, unless you obtain an order from a Federal court, immigration court, or the Board of Immigration Appeals staying execution of the removal order. Immigration regulations at 8 CFR 241.1 define when the removal order becomes administratively final. If you are granted voluntary departure and fail to depart the United States as required, fail to post a bond in connection with voluntary departure, or fail to comply with any other condition or term in connection with voluntary departure, you must surrender for removal on the next business day thereafter. If you do not surrender for removal as required, you will be ineligible for all forms of discretionary relief for as long as you remain in the United States and for ten years after departure or removal. This means you will be ineligible for asylum, cancellation of removal, voluntary departure, adjustment of status, change of nonimmigrant status, registry, and related waivers for this period. If you do not surrender for removal as required, you may also be criminally prosecuted under section 243 of the Act.

Request for Prompt Hearing

To expedite a determination in my case, I request an immediate hearing. I waive my right to a 10-day period prior to appearing before an immigration judge.

Before: _____

_____
(Signature of Respondent)

Date: _____

_____
(Signature and Title of Immigration Officer)

Certificate of Service

This Notice To Appear was served on the respondent by me on SEP 1 6 2011, in the following manner and in compliance with section 239(a)(1)(F) of the Act.

☐ in person   ☐ by certified mail, returned receipt requested   ☒ by regular mail
☐ Attached is a credible fear worksheet.
☒ Attached is a list of organization and attorneys which provide free legal services.

The alien was provided oral notice in the _____ language of the time and place of his or her hearing and of the consequences of failure to appear as provided in section 240(b)(7) of the Act.

MARIAN█████████████████████ ES OFFICER

_____
(Signature of Respondent if Personally Served)

_____
(Signature and Title of officer)

Form I-862 Page 2 (Rev. 08/01/07)

> ● **EXAMPLE**
>
> Iman from Yemen is seeking asylum to avoid being forced into a marriage with an elderly friend of her father's whom she is not attracted to. During her interview, Iman was extremely nervous, resulting in inconsistencies in her story. At the end of the interview, the asylum officer tells her that she must return to the office in 14 days to receive a decision on her application. Iman duly returns and is handed two things; first, a letter explaining why her application has not been granted; second, a notice to appear, advising her to appear at her local immigration court on a date to be arranged so that her asylum application can be reviewed by an immigration judge.

Special rules apply regarding service of the NTA when the respondent in proceedings is under 14 years old. Essentially, s/he cannot be served with the document directly. Instead, service "shall be made upon the person with whom ... the minor resides; whenever possible, service shall also be made on the near relative, guardian, committee, or friend."[4] Therefore, whenever there has been a failure to comply with this requirement, it should be brought to the attention of the immigration judge and a request to terminate proceedings for lack of proper service should be made.[5]

When an NTA is sent by mail, there is a presumption that it was delivered appropriately by the post office to the most recent address provided by the foreign national. The USCIS is also entitled to presume the last address it has on file is the correct one. Anyone who is not a citizen of the United States is required to furnish the USCIS with any new address within ten days of the change.[6] A foreign national is under a similar obligation with respect to the immigration court and BIA. Therefore, if the foreign national moves from the last address provided to the USCIS and does not provide a new address, the agency may still use the old one and the presumption of proper service will hold, even if mail is never received. However, it may be possible to challenge this, as discussed later.

The NTA is an important document, which should be carefully reviewed to ensure the information contained in it is accurate. Any inaccuracies should be challenged in court as it could affect the foreign national's ability to claim certain types of relief from deportation. In criminal court proceedings, the foreign national charged is referred to as the defendant. However, the term used in immigration proceedings is respondent.

The NTA will allege certain facts, the most important of which is that the respondent is not a U.S. citizen. This is because, if the respondent is in fact a citizen, then s/he would be protected from deportation and not subject to the jurisdiction of the EOIR. Instead, the NTA will state the citizenship of the foreign national, if known, and then state the legal capacity in which the person entered the country. Where the allegation is that the foreign national either entered as an

---

[4] 8 C.F.R. § 103.5a(c)(2)(ii).
[5] *Matter of Rosa Mejia Andino*, 23 I&N Dec. 533 (BIA 2002).
[6] INA § 265(a).

arriving alien[7] or entered without inspection, or EWI, the government need only allege that the respondent is inadmissible because of a breach of the requirement to possess appropriate immigrant visa documentation.[8] Where the foreign national has been admitted in a particular immigration category or paroled, then s/he will be charged with deportability and given more detail explaining the immigration violation, whether it relates to a criminal issue, failure to maintain an immigration status, violating his or her status by working without authorization, or any other violation.

Once all the allegations have been made, the NTA will state the basis on which the government believes the respondent is removable, either because an inadmissibility ground under INA § 212(a) or a deportation ground under INA § 237(a) applies. For example, the NTA in Figure 10.1 refers to a person who was previously admitted as a student but violated the terms of his visa and is charged with one of the grounds of deportation.

Case for Discussion 10.1

Recall Baraka from Yemen in Case for Discussion 9.1, who was stopped at the border when returning from his brother's wedding in the Dominican Republic because of his prior conviction for possession of marijuana. Following further questioning, he is placed into removal proceedings by a designated officer from CBP, even though he is a lawful permanent resident, or LPR.

- Will Baraka be charged as removable because he is inadmissible or deportable?

Understanding the charges in the NTA is essential because it will determine the applicable standard of proof and who has the burden to meet it. Any foreign national alleged to be inadmissible must prove that s/he is "clearly and beyond doubt entitled to be admitted and is not inadmissible"[9] or prove that "by clear and convincing evidence [s/he] is lawfully present in the United States pursuant to a prior admission."[10] In contrast, the government must prove by "clear and

---

[7] The term "arriving alien" is an important one in immigration law. Individuals apprehended at a border or within the United States who have not been given permission to enter have curtailed rights to immigration relief and are subject to detention. The foreign national may have arrived clandestinely or may have presented him or herself to an official who has yet to decide whether or not to allow entry into the country in the immigration status sought. Further discussion of this category of foreign national is in Section C.
[8] INA § 212(a)(7)(A)(i)(I). *See also* Section B.7 of Chapter 9, Grounds of Inadmissibility and Deportation.
[9] INA § 240(c)(2)(A).
[10] INA § 240(c)(2)(B).

convincing evidence," that a foreign national is deportable.[11] In either case, the government has the burden to prove that the foreign national is not a U.S. citizen.[12]

Reviewing the NTA carefully to ensure all information is correct is good practice. Also, strategically, the respondent should consider whether to admit or deny some or all of the allegations made. Where allegations are denied, the government will be required to provide "reasonable, substantial, and probative evidence" to support its case.[13] If the government alleges that a respondent has criminal convictions, then INA § 240(c)(3)(B) requires that only one of the following documents should be produced to meet the evidentiary requirement to prove the conviction exists:

- An official record of judgment and conviction;
- An official record of plea, verdict, and sentence;
- A docket entry from court records that indicates the existence of the conviction;
- Official minutes of a court proceeding or a transcript of a court hearing in which the court takes notice of the existence of the conviction;
- An abstract of a record of conviction prepared by the court in which the conviction was entered, or by a state official associated with the state's repository of criminal justice records, that indicates the charge or section of law violated, the disposition of the case, the existence and date of conviction, and the sentence;
- Any document or record prepared by, or under the direction of, the court in which the conviction was entered that indicates the existence of a conviction; or
- Any document or record attesting to the conviction that is maintained by an official of a state or federal penal institution, which is the basis for that institution's authority to assume custody of the individual named in the record.

The NTA orders the respondent to appear before an immigration judge at one of the immigration courts around the country on a given day and time or on one yet to be determined, as illustrated in Figure 10.1 by the designation "TBA" in the area allowed for the date and time. The appropriate immigration venue will depend on the location of the respondent's apprehension, regardless of where s/he lives. For example, someone who lives in New Jersey, but was apprehended and processed for removal in Atlanta, Georgia, may be ordered to appear in the immigration court in Atlanta. However, it is possible to request that the venue for proceedings be changed to a more convenient location by filing a

---

[11] INA § 240(c)(3).
[12] 8 C.F.R. § 1240.8(c).
[13] INA § 240(c)(3)(A).

Motion to Change Venue with the court requesting this, as discussed in Section E.3.

The second page of the NTA provides the respondent with important information, including the fact that the foreign national has the right to legal representation during the removal proceedings. Unlike criminal cases, a respondent with limited funds is not entitled to free representation, even though the immigration hearing could result in removal. Courts have acknowledged that deportation is a harsh penalty (*see Harisiades v. Shaughnessy*, 342 U.S. 580, 600 (1952), where the Supreme Court held that deportation "may deprive a man and his family of all that makes life worthwhile."). Supreme Court Justice Francis Murphy expressed the consequences in even starker terms:

> The impact of deportation upon the life of an alien is often as great, if not greater than, the imposition of a criminal sentence. A deported alien may lose his family, his friends, and his livelihood forever. Return to his native land may result in poverty, persecution, and even death.[14]

Despite these possible consequences, a respondent is required to find his or her own lawyer and pay whatever legal expenses are charged.

The NTA also provides a warning to the respondent that s/he must appear at every assigned hearing date. Failure to do so could result in an ***in absentia order*** of removal or deportation order being entered.[15] A removal order is a harsh consequence, since it means that a respondent with such an order will be barred from receiving most forms of immigration relief for which the foreign national may qualify, for a period of ten years.[16] However, if there are exceptional circumstances that can explain the failure to appear that led to the *in absentia* order (for example because the respondent was seriously ill or might have been stuck in a serious traffic incident), the immigration judge might be persuaded to reopen the proceedings to allow the respondent the opportunity to seek immigration relief. A **Motion to Reopen** the case in this instance must be filed within 180 days of the *in absentia* order being issued,[17] with evidence demonstrating the exceptional circumstance faced by the respondent that prevented appearance in court on the appointed date. Where a respondent can show failure to receive information regarding when to appear in court, possibly because any notice was sent to the wrong address despite the respondent having duly reported any changes, or where the notice was returned to the court as undelivered, or the foreign national can prove that s/he was incarcerated and the failure to appear

In Absentia Order: An order of removal entered by an immigration judge during court proceedings where the respondent fails to appear after oral warning of the consequences of so doing have been given in the foreign national's language or one s/he understands.

---

[14] *Bridges v. Wixon*, 326 U.S. 135, 164 (1945).
[15] INA § 240(b)(5).
[16] However, if the immigration judge fails to provide oral notice of the consequences of failing to appear, a foreign national may move to rescind the removal order within the time allowed, if s/he may now apply for relief that was previously unavailable at the time of the initial removal proceedings. *See Matter of M-S-*, 22 I&N Dec. 349 (BIA 1998).
[17] INA § 240(b)(5)(C).

was no fault of his or her own, then a Motion to Reopen an *in absentia* order may be filed at any time.[18]

The NTA also advises respondents of their responsibility to notify the court in the event of an address change. This should be done within five days of a move and can be filed on form EOIR 33/IC, Alien's Change of Address Form/Immigration Court, for the immigration court or EOIR 33/BIA, Alien's Change of Address Form/Board of Immigration Appeals, for the BIA, or in any other manner that makes clear the new address. Failure to provide the new address could mean that a respondent will not receive correspondence sent by the immigration court and therefore not know when to appear for a hearing, running the risk of an *in absentia* order being entered. However, before such an order can be made, a respondent must have been advised of the responsibility to keep the court aware of any address change. *See Matter of G-Y-R-*, 23 I&N Dec. 181 (BIA 2001). This is why, where possible, the government makes every effort to serve a respondent with an NTA in person and have him or her acknowledge personal service by obtaining a signature directly on the notice, as this provides strong evidence that the respondent was made aware of the requirement to provide the court with an up to date address. The fact that the NTA may be written in a language that the respondent cannot understand, since it is in English, is no defense to any failure to notify the court of an address change. However, the agency issuing the NTA is required to provide oral notice of its contents in a language that the foreign national understands.

A.2. Notice of Hearing

Once the NTA has been issued and served on the respondent, it must also be filed with the immigration court. Failure to do this will mean that a judge has no jurisdiction to consider whether or not the respondent should be deported and therefore must terminate proceedings. If the NTA is properly filed, the court will then issue a **Notice of Hearing**, informing the respondent of when to appear in court to answer the charges against him or her. A sample notice is in Figure 10.2.

INA § 239(b)(1) requires that the Notice of Hearing be addressed to the respondent at the address provided to the court by the USCIS or any other agency that processed the foreign national for removal. The notice will advise the respondent of the date and time to appear in court, unless his or her legal representative has already entered his/her appearance, or advised the court that s/he is acting on behalf of the respondent. In this case, the representative will receive the notice instead.

The respondent and/or his or her legal representative must be given at least ten days' notice that appearance in court is required. The respondent will also be reminded of the responsibility to update his or her address with the court, the

---

[18] INA § 240(b)(5)(C)(ii).

Figure 10.2

Notice of Hearing

```
              NOTICE OF HEARING IN REMOVAL PROCEEDINGS
                         IMMIGRATION COURT
                      900 MARKET STREET, SUITE 504
                         PHILADELPHIA, PA   19107
RE:
FILE:  A                                       DATE: Dec 3, 2015

TO:   HIAS & COUNCIL MIGRATION SERVICE OF PHILADELPHIA

      2100 ARCH STREET, 3RD FLOOR
      PHILADELPHIA, PA  19103
```

Please take notice that the above captioned case has been scheduled for a MASTER hearing before the Immigration Court on Oct ██, 2016 at 09:00 A.M. at:

    900 MARKET STREET, COURTROOM 2
    PHILADELPHIA, PA 19107

You may be represented in these proceedings, at no expense to the Government, by an attorney or other individual who is authorized and qualified to represent persons before an Immigration Court. Your hearing date has not been scheduled earlier than 10 days from the date of service of the Notice to Appear in order to permit you the opportunity to obtain an attorney or representative. If you wish to be represented, your attorney or representative must appear with you at the hearing prepared to proceed. You can request an earlier hearing in writing.

Failure to appear at your hearing except for exceptional circumstances may result in one or more of the following actions: (1) You may be taken into custody by the Department of Homeland Security and held for further action. OR (2) Your hearing may be held in your absence under section 240(b)(5) of the Immigration and Nationality Act. An order of removal will be entered against you if the Department of Homeland Security established by clear, unequivocal and convincing evidence that a) you or your attorney has been provided this notice and b) you are removable.

IF YOUR ADDRESS IS NOT LISTED ON THE NOTICE TO APPEAR, OR IF IT IS NOT CORRECT, WITHIN FIVE DAYS OF THIS NOTICE YOU MUST PROVIDE TO THE IMMIGRATION COURT PHILADELPHIA, PA THE ATTACHED FORM EOIR-33 WITH YOUR ADDRESS AND/OR TELEPHONE NUMBER AT WHICH YOU CAN BE CONTACTED REGARDING THESE PROCEEDINGS. EVERYTIME YOU CHANGE YOUR ADDRESS AND/OR TELEPHONE NUMBER, YOU MUST INFORM THE COURT OF YOUR NEW ADDRESS AND/OR TELEPHONE NUMBER WITHIN 5 DAYS OF THE CHANGE ON THE ATTACHED FORM EOIR-33. ADDITIONAL FORMS EOIR-33 CAN BE OBTAINED FROM THE COURT WHERE YOU ARE SCHEDULED TO APPEAR. IN THE EVENT YOU ARE UNABLE TO OBTAIN A FORM EOIR-33, YOU MAY PROVIDE THE COURT IN WRITING WITH YOUR NEW ADDRESS AND/OR TELEPHONE NUMBER BUT YOU MUST CLEARLY MARK THE ENVELOPE "CHANGE OF ADDRESS." CORRESPONDENCE FROM THE COURT, INCLUDING HEARING NOTICES, WILL BE SENT TO THE MOST RECENT ADDRESS YOU HAVE PROVIDED, AND WILL BE CONSIDERED SUFFICIENT NOTICE TO YOU AND THESE PROCEEDINGS CAN GO FORWARD IN YOUR ABSENCE.

A list of free legal service providers has been given to you. For information regarding the status of your case, call toll free 1-800-898-7180 or 240-314-1500. For information on Immigration Court procedures, please consult the Immigration Court Practice Manual, available at www.usdoj.gov/eoir.

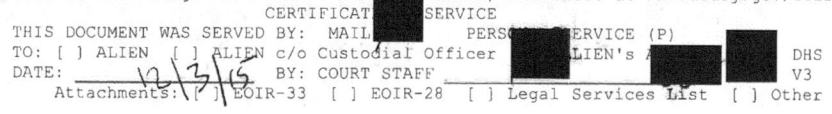

```
                       CERTIFICATE OF SERVICE
THIS DOCUMENT WAS SERVED BY:  MAIL (M)     PERSONAL SERVICE (P)
TO: [ ] ALIEN  [ ] ALIEN c/o Custodial Officer   [ ] ALIEN's ATT/REP  [ ] DHS
DATE:   12/3/15      BY: COURT STAFF                                    V3
    Attachments: [✓] EOIR-33  [ ] EOIR-28  [ ] Legal Services List  [ ] Other
```

Figure 10.2 (Continued)

```
ALIEN NUMBER: ████████        NAME: ████████

     /       LIMITATIONS ON DISCRETIONARY RELIEF FOR FAILURE TO APPEAR
(√)  1. You have been scheduled for a removal hearing, at the time and place
        set forth on the attached sheet. Failure to appear for this hearing
        other than because of exceptional circumstances beyond your control**
        will result in your being found ineligible for certain forms of
        relief under the Immigration and Nationality Act (see Section A.
        below) for a period of ten (10) years after the date of entry of the
        final order of removal.

( )  2. You have been scheduled for an asylum hearing, at the time and place
        set forth on the attached notice. Failure to appear for this hearing
        other than because of exceptional circumstances beyond your control**
        will result in your being found ineligible for certain forms of relief
        under the Immigration and Nationality Act (see Section A. Below) for a
        period of ten (10) years from the date of your scheduled hearing.

( )  3. You have been granted voluntary departure from the United States
        pursuant to section 240B of the Immigration and Nationality Act, and
        remaining in the United States beyond the authorized date will result
        in your being found ineligible for certain forms of relief under the
        Immigration and Nationality Act (see Section A. Below) for ten (10)
        years from the date of the scheduled departure. Your Voluntary
        departure bond, if any, will also be breached. Additionally, if you
        fail to voluntarily depart the United States within the time period
        specified, you shall be subject to a civil penalty of not less than
        $1000 and not more than $5000.
        **the term "exceptional circumstances" refers to circumstances such
        as serious illness of the alien or death of an immediate relative
        of the alien, but not including less compelling circumstances.

A.  THE FORMS OF RELIEF FROM REMOVAL FOR WHICH YOU WILL BECOME INELIGIBLE ARE:
    1)    Voluntary departure as provided for in section 240B of the
          Immigration and Nationality Act;
    2)    Cancellation of removal as provided for in section 240A of the
          Immigration and Nationality Act; and
    3)    Adjustment of status or change of status as provided for in Section
          245, 248 or 249 of the Immigration and Nationality Act.

    This written notice was provided to the alien in English. Oral notice of
the contents of this notice must be given to the alien in his/her native
language, or in a language he/she understands by the Immigration Judge.
Date:
Immigration Judge: _____        or Court Clerk: ████████
                            CERTIFICATE OF SERVICE
THIS DOCUMENT WAS SERVED BY:  MAIL (M)       PERSONAL SERVICE (P)
TO: [ ] ALIEN  [ ] ALIEN c/o Custodial Officer  [✓] ALIEN's ATT/REP  [✓] DHS
DATE:    1/29/15         BY:  COURT STAFF      ████████
     Attachments:   [ ] EOIR-33   [ ] EOIR-28   [ ] Legal Services List  [ ] Other
                                                                              N6
```

right to counsel at his or her own expense, consequences of failing to appear in court on an appointed date, and provided with a list of free or low cost legal service providers approved by the EOIR in the state that he or she might want to contact in order to obtain legal advice regarding his or her case.[19]

---

[19] This list can be found at https://www.justice.gov/eoir/find-legal-representation.

A.3. Authorized Legal Representatives

Only certain people may represent a respondent in immigration court proceedings under 8 C.F.R. §§ 292.1 and 1292.1. They are:

- Attorneys,
- Law students enrolled with an accredited law school through a legal aid or clinical program,
- Law graduates not yet admitted to the bar but supervised by a licensed attorney or accredited representative,
- *Accredited representatives,*
- Accredited official from the respondent's government, usually a consular official,
- Reputable individuals with a pre-existing relationship with the respondent, or
- Foreign attorneys.

Any person from this list who is the legal representative for the respondent must notify the court of this fact by filing Form EOIR 28, Notice of Entry of Appearance as Attorney or Representative, Before the Immigration Court, which is the EOIR equivalent of Form G-28, Notice of Entry of Appearance as Attorney or Representative, used with the USCIS. The representative must also deliver a copy of the form to the attorney for ICE who represents the U.S. government in immigration court. A sample of this form is in Figure 10.3. Paralegals are not authorized to appear in immigration court.[20]

Accredited Representatives: People of good moral character, employed by a BIA-recognized nonprofit religious, charitable, social services or similar organization who are approved as competent to represent individuals before certain immigration agencies.

B. Immigration Court Hearings

Hearings in immigration court take different formats and are for different purposes. Each are discussed in turn.

B.1. The Master Calendar Hearing

The Notice of Hearing will also advise the respondent of the type of hearing s/he will be attending, either a master or an individual calendar hearing. The ***master calendar hearing*** is the first hearing that a respondent will have before an immigration judge. It is similar to a status hearing held in other courts and is open to the public. A judge's docket for a master calendar hearing usually consists of several respondents who appear on the same day to update the court on the status of their case. Those who appear without an attorney or legal representative are referred to as appearing ***pro se***. There is no rule preventing litigants from representing themselves.

Master Calendar Hearing: A brief status hearing that permits an immigration judge to obtain preliminary information about a case and a respondent to plead to the charges against him or her.

Pro Se: An unrepresented respondent in court proceedings.

---

[20] The Office of the Chief Immigration Judge Practice Manual, Section 2.6.

Chapter 10: Immigration Court Practice and Relief from Removal

Figure 10.3

Notice of Entry of Appearance as Attorney or Representative Before the Immigration Court

Source: EOIR.

U.S. Department of Justice
Executive Office for Immigration Review
Immigration Court

OMB#1125-0006
Notice of Entry of Appearance as Attorney or Representative Before the Immigration Court

(Type or Print) NAME AND ADDRESS OF REPRESENTED PARTY	ALIEN ("A") NUMBER (Provide A-number of the party represented in this case.)
Ben _____ _____ Evolent (First) (Middle Initial) (Last) 226 Heavens Way _____ D (Number and Street) (Apt. No.) Nowhere City _____ PA _____ 61666 (City) (State) (Zip Code)	

Attorney or Representative (please check one of the following):

☑ I am an attorney eligible to practice law in, and a member in good standing of, the bar of the highest court(s) of the following states(s), possession(s), territory(ies), commonwealth(s), or the District of Columbia (use additional space on reverse side if necessary) and I am not subject to any order disbarring, suspending, enjoining, restraining or otherwise restricting me in the practice of law in any jurisdiction (if subject to such an order, do not check this box and explain on reverse).

Full Name of Court New York Court of Appeals   Bar Number (if applicable) N/A

☐ I am a representative accredited to appear before the Executive Office for Immigration Review as defined in 8 C.F.R. § 1292.1(a)(4) with the following recognized organization: _____

☐ I am a law student or law graduate of an accredited U.S. law school as defined in 8 C.F.R. § 1292.1(a)(2).
☐ I am a reputable individual as defined in 8 C.F.R. § 1292.1(a)(3).
☐ I am an accredited foreign government official, as defined in 8 C.F.R. § 1291.1(a)(5), from _____ (country).
☐ I am a person who was authorized to practice on December 23, 1952, under 8 C.F.R. § 1292.1(b).

Attorney or Representative (please check one of the following):

☑ I hereby enter my appearance as attorney or representative for, and at the request of, the party named above.
☐ EOIR has ordered the provision of a Qualified Representative for the party named above and I appear in that capacity.

I have read and understand the statements provided on the reverse side of this form that set forth the regulations and conditions governing appearances and representations before the Board of Immigration Appeals. I declare under penalty of perjury under the laws of the United States of America that the foregoing is true and correct.

SIGNATURE OF ATTORNEY OR REPRESENTATIVE	EOIR ID NUMBER	DATE
X _____	ER22222	_____

NAME OF ATTORNEY OR REPRESENTATIVE, ADDRESS, FAX & PHONE NUMBERS, & EMAIL ADDRESS

Name: Righteous _____ _____ Mess
          (First)   (Middle Initial)   (Last)
Address: 2100 Sweet Briar Avenue
                   (Number and Street)
         Nowhere City   PA   61666
         (City)   (State)   (Zip Code)

Telephone: 555 555 5555   Facsimile: 555 555 5111   Email: rmess@me.com

☑ Check here if new address

Form EOIR - 28
Rev. Oct. 2014

Figure 10.3 (Continued)

Indicate Type of Appearance:
☑ Primary Attorney/Representative ☐ Non-Primary Attorney/Representative
☐ On behalf of _____ (Attorney's Name) for the following hearing: _____ (Date)
I am providing pro bono representation. Check one: ☐ yes ☑ no

<u>**Proof of Service**</u>

I (Name) R. Mess _____ mailed or delivered a copy of this Form EOIR-28 on (Date) _____
to the DHS (U.S. Immigration and Customs Enforcement – ICE) at 900 Market Street, Suite 777, Nowhere City, PA 61664

X _____
 Signature of Person Serving

APPEARANCES - An appearance shall be filed on a Form EOIR-28 by the attorney or representative appearing in each case before an Immigration Judge (see 8 C.F.R. § 1003.17). When an appearance is made by a person acting in a representative capacity, his/her personal appearance or signature constitutes a representation that, under the provisions of 8 C.F.R. part 1003, he/she is authorized and qualified to represent individuals and will comply with the EOIR Rules of Professional Conduct in 8 C.F.R. § 1003.102. Thereafter, substitution or withdrawal may be permitted upon the approval of the Immigration Judge of a request by the attorney or representative of record in accordance with 8 C.F.R. § 1003.17(b). Please note that appearances for limited purposes are not permitted. *See Matter of Velasquez*, 19 I&N Dec. 377, 384 (BIA 1986). A separate appearance form (Form EOIR-27) must be filed with an appeal to the Board of Immigration Appeals (see 8 C.F.R. § 1003.38(g)). Attorneys and Accredited Representatives (with full accreditation) must first update their address in eRegistry before filing a Form EOIR-28 that reflects a new address.

FREEDOM OF INFORMATION ACT - This form may not be used to request records under the Freedom of Information Act or the Privacy Act. The manner of requesting such records is in 28 C.F.R. §§ 16.1-16.11 and appendices. For further information about requesting records from EOIR under the Freedom of Information Act, see How to File a Freedom of Information Act (FOIA) Request With the Executive Office for Immigration Review, available on EOIR's website at http://www.justice.gov/eoir.

PRIVACY ACT NOTICE - The information requested on this form is authorized by 8 U.S.C. §§ 1229(a), 1362 and 8 C.F.R. § 1003.17 in order to enter an appearance to represent a party before the Immigration Court. The information you provide is mandatory and required to enter an appearance. Failure to provide the requested information will result in an inability to represent a party or receive notice of actions in a proceeding. EOIR may share this information with others in accordance with approved routine uses described in EOIR's system of records notice, EOIR-001, Records and Management Information System, 69 Fed. Reg. 26,179 (May 11, 2004), or its successors and EOIR-003, Practitioner Complaint-Disciplinary Files, 64 Fed. Reg. 49237 (September 1999).

CASES BEFORE EOIR - Automated information about cases before EOIR is available by calling (800) 898-7180 or (240) 314-1500.

FURTHER INFORMATION - For further information, please see the *Immigration Court Practice Manual*, which is available on the EOIR website at *www.justice.gov/eoir*.

ADDITIONAL INFORMATION:

Under the Paperwork Reduction Act, a person is not required to respond to a collection of information unless it displays a valid OMB control number. We try to create forms and instructions that are accurate, can be easily understood, and which impose the least possible burden on you to provide us with information. The estimated average time to complete this form is six (6) minutes. If you have comments regarding the accuracy of this estimate, or suggestions for making this form simpler, you can write to the Executive Office for Immigration Review, Office of the General Counsel, 5107 Leesburg Pike, Suite 2600, Falls Church, Virginia 20530.

Form EOIR - 28
Rev. Oct. 2014

All proceedings in immigration court are recorded so that a full record is created.[21] It is always possible to request a copy of the recording from the court in order to be clear about what may have happened previously. This is especially important when there is a change of legal representation midway through a case. Listening to the recording of the proceedings enables a new representative to learn what has already happened. It is also important to review the judge's court file to make sure that all the documents filed with the court have been made available to the respondent. If there are any documents on the judge's file that may be useful in preparing the respondent's case, a limited number of copies may be requested from the court administrator.

Many respondents in immigration court do not speak or understand English. It is always the court's responsibility to provide a professional interpreter for any hearings before the immigration judge. During master calendar hearings, which tend to be short, the interpreter might be present in person or by telephone. However, an interpreter is usually physically present during the individual calendar hearing, also referred to as a merits hearing. Some practitioners or representatives bring their own interpreter as a safeguard in order to verify the accuracy of interpreting of the court appointed interpreter. This is often useful as there may be issues with different dialects or even simply with the quality of interpretation.

Because of the open nature of the master calendar hearing, some practitioners request a side bar conversation with the judge and the attorney for the government in order to share sensitive and confidential information that may relate to issues of domestic violence or sexual assault. Once all matters have been discussed and resolved, the judge can summarize the discussion on the record discreetly.

● **EXAMPLE**

Ismail is a Tunisian national who arrived as a student but never attended school as required by the terms of his visa. In late 2009, he began to assist the FBI in its investigations of a local drug ring. In return, they notified the USCIS of his cooperation and, as a consequence, he was granted permission to work and issued an employment authorization document, or EAD, because he was being useful to law enforcement. This continued for a number of years until Ismail realized that it was becoming too dangerous for him to continue his work and so he notified his FBI agent that he wanted to discontinue. A few months later, Ismail received a notice to appear, advising him to go to immigration court on a particular day as he had been placed into removal proceedings. He retained a lawyer to represent him. At the first master calendar hearing, the immigration judge asked a number of questions regarding how Ismail came to be placed into removal proceedings. The attorney is wary of disclosing Ismail's involvement with the FBI in open court as it may compromise his safety. Therefore, a sidebar is requested with the judge and government attorney so that this information can be disclosed discreetly.

---

[21] 8 C.F.R. § 1240.9.

In the event that a respondent's legal adviser is unable to appear in court in person, s/he may file a motion with the court to ask permission to appear by telephone. There must be exceptional reasons for this request and an immigration judge always has the discretion to refuse to grant it. Even when a legal representative is unable to appear in person, the respondent must still appear, unless the judge has previously waived his or her appearance. Failure to do so may result in an *in absentia* order being entered, as discussed in Section A.1. It is always possible to request that the appearance of minor children be excused if they are in removal proceedings jointly with a parent.

B.1.a. Obtaining a Copy of the Immigration File

It is often a good idea to request a copy of the respondent's immigration file from the USCIS as part of the work to be done to prepare his or her case for hearing. The request is made by filing Form G-639, **Freedom of Information/Privacy Act Request,** or **FOIA,** with the USCIS. Such a request should be made as soon as possible during preparations so that the legal representative obtains all relevant evidence concerning the client's immigration history before going into court for the master calendar hearing, if possible, and definitely before the individual hearing. It also takes time for the request to be fulfilled, so the sooner the request is made, the more likely the information will be provided in time.

Another way to speed up the request, where appropriate, is to alert the FOIA fulfillment department that this case is in immigration court proceedings. FOIA requests are divided into three tracks. Track one is for complex cases which will take the longest time. Track two is for limited requests that do not require an entire file. Track three relates to requests where removal proceedings are ongoing so will be dealt with as quickly as possible, recognizing the urgency of the situation. In order to prove that a request should be allocated track three status, it should be accompanied by a copy of a notice of hearing, indicating a court hearing date sometime in the future.

A foreign national typically has one immigration file that is used by all three immigration agencies, USCIS, ICE, and CBP. However, the USCIS has primary responsibility for fulfilling FOIA requests, disclosing information that it either prepared or has control over. Documents prepared by either ICE or CBP will be redacted when sent to the requester while the file is forwarded on to those agencies so that they can decide what they deem disclosable to the respondent. Any further documents from those agencies are then sent to the respondent or legal representative at a later date.

B.1.b. Pleadings

At the very first master calendar hearing, a respondent will be expected to plead to each of the allegations contained in the NTA, advising which ones are admitted or denied. This can be done orally or in writing. A sample of a written pleading is in Figure 10.4. After the respondent admits or denies specific allegations in the NTA, s/he will then be asked to designate a country for removal, if this becomes necessary. In most cases, respondents designate the country of their nationality.

Figure 10.4

Sample Written Pleading

Source: OCIJ Practice Manual.

Immigration Court
Practice Manual — Appendix L

APPENDIX L
Sample Written Pleading

Prior to entering a pleading, parties are expected to have reviewed the pertinent regulations, as well as Chapter 4 of the Immigration Court Practice Manual (Hearings before Immigration Judges).

[name and address of attorney or representative]

United States Department of Justice
Executive Office for Immigration Review
Immigration Court
[the court's location (city or town) and state]

In the Matter of:

[the respondent's name]   File No.: [the respondent's A number]

In removal proceedings

RESPONDENT'S WRITTEN PLEADING

On behalf of my client, I make the following representations:

1. The respondent concedes proper service of the Notice to Appear, dated _____.

2. I have explained to the respondent (through an interpreter, if necessary):

    a. the rights set forth in 8 C.F.R. § 1240.10(a);
    b. the consequences of failing to appear in court as set forth in INA § 240(b)(5);
    c. the limitation on discretionary relief for failure to appear set forth in INA § 240(b)(7);
    d. the consequences of knowingly filing or making a frivolous application as set forth in INA § 208(d)(6);
    e. the requirement to notify the court within five days of any change of address or telephone number, using Form EOIR-33/IC pursuant to 8 C.F.R. § 1003.15(d).

---

updates: www.justice.gov/eoir

Version released on February 4, 2016

3. The respondent concedes the following allegation(s) _____, and denies the following allegation(s) _____.

4. The respondent concedes the following charge(s) of removability _____, and denies the following charge(s) of removability _____.

5. In the event of removal, the respondent;

    ☐ names _____ as the country to which removal should be directed;

    OR

    ☐ declines to designate a country of removal.

6. The respondent will be applying for the following forms of relief from removal:

    ☐ Termination of Proceedings
    ☐ Asylum
    ☐ Withholding of Removal (Restriction on Removal)
    ☐ Adjustment of Status
    ☐ Cancellation of Removal pursuant to INA § _____
    ☐ Waiver of Inadmissibility pursuant to INA § _____
    ☐ Voluntary Departure
    ☐ Other (specify) _____
    ☐ None

7. If the relief from removal requires an application, the respondent will file the application (other than asylum), no later than fifteen (15) days before the date of the individual calendar hearing, unless otherwise directed by the court. The respondent acknowledges that, if the application(s) are not timely filed, the application(s) will be deemed waived and abandoned under 8 C.F.R. § 1003.31(c).

    If the respondent is filing a defensive asylum application, the asylum application will be filed in open court at the next master calendar hearing.

8. If background and security investigations are required, the respondent has received the DHS biometrics instructions and will timely comply with the instructions. I have explained the instructions to the respondent (through an interpreter, if necessary). In addition, I have explained to the respondent (through an interpreter, if necessary), that, under 8 C.F.R. § 1003.47(d), failure to provide biometrics or other biographical information within the time allowed will constitute abandonment of the application unless the respondent demonstrates that such failure was the result of good cause.

Figure 10.4 (Continued)

9. The respondent estimates that _____ hours will be required for the respondent to present the case.

10. ☐ It is requested that the Immigration Court order an interpreter proficient in the _____ language, _____ dialect;

OR

☐ The respondent speaks English and does not require the services of an interpreter.

_____   _____
Date   Attorney or Representative for the Respondent

RESPONDENT'S PLEADING DECLARATION

I, _____, have been advised of my rights in these proceedings by my attorney or representative. I understand those rights. I waive a further explanation of those rights by this court.

I have been advised by my attorney or representative of the consequences of failing to appear for a hearing. I have also been advised by my attorney of the consequences of failing to appear for a scheduled date of departure or deportation. I understand those consequences.

I have been advised by my attorney or representative of the consequences of knowingly filing a frivolous asylum application. I understand those consequences.

I have been advised by my attorney or representative of the consequences of failing to follow the DHS biometrics instructions within the time allowed. I understand those consequences.

I understand that if my mailing address changes I must notify the court within 5 days of such change by completing an Alien's Change of Address Form (Form EOIR-33/IC) and filing it with this court.

Finally, my attorney or representative has explained to me what this Written Pleading says. I understand it, I agree with it, and I request that the court accept it as my pleading.

_____   _____
Date   Respondent

Figure 10.4 (Continued)

CERTIFICATE OF INTERPRETATION

I, _____, am competent to translate and interpret from
    (name of interpreter)

_____ into English, and I certify that I have read this entire document to the
(name of language)

respondent in _____, and that the respondent stated that he or she understood
    (name of language)

the document before he or she signed the Pleading Declaration above.

_____
(signature of interpreter)

_____
(typed/printed name of interpreter)

OR

I, _____, certify that _____, a telephonic
(name of attorney or representative)   (name of interpreter)

interpreter who is competent to translate and interpret from _____ into English, read
    (name of language)

this entire document to the respondent in _____ and that the respondent stated
    (name of language)

that he or she understood the document before he or she signed the Pleading Declaration above.

_____
(signature of attorney or representative)

_____
(typed/printed name of attorney or representative)

Where the immigration relief sought is asylum, however, the respondent typically refuses to designate because agreeing to be removed to the country from which asylum is sought would be an incongruous position, calling into doubt whether the person truly has a fear of persecution. In these cases, either the government attorney or the immigration judge will designate the respondent's country of citizenship. Next, the foreign national will have to concede inadmissibility or deportability in order to seek any form of immigration relief and advise the court which relief is requested. If the respondent appears *pro se*, the proceedings are generally continued or delayed at least once to allow him or her to find legal representation. The immigration judge may even refer the respondent to the list of free or low-cost legal service providers maintained by EOIR. The number of times a judge will continue a case to allow a foreign national to find legal representation will vary from court to court. However, if a respondent is unable to find any representation, s/he will be required to move forward alone.

Where a respondent does qualify for and is seeking relief from removal, then the master calendar hearing allows a judge to learn more about the case, the type of relief sought, the amount of time required to prepare for a merits or individual hearing, and how long that hearing is expected to last. Some judges may treat master calendar hearings as merely an opportunity to schedule a merits hearing while others may schedule several master calendar hearings to allow either the respondent's attorney or the government attorney to prepare documents or memoranda of law concerning certain legal issues. Either way, a representative at these hearings should be fully prepared to provide as much information on the respondent and the facts of his or her case as the judge may require.

B.1.c. Pre-Hearing Voluntary Departure[22]

In the event that no immigration relief is available, a respondent may ask permission from the court to depart voluntarily in lieu of a removal order being entered against him or her.[23] This is known as pre-hearing ***Voluntary Departure,*** or VD.

Voluntary Departure: Permission given to a foreign national to depart the United States other than at government expense, within a specified time frame.

A respondent may also seek VD at the conclusion of a merits hearing. The conditions for granting VD at each stage of the proceedings are different and will be dealt with separately. In either case, VD will be granted at the judge's discretion.

VD may be requested at a master calendar hearing where it is clear that no immigration relief is available to a respondent in proceedings. By seeking VD at this stage, an immigration judge is able to grant a maximum of 120 days for a respondent to arrange his or her affairs and depart the United States voluntarily. This time ordinarily cannot be extended although if there are exceptional reasons why a person cannot comply, a request should be made to the ICE Enforcement and Removals Operations, or ERO, Field Office Director within the jurisdiction of the immigration court that issued the VD order.

---

[22] While in court VD is discussed here, it should be noted that both USCIS and ICE have authority to grant it also.
[23] INA § 240B.

Before an immigration judge can grant VD, s/he must be satisfied that the respondent does not have a conviction for significant criminal offenses and has sufficient resources to cover the cost of departing the United States.[24] No evidence is required to be submitted to substantiate this as the respondent's own assurances will be sufficient.

The benefit of accepting VD at this stage is that it ensures a respondent will not have a removal order entered against him or her. As a result, s/he is not legally barred from reentering the country based on having been deported and, theoretically, could seek to reenter the United States the very next day after s/he has departed. In reality, however there may be some problems for a foreign national who is seeking to return for a temporary purpose, particularly when past immigration history shows a violation of the terms of any prior visa issued or status granted or departing the United States may trigger the unlawful presence bar. Therefore, careful consideration should be given to the real value of requesting VD.

Case for Discussion 10.2

Miguel entered the United States from Mexico, crossing at the border in Texas. He was discovered by CBP agents within a week of his arrival, while he and others hid in a safe house, waiting for their guide to lead them to the local Greyhound bus station so that they could each continue to their destinations to find family and friends. Miguel is detained as an arriving alien and appeared before an immigration judge. He has no immediate family members here who can file a relative petition for his benefit and is not afraid to return to his native Mexico. Miguel is unhappy about the conditions of his detention and wants to leave as quickly as possible.

- What are his options?

B.2. The Individual Hearing

Once a judge is satisfied that the case is ready to be heard, s/he will schedule it for an *individual hearing*. This is when the judge will hear the merits of the claim for immigration relief. This hearing will be just for the respondent and his or her witnesses and whoever else s/he wants to be present during the hearing. It is not open to the public.[25] Individual hearings usually last one to three hours, although some may last longer if there are complicated facts or numerous witnesses involved.

Individual Hearing: A hearing held in immigration court where an immigration judge considers the merits of any application for immigration relief and renders a decision.

---

[24] 8 C.F.R. § 1240.26(b).
[25] 8 C.F.R. § 1240.32(a).

In order to prepare for an individual hearing, any application forms and appropriate fees related to a particular immigration relief must be properly completed and filed with the immigration court or with the USCIS. The immigration court does not have the ability to receive fees, therefore, the filing fee(s), together with copies of the application(s) to be submitted to the court, must be sent to the USCIS, either through the Texas or Nebraska Service Centers, using a special cover sheet prepared by EOIR. A sample of the cover sheet appeared in Figure 5.5.

Once filed, a fee receipt for the application will be issued by the USCIS and sent to the respondent or his or her legal representative, for submission to the court as proof that all fees have been paid. The respondent will also receive an appointment notice to appear at an **Application Support Center** for digital fingerprints and photographs to be taken as part of the necessary biometrics information collection process. Once obtained, this information will be used for comparison with several security and criminal databases maintained by the government, with the results presented to the court. Judges have no authority to issue a decision on an application for relief without first obtaining the results of these checks. Some immigration judges may even refuse to hear the merits of the case without this. Biometrics results are valid for only 15 months and therefore it may be necessary to have a client resubmit biometric information in the event that his or her hearing is scheduled beyond the validity period.

Notice of Intent to Offer Evidence: A cover sheet which acts as an index to documents submitted to the court as evidence.

Office of the Chief Immigration Judge Practice Manual: A guide to uniform procedures, recommendations, and requirements for practicing before the immigration court.

As part of the preparation for the individual hearing, a witness list, a request for an interpreter, if required, and any supporting documents, are required to be filed with the court in a *Notice of Intent to Offer Evidence* at least 15 days prior to the hearing. This requirement is set out in *the Office of the Chief Immigration Judge Practice Manual,* or OCIJ Practice Manual, issued by the Chief Immigration Judge and is available at the EOIR website.[26] Representatives should familiarize themselves with the manual's contents as it provides guidance on all aspects of court procedure, deadlines, and other facets of representation. There is a separate manual for representation before the BIA, which is the Board of Immigration Appeal Practice Manual.[27]

A judge is free to require documents to be filed in court in a different time frame from the manual. For instance, if a judge orders all documents to be submitted 30 days or more before the hearing, this is now the timeframe that must be followed. If after filing and before the date of the hearing new information comes to light, a legal representative may always request the court's permission to enter it into the record, right up until the date of the hearing. Whenever evidence is being offered out of time, a good explanation as to why it is late should be provided in the form of a motion to the court.

---

[26] *See* https://www.justice.gov/sites/default/files/pages/attachments/2016/02/04/practice_manual_-_02-08-2016_update.pdf.
[27] *See* https://www.justice.gov/sites/default/files/pages/attachments/2016/04/27/biapracticemanual_0.pdf#page=1.

B.2.a. Case Preparation

Practitioners can prepare a case for hearing in immigration court in many ways. Ultimately, the one chosen will depend on the type of case and the strategy that is being followed. Here are some general rules.

Each witness to testify at the hearing should prepare either an affidavit or statement of what they will testify to, or a **proffer of information or evidence**, which may be an outline or summary. Some practitioners prefer detailed statements so that the court is aware of the respondent's story and can see from documents submitted that there is evidence to corroborate it. This may be preferable where a respondent or witness can be relied upon to be consistent in the telling of his or her story and therefore questions regarding credibility are less likely to arise.

Typically, it is better to have witnesses come to court to testify in person. However, sometimes this is not feasible because of other commitments or the difficulty of traveling to a court that may be many miles away. Judges may be willing to agree to a witness testifying telephonically, although, this is usually with respect to those whose identities can be verified, such as professors or others who are testifying as experts. Before making a request for telephonic testimony, it may be useful to consider what advantages may be lost when a person's facial expressions, general demeanor, and physical responses cannot be seen by the judge. Testifying in person can provide a certain gravitas that may be an important component in the presentation of the case.

In some cases, a witness may be willing to provide a detailed statement but not to appear in court. This can be problematic because s/he is not available to be cross-examined by the attorney for the government regarding the content of the statement or affidavit. In such cases, an immigration judge has discretion to enter the statement into the record as evidence and to decide how much weight to give it, which may not be much where the affiant does not appear to testify in person. An alternative may be to enter the information as a letter of support rather than as a statement or affidavit.

Once all the documents to be filed with the court have been prepared, they must be copied, collated, tabbed, and paginated.[28] Paralegals are often responsible for properly collating and organizing an application package under the supervision of an attorney. A Notice of Intent to Offer Evidence should also be filed, identifying each document, its page number, and the tab letter assigned to it. There should also be a witness list, identifying each witness the respondent intends to call. Relevant sections or pages of documents addressing country conditions information should be highlighted. The documents are then filed with the immigration court, with the exact copy prepared for and sent to the attorney for the government. A proof or certificate of service, confirming how the government was served must also be included in the filing. A sample certificate is in Figure 10.5. All documents must be two-hole punched at the top.[29]

---

[28] OCIJ Practice Manual, Section 3.3.
[29] OCIJ Practice Manual, Section 3.3(c)(viii).

Figure 10.5

Sample Proof or Certificate of Service

Source: OCIJ Practice Manual.

Immigration Court
Practice Manual   Appendix G

Sample Proof of Service

_____
(Name of alien or aliens)

_____
("A number" of alien or aliens)

PROOF OF SERVICE

On _____, I, _____.
      (date)   (printed name of person signing below)

served a copy of this _____
                        (name of document)

and any attached pages to _____
                        (name of party served)

at the following address: _____
                        (address of party served)

_____
                        (address of party served)

by _____.
(method of service, for example overnight courier, hand-delivery, first class mail)

_____   _____
     (signature)   (date)

updates: www.justice.gov/eoir   G-2   Version released on February 4, 2016

The legal representative can make a decision about whether there are any issues in the case which should be addressed in a legal brief. It is not always necessary to file a brief in every case, but where the legal issue is relatively new or contentious, a brief can be helpful.

B.2.b. Case Proceedings

Proceedings at the merits or individual hearing are rather straightforward. They typically begin with the immigration judge identifying each document that is to be entered into the record and according it an exhibit number. This is for ease of reference of the parties. The government attorney and legal representative for the respondent will each be asked if they object to the admission of any document into the record with a discussion ensuing to explain why there is an objection before the judge rules on it. Once this is complete, the proceedings will begin.

Where the respondent has requested an interpreter, the judge will first swear in the chosen person and give him or her instructions on their role in the proceedings. A brief conversation between the interpreter and witness will follow to ensure they understand each other, as poor quality interpreting can lead to appeals asserting lack of due process.[30] Proceedings will then be turned over to the respondent's legal representative for him or her to begin questioning. Some judges allow opening statements to be made by either party first. However, it is not always necessary unless there are legal issues that need to be addressed at the beginning of the hearing.

The first set of questions in a hearing is known as ***examination in chief***. This is the opportunity for the legal practitioner to ask questions that will allow the respondent to tell his or her story. In doing so, it is important to think about the audience, i.e., the judge, and how s/he will respond to the evidence presented. Therefore, some work may need to be done in order to gather information on the personality of a particular immigration judge. Questions that might be asked of other practitioners in order to ascertain a sense of the judge might be: What is his or her manner? How does s/he like information to be presented? Does s/he prefer you to get to the point or is some latitude permitted in the giving of information? It is important to remember that judges may ask questions of respondents at any time during the proceedings and some judges may decide to question the witness extensively. Either way, the legal practitioner must be prepared to resume questioning from the next appropriate point, making sure not to repeat questions the judge may have already asked.

One of the advantages of providing a detailed affidavit or statement as part of the evidence filing is that it may allow you to waive examination in chief and

> **Examination in Chief:** Questions posed by the person calling a witness to testify under oath, which allows him or her to lay a foundation of pertinent facts for the case.

---

[30] *Matter of Tomas*, 19 I&N Dec. 464 (BIA 1987); *Perez-Lastor v. INS*, 208 F.3d 773 (9th Cir. 2000).

move directly to the next stage. Careful thought must be given to doing this, as it might be better for the respondent to testify in his or her own words first in order to become comfortable with the proceedings. However, bringing back memories of what happened in a case involving traumatic events can be extremely painful for some, therefore it might be appropriate to waive if this would help to minimize the retraumatization of the respondent.

The second round of questioning that takes place during proceedings is known as ***cross-examination*** and is conducted by the attorney for the government, whose role is to assist the judge in whatever decision s/he makes. This could mean that, where there is sufficient evidence to support an application for relief without negative factors, the government attorney may decide to concede or to alert the immigration judge that a grant of relief would be uncontested. However, where there are negative factors that the attorney determines should preclude the granting of relief, then s/he must present them. In such cases, the objective of cross-examination will be to challenge the respondent's credibility by trying to elicit the truth of what happened and to persuade the judge that relief should or should not be granted.

> **Cross-Examination:** The questioning of a witness by the opposing party in order to ascertain the veracity of information provided during examination in chief or to further develop testimony.

Following cross-examination, the legal representative for the respondent may choose to re-examine the respondent. This is done in order to address any information that may have been disclosed during cross-examination that had not been dealt with previously or to clarify certain matters that may be confusing. As a rule, this should only be considered if the answer the respondent will give is likely to be helpful.

Following the testimony of all witnesses in the case, either party may opt to make a ***closing argument*** to the judge. Some immigration judges encourage a legal representative and the government attorney to present a closing argument, while others do not.

> **Closing Argument:** A summary of the facts and applicable law as they relate to the case before the judge.

B.3. Evidence Rules in Immigration Court

While the **Federal Rules of Evidence** are applicable in immigration proceedings, they are used in a more relaxed format. Therefore, the judge may consider "any oral or written statement that is material and relevant to any issue in the case previously made by the respondent or any other person during any investigation, examination, hearing, or trial."[31] This means that the government may use any information it has to impugn a respondent's credibility. Therefore, as part of case preparation, it is important to review all prior statements made by the respondent during *any* interviews s/he may have had with *any* of the three DHS agencies s/he has come into contact with at any time. An immigration judge can also consider

---

[31] 8 C.F.R. § 1240.7(a).

hearsay evidence during proceedings, whereas under the Rules of Evidence, it can only be introduced in certain circumstances.[32]

Hearsay Evidence: The relaying of information by someone without firsthand knowledge of it.

● **EXAMPLE**

Zoyla is in removal proceedings and applying for asylum because she is afraid to return to her native Guatemala. Her husband has abused her for many years, with no recourse to protection from the government. When the worst of the abuse was happening, Zoyla finally broke down and told her friends and family because she was afraid of what her husband might do. They were the ones who encouraged her to leave him and seek protection in the United States. During her asylum hearing, Zoyla's friends and family can provide statements or letters, explaining what she told them about her husband's treatment of her. Even though this is hearsay evidence because they did not witness the abuse themselves, an immigration judge may allow it as evidence in Zoyla's case and decide what weight to give it.

Sometimes the government may introduce statements or evidence, either previously made or damaging to a witness, in order to challenge or impeach his or her credibility. If this is something that has not been previously made available to the respondent prior to the hearing, it is quite appropriate for the legal practitioner to request a short adjournment to allow review of the document and to confer with the respondent about its content.

B.4. Decision of the Immigration Judge

At the end of the proceedings, the immigration judge may issue an oral decision. Where all parties are agreed that the relief sought should be granted, it is very rare for there to be a written decision. Instead, the judge will issue a minute order, a sample of which is in Figure 10.6. This is merely written evidence of what was decided at the conclusion of the proceedings.

The immigration judge may also reserve his or her decision, electing to provide it at some later stage after all of the facts and evidence have been reviewed more thoroughly. The case may be continued to a master calendar hearing some months ahead to allow sufficient time for the decision to be prepared, while keeping it on the judge's docket.

B.5. Post-Hearing Voluntary Departure

As to the decision the judge makes, s/he could grant the relief sought, deny and order removal, or deny and grant voluntary departure. If the decision is to grant relief, then the respondent must contact the USCIS in order to complete any necessary paperwork to allow the foreign national to obtain documentation to prove the status given. Instructions on what to do will be

---

[32] *See* Federal Rules of Evidence § 801 et al.

Figure 10.6

Sample Minute Order

```
                    IMMIGRATION COURT
                900 MARKET STREET, SUITE 504
                    PHILADELPHIA, PA 19107

In the Matter of
                                    Case No.: A_____
_____
        Respondent              IN REMOVAL PROCEEDINGS

                ORDER OF THE IMMIGRATION JUDGE

This is a summary of the oral decision entered on Oct 30, 2014
This memorandum is solely for the convenience of the parties. If the
proceedings should be appealed or reopened, the oral decision will become
the official opinion in the case.
[ ]  The respondent was ordered removed from the United States to
     or in the alternative to .
[ ]  Respondent's application for voluntary departure was denied and
     respondent was ordered removed to  or in the
     alternative to .
[ ]  Respondent's application for voluntary departure was granted until
     upon posting a bond in the amount of $ _____
     with an alternate order of removal to .
Respondent's application for:
[ ]  Asylum was ( )granted ( )denied( )withdrawn.
[✓]  Withholding of removal was (W) granted ( )denied ( )withdrawn.
[X]  A Waiver under Section ___ was ( )granted ( )denied ( )withdrawn.
[ ]  Cancellation of removal under section 240A(a) was ( )granted ( )denied
     ( )withdrawn.
Respondent's application for:
[ ]  Cancellation under section 240A(b)(1) was ( ) granted ( ) denied
     ( ) withdrawn. If granted, it is ordered that the respondent be issued
     all appropriate documents necessary to give effect to this order.
[ ]  Cancellation under section 240A(b)(2) was ( )granted ( )denied
     ( )withdrawn. If granted it is ordered that the respondent be issued
     all appropriated documents necessary to give effect to this order.
[ ]  Adjustment of Status under Section ____ was ( )granted ( )denied
     ( )withdrawn. If granted it is ordered that the respondent be issued
     all appropriated documents necessary to give effect to this order.
[ ]  Respondent's application of ( ) withholding of removal ( ) deferral of
     removal under Article III of the Convention Against Torture was
     ( ) granted ( ) denied ( ) withdrawn.
[ ]  Respondent's status was rescinded under section 246.
[ ]  Respondent is admitted to the United States as a ____ until ____.
[ ]  As a condition of admission, respondent is to post a $ _____ bond.
[ ]  Respondent knowingly filed a frivolous asylum application after proper
     notice.
[ ]  Respondent was advised of the limitation on discretionary relief for
     failure to appear as ordered in the Immigration Judge's oral decision.
[X]  Proceedings were terminated.
[ ]  Other: _____
     Date: 10/8/14
                                            _____
                                              Immigration Judge

        Appeal: Waived/Reserved    Appeal Due By:
```

given to the respondent at the conclusion of the hearing and a sample of it is in Figure 10.7.

As an alternative, the immigration judge may deny relief but, rather than enter an order of deportation, grant voluntary departure instead. This is similar to VD granted during a master calendar hearing, but is issued post-proceedings. To be eligible for VD at the conclusion of a merits hearing, a respondent must prove that s/he has been present in the United States for at least one year before service of the NTA, has been a person of good moral character for five years prior to the VD request, has no aggravated felony convictions, and is not a national security risk.[33] The respondent must also demonstrate by clear and convincing evidence that s/he has the means and intent to depart the United States.[34] The maximum period given to leave the country is only 60 days, which contrasts with the 120 days available when VD is granted at the master calendar pre-hearing stage.[35]

In addition to these eligibility requirements, a person seeking post-hearing VD must post a bond of at least $500 with ICE within five business days of the issuance of the order.[36] Failure to do so will mean the VD order is no longer available and an order of removal will be substituted instead.

When a respondent accepts VD at the end of proceedings, s/he is entering into an agreement to leave as promised. There are serious consequences for failing to depart. The foreign national could be subject to a civil penalty of between $1,000 and $5,000 and be ineligible to receive any immigration benefits to which s/he may be entitled, for a period of ten years.[37] In some ways, these consequences are more harsh than those imposed by a removal order. Once a person is ordered deported,

---

[33] INA § 240B(b)(1).
[34] INA § 240B(b)(2).
[35] Id.
[36] 8 C.F.R. § 1240.26(c)(3).
[37] INA § 240B(d)(1)(A).

Figure 10.7
Post-Order Instructions for Individuals Granted Relief or Protection from Removal by Immigration Court

Source: USCIS.

POST-ORDER INSTRUCTIONS FOR INDIVIDUALS GRANTED RELIEF OR PROTECTION FROM REMOVAL BY IMMIGRATION COURT

Please follow the applicable instructions marked below.

If you fail to present yourself to the U.S. Citizenship and Immigration Services (USCIS) as instructed, and fail to follow USCIS instructions for providing your biometrics (such as fingerprints, photograph, and signature) and other biographical information, you may not receive your immigration documents.

☐ A. Instructions for Individuals with Final Orders	☐ B. Instructions for Individuals Without Final Orders
○ You have been granted permanent residence or asylum, and that decision is final. In order to receive a Permanent Resident Card or asylum and employment authorization documents, you must contact USCIS in one of the following ways: • You may schedule an appointment with your local USCIS office through INFOPASS, an internet-based online system at www.uscis.gov, or • In case of a true emergency, your local USCIS office will try to assist you without an appointment. **In order to allow sufficient time for the USCIS office to receive information about your court order, please do not make your appointment or visit USCIS any earlier than 3 business days after the date of your immigration court order.** *You **must** bring a copy of your final order granting you asylum or permanent residency when you come to USCIS to complete processing for your status and/or work authorization documents.* ○ You have been granted another form of relief or protection, such as withholding of removal, and you *may* be eligible for work authorization. You may obtain an I-765, Application for Employment Authorization, from the USCIS website at www.uscis.gov/graphics/formsfee/forms/index.htm, or by calling (800) 375-5283. Submit the application as directed in the instructions to the application.	Your application for relief/protection has been granted, but the decision is not final. Therefore, you will not receive a Permanent Resident Card or documentation of asylum at this time. • The government has 30 days to file an appeal of the Immigration Judge's decision with the Board of Immigration Appeals (BIA). You may check whether the government has filed an appeal by calling (800) 898-7180. • If the government does not file an appeal, the Immigration Judge's decision will become final after 30 days, and you may then schedule an appointment with USCIS to receive your immigration documents (*e.g.,* Permanent Resident Card or asylum and employment authorization). Follow the instructions on the left side (A) of this paper for making an appointment at your local USCIS office. Be sure to bring the judge's order to USCIS. • If the government files an appeal of the Immigration Judge's decision, the BIA will issue a filing receipt. You may consult the BIA Practice Manual at www.usdoj.gov/eoir for information on the appellate process. • While an appeal of your case is pending at the BIA, you may be eligible to apply to USCIS for an employment authorization document. For further information, *see* www.uscis.gov. • If the BIA issues an administratively final order granting you relief or protection, at that time you may schedule an appointment with USCIS to receive your immigration status documents. Be sure to bring your BIA order to USCIS.

(Eff. Date 4/1/05)

s/he cannot return to the United States for a period of ten years after his or her departure under that order.[38] Should there be a need to return before the ten-year period has expired, a waiver to re-enter the country must be obtained from the attorney general first.[39] Anyone returning to the United States during the ten-year period and without a waiver is subject to having the prior removal order reinstated without the opportunity to see an immigration judge unless s/he expresses a fear of returning to a country where s/he will be persecuted.[40]

A foreign national granted VD must present him or herself to a consular officer at an embassy or consular office on his or her return home as proof of departing the United States. The consular officer will then notify ICE that the foreign national has left the country, at which time any bond paid plus accrued interest will be released. If there is no such evidence of departure within the allotted time, the bond will be forfeited to the government. Again, theoretically the foreign national could apply for a visa to reenter the United States, but the likelihood of a grant may be quite slim.

C. Expedited Removal Proceedings

In most cases, a foreign national who is subject to removal is guaranteed due process rights, which allow the opportunity to argue his or her case before an immigration judge. However, that right may be denied in special and limited circumstances, where officers from either CBP or ICE may decide to remove the foreign national from the United States without a hearing. This process is known as expedited removal proceedings and is governed by INA § 235(b).

A CBP officer is authorized to place a foreign national into expedited removal if, at the time of applying for admission, s/he seeks to enter through fraud or misrepresentation[41] or because s/he does not have the appropriate documentation to support the type of immigration status sought.[42] Misrepresentation and lack of proper documents are the only grounds of inadmissibility that can result in expedited removal.[43] Foreign nationals in these types of proceedings for these reasons are referred to as arriving aliens and will only be

---

[38] INA § 212(a)(9)(A)(ii).
[39] INA § 212(a)(9)(A)(iii).
[40] INA § 241(a)(5). *See also* Section C of Chapter 5, Asylum and Other Related Humanitarian Relief, for a discussion on reasonable fear interviews.
[41] INA § 212(a)(6)(C). *See also* Section B.6.c of Chapter 9, Grounds of Inadmissibility and Deportation.
[42] INA § 212(a)(7). *See also* Section B.7 of Chapter 9, Grounds of Inadmissibility and Deportation.
[43] INA § 235(b)(1)(A)(i).

entitled to see an immigration judge if they pass a credible fear interview.[44] All other grounds of inadmissibility will result in the applicant for entry being placed into the more expansive removal proceedings, where any viable immigration benefit may be sought.

ICE officers also have authority to remove an arriving alien without permitting him or her to see an immigration judge. A foreign national who enters without inspection and cannot prove s/he has been in the United States for a continuous period of two years without any absences may be placed into expedited removal proceedings.[45] This provision has been expanded to include those who enter without inspection, or EWI, and have "spent 14 days or less in the United States, and are either apprehended within 100 miles of the border with Mexico or Canada or arrive by sea and are apprehended within 100 miles of a coastal border area."[46] Inadmissible or deportable Visa Waiver Program travelers[47] are also subject to expedited removal since, as a condition of their participation in the program, they are required to waive all rights to a hearing unless they are seeking asylum.[48]

A foreign national subject to expedited removal is subject to mandatory detention until removal can be effected.[49] S/he cannot apply to be freed on **bond** but release may be possible if it is "required to meet a medical emergency or is necessary for a legitimate law enforcement objective."[50] In such circumstances, parole into the United States will be granted, with a requirement to report to ICE on a regular basis. Return to the United States for those removed under expedited removal is prohibited for a period of five years.[51]

Arriving aliens who express fear of return to their country of origin are exempted from these rules, as they must be afforded an interview with an asylum officer.[52] If they are deemed to have demonstrated a credible fear of return, or the higher reasonable fear standard for those who are returning to the United States while a prior deportation order is still in effect, then s/he will be referred to an immigration judge for a hearing where the relief available to the respondent is limited to asylum, withholding of removal, or relief under the Convention Against Torture.

---

[44] INA § 235(b)(1)(A)(ii). *See also* Section C of Chapter 5, Asylum and Other Related Humanitarian Relief, for a discussion on credible fear interviews.
[45] INA § 235(b)(1)(A)(iii)(II).
[46] *See* U.S. Department of Homeland Security Press Office Press Release, dated January 30, 2006, "DHS Streamlines Removal Process Along Entire U.S. Border."
[47] *See* Section E.2.a of Chapter 2, Nonimmigrant Visas for Brief Stays, Studies, and Cultural Exchange.
[48] INA § 217(b).
[49] INA § 235(b)(1)(B)(iii)(IV).
[50] 8 C.F.R. § 235.3(b)(2)(iii).
[51] INA § 212(a)(9)(A)(i).
[52] INA § 235(b)(1)(B). *See also* Section C of Chapter 5, Asylum and Other Related Humanitarian Relief.

> **Case for Discussion   10.3**
>
> Solange arrives at JFK airport in New York from her native Democratic Republic of Congo, or DRC, where she had been a nurse. She wants to escape from her country because government soldiers raped her as punishment for medically treating fighters in the rebel forces. Solange is afraid to tell this to the CBP Officer because she believes she will be sent back home. She presents a passport that was given to her by a friend who helped her to escape the country. However, the CBP officer is able to recognize that the passport is fraudulent. During a search of Solange's luggage, officers discover her nursing diploma and letters of recommendation, which are to help her find work. A CBP supervisor determines that Solange tried to enter the United States illegally by using fraudulent documents and tells her that she is subject to expedited removal and will be put on the next plane back to the DRC. Solange is placed in a detention facility until there is a plane available to take her back home. While there, she learns about the asylum process and notifies an immigration officer in the detention center that she is afraid to return.
>
> - What should happen after Solange has disclosed this information? You may need to refer back to Section C of Chapter 5, Asylum and Other Related Humanitarian Relief, to assist you in answering this question.
> - Will Solange still be subject to expedited removal?

D. Detention

Any foreign national who is an arriving alien and found inadmissible at the border is subject to detention.[53] However, s/he may apply for release on parole under INA § 212(d)(5), where a determination must be made that such release would be in the public interest.

Foreign nationals who are not considered arriving aliens and are not subject to mandatory detention because of a qualifying criminal offense or on terrorism grounds, as discussed in Section D.1, may be released on bond.[54] The initial application is made to the ICE Field Office Director who can decide whether the person is eligible for release and, if a bond is to be set, the amount that is reasonable in the circumstances.

---

[53] *Shaughnessy v. U.S. ex. rel. Mezei*, 345 U.S. 206, 219 (1953).
[54] INA § 236(a).

When deciding whether to grant bond, the following are some of the factors that may be considered:

- Whether the foreign national is likely to appear at any immigration court hearing scheduled to determine his or her removability,
- Family and community ties in the United States,
- Medical need,
- Prior immigration history,
- Length of time in the United States,
- Whether there is any immigration relief available and what type, and
- The person's criminal and character history.[55]

While this is not an exhaustive list, a bond applicant should present suitable evidence to support the release request. If the bond amount is set at a level that the foreign national cannot meet, a request for redetermination may be made to the ICE Field Office Director or an application for review of the amount can be made to an immigration judge who has jurisdiction to hear bond requests,[56] even if jurisdiction to hear the overall immigration case has not lodged with the court because the NTA has not yet been filed.[57] In very rare circumstances, a person may be released on his or her own recognizance, thereby not requiring any bond to be paid. Bond hearings are completely separate from removal proceedings and can only be conducted by immigration judges who preside over hearings for those who are detained. These hearings are generally held in special courts within or close to the detention facility.

Once the bond amount has been set, it must be paid to the local ICE office, whether that is at the detention facility or some other location. A receipt is provided for the amount paid and bond papers given to the person responsible for paying the money. Only after all removal proceedings are complete and the bonded person removed or released, where appropriate, will the bond be repaid. If the foreign national absconds, however, the bond amount will be forfeited to the government.

It should be noted that an industry has developed to provide alternatives to detention, or ATD, to the immigration system in much the same way as that used in the context of pre-trial criminal proceedings. These methods can encompass electronic monitoring through ankle bracelets fitted with GPS tracking, unannounced home visits, biometric voice recognition software that will identify a caller, and regular in person supervision appointments. The main objective is to keep track of foreign nationals either while they navigate the immigration system and ensure compliance with court attendance, or post hearing orders before removal is carried out. There is also a group of foreign nationals who may be deportable, but whose removal cannot be effected for a number of reasons. Using

---

[55] *Matter of Patel,* 15 I&N Dec. 666 (BIA 1976).
[56] 8 C.F.R. § 1003.19(c).
[57] 8 C.F.R. § 1003.19(c)(1).

ATD to monitor these individuals is less expensive than detention and thus more cost-effective.

For-profit companies operate many of the ATD options available. With this myriad of choices, on average, foreign nationals now spend less time in actual detention than previously. However, the monitoring alternatives can be onerous for those trying to support themselves through working, because they often find themselves either having to be home at a particular time of day, so that they can receive a monitoring call or visit, or because they have to report frequently at an immigration or ATD office. Once a pattern of compliance has been established, however, modification of the reporting requirements can be requested and is often granted.

Not all detention facilities contain an immigration court. In these cases, hearings are conducted by video link. The immigration judge and government attorney are usually in one location while the respondent and his or her legal representative may be in another. The legal representative may also make the strategic decision to be in the courtroom with the judge rather than with his or her client, which adds another dimension to the removal proceedings. Once release from detention is complete, either on bond or on an ATD program, the government will then file a Motion to Change Venue, since courts presiding over detention facilities only have jurisdiction to hear immigration cases for those detained. The motion will request that the removal proceedings continue in the immigration court that covers the geographic area where the person now resides.

D.1. Mandatory Detention

Some detained individuals are not eligible to be released on bond and must be detained until a decision is made about whether they can remain in the United States or must leave. For those eligible for relief, this can be quite frustrating and points to a contradiction in a system that detains those who will ultimately be granted an immigration benefit. The detention of those ineligible for release is known as mandatory detention and can be divided into two categories: pre-issuance of a **final order of removal**, governed by INA § 236(c)(1), and post issuance of a final order of removal under INA § 241.

Foreign nationals subject to detention under INA § 236(c)(1) before a final order of removal has been issued include:

- Those inadmissible for committing two or more crimes involving moral turpitude, or CIMTs,[58]
- Those deportable for multiple criminal convictions,[59]
- Those deportable for aggravated felony crimes,[60]
- Those deportable for convictions involving controlled substances,[61]

---

[58] INA § 237(a)(2)(A)(i).
[59] INA § 237(a)(2)(A)(ii).
[60] INA § 237(a)(2)(A)(iii).
[61] INA § 237(a)(2)(B).

- Those inadmissible or deportable for security related grounds,[62]
- Those deportable for certain firearms offenses,[63] and
- Those deportable for miscellaneous crimes.[64]

After a final order of removal has been issued, foreign nationals subject to detention under INA § 241 include those who are inadmissible, such as arriving aliens denied asylum, or those who are or deportable for criminal or security-related issues, as listed above. However, even the use of detention here has some safeguards. Removal of these individuals must be carried out within a period of 90 days, known as the **removal period**,[65] which begins after the removal order becomes final. This period is generally after all administrative appeals have been exhausted,[66] or, where there is a federal court challenge, the circuit court issues its final decision in the case.[67] It can also begin when a foreign national who has been convicted of an offense completes any period of confinement imposed.[68]

During the removal period, the foreign national is expected to assist ICE in its efforts to obtain any documentation necessary to facilitate his or her removal to the designated country or country of nationality. This can involve completing paperwork to obtain a passport or other travel documents. Any acts of obstruction engaged in by the foreign national will extend the 90-day period.[69] There are times a foreign national cannot obtain a travel document, either because the United States does not have diplomatic relations with his or her government or because that government refuses to issue the necessary travel document. If at the end of the removal period the foreign national cannot be removed or it appears unlikely that removal will be imminent, then s/he will be released on an *order of supervision*.[70] One of the benefits of a supervision order is that a foreign national in this situation is, in most circumstances, able to apply for permission to work.[71] An application is filed on Form I-765, Application for Employment Authorization.

Order of Supervision: An order imposing conditions on an individual's release from detention, which may include reporting requirements, monitoring, and updating of biographic information within a certain time period.

Notwithstanding the requirement to release a foreign national after the removal period, certain individuals can be detained beyond that time.[72] This includes those who have been found inadmissible for any reason, those who are removable for committing certain crimes or for security related reasons, or anyone the Attorney General determines to be a risk to the community or a potential flight risk, unless the foreign national can demonstrate that these risks do not apply.[73]

---

[62] INA §§ 212(a)(3) and 237(a)(4)(A).
[63] INA § 237(a)(2)(C).
[64] INA § 237(a)(D).
[65] INA § 241(a)(1)(A).9
[66] INA § 101(a)(47)(B).
[67] INA § 241(a)(1)(B)(ii). Note that a foreign national can be deported while his or her judicial case is still pending in federal court. In order to prevent this, an order to stay removal must be requested from and granted by the court.
[68] INA § 241(a)(1)(B)(iii).
[69] INA § 241(a)(1)(C).
[70] INA § 241(a)(3).
[71] INA § 241(a)(7).
[72] INA § 241(a)(6).
[73] 8 C.F.R. §§ 241.4(d)(1), 1241.14.

Where a foreign national considers that his or her continued detention is unreasonable, a ***habeas corpus*** action in federal district court may be initiated to force release. The Supreme Court has held that the indefinite detention of foreign nationals is unconstitutional.[74] It has set a limit of six months in which removal must be arranged or the individual released. This provides some certainty in the process.

Habeas Corpus: Latin term that allows a court to hear constitutional challenges to a person's continued detention.

E. Motions Practice in Immigration Court

Immigration court practice allows for the filing of various motions. The OCIJ Practice Manual should be reviewed for guidance on format and content. There are a number of important motions that can be filed before the court, such as a Motion to Reopen and a Motion to Reconsider. Each serves a different purpose.

E.1. Motion to Reopen

A Motion to Reopen an immigration case may be filed after removal proceedings are complete and the immigration judge has entered a decision in the case. The motion is filed with the original judge, asking him or her to reopen the case so that previously unavailable or undiscoverable evidence may be considered.[75] Any request must be supported by relevant evidence.

Case for Discussion 10.4

Mariam from Pakistan has been in immigration removal proceedings for several years. She is married to a U.S. citizen and he has filed Form I-130, Petition for Alien Relative, on her behalf. However, the petition was denied by the USCIS because it was not satisfied that the couple had demonstrated that their marriage is *bona fide*. Because the petition has been denied and there is no readily available visa or other immigration relief from removal available for Mariam, the immigration judge has ordered her deported. Subsequent to her proceedings, Mariam became pregnant. Her husband files a new relative petition, providing information regarding the pregnancy as part of his application. The petition is approved, making way for Mariam to file a Form I-485, Application to Register Permanent Residence or Adjust Status. However, because she already has a deportation order entered against her, Miriam must take a number of steps before she can file this application.

- What steps must Mariam take in order to adjust her status to lawful permanent resident, or LPR?

---

[74] *Zadvydas v. Davis*, 533 U.S. 678 (2001).
[75] 8 C.F.R. § 1003.23(b)(3).

Only one Motion to Reopen may be filed by a foreign national in removal proceedings.[76] In addition, the motion should be filed within 90 days of the immigration judge's final order.[77] There are exceptions to these two requirements. For instance, if the motion is based on changed country conditions in an asylum case, then it may be filed outside the 90-day limit.[78] This is also true for a Motion to Reopen an *in absentia* order which can be filed, either within 180 days after the order was issued, or at any time if the respondent can prove the Notice of Hearing was never received. This is discussed in Section A.1.

A very useful tool is a Motion to Reopen filed jointly with the government because both parties agree that reopening would be an appropriate course of action to take. Obtaining government cooperation on such a motion generally requires a respondent to first make a detailed case supported by substantial evidence to explain why reopening would be appropriate. If the government agrees to join in the motion, then neither the number of motions previously filed nor the timing of the filing are of any consequence as joint motions may be filed at any time. If the government refuses to join in a motion, the legal practitioner can send a motion to the judge asking that the immigration case be reopened *sua sponte*, or on the judge's own motion.[79]

> *Sua Sponte*: Latin term acknowledging unilateral action.

E.2. Motion to Reconsider

A **Motion to Reconsider** asks an immigration judge to review his or her decision in a case because there has been an error in applying the law, some aspect in the case was overlooked, or there has been a change in the law that affects the judge's prior decision.[80] By filing the motion, the judge is asked to reexamine his or her ruling and make a different decision. For this motion, new evidence cannot be introduced as the questions raised are based on the record that existed at the time of the initial decision. Similar to a Motion to Reopen, only one Motion to Reconsider can be filed.[81] The time limit for this motion is 30 rather than 90 days.[82]

E.3. Motion to Change Venue

A respondent may request a change of venue from one court to another at any time. However, an immigration judge must decide whether to grant that request and may do so only if good cause is shown.[83] Typically, a respondent's move out of the jurisdiction of the court that has control of his or her case into an area where a different court has jurisdiction will precipitate a change. An immigration judge may deny a motion to change venue if s/he believes the respondent moved

---

[76] INA § 240(c)(7)(A).
[77] INA § 240(c)(7)(C)(i).
[78] 8 C.F.R. § 1003.23(b)(4)(i).
[79] 8 C.F.R. § 1003.23(b)(1).
[80] *Matter of Ramos*, 23 I&N Dec. 336 (BIA 2002).
[81] INA § 240(c)(6)(A).
[82] INA § 240(c)(6)(B).
[83] 8 C.F.R. § 1003.20(b).

in order to get the case heard before a perceived more favorable court, known as "forum shopping," or seeks to delay a hearing in his or her case. A respondent or his or her legal representative can submit a Motion to Change Venue at any time after the charging document or NTA has been filed with the court. The request must be made with the court with current jurisdiction over the case, requesting that venue be changed to a different one.[84] The attorney for the government typically files requests to change venue for those released from detention.

The OCIJ Practice Manual requires that each Motion to Change Venue include the following information:

- The date and time of the next scheduled hearing,
- An admission or denial of the factual allegations and charge(s) in the Notice to Appear if pleadings have not already been taken,
- A designation or refusal to designate a country of removal,
- If the alien will be requesting relief from removal, a description of the basis for eligibility,
- The address and telephone number of the location at which respondent will be residing if the motion is granted,
- If the address at which the alien is receiving mail has changed, a properly completed Form EOIR 33/IC, Aliens Change of Address Form, and
- A detailed explanation of the reasons for the request.[85]

At any time during preparation of a case, a legal representative may require more time to obtain documents from abroad, or to await approval of an underlying application or petition filed with the USCIS. In such cases, a request for a **continuance** may be made to the court, which then has the discretion to decide whether to grant it or not. The regulations permit an immigration judge to grant a continuance for "good cause shown."[86] The judge may do so unilaterally or at the request of either party. However, the time granted must be for a reasonable period, taking into account the reason for the adjournment in the first place.[87] Courts have frowned on denials of continuances simply because it will inconvenience the judge's docket.[88]

There are numerous other motions that may be filed in a removal proceeding. For instance, there might be motions filed to substitute or withdraw as counsel, to advance a calendar in order to bring a hearing date forward, to waive appearance of the respondent or a witness at a hearing, to request telephonic testimony, or to request that a witness be subpoenaed. A motion should also be filed when evidentiary documents in support of a case are to be submitted late or out of time.

---

[84] 8 C.F.R. § 1003.20.
[85] OCIJ Practice Manual Chapter 5.10(c).
[86] 8 C.F.R. §§ 1003.29.
[87] 8 C.F.R. § 1240.6.
[88] See *Rendon v Holder*, 588 F.3d 669 (9th Cir. 2009), *Hashmi v. Att'y Gen. of the U.S.*, 531 F.3d 256, (3d Cir. 2008).

Any request for action on a case that needs to be made to an immigration judge should be in the form of a written motion, which is required to be filed with the court (together with three copies of the order sought and a certificate confirming service on the government) within 15 days of the hearing date that is the subject of the motion. A sample proposed order is in Figure 10.8. Any responses to the motion must be filed within ten days of that date.[89] Judges can sometimes take a while to respond to the motion and may even rule on it on the day of the hearing itself. Motions can also be made orally at the hearing although presenting it in written form may be better if it deals with a complex issue.

● **EXAMPLE**

Recall Zoyla from Guatemala who is seeking asylum. Her attorney has requested letters from family members abroad that explain what they know about what was going on between Zoyla and her husband and any first- or second-hand knowledge they may have about the abuse she suffered. Despite all efforts, the mail arrives ten days before the hearing. It took another two days to have them translated from Spanish to English. Even though the OCIJ Practice rules require all documents to be filed 15 days before the hearing, the legal representative can file a motion with the court to request that the documents be filed out of time. Most likely, there will be insufficient time for the government attorney to file any objection to the filing or for the judge to rule on the request. However, a decision can be made on the day of the hearing.

F. Administrative Closure

Administrative Closure: A mechanism that assists immigration judges in managing their dockets by closing cases that are not considered a priority for hearing at the present time.

Sometimes, a case before an immigration judge will not proceed to full hearing. This is because either the judge or the parties decide there are special circumstances that warrant a hold being placed on the case. The legal term for this is *administrative closure*. Essentially, the judge agrees that the case should be given a lower priority for hearing and it will effectively go to the back of his or her list of cases to be heard. When administrative closure is granted, a removal case will not be listed for hearing again until one of the parties files a motion with the immigration judge, asking for it to be **re-calendared** or placed back onto the judge's docket for a hearing date. Using this method eliminates the need for the parties to continue to appear simply to request continuances.

Administrative closure can be used in many different situations. For example, if a respondent is seeking immigration relief to which an underlying petition has to be approved first, such as an adjustment of status based on marriage, a judge may decide to administratively close the case before the court until

---

[89] OCIJ Practice Manual Chapter 3.1(b).

Figure 10.8

Sample Proposed Order
Source: OCIJ Practice Manual.

APPENDIX Q

Sample Proposed Order

A proposed order is submitted with every motion filed. Prior to filing a motion, parties are expected to have reviewed the pertinent regulations, as well as Chapter 5 of the Immigration Court Practice Manual (Motions before the Immigration Court).

United States Department of Justice
Executive Office for Immigration Review
Immigration Court
[the court's location (city or town) and state]

In the Matter of: [the respondent's name]   A Number: [the respondent's A number]

ORDER OF THE IMMIGRATION JUDGE

Upon consideration of ["the respondent's" or "DHS's"] [title of motion], it is HEREBY ORDERED that the motion be ☐ **GRANTED** ☐ **DENIED** because:

- ☐ DHS does not oppose the motion.
- ☐ The respondent does not oppose the motion.
- ☐ A response to the motion has not been filed with the court.
- ☐ Good cause has been established for the motion.
- ☐ The court agrees with the reasons stated in the opposition to the motion.
- ☐ The motion is untimely per _____.
- ☐ Other:

Deadlines:

- ☐ The application(s) for relief must be filed by _____.
- ☐ The respondent must comply with DHS biometrics instructions by _____.

_____   _____
Date   [name]
                                                      Immigration Judge

---

Certificate of Service

This document was served by: [ ] Mail [ ] Personal Service
To: [ ] Alien [ ] Alien c/o Custodial Officer [ ] Alien's Atty/Rep [ ] DHS
Date: _____

By: Court Staff _____

Version released on February 4, 2016

such time as the required relative petition has been approved by the USCIS, which could take several months. It may be appropriate when the foreign national has been given permission to remain here in a temporary category such as Temporary Protected Status, or TPS,[90] or Deferred Action for Childhood Arrivals, or DACA.[91] Another situation where administrative closure is useful is when ICE decides to exercise its discretion and defer further prosecution of a case that is in immigration court. This is known as ***prosecutorial discretion***.

The Director for ICE has discretion to decide who to target for removal and who should be treated as a lower priority. This is because there are insufficient resources to pursue every single person who is in the United States in violation of immigration laws. Therefore, on June 17, 2011, the ICE Director issued a memorandum[92] providing guidance to all Chief Counsels, ICE Field Office Directors, and others about who should be considered a priority for removal and against whom ICE can decide "not to assert the full scope of the enforcement authority available to the agency in a given case."[93]

The factors for consideration when exercising prosecutorial discretion include:

- The agency's civil immigration enforcement priorities;
- The person's length of presence in the United States, particularly while in lawful status;
- The circumstances of the person's arrival in the United States and manner of entry;
- The person's pursuit of education in the United States;
- Whether the person, or the person's immediate relative, has served in the U.S. military, reserves, or national guard, with particular consideration given to those who served in combat;
- The person's criminal history;
- The person's immigration history;
- Whether the person raises a national security or public safety concern;
- The person's ties and contributions to the community, including family relationships;
- The person's ties to the home country and conditions in the country;
- The person's age, with particular consideration given to minors and the elderly;
- Whether the person has a U.S. citizen or permanent resident spouse, child, or parent;

Prosecutorial Discretion: The authority of an agency charged with enforcing a law to decide to what degree to enforce it against a particular individual.

---

[90] *See* Section G of Chapter 5, Asylum and Other Related Humanitarian Relief.
[91] *See* Section U of Chapter 8, Immigration Relief for Vulnerable Populations.
[92] *Exercising Prosecutorial Discretion Consistent with the Civil Immigration Enforcement Priorities of the Agency for the Apprehension, Detention, and Removal of Aliens*, John Morton, ICE Director, Policy No. 10075.1, FEA No. 306-112-0026 (June 17, 2011), available here: https://www.ice.gov/doclib/secure-communities/pdf/prosecutorial-discretion-memo.pdf.
[93] *Id.* at page 2.

- Whether the person or the person's spouse suffers from severe mental or physical illness; and
- Whether the person is likely to be granted temporary or permanent status or other relief from removal.[94]

● **EXAMPLE**

Francisco is a citizen of Venezuela. He arrived in the United States in 1972, when he was just three years old and always believed that he was here as an LPR. In fact, he came as a visitor and has overstayed the leave granted to him many years ago. Francisco enlisted in the U.S. Marines Reserve Unit claiming LPR status and served for five years on active duty before he was honorably discharged. Following his release, his life went through a rough patch, and he began taking drugs. He was arrested and convicted of possession of cocaine back in 1998. Several years later, Francisco is placed into removal proceedings and is ineligible for relief because his conviction makes him inadmissible with no waiver available for possession of a controlled substance other than 30 grams or less of marijuana.[95] He has a history of mental illness and has tried to commit suicide on at least three occasions. He suffers from bipolar disorder and a number of other physical ailments. He is married to a U.S. citizen and has one child from a previous marriage who does not live with him. All of these factors point to a strong argument that Francisco may be granted prosecutorial discretion, despite his conviction, which was several years ago, and because he has had no other contact with law enforcement.

Prosecutorial discretion can be a useful tool to prevent the removal of those who have no immigration relief available to them but have sympathetic factors and or family that warrant them remaining in the United States. However, it does not confer any immigration status and, on its own, does not grant the ability to obtain permission to work.

G. Appeals Practice

Either party to an immigration case may be dissatisfied with a decision of the immigration judge and want to appeal it. Recall Zoyla from Guatemala who is seeking asylum because of the abuse she suffered from her husband. Despite all the evidence presented, the immigration judge denies her application because she believes that Zoyla was not a credible witness. If Zoyla disagrees with this decision, she can challenge it by filing an appeal with the BIA, which is the appellate body with jurisdiction over immigration cases.

---

[94] *Id.* at page 4.
[95] INA § 212(h). *See also* Section B.2.b.ii of Chapter 9, Grounds of Inadmissibility and Deportation.

A decision by an immigration judge only becomes final if no appeal is lodged with the BIA within 30 days.[96] This period is strictly enforced. An appeal filed even one day late will be dismissed simply for that reason.[97] A properly filed appeal will consist of the following:

- Form EOIR 26, Notice of Appeal from a Decision of an Immigration Judge, indicating either in detail or briefly the reason why the judge's decision is being appealed,
- Form EOIR 27, Notice of Appearance as Attorney or Legal Representative,
- A copy of the decision of the immigration judge that is the subject of the appeal,
- A fee, where appropriate, and
- A certificate of service, confirming that the government has been served.

Whatever documents are filed with the BIA must also be filed with the government. Once the appeal has been received, the Board will prepare a written transcript of the proceedings for service on each of the parties to the appeal and issue a briefing schedule that will determine the deadline when each party is required to file his or her brief in the case. Where the respondent is not detained, the appealing party is required to file a brief within 21 days,[98] with a response from the other side due 21 days thereafter. An extension of the time to file the brief may be granted for good cause shown for up to 90 days.[99]

For those who are detained, briefs must be filed simultaneously by both parties within 21 days.[100] This can be extremely difficult if the government is the one bringing the appeal. Typically, the Notice of Appeal will be completed in very general terms, simply to preserve the right to appeal. For instance, it might state, "[T]he decision of the immigration judge is not in accordance with the facts or the law." While this sentence may be enough, details regarding the actual issues to be raised will not be available until they are explored in the brief in support of the appeal. With a requirement of simultaneous filing of a brief, the non-appealing party is unfortunately in the dark as to the legal issues to be addressed in their own brief in reply. In such circumstances, a legal practitioner should do his or her best to counter issues s/he thinks may come up. Once the government's brief has been filed, consideration should be given to filing a reply brief, if necessary, that addresses issues that may not have been raised or anticipated previously. However, this additional brief must be filed with the BIA, along with a Motion to Accept a Reply Brief, within 14 days of receipt of the initial reply brief.[101] The BIA Practice Manual Chapter 4.6(c)(iv) recommends that all briefs contain:

---

[96] 8 C.F.R. § 1003.38(b).
[97] 8 C.F.R. § 1003.1(d)(2)(i)(G).
[98] 8 C.F.R. § 1003.3(c)(1).
[99] *Id.*
[100] *Id.*
[101] BIA Practice Manual Chapter 4.7(a)(ii).

- A concise statement of facts and procedural history of the case,
- A statement of issues presented for review,
- The standard of review,
- A summary of the argument,
- The argument, and
- A short conclusion stating the precise relief or remedy sought.

Any decision of the BIA is final, unless the respondent files a Motion to Reconsider or Reopen and it is successful.[102] If the BIA issues a final order denying relief, a respondent may be deported any time after that, unless further action is taken in federal court. A respondent who departs the United States while an appeal is pending before the BIA is deemed to have withdrawn it.[103]

Most decisions of the BIA are non-precedential and therefore only affect the immediate parties in the case. However, the BIA does issue 30 or so precedential decisions a year. This means that the holding in those cases must be applied by all immigration judges around the country, unless there is a different decision by a higher court, either a federal district court, court of appeals controlling the circuit for the case, or the U.S. Supreme Court.

H. Federal Court Practice

A final order of removal issued by the BIA may only be challenged by filing a petition for judicial review with the U.S. Court of Appeals in the circuit of jurisdiction of the immigration court that issued the initial decision.[104] These are federal courts, divided into 13 circuits around the country.

A circuit court only has jurisdiction to hear a petition if certain criteria are present. The most important one is that all forms of administrative challenge must be exhausted first, unless there are strong arguments to show that this would be futile.[105] Therefore, a person who receives an adverse decision from an immigration judge ordinarily cannot directly appeal that decision to the circuit court without first bringing a challenge before the BIA. Jurisdiction of the circuit courts is limited by statute to considering "constitutional claims or questions of law."[106]

While paralegals who are also fully accredited representatives can try cases in immigration court and handle appeals before the BIA, only attorneys can represent respondents in federal court. However, it is helpful to understand what happens in those courts so that work done for the lower courts can take into account the possibility of federal action later.

---

[102] 8 C.F.R. §§ 1003.1(d)(7); 1241.31.
[103] 8 C.F.R. § 1003.4.
[104] INA § 242(b)(2).
[105] INA § 242(d).
[106] INA § 242(a)(2)(D).

The first step in challenging a BIA decision is to file a **petition for review** with the relevant circuit court of appeals. It must be filed within 30 days of the BIA's decision issuing a final order of removal.[107] This is a strict rule, and applies even if the respondent decides to file a Motion to Reopen or Reconsider and does not receive a decision on those motions before the 30 days for filing the petition for review would expire. In such circumstances, the petition should still be filed in order to preserve the opportunity to have the case heard, although a request to the circuit court to postpone consideration of the petition until the prior motions are decided may be a good idea to allow the court to review any adverse decisions from those motions as well.

Filing a petition for review, however, will not protect a respondent from deportation, since a final order of removal has been issued by the BIA.[108] Once entered, the removal order authorizes ICE to take appropriate steps to remove the person from the country. In order to prevent this from happening, a request for a stay of removal must be filed either with the Field Office Director for ICE and/or with the circuit court directly. The BIA will only have jurisdiction to consider a stay if there is still a case pending before it, either in the form of an appeal, a motion to reopen, or a motion to reconsider.[109] In any event, a strong case must be made to explain why a foreign national should remain in the United States while his or her petition is being considered. If a foreign national is removed, the appeal to the circuit court may still go forward, since removal will not result in the termination of the case. However, if a foreign national for whom a stay of deportation has been denied fails to appear when asked to do so because ICE is seeking to enforce the removal order, s/he is treated as an absconder. In such cases, there is an argument that his or her case before the circuit court should be terminated, since fugitives do not have the benefit of the law.[110]

A precedential or published decision issued by a circuit court is binding on all immigration courts within its jurisdiction. This can result in different courts interpreting the same statutory provision differently. Where there is a circuit court split, because one court applies the law differently from another, the legal issues may only be resolved by the U.S. Supreme Court, if it decides that it wants to review the questions that have arisen.

I. Relief Available in Removal Proceedings

Most respondents in removal proceedings request relief from deportation by applying for a particular immigration benefit. Asylum and other related humanitarian relief and adjustment of status as forms of relief have already

---

[107] INA § 242(b)(1).
[108] INA § 242(b)(3)(B).
[109] BIA Practice Manual Chapter 6.3(a).
[110] *Matter of Barocio*, 19 I&N Dec. (BIA 1985). *See also Arrozal v. INS*, 159 F.3d 429 (9th Cir. 1998).

been discussed in Chapters 5 and 6 respectively. Only adjustment of status applications have any significant difference when filed in immigration court.

I.1. Adjustment of Status

As previously discussed, an adjustment application is divided into two parts. The first is the filing of a relative or employment based petition, which the USCIS must approve before the second stage, adjustment of status, can be considered. Immigration judges do not have jurisdiction to consider the validity of immigrant petitions, only the ensuing adjustment of status application. Therefore, anyone seeking to become an LPR through adjustment of status in court must first file a family sponsored or employment-based immigrant petition with the USCIS. When necessary, judges will often grant requests to continue proceedings until the USCIS has adjudicated the petition.

Where a respondent seeks to adjust status based on a marriage entered into after removal proceedings have begun, a good faith exception must be requested as part of the immigrant petition filing.[111] INA § 245(e)(3) states that the respondent has the burden to prove by "clear and convincing evidence" that the marriage:

- Was entered into in good faith,
- Complied with the laws of the place where it took place, and
- Was not entered into merely to confer immigration benefits.

These petitions are subject to heightened scrutiny when compared to family petitions submitted by those not in removal proceedings and therefore require persuasive evidence to substantiate the marriage is *bona fide* before the petition will be approved.

I.2. Cancellation of Removal

Cancellation of removal is discretionary relief available to a foreign national who, though determined to be removable from the United States, is allowed to remain. In effect, if the request is granted, then the respondent's removal has been cancelled because s/he meets certain criteria and an immigration judge has exercised discretion in his or her favor. Cancellation is generally used as a form of relief where no other is available to protect a foreign national from deportation. However, it can only be granted once.[112] Cancellation of removal is available to certain LPRs, while an undocumented foreign national applies for non-LPR cancellation of removal. The distinctions between the two are discussed later.

---

[111] *See* Section C.1 of Chapter 6, Family Sponsored Immigration and Permanent Resident Status, for further discussion.
[112] INA § 240A(c)(6).

When a foreign national is granted cancellation of removal, the immigration status granted to him or her is lawful permanent residency. Therefore, an LPR placed into removal proceedings who is ultimately granted cancellation remains an LPR, without any break in the period of his or her residency. Consequently, if the respondent qualifies to become a U.S. citizen after the grant of relief, s/he will be able to go ahead and apply to naturalize.[113]

One of the difficulties with seeking cancellation of removal is that only an immigration judge can grant it during removal proceedings. However, many non-LPR individuals meet the eligibility requirements for this relief but have no avenue to have their cases heard because they have not been served with an NTA and therefore have not been placed into removal proceedings yet.

In some cases, a tactical decision has to be made whether to actively seek to have a foreign national placed into removal proceedings so that s/he might pursue this relief or to wait until the person comes to the attention of the immigration service at some later date. Even placing someone into removal proceedings can be difficult because ICE may be reluctant to spend its scarce resources on processing a person who does not come within its removal priorities, particularly when it is clear that the foreign national is really only seeking immigration relief through cancellation of removal. Either way, the options must be weighed very carefully because, if the cancellation application is denied, a deportation order will be issued instead.

There are four different groups who can apply for cancellation of removal. They are:

- LPRs who have not been convicted of an aggravated felony crime, who apply for LPR cancellation;[114]
- Undocumented foreign nationals, who apply for non-LPR cancellation;[115]
- Battered spouses and children, who apply for VAWA cancellation;[116] and
- Individuals from certain Central American and Eastern European countries, who apply for relief under the Nicaraguan Adjustment and Central American Relief Act, or NACARA.[117]

Each of the four types of cancellation of removal is discussed in detail, but first some common issues are addressed.

Continuous Presence

Those seeking LPR and non-LPR cancellation of removal must show continuous presence and residence in the United States for seven and ten years respectively. There are special rules that apply to how those periods are counted. However,

---

[113] Detailed discussion is in Chapter 11, Citizenship and Naturalization.
[114] INA § 240A(a).
[115] INA § 240A(b)(1).
[116] INA § 240A(b)(2).
[117] Nicaraguan Adjustment and Central American Relief Act of 1997, Pub. L. 105-100, 111 Stat. 2160 (1997).

the foreign national must have accrued the relevant period prior to being served with the Notice to Appear.[118]

Even though an applicant must be continuously present for a period of time, this does not mean no absences at all are permitted. In fact, absences that do not exceed 90 days during any one trip or more than 180 days in aggregate throughout the total seven or ten year period will not disqualify an applicant from this relief.[119]

When a foreign national commits one of the offenses listed in INA § 212(a)(2) (criminal grounds) or INA § 237 (a)(2) or INA § 237 (a)(4) (security and terrorism grounds) accrual of the relevant time period stops. This is known as the "stop-time" rule and applies on *commission* of the offense, *not* on conviction or sentencing.[120] This may make it impossible for a person with a criminal history to qualify for cancellation of removal, even if the foreign national meets all other criteria. S/he cannot begin to count the continuous period afresh from the date of the commission of the crime or by departing the United States and reentering either. Therefore, if the required period has not been accrued prior to the crime's commission, the foreign national will be prevented from qualifying for relief for this reason alone.

Case for Discussion 10.5

Yang is from China. He has been an LPR since he arrived here in 1989, after the relative petition his brother filed for him was approved. Recently, Yang was diagnosed with bipolar disorder and placed on medications. However, he would not take them regularly because he complained they made him drowsy. On January 1, 2012, Yang was in a local grocery store when he started yelling at one of the customers, accusing him of being the devil. When the customer tried to move away, Yang lunged at him and began to strangle him violently with his hands, causing the customer to choke. Eventually Yang was wrestled off and the police came to arrest him. He was charged with assault and sentenced to 364 days in prison with five years' probation. Following completion of his sentence, Yang traveled to visit his family in China. On his return two weeks later, he was questioned about his conviction and placed into removal proceedings by CBP.

- Would Yang be eligible for LPR cancellation or will the "stop time" rule apply to prevent Yang from demonstrating the requisite continuous presence requirement?
- Assume Yang only arrived six years ago, with all other facts the same. Would your answer be different and if so, why?

---

[118] INA § 240A(d)(1).
[119] INA § 240A(d)(2).
[120] *Matter of Perez,* 22 I&N Dec. 689 (BIA 1999).

Crimes Barring Eligibility for Cancellation of Removal

The only convictions that make an LPR ineligible for cancellation of removal are aggravated felony offenses, as defined in INA § 101(a)(43) and discussed in Section C.2.a of Chapter 9, Grounds of Inadmissibility and Deportation. This means that a foreign national who may be removable because s/he has a number of convictions for crimes involving moral turpitude may still remain in the United States if an immigration judge decides to grant cancellation of removal. However, convictions that exclude a non-LPR from receiving cancellation are broader and include:

- Any inadmissibility crime offense under INA § 212(a),
- Any deportability crime offense under INA § 237(a)(2), and
- Any offense under INA § 237(a)(3).

In addition to these criminal disqualifiers, INA § 240A(c) also bars the following classes of foreign nationals from receiving *any* type of cancellation of removal:

- People who entered the United States as crewman after June 30, 1964,
- Nonimmigrants who enter in J category,[121] whether or not they are subject to the two year residency requirement,
- People who are inadmissible or deportable for engaging in terrorist activities,[122]
- People who have persecuted others, as described in INA § 208,[123] and
- People who have received cancellation of removal or similar relief previously.

All grants of cancellation of removal, other than NACARA applications, are subject to an overall limit of 4,000 cases to be granted per year.[124] Therefore, in the event that the limit is reached before the end of the government's fiscal year on September 30, a waiting list of potential grants is collated by EOIR until the beginning of the next year, beginning on October 1, when remaining cases can finally be adjudicated.

Having outlined factors these applications have in common, we now review eligibility and application process for each individually.

I.3. Cancellation of Removal for LPRs

Cancellation of removal is an avenue for an LPR with convictions for certain crimes or immigration violations to retain his or her immigration status. To be eligible, INA § 240A(a) requires that the LPR must show that s/he has:

---

[121] *See* Section E.4 of Chapter 2, Nonimmigrant Visas for Brief Stays, Study, and Cultural Exchange.
[122] *See* Section B.3 of Chapter 9, Grounds of Inadmissibility and Deportation.
[123] *See* Section A.5.b of Chapter 5, Asylum and Other Related Humanitarian Relief.
[124] INA § 240A(e)(1).

- Resided in the United States continuously for seven years after having been admitted in any status,
- Been an LPR for at least five of those seven years, and
- Not been convicted of an aggravated felony crime.

Once these requirements have been met, a foreign national will still need to persuade an immigration judge to exercise discretion in his or her favor and allow the respondent to remain in the United States. The discretionary factors to be considered can be ones directly affecting the foreign national and may include the following:

- Family ties within the United States,
- Residence of long duration in this country, particularly when the start of residence occurred while the respondent was still of a young age,
- Evidence of hardship to the respondent and family if deportation occurs,
- Service in this country's Armed Forces,
- A history of employment,
- The existence of property or business ties,
- Evidence of value and service to the community,
- Proof of a genuine rehabilitation if a criminal record exists, and
- Other evidence attesting to a respondent's good character.

These factors were provided by the BIA in *Matter of Marin*, 16 I&N Dec. 581, 584-585 (BIA 1978), where the BIA reversed a decision of an immigration judge to deny relief to a foreign national convicted of a drug offense. Essentially, the BIA held that the positive and negative factors must be balanced for there to be an "equitable application of discretionary relief"[125] when deciding whether to cancel removal. The BIA went on to suggest adverse factors for consideration might include:

- The nature and underlying circumstances of the removal ground,
- The presence of additional significant immigration law violations,
- The existence of a criminal record and, if so, its nature, recency, and seriousness, and
- The presence of other evidence indicative of a respondent's bad character or undesirability as an LPR.[126]

A decision in the LPR respondent's favor will result in the retention of immigration status as an LPR.

---

[125] *Matter of Marin*, 16 I&N Dec. 581(BIA 1978).
[126] *Id.*

Relief Under INA § 212(c)

A foreign national convicted of a crime prior to the enactment of the Illegal Immigration Reform and Immigrant Responsibility Act, or IIRAIRA, in 1996, could apply for relief under INA § 212(c). The discretionary provision permitted LPRs with criminal convictions, including some offenses classified as aggravated felony crimes, so long as less than five years in prison had been served for one or more of these types of crimes, to seek relief from removal, applying a more relaxed evidentiary standard.[127] Although repealed, the relief remains available in certain circumstances.[128] The law in this area is complex and requires the expertise of an attorney experienced in both immigration and criminal law. The following section describes how to identify cases that may qualify for this waiver.

Prior to the passage of IIRAIRA on April 24, 1996, an LPR could apply to waive any ground of inadmissibility or deportability by applying for relief under INA § 212(c). It was available only to those LPRs who had pled guilty in their criminal proceedings, although convictions for some crimes, such as firearms offenses under INA § 237(a)(2)(C) or entry without inspection, were not covered. Following IIRAIRA's repeal of INA § 212(c), the relief was no longer available and those seeking relief were required to apply for the more stringent cancellation of removal for LPRs discussed previously. The result was that many longtime LPRs were barred from obtaining relief in immigration court, and, with no other legal options, were deported. However, the Supreme Court in *St. Cyr*,[129] held that the relief still existed for a small class of LPRs with certain kinds of convictions and under certain conditions.

As applied today, INA § 212(c) is generally available to longtime LPRs with convictions prior to IIRAIRA's enactment. There are complicated rules that must be reviewed to determine just who is covered, which make it all the more important that initial assessments and referrals are made to practitioners with appropriate experience who can protect those who would otherwise have few prospects to ameliorate their deportation.

I.4. Non-LPR Cancellation of Removal

A foreign national who is not an LPR may qualify for cancellation of removal under INA § 240A(b), if s/he can demonstrate the following:

- Continuous presence in the United States for a period of ten years;
- S/he is a person of good moral character;
- S/he has a qualifying relative who is either a U.S. citizen or LPR parent, spouse, or child;

---

[127] *Id.*
[128] *See INS v. St. Cyr*, 533 U.S. 289 (2001).
[129] *Id.*

- S/he has not been convicted of certain crimes, as discussed in Section I.2., and
- Removing the foreign national from the United States will cause exceptional and extremely unusual hardship to that qualifying relative.[130]

Of the factors listed, demonstrating good moral character, or GMC, is an extremely important one that only non-LPRs are required to satisfy. INA § 101(f) lists a number of behaviors that prevent a person from demonstrating GMC. These include:

- Classification as a habitual drunkard,
- Aggravated felony convictions,
- Prostitution,
- Two or more convictions for or income derived from illegal gambling,
- Spending more than 180 days confined in a prison following a conviction,
- Participation in genocide or Nazi persecution, and
- Falsely claiming U.S. citizenship.[131]

While these are the statutory grounds precluding a finding of good moral character, there are other acts that an immigration judge, in the exercise of discretion, may take into account to determine if a positive finding should be made. Examples of these might be failing to file tax returns or pay any taxes owed, delinquent child support payments, or failing to contribute to the maintenance of a child. When reviewing these factors, however, the immigration judge is required to consider the totality of the circumstances. In other words, s/he must weigh the good facts against the bad before making a final decision. A foreign national is required to show that s/he has been a person of good moral character for the period of ten years necessary to qualify for cancellation of removal, calculated back from the date the immigration judge decides the case.

A non-LPR seeking cancellation of removal must have a qualifying relative who is likely to suffer exceptional and extremely unusual hardship if the applicant is not permitted to remain in the United States. This is another difference between non-LPR cancellation and the available relief for LPRs, who can demonstrate that they themselves will suffer hardship if they are deported. In contrast, a non-LPR must show that s/he has a parent, spouse, or child less than 21 years of age, who is either a U.S. citizen or an LPR, who will suffer as a result of the deportation. Direct hardship to any other relatives cannot be considered unless it will contribute to the hardship of the qualifying relatives.

The "exceptional and extremely unusual" hardship that a qualifying relative must experience in the event a foreign national is not allowed to remain in the United States is the most extreme standard applied in immigration law.

---

[130] INA § 240A(b)(1).
[131] In *Matter of Guadarrama*, 24 I&N Dec. 625 (BIA 2008), the BIA held that a false claim to citizenship made on an I-9 form is not an automatic bar to demonstrating good moral character.

The BIA has provided some guidance on how to interpret it.[132] In *Matter of Monreal*, the BIA held that a foreign national seeking cancellation must show qualifying relatives would experience hardship that was more than extreme, but not necessarily "unconscionable."[133] However, the BIA has also made it clear that, while Congress, by applying this strict standard, intended to limit the number of people who would qualify for cancellation relief, "the hardship standard is not so restrictive that only a handful of applicants, such as those who have a qualifying relative with a serious medical condition, will qualify for relief."[134]

While serious medical conditions suffered by qualifying relatives are relevant considerations, they are just one factor out of a possible array. Other factors for consideration might include: how old is the qualifying child and what connection does s/he have to the country where the foreign national will be deported? It may be more difficult for children over 12-years old to assimilate into a new country and culture. However, this does not automatically preclude a similar finding for younger children. Has the child ever been to the country of deportation or does s/he even speak the language? Perhaps English is spoken in the home, limiting the opportunity for exposure to the foreign language. How easy will it be for the child to adapt to this new environment? Could removal to that country create or exacerbate health conditions already suffered? Does the child have any learning issues and, if so, will they be adequately addressed in this new country? How easy will it be for the foreign national to find suitable work that will allow him or her to support family members in this new environment? What support network through family or other means will be available for the foreign national once s/he arrives in the country of deportation? Perhaps the family members there relied on remittances sent to them by the foreign national from abroad and so they will not be able to assist him or her with transitioning back because they no longer have this additional income. Are there any alternative methods for the foreign national to immigrate to the United States? Even if there are, how long might that process take, causing separation of the family? These are just some factors that might be addressed.

● EXAMPLE

Samba, a citizen of Mauritania, has been undocumented in the United States for over 15 years. Recently, Samba was placed into removal proceedings following a traffic stop that identified him as a person present without lawful status. He has three U.S. citizen children, aged 13, 10, and 9. Two of his children are on the honor role at school and one is dyslexic. None of his children have ever traveled to Mauritania and, while they understand the language Samba speaks, they cannot speak it themselves and cannot read it. One of the children suffers from skin disorders and has problems with digestion. Samba may be eligible to apply for non-LPR cancellation of removal. In support of this application, he could present evidence of his children's school records, medical conditions, and lack of treatment

---

[132] *Matter of Monreal*, 23 I&N Dec. 56 (BIA 2001).
[133] *Id.* at 60.
[134] *See Matter of Recinas*, 23 I&N Dec. 467, 470 (BIA 2002).

opportunities in Mauritania, as well as their inability to communicate in a foreign language, which could severely hamper their ability to study in school, as proof of the equities in his case to support his request to remain here.

Typically, in cancellation of removal cases, hardship to the foreign national is not a factor an immigration judge can consider as direct evidence. However, if it can be argued that the hardship the foreign national experiences would affect the level of hardship the qualifying relatives will experience if cancellation is not granted, then it can be introduced into evidence for that purpose. For example, it may be possible to introduce information on health problems suffered by a foreign national as evidence that they will limit his or her ability to work and therefore support himself or herself abroad, requiring greater reliance on the qualifying relative in the United States for financial assistance. This may be an exceptional and extremely unusual hardship on the relative here if s/he was not the breadwinner previously and may not have the skills to work in a job that provides income for him or her to maintain two households.

It is prudent to provide supporting evidence for any factor offered for consideration as a hardship. This may be in the form of medical, financial or school records, and letters of support from employers, religious leaders, or members of the community who are able to express an opinion on such matters. Conditions in the country of deportation may also be documented, including how they will affect the foreign national or any family member who may travel with him or her. It is useful to include an evaluation focused on the psychological effects, if any, of the deportation on relevant family members. A sample Notice of Intent to Offer Evidence listing possible documents in support of an application for cancellation of removal is in Figure 10.9.

I.5. Cancellation of Removal Under the Violence Against Women Act, or VAWA

In Chapter 8, Immigration Relief for Vulnerable Populations, we reviewed the different types of relief available to vulnerable populations, one of which was VAWA relief for battered spouses. Cancellation of removal is the defensive or in court equivalent of the abused spouse petition discussed in that chapter. The eligibility requirements for this relief as set out in INA § 240A(b)(2) are significantly relaxed compared to those required for other groups seeking cancellation of removal. To qualify, an abused foreign national must demonstrate:

- Physical presence in the United States for a continuous period of at least three years,
- S/he has been battered or subjected to extreme cruelty by a spouse or parent who is a U.S. citizen or LPR,
- Good moral character during the three-year period,
- S/he has not been convicted of an aggravated felony, and
- Removal would cause extreme hardship to the foreign national directly or any child or a parent.

Figure 10.9

Sample Notice of Intent to Offer Evidence in Cancellation of Removal Case

A. T. Torney, Esq.
A Law Firm, LLC
Follow the Yellow Brick Road
Kansas, MO 19103

UNITED STATES DEPARTMENT OF JUSTICE
EXECUTIVE OFFICE OF IMMIGRATION REVIEW
OFFICE OF THE IMMIGRATION JUDGE
KANSAS CITY, MISSOURI

In the Matter of: :
                            :
DOE, JOHN   :   File No.: A 200 000 000
                            :
In Removal Proceedings   :
                            :

Immigration Judge Decider   Next Hearing: April 29, 2013, 8.30 A.M.
                                   Master Calendar

NOTICE OF INTENT TO OFFER EVIDENCE

TAB		PAGE
A.	Form EOIR 42B, with addendum	1–10
B.	Receipt from Texas Service Center	10A
C.	Birth certificates for respondent's children, as qualifying relatives	11–13
D.	Copy of I-94 card as evidence of respondent's date of entry	14
E.	FBI report indicating respondent has no arrest record	15
F.	Evidence of respondent's presence in the United States for requisite 10 years	16–46
G.	Medical information regarding respondent's son, Full of Life Doe	47–49
H.	Information on Spondiloepiphyseal dysplasia	50–54
I.	Information on Restrictive Lung Disease	55

Figure 10.9 (Continued)

TAB		PAGE
J.	Information on Club Feet	56–60
K.	Information on Gastroesophageal Reflux Disease	61–66
L.	Information on Bilateral Hearing Loss	67–70
M.	Information on G6PD Deficiency	71–73
N.	Information on Hypertonica	74–75
O.	Information on Hypertonicity	76–77
P.	Information on Developmental Delays	78–82
Q.	Encyclopedia of the Nations Report on Healthcare in Mali	83–87
R.	U.S. State Department Human Rights Report on Mali, 2012	88–110

Counsel reserves the right to present further documents as determined necessary in support of respondent's application.

_____   _____
A.T. Torney, Esq.   Date

A Law Firm, LLC

Follow the Yellow Brick Road

Kansas, MO 19103

Foreign nationals are ineligible for VAWA cancellation relief if they are subject to the criminal or security grounds of inadmissibility under INA § 212(a)(2) or INA § 212(a)(3), respectively, or are deportable for engaging in marriage fraud under INA § 237(1)G(2), being convicted of certain crimes under INA § 237(2), failing to register or engaging in document fraud under INA § 237(3), or security related grounds under INA § 237(4).[135]

Those seeking relief in this category need only show continuous presence for a period of three years. However, unlike rules regarding the seven or ten years required for other forms of cancellation, this period can continue to be accrued *after* the NTA has been served, right up until the day of the judge's decision.[136] Therefore, someone who has been continuously present for only two years at the time of service of the NTA can continue to accrue the additional year needed to qualify for VAWA cancellation by adding the time s/he is in removal proceedings

---

[135] INA § 240A(b)(2)(iv).
[136] INA § 240A(d)(1).

before a judge. Absences of more than 90 days in a single trip or over 180 days in aggregate will not prevent a foreign national from fulfilling the continuous presence requirement if a connection between the abuse suffered and the absence can be demonstrated.[137]

Applicants for VAWA cancellation of removal must show that they have either been battered or subjected to extreme cruelty, which is defined in 8 C.F.R. § 204.2(c)(1)(vi) to include threats or acts of violence resulting in physical or mental injury. Acts such as rape, forced prostitution, and psychological abuse are some forms of treatment recognized as extreme cruelty.[138] Any credible evidence may be presented to document the harm suffered.[139]

Although VAWA cancellation proceedings are under the jurisdiction of the EOIR, a determination that the respondent seeking this relief is indeed an abused spouse must still be made by the VAWA unit within the USCIS. Therefore, a battered spouse self-petition on Form I-360, Petition for Amerasian, Widow(er), or Special Immigrant, must be filed and approved as a prerequisite to seeking this relief in immigration court. This is similar to the way a Form I-130, Petition for Alien Relative in family sponsored cases or Form I-140, Immigrant Petition for Alien Worker in employment-based cases is filed as prerequisites to adjustment of status applications. Once the petition is approved, an immigration judge has no jurisdiction to readjudicate it. However, the judge can still determine whether the respondent is eligible for adjustment of status.

The foreign national has the burden to show that his or her abuser is a U.S. citizen or LPR. Sometimes a relative petition may have been filed with the USCIS by the abuser who later withdraws it as a form of control or psychological abuse or because the marriage breaks down. The filed immigrant petition may not be accessible to the foreign national seeking immigration relief because it was filed by the abuser as petitioner and therefore is not available to the abuse survivor or beneficiary. Nevertheless the foreign national may reference this prior petition and the citizenship documents filed in support of it as evidence of the abuser's immigration status if no other documentation is available.

INA § 240A(b)(2)(i) permits applications to be filed even in the event that the abuser subsequently loses citizenship or LPR status. Similarly, a marriage that may be deemed invalid because the U.S. citizen or LPR is a bigamist would still be a valid marriage for the purposes of this relief.[140] The language of the statute makes clear that foreign nationals can apply for cancellation of removal even if they are no longer married to the abuser, so long as the application is filed within two years of the termination.

One of the critical elements of this application is demonstrating that the marriage was not entered solely to obtain immigration benefits. This requires sufficient evidence to show that the couple was actually living together as

---

[137] INA § 240A(b)(2)(B).
[138] 8 C.F.R. § 204.2(c)(2)(vi). A more in depth discussion of these terms can be found in Chapter 8, Immigration Relief for Vulnerable Populations.
[139] INA § 240A(b)(2)(D).
[140] INA § 240A(b)(2)(i)(III).

spouses at some point in the marriage. As with self-petition applications for abused spouses,[141] documents such as leases or mortgages, car or life insurance policies, utility bills, or tax returns filed jointly or any other evidence that might suggest a comingling of the couple's life, may help to prove this.

There are special rules that apply to the good moral character requirement for VAWA cancellation. An immigration judge has discretion to waive any act or conviction that is not an automatic bar to relief but would otherwise prevent an applicant from demonstrating good moral character, so long as the foreign national can show it was directly connected to the abuse.[142]

Case for Discussion 10.6

Hyacinth came to the United States on vacation as a visitor. While here, she met Ronald and they fall deeply in love and marry. Shortly after, Ronald began to abuse Hyacinth, first psychologically by refusing to file her immigration papers, then by withholding money that she needed to maintain the household, then by physically abusing her by beating her whenever he was drunk, which is most nights of the week. Hyacinth remained in this situation for 18 months, not knowing what to do. Finally, her family in Jamaica encouraged her to leave Ronald and return home so that they might help her heal. While she was there, Ronald contacted Hyacinth, begging her to come back. He promised that he would change and would file her papers so that she can finally find work and that if she did not return, he would kill himself. Hyacinth, concerned for Ronald's safety, decided to return. Because her visitor's visa had expired, she re-entered the United States using a friend's passport. However, soon after her return, Ronald's brutal treatment resumed. Hyacinth finally left and sought refuge in a shelter for survivors of domestic violence. The agency referred her case to an immigration agency to see if there was a way for them to assist her in legalizing her status.

- Are there any inadmissibility issues that should be addressed as part of Hyacinth's application?
- If so, how?

Similar to cancellation of removal for LPRs, VAWA cancellation of removal also requires a judge to exercise discretion when deciding whether or not to grant relief to the respondent. However, the foreign national need only show that deportation from the United States will cause extreme hardship to him

---

[141] *See* Chapter 6, Family Sponsored Immigration and Permanent Resident Status.
[142] INA § 240A(b)(2)(C).

or her individually, or to *any* children or parents. Hardship factors that might be considered are the effects of the abuse or psychological harm on the respondent's functioning, his or her ability to obtain treatment for the abuse in the country of deportation, lack of access to courts in the United States in order to pursue or defend custody or other legal hearings, or the lack of protections available in the event the abuser or his or her family and friends seek to continue to abuse the foreign national should s/he return to a country they have in common. The old Immigration and Naturalization Service, or INS, produced a memorandum entitled "'Extreme Hardship' and Documentary Requirements Involving Battered Spouses and Children."[143] It is a helpful guide to how this component of the abused spouse cancellation application criteria is considered.

Unlike VAWA self-petitioners, a foreign national granted VAWA cancellation cannot apply for derivatives to come and join them in the United States. Instead, any children under 21 at the time the application is filed will be paroled into the United States under INA § 212(d)(5), until such time that s/he is able to adjust his or her status through a relative petition filed by the parent granted VAWA relief.[144] Generally, a relative petition can be filed straight away because a grant of cancellation of removal in court means that the respondent immediately becomes an LPR. Any petition filed for the child will be in the second preference category applicable to LPRs.[145] Those for whom a visa is not yet available because their priority date is not yet current, will remain in parole status until they can adjust to LPRs in their own right.[146] While the child waits to adjust to become an LPR, s/he can apply for permission to work as one of the benefits available to parolees.[147]

Children who have been abused by a parent may themselves apply for cancellation of removal in proceedings. This provision is not limited to those under 21 years of age at the time the application is adjudicated.[148] Where a child is granted relief and has been abused by only one parent, s/he can apply for the non-abusing parent to enter the United States on parole until such time as the parent can adjust to LPR status through the child or any other available means.[149]

---

[143] The memorandum was issued on October 16, 1998 and is available at http://iwp.legalmomentum.org/immigration/vawa-self-petition-and-cancellation/government-memoranda-and-factsheets/VAWA_Virtue%20Extreme%20Hardship%20memo_8.16.98.pdf/view.
[144] INA § 240A(b)(4).
[145] *See* Section A.2 of Chapter 6, Family Sponsored Immigration and Permanent Resident Status, for further details.
[146] INA § 240A(b)(4)(B).
[147] 8 C.F.R. § 274a.12.(c)(11).
[148] INA § 201(f)(4).
[149] INA § 240A(b)(4)(A)(ii).

J. NACARA and Other Forms of Cancellation of Removal

Sometimes, special immigration rules apply to nationals of certain countries. This is the case with NACARA. Introduced in 1997, Congress permitted Nicaraguan and Cuban nationals who had been physically present in the United States continuously since December 1, 1995 to become permanent residents. Although applications had to be filed by April 1, 2000, a few still remain.

Another provision of the legislation provided relief to Guatemalans, Salvadorans, and nationals from the former Soviet bloc and other Eastern European countries.[150] Those who first entered the United States by a certain date and were known to the then INS, now the USCIS, through specific applications for relief already filed, are able to apply for a special rule cancellation of removal under similar provisions to cancellation of removal for LPRs. Therefore, this group of foreign nationals is subject to the more relaxed criteria for relief.

The Haitian Refugee Immigration Fairness Act of 1998, or HRIFA,[151] provided similar relief to Haitian nationals who filed for relief between June 11, 1999 and March 31, 2000. Again, few of these applications remain.

K. Conclusion

Immigration court practice requires a great deal of attention to detail and familiarity with court practice rules. While procedures in immigration court are somewhat more relaxed than in federal courts, it is still important to comply with them and to review carefully any documents submitted by the government for use against a foreign national. Ensuring accuracy is paramount, since a simple mistake could result in a limiting of immigration relief available for a person challenging his or her deportation.

Now that we have reviewed immigration court practice and forms of immigration relief available in removal proceedings, we are ready to analyze the citizenship and naturalization process, which provides the ultimate protection to any foreign national.

---

[150] NACARA § 203.
[151] Pub. L. 105-277 (1998).

Citizenship and Naturalization

Key Terms and Acronyms

Citizenship by Acquisition
Continuous Residence
Denaturalization
Derivative Citizenship
Expatriation
Form N-400
Form N-600
Form N-648
Good Moral Character
Jus Sanguinis
Jus Soli
Naturalization
Physical Presence
Relinquishment of Citizenship
Section 322 Citizenship
Statutory Period

Chapter Objectives

- Understand the legal requirements for U.S. citizenship
- Understand how citizenship is acquired or derived through parents or grandparents
- Understand the naturalization application process
- Analyze the effects of good moral character in the naturalization application
- Review the ways in which citizenship can be lost

Throughout this book, we have introduced various immigration concepts that have either provided temporary or permanent permission to remain in the United States. We have also reviewed the impediments to gaining entry or requiring a person to leave. However, the ultimate goal for many foreign nationals is to become a U.S. citizen. For some, making the decision to become a citizen can be a complex one because it may mean losing not only the citizenship of their country of birth, but also land or inheritance rights enjoyed there. A decision to become a citizen is rarely taken lightly. As mentioned in Chapter 10, Immigration Court Practice and Relief from Removal, citizens are generally protected from being deported from the United States, except in certain narrow circumstances where a person must be denaturalized first.[1] U.S. citizens also have the right to vote in all federal and state elections. Citizenship can be a requirement for eligibility for certain government jobs.

This chapter reviews the various ways a foreign national can become a U.S. citizen, whether by birth, naturalization, or through parents and grandparents. It reviews the criteria that must be satisfied in order to qualify for citizenship, particularly good moral character. The laws on eligibility for citizenship, particularly for those who acquire citizenship through their parents, have changed several times over the years. While this chapter's focus is on current citizenship laws, it is important to note that, when analyzing whether a foreign national is a citizen or not, it is necessary to review prior laws that may have been applicable at the time of the person's birth. This can be a complicated process; however, there are a number of charts that may be helpful for this analysis. This chapter discusses how to use charts provided by the government that help to track the various changes in order to apply the law applicable at the time of birth to determine if an applicant has acquired citizenship through his or her parents or grandparents. Finally, this chapter discusses the limited situations when a foreign national can be stripped of citizenship and the consequences of such a serious action.

A. Overview of Citizenship

A.1. Sources of law

Jus Soli: Latin term meaning right of the soil, that defines the ability of a person to acquire citizenship simply by virtue of being born in a particular country.

Jus Sanguinis: Latin term meaning right of the blood that defines the acquisition or derivation of citizenship through specific family members.

Two main concepts determine a person's citizenship. The first, derived from the Latin term ***jus soli***, stands for the principle that a person obtains citizenship in the country where they were born. The second concept, ***jus sanguinis,*** is when a person obtains citizenship through his or her relationship with parents or grandparents.

Many countries, including the United States, adopt a mixture of these principles in determining whether or not a person is a citizen. The Immigration and Nationality Act, or INA, sets out five ways a person can achieve U.S. citizenship:

- Birth in the United States.[2] This is the most common way that citizenship is acquired and is available, regardless of the immigration status of the child's parents at the time of his or her birth. This is an example of *jus soli.*

---

[1] Section H.2 discusses this.
[2] INA § 301.

- **Naturalization.**[3] This requires an eligible person to file an application with the United States Citizenship and Immigration Service, or USCIS.
- **Derivative Citizenship.**[4] This is when a foreign national minor child automatically derives citizenship when a parent becomes a citizen before the child reaches the age of 18 years. This is an example of *jus sanguinis*.
- **Citizenship by acquisition.**[5] This is when a foreign national, born and residing abroad, acquires citizenship at birth because s/he is born to a U.S. citizen parent or parents. This is another example of *jus sanguinis*.
- **Section 322 Citizenship.**[6] This is designed for minor children, under 18 years of age, born to a U.S. citizen parent who may not have lived in the country for the requisite period. If this is the case, then the child can look to the length of time his or her grandparent has lived in the country in order to be eligible for citizenship. This is used when no other option is available and is the final example of *jus sanguinis*.

A.2. Advantages of Citizenship

As previously mentioned, the goal for many foreign nationals is to become citizens of the United States. The advantages of obtaining citizenship status include:

- The right to vote in all federal and state elections,
- Eligibility to work in certain government jobs,
- The right to run for and hold political office,
- The ability to petition for a broader spectrum of relatives to immigrate to the United States or to achieve faster family reunification with spouses and minor children,[7]
- Protection from deportation, although some naturalized citizens can be denaturalized under limited circumstances,
- The ability to travel outside of the United States for unlimited periods of time without losing citizenship status,
- Protection of the U.S. Department of State when abroad, and
- Entitlement to certain means tested public benefits that are not available at all or only available for a limited time to lawful permanent residents, or LPRs, who entered the United States after August 22, 1996.[8]

---

[3] INA § 310.
[4] INA § 320.
[5] INA §§ 301(c) and (d).
[6] INA § 322.
[7] For example, as explained in Chapter 6, Family Sponsored Immigration and Permanent Resident Status, only U.S. citizens can file for children over 21-years of age, married children, or siblings to become lawful permanent residents. At the same time, U.S. citizens can bring spouses and minor children to the U.S. without regard to the quota system.
[8] The relationship of immigration status to eligibility for means tested public benefits is complex and changed dramatically with the passage of the Personal Responsibility and Work Opportunity Reconciliation Act (PRWORA) of 1996, Pub. L. No. 104-193, 110 Stat. 2105 (1996) (codified as 8 USC §§ 1601 et seq.). Certain immigrants, even those who fail to naturalize, who were lawfully present before the passage of PRWORA and already receiving benefits were "grandfathered in" and therefore remain eligible for benefits. For more information, see the National Immigration Law Center website at https://www.nilc.org/issues/economic-support/.

B. Citizenship Based on Birth in the United States

Birth in the United States is the most common way of acquiring citizenship. However, this was only guaranteed to those born here after a change was made to the U.S. Constitution. In 1868, the Fourteenth Amendment was passed in order to guarantee additional rights to slaves freed after the civil war and to overturn the Dred Scott decision, which held that slaves could never become U.S. citizens.[9] The key language that confers citizenship on those born on U.S. soil is:

> All persons born or naturalized in the United States, and subject to the jurisdiction thereof, are citizens of the United States and the State wherein they reside.[10]

The U.S. Supreme Court, applying the Amendment in *United States v. Wong Kim Ark*, 169 U.S. 649 (1898), upheld the citizenship of a child born in the United States to non-citizen parents and thereby confirmed the child was not subject to the Chinese Exclusion Act.[11]

With few exceptions, such as the children of diplomats,[12] all children born on United States soil[13] or its ***outlying possessions*** are U.S. citizens, regardless of their parents' citizenship or immigration status. Also known as "birthright citizenship," the conferring of citizenship at birth to children born in the United States is not without recent controversy. Some groups and political leaders claim that this policy is an incentive for undocumented or nonimmigrant women and families who come to the United States to give birth. There is a movement to abolish "birthright" citizenship to children born to parents who lack permanent immigration status. Most legal scholars agree that birthright citizenship has a strong basis in the Constitution and precedential legal decisions, and many who are in favor of it argue that this right has promoted the rapid integration of immigrants into United States society.

Outlying Possessions: Countries such as American Samoa and Swain Island that are possessions of the United States.

---

[9] *Dred Scott v. Sandford*, 60 U.S. 393 (1857).
[10] U.S. Constitution, Amendment XIV, § 1.
[11] Discussed in Chapter 1, Historical Background and Introduction to the U.S. Immigration System.
[12] Children of diplomats who are born in the United States do not benefit from the *jus soli* rule and therefore are not citizens at birth. This is because, under international law, foreign diplomatic officers are not subject to the jurisdiction of the United States and therefore their children cannot benefit from being born here. Those children may be considered LPRs instead. *See* 8 C.F.R. § 101.3(a)(1).
[13] Puerto Rico, the Virgin Islands, and Guam are considered to be part of U. S. soil and therefore anyone born in those countries is also a U.S. citizen.

> **Case for Discussion 11.1**
>
> Leon's mother came to the United States on an H-2B visa to work on landscaping a golf course. She did not realize she was pregnant until after she arrived here. She gave birth to Leon seven months after she entered the country, by which time her visa had expired. When Leon was one-year old, his mother took him with her when she returned to Mexico.
>
> - Is Leon a United States citizen?
> - How would he prove it?

C. Citizenship Through Naturalization

In order to obtain citizenship through naturalization, there are many criteria that must be satisfied. A foreign national wishing to become a U.S. citizen must prove that s/he:

- Is 18 years or older at the time of the application,
- Has been a resident of the United States for the **statutory period,**
- Any absences from the country do not exceed stated limits,
- Meets the requirements of physical presence in the United States,
- Is a person of good moral character,
- Understands the English language, history, principles, and form of government of the United States, and
- Is willing to take the Oath of Allegiance to the United States.[14]

We address each of these criteria in turn.

C.1. The Applicant Must Be at Least 18-Years Old

In order to apply for citizenship, an applicant must be at least 18-years old at the time of filing the application[15] unless s/he is serving in the military during a period of hostility.[16] For those minors who are under 18, they may be able to derive citizenship if a parent naturalizes before the child's 18th birthday.[17]

---

[14] INA §§ 316, 312 and 334(b).
[15] INA § 334(b).
[16] INA § 329(b)(1).
[17] INA § 320.

C.2. The Applicant Must Be a Lawful Permanent Resident for a Continuous Period

In general, a foreign national seeking to naturalize must first be an LPR. That status must usually be held for a continuous period of either three or five years before s/he can become eligible for this benefit.[18] The periods required to qualify for naturalization are known as the statutory period. Those who are married to citizens may naturalize after a continuous period of three years of marriage and as LPRs, regardless of how LPR status was acquired, but only, if they remain living with their U.S. citizen spouse throughout that time and immediately before filing the application.[19] For example, a foreign national who gains LPR status as a refugee but subsequently marries a U.S. citizen would be required to wait only three years as an LPR before qualifying to naturalize because of that marriage, even if some of that three year period accrued before the marriage took place. There is an exception for those spouses who were granted LPR status after filing a Violence Against Women Act, or VAWA, battered spouse self-petition.[20] In these cases, the self-petitioner can still apply for citizenship in three years, even though she may no longer live with her abuser or have done so for the requisite three-year period.[21] With the exception of members of the military, all other foreign nationals who are not married to U.S. citizens must wait until they have been LPRs for at least five years to meet the statutory period.[22]

> **Case for Discussion 11.2**
>
> Rosa, a national from Argentina, originally entered on a B-2 nonimmigrant visa as a visitor, and met her husband, a U.S. citizen, who never petitioned for her to become an LPR. In fact, he became very abusive towards her, especially after she became pregnant. When her baby was six-months old, the abuse forced Rosa to leave their apartment and stay in a shelter. She successfully filed a petition under VAWA as a battered spouse and received her LPR status two and a half years ago. Rosa wants very much to become a citizen so she can petition for her mother to come here to help her take care of her baby so that Rosa can go out to work to support them all.
>
> - When will Rosa be eligible to apply for naturalization?
> - What is the basis for your answer?

---

[18] INA §§ 319 and 316.
[19] INA § 319(a).
[20] *See* Chapter 8, Immigration Relief for Vulnerable Populations, for more details.
[21] INA § 319(a).
[22] INA § 316(a).

Case for Discussion 11.3

Recall Akinbola, the Nigerian citizen in Case for Discussion 5.4, in Chapter 5, Asylum and Other Related Humanitarian Relief, who wishes to apply for asylum based on his sexual orientation. Assume that he is granted status in September 2012 and one year later applies for LPR status, which is granted in April 2014. Shortly after the U.S. Supreme Court declares same sex marriage legal in all 50 states, Akinbola and his U.S. citizen partner, Eric, who have been together for 5 years now, decide to get married on August 1, 2015.

- Which is the earliest year that Akinbola will qualify to apply to become a U.S. citizen?
- Would your answer be the same if they had not married?

Foreign nationals may apply for citizenship 90 days before the anniversary of their statutory period is complete.[23] In addition, they must have residency within the jurisdiction of the USCIS office that adjudicates their naturalization application for at least three months prior to the interview.[24]

● EXAMPLE

Frieda is from Sweden. She became an LPR in May 2010 through employment with a software engineering firm in New York. She wants to apply for citizenship and will be eligible to apply four years and nine months after her grant of LPR status. However, Frieda's work requires her to travel to different states for months at a time while she supervises different projects. So long as she maintains a permanent residence in one location, despite her travels, for more than three months prior to her interview within the jurisdiction of the USCIS Field office location that will adjudicate her naturalization application, she will be eligible to naturalize.

INA, §§ 328 and 329 provide special exceptions for members of the U.S. armed forces, so that those serving an aggregate of one year during periods of peacetime or any length of time, even only one day, during periods of designated hostilities, are immediately eligible to apply to naturalize. On July 3, 2002, President George W. Bush, by Executive Order, ruled that anyone serving in the military since September 11, 2001, is serving during a period of hostility. That order remains in effect today.[25] Those who serve during hostilities do not need to be LPRs before applying for citizenship.[26] Those no longer serving in the military

---

[23] *Id.*
[24] 8 C.F.R. § 316.2(a)(5).
[25] Executive Order, President George W. Bush, July 3, 2002, available at http://georgewbush-whitehouse.archives.gov/news/releases/2002/07/20020703-24.html.
[26] INA § 329.

must have been honorably discharged in order to qualify for naturalization under these sections.[27]

Family members may also petition for the posthumous citizenship of members of the military who died during a period of hostility, so long as the petition is filed within two years of the service member's death.[28] Surviving spouses, children, or parents of a U.S. citizen who serve honorably and die during active duty may also qualify to naturalize without fulfilling any of the residence requirements.[29] Spouses and children of military members serving during hostilities can also naturalize as long as they are LPRs and reside with their spouses abroad pursuant to official orders.[30] Any time spent abroad living in marital union with the service member will count towards meeting any required residence period in the United States and within the jurisdiction of a USCIS office.[31] There are special naturalization ceremonies held abroad for military members and their eligible spouses and children.

Another important difference in the treatment of military members is that they may file an application to naturalize even if they are removable.[32] All other applicants cannot apply for citizenship while removal proceedings are pending or a deportation order has been entered against them.[33] In addition, where a foreign national is *prima facie* eligible to naturalize and this has been affirmatively communicated by the government, an immigration judge can exercise his or her authority to terminate proceedings under 8 C.F.R. § 1239.2(f) to enable the naturalization application to be pursued.[34]

C.3. Absences from the United States: Continuous Residence and Physical Presence Requirements

To be eligible to naturalize, a foreign national must meet both a **continuous residence** and a **physical presence** requirement. These relate to two different criteria.

C.3.a. Continuous Residence

Continuous residence refers to unbroken periods of time, which in most cases means that the applicant has not been away from the United States beyond a set length of time. As discussed previously, the general rule is that in order to be eligible for citizenship, a person must reside in the United States as an LPR for five years, or three years if s/he is the spouse of a U.S. citizen.

While LPRs are expected to make their home in the United States, they are permitted to travel freely. However, leaving for a protracted period could raise problems for a foreign national. Individuals who depart the United States and are

---

[27] INA § 329(a).
[28] INA § 329A.
[29] INA § 319(d).
[30] INA § 319(e).
[31] INA § 319(b).
[32] INA §§ 328(b)(2) and 329(b)(1).
[33] INA § 318.
[34] *Matter of Acosta Hidalgo*, 24 I&N Dec. 103 (BIA 2007).

abroad for six months or more but less than one year are presumed to have broken their continuous residency.[35] However, that presumption can be rebutted by evidence that the person did not actually interrupt his or her residency. Factors that may tend to support this include immediate family members who remained in the United States during the LPR's travel abroad, property and or bank accounts that remained opened, employment that has not been relinquished, or evidence that the foreign national is paying taxes or attending school here. Any proof available to show why a person's visit abroad was for such a long period may also be helpful in demonstrating that there was no intent to abandon residency in the United States. This might include evidence of a lengthy illness of the foreign national or a family member, or of civil unrest that made it difficult to travel. This requirement applies equally to those whose statutory period for eligibility is three or five years.

Individuals who are abroad for one year or more are almost always considered to have broken the continuous residency requirement[36] However, such foreign nationals do not have to establish a new period of five years of continuous residency before they can apply for citizenship. Instead, they need only wait four years and a day after their return to be eligible to apply.[37] In the case of foreign nationals married to U.S. citizens and therefore eligible to naturalize after three years in LPR status, they must wait two years and a day before they can apply.

Case for Discussion 11.4

Yessenia, a national from Panama, originally entered on a B-2 nonimmigrant visa as a visitor, and met her husband, a U.S. citizen, who petitioned for her to become an LPR. Her application was approved. They have one daughter, aged two. Three years after she became an LPR, Yessenia had to leave the country to return to Panama to take care of her sick mother. The visit was supposed to last for three months, but her mother's health was worse than anticipated and eventually she passed away. Yessenia had to take care of her mother's property and remained in Panama for seven months, after which she returned to the United States.

- Has Yessenia broken her continuous residence?
- What evidence would be helpful in this case?

Applying for citizenship after being abroad for more than six months also places a foreign national at risk of losing his or her LPR status. The naturalization application asks applicants to list all trips abroad in the last five years. This information highlights the possibility of breaks in continuous residency. Where this is

---

[35] INA § 316(b).
[36] *Id.*
[37] 8 C.F.R. § 316.5(c)(1)(ii).

Abandonment of Lawful Permanent Resident Status: Results from an LPR's frequent and extended absences from the United States when there are limited ties to demonstrate an intent to maintain residence here.

the case, the foreign national could also be subject to charges of ***abandonment of LPR status***.

If an LPR is determined to have abandoned his or her LPR status, the foreign national would not only be denied naturalization but could be placed in removal proceedings for an immigration judge to decide if LPR status was indeed abandoned.[38] If this is the case, the foreign national will be ordered removed. The government has a high burden in these cases, however, and must show by "clear, unequivocal and convincing evidence"[39] that LPR status has in fact been abandoned. In order to defend against such a charge, some of the same factors that might be produced to prove that an LPR did not intend to disrupt his or her continuous residency might also be produced, including the presence of relatives in the United States, employment that has not been relinquished, or other evidence of strong ties to the country. Foreign nationals planning to be abroad for a period of one year or more can obtain a special travel document, known as a Reentry Permit, using Form I-131, Application for Travel Document, which can be helpful in demonstrating that s/he intends to return to the United States. The abandonment of LPR status is distinct from the disruption of continuous residence. It is important to analyze both issues when applying for citizenship to ensure no possible risk of removal exists.

Those in the armed forces are not subject to the continuous residency requirements.[40] There are additional exceptions available for employees who work for the U.S. government, certain U.S. companies, certain research institutions, and international organizations, where they are regularly required to work abroad.[41] Those individuals who are employees of such organizations and have lived in the United States for an uninterrupted period of at least one year as LPRs can be absent from the United States for one year or more without breaking continuous residency if they file Form N-470, Application to Preserve Residency for Naturalization Purposes.[42] Spouses of U.S. citizen employees who work for the government, certain companies, or certain research institutions that require them to be regularly stationed abroad, may naturalize without any prior residence in the United States or completing Form N-470, so long as they are in the United States at the time of naturalization and declare an intent to take up residency in the United States immediately after their citizen spouse completes the work abroad.[43]

---

[38] *See* Chapter 10, Immigration Court Practice and Relief from Removal, for further discussion.
[39] *Matter of Huang*, 19 I & N Dec. 749,754 (BIA 1988).
[40] INA §§ 328 and 329.
[41] INA § 316(b).
[42] 8 C.F.R. § 316.5(d)(1)(i).
[43] INA § 319(b).

Religious workers who have lived in the United States as LPRs for an uninterrupted period of one year are also exempt from the continuous residency requirements, if they leave the country in order to perform religious duties abroad.[44] However, they must also preserve residency for naturalization by completing Form N-470, Application to Preserve Residency for Naturalization.[45]

C.3.b. Physical Presence

Physical presence is related to but different from continuous residence as it refers to how much time in the aggregate the foreign national must spend in the United States in order to qualify to become a U.S. citizen. Regardless of the applicable statutory period, a foreign national must have been physically present in the United States for at least 50 percent of the requisite time, effectively 18 months for those with a three-year statutory period and 30 months for those with five years.

● EXAMPLE

Marilyn, who received her permanent residency based on the sponsorship of her father, often travels to her home country of Barbados to see old friends and family. While she has never been gone more than 6 months at any one time, she has taken 30 trips in the last 5 years totaling 32 months. Since Marilyn is required to have continuous presence of 5 years in order to be eligible for citizenship, she must show that she has been in the United States an aggregate of 30 months. Therefore, because she has been absent for an aggregate of 32 months, she does not meet the physical presence requirements. Marilyn can cure this problem by remaining in the United States for a period of time so that she is physically present 30 months or more out of the 60-month requisite statutory period.

Exceptions to the physical presence requirement for members of the armed forces, certain government employees and their spouses, religious workers, and others described earlier are also permitted in a similar way to continuous residence.

---

[44] INA § 317.
[45] 8 C.F.R. § 316.5(d)(2).

> **Case for Discussion 11.5**
>
> Francesca is from Italy and became an LPR in 2008 through her work as a graphic designer for an international company based in the United States. Her work requires her to travel a great deal and so she is frequently out of the country on business. She now wants to naturalize so that she can vote in the 2016 presidential elections as she has been paying close attention and wants desperately to vote for her favorite candidate. On the naturalization form, she lists her absences as follows:
>
> 2016, Feb–Apr: 90 days
> 2015, Oct–Nov: 45 days
> 2015, Jun–Jul: 30 days
> 2015, Jan–May: 120 days
> 2013, Feb–Aug: 180 Days
> 2012, Aug–Nov: 90 Days
> 2012, Jan–May: 120 Days
> 2011, Mar–Nov: 240 Days
>
> - Does Francesca meet the physical presence requirement?
> - If not, when is the earliest time she can file for citizenship?
> - Are there any other issues that Francesca might have to address before she decides to file her application?

C.4. Good Moral Character

An individual applying for citizenship must be a person of good moral character, or GMC.[46] Specific statutory provisions regarding this are found in INA § 101(f), and at 8 C.F.R. § 316.10. Some of the factors listed in these provisions that tend to show a lack of GMC are mandatory, leading to a permanent bar to citizenship, while others are conditional and left to the **adjudicating officer**'s, or **AO**'s, discretion. The conditional bars to naturalization usually relate to actions and behavior that occur during the requisite statutory period needed to establish eligibility to file the citizenship application. However, the government may take into consideration behavior outside that period if the applicant does not "reflect a reform of character" or if they have a bearing on the applicant's moral character.[47] The mandatory provisions that demonstrate lack of GMC and that can never be overcome are:

---

[46] INA § 316(a).
[47] 8 C.F.R. § 316.10 (a)(2). Interestingly, INA § 329 does not impose a good moral character requirement for those applying to naturalize based on their military service. However, 8 C.F.R. § 329(2)(d) does impose the requirement, but only for a period of one year prior to filing the application and continuing through adjudication of the application.

- Conviction for murder at any time, and
- Conviction of an aggravated felony as defined in section 101(a)(43) of the [Immigration and Nationality] Act on or after November 29, 1990.[48]

Good moral character cannot be established if any of the following have been committed during the statutory period:

- Commission of one or more crimes involving moral turpitude or CIMT, other than a purely political offense, for which the applicant was convicted, except as specified in section 212(a)(2)(ii)(II) of the [Immigration and Nationality] Act;
- Commission of two or more offenses for which the applicant was convicted and the aggregate sentence actually imposed was five years or more, provided that, if the offense was committed outside the United States, it was not a purely political offense;
- Violation of any law of the United States, any State, or any foreign country relating to a controlled substance, provided that the violation was not a single offense for simple possession of 30 grams or less of marijuana;
- Admits committing any criminal act under 8 C.F.R §§ 316.10(b)(2)(i), (ii), or (iii) for which there was never a formal charge, indictment, arrest, or conviction, whether committed in the United States or any other country;
- Confinement to a penal institution for an aggregate of 180 days pursuant to a conviction or convictions (provided that such confinement was not outside the United States due to a conviction outside the United States for a purely political offense);
- The giving of false testimony to obtain any benefit from the [Immigration and Nationality] Act, if the testimony was made under oath or affirmation and with an intent to obtain an immigration benefit regardless of whether the information was material;
- Involvement in prostitution or commercialized vice as described in section 212(a)(2)(D) of the [Immigration and Nationality] Act;
- Involvement in the smuggling of a person or persons into the United States as described in section 212(a)(6)(E) of the [Immigration and Nationality] Act;
- Practiced or is practicing polygamy;
- Commission of two or more gambling offenses for which the applicant was convicted;
- Income earned principally from illegal gambling activities; or
- Being a habitual drunkard.[49]

It may be helpful to see these conditional bars to GMC in Table 11.1.

---

[48] 8 C.F.R. § 316.10 (a)(1).
[49] 8 C.F.R. § 316.10(b)(2).

Table 11.1 Conditional Bars to Good Moral Character for Acts Committed in Statutory Period

Offense	Citation	Description
One or More CIMTs	8 C.F.R. § 316.10(b)(2)(i), (iv) INA § 101(f)(3)	Conviction or admission of one or more CIMTs (other than political offense), except for one petty offense
Aggregate Sentence of Five Years or More	8 C.F.R. § 316.10(b)(2)(ii), (iv) INA § 101(f)(3)	Conviction of two or more offenses with combined sentence of five years or more (other than political offense)
Controlled Substance Violation	8 C.F.R. § 316.10(b)(2)(iii), (iv) INA § 101(f)(3)	Violation of any law on controlled substances, except for simple possession of 30g or less of marijuana
Incarceration for 180 Days	8 C.F.R. § 316.10(b)(2)(v) INA § 101(f)(7)	Incarceration for a total period of 180 days or more, except political offense and ensuing confinement abroad
False Testimony Under Oath	8 C.F.R. § 316.10(b)(2)(vi) INA § 101(f)(6)	False testimony for the purpose of obtaining any immigration benefit
Prostitution Offenses	8 C.F.R. § 316.10(b)(2)(vii) INA § 101(f)(3)	Engaged in prostitution, attempted or procured to import prostitution, or received proceeds from prostitution
Smuggling of a Person	8 C.F.R. § 316.10(b)(2)(viii) INA § 101(f)(3)	Involved in smuggling of a person to enter or try to enter the United States in violation of law
Polygamy	8 C.F.R. § 316.10(b)(2)(ix) INA § 101(f)(3)	Practiced or is practicing polygamy (the custom of having more than one spouse at the same time)
Gambling Offenses	8 C.F.R. § 316.10(b)(2)(x)–(xi) INA § 101(f)(4)–(5)	Two or more gambling offenses or derives income principally from illegal gambling activities
Habitual Drunkard	8 C.F.R. § 316.10(b)(2)(xii) INA § 101(f)(1)	Is or was a habitual drunkard

Offense	Citation	Description
Failure to Support Dependents	8 C.F.R. § 316.10(b)(3)(i) INA § 101(f)	Willful failure or refusal to support dependents, unless extenuating circumstances are established
Adultery	8 C.F.R. § 316.10(b)(3)(ii) INA § 101(f)	Extramarital affair tending to destroy existing marriage, unless extenuating circumstances are established
Unlawful Acts	8 C.F.R. § 316.10(b)(3)(iii) INA § 101(f)	Unlawful act that adversely reflect upon GMC, unless extenuating circumstances are established

Source: USCIS.

Since many of the mandatory bars to naturalization are also grounds for deportation, it is extremely important to do a complete assessment of an applicant's history as it relates to GMC because individuals who have difficulty establishing it may not only be denied citizenship, but may also be placed into removal proceedings.

With respect to the discretionary bars to GMC, an AO is required to conduct a balancing test, where the positive GMC factors are weighed against the negative to determine whether the criteria has been established.[50] Where establishing GMC may be a problem, it is important to present evidence of things that are likely to indicate a repair of the foreign national's moral character, which can include:

- Family in the United States,
- Length of time in the United States, both legally and in undocumented status,
- Ties to the community,
- Employment history,
- Volunteer work,
- Circumstances leading to the act of poor moral character,
- Any actions taken to rectify that act, and
- Any rehabilitation work on the part of the applicant.

All of these things may help to show, in the totality of the evidence, that the foreign national is a person with GMC.

---

[50] *Matter of B*, 1 I. & N. Dec. 611, 612 (BIA 1943), "We do not think [good moral character] should be construed to mean moral excellence, or that it is destroyed by a single lapse. Rather we think it is a concept of a person's natural worth derived from the sum total of all his actions in the community."

C.4.a. Individuals on Probation or Parole

Foreign nationals who are performing a period of probation or parole, or a suspended sentence at the time they apply for citizenship, are not automatically ineligible for naturalization. While the application cannot be approved during this period, a final decision on the application will be withheld until evidence is presented to prove satisfactory completion of all requirements.[51]

Several jurisdictions have prison diversionary programs that allow a person to avoid incarceration and instead pay a fine and/or perform community service without admitting to committing a crime. In these cases, the foreign national is not considered to have been convicted and therefore can also naturalize once the alternative sentencing program is completed.[52] Those who have been convicted of a crime that tends to show lack of GMC must count their requisite statutory period from the date of conviction, which is determined to be the date of sentencing and not the guilty plea.[53]

> **Case for Discussion 11.6**
>
> Tatyana, an LPR from Croatia was arrested for shoplifting seven years ago. She took some make-up and a scarf. She was arrested and charged with a summary offense of retail theft. Tatyana was not "convicted" of the offense, because she was placed in a sentencing diversion program that did not require her to plead guilty. Tatyana had to complete 20 hours of community service, which she did. She is now applying for citizenship.
>
> - Review 8 C.F.R. § 316.10 (a) and (b) to determine why, despite the shoplifting offense, she can still meet the good moral character requirement for citizenship.
> - What documents should Tatyana submit in support of her application?

C.4.b. Selective Service

Although not in the regulations, the stated policy of the government is to consider male applicants who fail to register for the selective service if present in the United States between the ages of 18 and 26 on other than nonimmigrant visas, as lacking GMC. This failure can be cured, however, by the foreign national registering before he applies for naturalization, if still eligible to do so. Otherwise,

---

[51] 8 C.F.R. § 316.10(c)(1).
[52] *See* Section B.2.a of Chapter 9, Grounds of Inadmissibility and Deportation, for further discussion.
[53] *Puello v. BCIS*, 511 F.3d 324 (2d Cir. 2007).

he must show that the failure to register was not done willfully and knowingly. A signed statement or affidavit by the applicant stating this is often sufficient.

C.4.c. Payment of Taxes

Individuals who fail to pay taxes will be considered as lacking GMC. The USCIS is willing to accept evidence that the foreign national has entered into a formal agreement with the Internal Revenue Service, or IRS, or other taxing authority, to repay any taxes owed and is current on those payments. Those exempt from filing a tax return need only provide evidence of this to prove compliance with the tax requirements.

C.4.d. Dependent Support

We have already established that willfully failing to support dependents can be considered a factor in assessing a person's GMC.[54] If an applicant is under a court order to provide child support but fails to do so, it is likely, unless there are extenuating circumstances, to lead to a finding of lack of GMC. The more difficult case is when a foreign national parent has children in the home country or where there are children in the United States but no formal support order. In many jurisdictions, AOs will ask to see proof that the applicant is supporting the child, perhaps by providing receipts for remittances sent abroad for the child's maintenance. Often, a letter from the parent or guardian with whom the child lives confirming support will suffice, but this can be difficult where the relationship between the parents is strained. Other evidence of support can include receipts for school or other fees paid for the child's benefit. If the officer finds the applicant *willfully* failed to support his or her dependents, the application for naturalization can be denied, depending on what factors are presented to explain that failure.

Case for Discussion   11.7

Oscar, an LPR, is separated from his wife. They have two U.S. citizen children. He was sending money to his wife regularly for their support but was recently laid off from his job, so he reduced his payments. He is actively looking for work.

- What arguments would you make that Oscar is a person of good moral character?
- What evidence would you gather to support this argument?

---

[54] 8 C.F.R. § 316.10(b)(3)(i).

C.4.e. Voting

Immigrants who register to vote when they are not eligible to do so may be said to violate INA § 237(a)(3)(D), which makes false claims to citizenship a removable offense. This is because, in most cases, only U.S. citizens can vote and so by voting, even in error, the foreign national could be charged with holding him or herself out to be a citizen. However, LPRs who mistakenly register to vote can have their names removed from the voting rolls and, if able to demonstrate lack of intent to make a false claim to citizenship, may retain their eligibility to naturalize. LPRs who actually vote face a major barrier, since the act of voting in violation of any federal, state, or local law or regulation is a deportable offense with no waiver available.[55] Therefore, where a foreign national admits to this, careful thought should be given to whether or not an application to naturalize should be filed in the first place because of the possible risk of the person being placed into removal proceedings.

C.4.f. Marriage Fraud

The citizenship interview provides an opportunity for the USCIS to re-examine a foreign national's immigration history, including where a spouse may have received LPR status through marriage. There are many questions on Form N-400, Application for Naturalization, that delve into the status of the marriage in order to determine if it is valid. For example, the government may look once again into how an applicant became an LPR or even examine how the LPR's spouse received his or her immigration status, where applicable. If it is determined that fraud was involved in any way, the naturalization candidate could be placed into removal proceedings.

> ● **EXAMPLE**
>
> Fatima, from Senegal, married a U.S. citizen solely to remain in the country. The fraud was not discovered at the time she applied to adjust her status to an LPR and was granted status based on the marriage. She applied to become a U.S. citizen after three years, but actually never lived with her husband. At the naturalization interview, the officer asked for evidence she still lived with him, but she could not produce any documents. This raised the suspicion of the AO who then questioned her extensively about the nature of her relationship with her husband. Fatima was not prepared for this line of questioning. She became flustered and could not remember simple details, such as where she and her husband were married, where they had lived together, and other basic information. An investigation into possible marriage fraud was triggered and her citizenship application is on hold, pending any adverse findings from the investigation.

---

[55] INA § 237(a)(6).

C.4.g. Evidence to Demonstrate Good Moral Character

Individuals applying for naturalization bear the burden to establish good moral character. When there has been contact with the criminal justice system, applicants should gather certified dispositions from the court that presided over their case, which will provide information about the nature of the offense and outcome of the proceedings. In some cases, a person may be eligible to have their criminal history expunged or removed from the court record. This may be done automatically by the court or by application and is advantageous because the foreign national is now free to declare that s/he has never been arrested. While this is possible under the criminal law, any arrest or conviction, even though expunged, must *always* be disclosed for immigration purposes. However, obtaining the disposition for an expunged case may not be straightforward. Prior to a request for expungement, foreign nationals who remain eligible to naturalize despite their convictions should request a certified disposition of the court records to avoid the difficulties of requesting one after the record is clear. If this is not possible, then every effort should be made to trace the case through proper channels or, where unsuccessful, obtain a letter from the court or prosecutor's office confirming that there is no record available.

For those on parole, probation, or a diversion program, proof of satisfactory completion of the program from a probation or other suitable officer is required. Copies of past tax filings or a written agreement with the IRS to pay past taxes owed is necessary where there are tax issues. For child support payments, the applicant can obtain payment printouts from the responsible family court or provide evidence of payments through payroll deductions, money orders, or cancelled checks. Evidence of a *bona fide* marriage and living together to demonstrate fulfilment of the shortened statutory period can be provided by using many of the same documents submitted in support of the immediate relative petition, such as marriage certificate, prior divorce decrees, and joint tax filings.[56]

C.4.h. Literacy and Civics

Individuals applying for citizenship must demonstrate an ability to read, write, and speak English.[57] The foreign national is tested on his or her ability to understand English by an AO, who may review the contents of the application with the applicant after s/he has been sworn in or affirmed to tell the truth, under penalty of perjury. The Form N-400, Application for Naturalization, includes questions about family and seeks information on all addresses where the applicant has lived in the United States. It also asks applicants to provide their work history, as well as questions about GMC and loyalty to the United States. By reviewing the application with the foreign national, the AO is able to assess the applicant's ability to speak and understand basic English. In order to check the applicant's

---

[56] *See* Section C of Chapter 6, Family Sponsored Immigration and Permanent Resident Status, for further discussion of marriage *bona fides*.
[57] INA § 312(a)(1).

proficiency in reading and writing, the applicant will be asked to read a sentence and write another that is dictated. S/he will be given up to three sentences, if there is difficulty with the first one. Additionally, the applicant must demonstrate an understanding of United States history, form of government, and civics. There is a selection of 100 questions that may be asked to test the applicant's knowledge of this.[58] Ten are randomly selected by an AO, and the applicant must answer six correctly in order to pass the test.

C.5. Exemptions, Waivers, and Reasonable Accommodation

The INA provides for certain applicants for naturalization to qualify for waivers and to be afforded reasonable accommodations, where appropriate.[59] Foreign nationals who are 50 years of age or older at the time of their naturalization interview and who have been LPRs for 20 years or more, or who are 55-years old and have been LPRs for at least 15 years, may take the government and civics test orally in their own language.[60] They are required to bring their own interpreter with them. Those who are 65 and over and have been LPRs for at least 20 years are given special consideration, as they are required to study only 20 of the 100 questions.[61] All waiver eligible applicants are required to get six out of ten questions correct from that list. Additionally, congress enacted the Hmong Veterans' Naturalization Act of 2000,[62] exempting Laotian nationals who supported U.S. troops in the Vietnam War from the English comprehension and literacy requirements.

Case for Discussion 11.8

Paola was sponsored by her U.S. citizen daughter for LPR status. She entered the United States in 1990 from Colombia on a visitor's visa and received her green card in 2005. Assume it is 2015. Paola is now 65-years old; she cannot read, write, or speak English.

- Is Paola exempt from the English or government and civics requirement?
- Would your answer be the same if she obtained her LPR status in 1995?

---

[58] A copy of the questions can be found at http://www.uscis.gov/sites/default/files/USCIS/Office%20of%20Citizenship/Citizenship%20Resource%20Center%20Site/Publications/100q.pdf. The USCIS now has many resources in many different interactive mediums to help an applicant learn the information necessary to do well on the tests. More information can be found at http://www.uscis.gov/citizenship/learners/study-test/study-materials-civics-test.
[59] INA § 312(b).
[60] Id. The learning materials are available in English, Spanish, and Chinese.
[61] A copy of the questions can be found at http://www.uscis.gov/sites/default/files/USCIS/Office%20of%20Citizenship/Citizenship%20Resource%20Center%20Site/Publications/PDFs/65-20q.pdf.
[62] Pub. L. 106-207, 114 Stat. 316 (2000).

Foreign nationals who suffer from a physical or mental disability do not have to meet the language or civics requirements, if they can show that their inability to learn the material for the citizenship test is directly related to this condition.[63] The connection between the diagnosis and the inability to learn English and civics is referred to as the nexus, which must clearly demonstrate how the physical or mental disability prevents an applicant from completing this portion of the examination. It is important to show the effect of the disability on both the English language *and* civics requirement of the citizenship examination, if applicable. Waivers can be applied for either the language or civics portion alone, though in practice most applicants apply to waive both.

A Medical Doctor, or M.D., Doctor of Osteopathy, or D.O., or licensed clinical psychologist must sign Form N-648, Medical Certification for Disability Exceptions, which describes the disability and explains its connection to the person's inability to learn English and the government and civics portion of the test. Other medical staff may assist in completing the form but it must be signed as a means of certifying it by the specified professionals. Where possible, a Diagnostic and Statistical Manual of Mental Disorder, or **DSM-V** code explaining the diagnosis should be included along with a description of the condition. A sample Form N-648, Medical Certification for Disability Exceptions, is in Figure 11.1.

DSM-V: Diagnostic and Statistical Manual of Mental Disorder that defines and classifies mental disorders as an aid to diagnosis.

It is preferable to have the applicant's treating physician complete the N-648, Medical Certification for Disability Exceptions, but it is certainly acceptable to have another medical professional or specialist evaluate the applicant, especially if the treating physician feels that the applicant's impediments are outside his or her area of expertise. For example, an internist treating a patient for a physical problem may not be able to evaluate the patient for the post-traumatic stress disorder, or PTSD, that affects his or her ability to study, or explain *why* it interferes with the ability to learn English and civics. The Form N-648 can be submitted with the citizenship application at the time of filing or later at the interview. As with other immigration forms, it is important to check the USCIS website for the most current version since they are frequently updated or changed. It is also essential to check the site for the appropriate address to send the form since this also changes periodically.

There are applicants who have conditions that do not rise to the level of a medical waiver but require special accommodations in order to take the citizenship test. For example, a deaf person could require a sign language interpreter. A person with a mental or behavioral disability who can still take the test may need to bring in a social worker or family member to the interview to alleviate anxiety. Both of these accommodation needs can be noted on the Form N-400, Application for Naturalization, and should be permitted by the USCIS under the Rehabilitation Act of 1973, which prohibits discrimination by government agencies on the basis of disability.

---

[63] INA § 312(b)(1).

Figure 11.1

Sample Form N-648, Medical Certification for Disability Exceptions

OMB No. 1615-0060; Expires 03/31/2017

Department of Homeland Security
U.S. Citizenship and Immigration Services

Form N-648, Medical Certification for Disability Exceptions

ALL parts of this form, except the "APPLICANT ATTESTATION" and "INTERPRETER'S CERTIFICATION" must be certified by a licensed medical professional as provided in the instructions for Form N-648. Before certifying this form, the medical professional must conduct an in-person examination of the applicant. (See instructions for Form N-648 for additional information which is also located in the "FORMS" section at www.uscis.gov.)

Reminder About Eligibility Requirements

This form is intended for an applicant who seeks an exception to the English and/or civics requirements due to a physical or developmental disability or mental impairment that has lasted, or is expected to last, 12 months or more. An applicant who with reasonable accommodations provided under the Rehabilitation Act of 1973 can satisfy the English and civics requirements does not need to submit this form. Reasonable accommodations include, but are not limited to, sign language interpreters, extended time for testing, and off-site testing.

Completing and Certifying This Form

All questions or items must be answered fully and accurately. Responses should utilize common terminology, without abbreviations, that a person without medical training can understand. U.S. Citizenship and Immigration Services (USCIS) recommends that the certifying medical professional use the electronic Form N-648 located in the "FORMS" section www.uscis.gov. If the medical professional completes the form by hand, then responses must be legible and appear in black ink.

Type or print clearly in black ink.

Part I. APPLICANT INFORMATION

I certify that I have examined:

Last Name	First Name	Middle Name	USCIS A-Number
			A-

Address (Street Number and Name)		U.S. Social Security Number

City	State or Province	Zip Code or Postal Code
Philadelphia	PA	19131

Telephone Number	E-Mail Address (if any)	Date of Birth	Gender
(215)	none	01/22/	☐ Male ☒ Female

USCIS USE ONLY

This N-648 is:
☐ Sufficient
☐ Insufficient
☐ Continued/RFE

Reviewer

Location & Date

Part II. MEDICAL PROFESSIONAL INFORMATION

Type or print clearly in black ink. If you need more space to complete an answer, use a separate sheet of paper. Write the applicant's name and Alien Registration Number (A-Number), at the top of each sheet of paper and indicate the part and number of the item to which the answer refers. You must sign and date each continuation sheet. You must answer and complete each question since USCIS will not accept an incomplete Form N-648. You may, but are not required to, attach to this completed form supportive medical diagnostic reports or records regarding the applicant.

NOTE: Only medical doctors, doctors of osteopathy, or clinical psychologists licensed to practice in the United States (including the U.S. territories of Guam, Puerto Rico, and the Virgin Islands) are authorized to certify the form. While staff of the medical practice associated with the medical professional certifying the form may assist in its completion, the medical professional is responsible for the accuracy of the form's content.

Last Name	First Name	Middle Name

Business Address (Street Number and Name)	City	State or Province	Zip Code or Postal Code	Telephone Number
	Philadelphia	PA	19116	(215)

License Number	Licensing State	E-Mail Address (if any)
	PA	none@example.com

1. **Currently licensed as a** *(Check all that apply):* ☒ Medical Doctor ☐ Doctor of Osteopathy ☐ Clinical Psychologist

2. **Medical practice type:** internal medicine

Form N-648 03/11/15 Y Page 1

C: Citizenship Through Naturalization   591

Figure 11.1
(Continued)

Applicant's Name	USCIS A-Number
▮▮▮▮▮	A- ▮▮▮▮▮

9. What clinical methods did you use to diagnose the applicant's medical disability and/or impairment(s) listed in number 1?

Blood tests
EKG
CT Brain
X-ray Chest, extremities
Monthly examinations

10. Clearly describe how the applicant's disability and/or impairment(s) affect his or her ability to demonstrate knowledge and understanding of English and/or civics.

Ms. ▮▮▮▮▮ has suffered from chronic diseases for many years. Patient's Coronary Artery Disease, Hypertension, Congestive Heart Failure, and Diabetes have resulted in poor blood circulation of heart and brain vessels, and abnormal oxygen supply of these organs. All these factors brought to Dementia, a chronic global irreversible deterioration of mental functions including memory impairment, cognition and behavioral changes. It affects patient's brain functioning: such as attention and orientation deficit, marked short-term memory loss, and low concentration. Her brain functions are irreversible, and her decline became progressive.

It is my professional opinion that Ms. ▮▮▮▮▮ will not be able to to learn English, US History and Civics. Therefore we request an exemption due to medical condition.

11. In your professional medical opinion, does the applicant's disability or impairment(s) prevent him or her from demonstrating the following requirements? *(Check all that apply. If none applies, the applicant is not eligible for this exception.)*

The ability to:

- [x] Read English
- [x] Write English
- [x] Speak English
- [x] Answer questions regarding United States history and civics, even in a language the applicant understands.

Form N-648 03/11/15 Y Page 4

Figure 11.1 (Continued)

Applicant's Name	USCIS A-Number
Ms. ▮▮▮▮▮▮▮	A- ▮▮▮▮▮▮▮

Part III. INFORMATION ABOUT DISABILITY and/or IMPAIRMENT(S)

1. Provide the clinical diagnosis and DSM IV code (*if applicable*) of the applicant's disability and/or impairment(s) that form the basis for seeking an exception to the English and/or civics requirements; e.g., *DSM-IV 318.0 Down syndrome.* If you cannot provide a DSM IV code, write "N/A" and explain why you cannot provide a DSM IV code.

Ms. ▮▮▮▮▮ suffers from
125.10 Coronary Artery Disease;
150.9 Congestive Heart Failure;
E11.9 Diabetes Mellitus;
E78.5 Hyperlipidemia;
I10 Hypertension;
F03.90 Dementia;
S/P Left hip fracture;

2. Provide a basic description of the disability and/or impairment(s), e.g., "Down syndrome is a genetic disorder that causes lifelong intellectual disability (also referred to as mental retardation), developmental delays, and other problems."

Coronary Artery Disease is the end result of the accumulation of the atheromatous plaques within the walls of the coronary arteries that supply the myocardium (muscle of the heart) with oxygen and nutrients.
Hypertension is a condition in which the blood pressure in the arteries is chronically elevated. With every heart beat the heart pumps blood though the arteries to the body. If the pressure is too high, the heart has to work harder to pump, and this could lead to organ damage.
Congestive heart failure means that the heart's pumping power is weaker than normal. With heart failure, blood moves through the heart and body at a slower rate, and pressure in the heart increases. As a result, the heart cannot pump enough oxygen and nutrients to meet the body's needs.
Dementia is a chronic global irreversible deterioration of mental functions including memory impairment, cognition and personality changes.

3. Date you first examined the applicant regarding the condition(s) listed in number 1.

Date *(mm/dd/yyyy)*	Location (if different from business address on Page 1; otherwise write "same as business address")
06/16/2011	same as business address

4. Date you last examined the applicant regarding the condition(s) listed in number 1, if different from above.

Date *(mm/dd/yyyy)*	Location (if different from business address on Page 1; otherwise write "same as business address")
09/10/2015	same as business address

5. Are you the medical professional regularly treating this applicant for the condition(s) listed in Item Number 1?

[X] Yes *(If "Yes," indicate duration of treatment.)*   Years 4   Months 3

[ ] No *(If "No," provide the name of the applicant's regularly treating medical professional on the next page and explain why you are certifying this form instead of the regularly treating medical professional.)*

C: Citizenship Through Naturalization

Figure 11.1
(Continued)

Applicant's Name	USCIS A-Number
	A-

Name of Regularly Treating Medical Professional and Address.

Last Name	First Name		Middle Name	
Business Address (Street Number and Name)	City	State or Province	Zip Code or Postal Code	Telephone Number

Explanation

_____
_____
_____
_____
_____
_____
_____
_____
_____
_____

6. Has the applicant's disability and/or impairment(s) lasted, or do you expect it to last, 12 months or more?

   [X] Yes *(If "Yes," continue to complete this form.)*

   [ ] No *(If "No," the applicant is not eligible for this exception and you need not complete the remainder of the questions. Please go directly to the "Medical Professional's Certification.")*

7. Is the applicant's disability and/or impairment(s) the result of the applicant's illegal use of drugs?

   [ ] Yes *(If "Yes," the applicant is not eligible for this exception and you need not complete the remainder of the questions. Please go directly to the "Medical Professional's Certification.")*

   [X] No *(If "No," continue to complete this form.)*

8. What caused this applicant's medical disability and/or impairment(s) listed in number 1, if known?

The cause of the disability is unknown.
_____
_____
_____
_____
_____
_____
_____
_____
_____
_____
_____
_____

Form N-648 03/11/15 Y Page 3

Figure 11.1 (Continued)

Applicant's Name	USCIS A-Number
▇▇▇▇▇▇▇	A- ▇▇▇▇▇▇▇

INTERPRETER'S CERTIFICATION

An interpreter must complete, and certify, the section below if an interpreter translated communications between the applicant and medical professional on the day of the examination that formed the basis of this Form N-648 certification.

Interpreter Information

Last Name	First Name	Middle Name	

Address (Street Number and Name)	City	State or Province	Zip Code or Postal Code

Was a phone interpreter used?

☐ Yes *(If yes, the interpreter is not required to complete the information below.)*

☐ No *(If no, the interpreter is required to complete the information below.)*

Interpreter Certification

I am fluent As the interpreter, I certify that I am fluent in English and the following language: _____.
I further certify that I have accurately and completely translated all communications between the medical professional and the applicant that occurred on _____, the date(s) of the examination(s) that form the basis of this certification.

Interpreter Signature   **Date** *(mm/dd/yyyy)*

APPLICANT (PATIENT) ATTESTATION/RELEASE OF INFORMATION

I, ▇▇▇▇▇▇▇▇▇▇▇▇▇▇▇▇▇▇▇▇▇ , authorize _____
         (Applicant's Name)   (Licensed medical doctor, doctor of osteopathy, or clinical psychologist)

to release to U.S. Citizenship and Immigration Services all relevant physical and mental health information related to my medical status for the purpose of applying for an exception from the English language and U.S. civics requirements for naturalization. I certify under penalty of perjury, pursuant to Title 28, U.S.C. Section 1746, that the information I provided to the medical professional is true and correct. I am aware that the knowing placement of false information on Form N-648 and related documents may also subject me to civil penalties under Title 8, U.S.C. Section 1324c. I understand that if this form is not completely filled out or if I fail to submit any required documentation, I may not be found eligible for the requested disability exception.

Applicant or Applicant's Authorized Representative Signature   **Date** *(mm/dd/yyyy)*

Figure 11.1 (Continued)

Applicant's Name	USCIS A-Number
▮▮▮▮▮▮	A- ▮▮▮▮▮▮

12. Was an interpreter used during your examination of the applicant?

☐ Yes *(If "Yes," the interpreter must complete the "Interpreter Certification" section.)*

☒ No

Additional Comments *(Optional)*

_____

MEDICAL PROFESSIONAL'S CERTIFICATION

Complete the following if an interpreter was not used during your examination of the applicant between the applicant and medical professional pertaining to the examination(s) that form the basis of this Form N-648 certification.

I am fluent in English and _____Russian_____, the language spoken by this patient. Therefore, an interpreter was not used during my examination(s) of this applicant.

All medical professionals **must** complete the certification below.

I certify that this applicant's identity has been verified through the following United States or State government-issued photographic identity document:

☒ Permanent Resident Card ☐ State ID Number: _____

☐ Other Identification (State type and ID Number): _____

I certify, under penalty of perjury under the laws of the United States of America, that the information on this form and any evidence submitted with it are all true and correct. I will furnish relevant medical records to USCIS, if requested to do so by USCIS, based on the applicant's consent. I am aware that the knowing placement of false information on Form N-648 and related documents may also subject me to criminal penalties including under Title 18, U.S.C. Section 1546, civil penalties under Title 18, U.S.C. Section 247c of the Immigration and Nationality Act, and civil license suspension or revocation by the appropriate authorities.

Licensed Medical Professional Signature **Date** *(mm/dd/yyyy)*

_____

Form N-648 03/11/15 Y Page 5

● EXAMPLE

Lilibeth, a Filipino national, has been diagnosed with schizophrenia, which is controlled by medication. She is able to speak English and learn civics, but suffers from high anxiety in stressful situations and cannot handle crowds. She also responds slowly to questions as a result of her medication. Lilibeth is much calmer when her sister is in the room with her. Under the rule for special accommodations, the USCIS should allow her sister into the interview. The AO should be prepared to repeat questions slowly and give Lilibeth sufficient time to answer because of her condition. Lilibeth can also request that she be sworn in at a private oath swearing ceremony held immediately after the interview or at a later date instead of being invited to a group citizenship ceremony where she may react negatively to the large crowd of people.

C.6. Bars to Naturalization and the Oath of Allegiance

Applicants for naturalization must show they are attached to the principles of the U.S. Constitution.[64] This does not mean those who advocate social reform are ineligible. However, those who advocate the violent overthrow of the government or are members of totalitarian organizations are ineligible,[65] as are members of the Communist Party, unless membership was involuntary or required for employment or other essentials for living.[66]

Deserters from the U.S. military or those who fled to avoid the draft in time of war are permanently barred from naturalization, if convicted of these offenses by a court martial or civil court.[67] However, a presidential pardon may allow a deserter or draft evader to qualify nevertheless. One example of such a pardon is when President Carter granted blanket pardons to those who violated selective service laws during the Vietnam War from August 4, 1964 to March 28, 1973.[68] A foreign national who sought and received an exemption or discharge from training or service in the United States military on the ground that s/he is a foreign national is also permanently ineligible for citizenship, unless s/he served in the armed forces in his or her country of nationality previously and sought the exemption pursuant to the terms of a treaty permitting this.[69]

Applicants must also take an oath or provide an affirmation of allegiance to the United States that includes a willingness to bear arms or fight in combat.[70] However, those whose religious or moral beliefs prevent them from performing combat services can demonstrate their allegiance by affirming their intention to

---

[64] INA § 316(a).
[65] INA § 313(a)(1).
[66] INA § 313(d).
[67] INA § 314.
[68] Exec. Order No. 11,967, 42 Fed. Reg. 4393 (1977); Proc. No. 4483, 42 Fed. Reg. 4391 (1977).
[69] INA § 315.
[70] INA § 337(a).

perform non-combatant services instead.[71] Individuals who are mentally or physically disabled are relieved from taking the oath.[72]

D. The Naturalization Application Process

The naturalization application process begins with the completion of the Form N-400, Application for Naturalization, which is lengthy and should be completed in full.

D.1. Compiling the Application for Naturalization

The naturalization application package should include:

- Form N-400, Application for Naturalization
- Form G-28, Notice of Entry of Appearance as Attorney or Accredited Representative, if the applicant is represented
- Two passport style photographs; it is a good idea to write the A# and name of the applicant on the back of both photographs and place them in an envelope with the name and A# written on it as well
- A photocopy, front and back, of the I-551, Permanent Residency card
- A check or money order for the immigration fee, made out to the Department of Homeland Security, or
- Form I-912, Request for Fee Waiver, with supporting documents to demonstrate financial hardship, where appropriate
- Foreign nationals applying based on marriage to a U.S. citizen should also include a marriage certificate and evidence of the spouse's citizenship. Where either party has been married before, evidence of the termination of a marriage prior to this one should also be included as evidence that the couple was free to marry
- Those with a criminal record should include certified dispositions for each and every arrest, regardless of the manner in which the case was disposed
- For those applying for citizenship based on service in the armed forces, an additional Form N-426, Request for Certification of Military or Naval Service, is required
- For those who are unable to take the English and Civics exam due to a physical or mental disability, Form N-648, Medical Certification for Disability Exceptions, completed by a doctor or clinical psychologist, must be submitted

A complete checklist of documents is available in the USCIS's Citizenship Resource link at http://www.uscis.gov/us-citizenship/citizenship-through-naturalization/guide-naturalization.

---

[71] INA § 337(a)(5)(B).
[72] INA § 337(c).

Form N-400, Application for Naturalization, asks many biographical questions. The foreign national must be prepared to list all marriages, places of employment, and residences for the last three or five years, depending on the applicable requisite statutory period. There are currently more than 50 questions on the form in all that seek to determine if the applicant can establish GMC. Legal practitioners should stress the importance of completing each question and answering honestly, particularly since every applicant will be required to present him or herself for biometrics, when fingerprints and pictures are captured digitally and then cross-referenced against several government databases as part of criminal and national security background checks. All criminal charges, whether dismissed, dropped, or expunged, must be listed on the application and documented.

● EXAMPLE

Tatyana, who was arrested and charged with the summary offense of shoplifting in Case for Discussion 11.6 is completing her citizenship application. One of the questions asks, "Have you ever been arrested, cited, or detained by any law enforcement officer (including any and all immigration officials or the U.S. Armed Forces) for any reason?" Tatyana is afraid to answer "yes" because she thinks she will be denied citizenship, so she checks "no," thinking the USCIS will not discover the shoplifting incident. However, since Tatyana's fingerprints were taken when she was arrested, it is likely that the arrest will in fact be discovered, since she will have to submit for biometrics as part of her application. While the shoplifting offense may not bar her from citizenship, Tatyana's efforts to hide it raise issues of her GMC and her application could be denied if she lied under oath.

Low-income applicants who receive means tested public benefits such as food stamps or medical assistance, or whose income is 150 percent of the poverty level or below, or those experiencing temporary financial hardship, are eligible to apply for a fee waiver on Form I-912, Request for Fee Waiver, to avoid paying the naturalization application fee. The USCIS also publishes Form I-912P, which lists the poverty guidelines for fee waiver eligibility.

Applications are mailed to one of two USCIS Lockboxes, depending on where the applicant lives, which processes the fees or reviews the fee waiver request before sending it to the appropriate USCIS Field office for adjudication. Applications should be sent by certified mail, return receipt requested, or by private courier service, with a copy retained for the file.

Once the application is received, the applicant and any legal representative are sent a receipt. If a fee waiver was filed and approved, the receipt will reflect "$0." A few weeks later, the applicant will then receive a biometrics appointment notice to report to a designated **Application Support Center** that serves the jurisdiction where the interview will occur. At the appointment, the applicant's picture and fingerprints will be taken digitally for review against government databases.

Following the biometrics appointment, a pre-interview notice will sometimes be sent, reminding the applicant that an interview is pending and advising of any documents that s/he should bring along. The interview notice follows, inviting the applicant to appear at a particular time and date for the citizenship interview.

If Form G-28, Notice of Entry of Appearance as Attorney or Accredited Representative, is filed, both the applicant and the legal representative should receive copies of all correspondence from the USCIS. However, this may not always happen. The better practice would be for both parties to inform the other whenever correspondence is received, to ensure nothing gets missed.

D.2. The Final Steps of the Naturalization Application

As part of the naturalization process, a foreign national may decide to legally change his or her name.[73] S/he can express this wish either on the application form or during the interview, when the AO specifically asks this question. This offers an inexpensive option for individuals to change their name without the complication of going into state court, which may be a lengthy and costly process. If the foreign national does request this, s/he will be required to be sworn in as a U.S. citizen with the new name at an oath swearing ceremony conducted by a federal court judge. As these appointments are infrequent, the foreign national may have to wait longer for a ceremony to take place and naturalization to be finalized. Most other applicants attend ceremonies administered by the USCIS Field office, which can occur fairly quickly after the interview has been completed.

An applicant who is missing documents at the time of the interview, or who is unable to pass the English and/or civics portion, is given another opportunity to either submit the missing information or take the examination again at no additional fee. This is known as a reexamination and cannot take place less than 60 days after the initial interview.[74] If the problem with passing the examination is based on a mental or physical disability, the applicant should consider submitting Form N-648, Medical Certification for Disability Exceptions, for consideration at the time of the second interview.

Following the interview, the AO has 120 days to make a decision on the application.[75] If no decision is made within that time frame, the applicant can request a hearing in federal district court, asking a judge to determine his or her application for citizenship, or to remand it back to the USCIS with instructions on how to resolve any issues that may exist.[76]

If the foreign national's application to naturalize is denied, s/he must be given written notice of that denial and afforded a period of 30 days in which to appeal using Form N-336, Request for a Hearing on a Decision in Naturalization Proceedings (Under Section 336 of the INA).[77] That hearing must take place no later than 180 days later[78] and must be conducted by a different officer from the one how made the initial decision. It can include submission of

---

[73] INA § 336(e).
[74] 8 CFR § 335.3(b).
[75] INA § 336(b).
[76] Id.
[77] 8 C.F.R. §§ 336.1(b) and 336.2(a).
[78] 8 C.F.R. § 336.2(b).

additional evidence or a review of the entire administrative record.[79] Sometimes it makes sense to file a new application for naturalization, since the fee for an appeal is similar to that of a new application. This is especially true if the denial was based on a missing document that can now be obtained, or lack of English and civics knowledge, which could be overcome through study or a medical waiver. Individuals can apply for naturalization numerous times, and each application will be considered on its individual merit.

If the appeal is denied, the foreign national can seek judicial review of the decision before the United States District Court with jurisdiction over where the foreign national lives.[80] This will require the expertise of a lawyer with experience in this type of work.

If the applicant passes the citizenship examination, s/he will then be invited to an oath swearing ceremony at the USCIS Field office, unless s/he has opted for a name change, where the Oath of Allegiance will be administered and the foreign national sworn in as a citizen. Prior to the ceremony, applicants will have to complete a form declaring that they have not engaged in any disqualifying acts between the time of the examination and the oath ceremony. The foreign national can choose to either swear to the oath or provide an affirmation of allegiance to the United States, which includes a willingness to bear arms or fight in combat. However, those whose religious or moral beliefs prevent them from performing combat services can demonstrate their allegiance by affirming their intention to perform non-combatant services. As noted in Section C.6., the oath may be waived for some severely disabled individuals, but a legal guardian, surrogate, or eligible designated representative must present specific medical documents and complete the process for the applicant. This is not available for all disabled individuals. At the end of the ceremony, the new citizen will receive a certificate of citizenship.

Case for Discussion 11.9

Stanley is from Germany and follows the Mennonite faith; his religion forbids him to engage in combat. Stanley wishes to apply for naturalization but he wants to explain that while he is loyal to the United States, his beliefs mean he cannot take up arms. Find the question on Form N-400, Application for Naturalization, that relates to "bearing arms."

- How should Stanley answer that question?
- What evidence would you prepare to support Stanley's request that he be exempt from bearing arms on behalf of the United States?

---

[79] *Id.*
[80] 8 C.F.R. § 336.9.

E. Derivative Citizenship: INA § 320

INA § 320 allows children to derive citizenship through their parents. The requirements for this have changed significantly over time. Which provision applies will in most cases depend on the year the child was born. Because the old rules can be complex, we pay particular attention here to the law after the enactment of the Child Citizenship Act of 2000, or CCA, effective February 27, 2001.[81] For those who do need to understand the old law, the USCIS publishes a chart that contains the requirements for derivation of citizenship based on the law existing at various historical periods, which is shown in Figure 11.2.[82]

> **Case for Discussion 11.10**
>
> Victor is from Costa Rica and was born on January 1, 1980. His mother, Rosa, never married Victor's father, Manuel. Manuel remained in Costa Rica and married another woman. Rosa received her LPR status through employment and petitioned for Victor in 1988, when she was an LPR. Victor arrived in 1990, at the age of ten, as an LPR. That same year, Rosa became a U.S. citizen.
>
> - Using the chart in Figure 11.2, determine if Victor can derive citizenship.

Today, children whose parents naturalize prior to their 18th birthday may derive citizenship from one or both parents. This is governed by the CCA and has been codified into INA § 320. Under this section, if one parent naturalizes before the child is 18, and the child is residing in the United States as an LPR, in the physical and legal custody of the newly naturalized citizen parent, the child will automatically derive citizenship. All of these requirements must be met on or after the CCA was enacted. If an individual was already 18 when CCA was enacted, s/he must refer to the chart in Figure 11.2 to see which requirements were in place at the time of the child's birth.

The CCA makes it possible for a biological or adopted child under the age of 18, who has a visa to enter the United States as an LPR in order to live with a U.S. citizen parent, to automatically derive citizenship upon entry to the United States because all the requirements of INA § 320 will be fulfilled at the time of entry.

---

[81] Pub. L. 106-395, 114 Stat. 163 (2000).
[82] This chart is available at http://www.uscis.gov/policymanual/PDF/NationalityChart3.pdf.

Figure 11.2
USCIS Chart 3 on Derivative Citizenship: INA § 320
Source: USCIS.

Nationality Chart 3
Derivative Citizenship of Children

A child may derive U.S. citizenship during the below listed historical periods if such child was under the statutory age, AND the child was lawfully admitted for permanent residence, AND the parent(s) naturalized. It does not matter in which order the actions occurred.

PERIOD IN WHICH LAST ACTION TOOK PLACE	CHILD BECAME AN LPR BEFORE STATUTORY AGE OF:	NATURALIZATION OF PARENT(S) PRIOR TO CHILD'S STATUTORY AGE	ADDITIONAL REMARKS
Prior To May 24, 1934	Age 21	At least one parent naturalized	None
On or After May 24, 1934 and Prior To Jan. 13, 1941	Age 21	At least one parent naturalized	U.S. citizenship effective 5 years from date child becomes an LPR **
	Age 21	Both parents* naturalized	None
On or After Jan. 13, 1941 and Prior To Dec. 24, 1952	Age 18	Both parents* naturalized	Child born out of wedlock derived on 12/14/52 if under age 16 and had remained an LPR
On or After Dec. 24, 1952 and Prior To Oct. 5, 1978	Age 18	Both parents* naturalized	Child unmarried
On or After Oct. 5, 1978 and Prior To Feb. 27, 2001	Age 18	Both parents* naturalized	Child unmarried (includes child adopted before age 16 who is residing with adoptive parent(s) at time of their naturalization
On or After Feb. 27, 2001	Age 18	At least one parent is a USC by birth or naturalization	Child resides in U.S. in legal and physical custody of USC parent (includes adopted child of USC ; must meet INA 101(b)(1) requirements for adopted children)

Notes

* The definition of "both parents" includes the:

- Surviving parent should one die; or
- Parent having legal custody where there has been a legal separation or divorce; or
- Alien parent who naturalizes when the other parent is already a USC; or
- Mother of a child born out of wedlock (as long as the child has not been legitimated).

Exceptions: child born on or after 1/13/41 and prior to 12/24/52; and child born on or after 2/27/01.

** Child relieved of the remainder of the 5-year wait if the naturalized parent comes to meet definition of "both parents."

Figure 11.2 (Continued)

● EXAMPLE

Patrick, a Liberian national, recently naturalized. He is separated from his wife who agreed he would have custody of their child, Lorena. She currently lives in Liberia. Patrick then petitioned for his daughter, who is 14-years old, to come and join him here. Lorena enters the United States on an immigrant visa as an LPR. She immediately derived citizenship on entry because she is under 18 years old, became an LPR on entry, and resides with her father, a naturalized U.S. citizen, who has physical and legal custody of her.

E.1. Compiling the Application for Proof of Derivation

Children who derive citizenship can obtain proof of this by filing Form N-600, Application for Certificate of Citizenship. Parents may complete this form for their minor children. Alternatively, children who derive citizenship from their parents can file an application for a U.S. passport, which also serves as proof of citizenship. While obtaining a passport is less expensive and often a faster application process, the better practice is also to obtain a certificate, which, unlike a passport, does not expire.

The N-600 application package should contain:

- Form N-600, Application for Certificate of Citizenship
- Form G-28, Notice of Entry of Appearance as Attorney or Accredited Representative
- Two passport style photographs
- The requisite fee, or
- Form I-912, Request for Fee Waiver, with supporting evidence of qualification, where appropriate
- The birth certificate of the applicant, or alternative proof of birth listing the parents names
- Proof of LPR status of the child
- Proof of applicant's parent(s) citizenship

- Proof that parent(s) had physical and, if relevant, legal custody of the applicant when the applicant was under 18 years old

Unlike the naturalization application, a Form N-600, Application for Certificate of Citizenship, is merely proof of derivative citizenship status and therefore does not ask any questions about the child's GMC. The only questions on the form pertain to the child's relationship to the U.S. citizen parent(s) and whether the parent(s) have the requisite status required for the child to derive citizenship.

Derivative citizenship is often very important to individuals who may have entered the United States as LPRs as young children and grew up believing themselves to be U.S. citizens only to realize that they may not be when they are convicted of an aggravated felony crime[83] for which the only effective remedy against deportation is to be a citizen. The ability to show that citizenship was derived sometime before the crime was committed is a lifeline that prevents any further steps towards deportation because, in general, citizens cannot be deported, although denaturalization is discussed further in Section H. A person can prove derivation of citizenship at any age so long as all the requirements for this benefit were met before s/he reached the age of 18.

F. Citizenship by Acquisition: INA § 301

Citizenship by acquisition is a similar but distinct concept from derivation. Individuals born outside of the United States to one or both U.S. citizenship parents may *acquire* citizenship *at the time of* birth, while those who derive citizenship do so *after* birth. The Form N-600, Application for Certificate of Citizenship, used to prove derivation of citizenship, is also used for those in the United States who assert they acquired citizenship at birth. Parents may complete this form for their children.

All the requirements needed for acquisition must have been fulfilled *before* the birth of the child. The requirements for acquisition of citizenship have also changed over time and depend on: the year the child was born; whether or not the child's parents were married at the time of the child's birth; the citizenship status of one or both parents; or the length of time the child's citizen parent or parents resided in the United States. Adopted children born on or after February 27, 2001, the date of enactment of the CCA, cannot acquire citizenship at birth, but may acquire citizenship as soon as the child is granted LPR status.[84] Stepchildren must be adopted by the U.S. citizen parent in order to acquire citizenship after being granted LPR status. Without adoption, they are not considered to be a child of that parent under INA § 101(b)(1)(B), and therefore ineligible to acquire that benefit.

---

[83] *See* Section C.2.a of Chapter 9, Grounds of Inadmissibility and Deportation, for a more detailed discussion on aggravated felony crimes.
[84] INA § 320(b), as amended by the Child Citizenship Act of 2000.

The USCIS has also prepared charts that track the eligibility requirements for the acquisition of citizenship in various periods. These charts use the term "born in wedlock" to describe children born during their parents' marriage. Children born to unmarried parents are considered "born out of wedlock." While these terms are rarely used in modern discourse, they are descriptive for immigration purposes. The chart in Figure 11.3 is used for children born in wedlock.[85] The chart in Figure 11.4 is used for children born out of wedlock.[86]

A U.S. citizen parent who gives birth abroad can file Form DS-2029, Application for Consular Report of Birth Abroad of a Citizen of the United States of America, with the appropriate consular office with jurisdiction over the country of the child's birth. The approved application is proof of U.S. citizenship of the child.

● **EXAMPLE**

Luiz, a citizen of Brazil, married Erma, a U.S. citizen, in 1982. Erma was 21 at the time of the marriage. She was born in the United States and spent her entire life here prior to their marriage. Luiz became an LPR in 1982, but never naturalized. In 1983, the couple moved to Brazil, and in 1984, their daughter Corliss was born. Reviewing Chart 1 in Figure 11.3, it can be determined that Corliss acquired citizenship at birth. This chart is used because the couple is married. Examining the requirements for a child born between 1952 and 1986 where one parent is a U.S. citizen and the other is not, the U.S. citizen parent must have resided in the United States for a period of ten years, five of which were after the age of 14. Since Erma was born in the United States and never left until she was over 21 years of age, she meets those requirements.

Case for Discussion   11.11

Lucas is a U.S. citizen who met Mercedes in Spain when he studied there in 1990. Unknown to him, Mercedes became pregnant with his child and gave birth to Lucia in 1991, after Lucas returned to the United States. Lucas did not legitimize Lucia or promise to pay support during her childhood.

- Using the chart in Figure 11.4 that deals with children born out of wedlock, determine if Lucia acquired U.S. citizenship at birth through her father.

Now assume Mercedes was a U.S. citizen studying in Spain and met Lucas, a Spanish national, and gave birth to Lucia before returning to the United States. She left Lucia with Lucas and his mother. Lucas followed the legal process in Spain to legitimate his daughter.

- Using the chart in Fig. 11.4, determine if Lucia acquired U.S. citizenship at birth.

---

[85] This chart is available at http://www.uscis.gov/policymanual/PDF/NationalityChart1.pdf.
[86] This chart is available at http://www.uscis.gov/policymanual/PDF/NationalityChart2.pdf. The abbreviation "OLP" in Figures 11.3 and 11.4 means Outlying Possession.

Figure 11.3

USCIS Chart 1 on Acquisition of Citizenship for Children Born in Wedlock: INA § 301

Source: USCIS.

Nationality Chart 1
Children Born Outside U.S. in Wedlock

PERIOD IN WHICH CHILD WAS BORN	CITIZENSHIP OF PARENTS AT TIME OF CHILD'S BIRTH	PARENTS' RESIDENCE & PHYSICAL PRESENCE PRIOR TO CHILD'S BIRTH	CHILD'S RETENTION REQUIREMENT
STEP 1: Determine period in which child was born	*STEP 2:* Determine parents' citizenship at time of child's birth	*STEP 3:* Did USC parent meet residence or physical presence requirement prior to birth? (If Yes, child was a USC at birth)	*STEP 4:* Did child meet retention requirement (if any)? (Child lost citizenship on date it became impossible to meet requirement)
Prior To May 24, 1934	Either parent a USC*	USC parent resided in U.S.	Not Applicable
On or After May 24, 1934 and Prior To Jan. 13, 1941	Both parents USCs	At least one USC parent resided in U.S.	Not Applicable
	One USC parent and one alien parent	USC parent resided in U.S.	** 5 years residence in U.S. or OLP between ages 13 and 21 (must start before age 16) OR ** 5 years continuous physical presence in U.S. between ages of 14 and 28 (must start before age 23) OR ** 2 years continuous physical presence in U.S. between ages of 14 and 28 (must start before age 26) OR Exempt, if at time of child's birth, USC parent was employed by U.S. Government or specified organization (Exemption does not apply if parent used a special provision). *See Notes 1, 2, 4*
On or After Jan. 13, 1941 and Prior To Dec. 24, 1952	One USC parent and one alien parent	USC parent resided in U.S. or OLP for 10 years, at least 5 after age 16. Special provisions for parents with honorable service in U.S. armed forces: (1) Between 12/7/41 & 12/31/46, 10 years of residence, at least 5 after age 12 (2) Between 1/1/47 & 12/24/52, 10 years of physical presence, at least 5 after age 14. *See Note 3*	5 years residence in U.S. or OLP between ages 13 and 21 (must start before age 16) OR 5 years continuous physical presence in U.S. between ages 14 and 28 (must start before age 23) OR 2 years continuous physical presence in U.S. between ages of 14 and 28 (must start before age 26) OR Exempt, if at time of child's birth, USC parent was employed by U.S. Government or specified organization (Exemption does not apply if parent used a special provision). *See Notes 1, 2, 4*
	Both parents USCs	At least one USC parent resided in U.S. or OLP *See Note 3*	Not Applicable

Figure 11.3 (Continued)

Nationality Chart 1
Children Born Outside U.S. in Wedlock

PERIOD IN WHICH CHILD WAS BORN	CITIZENSHIP OF PARENTS AT TIME OF CHILD'S BIRTH	PARENTS' RESIDENCE & PHYSICAL PRESENCE PRIOR TO CHILD'S BIRTH	CHILD'S RETENTION REQUIREMENT
STEP 1: Determine period in which child was born	**STEP 2:** Determine parents' citizenship at time of child's birth	**STEP 3:** Did USC parent meet residence or physical presence requirement prior to birth? (If Yes, child was a USC at birth)	**STEP 4:** Did child meet retention requirement (if any)? (Child lost citizenship on date it became impossible to meet requirement)
On or After **Dec. 24, 1952** *and Prior To* **Nov. 11, 1986**	Both parents USCs	At least one USC parent resided in U.S. or OLP *See Note 3*	Not Applicable
	One USC parent and one alien parent	USC parent physically present in U.S. or OLP 10 years, at least 5 after age 14. *See Note 3*	Not Applicable
On or After **Nov. 11, 1986**	Both parents USCs	At least one USC parent resided in U.S. or OLP *See Note 3*	Not Applicable
	One USC parent and one alien parent	USC parent physically present in U.S. or OLP 5 years, at least 2 after age 14. *See Note 3*	Not Applicable

Notes

* USC mother added by Immigration and Nationality Technical Corrections Act of 1994 (INTCA 94).

Note 1: Absence of less than 12 months in the aggregate during the 5-year period will not break continuity of residence or physical presence; absence of less than 60 days in the 2-year period in the aggregate will not break continuity of physical presence. Honorable service in the U.S. armed forces counts as residence or physical presence.

Note 2: A child is relieved from the retention requirements if, prior to his 18th birthday, the child begins to reside permanently in the United States and the alien parent naturalizes.

Note 3: Includes periods spent abroad while employed by the U.S. government or an international organization OR as the dependent unmarried son or daughter member of the household of such employee.

Note 4: Public Law 95-432 of October 10, 1978 repealed retention requirements prospectively only. Anyone born on or after 10/11/52 (i.e., not age 26 on 10/10/78) no longer had retention requirements. The amending legislation was prospective only and did not restore citizenship to anyone who, prior to its enactment, had lost citizenship for failing to meet the retention requirements.

Figure 11.4
USCIS Chart 1 on Acquisition of Citizenship for Children Born Out of Wedlock: INA § 301
Source: USCIS.

Nationality Chart 2 (3 tables below)
Children Born Outside the U.S. Out of Wedlock

Child Born Out Of Wedlock to U.S. Citizen Mother (Table 1 of 3)

PERIOD IN WHICH CHILD WAS BORN	ELIGIBILITY REQUIREMENTS
Prior To May 24, 1934	The child was born an alien. **HOWEVER**, the child became a U.S. citizen retroactively to birth on 01/13/41 if the child's mother resided in the U.S. or OLP prior to the child's birth, **UNLESS**, the child was legitimated by alien father prior to 1/13/41.
On or After May 24, 1934 *and Prior To* Dec. 24, 1952	Mother resided in U.S. or OLP at any time prior to the child's birth
On or After Dec. 24, 1952	Mother had at least one year of continuous physical presence in U.S. or OLP at any time prior to child's birth

Child Born Out Of Wedlock to U.S. Citizen Father and Alien Mother
Child Legitimated by Father (Table 2 of 3)

PERIOD IN WHICH CHILD WAS BORN	ELIGIBILITY REQUIREMENTS
Prior To May 24, 1934	Child legitimated at any time after birth under laws of father's domicile; USC father resided in U.S. prior to child's birth; and No residence required for child to retain U.S. citizenship. *See Nationality Chart 1*
On or After May 24, 1934 *and Prior To* Jan. 13, 1941	Child legitimated at any time after birth under laws of father's domicile; USC father resided in U.S. prior to child's birth; and Child met retention requirements. *See Nationality Chart 1*
On or After Jan. 13, 1941 *and Prior To* Dec. 24, 1952	Child legitimated before age 21 under laws of father's or child's domicile; USC parent(s) had the required residence at time of child's birth; and Child met retention requirements. *See Nationality Chart 1*
On or After Dec. 24, 1952 *and Prior To* Nov. 14, 1986	Child legitimated before age 21 under law of father's or child's domicile; Child legitimated PRIOR to 11/14/86; Child must be unmarried; USC parent(s) had the required residence at time of child's birth; No residence required for child to retain U.S. citizenship. *See Nationality Chart 1*

G: Acquisition of Citizenship for Children Whose Parents Regularly Live Abroad: INA § 322

Figure 11.4
(Continued)

Child Born Out Of Wedlock to U.S. Citizen Father and Alien Mother **Child Legitimated or Acknowledged by Father** (Table 3 of 3)	
DATE RELATIONSHIP ESTABLISHED	**ELIGIBILITY REQUIREMENTS**
On or After *Nov. 14, 1986*	Child legitimated OR acknowledged before age 18* (Legitimated under law of child's residence or domicile; or Paternity acknowledged in writing under oath; or Paternity established by court order); Blood relationship established; Father, unless deceased, has agreed in writing under oath to provide financial support until child reaches age 18 if not married to the mother; Child must be unmarried; USC parent(s) had the required residence at time of child's birth (*See Nationality Chart 1*). *A child 18 or over on 11/14/86 could use the old law. A child at least age 15, but under 18, could use either law (DOB on/after 11/15/68).*

G. Acquisition of Citizenship for Children Whose Parents Regularly Live Abroad: INA § 322

Enacted by the CCA, INA § 322 enables children born to U.S. citizen parents living abroad who do not automatically acquire or derive citizenship, and who are in the United States temporarily pursuant to a lawful admission, to acquire citizenship. In order to qualify, the child's citizen parent must have lived in the United States for a period of five years, at least two of which were after attaining the age of 14.[87] If the child's citizen parent does not meet the residency requirement, then a grandparent, whether alive or deceased, who does meet the requirement may be substituted to enable the child to acquire citizenship.[88] The child must be residing outside of the United States in the legal and physical custody of the U.S. citizen parent or, if deceased, a person who does not object to the application.[89] Chart 4 in Figure 11.5 may be a helpful guide to this provision.[90]

---

[87] INA § 322(a)(2)(A).
[88] INA § 322(a)(2)(B).
[89] INA § 322(a)(3).
[90] This chart is available at http://www.uscis.gov/policymanual/PDF/NationalityChart4.pdf.

Figure 11.5

USCIS Chart on the Acquisition of Citizenship for Children Whose Parents Regularly Live Abroad: INA § 322

Source: USCIS.

Nationality Chart 4
Children of U.S. Citizens Regularly Residing Abroad (INA 322)

CHILD	GENERAL REQUIREMENTS	PHYSICAL PRESENCE OF PARENT OR GRANDPARENT
Genetic or Legitimated Child *Must meet definition of child in INA 101(c)(1). This means a biological or legitimate child, or a child legitimated before their 16th birthday. Benefits under this law are not available for stepchildren or for illegitimate children.* **OR** **Adopted Child** *Must meet definition of adopted child in INA 101(b)(1). This means the child must either have approved I-600 or be eligible to have an I-130 (which does not have to be filed) approved under INA 101(b)(1)(E).*	• Child has at least one U.S. citizen parent by birth or through naturalization, (including an adoptive parent). Adoptive parent must meet requirements of either INA 101(b)(1)(E), INA 101(b)(1)(F), or INA 101(b)(1)(G). • Child's USC parent or USC grandparent meets physical presence requirements. • Child is under 18 years of age (adjudication and the taking of the Oath, unless waived because the child is unable to understand its meaning by reason of mental incapacity or young age, must be completed before the child's 18th birthday). • Child is residing outside of U.S. in the legal and physical custody of the USC parent, or a person who does not object to the application if the USC parent is deceased. • Child is lawfully admitted, physically present, and maintaining a lawful status in U.S. at the time the application is approved and time of naturalization. Both the child and the citizen parent must appear at an interview.	**U.S. Citizen Parent** U.S. citizen parent was physically present in the U.S. or its outlying possessions for at least 5 years (2 after age 14) *If the child's parent does not meet the physical presence requirement, the child may rely on the physical presence of the child's U.S. citizen grandparent (5 yrs, 2 after age 14)* **OR** **U.S. Citizen Grandparent or Legal Guardian** *If the U.S. citizen parent has died, the child's USC grandparent or USC legal guardian may file on the child's behalf within five years of parent's death.* *At time of death, the USC parent (or grandparent) must have met physical presence requirements.*

The application for citizenship under this provision is filed on Form N-600K, Application for Citizenship and Issuance of Certificate Under Section 322, and can be filed from abroad. However, the child and, if needed, the parent, must be legally in the United States at the time the interview is conducted. The child must take an oath of allegiance before an immigration officer as part of the application process. In the case of a child of a U.S. citizen who is a member of the armed forces, there is no requirement that the child be physically present in the United States due to a lawful admission.[91] The parent's time abroad while

---

[91] INA § 322(d)(2).

in the military counts towards his or her acquiring the requisite physical presence in the United States[92] and the oath of allegiance can be administered abroad.[93]

> **Case for Discussion 11.12**
>
> Steven was born in the United States in 1978 to U.S. citizen parents who lived in Southern California all their lives. At the age of 11, his parents divorced. His father, Joe, moved to Mexico and Steven stayed with his mother, Jodi. He went to live with his father when he was 13-years old, and visited his mother in the United States during the holidays. At 15, Steven went to a boarding school in Mexico and visited his mother less often. When he was 20, he met and married Isabel, a Mexican national. They have decided to remain in Mexico for the time being. They had a daughter, Cynthia, in 2000. Steven obtained a ten-year multi-entry B-2 visa for Cynthia when she was 12-years old so that she could visit her grandmother Jodi, Steven's mother. Cynthia often spends a month in the summer with Grandma Jodi. Steven wants his daughter to obtain citizenship through him.
>
> - Does Cynthia qualify to derive citizenship under INA § 320?
> - If not, can she qualify to acquire citizenship solely through her father under either INA § 301 or § 322?
> - What impediments might exist for this application and how might you overcome them?

H. Loss of Citizenship

A person can lose U.S. citizenship in two ways. The first is to voluntarily give it up through an act that demonstrates allegiance to another country *and* an intent to give up citizenship in order to **expatriate** to another country. The second way is through denaturalization, which is when the U.S. government strips a naturalized person of his or her citizenship. We explore each in turn.

H.1. Expatriation

The act of voluntarily relinquishing citizenship is known as an act of expatriation. Acts that would suggest expatriation are set forth in INA § 349 and include:

---

[92] INA § 322(d)(1).
[93] INA § 322(d)(3).

- Obtaining naturalization in a foreign state after age 18;
- Taking an oath or making an affirmation or other formal declaration of allegiance to a foreign state or a political subdivision;
- Entering, or serving in, the armed forces of a foreign state if (A) the armed forces are engaged in hostilities against the United States, or (B) the person serves as a commissioned or non-commissioned officer; or
- Accepting, serving in, or performing the duties of any office, post, or employment under the government of a foreign state or a political subdivision if the person has or acquires the nationality of such foreign state or an oath, affirmation, or declaration of allegiance is required for the position;
- Making a formal renunciation of nationality before a diplomatic or consular officer of the United States in a foreign state;
- Making a formal written renunciation of nationality in the United States when the country is in a state of war and the attorney general approves the renunciation as not contrary to the interests of national defense; or
- Being convicted of an act of treason or conspiracy to overthrow the U.S. government.

Since citizenship by birth has been guaranteed by the Fourteenth Amendment of the U.S. Constitution, it cannot be easily revoked, even by Congress. Those seeking to relinquish their citizenship must clearly consent to expatriation by demonstrating that each of these acts have been performed with the intent of relinquishing U.S. citizenship to effect a loss of nationality. The U.S. Supreme Court, in *Afroyim v. Rusk*, 387 U.S. 253, 257 (1967), set a high standard for relinquishment. It must be done *knowingly, voluntarily, and with full knowledge of the consequences*. Regulations at 22 C.F.R. § 50.40 further provide that there is a presumption that a person seeks to retain citizenship even if s/he commits the following acts as described in INA § 349:

- Naturalized in a foreign state,[94]
- Takes an oath of allegiance to a foreign state,[95]
- Serves in the armed services of a foreign state as a commissioned or noncommissioned officer of a foreign state not engaged in hostilities against the United States,[96] or
- Accepts non-policy level employment with a foreign government and is either a dual national of the state of employment or has taken an oath or affirmation of allegiance in connection with the position.[97]

---

[94] INA 349(a)(1).
[95] INA 349(a)(2).
[96] INA 349(a)(3).
[97] INA 349(a)(4).

Case for Discussion 11.13

Ari was born in the United States and holds both Israeli and U.S. citizenship. He went to Israel when he was 18 and lived there until he was 30. From age 19 to 24, he served in the Israeli army where he rose to the position of the equivalent of Sargent First Class. Following the army, he served in Israel's Ministry of Health as a planner. When he was 28, he went to renew his U.S. passport at the consulate and mentioned to the consular officer how he felt more Israeli than American and thought that American society had grown too soft. Ari returned to the United States when he was 32 with plans to reside in New York for most of the year, with frequent travels to Israel.

- Could Ari's prior actions and statements be sufficient to subject him to charges that he has relinquished his citizenship through expatriation?

H.2. Denaturalization

In cases where naturalization has been obtained illegally due to the concealment or willful misrepresentation of a material fact, the U.S. government, through the federal courts, can initiate the revocation of a person's citizenship.[98] Individuals who become members of organizations that call into question their allegiance and loyalty to the United States within five years following naturalization are specifically subject to revocation.[99] The revocation procedure is described in INA § 340. If the citizenship of a person is revoked, any spouse or minor who obtained citizenship through the denaturalized individual will also have their citizenship revoked.[100]

● EXAMPLE

Mustafa was born in Morocco but entered the United States as an LPR back in 1998, following a fraudulent marriage with a U.S. citizen friend. They never lived together as husband and wife. Three years later, he filed an application for citizenship based on that marriage, which was granted. Subsequently, he and the friend got divorced. Five years later, Mustafa met and married his current wife, an old girlfriend from Morocco, who was granted LPR status in 2005 as a refugee. They are very happy together and have three U.S. citizen children. She finally applied for and received her citizenship in 2008, based on her marriage to a U.S. citizen. A year later, a disgruntled friend alerted the immigration service to Mustafa's fraudulent first marriage. He is

---

[98] INA § 340.
[99] INA § 340(c).
[100] INA § 340(d).

arrested and admits to committing marriage fraud. Following his conviction and denaturalization in federal district court that strips Mustafa of his citizenship, ICE places him into removal proceedings so that an immigration judge can decide if he should be deported because of the fraud he perpetrated on entry to the United States. Because Mustafa's wife obtained her citizenship based on the three-year statutory period available to those married to U.S. citizens, her citizenship will be revoked and she will revert back to an LPR. If she had waited five years to apply for citizenship instead of three, then she would not have been affected by Mustafa's denaturalization because she would have completed the five-year statutory period and could be considered to have applied separately from her husband's status. Had she acquired her LPR status through her marriage to Mustafa rather than independently as an asylee, her LPR status might also be in jeopardy, requiring removal proceedings to be initiated so that an immigration judge can decide the issue.

The U.S. government must meet a high standard of proof to revoke a person's citizenship. It must show by "clear, unequivocal, and convincing evidence" that does not leave the issue in doubt that the applicant is subject to denaturalization.[101]

> **Case for Discussion 11.14**
>
> Igor from the Ukraine entered the United States in 1952 on a visa available for internally displaced individuals during WWII. He did not disclose that he was captured by the Germans and forced to serve as a guard in a concentration camp in Poland. Individuals who voluntarily assisted the Nazis are not entitled to visas to the United States. In 1970, Igor applied for naturalization and received U.S. citizenship. He again did not disclose his work as a guard. After he obtained citizenship, the government discovered this withheld information and sought to revoke his citizenship.
>
> ▪ What are the arguments for and against denaturalization in this case?

I. Conclusion

Citizenship is the last step for many foreign nationals seeking to become full members of U.S. society. Apart from denaturalization, which is a rare occurrence, citizenship provides the final opportunity the U.S. immigration system

---

[101] *See Fedorenko v. United States*, 449 U.S. 490 (1981) at 505-7.

has to review the applicant's immigration history and determine that information provided previously is accurate and immigration status was granted appropriately. An AO reviewing the naturalization application can not only determine an applicant's eligibility for citizenship, but also delve into whether the applicant has engaged in any behavior making him or her ineligible for the predicate LPR status, or even removable. It is therefore very important for practitioners to go over each item in the Form N-400, Application for Naturalization, with the applicant, carefully and thoroughly, obtaining background documents such as court records or past immigration applications when needed, to ensure a proper review of the circumstances to confirm the foreign national is eligible to naturalize and is not placing him or herself at risk of removal proceedings. Once all the information is obtained, the legal practitioner can then discuss the options with the applicant, weighing the advantages of filing over the potential risk to the foreign national who must ultimately make the final decision about what s/he wants to do.

12

Managing an Immigration Practice

Key Terms and Acronyms

BIA recognized Organizations
Case Management System
Dual Representation
Intake
Model Rules of Professional Conduct
Records Retention
Release of Information
Representation Agreement
Retainer Agreement
Tickler System

Chapter Objectives

- Provide an overview of immigration law practice
- Provide a framework for case assessment and case management
- Consider ethical issues in immigration practice
- Address the role of paralegals and accredited representatives

This chapter briefly discusses immigration practice within a private law firm or a nonprofit organization that is recognized as capable of providing immigration services before government administrative agencies. It begins with providing the framework for case assessment, which may vary depending on the type of immigration practice involved. The chapter considers the management of immigration cases along with some of the ethical issues associated with the various actors who practice immigration law and their relationships with clients. It concludes with a summary of the role of the paralegal and accredited representatives, while also suggesting other opportunities in the immigration field.

A. Types of Immigration Practices

A.1. The Private Immigration Law Firm and Corporate Offices

A private law firm may be exclusively dedicated to the practice of immigration and nationality law or may have a department that handles immigration matters. Law firms exclusively devoted to this area may further specialize, concentrating on either removal defense, family petitions, or employment and investor-based immigration matters. However, most handle a range of immigration cases. In order to manage the volume of work that it receives, the firm may need paralegals or junior associates to specialize in one particular area of immigration law. In other situations, a large firm servicing clients in many different legal areas may develop an immigration practice in order to address the needs of its client base that may be raising a number of immigration questions. In this situation, an immigration practice group may be set up to work within the structure of the larger firm. Alternatively, a firm that does not offer immigration advice to its clients might develop a relationship with a private, specialized firm and refer clients with immigration questions to them instead. The rationale behind this can be many. For instance, the larger firm might believe that, because it does not have the appropriate expertise needed to address its client's immigration interests, the more prudent approach would be to enter into a referral arrangement with a legal practice that does and is competent to perform the immigration legal work for their mutual clients.

Some corporations who have a large number of foreign national employees have in-house counsel and practitioners that directly handle employment-based immigration applications and petitions for their workers. This can often be quite cost effective and efficient, depending on the volume of employees.

A.2. Nonprofit Organizations Recognized by the Board of Immigration Appeals and Accredited Representatives

As previously discussed in Section A.3 of Chapter 10, Immigration Court Practice and Relief from Removal, the Board of Immigration Appeals, or BIA, which is part of the Executive Office for Immigration Review, or EOIR, within the Department of Justice, or DOJ, can recognize certain nonprofit religious, charitable, social services, or similar organizations to represent foreign nationals in immigration matters.[1] Reputable organizations or agencies seeking to provide immigration services should undergo a process where they receive recognition from the BIA. This permits an agency to host individuals who can separately

---

[1] 8 C.F.R. §§ 292.1(a)(4), 1292.1(a)(4).

become accredited or approved by the BIA as representatives for a renewable period of three years.[2] Accredited representatives may be authorized to handle all types of immigration matters in any administrative forum before the U.S. Citizenship and Immigration Service, or USCIS, Immigration and Customs Enforcement, or ICE, Customs and Border Protection, or CBP, immigration court, and before the BIA.[3] They may also request limited accreditation, which gives permission only to complete immigration forms and represent individuals before the administrative agencies of the Department of Homeland Security, or DHS.[4] Because they are not licensed attorneys, accredited representatives cannot represent a foreign national in any proceeding in the U.S. circuit or federal district courts.

Only nonprofit organizations can obtain BIA recognition and therefore host accredited representatives.[5] If non-attorney members of a nonprofit organization that is not recognized by the BIA engage in the practice of immigration law, which includes assisting individuals in the completion of immigration forms, the person or organization might be considered to be engaging in the unauthorized practice of law and therefore subject to civil or other penalties.

The BIA recognition and accreditation process was established out of a concern that unqualified, or worse, unscrupulous individuals or organizations would take advantage of low-income refugees and immigrants who seek assistance with immigration matters. The process also permits some monitoring of agencies and individuals who provide immigration services. In achieving recognition, these organizations must agree to charge only nominal fees, which, while not defined, should be below those charged by private practitioners. Because of the focus of BIA recognized agencies on service to refugees and low-income immigrants, most do not handle employment-based immigration cases.

Accredited representatives can complete Form G-28, Notice of Entry of Appearance as Attorney or Accredited Representative, or Form EOIR 28, Notice of Entry of Appearance as Attorney or Representative Before the Immigration Court, on their own and also be the primary case handler for matters before the various immigration agencies and courts.[6] In this regard, accredited representatives engage in activities that are broader than those of paralegals in private law firms who may not complete these forms under their own signature but instead must have them signed by an attorney, even if the paralegal prepares the form and manages many aspects of a case. Accredited representatives can conduct research, discuss strategy options with clients, and file appeals, memoranda, and briefs under their own names before immigration agencies within the DHS and the EOIR, as well as represent clients at interviews and hearings before the USCIS and in immigration court.

---

[2] 8 C.F.R. §§ 292.2(d) and 1292.2(d). A list of recognized organizations is published on the EOIR website at http://www.justice.gov/eoir/recognition-accreditation-roster-reports.
[3] *Id.*
[4] *Id.*
[5] 8 C.F.R. §§ 292.2(a) and 1292.2(a).
[6] 8 C.F.R. §§ 292.4 and 1292.4.

The Code of Federal Regulations also allows law students and law graduates not yet admitted to the bar to represent individuals before agencies of the DHS and the EOIR.[7] Law students and graduates must be under "the supervision of a faculty member, licensed attorney, or accredited representative, in a legal aid program or clinic conducted by a law school or nonprofit organization, and that he or she is appearing without direct or indirect remuneration from the alien he or she represents."[8] The law student or law graduate's appearance must be permitted by the DHS official before whom s/he appears.[9] Reputable individuals may also appear on behalf of an individual with permission, provided there is no direct or indirect financial remuneration from the foreign national and a statement to that effect is filed with the appropriate agency.[10]

B. Case Assessment

The first step in handling an immigration matter is to thoroughly assess a case, which includes identifying the client's goal and determining whether it can be achieved, or whether there are alternatives available. In engaging in an assessment, the legal practitioner applies all the knowledge of immigration law s/he has to understand what options, if any, are available to the foreign national.

In all immigration cases, basic information about the foreign national must be gathered, including:

- Name of client, and if there is a sponsorship relationship, name of both petitioner and beneficiary,
- Gender,
- Country of citizenship of foreign national,
- Address, phone numbers, and e-mail, if available, of relevant parties,
- Manner, date, and place of entry into the United States,
- Relevant or possible derivative qualifying family members and their immigration status
- Other government issued information such as Social Security number and/or Alien Registration Number, where issued,
- Current immigration status of foreign national,
- Preferred language,
- Any prior immigration history, and
- Any prior criminal history.

---

[7] 8 C.F.R. §§ 292.1(a)(2) and 1292.1(a)(2).
[8] 8 C.F.R. §§ 292.1(a)(2)(ii) and 1292.1(a)(2)(ii).
[9] 8 C.F.R. §§ 292.1(a)(2)(iv) and 1292.1(a)(2)(iv).
[10] 8 C.F.R. §§ 292.1(a)(3)(ii) and 1292.1(a)(3)(ii).

Additional information must be gathered, depending on the requirements of the visa or immigration status sought by the foreign national. For example, in cases involving H1-B specialty occupation nonimmigrant visas, information about the employer petitioner must also be gathered, including, but not limited to:

- The position being offered,
- The qualifications necessary for the position, including educational degree requirements,
- The salary for the position,
- The financial capacity of the employer to offer the position, and
- The number of foreign nationals the employer has already hired.

● EXAMPLE

Holtime is a growing internet security company that seeks to file an H-1B petition for Noah, a South African national who is currently working at the company on Optional Practical Training following his graduation from MIT. Holtime seeks the advice of the Green Card Law Firm on how to petition for Noah. Both Holtime and Noah are clients of the firm. An assessment of the case will involve information on the background of the company, the financial capacity of the company, a description of the position, and the salary being offered to Noah, to ensure the position meets the requirements as a specialty occupation and prevailing wage standards. Information must also be obtained from Noah, including the educational degrees he has obtained, and/or other experience he has had that makes him eligible to work in the offered position. Information about Noah's past immigration history is also required and, if relevant, about any criminal history.

Case for Discussion 12.1

Recall Edward, the U.S. citizen, and Ana, his girlfriend from El Salvador, in Case for Discussion 6.2 from Chapter 6, Family Sponsored Immigration and Permanent Resident Status. They do get married while Ana is here on her visit to the United States and now want to apply for her to remain here permanently. They both contact the Green Card Law Firm for an appointment and are referred to a junior associate for a consultation.

- What documents and information should the practitioner advise Ana and Edward to bring to the appointment? You may wish to review Chapter 6, Family Sponsored Immigration and Permanent Resident Status, before deciding your answer.

For those who may have been placed into removal proceedings, the information gathering process will again be different as the need to explore available options will have a different focus.

> ● **EXAMPLE**
>
> **Felix, who entered the United States 23 years ago, comes into the Green Card Law Firm seeking advice. He has never legalized his immigration status. Felix is separated from his wife and they have three children. He was picked up by the police for driving under the influence of alcohol and this brought him to the attention of ICE who served him with a Notice to Appear before an immigration judge, placing him into removal proceedings to decide if he should be deported. He wants to remain in the United States permanently. In order to assist him in his goal, it will require exploring what immigration options might be available to him to achieve this and the evidence available to support the application.**

Here, important key information must be gathered. Felix's country of origin is important. If he is from a country that is experiencing turmoil, immigration relief such as asylum or withholding of removal[11] may be possible long-term options, although he will have to explain why he did not file for relief within one year of his arrival in the United States. If the upheaval in the country is a recent event, he may be able to claim change in country conditions as his reason. In the short term, he may be eligible for Temporary Protected Status, or TPS, if his country was recently designated and he is still within the application period or has a good explanation as to why he needs to file out of time.[12]

Determining Felix's manner of entry to the United States is essential to the assessment as it could affect the types of immigration options available to him. If Felix is a visa overstay, there may be an opportunity for adjustment of status through family sponsorship if a U.S. citizen qualifying family member exists and is willing to file for him.[13] If that person is his wife, their separation may not matter, if the couple can show they are trying to resolve their differences and save their marriage. Verifying the age and status of his children is also very important, because if he has a daughter or son over 21-years old who is a U.S. citizen, s/he can potentially sponsor Felix and file a relative petition that, if approved, will allow him to adjust his status to an LPR. Again, Felix's manner of entry will be key here, because he may be ineligible to file while in the United States if he entered EWI by walking across the border rather than presenting himself to an immigration official at a port of entry.[14]

Alternatively, if the children are LPRs or U.S. citizens under 21 and Felix can demonstrate that they would suffer "exceptional and extremely unusual

---

[11] *See* Chapter 5, Asylum and Other Related Humanitarian Relief, for a discussion of this relief.
[12] *Id.* at Section G.
[13] *See* Section 6, Family Sponsored Immigration and Permanent Resident Status.
[14] *See* Section G.3.b of Chapter 6, Family Sponsored Immigration and Permanent Resident Status.

hardship" if he were deported, he may be eligible for cancellation of removal,[15] regardless of his manner of entry. A review of the NTA is essential to determine if the information in it is correct and especially to determine Felix's date of entry and if any criminal charges used support removal. Finally, understanding whether there is a prior immigration or criminal history that may hinder any potential application is always key.

B.1. Filing a FOIA

Obtaining and comprehending a foreign national's full immigration history may require multiple interviews and investigation beyond the information provided by the client. In Felix's case, if he is from Latin America, he may have tried to enter the United States on several occasions previously by seeking to cross at a land border before he was successful in entering. As he provides information to you, he may not understand that any prior interactions he may have had with CBP officers, where he was removed from the United States into the bordering country, constituted an expedited removal[16] or deportation, even without an order from an immigration judge. Alternatively, Felix may have been apprehended and sent to immigration court but did not appear when he was supposed to and so was issued an *in absentia* deportation order.[17] Perhaps he did appear and was granted voluntary departure but never left.[18] All of these things may not be fully understood and therefore cannot be properly disclosed. It is the responsibility of the legal practitioner to uncover as much information about this past history as s/he can so that effective representation can be offered.

Under the Freedom of Information Act, or FOIA, an individual is entitled to access any information held on him or her by the government following a request for the same. Therefore, in order to obtain Felix's complete immigration history, the legal practitioner should file a Form G-639, Freedom of Information Act/Privacy Act Request, which can now be submitted electronically at USCIS.FOIA@uscis.dhs.gov. Generally, the USCIS will release documents in the file that it has prepared and redact any created by ICE or CBP, at which point the file will be referred to those agencies so that they can make their own decisions about which of their documents can be released. Direct requests to CBP must be submitted online.[19] Each agency's policy regarding submission of FOIA requests should be reviewed on their website.

B.2. Obtaining Criminal Records

If a person has had any interactions with the police, part of the evaluation process should be to obtain past criminal records, including police reports

---

[15] *See* Section I.2 of Chapter 10, Immigration Court Practice and Relief from Removal.
[16] See Section C of Chapter 10, Immigration Court Practice and Relief from Removal.
[17] *See* Section A.1. of Chapter 10, Immigration Court Practice and Relief from Removal.
[18] *See* Sections B.1.c and B.4.a of Chapter 10, Immigration Court Practice and Relief from Removal.
[19] The site can be accessed at https://foiaonline.regulations.gov/foia/action/public/request/publicPreCreate.

and particularly certified court dispositions. The procedure to obtain such records varies from jurisdiction to jurisdiction so an inquiry must be made to determine where an arrest was made or trial held. Sending for the client's FBI records will enable the legal practitioner to find, through one source, arrests and convictions for someone who has lived in multiple jurisdictions. Instructions about how to obtain records from the FBI are on their website.[20] A fee is required for this record.

Case for Discussion 12.2

Felix initially tells the legal practitioner that he has not had any other arrests other than for the DUI. However, he later remembers that 12 years ago he was in a fight at work and the police were called, arrested him, and he spent the night in jail. He says the judge dismissed the charges.

- Would it be appropriate for the legal practitioner to send for his criminal records?
- If so, how should the worker explain this to Felix so that he continues to have confidence and trust in the firm or agency?

C. Conducting the Intake or Initial Consultation

In many cases, a law firm or immigration service agency will have a brief conversation with the potential client over the telephone to get a general idea of what the case may be about and then schedule an in-person consultation or intake, where more in-depth information will be gathered and documents reviewed. Both preliminary and in-depth information can be captured on an intake form, or as is increasingly the practice, a web-based form which is part of an electronic case management system.

The practice of immigration law today is very reliant on Internet technology. Many applications are submitted through a web portal and, increasingly, applications for immigration benefits must be submitted through the Internet. The USCIS now acknowledges receipt of applications by email for certain applications, if requested on Form G-1145, E-Notification of Application/Petition Acceptance. It also provides electronic access to case tracking when it sends out receipt notices. A sample of such a notice appears in Figure 12.1.

---

[20] The site can be accessed at https://www.fbi.gov/about-us/cjis/identity-history-summary-checks/submitting-an-identity-history-summary-request-to-the-fbi.

C: Conducting the Intake or Initial Consultation

Figure 12.1
Form I-797C, Notice of Action Receipt with Electronic Tracking

---

Department of Homeland Security
U.S. Citizenship and Immigration Services

FEB 2 5 2016

Form I-797C, Notice of Action

THIS NOTICE DOES NOT GRANT ANY IMMIGRATION STATUS OR BENEFIT.

Receipt Number	USCIS Online Account Number	Case Type
N/A		I90 - APPLICATION TO REPLACE PERMANENT RESIDENT CARD
Receipt Date	**Priority Date**	**Applicant**
11/16/2015	11/15/2015	
Notice Date	**Page**	
02/17/2016	1 of 1	

HIAS PENNSYLVANIA
HIAS PENNSYLVANIA
2100 ARCH STREET FL 3RD
PHILADELPHIA PA 19103

Notice Type: USCIS Account Access Notice
Online Access Code:

Welcome to USCIS!

Thank you for your recent benefit request submission. We have created a USCIS online account for you. With this account you can:

- check the status of your clients' cases.
- sign up to receive email notifications and text messages.
- manage your clients' contact information.
- manage your account preferences and contact information.

Log on and confirm your account within 30 days.

To access your account, please follow the steps below:

1. Visit us online at *https://myaccount.uscis.dhs.gov*
2. Select the "**Create a New Account**" icon on the upper right side of the screen, and follow the on-screen instructions for creating a new account in order to login to the system.
3. Once you have created a new account, the system will automatically bring you to a profile entry page.
4. At the top of the profile entry page, click the "Check here if you received an Online Access Code in your USCIS Account Access Notice."
5. Where prompted, click on your account type (i.e.,"Attorney" or "Accredited Representative"). Then enter your "Online Access Code" (found on the upper right side of this notice) and the additional information requested for your account type. Then, select "**Submit.**" If the information you entered is correct, you will return to the "**Customer Home Page**" and see a message indicating that you have successfully linked your case(s) to your account. Information regarding your case(s) will now appear at the lower left side of the application, under "**Recent Cases.**"

NOTE: Access to your USCIS Online Account will expire 30 days from the receipt date listed at the top of this letter. We will continue processing your application whether or not you access your USCIS Online Account. We strongly encourage you to confirm your USCIS Online Account as soon as possible and then use it in the future as your preferred method for interacting wth USCIS.

Additional Information

If you still have questions about how to confirm your USCIS Online Account or need technical support, please visit us online at https://egov.uscis.gov/cris/contactus

Please see the additional information on the back. You will be notified separately about any other cases you filed.

Department of Homeland Security
National Benefits Center
P.O. BOX 25920
Overland Park KS 66225

Customer Service Telephone: 800-375-5283

If this is an interview or biometrics appointment notice, please see the back of this notice for important information.   Form I-797C 07/11/14 Y

Law firms and nonprofit organizations use a variety of computer based case management systems to assist them in their work. Most allow legal practitioners to enter biographic information on the foreign national and/or the petitioner into separate sections, which then populates into various immigration applications. This is very efficient because the information will be entered only once and then used for several forms, rather than having to reenter it each time. For example, in the case of an immediate relative family sponsored relative petition filed by a U.S. citizen for the benefit of a spouse, the same biographic information entered for both parties would be needed for a variety of immigration forms, including Form I-130, Petition for Alien Relative; Form I-485, Application to Register Permanent Residence or Adjust Status; Form I-765, Application for Employment Authorization; Form G-28, Notice of Entry of Appearance as Attorney, and other documents.

Case management systems also enable legal practitioners to carefully track a case, enter deadlines and reminders, keep track of time spent on a case for billing purposes, and allow other members of the firm or organization to view the status of a case or work on it at the same time. Using a case management system also allows for firm- or agency-wide communication. Its use allows review to ensure there is no conflict of interest in representing a client due to prior representation of another client with an adverse interest.

● EXAMPLE

Community Immigration Services is a BIA recognized agency serving low-income foreign nationals. It previously represented Esperanza, a national from Costa Rica, in her VAWA self-petition to get a green card because her former LPR spouse, Eduardo, abused her. Esperanza calls again seeking assistance. The receptionist, following protocol, asks if Esperanza is currently a client of the agency. Esperanza explains she is and that she recently returned to the agency to apply for naturalization. Esperanza asks for the status of her citizenship application. She does not remember the name of the person representing her in the office. The receptionist answering the telephone searches for Esperanza in the case management system and finds the name of the accredited representative who is helping her. The receptionist discovers through the case notes that the Form N-400, Application for Naturalization, has not been mailed because Esperanza wants a fee waiver but has not brought in sufficient evidence to support her request. This information is shared with Esperanza and the receptionist can write a note in the case management system memorializing the call. She will also contact the accredited representative to let her know about Esperanza's concern and the information given to her about documentation required, based on the earlier file note in the system.

Two days after Esperanza calls, Eduardo contacts Community Immigration Services seeking representation in his removal case, arising from an assault stemming from domestic violence charges involving Esperanza. Following protocol, the receptionist looks up Eduardo in the case management system and sees that his name comes up as the abusive spouse in Esperanza's VAWA self-petition that was the basis of her grant of LPR status. The receptionist then notes

this connection and refers the matter to an accredited representative or attorney who will ultimately determine if a conflict of interest exists. If it does, then the accredited representative or attorney must contact Eduardo to explain why the agency is unable to represent him. However, in providing this explanation, it cannot be disclosed that Esperanza is a client of the firm because that would violate attorney-client privilege.

D. Retainer or Representation Agreements

After an in-depth consultation or intake, the firm or agency legal practitioner should develop a retainer or representation agreement that describes the scope of the representation and any fees involved, along with a schedule for payment, if applicable. This can also take the form of an engagement letter. In immigration matters, since the payment of government fees are necessary and apart from attorney fees, the agreement should clearly state who will be responsible for them.

Immigration law firms generally charge a flat fee for work they will do for a client, which is dependent on the type of representation to be provided. Others may charge an hourly fee or a combination of the two. Whatever method is used, the manner in which fees are charged and the amount should be clearly stated and included in the retainer or representation agreement. They should also make clear the responsibilities of the client, such as to respond diligently to requests for information or documents and to be truthful in providing information. Because this is clearly stated in the agreement, if an unfortunate event occurs where it appears that the client is being obstructive to efforts to attain his or her goal, the legal practitioner can point to the obligations agreed to but not met to explain the reasons for withdrawing representation, if that course of action is to be taken.

Immigration practice often involves the representation of two parties at the same time, a petitioner and beneficiary. In most cases, this is unlikely to pose a problem as both are seeking the same goal. However, this is not always the case. Best practice is to include the firm or agency's conflict of interest policy so that both clients understand from the outset the impact of any conflict that may arise during the course of representation. This is discussed further in Section I. on Ethical Issues.

When a foreign national's preferred language is other than English, in order to ensure informed consent, a translated version of the agreement by a competent translator into the language best understood by the client should be provided. The original signed copy of the agreement should be kept in the file with a copy given to the client for his or her records. A sample retainer agreement or engagement letter, for an employment-based immigration case appears in Figure 12.2, while a sample service fee agreement used by a nonprofit organization appears in Figure 12.3.

Figure 12.2

Sample Engagement Letter Used in Employment-Based Immigration Cases

DATE
COMPANY NAME
COMPANY ADDRESS

Re: Immigration Legal Services to COMPANY

Dear COMPANY REPRESENTATIVE:

Thank you for selecting our firm to provide legal services to COMPANY ("the Company") in immigration matters. Please excuse the formality, but we have found it helpful at the beginning of an engagement to set forth our expectations regarding billing and our understanding of the scope of our representation and the services you expect us to perform. If you do not understand or have questions or concerns about any part of this letter, please let me know immediately.

General Scope of this Letter

Unless expressly modified or revoked in writing, this letter will govern all work that we perform for the Company regarding immigration law matters that we begin to handle for identified employees and for their family members. Because our practice emphasizes immigration law matters, we do not undertake work unrelated to immigration law and will not function as your counsel for any nonimmigration law matters.

We will not send you a new engagement letter each time you send us a new matter to handle. By sending us information on behalf of an employee or prospective employee, you are requesting that we evaluate your options for employment of that individual in the United States. We will agree with you on a strategy to be pursued on behalf of that employee at the outset of the matter.

Client Identification

As you know, the Company will be a client of this firm in each of these matters. In the immigration law context, however, it is generally appropriate for the same firm to represent the individual employee and his or her family members in visa matters as well. When you ask us to handle such a matter, we will assume that you intend a joint representation, where appropriate, unless you advise us to the contrary at the outset of the matter. We will, however, inform the employee of the limitations on our representation and the confidentiality of information provided by the employee, as described below.

Because of this joint representation, there are a number of matters that need to be addressed:

- Subject only to the limitations noted in this letter with regard to termination of our services, the Company, and not the employee or his or her family members, will be responsible for all of our firm's bills.

- Our firm can represent more than one client in a matter only if their interests are consistent. You should not ask me to represent an employee or his or her family members if you are aware at the outset of the matter of any interests of the Company that are inconsistent with those of the employee, and you must let me know if you come to believe that any actual or potential conflicts develop after a representation begins. If significant conflicts develop, it may be that we will have to stop representing some or all of our clients in a particular matter, with the result that some or all of you may need to hire new counsel at that time.

- Whenever a lawyer represents multiple clients, there is a potential conflict between the lawyer's duty to keep client confidences and the lawyer's duty to represent the interests of the other clients in the matter. As noted above, at the outset of each matter, we will inform the employees on whose behalf we will provide services that our representation is limited to assisting the employees in connection with his or her employment with the Company. We will also inform the employees that any information they share with us will be kept confidential from third parties, but will not be confidential from the Company. If you think it likely at any time that you will or may want to tell us things that you would not want the employee in a matter to know, the Company must advise our firm before saying anything substantive to us.

Services to be Performed and Billing for Services

Our understanding is that you will look to us for representation in connection with general immigration advice and preparation of immigration petitions and applications for specific employees. The fee schedule for various matters is attached. Should any particular matter present complicating factors or require services outside the scope of the flat fee agreement, we will agree to an appropriate fee with you prior to commencing work on a matter.

In addition to legal fees, the Company is also responsible for costs, expenses, and services reasonably necessary for the handling of a matter that you refer to us. If expenses must be incurred, including but not limited to such things as express delivery and certified postage charges, toll telephone calls, faxes, photocopying, notary fees, government filings fees, advertising costs, translations, or travel expenses, in some cases the Company will be asked to pay for these expenses directly. Where our law firm pays the expenses, we will ask the Company to reimburse us at the time these expenses are billed.

The Company authorizes us to incur all such costs as are reasonable and necessary to our representation. You should feel free to ask us for an approximation of the applicable costs in each matter.

Electronic Communication of Confidential Information

While we and our clients appreciate the convenience of electronic communication, we would like to warn you that confidentiality and the attorney/client privilege cannot be guaranteed with respect to communications sent and received electronically over the Internet or other media. Services such as Gmail, Yahoo!, Hotmail, and other providers may not be secure and could be subject to third-party intrusion. Unless messages are encrypted or a secure, alternative direct file transfer is maintained, messages may be reviewed by someone other than the intended recipient. Until and unless you instruct us otherwise, you authorize us to send written privileged and confidential communications via facsimile, text message, and/or e-mail, and to communicate with you orally on cell phones. Should you need to send us documentation securely, please ask us for a login to our firm's Sharefile system, or send us hard copies by fax, mail, or courier.

Termination of Our Relationship and Related Duties

The Company has the right to terminate our representation at any time and for any reason. We reserve the right to terminate our services to any or all of our clients in a matter for any reasons permitted by the applicable Rules of Professional Conduct ("the Rules").

To the extent permitted by the Rules, our firm will be entitled to receive any unpaid basic fees, to receive compensation for hourly work performed by the firm up to the time that our withdrawal has been completed, and to receive compensation or reimbursement for costs and other charges incurred up to the time that our withdrawal has been completed. To the extent permitted by the Rules, the Company will also be liable, on the same basis that would have applied if our relationship had not terminated, for any post-termination services that we provide to an employee and his or her family if we are unable either to withdraw from that representation or we cannot make what we believe to be suitable alternative arrangements for payment. We acknowledge that depending in part upon the factual and legal circumstances surrounding the termination, there may be times when we will have to write off some or all unpaid fees or refund some or all fees that may already have been paid and we invite discussion with you on this subject if the need for it should arise.

Unless the Company hires us to do so, we have no responsibility to inform you of subsequent factual or legal developments once our work on a particular matter has been completed.

Conclusion

We look forward to a positive and productive relationship. We therefore encourage you to let us know if, at any time, you have any questions or concerns about any matter.

Very truly yours,

_____

For the Firm

We have reviewed this engagement letter and accept its contents.

By: _____

For the Company

Figure 12.2 (Continued)

Figure 12.3

Sample Service Fee Agreement Used by a Nonprofit Organization

HIAS Pennsylvania
2100 Arch Street 3rd Floor
Philadelphia, PA 19103
Tele: 215-832-0900 Fax: 215-832-0919
www.hiaspa.org

This agreement is made between HIAS Pennsylvania ("the Agency') and Client(s): _____CLIENT NAME_____

This agreement specifies the services requested by the Client(s) of the Agency, applicable service fees, the terms of payment and responsibilities of the Agency and Client(s).

Charges and Fees

- Client(s) are responsible for Agency fees in effect at the time of signing of agreement for each service. In exceptional circumstances fees may be paid according to a payment plan mutually agreed upon. In extreme hardship cases fees may be waived upon the approval of the Executive Director. Client(s) whose income exceeds our sliding fee schedule will be surcharged an additional 25%.

- **Client(s) are responsible for all express mail, specified certified mail, extraordinary long distance telephone and fax costs, especially those overseas, translation of documents.**

- Client(s) are responsible for payment of required fees to United States Immigration and Citizenship Service (USCIS), United States Immigration and Customs Enforcement (ICE) and the Executive Office of Immigration Review (EOIR). As these fees are subject to increases, the fees charged will be those in effect at the time of filing of any application, petition, motion or court pleading. All medical examination fees required by applications, evaluations of foreign credentials and other incidental costs will be paid by the Client(s). **All government and required fees must be paid in advance of the submission of documents and/or representation.**

Compliance with Regulations and Ethical Standards

- Client(s) have an obligation to notify the Agency and USCIS, ICE and EOIR when they change their address. A copy of an AR-11 change of address form used to notify USCIS with instructions will be given to Client(s) upon signing of the Service Fee Agreement.

- Client(s) understand(s) that members of the Agency's staff provide service in accordance with applicable laws, regulations and accepted standards of professional ethics. The Agency reserves the right to terminate service in the event that the Client(s) is unwilling to cooperate fully with the Agency's efforts on his/her behalf. Actions which may result in the termination of representation include, but are not limited to: the failure to submit documents in a timely manner, the failure to keep appointments, the failure to supply information the Agency professional deems is critical to the application or case, verbal abuse or threats of harm.

- The Agency can undertake the representation of both an applicant for benefits and sponsor in family and employment-based cases as long as the parties in such representation have mutually aligned interests. In the case of a conflict, the Agency must either obtain the parties written consent to continue the representation or withdraw from representing all parties involved in the conflict.

D: Retainer or Representation Agreements

Figure 12.3 Continued

Agency Responsibilities

- The Agency agrees to specify the services it will offer, the fees for the service and to adhere to all applicable laws, regulations and accepted standards of professional service.

- Clients who believe they have been unfairly charged or terminated can have the decision reviewed by the Executive Director. A request for review must be made within 15 days after the decision.

- The Client(s) acknowledge(s) that s/he has been advised the acceptance of a case and the provision of service in no way guarantees a positive outcome of the Client(s) petition, application, or immigration matter/case. Refunds will not be given for work completed, regardless of whether client(s) terminate service prior to the completion of the petition/application or case.

Agency Document Retention Policy

- The Agency will maintain the client(s) file for a period of ten (10) years after the matter has been closed by the Agency. After this period the Agency will destroy the file. The Agency reserves the right to maintain the Client(s) closed file on-site or at a remote location. The Client has the right at any time within the 10 year period after the matter has been closed to request a copy of the file. The Agency reserves the right to charge the Client for any reasonable file recovery and copying charges applicable at that time.

Client Grievance Procedure

- Client(s) who have concerns about how they were treated by Agency staff have the right to file a complaint with the Agency through the Agency's formal client grievance procedure.

The Agency is requested to and agrees to provide the following services to the Client(s):

Service Type	HIAS Fee	USCIS/Other Fee
Administrative fee		
TOTAL		

It is agreed that payment will be made in the following manner:

_____   _____
For HIAS PA   Client

Date: _____

My primary language is _____, and I am/am not fluent in English_____

This has been explained to me in my primary language and I fully understand its contents.

D.1. Payment of Fees

Where it has been agreed that a client can pay legal fees in installments, it is important to keep track of all payments made, as this allows a legal practice to remain aware of any arrears that may be accruing for a particular client. Maintaining a fee schedule that is consistent and understood by all staff involved in billing avoids errors and promotes accountability and transparency. Private law firms often have specialized staff and/or computerized billing capacity and provide printed invoices and receipts for clients. Small practitioners or nonprofit organizations may track the payment of fees through paper receipts. In this case, a copy should be maintained in the file and one given to the client so there is no dispute about what has been paid.

E. Gathering Evidence for Submission

Throughout this book, we have discussed the type of evidence needed in specific immigration matters. Often, a paralegal is tasked with preparing documents and gathering evidence to support an immigration case. 8 C.F.R. § 103.2 lists mandatory actions and documents needed in applying for immigration benefits and provides a useful checklist. It also reminds the legal practitioner that all forms must be executed and submitted in accordance with form instructions and filed with a non-refundable fee, unless no fee is required.[21] It cannot be stressed enough that all legal practitioners must check the USCIS website constantly to make sure the proper version of the form is being used, the correct fee is paid, and the form is mailed to the proper location. All forms have separate links to instructions on how to complete them.

All USCIS applications and petitions must be signed by the applicant or petitioner unless the person is under 14-years old, in which case a parent or guardian may sign on the child's behalf.[22] Documents in a foreign language must be translated into English with a certification that the translator is competent in both the target language and English and that the translation is accurate.[23] The translator need not be a professional but cannot be a party to the application or petition.

Obtaining supporting documents, especially for those who fled conflict zones, may present a major challenge. When a required document such as a birth certificate or marriage certificate is not available, secondary evidence

---

[21] 8 C.F.R. § 103.2 (a)(1).
[22] 8 C.F.R. § 103.2(a)(2).
[23] 8 C.F.R. § 103.2 (b)(3).

such as church and school records may be acceptable. The Department of State, or DOS, maintains a record of which documents can and cannot be obtained from foreign jurisdictions and which government offices need to be approached to obtain them. This is maintained in the Foreign Affairs Manual, or FAM. Where documents that the FAM says are available cannot be obtained, the applicant or petitioner must demonstrate why and also provide affidavits from two people who have direct knowledge of the event in question.[24] Furthermore, when a record does not exist, the applicant or petitioner must submit "an original written statement" on government letterhead from the proper authority confirming this. The statement is not required if the FAM indicates the document does not generally exist.[25]

● **EXAMPLE**

Bindu, a Liberian national, entered the United States in 2002 during the Liberian Civil War and sought help that same year from accredited representative Jeremiah to bring her daughter, Suah, here. Bindu was granted asylum. Bindu had left Suah behind with her grandmother. She now wishes to file Form I-730, Refugee/Asylee Relative Petition, for Suah, but she was born at home and no birth certificate was ever issued, so she is not able to produce an important document in support of the application. Jeremiah reviews the DOS FAM rules when preparing the petition and finds that during the war, birth certificates were in fact unavailable. Therefore, Bindu is permitted to supply secondary evidence of Suah's birth. Bindu has several relatives who now live near her in the United States and who have personal knowledge that she is Suah's mother. Bindu can obtain affidavits from them to demonstrate her relationship to her daughter. She and her daughter may have to undergo DNA testing[26] as well in order to conclusively establish their relationship.

Affidavits are regularly used in immigration cases, not only for secondary evidence when documents are missing, but as primary evidence in cases such as asylum, cancellation of removal, and relief under VAWA. They allow the foreign national to tell his or her story in a logical, coherent way. In asylum cases, paralegals, accredited representatives, or junior associates may be assigned to interview the applicant, so that a detailed affidavit or personal statement about why the applicant fears returning to his or her home country may be prepared. Additional affidavits from expert witnesses or individuals who have knowledge of the applicant's situation may also be his or her responsibility.

---

[24] 8 C.F.R. § 103.2 (b)(2)(i).
[25] 8 C.F.R. § 103.2 (b)(2)(ii).
[26] *See* Section C.3 of Chapter 6, Family Sponsored Immigration and Permanent Resident Status, for further discussion on DNA testing.

Those who draft these affidavits must make sure to ask open-ended questions that do not lead the foreign national to a particular response, to follow-up on potential issues raised by the affiant, and to ensure that the affidavits reflect the affiant's own words and situations. Best practice is to include a statement at the end of the affidavit that states that the person making the affidavit or statement has read and understands its contents. If the person does not speak English, it can be translated into his or her language to assist in understanding its contents and then can be submitted, along with an English language version, with a certification from an interpreter or translator regarding his or her competency in the foreign language and English and an attestation as to his or her accuracy. A sample certificate of translation is shown on page four of Figure 10.4 in Chapter 10, Immigration Court Practice and Relief from Removal.

There is some debate about whether an attestation should be provided that a client has read and understood the contents of his or her statement. This is because, even though it may have been translated into a language that the foreign national understands, there is no guarantee that s/he can even read or that the translated document accurately conveys his or her story. Relationship dynamics often mean that a client is reluctant to express a view that may oppose or challenge that of the legal practitioner, who may be seen to be in a superior position. Every effort should be made to encourage the client to feel comfortable and express his or her own view, although this may not always be successful. Clients also may not take the time needed to read through documents, even after their importance have been explained. Careful thought should be given as to whether the client should attest to having read and understood something that will be submitted to the government, because once it is, then it is reasonable for a judge to assume that it accurately states the foreign national's position.

In some cases, medical records may need to be obtained. Care should be taken to ensure that a release of information form for the designated agency is signed as soon as possible so that the documents can be released to the legal practitioner for review. Forms requesting medical records must be compliant with the confidentiality provisions of the American Health Insurance Portability and Accountability Act, abbreviated as HIPAA. Often hospitals or health care providers have their own release forms that are compliant with these requirements that must be signed before any records will be released.

● EXAMPLE

Valentina, from the Dominican Republic, or DR, is applying for non-LPR cancellation and must show her removal would cause "exceptional and extremely unusual hardship" to her three U.S. citizen children. Paralegal Mandisa has been asked to begin the process of drafting an affidavit and gathering evidence, which focuses on the hardship to Valentina's children. After learning that the girls are aged 15, 12,

and 7, Mandisa asks about their education. Valentina reports they are doing well, but the 12-year-old has a lot more absences than the others. Mandisa then notes that all the girls are doing well in school, earning A's and B's, and copies the report cards that Valentina has brought in. Instead of asking further questions to learn why the child is missing school so often, Mandisa moves on to ask about their extracurricular activities. As a result, she fails to learn that the 12-year-old has cystic fibrosis and therefore cannot ascertain that the medical care in the DR for this condition is very expensive and would be unaffordable to Valentina. This is very important evidence since it could establish that Valentina's daughter would suffer exceptional and extremely unusual hardship if she had to return to the DR with her mother. The information about cystic fibrosis should have led Mandisa to ask Valentina to sign medical release forms so that the records could be obtained and included as evidence in the case, and would also permit research to focus on health care delivery in the DR, all of which might support a successful application for immigration relief.

A good way to approach evidence gathering is to review the requirements for each immigration benefit, make a list of what is needed, check it against what is available, and develop a plan and a timeline to obtain the needed items. Many firms and BIA recognized agencies have developed checklists that can be given to clients so the gathering of evidence is done in an organized and efficient manner. By using a checklist, the legal practitioner can quickly determine if alternative evidence must be gathered because a preferred document is not available.

Case for Discussion 12.3

Recall Marie, a native of Haiti, from the example in Section G of Chapter 5, Asylum and Other Related Humanitarian Relief, who applied for and received Temporary Protected Status, or TPS, and employment authorization because of the devastation caused by the earthquake in her country. While she was filing her application, she realized that she did not have a birth certificate because she was born in a rural area and no certificates were issued in her village, but she had her baptismal papers. Marie also had a national identification card with her photo on it, as well as an I-94 Arrival/Departure Record card showing her date of entry.

- Using the USCIS website, www.uscis.gov, link to instructions for the Form I-821, Application for Temporary Protected Status, and Form I-765, Application for Employment Authorization, determine what documents/evidence can be gathered and included to support Marie's application package.

F. Examining Immigration Options

In some cases, an immigration option is straightforward because the foreign national and/or petitioner is seeking a specific status or visa, and the scope of the retainer or representation agreement will reflect that. In the previous examples and Case for Discussion in this chapter, Noah is seeking an H-1B Specialty Occupation nonimmigrant visa, and Valentina is seeking cancellation of removal based on her daughter's health condition. Other situations, such as the one faced by Felix, require a broader analysis and may result in applying for multiple immigration benefits simultaneously, such as asylum and cancellation of removal. The work needed for each form of relief should be spelled out in the retainer or representation agreement. The agreement should summarize the activities that will be conducted immediately on behalf of the foreign national or client.

Many foreign nationals and their U.S. citizen relatives are interested in learning all of their options, including those that may be available in the future. These options may be presented in the in-depth consultation and intake sessions. Sometimes, additional appointments will be necessary to research and determine all possible relief available, especially if critical documentation, including immigration records, is not available at the beginning to clarify that certain requirements can be met.

In private firms, an attorney generally examines immigration options, but an experienced paralegal or accredited representative under the supervision of an attorney may conduct the interview to gather the information that forms the basis of determining the client's options.

● EXAMPLE

In June 2012, Hee-Young from South Korea completed her Bachelor of Science Degree at age 21. Hee-Young was brought to the United States at the age of ten on a visitor's visa and remained beyond the limits specified for her stay. Her mother and father are divorced and her father remarried a U.S. citizen. Her father is now an LPR. Hee-Young has a job offer, but lacks employment authorization. An evaluation shows that Hee-Young currently has a short-term immigration option available through Deferred Action for Childhood Arrivals, or DACA,[27] which will allow her to work legally in the United States. In the longer term, if Hee-Young enters into a *bona fide* marriage with a U.S. citizen, she can apply to adjust her status as an immediate relative so that she can become an LPR.

---

[27] This relief is discussed in Section U. of Chapter 8, Immigration Relief for Vulnerable Populations.

F: Examining Immigration Options

Case for Discussion 12.4

Recall Gilberto from Angola in Section A.4 of Chapter 5, Asylum and Other Related Humanitarian Relief, who sought to protect the boys in the orphanage he managed from being forcibly recruited into the army. After speaking out against the government recruitment of child soldiers, he was imprisoned. Conditions in the prison were very poor, and he developed a rare parasite, which continues to affect his health. He managed to escape and flee the country. After he entered the United States, he did not apply for asylum because he was afraid of being returned to his country. Instead, he decided to live here undocumented. He remains fearful that other Angolans will denounce him, causing him to be returned there. Gilberto has a brother in the United States who just became a citizen. Gilberto later married a U.S. citizen. They have one son together, now aged 14. Four months ago, Gilberto's wife's mental health problems surfaced and she actually tried to attack both Gilberto and their son with a knife. He took out a restraining order against her and moved out of the family home with their son, who now lives with him. Gilberto has been a very involved father to his son, who suffers from childhood diabetes. However, he has been unable to find work recently due to his immigration status and is worried he will no longer be able to support his son. He comes to your firm seeking to learn of his immigration options.

- What are the possible short- and long-term options that might be available to Gilberto?

Case for Discussion 12.5

Recall Paula from Case for Discussion 3.7 from Chapter 3, Nonimmigrant Visas for Intracompany Transferees, Trade and Investment, and Professional Employment. She is the German graduate student with a degree in Finance that the River City Law Firm in Pittsburgh, PA wants to hire as an accountant. Assume her application for H-1B nonimmigrant status was approved and, during her time here, she met and married a U.S. citizen. She is now a U.S. citizen through her marriage and is pregnant, expecting the couple's first child. Her father works for an international corporation that does more than 50 percent of its business in the United States. Her parents would like to be present for the birth of their first grandchild. They are also considering moving to the United States for at least a year and are open to relocating permanently to be near Paula and help with the baby and provide some financial support to her and her husband.

- What are Paula's parents' short- and long-term options?

G. Managing an Immigration Case and Responding to Requests from the USCIS

Immigration cases can involve multiple agencies. Therefore, carefully documenting each action, application and petition must be ensured. Copies of all documents filed, correspondence, and receipts received should be maintained in the client file. Firms or agencies that do not use a case management system should keep notes related to each petition or application submitted in chronological order. It is advisable when documents are filed by mail with a government agency that they be sent certified mail or by other forms of delivery that can track the item and prove receipt. Clients should be provided with copies of all key applications. Best practice is to agree that whenever correspondence is received from the USCIS, both client and legal practitioner will inform the other as a failsafe against the times the government forgets to notify one or other of them.

Many immigration forms and procedures have strict deadlines and these must be adhered to or else the foreign national may lose the opportunity to apply for a particular benefit. Some law firms develop a tickler system, which contains reminders with sufficient time prior to the deadline to file a document, appear in court or at an interview, or perform other tasks. Computer calendars offer a fast and inexpensive way to maintain this. Case management systems also contain reminders and notifications.

G.1. Responding to USCIS Requests for Evidence or Notices of Intent to Deny

When an application or petition is filed with the USCIS, the agency can either approve or deny it, request more information or evidence be submitted, or notify the applicant or petitioner of an intent to deny it.[28] The request for more evidence and Notice of Intent to Deny, or NOID, serve specific and distinct purposes.

Applications or petitions that are considered lacking in certain evidence tend to receive a request for evidence, also known as an RFE. It will list the specific information or documents required and the date by which they must be submitted. William Yates, in a memo to Regional Service Centers and District Directors and Officers-in-Charge,[29] sought to provide guidance on when to issue RFEs and NOIDs. He advised that a "RFE is most appropriate when a particular piece or pieces of necessary evidence are missing, and the highest quality RFE is one that limits the request to the missing evidence," strongly advising against

---

[28] 8 C.F.R. §§ 103.2(b)(8)(i) and (iv).
[29] William R. Yates Memorandum, Requests for Evidence (RFE) and Notices of Intent to Deny (NOID), dated February 16, 2005, HQOPRD 70/2; available at http://www.uscis.gov/sites/default/files/USCIS/Laws/Memoranda/Static_Files_Memoranda/Archives%201998-2008/2005/rfe021605.pdf.

generalized requests. The maximum period allowed for a response is 12 weeks.[30] Failure to respond by the RFE deadline usually results in the denial of a petition or application. The legal practitioner should write down the deadline for submitting the information and enter it into a tickler or reminder system to ensure that it is met.

On the other hand, the Yates memo states that a NOID "is designed to provide a poignant taste of denial without its immediate consequences, so that the filer can understand why the evidence submitted has not been persuasive and can have the best chance to overcome the deficiency if possible."[31] The memo went on to say that a

> NOID is more appropriate than a RFE when initial evidence is predominantly present, but:
>
> - the filing does not appear to establish eligibility by the preponderance of the evidence;
> - the case appears to be ineligible for approval but not necessarily incurable; or
> - the adjudicator intends to rely for denial on evidence not submitted by the filer.

After receiving a NOID, a legal practitioner should review it carefully to determine what additional evidence is needed or what items from the submission were not considered by the USCIS. There is usually a 30-day deadline in which to reply to the NOID.[32]

Case for Discussion 12.6

Natasha is a paralegal with the Integrity Law Firm. The firm has undertaken the representation of Diego in an H1-B specialty occupation petition. Natasha is managing documents and coordinating information needed for the case. She also reviews the mail in the office and notices an RFE was received pertaining to Diego's case, asking for his college transcript. The deadline for obtaining these documents is in 45 days.

- What should Natasha do?

---

[30] 8 C.F.R. §§ 103.2(b)(8)(iv).
[31] Yates memo, *supra*.
[32] 8 C.F.R. § 103.2(b)(8)(iv). However, 8 C.F.R. § 103.5a(b) requires that an additional three days be added whenever a notice is served by mail, effectively allowing 33 days to respond.

H. Filing Systems

Every firm or agency has its own method of maintaining its files. In some cases, they are color coded to match the type of case being handled, perhaps with H1-B specialty occupation cases one color folder or tab, family sponsored relative petitions another, and so forth. Files can be kept alphabetically, or chronologically and then alphabetically.

Another aspect of file management is within the case file itself. Some firms and agencies have specific rules on how a paper file should be kept. For example, the firm or agency may place biographic information in one section, government immigration forms and receipts in another, documents from clients in a different section, and background evidence and research in yet another section. Whatever the system, it should be logical and done in a manner that allows for the quick retrieval of files and information from anyone looking at it, especially given the emphasis on deadlines. Additionally, most firms and agencies have record retention policies that provide guidance on how long files are stored in the office, whether files are sent to an off-site storage facility after a certain date, and the length of time files are retained before they might be destroyed.

After a case is closed, any original documents that might be in the file that belong to the client should be returned and a closing letter sent so that s/he is clear that the attorney-client or agency-client relationship has ended. Some firms and agencies include their record retention policy in such a letter so that clients are clear when their records will be sent to storage or destroyed.

I. Ethical Issues Arising During the Course of Representation

In all aspects of interactions with clients and in the development of case management procedures, care must be taken to ensure that ethical standards of the legal profession are always met. The National Association of Legal Assistants, or NALA, a leading professional organization for paralegals and legal assistants, has a Code of Ethics and Professional Responsibility available on their website that provides guidance on the scope of the paralegal's role.[33]

Canon 4 provides that the paralegal "must not render independent legal judgment in place of an attorney." However, paralegals who are accredited representatives working in BIA recognized organizations can render independent judgment with respect to immigration legal matters. Canon 3 holds that paralegals cannot engage in the unauthorized practice of law, while Canon 2 states

---

[33] The code can be accessed at https://www.nala.org/certification/nala-code-ethics-and-professional-responsibility.

that a "paralegal may perform any task that is properly delegated and supervised by the attorney, as long as the attorney is ultimately responsible to the client."

● **EXAMPLE**

Spencer has been a paralegal for 20 years at the Green Card Law Firm, focusing on family petitions and deportation defense. Mr. Blue, the attorney and founder of the firm, asks Spencer to conduct a consultation with Gilberto from Case for Discussion 12.4. Because of his experience as an interviewer and legal practitioner, Spencer is able to identify several possible immigration options and convey these to Gilberto. If Spencer explains to him that these options are possibilities, but that Spencer will have to review these options with Mr. Blue first before pursuing anything, Spencer has not engaged in the unauthorized practice of law. If, however, Spencer identifies the options and tells Gilberto he will begin working on one or more options that week, he may be. If Spencer were an accredited representative, he could identify the options, draw up a retainer or representation agreement, and begin working on the agreed upon options.

Attorneys are governed by the rules of professional conduct that are in operation in the jurisdiction where they practice. Although each state has its own rules of professional conduct, the overwhelming number of states base their rules on the American Bar Association's, or ABA's, Model Rules of Professional Conduct.[34]

Unlike paralegals, attorneys can provide "candid advice" to a client when reviewing options available to him or her.[35] The legal representation must be competent[36] and performed reasonably diligently and prompt.[37] Attorneys also have a duty to ensure that the scope of representation and allocation of authority between client and lawyer is clearly stated;[38] client information is kept confidential;[39] and that they adhere to the code of conduct when a conflict of interest arises between current or former clients,[40] among other responsibilities. An important duty of attorneys is candor to the tribunal,[41] which requires that s/he will not knowingly:

- Make a false statement of fact or law to a tribunal or fail to correct a false statement of material fact or law previously made to the tribunal by the lawyer;
- Fail to disclose to the tribunal legal authority in the controlling jurisdiction known to the lawyer to be directly adverse to the position of the client and not disclosed by opposing counsel; or

---

[34] These are available at http://www.americanbar.org/groups/professional_responsibility/publications/model_rules_of_professional_conduct.html.
[35] American Bar Association Model Rules of Professional Conduct, Rule 2.1.
[36] *Id.* ABA Model Rule 1.1.
[37] *Id.* ABA Model Rule 1.3.
[38] *Id.* ABA Model Rule 1.2.
[39] *Id.* ABA Model Rule 1.6.
[40] *Id.* ABA Model Rules 1.7 and 1.8.
[41] *Id.* ABA Model Rule 3.3.

- Offer evidence that the lawyer knows to be false. If a lawyer, the lawyer's client, or a witness called by the lawyer, has offered material evidence and the lawyer comes to know of its falsity, the lawyer shall take reasonable remedial measures, including, if necessary, disclosure to the tribunal. A lawyer may refuse to offer evidence, other than the testimony of a defendant in a criminal matter, that the lawyer reasonably believes is false.

In addition:

- A lawyer who represents a client in an adjudicative proceeding and who knows that a person intends to engage, is engaging, or has engaged in criminal or fraudulent conduct related to the proceeding shall take reasonable remedial measures, including, if necessary, disclosure to the tribunal . . .
- In an ex parte proceeding, a lawyer shall inform the tribunal of all material facts known to the lawyer that will enable the tribunal to make an informed decision, whether or not the facts are adverse.

Model Rule 5.3 establishes that attorneys bear the ultimate responsibility to ensure that non-lawyers they supervise or employ, who act as their agents, conduct themselves in a manner that is consistent with the attorney's professional obligations. Without proper delegation or supervision, the attorney may be assisting in the unauthorized practice of law, contrary to Model Rule 5.5. Attorneys who violate the Professional Rules in their jurisdiction face fines, temporary or permanent suspension from the practice of law, or, in more serious cases, criminal charges.

● **EXAMPLE**

There are discussions in Congress to permit U.S. citizens to petition for their spouses who entered without inspection so that they can become LPRs without leaving the country. In return, applicants would pay a fine and adjust their status following an interview with the USCIS. Attorney Sam, who runs a small immigration law firm, offers to conduct workshops at area churches where he encourages immigrants to secure their place in line, even though the law has not passed yet, so there is actually no line. Sam further promises applicants they will get a green card in six months. Sam charges $1,500 to complete and file Form I-130, Petition for Alien Relative, and instructs his paralegal to assist in this unethical endeavor. Although Sam submits Form G-28, Notice of Entry of Appearance as Attorney or Accredited Representative, under his signature for all of the applications, the form is completed entirely by paralegal Pina who also knows that under the current law, the undocumented spouse cannot adjust status in the United States because of the manner of entry. Therefore, her actions implicate her in the conduct of unethical behavior.

Sam's actions are serious violations of a number of the Model Rules of Professional Conduct. He engaged in misleading communication (Model Rule 7.1), and did not specifically explain he was advertising his services (Rules 7.2 and 7.3). Instead, he clothed his solicitation of clients as "workshops." Additionally, Sam did not demonstrate competence because he is advocating that immigrants apply for a provision that has not yet passed into law and so is not even available. (Model Rule 1.1). As discussed in Part II and Section G.1. of Chapter 6, Family Sponsored Immigration and Permanent Resident Status, spouses who entered without inspection, or EWI, must leave the United States and apply for an immigrant visa to enter the country from abroad. They are also subject to the three- or ten-year bar to re-entry if they have been present in the United States for over 180 days to 1 year or more without permission, unless they receive a waiver to reenter first.[42] Under a policy of the Obama administration, spouses facing the three- and ten-year bar due to unlawful presence can apply for a waiver while in the United States but, even if the waiver is approved, must return to the home country and obtain a family sponsored immigrant visa through consular processing before returning.[43] Sam is either unaware of the immigration law related to family petitions, or worse, is simply not providing truthful information, hoping to gain financially through the procedure he is offering.

If Sam had considered filing a Form I-130, Petition for Alien Relative, with an in-country Form I-601A, Application for Provisional Unlawful Presence Waiver, which is available, then the fee of $1,500 might be reasonable. However, in this example it is not, since it is being paid to achieve an impossible result, violating Model Rule 1.5 against collecting an unreasonable fee. In fact, Sam could be said to have engaged in misconduct, because his claim that spouses can adjust in the United States is currently false and misleading, in violation of Model Rule 8.4(c), which discourages engaging in conduct involving dishonesty, fraud, deceit, or misrepresentation. This is because the path he is offering is presented as something that will happen, when it is simply something that is under discussion.

Sam can delegate the completion of a Form I-130, Petition for Alien Relative, to a paralegal, which is the practice in many immigration firms. However, he has a responsibility, under Model Rule 5.3, to provide adequate supervision and ensure that the paralegal does not violate the rules of professional conduct, including engaging in the unauthorized practice of law, prohibited by Model Rule 5.5. While the ultimate responsibility for these misdeeds lies with Sam, case law and some States have concluded that regardless, a paralegal has an independent obligation to engage in appropriate professional conduct. For example, Kentucky Supreme Court Rule 3.7 states "the paralegal does have an independent obligation to refrain from illegal conduct." Therefore, Pina should have refused to assist in completing the forms.

In this case, Sam had purely financial motives to conduct "workshops" in the community and mislead his audience. However, many immigration lawyers and accredited representatives, as a public service, do provide programs and presentations as a way of educating the community about new immigration programs

---

[42] Section G.3.a of Chapter 6, Family Sponsored Immigration and Permanent Resident Status.
[43] Section H of Chapter 6, Family Sponsored Immigration and Permanent Resident Status.

or changes in the law. This type of public service should be encouraged, as it not only informs the community but also serves as a vehicle to promote civic engagement in immigration policy. Legal practitioners should look to their state rules to determine what role they can play in community educational presentations, because some jurisdictions have deemed presentations that provide specific information about an area of law and answering audience questions to equate to the unauthorized practice of law.[44]

J. Conflict of Interest

One of the most vexing ethical areas in immigration law relates to conflict of interest. As we have seen in both family sponsored relative petitions and employment-based cases, an attorney generally represents both the petitioner and beneficiary. There is nothing to prevent dual representation in such cases, so long as the interests of both parties and the representation of one client will not be directly adverse to another, or materially limit the representation of one or more clients. The lawyer must reasonably believe that s/he can provide competent and diligent representation to each affected client.[45] Additionally, the attorney or paralegal acting on the attorney's behalf receives confidential information from both parties in dual representation cases. If the attorney uses information obtained in a confidential setting from current clients[46] in representing another client without his or her consent, the hallmark rule of professional responsibility on confidentiality is violated. Attorneys also have duties to former clients[47] and cannot represent another person whose interests are adverse to the former client without his or her informed consent, confirmed in writing. Some immigration firms handle this thorny area by making sure the retainer or representation agreement contains clear language on what the firm intends to do if a conflict arises. The sample engagement letter in Figure 12.2 is a good example of this.

In an article written for the American Immigration Lawyers Association, attorney Bruce Hake maintains, "It should be explained in writing that representing two parties simultaneously in one matter requires the lawyer to disclose information and to be equally loyal to both parties."[48] Hake explains that when a conflict of interest develops, the attorney must be neutral but not

---

[44] *See Doe v. Condon*, 532 S.E.2d 879 (S.C. 2000), where the court held that it is the unauthorized practice of law for a paralegal to conduct educational seminars and answer estate planning questions because s/he will be implicitly advising participants that they require estate planning services.
[45] ABA Model Rule 1.7.
[46] ABA Model Rule 1.6.
[47] ABA Model Rule 1.9.
[48] Hake, *Dual Representation in Immigration Practice*, AILA Doc. No 05060724, June 7, 2005, p. 28, available at http://www.aila.org/practice/ethics/ethics-resources/2005-2011/dual-representation-in-immigration-practice.

pretend that a conflict does not exist. "The lawyer must try to resolve the conflict, and if that is impossible, withdraw from the case."[49]

Writing for the web-based Immigration Daily, Cyrus Mehta, a well-known immigration attorney, proposes another approach: anticipating a conflict and limiting representation to one party if it arises, asking the party who will then be unrepresented if the conflict arises, to sign a waiver from the outset of the representation.[50] Mehta uses the case example where a foreign national wife, who has conditional LPR status based on marriage to a U.S. citizen, approaches an attorney for advice on lifting the conditions through a joint Form I-751, Petition to Remove Conditions on Residence. She says the marriage is having problems, but her husband is willing to participate in filing a joint petition to remove the conditional status of her permanent residency. Mehta proposes the husband should sign a waiver in the retainer or representation agreement at the beginning of the case, acknowledging that if the marriage dissolves during the pendency of the petition process, the attorney will continue to represent his wife.

Whether an attorney seeks to limit representation through a waiver, withdrawing from a case might still be the only option to preserve client confidence so as not to run afoul of Model Rule 1.6 requiring confidentiality, or Model Rule 1.7, regarding conflict of interest, or Model Rule 1.9 regarding duties to former clients.

In Mr. Mehta's Form I-751, Petition to Remove Conditions on Residence, case, it can be surmised that the U.S. citizen spouse did not feel that participating in a joint petition to remove conditions, or even the possibility of a divorce, was adverse to his interests. However, this might not be the situation in other family sponsored or employment-based cases. For example, if a couple seeks dual representation in a marriage case but then the foreign born spouse reveals she is being abused, it would not be possible to be loyal to both parties and continue the representation because clearly information that is adverse to one party must be disclosed. It might also not be in the best interests of the victim to continue to be represented by the same attorney, as the legal practitioner may have learned confidential information from the abusive spouse in the course of dual representation that cannot ethically be divulged, thus limiting representation available to the victim. For example, the U.S. citizen spouse may have confided to the attorney or to the paralegal as his or her agent that this marriage showed he was a changed man. He explained that he used to have a drinking problem, which caused a prior marriage to fail because of abuse, but now he only drinks once in a while. This might be key evidence of a pattern of abuse that could not be included by an attorney who once represented both parties as part of the victim's case without violating the attorney's confidential

---

[49] Id, at p. 29.
[50] Mehta, *Counterpoint: Ethically Handling Conflicts Between Two Clients Through the "Golden Mean,"* ILW.com, available here: www.ilw.com/articles/207,1009-mehta.shtm.

relationship with the U.S. citizen spouse or duty of loyalty to him as a former client.

> ● **EXAMPLE**
>
> The Preciso Engineering Company sponsored Diego, an Ecuadoran national, for an H-1B Specialty Occupation nonimmigrant visa and it now needs to be renewed. Both Preciso and Diego are represented by the Integrity Law Firm. Diego signed a retainer or representation agreement with Integrity that said if a conflict arises relating to issues of employment, Integrity would continue to represent Preciso only. In the course of representation, Diego informs the paralegal of Integrity that in the last year he discovered he has diabetes and his health care coverage at Preciso has been critical to his health. He explains that he believes he could not get this level of care in Ecuador and that, in his words, having to return to Ecuador would be a "death sentence." He asks the paralegal to keep information about his health confidential. A member of Preciso's human resources team tells the paralegal that the company is thinking of restructuring and wishes to eliminate Diego's position. They seek advice from the Integrity firm on how to do this in a way that is least harmful to Diego. If they eliminate the position, Diego may lose his immigration status in the United States and health insurance and would have to return to his home country.

Even though Diego signed a waiver, in this example, some clear conflicts exist that arose after the waiver was signed. Diego wishes to remain at the firm, and, since his status is dependent on an employer sponsoring him, if Preciso eliminates his position he faces both loss of health care and the need to return to Ecuador. It is in Diego's best interest to remain under Preciso's sponsorship. Preciso may have financial or workforce reasons for restructuring, and it might be in their best interest to do so. If an attorney from the Integrity Law Firm receives informed consent from both parties to disclose their information and sets up a meeting where a mutually beneficial arrangement is made, a conflict may be avoided. However, if either party insists on confidentiality, the Integrity Law Firm cannot reveal the confidential information each party shared with the firm's paralegal. In that case, the prudent course would be for Integrity Law Firm to withdraw from representing both parties.

K. Special Professional Conduct Rules for Practitioners of Immigration Law

Since accredited representatives are not attorneys and need not be paralegals, it is unclear whether they are covered by the Model Rules of Professional Conduct or NALA's Code of Ethics and Professional Responsibility. However, there are very specific rules of conduct for those practicing before the agencies of the DHS or the EOIR, many of which incorporate the principles of the Model Rules. Under 8 C.F.R § 1003.101(a), an adjudicating official of the BIA may impose disciplinary sanctions against any practitioner, including an attorney or accredited representative, when the person engages in criminal, unethical, or unprofessional conduct before the BIA, immigration courts, or DHS. Specific acts that give rise to disciplinary action are set forth in 8 C.F.R. § 1003.102 and include, but are not limited to:

- Charging grossly excessive fees; accredited representatives must be paid by their organization which is bound to charge only nominal fees as a requirement for BIA recognition under 8 C.F.R. § 1292.1(a)(4);
- Accepting bribes or attempting to bribe or coerce any party to a case or officer or employee of the Department of Justice;
- Knowingly or with reckless disregard for the truth, making a false statement of material fact or law, or willfully misleading any party or official or employee of the Department of Justice regarding a case;
- Soliciting clients for financial gain, unless the practitioner includes "Advertising Material" on the outside of envelopes that include written materials sent to prospective clients;
- Practicing when disbarred or suspended;
- Knowingly or with reckless disregard, making a false communication about his or her qualifications;
- Having been found guilty of, or pleading guilty or *nolo contendere* to a serious crime in any federal, state, possession, territory or commonwealth, or the District of Columbia;
- Knowingly or with reckless disregard, falsely certifying a document as a true copy;
- Engaging in frivolous conduct before the BIA, immigration court, and any other administrative body under title II of the INA, which includes pursuing courses of action that have no basis in law or fact;
- Engaging in conduct that constitutes ineffective assistance of counsel;
- Repeatedly failing to appear for pre-hearing conferences and scheduled hearings in a timely manner without good cause;
- Failing to provide competent representation to a client;
- Assisting any person in the unauthorized practice of law;
- Engaging in conduct that is prejudicial to the administration of justice or undermining the integrity of the adjudicative process;
- Failing to abide by a client's decision concerning the objectives of representation and failing to consult with the client as to the means by which those objectives will be pursued; and
- Failing to disclose known adverse controlling legal authority to an adjudicator.

Case for Discussion 12.7

Junior Associate Sandra has been asked to interview a couple in a potential marriage case. The petitioner is a U.S. citizen and pregnant from a former relationship. She has not completed high school and has erratic work history. Although she is not working, she states she has recently come into a substantial amount of money and can support her husband. The beneficiary spouse has a Master's degree from his home country of Turkey. He is about 15 years senior to his wife. In preparing to demonstrate the *bona fides* of the marriage, Sandra asks the couple how they met, what they like to do together, and how their finances are arranged. The couple cannot identify what they do together or what they have in common. The foreign national says he supports his U.S. citizen wife because she is pregnant and that they have a joint bank account. However, they describe the home where they reside differently; the U.S. citizen says it has two bathrooms and the foreign national only recalls one. He then offers to pay the firm money beyond its regular fee to handle the case because he explains, "it may be a hard case."

- What issues, if any, does this case raise?
- What, if any, ABA Model Rules of Conduct, or grounds enumerated in 8 C.F.R. § 1003.102, might be relevant in this situation?

Case for Discussion 12.8

David is an accredited representative in a nonprofit organization that has a very high caseload. He is working on getting TPS for a Syrian national who desperately needs it to work. The client is very low income and cannot even afford a cell phone. It took several weeks to set up the appointment to meet with the client, including arranging for an Arabic interpreter to assist with communications between them. All the paperwork is now complete and the client leaves the office. Just before mailing the forms, David notices that the client did not sign the Form I-821, Application for Temporary Protected Status. David knows the client really wants the application mailed immediately and that the client has reviewed all of the information and would certainly approve of David signing on his behalf. Additionally, the client would be very upset to learn there was a delay in mailing the application.

- What should David do?

> **Case for Discussion 12.9**
>
> The Competent Law Firm is very busy because it has developed a sound reputation in deportation defense cases. The phones are constantly ringing. Because the firm is busy responding to new callers, existing clients often leave many messages before their calls are returned, if at all.
>
> - Does this conduct violate any of the professional conduct rules in 8 C.F.R. § 1003.102?
> - How can the violation, if any, be rectified and avoided?

L. Conclusion

Paralegals, accredited representatives, and junior associate attorneys play an essential role in an immigration practice. Their duties can vary depending on the skills they bring and the cases they handle. Bilingual or multilingual paralegals, accredited representatives, and junior associates often act as interpreters during interviews and can translate documents into English or into another language for clients to read. They are often the "front-line" communicators with clients, obtaining client history, information, and relevant documents. Many research the availability of documents from other countries and obtain them or assist clients in doing so, where necessary.

For those that work on employment-based cases, paralegals and junior associates may assist attorneys in developing job descriptions, seeking evaluations of foreign degrees, coordinating the filing of immigration documents among various government agencies, or tracking deadlines. They also research statutes, regulations, and case law and act as a liaison to the many agencies connected to an immigrant benefit and/or visa application or petition, including the DOL, the USCIS, and the DOS. It is rare for nonprofit organizations to provide representation in employment-based immigration matters, so the role of an accredited representative in this sphere is limited. Additional duties include drafting letters to clients and monitoring correspondence.

Those who work in litigation firms also take client history, develop affidavits, gather records, including a person's past criminal history, perform legal research, communicate with the clients, and track deadlines that arise in a case. Paralegals, accredited representatives, and junior associates must be well versed in database management and web-based systems in order to submit and track various immigration applications and forms. Those who pay close attention to detail and have a high degree of organizational management skills are highly sought after.

Accredited representatives working in BIA recognized agencies are unique to immigration practice, and have additional duties to those traditionally performed by paralegals, since they also represent clients independently, manage their own caseloads, and often must exercise their own judgment regarding a strategy or procedure in a case. Their role in this regard is very similar to that of an attorney.

The knowledge of immigration law opens up many employment opportunities apart from direct representation of foreign nationals, particularly within institutions of higher education and the government. Colleges and schools that admit foreign students must have a designated foreign student office, which includes a designated school official whose primary tasks include advising on F-1/J-1 student visa issues, tracking compliance of students in the Student and Exchange Visitor Information System, or SEVIS,[51] along with nonimmigration related tasks. Many offices that serve foreign students provide additional information on immigration issues to their international students. A national organization, the Association of International Educators, has a website[52] that provides information for student advisors and other interested individuals. It also contains an online Student Advisor's Manual that provides updated information on immigration law and policy pertaining to international students.

Non-attorneys with knowledge of immigration laws have additional opportunities in government. These include paralegal positions for the USCIS, ICE, and to counsel in various branches of the EOIR. Additionally, knowledge of immigration law is required for a career as a Foreign Service Officer with the DOS for those posted overseas at U.S. consulates. The DOS has a website further explaining the type of careers it has available together with educational and experience requirements for such careers. It often administers competitive examinations and conducts extensive background security checks as part of the recruitment process.

Immigration law is in constant flux. No one textbook can cover in detail all of its aspects. Readers are encouraged to attend additional training and to read in-depth materials focused on particular elements of immigration law if they intend to join this growing and interesting field.

---

[51] *See* Section E.3.a of Chapter 2, Nonimmigrant Visas for Brief Stays, Studies, and Cultural Exchange, for further discussion on this topic.
[52] Available at www.nafsa.org.

Glossary

AAO—Administrative Appeals Office: Administrative office that reviews appeals of decisions made by the USCIS for certain categories of immigration benefits, issuing non- or precedential decisions.

Abandonment of Lawful Permanent Resident Status: Results from an LPR's frequent and extended absences from the United States when there are limited ties to demonstrate an intent to maintain residence here.

Academic Field: A body of specialized knowledge offered for study at an accredited U.S. university or institution of higher education.

Accompanying Relative: A type of visa in which family members travel with the principal applicant which, in immigrant visa cases, must be within six months of issuance of an immigrant visa to the principal applicant.

Accredited Representatives: People of good moral character, employed by a Board of Immigration Appeals-recognized nonprofit religious, charitable, social services, or similar organization who are approved as competent to represent individuals before certain immigration agencies.

Actual Wage: The wage paid to similarly qualified U.S. workers for similar work.

Adjudicating Officer: *See* **AO**.

Adjudicator's Field Manual: A USCIS publication that details its policies and procedures for adjudicating applications and petitions.

Adjustment of Status: An application by a foreign national already in the United States to become a lawful permanent resident, allowing him or her to live here permanently.

Administrative Appeals Office: *See* **AAO**.

Administrative Closure: A mechanism that assists immigration judges in managing their dockets by closing cases that are not considered a priority for hearing at the present time.

Admission or **Admitted:** The lawful entry of a foreign national into the United States after inspection and authorization by an immigration officer.

Admissions Plan: A plan presented to the President and Congress regarding the number, nationalities, and geographic region of origin of the refugees to be admitted to the United States.

Advanced Degree: Any U.S. academic or professional degree or a foreign equivalent degree above that of baccalaureate.

Advanced Parole: Prior permission to leave and re-enter the United States before any travel outside of the country takes place.

Adverse Effect Wage Rate: Minimum hourly wage, as determined by the Department of Labor, that must be paid by the employer to the foreign agricultural employee in a given area so that U.S. workers are not adversely affected.

Advisory Opinion: An opinion providing guidance on legal interpretation regarding a point of law requested from and issued by the government before an application or petition is submitted and adjudicated.

Affidavit of Relationship: *See* **AOR**.

Affidavit of Support: A contractually binding pledge by a petitioner and, where necessary, a joint sponsor, that pledges to financially support a foreign national or family member who intends to enter the United States as a sponsored immigrant.

Affiliate: One of two subsidiaries, both of which are owned and controlled by the same parent or individual, or one of two legal entities owned and controlled by the same group of individuals, each owning and controlling approximately the same share or portion of each entity.

Affirmative Asylum Request: An application for asylum filed directly with the USCIS as opposed to an immigration judge.

Agents: The actual employers of the beneficiary who will perform at an event, the representatives of both the employer and the beneficiary of the petition, or a person or entity authorized by an employer to act for, or in place of, the employer as its agent.

Glossary

Aggravated Felony Crimes: A term used to describe certain offenses that severely limit immigration relief available to those convicted of such crimes.

AO—Adjudicating Officer: An immigration officer who adjudicates applications for immigration benefits.

AOR—Affidavit of Relationship: An affidavit completed by a refugee of a designated P-3 country who is seeking to have qualifying family members join him or her in the United States.

Application Support Center: Designated USCIS centers that take digital fingerprints of foreign nationals who are applying for certain immigration benefits.

Arriving Alien: An applicant for admission who either arrives clandestinely and is apprehended at or near a border or within the United States, or who presents him or herself to an official at a designated port of entry, and who has not yet been given permission to enter in the immigration status sought.

Arts: Any field of creative activity or endeavor such as, but not limited to, fine, visual, culinary, and performing arts.

Asylee: A foreign national physically present in the U.S. who has been granted asylum status.

Asylum: Legal protection offered to foreign nationals in the U.S. who have a well-founded fear of persecution on account of race, religion, national origin, membership in a particular social group, or political opinion.

Asylum EAD Clock: Measures the length of time an application for asylum has been pending either with the USCIS or the EOIR before an asylum applicant is eligible to apply for an Employment Authorization Document.

Authorized Entity: An individual person, agent, or corporate organization that is permitted to file a nonimmigrant visa petition on behalf of a foreign national.

BALCA—Board of Alien Labor Certification Appeals: Administrative appeals unit of the Department of Labor that hears appeals from the denials of temporary or permanent labor certification applications.

Benching: Failure to pay a worker his or her salary when no active work is available, in violation of the Department of Labor's regulations regarding the attestations made in the signed Labor Certificate Application.

Beneficiary: The foreign national, family member, or employee who will receive an immigration benefit from a family sponsored or employer-based petition for his or her benefit.

BIA—Board of Immigration Appeals: Appellate division of the Executive Office for Immigration Review, where appeals of decisions of immigration judges or other immigration decisions are reviewed.

Biometrics: The digital capturing of an individual's fingerprints, photograph, eye scan, and signature for submission and search through several government databases for background security checks and identity verification.

Board of Alien Labor Certification Appeals: *See* **BALCA.**

Board of Immigration Appeals: *See* **BIA.**

***Bona Fide* Nonprofit Religious Organization:** A tax exempt religious organization as cited in Section 501(c)(3) of the Internal Revenue Code of 1986, possessing a currently valid determination letter from the Internal Revenue Service, confirming the tax-exempt status.

***Bona Fide* Relationship:** A familial relationship between spouses that is authentic and not simply entered into in order to obtain immigration benefits.

Bond: An amount of money set by ICE or by an immigration judge that, if paid, will allow a detained foreign national to be released from detention.

Branch: Any office or operating division not established as a separate business entity.

Bureau of Population, Refugees, and Migration: *See* **PRM.**

Business Necessity: An employer's requirements for a position that exceeds those listed in the O*Net classification, the need for which must be justified before they can be included in the job description.

Business Plan: An outline set forth by an enterprise that explains its goals and strategy for reaching them.

CAM—Central American Minors Refugee/Parole Program: A program created in 2015 to permit children who live in El Salvador, Guatemala, and Honduras and whose parent(s) are in lawful status in the United States, to apply and enter as refugees to reunite with that parent(s).

Cancellation of Removal: A discretionary relief available to a foreign national who, though determined to be removable from the United States, is allowed to remain, and either retain or obtain lawful permanent resident, or LPR, status because to deport him or her would cause hardship to an LPR or exceptional and extremely unusual hardship to a qualifying relative of a non-LPR.

Cap Gap: A provision created by the USCIS whereby a student in F-1 status with Optional Practical Training may continue to work with permission if the foreign national's H-1B petition is selected for adjudication.

Capital: Cash, equipment, inventory, other tangible property, cash equivalents, and indebtedness secured by assets owned by a foreign national entrepreneur, provided that s/he is personally and primarily liable and that the assets of the new commercial enterprise upon which the petition is based are not used to secure any of the indebtedness.

CBP—Customs and Border Protection: Agency within the Department of Homeland Security that protects the U.S. borders.

Central American Minors Refugee/Parole Program: *See* **CAM.**

Certified Disposition: An official document issued by a court that adjudicated a case, bearing its seal or stamp, providing an official explanation of the case outcome.

Changed or **Extraordinary Circumstances:** Facts and situations that excuse the filing of an asylum application after the One-Year Deadline.

Child Status Protection Act: *See* **CSPA.**

Citizenship and Immigration Service: *See* **USCIS.**

Citizenship by Acquisition: A process by which a foreign national, born and residing abroad, acquires citizenship at birth because s/he is born to a U.S. citizen parent(s).

Civil Surgeon: A physician selected by the immigration service to conduct medical examinations of foreign nationals seeking lawful permanent resident status in the United States.

Class A Port of Entry: A location where all travelers, including foreign nationals, lawful permanent residents, and United States citizens, can apply for entry to the United States.

Closing Argument: A summary of the facts and applicable law as they relate to the case before the judge.

Code of Federal Regulations: Specific guidelines, directives, or requirements issued by federal agencies in order to implement legislation.

Conditional Lawful Permanent Resident Status: A conditional status granted to foreign nationals who obtain Lawful Permanent Resident status through a marriage that is less than two-years old at the time of adjudication of the application or entry into the United States.

Consular Officers: Members of the foreign service of the Department of State who can rule on visa applications, assist U.S. citizens abroad, and represent the interests of the United States in foreign countries.

Consular Processing: Applying for an immigrant or nonimmigrant visa at a consular office abroad.

Continuance: A decision to delay hearing a case until a future date.

Continued Presence: Provision of temporary immigration relief to individuals who are identified by Federal, State, local, tribal, or territorial law enforcement as victims of human trafficking.

Continuous Residence: The continuous period of time a foreign national resides in the United States without leaving the country.

Control: The right and authority to direct the management and operations of a business entity.

Convention or **Protocol:** An agreement between states and nations on the regulation of particular matters between them.

Convention Against Torture: A form of humanitarian relief directly related to international law emanating from the UN Convention Against Torture and Other Cruel, Inhuman, or Degrading Treatment or Punishment that contains an absolute prohibition against expelling, returning, or extraditing a foreign national to a country where there are "substantial grounds for believing that he would be in danger of being subjected to torture."

Credibility: The truthfulness or believability of a person's version of events.

Glossary

Credible Fear Interview: An interview or screening conducted by an Asylum Officer to determine whether an arriving alien has demonstrated that the fear s/he has of returning to his or her country of nationality is credible or not.

Crime of Violence: an offense that has as an element the use, attempted use, or threatened use of physical force against the person or property of another, or a felony offense that, by its nature, involves a substantial risk that physical force against the person or property of another may be used in the course of committing the offense.

Cross-Examination: The questioning of a witness by the opposing party in order to ascertain the veracity of information provided during examination in chief or to further develop testimony.

CSPA—Child Status Protection Act: An act that permits certain unmarried derivative children of U.S. citizen or lawful permanent resident applicants or petitioners to continue to be treated as though they were under 21 years old even after they reach their 21st birthday.

Cultural Exchange Program Sponsor: A legal entity designated by the Secretary of State to conduct an exchange visitor program.

Culturally Unique: Style of artistic expression, methodology, or medium that is unique to a particular country, nation, society, class, ethnicity, religion, tribe, or other group of persons.

Customs and Border Protection: *See* **CBP.**

DACA—Deferred Action for Childhood Arrivals: An immigrant benefit available to youth and young adults who are in or have completed high school or an equivalent diploma; who entered the United States before the age of 16, and were under the age of 31 as of June 15, 2012; and have been living in the United States continuously since June 15, 2007.

De Novo: Review of a previously decided case as though it has never been considered before.

DED—Deferred Enforced Departure: Similar to Temporary Protected Status, or TPS, DED allows foreign nationals granted this status to work legally with protection from removal while it is in effect.

Defensive Asylum Applications: Claims for asylum as a defense to removal, filed initially with a judge in a U.S. Immigration Court.

Deferred Action for Childhood Arrivals: *See* **DACA.**

Deferred Action Status: A discretionary decision taken by the USCIS not to prosecute a foreign national known to be present in the United States without legal status, formally acknowledging that the recipient is of lower priority for removal proceedings.

Deferred Enforced Departure: *See* **DED.**

Denaturalization: A process by which a person who became a U.S. citizen by application can be stripped of that status, typically because citizenship was acquired fraudulently or through some withholding of critical relevant information.

Department of Health and Human Services: *See* **HHS.**

Department of Homeland Security: *See* **DHS.**

Department of Justice: *See* **DOJ.**

Department of Labor: *See* **DOL.**

Department of State: *See* **DOS.**

Department of State Foreign Affairs Manual: *See* **FAM.**

Dependency Order: A predicate order to Special Immigrant Juvenile status issued by a state juvenile court that states a child lacks parental care and control.

Deported: More recently referred to as removal, it is the physical removal or expulsion from the United States of a foreign national by immigration officials.

Derivative Citizenship: A process by which a foreign national minor child automatically derives citizenship when a parent becomes a citizen before the child reaches the age of 18 years.

Derivative Relatives: The spouse and unmarried children under 21 years old of preference relatives.

Designated School Official: *See* **DSO.**

Development, Relief, and Education for Alien Minors: *See* **DREAM ACT.**

DHS—Department of Homeland Security: A cabinet office created in 2003 that consolidates many enforcement agencies in order to protect the United States from attack and harm while overseeing the functions of the main agencies that either enforce or administer immigration laws, which are Customs and Border Protection, or CBP; Immigration and Customs Enforcement, or ICE; and the U.S. Citizenship and Immigration Service, or USCIS.

Direct Victim: A foreign national who has suffered direct and proximate harm as a result of the commission of a U Nonimmigrant visa qualifying criminal activity.

Doctrine of Consular Nonreviewability: The doctrine that a decision by a consular officer is final and cannot be appealed.

DOJ—Department of Justice: A cabinet level office, it enforces federal law and is charged with the administration of justice including overseeing the Executive Office for Immigration Review, or EOIR, that consists of the Board of Immigration Appeals, or BIA, and U.S. Immigration Courts.

DOL—Department of Labor: A cabinet office with the mission to foster, promote, and develop the welfare of the wage earners, job seekers, and retirees of the United States; improve working conditions; advance opportunities for profitable employment; and assure work-related benefits and rights.

DOS—Department of State: A cabinet office that oversees the foreign affairs of the United States.

DREAM ACT—Development, Relief, and Education for Alien Minors: Proposed congressional legislation that, if passed, would enable certain youth who arrived in the United States before a certain age, who are in or have completed high school or the equivalent, to apply for lawful permanent resident status.

D/S—Duration of Status: Admission to the United States for an unspecified duration as long as the underlying nonimmigrant status is maintained.

DSM-V: Diagnostic and Statistical Manual of Mental Disorder that defines and classifies mental disorders as an aid to diagnosis.

DSO—Designated School Official: A responsible employee of an educational institution that is charged with assisting students in obtaining and maintaining F-1 and M-1 status as well as entering student information into SEVIS.

Dual Intent: The simultaneous intent to remain either temporarily or permanently in the United States.

Due Process Clause: A clause in the Fourteenth Amendment of the U.S. Constitution that provides that no person should be deprived of life, liberty, or property without legal safeguards.

Duration of Status: *See* **D/S.**

E-Verify: An optional electronic program offered by the U.S. Department of Homeland Security to assist employers in ensuring the employment eligibility of new hires.

EAD—Employment Authorization Document: A document issued by the USCIS that confirms the ability of a foreign national to work in the United States.

EIN—Employer Identification Number: A unique number assigned to a business by the Internal Revenue Service.

Employer Identification Number: *See* **EIN.**

Employment Authorization Document: *See* **EAD.**

Enforcement and Removal Operations: *See* **ERO.**

Entered Without Inspection: *See* **EWI.**

Enumerated Grounds: Grounds of race, nationality, religion, membership in a particular social group, or political opinion on which an application for asylum must be based.

EOIR—Executive Office for Immigration Review: A Department of Justice agency responsible for adjudicating immigration cases by fairly, expeditiously, and uniformly interpreting and administering the nation's immigration laws through conducting immigration court proceedings, appellate reviews, and administrative hearings.

ERO—Enforcement and Removal Operations: Section of ICE responsible for detaining and removing foreign nationals who have violated U.S. immigration laws.

Essential Skills Employee: An employee with special qualifications that make the service s/he renders essential to the efficient operation of an enterprise.

Event: An activity such as, but not limited to, a scientific project, conference, convention, lecture series, tour, exhibit, business project, or engagement.

EWI—Entered Without Inspection: Entering the United States at a place other than a designated port of entry without being inspected or paroled by an immigration officer.

Glossary

Examination in Chief: Questions posed by the person calling a witness to testify under oath, which allows him or her to lay a foundation of pertinent facts for the case.

Executive Capacity: An assignment within an organization in which the employee primarily directs the management of the organization or a major component or function of it; establishes the goals and policies of the organization, component, or function; exercises wide latitude in discretionary decision making; and receives only general supervision or direction from higher level executives, the board of directors, or stockholders of the organization.

Executive Office for Immigration Review: *See* **EOIR.**

Exclusion Grounds: Now referred to as inadmissibility, former term used to refer to foreign national who could be denied permission to enter the United States.

Expatriate: One who voluntarily relinquishes citizenship through an act that demonstrates allegiance to another country *and* an intent to give up U.S. citizenship.

Expedited Removal: A procedure used by the Department of Homeland Security to remove certain foreign nationals who arrive at the U.S. border without proper documents or who have other problems causing them to be barred from entering or remaining in the United States, without the opportunity to present a case to an immigration judge.

Extraordinary Ability: A term used to describe foreign nationals who are truly the best and brightest in their field.

FAM—Department of State Foreign Affairs Manual: A publication that contains statutes, regulations, policies, organizational structure, and operations of the DOS, Foreign Office, and other federal agencies.

Federal Register: A legal newspaper of the federal government published every business day by the National Archives and Records Administration, which contains federal agency regulations, proposed rules, and public notices, as well as executive orders and other presidential documents.

Federal Rules of Evidence: Rules enacted by the U.S. Supreme Court, which can be amended by Congress, that set forth the procedures in civil and criminal matters before the federal courts.

Female Genital Mutilation: *See* **FGM.**

FGM—Female Genital Mutilation: The total or partial alteration of the external female genitalia for non-medical purposes.

Final Order of Removal: A decision by an immigration judge or the Board of Immigration Appeals to remove a foreign national from the United States that can no longer be challenged.

Firm Resettlement: A state achieved by a foreign national who has lived in another country where s/he could be considered as having received an offer of permanent residency, citizenship, or other type of permanent resettlement in that other country.

FLCDC—Foreign Labor Certification Data Center: A Department of Labor Online Wage Library used to determine prevailing wage determinations.

FOIA—Freedom of Information/Privacy Act Request: A formal request to the government for records pertaining to an individual case or government action.

Following to Join: A qualifying derivative family member who derives immigration benefits from a principal beneficiary and joins him or her in the United States within six months after the beneficiary immigrates.

Foreign Affairs Manual: *See* **FAM.**

Foreign Labor Certification Data Center: *See* **FLCDC.**

Fourteenth Amendment: An Amendment to the U.S. Constitution which grants U.S. citizenship to "all persons born or naturalized in the United States."

Freedom of Information/Privacy Act Request: *See* **FOIA.**

Frivolous Asylum Application: An asylum application where the applicant has deliberately lied or misrepresented a material or key fact in his or her claim to protection before an immigration judge after oral or written warning of the consequences of so doing have been given in the foreign national's language or one s/he understands.

Functional Managers: Those in charge of a key function or division in an organization that do not have any subordinates reporting to them.

GMC—Good Moral Character: A finding that an applicant for certain immigration benefits has behaved according to the moral standard of the community.

Good Moral Character: *See* **GMC**.

Green Card: Colloquial term for a Permanent Resident card, proving the holder is a lawful permanent resident, or LPR.

Habeas Corpus: Latin term that allows a court to hear constitutional challenges to a person's continued detention.

Hearsay Evidence: The relaying of information by someone without firsthand knowledge of it.

HHS—Department of Health and Human Services: Cabinet level agency created to protect the health of the American people and to provide human services and assistance to vulnerable populations.

High School Education: The successful completion of a formal course of elementary and secondary education comparable to completion of a 12-year course in the United States.

Homeland Security Investigations: *See* **HSI**.

Household Member Sponsor: A household member of a petitioner or sponsor who signs Form I-864A, Contract Between Sponsor and Household Member, as a supplement to Form I-864, Affidavit of Support, binding the household member to a promise that his or her income and assets will be made available to support the foreign national and any qualifying family members who are the subject of the affidavit of support.

HSI—Homeland Security Investigations: Section of ICE responsible for investigating a wide range of domestic and international activities arising from the illegal movement of people and goods into, within, and out of the United States.

Humanitarian Parole: Permission granted by the Department of Homeland Security to an individual who is otherwise inadmissible into the United States to enter for a temporary period of time due to a compelling emergency.

ICE—Immigration and Customs Enforcement: Agency of the Department of Homeland Security that is charged with enforcing federal laws governing border control, customs, trade, and immigration to promote homeland security and public safety.

iCERT: The Department of Labor's Visa Portal System website that is used to electronically determine the prevailing wage of a position.

IGA—Interested Government Agency: U.S. government agency that provides a waiver to a J-1 visa holder, attesting to the significant contributions s/he made to the United States and affirming that it would be contrary to U.S. interests to send the foreign national back to his or her home country.

IIRAIRA—Illegal Immigration Reform and Immigrant Responsibility Act: An act passed by Congress in 1996 to tighten border control and internal enforcement of immigration laws that increased penalties for those using fraudulent documents and lawful permanent residents who committed certain types of crimes, while also making it more difficult for undocumented immigrants to achieve lawful permanent resident status.

Illegal Immigration Reform and Immigrant Responsibility Act: *See* **IIRAIRA**.

Immediate Relative: An immigration category referring to the spouse, parent, or unmarried minor child (under 21) of a U.S. citizen.

Immigration and Customs Enforcement: *See* **ICE**.

Immigration and Nationality Act: *See* **INA**.

Immigration and Naturalization Service: *See* **INS**.

Immigration Judge: An administrative law judge under the Department of Justice, Executive Office for Immigration Review, tasked with presiding over immigration hearings that determine whether a foreign national should be removed from the United States.

Immigration Status: A classification used to describe a foreign national's eligibility to enter or remain in the United States, perform work, access certain government benefits, and access other privileges normally afforded to U.S. citizens.

Immutable Characteristic: An unchangeable physical attribute.

Imputed or **Perceived Political Opinion:** A political view attributed to a person that he or she does not actually hold.

In Absentia Order: An order of removal entered by an immigration judge during court proceedings where the respondent fails to appear, after oral warning of the consequences of so doing have been given in the foreign national's language or one s/he understands.

INA—Immigration and Nationality Act: An act codifying the U.S. immigration laws and procedures.

Inadmissible: The inability to demonstrate eligibility for lawful entry into the United States, either abroad, at the border, or during an application to adjust status to a lawful permanent resident, because of a failure to meet the criteria of one or more of the grounds enumerated in § 212(a) of the Immigration and Nationality Act.

Indirect Victim: The eligible family members of a direct victim of U Nonimmigrant visa qualifying criminal activity who has died as a result of murder or manslaughter, or is incapacitated or incompetent and therefore cannot provide information or be helpful in the investigation or prosecution of that crime.

Individual Hearing: A hearing held in immigration court where an immigration judge considers the merits of any application for immigration relief and renders a decision.

INS—Immigration and Naturalization Service: A U.S. government agency that existed prior to the creation of the Department of Homeland Security in 2003, responsibile for both adjudication of immigration benefits, as well as internal enforcement of immigration laws.

Integration: A plan to allow refugees to remain in a country, other than that of their nationality, where they currently reside, integrating them into the legal, social, and economic fabric of that country.

Intending or **Sponsored Immigrant:** A foreign national abroad or in the United States who is sponsored for lawful permanent residency by a family member or employer petitioner.

Interested Government Agency: *See* **IGA**.

Internal Relocation: The ability of an individual who may have suffered persecution to relocate to a safe place within his or her own country.

Internally Displaced People: People who, because of conflict or other disruption to their lives, have been forced to leave their homes and find refuge in another area of their country.

Job Zone: A classification created by the Department of Labor and listed in its O*NET portal that identifies the amount of education, experience, and on-the-job training it believes is necessary to perform work for which a labor certification is required.

Joint Sponsor: An individual willing to obligate him or herself, under the terms of Form I-864, Affidavit of Support, to help a petitioner or sponsor support the family member beneficiary.

Judicial Review: The authority of a court to review the policies and actions of the legislative or executive branch of government.

Jus Sanguinis: Latin term meaning right of the blood, that defines the acquisition or derivation of citizenship through a specific family member at birth.

Jus Soli: Latin term meaning right of the soil that defines the ability of a person to acquire citizenship simply by virtue of being born in a particular country.

Juvenile Court: A state court that has jurisdiction to rule on the custody and care of children.

Labor Condition Application: *See* **LCA**.

Lawful Permanent Resident: *See* **LPR**.

Lawful Status: Foreign nationals who may remain in the United States with permission of the government.

LCA—Labor Condition Application: An application filed with the Department of Labor that demonstrates an employer's ability to pay a foreign national the prevailing wage for the position offered, that no American worker is available and willing to accept the position offered, and that hiring the foreign national will not adversely affect the working conditions of similarly situated workers.

Limited Liability Entity: A particular type of corporate formation with no shareholders, where the owners are protected from liability, but can gain some benefits of profits and losses by being treated as individuals.

LPR—Lawful Permanent Resident: Status given to a foreign national who has immigrated to and intends and is authorized to reside permanently and indefinitely in the United States, with rights to work, travel, and petition for certain qualifying relatives to also be granted LPR status.

Managerial Capacity: An assignment within an organization in which the employee primarily manages the organization, or a department, subdivision, function, or component of the organization, along with other managerial functions.

Marginal Enterprise: An enterprise that does not have the present or future capacity to generate more than enough income to provide a minimal living for the treaty investor and his or her family.

Marriage Fraud: A marriage entered into for the purpose of evading the immigration laws.

Master Calendar Hearing: A brief status hearing that permits an immigration judge to obtain preliminary information about a case and a respondent to plead to the charges against him or her.

Means-Tested Federal Public Benefits: Federal benefits such as food stamps, Supplemental Security Income (SSI), Temporary Assistance to Needy Families (TANF), and Medicaid that are allocated based on a person's income.

Motion to Change Venue: A motion to change the hearing from one geographical location to another.

Motion to Reconsider: A motion that asks an immigration judge to review his or her decision in a case because there has been an error in applying the law, some aspect of the case was overlooked, or there has been a change in the law that affects the judge's prior decision.

Motion to Reopen: A motion made to a USCIS adjudicator, Immigration Court, or the Board of Immigration Appeals, asking them to reconsider a decision based on new evidence that was previously unavailable or undiscoverable.

National Security Entry-Exit System: *See* **NSEERS.**

Naturalization: The process by which a foreign national becomes a citizen of the United States.

New Enterprise: A commercial enterprise established after November 29, 1990.

New Office: The U.S. entity of a multinational company that has been doing business for less than one year.

No Objection Statement: A letter from the J-1 visa holder's home country's government stating that it does not object to the visa holder remaining in the United States rather than returning home as initially required.

NOID—Notice of Intent to Deny: A notice received by a petitioner or applicant from the USCIS indicating that the petition or application already filed is inadequate and that the USCIS intends to deny it unless the recipient provides additional information that may overcome the deficiency.

Nolo Contedere: Latin term meaning "no contest," allowing a defendant in criminal proceedings to neither admit nor deny levied charges, even though s/he will be sentenced as though a guilty plea was entered.

Non-Governmental Organization: An organization that operates independently from the government and, in some cases, may supplement its offerings.

Nonimmigrant: The classification used for foreign nationals with temporary visas designated for specific purposes.

Nonimmigrant Intent: A foreign national's proven intent to return to the country of origin following expiration of period of stay in the United States.

Nonimmigrant Visa: A visa issued to a foreign national who has a permanent residence abroad, but enters the United States for a specific time-limited purpose or activity such as tourism, study, and temporary employment.

Nonimmigrant Waiver: A waiver that allows a foreign national to overcome a ground of inadmissibility for temporary stays in the United States.

Non-refoulement: Fundamental principle of international refugee law that prevents the return of a foreign national to a country where there is reason to believe s/he will be persecuted.

Notice of Hearing: A notice sent to a respondent listing the date, time, and location of an immigration hearing in his or her case.

Notice of Intent to Deny: *See* **NOID.**

Notice of Intent to Offer Evidence: A cover sheet that acts as an index to documents submitted to immigration court as evidence.

Notice of Intent to Revoke: Notice sent to a petitioner by the USCIS with an explanation as to why an approved petition is to be revoked unless the petitioner can provide additional evidence to overcome this.

Notice to Appear: *See* **NTA.**

NSEERS—National Security Entry-Exit Registration System: Also known as special registration, the requirement that foreign citizens entering and exiting the United States register under this system.

NTA—Notice to Appear: A charging document served on a foreign national that begins removal proceedings and notifies him or her of the immigration violations with which s/he is being charged.

Office of Refugee Resettlement: *See* **ORR.**

Office of the Chief Immigration Judge Practice Manual: A guide to uniform procedures, recommendations, and requirements for practicing before the immigration court.

O*NET: Also known as the Occupational Information Network, O*NET is a database developed by the Department of Labor that contains information on hundreds of standardized and occupation-specific classifications, describing skills needed to perform particular jobs and the specific vocational preparation required.

One-Year Deadline: The requirement in immigration law for applicants for asylum to file their application within one year of arrival in the United States

Order of Supervision: An order imposing conditions on an individual's release from detention, which may include reporting requirements, monitoring, and updating of biographic information within a certain time period.

ORR—Office of Refugee Resettlement: A federal office within the Department of Health and Human Services that administers programs and assistance to refugees, unaccompanied children, and victims of torture and trafficking.

Outlying Possessions: Countries such as American Samoa and Swain Island that are possessions of the United States.

Overstayer: A foreign national who remains in the United States longer than the time permitted by the period of stay granted to him or her on entry, without seeking an extension.

Parent-Subsidiary Relationship: An entity that is directly and majority-owned by another entity.

Paroled: Grant of permission to enter the United States to an ineligible foreign national under the legal fiction that s/he is standing at the border waiting for a decision to be made as to whether s/he will be given permission to enter in a particular immigration category.

Parolee: A person granted parole.

Particularly Serious Crime: A crime that, by its nature, indicates that the foreign national poses a danger to the community.

Peer Group: A group or organization comprised of practitioners of the foreign national's occupation.

PERM: The Labor Certification Application requirements for those seeking permanent resident status through employment that involves the Program Electronic Review Management process, or PERM.

Permanent Research Position: Positions that are either tenured, tenure-track, or for a term of unlimited duration, in which the employee will ordinarily have an expectation of continued employment.

Persecution: Suffering that is inflicted on a person that can include actual or threats of physical or other serious harm, such as deprivation of liberty, food, housing, and employment.

Persecution Waiver: A waiver available to a J-1 visa holder who can demonstrate that returning to his or her home country would result in the foreign national being subject to persecution on account of his or her race, religion, or political opinion.

Persecutor Bar: A bar to asylum for anyone found to have ordered, incited, assisted, or participated in any way in the persecution of others on account of one of the enumerated grounds.

Petition: An application filed with the USCIS that must first be approved before a foreign national can apply for a visa to enter the United States or seek particular immigration benefits.

Petition for Review: A request to a United States Court of Appeals to review a decision of the Board of Immigration Appeals or, in limited cases, a decision by Immigration and Customs Enforcement that involves removal, deportation, or exclusion.

Petitioner: A U.S. citizen or lawful permanent resident relative or employer who seeks to sponsor a foreign national family member or employee.

Petty Offense Exception: A waiver that excuses a foreign national from inadmissibility for a crime considered minor because it was either when s/he was under 18 years old and it occurred more than five years before an application for entry to the United States, *or* the maximum penalty for the crime does not exceed one-year of imprisonment *and* the foreign national served six months or less of incarceration.

Physical Presence: The amount of time a person is physically present in the United States.

Polygamous Marriage: A marriage to more than one person at the same time.

Portability: The ability to change employers after a prospective employer files a petition for a change of status and receives proof of that filing from the USCIS, without waiting for the petition to be approved first.

Preemption: Supremacy Clause of the U.S. Constitution requiring federal law to preempt or supersede any inconsistent state or local laws.

Preference Categories: Categories in the immigration system to allocate family sponsored and employment-based visas in order of priority, taking into account a number of different factors such as familial relationship, employment skills, and nationality.

Premium Processing Service: The opportunity to expedite the processing of certain applications with the USCIS for an additional fee.

Prevailing Wage Determination: *See* **PWD**.

Prevailing Wage Rate: The wage that is considered average for a given occupation in the area of intended employment, obtained either through requesting a determination from the Department of Labor, known as a Prevailing Wage Determination, or PWD, or from other legitimate sources.

Prima Facie **Eligibility:** An application filed with the USCIS that meets basic eligibility requirements regarding documents to be submitted without a formal assessment of its factual contents.

Principal Applicant: The main applicant applying for an immigration benefit.

PRM—Bureau of Population, Refugees, and Migration: Bureau within the Department of State that works with the international community and UNHCR to provide durable solutions including repatriation, integration, and resettlement to third countries including the United States, to those who have been displaced and uprooted, while promoting humanitarian practices for refugees.

Priority 1 Refugees: Individuals of any nationality who have a compelling need for protection.

Priority 2 Refugees: Vulnerable groups of special humanitarian concern to the United States that generally includes refugees living in third countries who cannot return to their country of origin and have been identified by the United States Refugee Admissions Program.

Priority 3 Refugees: Foreign nationals of designated nationalities outside of the United States whose family members have already been admitted as refugees, asylees, or lawful permanent residents, who may be permitted to enter as refugees in an attempt to achieve family reunification.

Priority Date: Date a relative or employer-based petition was filed with the USCIS.

Pro Se: An unrepresented respondent in court proceedings.

Productive Work: Duties or activities that would normally be performed by a U.S. worker and/or activities that result in financial gain for the U.S. employer.

Professionals: Members of the professions whose jobs require at least a baccalaureate degree from a U.S. university or college or its foreign equivalent degree and which may ultimately enable the foreign nationals to obtain lawful permanent resident status in the third preference EB-3 category.

Proffer of Information or **Evidence:** An offer or description of evidence used to support facts or arguments in a specific court case

Prosecutorial Discretion: The authority of an agency charged with enforcing a law to decide to what degree to enforce it against a particular individual.

Proximate Harm: Harm suffered immediately as a direct result of the actions of another.

Proxy Marriage: A marriage conducted when one of the contracting parties is not physically present.

Public Access File: A file that maintains documentation pertaining to the Labor Certification Application for a given foreign national employee as well as evidence of the compensation and benefits provided.

PWD—Prevailing Wage Determination: A prevailing wage rate determination issued by the Department of Labor.

Qualifying Derivative Family Members: Specific members of a foreign national's family who can derive immigration benefits and status from the principal applicant or petitioner.

Reasonable Fear Interview: An interview or screening of a previously removed arriving alien, to determine whether s/he shows a reasonable possibility of persecution for one of the five enumerated grounds if returned to his or her country of origin.

Reciprocity Fee: An additional fee a visa applicant must pay depending on the visa classification and nationality of the applicant.

Re-calendared: An action placing an administratively-closed case back on an immigration judge's hearing calendar.

Reciprocity Table: A list maintained by the Department of State in its Foreign Affairs Manual that catalogues which identity and government-issued documents are available in particular countries and the length of time visas can be given to foreign nationals of particular countries, based on the foreign national's own country's issuance of similar visas to U.S. citizens.

Refugee: Any person who is outside any country of such person's nationality or, in the case of a person having no nationality, is outside any country in which such person last habitually resided, and who is unable or unwilling to return to, and is unable or unwilling to avail himself or herself of the protection of that country, because of persecution or a well-founded fear of persecution on account of race, religion, nationality, membership in a particular social group, or political opinion.

Refugee Support Centers: Agency funded by the Bureau of Population, Refugees, and Migration, or PRM, and run by a non-governmental organization with specially trained staff who prepare the case for consideration for a resettlement request.

Regional Center: A business entity that coordinates investments, which can include both foreign and domestic financing, within a defined geographical area in compliance with the EB-5 preference category requirements.

Relative Petition: A petition filed by a parent, spouse, or adult child (petitioner) for the benefit of a foreign national (beneficiary) who can demonstrate a legal family relationship that then forms the basis of an application by the beneficiary to either apply for an immigrant visa at a consular office abroad or adjust status to become a lawful permanent resident in the United States, once a visa number is available

Religious Occupation: Engagement in activities that relate to a traditional religious function.

Religious Vocation: A position where the foreign national has undertaken a lifelong commitment to a religious denomination, demonstrated by the adoption of vows such as for a nun or a monk.

Religious Workers: A minister or person working in a professional religious occupation or vocation, or has worked for the religious group in a religious occupation for at least two years immediately preceding the filing of a petition.

Remanded: Returning a case back to a lower court for reconsideration, taking into account the decision and guidance of the higher court.

Removal: Formerly referred to as deportation, the administrative process by which the U.S. government determines whether a noncitizen can be expelled from the United States due to a violation of federal immigration law.

Removal Period: A 90-day period after a final order of removal has been issued, when a foreign national in detention is to be returned to his or her home country or released on an Order of Supervision.

Removal Proceedings: An administrative proceeding in U.S. immigration court to determine whether a foreign national should be removed from the United States.

Repatriation: The safe return of refugees to their country of origin or citizenship based on a plan developed by the UNHCR, if involved, the U.S. Department of State, and other governments.

Request for Evidence: *See* **RFE.**

Respondent: A foreign national placed into removal proceedings because of a violation of immigration laws.

RFE—Request for Evidence: A request from the USCIS to provide supplemental or missing evidence to assist in adjudication of an application or petition before the agency.

Section 322 Citizenship: A process designed for minor children under 18 years of age, born to a U.S. citizen parent who may not have lived in the country for the requisite period, to acquire citizenship by looking to the length of time his or her grandparent has lived in the United States in order to be eligible for citizenship.

SEVIS—Student and Exchange Visitor Information System: A database managed by ICE used to track student information such as enrollment, graduation, changes to program, maintenance of required course load, etc.

SEVP—Student and Exchange Visitor Program: A branch of U.S. Immigration and Customs Enforcement, or ICE, which manages schools, nonimmigrant students in the F and M visa classifications, and their dependents through a Designated School Official whose role is to guide the foreign student through the visa application process.

SIJ—Special Immigrant Juvenile: An immigration status obtained through self-petition provided to abused, neglected, or abandoned juveniles who cannot be reunited with one or both parents.

Skilled Workers: Foreign nationals whose jobs require a minimum of two years of training or work experience that is not temporary or seasonal, and which may ultimately enable the foreign nationals to obtain lawful permanent resident status in the third preference EB-3 category.

Skills List: A list of skills cited by a foreign country that subject a J-1 visa holder to the two-year home residency requirement.

Special Immigrant Juvenile: *See* **SIJ.**

Specialized Knowledge: Special knowledge of a company's products, services, equipment, techniques, management, or other interests and its application in international markets; or an advanced level of knowledge or expertise in the organization's processes and procedures.

Specialty Occupation: A position that requires theoretical and practical application of a body of highly specialized knowledge in fields of human endeavor, and which requires the attainment of a bachelor's degree or higher in a specific specialty, or its equivalent, as a minimum for entry into the occupation in the United States.

Specific Vocational Preparation: *See* **SVP.**

Sponsor: *See* **Petitioner.**

Stateless: A person with no legal or formal nationality or citizenship who therefore cannot receive protection from any government.

Statutory Period: The length of time required to qualify for naturalization, which can generally be either a three- or five-year period.

STEM: Acronym for Science, Technology, Engineering, and Math educational subjects.

Student and Exchange Visitor Information System: *See* **SEVIS.**

Student and Exchange Visitor Program: *See* **SEVP.**

Sua Sponte: Latin term acknowledging unilateral action.

Subsidiary: A firm, corporation, or other legal entity of which a parent owns, directly or indirectly, more than half and exercises control; or owns, directly or indirectly, 50 percent of a 50-50 joint venture and has equal control and veto power over the entity; or owns, directly or indirectly, less than half of the entity, but in fact controls the entity.

SVP—Specific Vocational Preparation: The amount of time required by a typical worker to learn the techniques, acquire the information, and develop the abilities needed for average performance in a specific work situation.

Targeted Employment Area: An area that, at the time of investment by an EB-5 investor, is rural or has experienced unemployment of at least 150 percent of the national average.

Temporary Protected Status: *See* **TPS**.

TN Professional: A citizen of Mexico or Canada who meets the qualifications of a professional and can obtain a TN visa created by the North American Free Trade Agreement, or NAFTA, to work in the United States.

TPS—Temporary Protected Status: Temporary immigration status that allows foreign nationals of countries affected by civil war, environmental disasters such as earthquakes, major health concerns, or other temporary emergency conditions that make it unsafe to return home, to remain in the United States legally with permission to work and travel on advanced parole for a specified but extendable period of time.

Trafficked: The trafficking of a foreign national into the United States to perform acts in which a commercial sex act is induced by force, fraud, or coercion, or in which the person induced to perform such act has not attained 18 years of age; or the recruitment, harboring, transportation, provision, or obtaining of a person for labor or services, through the use of force, fraud, or coercion for the purpose of subjection to involuntary servitude, peonage, debt bondage, or slavery.

Travel Document: An official U.S. government issued document used to facilitate the international travel of individuals that can include a passport or other government-issued identity document authorizing travel.

Treaty Investor: A national of a treaty country with which the United States maintains a treaty of commerce and navigation who is admitted to the United States solely to develop and direct the operations of an enterprise in which he has invested, or of an enterprise in which he is actively in the process of investing, a substantial amount of capital.

Treaty Trader: A national of a treaty country with which the United States maintains a treaty of commerce and navigation who is admitted to the United States solely to carry on substantial trade, including trade in services or trade in technology, principally between the United States and the foreign state of which he is a national.

Troubled Business: A business that has been in existence for a least two years, has incurred a net loss for accounting purposes during the 12- or 24-four month period prior to the date the foreign national's Form I-526, Immigrant Petition by Alien Entrepreneur is accepted by the USCIS, and the loss for such period is at least equal to 20 percent of the troubled business' net worth prior to such loss.

Two-Year Home Residency Requirement: The requirement that J-1 visa holders return to their home country or place of last residence abroad for a two-year period after completing a J-1 program before seeking other immigration benefits.

Unaccompanied Minors or Children: Any child under the age of 18 without legal immigration status in the United States who arrives without a parent or legal guardian capable of providing care and physical custody.

Undocumented or **Unauthorized Foreign National:** A foreign national who is without legal immigration status in the United States.

UNHCR—United Nations High Commissioner for Refugees: A body created by the United Nations and given the responsibility to lead and coordinate international action for the worldwide protection of refugees.

United Nations High Commissioner for Refugees: *See* **UNHCR.**

United States Citizen: A status that enables a person to have all the benefits and protection of the U.S. government, obtained either at birth, through adoption or naturalization, or by acquiring or deriving status through parents or grandparents.

United States Refugee Admissions Program: *See* **USRAP.**

Unlawful Presence: Present in the United States without permission, which can include a foreign national who entered without being admitted, inspected, or paroled, or someone who entered legally but remained beyond the admission period initially granted without requesting permission to extend that stay or to change to a different category.

Unskilled or **Other Workers:** Foreign nationals capable of filling positions that require less than two years' training or experience that is not temporary or seasonal, which may lead to a grant of lawful permanent resident status in the third preference EB-3 category.

U.S. Workers: U.S. citizens, lawful permanent residents, asylees, refugees, or any other person granted permission to work by the USCIS.

USCIS or **CIS—U.S. Citizenship and Immigration Service:** An agency of the Department of Homeland Security overseeing legal immigration to the United States by approving petitions, affirmative asylum applications, applications for adjustment of status, citizenship, and other immigration benefits.

USCIS Service Center: Service centers located in various parts of the country that process particular immigration applications depending on the type of form and the geographical location of the applicant or petitioner.

USRAP—The United States Refugee Admissions Program: An agency made up of three other government agencies: the Bureau of Population, Refugees, and Migration, or PRM, within the Department of State; the USCIS within the Department of Homeland Security; and the Office of Refugee Resettlement within the Department of Health and Human Services and representatives from Non-Governmental Organizations that oversees refugee admissions.

VAWA—Violence Against Women Act: Federal legislation first passed in 1994 to provide federal protection to victims of domestic violence, including immigrants, enabling abused spouses of U.S. citizens or LPRs to self-petition for lawful status without the need for spousal sponsorship.

Violence Against Women Act: *See* **VAWA.**

Visa: An official U.S. government-issued document placed in a foreign national's passport that allows him or her to travel to and apply for admission to the United States at a designated border or port of entry.

Visa Bulletin: A document prepared and published by the U.S. Department of State that provides information on the processing dates and allocation and availability of immigration visas.

Visa Exempt: The ability to enter the United States temporarily from particular countries, such as Canada or Bermuda, without the need for a foreign national to obtain a visa stamp.

Visa Waiver Program: *See* **VWP.**

Voluntary Departure: Permission given to a foreign national to depart the United States, other than at government expense, within a designated period of time.

VWP—Visa Waiver Program: A program that allows citizens from designated countries to travel to the United States without a visa for stays of 90 days or less, when they meet certain eligibility requirements.

Waiver: Permits an otherwise ineligible foreign national, i.e. who is inadmissible or removable, to enter or remain in the United States because of special circumstances that apply to his or her case.

Withholding of Removal: An order by an immigration judge forestalling a foreign national's removal to a country where it has been shown it is more likely than not that harm based on one of the enumerated grounds will occur, yet allowing removal to a third country that provides assurances it will not return the person to the country where harm is feared.

Index

A-1/A-2 nonimmigrant visa (Foreign government officials), 178
AAO. *See* Administrative Appeals Office
ABA. *See* American Bar Association
Abandonment of lawful permanent resident status, 578
Academic field, EB-1B immigrant visa, 317
Accelerated Rehabilitative Disposition, 465
Accompanying relative, 261
Accredited representatives
   generally, 30
   defined, 517
   practice of immigration law and, 618–620
   removal proceedings and, 517
Acquisition, citizenship by, 604–608
   generally, 571
   children born in wedlock outside United States, 606–607
   children born out of wedlock outside United States, 608–609
   N–600, Application for Certificate of Citizenship, 604
Actual wage
   defined, 122
   H-1B nonimmigrant visa, 127–128
ACWIA (American Competitiveness and Workforce Improvement Act of 1998), 121, 343
AC21 (American Competitiveness in the 21st Century Act of 2000), 130
Adam Walsh Child Protection and Safety Act of 2006 (AWA)
   family-sponsored immigration, 259
   fiancé(e)s, 300
Adjustment of status, 270–290
   advanced parole. *See* Advanced parole
   affidavit of support. *See* Affidavit of support
   asylees. *See* Asylees and refugees
   battered spouse petitions and. *See* Violence Against Women Act
   certified dispositions and, 274, 282
   Child Status Protection Act. *See* Children
   death of petitioner and, 265–268
   employment-based, 312, 317, 326, 363, 369, 374
   family-sponsored, 270–290
   household members, 279
   INA § 245(i), 287–290
      approvable when filed, defined, 288
      grandfathered, 288
      derivative qualifying family members for, 288
      petition or labor certification application, 288
   inadmissibility issues, 284–290
   ineligible persons for, 272
   joint sponsors, 279. *See* Affidavit of support
   medical examinations, 276–278
   overview, 270–271
   provisional waiver, 284–287
   refugees, 240–241. *See* Asylees and refugees
   relief from removal, 553
   religious workers, 368–375
   Special Immigrant Juveniles, 445–448
   sponsored immigrants, 278
   T nonimmigrant visa, 439–441
   U nonimmigrant visa, 422–426
   unlawful presence bar and, 284–287
   waivers, 284–290
   widow(er)s, 266–269
Administrative Appeals Office (AAO), 18, 264
Administrative closure, 546–549
Admission and admitted,
   defined, 457
   lawful permanent residents and, 458–459
Advanced degree, 327
Advanced degree professionals (EB-2 immigrant visa), 327–364
Advanced parole, 235
Adverse effect wage rate, 173
Advisory opinion, 86
Affidavit of Relationship (AOR), 239–240. *See also* Asylees and refugees
Affidavit of support,
   generally 265–266
   household member, 279
   intending immigrant, 278
   joint sponsor, 279
   petitioner and, 278–282
   public charge and, 474–475
   substitution of petitioner, 266
Affiliate, L-1A/L-1B nonimmigrant visa, 109
Affirmative asylum 216–222. *See also* Asylees and refugees
Affirmative VAWA petitions, 403
Afghanistan, translators and interpreters, 368
Ageing out. *See* Child Status Protection Act
Agents as petitioners for O and P nonimmigrant visa, 140, 142, 146, 157
Age requirements for naturalization, 573
Aggravated felony crimes
   as bar to asylum, 200
   defined, 481
   inadmissibility for, 481
Agricultural work of temporary or seasonal nature. *See* H-2A nonimmigrant visa, 172–174
Aliens with extraordinary ability, 314–317. *See also* EB-1A immigrant visa
American Bar Association (ABA), 641
American Competitiveness and Workforce Improvement Act of 1998 (ACWIA), 121, 343
American Competitiveness in the 21st Century Act of 2000
   EB-2/EB-3 immigrant visa, 364
   H-1B nonimmigrant visa, 130, 133
American Immigration Lawyers Association, 644
Amnesty International, 216
Antiterrorism and Effective Death Penalty Act of 1996 (AEDPA), 11
AOR (Affidavit of Relationship). *See* Asylees and refugees
Appeals
   to Board of Immigration Appeals, 549–551
   EOIR-26, Notice of Appeal from a Decision of an Immigration Judge, 550
   EOIR 27, Notice of Appearance as Attorney or Legal Representative, 550
   to Federal Courts, 551–552
   from Immigration Court, 549–551
Appeals practice, 549

667

AR-11, Change of Address, 495
Armed forces members
    EB-4 immigrant visa, 368
    naturalization of, 575–576, 578
Arriving aliens, 11
    asylum, 222
    defined, 222
Artists and entertainers, 156–166. *See also* P-2/P-3 nonimmigrant visa
Arts
    employment-based immigration of aliens with extraordinary ability in, 314–317. *See also* EB-1 immigrant visa (Priority workers)
    individuals with extraordinary ability in, 140–155. *See also* O-1B nonimmigrant visa
Asylees and refugees
    adjustment of status
        asylees, 230
        refugees, 240–241
    admissions plan, 237
    Affidavit of relationship for refugees, 239–240
    affirmative asylum requests, 216–222
        compiling the application, 216–221
    agents of persecution, 187
    aggravated felonies and, 200
    arriving aliens and, 222
    bars to eligibility, 197–202
    benefits of, 230–231
    burden of proof, 196–197
    Central American Minors Refugee/Parole Program. *See* Central American Minors Refugee/Parole Program
    changed circumstances, 198
    children, 217
    compared, 241–243
    Convention Against Torture compared, 233–234
    credibility, 196–197
    credible fear interviews, 229–230
    defensive asylum claims, 221–226
    definitions, 183–190
        agents of persecution, 187
        past persecution,187–189
        persecution,184–186
        well-founded fear of future persecution,189–190
    denial of, 202–203
    de novo review, 221
    determination of status, 237–239
    DNA testing, 240
    DS-7656, Affidavit of Relationship (AOR), 239
    Employment Authorization Document for asylum applicants, 228–229
    Employment Authorization Document clock, 228
    enumerated grounds for, 190–196
    EOIR-28, Notice of Entry of Appearance as Attorney or Representative Before the Immigration Court, 223
    expedited removal procedures, 223
    extraordinary circumstances, 198
    family reunification, 239–240
    firm resettlement bar, 200–201
    frivolous applications, 226–227
    future persecution, 198–190
    humanitarian, 188–189
    I-730, Refugee/Asylee Relative Petition, 240
    in-country processing, 238
    individual hearings, 226
    integration, 238
    internally displaced persons, 183
    internal relocation, 188
    membership in a particular social group as grounds for, 192–194
        clan membership, 192–193
        domestic violence, 194
        family, 193
        female genital circumcision or mutilation, 4,192–193
        gender-based, 193
        Homosexuality, 193
        immutable characteristics, 192
        particularity, 194
        sexual orientation, 193
        social distinction, 194
    multiple applications as bar, 202
    nationality as grounds for, 192
    nexus of grounds for, 190
    non-governmental organizations, 237
    Office of Refugee Resettlement, 13–14, 237
    one-year deadline, 198–199
        changed circumstances exception, 198
        extraordinary circumstances exception, 198
        unaccompanied minors or children and, 198
    overstayers and, 222
    particularly serious crimes and, 200
    past persecution, 187–189
    persecution, 184–186
    persecutor bar, 199–200
    political opinion as grounds for, 195–196
        imputed or perceived political opinion, 195
    Priority 1 refugees, 238
    Priority 2 refugees, 238
    Priority 3 refugees, 238–239
    PRM. *See* Bureau of Population, Refugees, and Migration
    procedure, 203–229
    race as grounds for, 191
    reasonable fear interviews, 229–230
    Reception and Placement Program, 241
    Refugee Processing Center, 240
    Refugee Support Centers, 238
    refugees compared, 241–243
    religion as grounds for, 191–192, 215–216
    repatriation, 238
    revocation of, 202–203
    safe third country as bar, 201–202
    security danger as bar, 202
    sexual orientation, 192–193
    social group membership, 192–194
    sources of law, 182–183
    spouses, 217
    stateless persons, 183
    termination of, 202–203
    terrorism bar, 202
    United States Refugee Admissions Program, 237–238
    Volags (voluntary agencies), 240
    well-founded fear of future persecution, 189–190
    withholding of removal compared, 233–234
Asylum Office, 203, 507
Athletes,
    employment-based immigration of aliens with extraordinary ability in, 314–317. *See also* EB-1 immigrant visa (Priority workers)
    O-1A nonimmigrant visa, 140–155. *See also* O-1A nonimmigrant visa
    P-1 nonimmigrant visa, 156–166. *See also* P-1 nonimmigrant visa
Attestation letters for EB-4 immigrant visa, 371

Attorneys. *See* Practice of immigration law
Attorneys' fees
  payment of, 632
  representation agreements, 627
  service fee agreements, 630–631
Au pair program, 81
Audits in PERM process, 352
Australia, E-3 nonimmigrant visa, 134
Authorized entity, 140
Authorized legal representatives in removal proceedings, 517
AWA. *See also* Adam Walsh Child Protection and Safety Act of 2006
  family-sponsored immigration, 259
  fiancé(e)s, 300

B-1 nonimmigrant visa (Temporary visitors for business), 61–70
  applications, 69–70
  commercial workers, 68
  consulates and consular processing, 60–65
  DS-160, Online Nonimmigrant Visa Application, 70
  industrial workers, 68
  investors, 68–69
  in lieu of H-1B nonimmigrant visa and, 67–68
  overview, 61–64
  productive work, 61, 63
  prohibited reasons for entry, 67
  purposes, 63
  reasons for seeking classification, 66–69
  requirements for entry, 64–66
  valid uses of, 66
  Visa Waiver Program, 64–65
B-2 nonimmigrant visa (Temporary visitors for pleasure), 61–70
BALCA. *See* Board of Alien Labor Certification Appeals
Battered spouse self-petition. *See* Violence Against Women Act
BEA (Bureau of Economic Analysis), 378
Benching, defined, 128
Beneficiary, defined, 94
Bermuda, visa exempt status, 48–49
BIA. *See* Board of Immigration Appeals
BIA recognized organizations, 618–619
Biometrics, 12
Birthright citizenship, 572
Blanket L nonimmigrant visa, 117–118

Board of Alien Labor Certification Appeals (BALCA)
  employment-based immigration, 307
  overview, 18
  PERM process, 345, 352
Board of Immigration Appeals (BIA)
  Board of Immigration Appeals Practice Manual, 528, 550
  appeals to, 549–551
  authority of, 13, 15
  case law, 18
  deportation, 491
  EOIR-33/BIA, Alien's Change of Address Form/Board of Immigration Appeals, 514
  ethical issues, 640
  forms, 30
  individual hearings, 528
  nonprofit organizations recognized by, 618–620
  Notice to Appear, 510
  paralegals, 650
  relief from removal, 557, 560
  removal proceedings, 506. *See also* Removal proceedings
  rules of conduct, 647
Bona fide nonprofit religious organizations, 167
Bona fide relationships
  defined, 253
  family sponsored immigration, 253–254
Bonds
  detention and, 539–531
  expedited removal and, 538
  mandatory detention, and, 541
  Voluntary Departure, and, 535–537
Bracero Program, 9
Branch of business for L-1A/L-1B nonimmigrant visa, 109
Brazil, E-1/E-2 nonimmigrant visa, 97
Burden of proof in asylum claims, 196–197
Bureau for Democracy, Human Rights, and Labor, 215
Bureau of Consular Affairs. *See also* Consulates and consular processing
  generally, 15
  nonimmigrant visas, 52
  website, 19
Bureau of Immigration and Naturalization, 8
Bureau of Labor Statistics, 127

Bureau of Population, Refugees, and Migration (PRM)
  Central American Minors Refugee/Parole Program, 453
  refugees, 237, 240
  role of, 14–15
Burlingame-Seward Treaty of 1868, 6
Business necessity in PERM process, 332–334
Business plan for E-1/E-2 nonimmigrant visa, 101

C-1 nonimmigrant visa (Transit), 70
CAM. *See* Central American Minors Refugee/Parole Program
Canada
  professionals with TN nonimmigrant visa, 135–137. *See also* TN nonimmigrant visa
  visa exempt status, 48–49
Cancellation of removal
  battered spouses, children and parents, 561–565
  LPR, 556–558
  NACARA cancellation, 567
  non-LPR cancellation, 558–561
Cap-exempt occupations, 129
Cap gap, 131
Capital of investors, 376–377
Cap on H-1B nonimmigrant visa, 129–130
Case assessment, 620–624
Case management system, 638–639
Case preparation in removal proceedings, 529–531
CBP. *See* Customs and Border Protection
Central American Minors Refugee/Parole Program (CAM), 451–453
  DS-7699, Affidavit of Relationship, 452–453
  I-134, Affidavit of Support, 452
Certified dispositions and adjustment of status applications, 274, 282
Change of address, deportation for failure to file, 495
Change of venue in removal proceedings, 513, 544–546
Changing nonimmigrant visa status, 54–60
Chargeability, family sponsored immigration and, 250–251
Child Citizenship Act of 2000
  acquisition, citizenship by, 604
  derivative citizenship, 601

Index

Child Status Protection Act of 2002 (CSPA)
  asylum, 217–218, 231
  children, petitions by, 390
  family-sponsored immigration, 262–264
  lawful permanent residents, children of, 263–264
  refugees, 240
  U.S. citizens, children of, 262–263
Child support, effect of nonpayment on naturalization, 585
Children,
  acquisition of citizenship, 604–611
  adopted, 257
    eligibility for citizenship, 601–602, 604, 610
    eligibility for VAWA, 384, 389–403
  aged-out. *See* Child Status Protection Act
  asylum applications, 217
  cancellation of removal and, 558–561
  Central American Minors Refugee/Parole Program. *See* Central American Minors Refugee/Parole Program, 451–453
  Child Status Protection Act. *See* Child Status Protection Act of 2000
  DACA. *See* Deferred Action for Childhood Arrivals
  dependency order for, 443–444
  derivative citizenship for, 601–603
  derivative of immediate relative, 267
  family preference category, 247–250
  family-sponsored immigration, 257–259, 261
  immediate relative petition, 251, 253–261
  INA § 245(i), grandfathering, 288
  INA § 322 citizenship, 609–611
  orphans, defined as child, 257
  relative petition for, 257
  son or daughter as preference relative, 247–250
  Special Immigrant Juvenile, 443–448
  step-children, 257, 604
  T nonimmigrant visas and, 427–430
  U nonimmigrant visas and, 409–410
  unaccompanied minor or child
    asylum, 198
    defined, 198

Chile and H-1B1 nonimmigrant visa, 133–134
China
  Cultural Revolution, 188
  E-1/E-2 nonimmigrant visa, 97
  EB-2 immigrant visa, 363
  family planning policy as social group, 195–196
  family sponsored immigration, 249
  reciprocity fees, 53
Chinese Exclusion Act of 1882, 6–7, 572
Citizenship
  by acquisition, 604–608. *See also* Acquisition, citizenship by
  advantages of, 571
  birth in United States, based on, 572
  birthright citizenship, 572
  children whose parents regularly live abroad, 608–611. *See also* Section 322 citizenship
  denaturalization, 613–614
  derivative citizenship, 601–604. *See also* Derivative citizenship
  DS-2029, Application for Consular Report of Birth Abroad of a Citizen of the United States of America, 605
  expatriation, 611–613
  INA § 322 citizenship, 608–611. *See also* Section 322 citizenship
  inadmissibility based on ineligibility for, 480
  jus sanguinis, 570–571
  jus soli, 570
  loss of, 611–614
  naturalization, based on, 573–597. *See also* Naturalization
  outlying possessions, 572
  overview, 569–570, 614–615
  relinquishment of. *See* Expatriation
  sources of law, 570–571
Citizenship and Immigration Service. *See* United States Citizenship and Immigration Service
Civics requirement for naturalization, 587–588
Civil Rights Act of 1964, nonimmigrant visas, 46
Civil surgeon, defined, 277
Civil war and asylum, 186
Clan or tribe affiliation and asylum, 192–193
Class A point of entry, 107

Closing argument in removal proceedings, 532
Code of Ethics and Professional Responsibility, 640–641, 645
Code of Federal Regulations, 18
Commerce Clause, 16
Commercial enterprise, 375–377
Commercial workers with B-1 nonimmigrant visa, 68
Compensation for R-1 nonimmigrant visa religious workers, 167
Computer systems analysts, TN nonimmigrant visa for, 135
Conditional lawful permanent resident status, 295–298
Confidentiality of VAWA proceedings, 403
Conflicts of interest, 644–646
Congress, authority of, 2, 13
Constitution, U.S.
  citizenship, 572
  Commerce Clause, 16
  Due Process Clause, 5
  expatriation, 611
  inadmissibility, 464
  naturalization, 596
  Naturalization Clause, 16
  as source of law, 16–17
  Supremacy Clause, 17
Consulates and consular processing
  admission applications, 15, 457, 485
  authorized legal representatives, 517
  defined, 48
  Diversity Immigrant Visa Program, 380–381
  doctrine of consular nonreviewability, 61
  DOS maintaining, 14
  I-797, Notice of Action Approval, 36
  immigrant visas, 24–26, 264, 290–295
  inadmissibility or deportation, 457, 469, 485, 488, 501
  nonimmigrant visas, 20, 46, 48–53, 55
  practice of immigration law, 643, 650
  Voluntary Departure, 537
  waiver to facilitate temporary admission, 488
Consultations for O-1A nonimmigrant visa, 143–144
Continuances in removal proceedings, 545
Continued presence
  relief from removal, 554–555
  T nonimmigrant visa, 429–430

Continuous residency requirement for naturalization, 576–579
Control as factor in qualifying for L-1A/L-1B nonimmigrant visa, 109
Controlled Substances Act of 1970, 463
Controlled substances offenses
   deportation, 493
   inadmissibility, 469
Convention, defined, 182
Convention Against Torture and Other Cruel, Inhuman, or Degrading Treatment or Punishment, 232–234
   asylum and withholding of removal compared, 233–234
   deportation, 492
   expedited removal proceedings, 538
Convention Relating to the Status of Refugees (1951), 20, 182–184, 191
Convictions,
   defined, 464–465
   effect of probation on, 466
   inadmissibility for, 464–466
   juvenile delinquency and, 465
Corporate offices, practice of immigration law in, 618
CPT (Curricular Practical Training) in F-1/M-1 nonimmigrant visa, 77
Credibility in asylum claims, 196–197
Credible fear
   defined, 229
   interviews, 229–230
Crew members (D nonimmigrant visa), 70
Crimes of moral turpitude
   deportation for, 490, 492
   inadmissibility for, 467–468
Crimes of violence, deportation for, 494
Criminal offenses. See also Aggravated felony crimes; specific offense
   deportation, 490–494
   inadmissibility, 464–472
Criminal records, obtaining, 623–624
Cross-chargeability in family petitions 250–251
Cross-examination in removal proceedings, 532
CSPA. See Child Status Protection Act of 2002
Cuba, relief from removal for persons from, 567

Cultural exchange
   H-3 nonimmigrant visa, 90–91
   program sponsors for J-1 nonimmigrant visa, 83
   Q nonimmigrant visa, 89–90
Culturally unique programs for P-2/P-3 nonimmigrant visa, 164–165
Curricular Practical Training (CPT) for F-1/M-1 nonimmigrant visa, 77
Customs and Border Protection (CBP)
   generally, 3
   admission, 457
   authority of, 14–16
   deportation, 460, 502
   expedited removal proceedings, 537
   Freedom of Information Act, 623
   I-94, Arrival/Departure Card, 23, 36
   immigration file, obtaining copy of, 521
   inadmissibility, 480, 502
   Notice to Appear, 507
   removal proceedings, 507. See also Removal proceedings
   withholding of removal, 232

D nonimmigrant visa (Crew member), 70
DACA. See Deferred Action for Childhood Arrivals
Death, effect on family sponsored immigration. See also Widow(er)s.
   benefits available upon death after petition filed, 268–269
   benefits available upon death before petition filed, 266–268
Death threats as persecution, 185
DED (Deferred Enforced Departure), 235–237
Defensive asylum claims, 221–226
Defensive VAWA applications, 403
Deferral of removal, 233
Deferred Action for Childhood Arrivals (DACA), 449–451
   generally, 548
   advanced parole, 235
   I-131, Application for a Travel Document, 450
   I-765, Application for Employment Authorization, 450
   I-821D, Consideration of Deferred Action for Childhood Arrivals, 450
   overview, 384

Deferred action status in VAWA proceedings, 401–402
Deferred Enforced Departure (DED), 235–237
   Temporary protected status compared with, 236–237
Degree equivalency, 123–124, 329, 336, 364
Denaturalization, 506, 613–614
De novo review in removal proceedings, 221
Department of Homeland Security (DHS), 13
   generally, 2
   Administrative Appeals Office. See Administrative Appeals Office
   authority of, 14–15
   CBP. See Customs and Border Protection
   ICE. See Immigration and Customs Enforcement
   nonprofit organizations recognized by, 619–620
   regulations, 18
   rules of conduct, 647
   USCIS. See United States Citizenship and Immigration Service
Department of Justice (DOJ)
   generally, 8, 10
   Board of Immigration Appeals. See Board of Immigration Appeals
   Executive Office for Immigration Review. See Executive Office for Immigration Review
   rules of conduct, 647
   T nonimmigrant visa, 430–431
Department of Labor (DOL)
   generally, 2
   adjustment of status, 288
   authority of, 14–15
   BALCA. See Board of Alien Labor Certification Appeals
   Bureau of Labor Statistics, 127
   Employment and Training Administrative Office of Foreign Labor Certification, 15, 307
   employment-based immigration, 306–307, 311–313
   Foreign Labor Certification Data Center, 127–128
   Foreign Labor Certification Permanent Online System, 351

Labor Condition Application. *See*
    Labor Condition Application
National Interest Waiver, 365
National Prevailing Wage Center,
    338, 343
Occupational Employment Statistics,
    338, 343
O*Net. *See* Occupational Information
    Network
paralegals, 649
PERM process, 329–364. *See also*
    PERM process
regulations, 18
Wage and Hour Division, 48, 126
Department of State (DOS)
  generally, 2
  advisory opinions, 86
  authority of, 14–16
  B-1/B-2 nonimmigrant visa, 64
  Bureau of Consular Affairs. *See*
    Bureau of Consular Affairs
  Consular Office, 15
  consular processing of immigrant
    visas, 291, 293
  Doctrine of Consular
    Nonreviewability, 61
  Foreign Affairs Manual. *See* Foreign
    Affairs Manual
  nonimmigrant visas, 44, 48, 51–52,
    54–55
  paralegals, 649–650
  regulations, 18
Dependency orders for Special
    Immigrant Juveniles, 443–444
Dependent support, effect of
    nonpayment on naturalization,
    585
Deportation
  agencies involved, 500–502
  AR-11, Change of Address, 495
  change of address, failure to file, 495,
    514
  consulates and consular processing,
    457, 469, 485, 488, 501
  controlled substances offenses, 493
  crimes of moral turpitude, 490, 492
  crimes of violence, 494
  criminal offenses, 490–494
  domestic violence offenses, 494
  drug offenses, 493
  entered without inspection, or EWI,
    3, 222, 271, 402, 417, 448, 476, 481,
    511, 531, 558
  EOIR 33/IC, Alien's Change of
    Address Form, 514
  failure to register, 495
  false claim to citizenship, 479, 495,
    497, 499, 586
  false documents, 495
  firearms offenses, 493
  general crimes, 490–493
  grounds for, 488–496
  inadmissibility at time of entry or
    adjustment of status, 489–490
  inadmissibility compared, 496–500,
    502
  miscellaneous crimes, 494
  overview, 455–456, 503
  public charges, 495–496
  removal proceedings. *See* Removal
    proceedings
  security-related grounds, 495
  voting unlawfully, 496
  weapons offenses, 493
Derivative citizenship, 601–604
  generally, 571
  chart, 602
  I-912, Request for Fee Waiver, 603
  N-600, Application for Certificate of
    Citizenship, 603–604
  petitions, 603–604
Derivative relatives. *See also* Children;
    Spouses
  in asylum applications, 217
  in family-sponsored immigration, 261
Designated school officials in F-1/M-1
    nonimmigrant visa, 71
Detention, 539–543
  alternatives to detention, 540–541
  bond. *See* Bonds
  factors considered, 540
  final order of removal, 541
  habeas corpus, 543
  I-765, Application for Employment
    Authorization, 542
  mandatory detention, 541–543
  order of supervision, 542
  removal period, 541
  terrorism, 539
Detention without trial, as persecution,
    185
Development, Relief, and Education for
    Alien Minors Act (DREAM
    ACT—proposed), 449–450
DHS. *See* Department of Homeland
    Security
Diagnostic and Statistical Manual of
    Mental Disorder (DSM-V), 589
Dillingham Commission, 7
Director's Guild Awards recipients, 150
Direct victims for U nonimmigrant visa,
    409
Disability exception to naturalization
    requirements, 589–595
Disciplinary actions, 647
Discrimination
  nationality as basis of, 192
  on racial grounds, 191
  religious, 191–192
Displaced Persons Act of 1948, 8
Diversity Immigrant Visa Program,
    380–381
DNA testing
  family-sponsored immigration, 260,
    269
  refugees, 240
  T nonimmigrant visa, 438
Doctrine of consular nonreviewability,
    61
Document fraud, 479, 495, 563
Document retention in PERM process,
    351–352
Documents. *See specific document*
DOJ. *See* Department of Justice
DOL. *See* Department of Labor
Domestic violence
  deportation, 494
    VAWA proceedings. *See* Violence
      Against Women Act of 1994
DOS. *See* Department of State
DREAM Act (Development, Relief, and
    Education for Alien Minors
    Act—proposed), 449–450
Drug addicts, inadmissibility of, 463
Drug offenses
  deportation, 493
  inadmissibility, 469
DS-156E, Nonimmigrant Treaty
    Trader/Investor Visa
    Application, 105
DS-160, Online Nonimmigrant Visa
    Application
  generally, 52
  B-1/B-2 nonimmigrant visa, 70
  E-1/E-2 nonimmigrant visa, 105
  F-1/M-1 nonimmigrant visa, 71, 75
  T nonimmigrant visa, 437
DS-260, Immigrant Visa and Alien
    Registration, 292
DS-261, Online Choice of Address and
    Agent, 291
DS-2019, Certificate of Eligibility for
    Exchange Visitor (J-1)
    Nonimmigrant visa, 83–84,
    86, 89

DS-2029, Application for Consular Report of Birth Abroad of a Citizen of the United States of America, 605
DS-7002, Training/Internship Placement Plan, 84
DS-7656, Affidavit of Relationship (AOR), 239
DS-7699, Affidavit of Relationship, 452–453
DSM-V (Diagnostic and Statistical Manual of Mental Disorder), 589
Dual intent, 115
Dual representation, 644–645
Due Process Clause, 5
Due process in removal proceedings, 506
Duration of status
    defined, 75
    E-1/E-2 nonimmigrant visa, 106
    F-1/M-1 nonimmigrant visa, 75–76
    H-1B nonimmigrant visa, 130
    L-1A/L-1B nonimmigrant visa, 115–116
    O-1A/O-1B nonimmigrant visa, 147
    R-1 nonimmigrant visa, 168
    TN nonimmigrant visa, 136–137

E-Verify, 78
E-1/E-2 nonimmigrant visa (Treaty traders/Treaty investors), 95–106
    applications, 104–105
    business plans, 101
    children, 106
    compiling the application, 104–105
    consulates and consular processing, 95–99, 101–106
    DS-156E, Nonimmigrant Treaty Trader/Investor Visa Application, 105
    DS-160, Online Nonimmigrant Visa Application, 105
    duration, 106
    E-1 Visa requirements, 98–100
    E-2 Visa requirements, 100–102
    essential skills employees, 102–104
    executive employees, 102–104
    50 percent rule, 98
    I-129, Petition for a Nonimmigrant Worker, 106
    I-765, Application for Employment Authorization, 106
    irrevocably committed funds, 100
    limited liability entities, 98
    marginal enterprises, 100
    overview, 95
    principal investors, 102–104
    requirements, 97–102
    shared requirements, 97–98
    sources of law, 95–97
    spouses, 106
    substantial investments, 101
    supervisory employees, 102–104
    treaty investors, 100–102
    treaty traders, 98–100
    visa acquisition maps, 96
E-3 nonimmigrant visa (Specialty occupation professionals from Australia), 134
EAD. *See* Employment Authorization Document
Eastern Europe, relief from removal for persons from, 567
EB-1 immigrant visa (Priority workers), 313–326
    compiling the application, 325–326
    EB-1A immigrant visa, 314–317. *See also* EB-1A immigrant visa
    EB-1B immigrant visa, 317–322. *See also* EB-1B immigrant visa
    EB-1C immigrant visa, 322–324. *See also* EB-1C immigrant visa
    I-140, Immigrant Petition for Alien Worker, 325–326
    I-485, Application to Register Permanent Residence or Adjust Status, 326
    I-864, Affidavit of Support, 326
    overview, 308
EB-1A immigrant visa (Aliens with extraordinary ability), 314–317
    compiling the application, 325–326
    evidentiary criteria, 315
    Kazarian test, 314–317
EB-1B immigrant visa (Professors and researchers), 317–322
    academic field, 317
    compiling the application, 325–326
    evidentiary criteria, 320
    I-140, Immigrant Petition for Alien Worker, 320
    Kazarian test, 320–321
    offers of employment, 318
    permanent research positions, 318
EB-1C immigrant visa (Multinational executives and managers), 322–324
    compiling the application, 325–326
    evidentiary criteria, 323
    executive capacity, 323
    managerial capacity, 324
EB-2 immigrant visa (Advanced degree professionals), 327–364
    advanced degrees, 327
    compiling the application, 364
    ETA 9809, Application for Permanent Employment Certification, 363–364
    I-140, Immigrant Petition for Alien Worker, 327, 363–364
    I-485, Application to Register Permanent Residence or Adjust Status, 363–364
    labor certification, 329–364. *See also* PERM process
    National Interest Waiver, 365–367
    overview, 308, 327–328
    Schedule A occupations, 367–368
EB-3 immigrant visa (Skilled workers, professionals, and other workers), 327–362
    compiling the application, 364
    ETA 9809, Application for Permanent Employment Certification, 363–364
    I-140, Immigrant Petition for Alien Worker, 363–364
    I-485, Application to Register Permanent Residence or Adjust Status, 363–364
    labor certification, 329–364. *See also* PERM process
    other workers, 329
    overview, 308, 328–329
    professionals, 329
    Schedule A occupations, 367–368
    skilled workers, 329
    unskilled workers, 329
EB-4 immigrant visa (Special immigrants including religious workers), 368–375
    attestation letters, 371
    compiling the application, 372–374
    I-360, Petition for Amerasian, Widow(er), or Special Immigrant, 372–374
    I-485, Application to Register Permanent Residence or Adjust Status, 373–374
    I-864, Affidavit of Support, 373
    non-profit religious organizations, 370

overview, 308, 368–372
religious workers, 368–375
Special Immigrant Juveniles. *See*
Special Immigrant Juveniles
EB-5 immigrant visa (Investors),
375–380
capital of investors, 376–377
compiling the application, 379–380
I-485, Application to Register
Permanent Residence or Adjust
Status, 380
I-526, Immigrant Petition by Alien
Entrepreneur, 379–380
I-829, Petition by Entrepreneur to
Remove Conditions, 380
I-864, Affidavit of Support, 380
new enterprises, 376
overview, 308, 375–389
regional centers, 375–379
targeted employment areas, 376
troubled businesses, 376
Education
employment-based immigration of
aliens with extraordinary ability
in, 314–317. *See also* EB-1
immigrant visa (Priority workers)
individuals with extraordinary ability
in (O-1A nonimmigrant visa),
140–155. *See also*
O-1A nonimmigrant visa
Student and Exchange Visitor
Information System (SEVIS), 71,
75, 79, 650
Student and Exchange Visitor
Program (SEVP), 71
students. *See* F-1/M-1 nonimmigrant
visa (Study)
EEOC (Equal Employment Opportunity
Commission), 408
EIN (Employer Identification Number),
122
Electronic Immigration System (ELIS),
293
Electronic System for Travel
Authorization (ESTA), B-1/B-2
nonimmigrant visa, 65
El Salvador
Central American Minors
Refugee/Parole Program,
451–452
EB-4 immigrant visa, 374
relief from removal for persons
from, 567
Special Immigrant Juveniles, 445

Emergency Quota Act of 1921, 7
Emmy Awards
employment-based immigration of
recipients, 314
O-1B nonimmigrant visa of
recipients, 150
Employees of international organizations
and NATO, G nonimmigrant visa
for, 179
Employer Identification Number (EIN)
for H-1B nonimmigrant visa, 122
Employment and Training
Administrative Office of Foreign
Labor Certification, 15, 307
Employment Authorization Cards,
27, 29
Employment Authorization Document
(EAD)
adjustment applications, 282–283
asylum, 228–229
defined, 77
F-1/M-1 nonimmigrant visa, 77–78
VAWA proceedings, 401
Employment-based immigration,
305–382
consulates and consular processing,
307, 312, 326, 374, 380
Diversity Immigrant Visa Program,
380–381
EB-1 immigrant visa, 313–326.
See also EB-1 immigrant visa
EB-2 immigrant visa, 327–364.
See also EB-2 immigrant visa
EB-3 immigrant visa, 327–362.
See also EB-3 immigrant visa
EB-4 immigrant visa, 368–375.
See also EB-4 immigrant visa
EB-5 immigrant visa, 375–380.
See also EB-5 immigrant visa
high school education requirement,
381
I-130, Petition for an Alien Relative,
1-140 compared to, 312
I-140, Immigrant Petition for Alien
Worker, 312, 325–327, 352,
363–365, 367, 382
I-360, Petition for Amerasian,
Widow(er), or Special Immigrant,
312, 372–374
I-485, Application to Register
Permanent Residence or Adjust
Status, 312, 326, 363–364,
373–374, 380–381
National Interest Waiver, 365–367

overview, 305–306, 381–382
PERM, 330, 337, 345, 353–362
religious workers. *See* EB-4
Schedule A occupations, 367–368
shared requirements, 311–313
sources of law, 306–311
visa bulletins, 309–313
Enforcement and Removal Operations
(ERO), 14, 526
Engagement letters, 628–629
Enhanced Border Security and Visa
Entry Reform Act of 2002, 12
Entered Without Inspection (EWI)
generally, 3
adjustment of status, 284
DACA, 451
defensive asylum claims, 222
expedited removal proceedings, 538
inadmissibility, 476, 486
Notice to Appear, 511
Entertainers, 156–166. *See also* P-2/P-3
nonimmigrant visa
Enumerated grounds. *See* Asylees and
refugees
EOIR. *See* Executive Office for
Immigration Review
EOIR 26, Notice of Appeal from a
Decision of an Immigration Judge,
550
EOIR 27, Notice of Appearance as
Attorney or Legal Representative,
550
EOIR 28, Notice of Entry of Appearance
as Attorney or Representative
Before the Immigration Court
asylum, 223
nonprofit organizations, 619
removal proceedings, 517
EOIR 33/BIA, Alien's Change of Address
Form/Board of Immigration
Appeals, 514
EOIR 33/IC, Alien's Change of Address
Form/Immigration Court, 514,
545
Equal Employment Opportunity
Commission (EEOC), 408
ERO (Enforcement and Removal
Operations), 14, 526
Essential skills employees
defined, 99
E-1/E-2 nonimmigrant visa, 102–104
Essential support for O1A/O-1B visa
holders, O-2 nonimmigrant visa,
154–155

ESTA (Electronic System for Travel Authorization), 65
ETA 9141, Application for Prevailing Wage Determination, 338–342
ETA 9809, Application for Permanent Employment Certification
  EB-2/EB-3 immigrant visa, 363–364
  PERM process, 330, 337, 345, 353–362
  Schedule A occupations, 367
Ethical issues, 640–644
E-Verify, 78
Evidence, Federal Rules of, 532–533
EWI. *See* Entered Without Inspection
Examination for naturalization, 599–600
Examination in chief in removal proceedings, 531
Exceptional and extremely unusual hardship, 559–561
Exchange visitors, 81–82. *See also* J-1 nonimmigrant visa
Exclusion grounds, 11
Executive branch, authority of, 13–15
Executive capacity in relation to L-1 visa, 113
Executive Office for Immigration Review (EOIR)
  generally, 17
  authority of, 14–16
  case law, 18
  defined, 506
  nonprofit organizations recognized by, 619–620
  paralegals, 650
  removal proceedings, 506. *See also* Removal proceedings
  rules of conduct, 647
Executives
  E-1/E-2 nonimmigrant visa, 102–104
  intracompany transferees, 107–120. *See also* L-1A/L-1B nonimmigrant visa
  multinational, 322–324. *See also* EB-1C immigrant visa
Expatriation, 611–613
Expedited removal, 537–539
  generally, 11
  asylum cases, 223
  defined, 223
  release on bond, 538
Expungement of criminal record, 465
Extension of stay, 54–60

Extraordinary ability
  aliens with, 314–317. *See also* EB-1A immigrant visa
  defined, 142–143
  O-1A nonimmigrant visa, 147–149
  O-1B nonimmigrant visa, 149–151
Extraordinary circumstances and one-year deadline, 198
Extreme cruelty, VAWA proceedings based on, 391–392
Extreme hardship,
  cancellation of removal and, 561, 565–566
  T nonimmigrant visas, 432, 439–442
  VAWA, 385
  waivers and, 256, 284–286, 296–297, 299

F-1 nonimmigrant visa (Student), 70–81
  compiling the application, 71, 75
  children, 79
  consulates and consular processing, 70–71, 75, 79
  Curricular Practical Training, 77
  DS-160, Online Nonimmigrant Visa Application, 71, 75
  duration of status, 75–76
  Employment Authorization Document, 77–78
  employment eligibility, 76–79
  E-Verify, 78
  I-20, Certificate of Eligibility for Nonimmigrant Student Status, 71–77, 79–80
  I-538, Certification by Designated School, 78
  I-539, Application to Extend/Change Nonimmigrant Status, 75, 80
  I-765, Application for Employment Authorization, 77
  international organizations, 78
  off-campus employment, 77
  on-campus employment, 77
  Optional Practical Training, 76, 78, 80
  overview, 70–71
  reinstatement of status, 80–81
  requirements, 71, 75
  spouses, 79
  travel considerations, 79–80
  vocational education, 70–71
Failure to register, deportation for, 495
False documents, deportation for using, 495

FAM. *See* Foreign Affairs Manual
Family planning, involuntary, as grounds for asylum, 195–196
Family reunification. *See also* Derivative relatives
  of refugees, 239–240
Family sponsored immigration, 246–270
  Adam Walsh Child Protection and Safety Act, 259
  affidavit of support, 265–266. *See also* Affidavit of support
  benefits available upon death after petition filed, 268–269
  benefits available upon death before petition filed, 266–268
  bona fide relationships, 253–254
  chargeability, 250–251
  children, 257–259, 261, *See also* Children
  Child Status Protection Act, 262–264
  consular offices and consular processing, 246, 252, 255–256, 260
  cross-chargeability, 250–251
  death after petition filed, effect of, 268–269
  death before petition filed, effect of, 266–268
  DNA testing, 260, 269
  documentation, 260–262
  F-1 Preference, 247
  F-2A Preference, 247
  F-2B Preference, 247
  F-3 Preference, 247
  F-4 Preference, 247
  family preference categories, 247–250
  following to join, 261
  G-325A, Biographic Information, 256, 269
  I-130, Petition for an Alien Relative, 252–264, 269
  I-360, Petition for Amerasian, Widow(er), or Special Immigrant, 267
  I-730, Refugee/Asylee Relative Petition, 268
  I-797, Notice of Action Approval, 269
  immediate relatives, preferential treatment, 252
  under immigration law, 251–252
  lawful permanent residents, children of, 263–264
  Notice of Intent to Revoke, 264

petitions, 252–264. *See also* Relative petitions
priority date, 247
proxy marriages, 253
quotas, 246–250
relative petitions, 252–264. *See also* Relative petitions
revocation of immigrant visas, 264–266
siblings, 257–259
sources of law, 246–247
spouses, 253–256, 261
termination of immigrant visas, 264–266
U.S. citizens, children of, 262–263
validity of marriage, 253–256
visa bulletins, 247–250
"widow's penalty," 267
FDNS (Fraud Detection and National Security Directorate)
family-sponsored immigration, 254–255
overview, 48
Fear, credible and reasonable, 229–230
Fear of persecution, 87
Federal Bureau of Investigation (FBI)
criminal records, obtaining, 624
T nonimmigrant visa, 429, 431
VAWA proceedings, 393
Federal Courts
appeals to, 551–552
petition for review, 552
practice and procedure, 551–552
Federal Register, 18
Federal Rules of Evidence, 532–533
Fees
adjustment of status, 284
attorneys' fees. *See* Attorneys' fees
reciprocity fees, 52–53
Felonies. *See* Aggravated felony crimes
Female genital mutilation, 184–185, 192–193
Fiancé(e)s, 298–303. *See also* K-1 nonimmigrant visas
50 percent rule for E-1/E-2 nonimmigrant visa, 98
Filing systems, 640
Final order of removal, 541
Firearms offenses, deportation for, 493
Firm resettlement bar to asylum, 200–201
First preference category, 247
FLCDC (Foreign Labor Certification Data Center), 127–128

FOIA. *See* Freedom of Information Act of 1966
Following to join, family sponsored immigration, 261
Foreign Affairs Manual (FAM)
generally, 19
B-1/B-2 nonimmigrant visa, 62, 66–67
consular processing of immigrant visas, 292
E-1/E-2 nonimmigrant visa, 95, 101, 103
evidence, gathering of, 633
family-sponsored immigration, 260
H-1B nonimmigrant visa, 121
L-1A/L-1B nonimmigrant visa, 109
overview, 60
Foreign government officials, visas for, 178
Foreign Labor Certification Data Center (FLCDC), 127–128
Foreign Labor Certification Permanent Online System, 351
Forms. *See specific form designation*
Fourth preference category, 247
Employment based, 306
Fourteenth Amendment
citizenship, 572
Due Process Clause, 5
expatriation, 611
as source of law, 17
Fraud and misrepresentation
inadmissibility for, 477–480
marriage fraud, 10, 256, 295, 586
naturalization, 586
Fraud Detection and National Security Directorate (FDNS)
family-sponsored immigration, 254–255
overview, 48
Freedom of Information Act of 1966 (FOIA)
determining immigrant status, 41
practice of immigration law, 623
removal proceedings, 521
Frivolous asylum applications, 226–227
Functional managers for L-1A/L-1B nonimmigrant visa, 113

G nonimmigrant visa (Employees of international organizations and NATO), 179

G-28, Notice of Entry of Appearance as Attorney or Accredited Representative, 30–34, 274–276
G-325, Biographic Information
family-sponsored immigration, 256, 269
Special Immigrant Juveniles, 445–446
T nonimmigrant visa, 441
U nonimmigrant visa, 423
G-325A, Biographic Information
adjustment of status, and marriage-based, 273, 276
G-639, Freedom of Information Act/Privacy Act Request
determining immigrant status, 41
Immigration Court, 521
practice of immigration law, 623
G-1145, E-Notification of Application/Petition Acceptance, 624
Geary Act of 1892, 6
GMC. *See* Good moral character
Good moral character
civics requirement, 587–588
dependent support, effect of nonpayment, 585
disqualifying conditions, 581–583
evidence, 587
literacy requirement, 587–588
marriage fraud, effect of, 586
naturalization, 580–588
parole, effect of, 584
probation, effect of, 584
relief from removal, 559
selective service, effect of failure to register, 584–585
statutory grounds, 580–583
taxes, effect of nonpayment, 585
VAWA proceedings, 392–394
voting unlawfully, effect of, 586
Government persecution, 187
Grammy Awards
employment-based immigration of recipients, 314
O-1B nonimmigrant visa of recipients, 150
P-1B nonimmigrant visa of recipients, 161
Grandfathered. *See* INA § 245(i)
Green card, 45. *See also* Lawful permanent residents
Guatemala
Central American Minors Refugee/Parole Program, 451–452
EB-4 immigrant visa, 374

relief from removal for persons from, 567
Special Immigrant Juveniles, 445

H-1B nonimmigrant visa (Professional specialty occupations), 120–134
actual wage, 127–128
compiling the application, 131–132
B-1 nonimmigrant visa in lieu of, 67–68
benching, 128
beneficiary qualifications, 123–125
cap, 129–130
"cap gap," 131
changes in employment, 130–131
children as derivatives, 133
duration, 130
Employer Identification Number, 122
I-129, Petition for a Nonimmigrant Worker, 131–132
I-140, Immigrant Petition for Alien Worker, 133
iCert, 121
job flexibility, 130–131
Labor Condition Application, 121, 125–128
numerical limitations, 129–130
Optional Practical Training, 122
overview, 120–122
portability, 131
prevailing wage, 127–128
public access files, 126
qualifying employers, 122
qualifying positions, 123
requirements, 122–129
similar working conditions, 128–129
sources of law, 120–122
spouses, 133
termination of status, 132–133
TN nonimmigrant visa compared, 136
transition from student, 130–131
visa acquisition map, 121
H-1B Visa Reform Act of 2004, 129
H-1B1 nonimmigrant visa (Specialty workers from Singapore and Chile), 133–134
H-2 nonimmigrant visa (Temporary nonimmigrant workers), 171–176
applications, 176
G-28, Notice of Entry of Appearance of Attorney or Accredited Representative, 176

I-129, Petition for a Nonimmigrant Worker, 176
overview, 171–172
H-2A nonimmigrant visa (Agricultural work of temporary or seasonal nature), 172–174
H-2B nonimmigrant visa (Non-agricultural work of temporary or seasonal nature), 174–175
H-3 nonimmigrant visa (Cultural exchange or training), 90–91
Habeas corpus
defined, 543
detention, 543
Haiti, relief from removal for persons from, 567
Haitian Refugee Immigration Fairness Act of 1998 (HRIFA), 12, 567
Hardship, relief from removal for, 561
Health and Human Services Department (HHS)
Administration for Children and Families, 14
authority of, 13–14
inadmissibility, 461–462
J-1 nonimmigrant visa, 88
National Interest Waiver, 366–367
Office of Refugee Resettlement. *See* Office of Refugee Resettlement
refugees, 237
Special Immigrant Juveniles, 447. *See also* Special Immigrant Juveniles
T nonimmigrant visa, 429–430
Health Insurance Portability and Accountability Act of 1996 (HIPAA), 634
Health-related grounds for inadmissibility, 461–463
Hearsay evidence in removal proceedings, 532–533
HHS. *See* Health and Human Services Department
High school education requirement for employment-based immigration, 381
HIPAA (Health Insurance Portability and Accountability Act of 1996), 634
Historical background, 4–13
Hmong Veterans' Naturalization Act of 2000, 588
Homeland Security Act of 2003, 13

Homeland Security Investigations (HSI), 14, 429
Homosexuality as social group, 193
Honduras
Central American Minors Refugee/Parole Program, 451–452
EB-4 immigrant visa, 374
Special Immigrant Juveniles, 445
Household members, adjustment of status, 279
HRIFA (Haitian Refugee Immigration Fairness Act of 1998), 12, 567
HSI. *See* Homeland Security Investigations
Humanitarian asylum grant, 188–189
Humanitarian parole, 243
Human Rights Watch, 216
Human trafficking, 384
T nonimmigrant visa, 427–441. *See also* T nonimmigrant visa

I nonimmigrant visa (Media representatives), 170–171
I-20, Certificate of Eligibility for Nonimmigrant Student Status, 71–77, 79–80, 84
I-94, Arrival/Departure Record
adjustment of status, 273, 276
asylum, 219
overview, 20, 23–24
visa applications, 50
I-102, Application for Replacement/Initial Nonimmigrant Arrival-Departure Document, 276
I-129, Petition for a Nonimmigrant Worker
E-1/E-2 nonimmigrant visa, 106
H-1B nonimmigrant visa, 131–132
H-2 nonimmigrant visa, 176
L-1A/L-1B nonimmigrant visa, 118
O-1A/O-1B nonimmigrant visa, 142, 144, 152–153
P-1/P-2/P-3 nonimmigrant visa, 157–158, 165
Q nonimmigrant visa, 89–90
R-1 nonimmigrant visa, 166, 169
visa applications, 57–58
I-129F, Petition for Alien Fiancé(e), 299–300
I-130, Petition for Alien Relative
adjustment of status, 270, 274, 284–285
employment-based immigration and, 312

ethical issues, 643
family-sponsored immigration, 252–264, 269
fiancé(e)s, 299–300
intake or initial consultation, 626
relief from removal, 564
I-131, Application for Travel Document
　adjustment of status, 274, 283
　DACA, 450
　humanitarian parole, 243
　naturalization, 578
I-134, Affidavit of Support
　Central American Minors Refugee/Parole Program, 452
　humanitarian parole, 243
I-140, Immigrant Petition for Alien Worker
　EB-1 immigrant visa, 325–326
　EB-1B immigrant visa, 320
　EB-2 immigrant visa, 327, 363–364
　EB-2/EB-3 immigrant visa, 363–364
　EB-3 immigrant visa, 363–364
　employment-based immigration, 312
　H-1B nonimmigrant visa, 133
　National Interest Waiver, 365–367
　PERM process, 352
　relief from removal, 564
　Schedule A occupations, 367
I-192, Application for Advance Permission to Enter as Nonimmigrant
　inadmissibility, 488
　T nonimmigrant visa, 432, 437, 440
　U nonimmigrant visa, 411, 416–418, 422
I-193, Application for Waiver of Passport and/or Visa, 411, 417
I-212, Application for Permission to Reapply for Admission into the United States After Deportation or Removal, 480, 486
I-360, Petition for Amerasian, Widow(er), or Special Immigrant
　adjustment of status, 285
　EB-4 immigrant visa, 372–374
　employment-based immigration, 312, 372–374
　family-sponsored immigration, 267,285
　Special Immigrant Juveniles, 445, 448
　VAWA proceedings, 397–400, 402

I-485, Application to Register Permanent Residence or Adjust Status
　adjustment of status, 270, 273–274, 284
　asylum, 230
　Diversity Immigrant Visa Program, 381
　EB-1 immigrant visa, 326
　EB-2/EB-3 immigrant visa, 363–364
　EB-4 immigrant visa, 373–374
　EB-5 immigrant visa, 380
　employment-based immigration, 312, 326, 363–364, 373–374, 380–381
　intake or initial consultation, 626
　refugees, 240
　Special Immigrant Juveniles, 445–446
　T nonimmigrant visa, 439, 441
　U nonimmigrant visa, 423
　VAWA proceedings, 398
I-526, Immigrant Petition by Alien Entrepreneur, 379–380
I-538, Certification by Designated School, 78
I-539, Application to Extend/Change Nonimmigrant Status
　generally, 55, 57–58
　F-1/M-1 nonimmigrant visa, 75, 80
　R-1 nonimmigrant visa, 169
　U nonimmigrant visa, 422–423
I-551, Permanent Resident Card
　asylum, 230
　conditional lawful permanent resident status, 297–298
　consular processing of immigrant visas, 293
　form, 28
　naturalization, 597
　overview, 26
　VAWA proceedings, 404
I-589, Application for Asylum and for Withholding of Removal, 203–212, 216, 218, 223
I-601, Application for Waiver of Ground of Inadmissibility
　adjustment of status, 285
　inadmissibility, 463, 472, 480, 485
　Special Immigrant Juveniles, 445–446
I-601A, Application for Provisional Unlawful Presence Waiver
　adjustment of status, 286
　ethical issues, 643
I-693, Report of Medical Examination and Vaccination Record, 277–278

I-730, Refugee/Asylee Relative Petition
　asylum, 231
　family-sponsored immigration, 268
　refugees, 240
I-751, Petition to Remove Conditions on Residency
　conditional lawful permanent resident status, 295–296
　conflicts of interest, 645
　VAWA proceedings, 404
I-765, Application for Employment Authorization
　adjustment of status, 274, 282–283
　asylum, 228–229
　DACA, 450
　detention, 542
　E-1/E-2 nonimmigrant visa, 106
　E-3 nonimmigrant visa, 134
　F-1/M-1 nonimmigrant visa, 77
　intake or initial consultation, 626
　Special Immigrant Juveniles, 445–446
　VAWA proceedings, 398
I-797, Notice of Action Approval
　adjustment of status, 274
　consulates and consular processing, 36
　family-sponsored immigration, 269
　notice of action, 36, 39
I-797A, Notice of Action Approval, Status Grant, 40
I-797C, Notice of Action Receipt Notice
　asylum, 220
　overview, 35–36
　practice of immigration law, 625
　U nonimmigrant visa, 426
I-821D, Consideration of Deferred Action for Childhood Arrivals, 450
I-829, Petition by Entrepreneur to Remove Conditions, 380
I-864, Affidavit of Support
　adjustment of status, 274, 278–282
　consular processing of immigrant visas, 291
　EB-1 immigrant visa, 326
　EB-4 immigrant visa, 373
　EB-5 immigrant visa, 380
I-864A, Contract Between Sponsor and Household Member, 279
I-907, Request for Premium Processing Service, 153

I-912, Request for Fee Waiver
  asylum, 230
  derivative citizenship, 603
  naturalization, 597–598
  Special Immigrant Juveniles, 445–446
  T nonimmigrant visa, 432, 441
  U nonimmigrant visa, 424
  VAWA proceedings, 404
I-912P, HHS Poverty Guidelines for Fee Waiver Request, 598
I-914, Application for T Nonimmigrant Status, 431, 437
I-914, Supplement A, Application for Immediate Family Member of T-1 Recipient, 432, 437
I-914, Supplement B, Declaration of Law Enforcement Officer for Victim of Trafficking in Persons, 431–432
I-918, Petition for U Nonimmigrant Status, 413
I-918, Supplement A, Petition for Qualifying Family Member of U-1 Recipient, 417
I-918, Supplement B, Law Enforcement Certification Form, 408, 410–411, 413–414, 423
ICE. *See* Immigration and Customs Enforcement
IGA (Interested government agency) waiver, 87–88
Illegal entrants, inadmissibility, 476–480
Illegal Immigration Reform and Immigrant Responsibility Act of 1996 (IIRAIRA)
  admission, 458
  asylum, 198
  deportation, 456, 493, 495
  inadmissibility, 456, 480
  overview, 11–12
  relief from removal, 558
Illness, inadmissibility based on, 461–463
IMBRA (International Marriage Broker Regulation Act of 2005), 301–302
IMFA (Immigration Marriage Fraud Amendments Act of 1986), 10, 295
Immediate relatives, preferential treatment, 252
Immigrant visas.
  adjustment of status, 270–290. *See also* Adjustment of status
  conditional lawful permanent resident status, 295–298
  consular processing, 24–26, 290–294

consulates and consular processing, 24–26, 264, 290–295
employment-based immigration, 305–382. *See also* Employment-based immigration
family-sponsored immigration, 246–270. *See also* Family-sponsored immigration
fiancé(e)s, 298–303
nonimmigrant visas compared, 45–48
overview, 24–26
post-interview proceedings, 295–298
revocation of, 264–266
termination of, 264–266
Immigration Act of 1882, 6
Immigration Act of 1891, 7
Immigration Act of 1917, 7
Immigration Act of 1990, 10–11, 489
Immigration and Customs Enforcement (ICE)
  authority of, 13–16
  authorized legal representatives, 517
  Chief Counsels, 548
  deportation, 460, 492, 502
  Enforcement and Removals Operations, 526
  expedited removal proceedings, 537–538
  Field Office Directors, 539–540, 548, 552
  Freedom of Information Act, 623
  Homeland Security Investigations, 14, 429
  immigration file, obtaining copy of, 521
  Law Enforcement Parole Unit, 429
  Notice to Appear, 507
  paralegals, 650
  petitions for review, 552
Immigration and Nationality Act of 1952 (INA)
  acquisition, citizenship by, 604
  adjustment of status, 271–272, 284, 286–290
  admission, 458–459
  asylum, 183, 199, 202
  children, petitions by, 390
  citizenship, 570
  codification of, 17
  conditional lawful permanent resident status, 296
  DACA, 451
  denaturalization, 613
  deportation. *See* Deportation

  derivative citizenship, 601
  detention, 539, 541–542
  E-1/E-2 nonimmigrant visa, 95
  employment-based immigration, 306–307
  enactment of, 8–9
  expatriation, 611–612
  expedited removal proceedings, 537
  F-1/M-1 nonimmigrant visa, 80
  family-sponsored immigration, 246–247, 256–257, 264, 268–269
  fiancé(e)s, 300
  H-1B nonimmigrant visa, 121
  H-2A nonimmigrant visa, 173
  humanitarian parole, 243
  inadmissibility. *See* Inadmissibility
  L-1A/L-1B nonimmigrant visa, 107
  National Interest Waiver, 365–367
  naturalization, 580–581, 586, 588, 599
  nonimmigrant visas, 44
  nonimmigrant waivers, 51
  notice of hearing, 514
  Notice to Appear, 511–512
  O-1A/O-1B nonimmigrant visa, 140
  P-1/P-2/P-3 nonimmigrant visa, 156
  PERM process, 329
  refugees, 238
  regulations, 18
  relief from removal, 553, 555–556, 558–559, 561, 563–564, 566
  rules of conduct, 647
  Special Immigrant Juveniles, 443–444
  T nonimmigrant visa, 428, 439–440
  Temporary Protected Status, 236
  U nonimmigrant visa, 405–406, 422
  VAWA proceedings, 402
  withholding of removal, 231
Immigration and Nationality Act of 1965, 8–9
Immigration and Nationality Act of 1990, 306
Immigration and Naturalization Service (INS—former)
  asylum, 192
  creation of, 8
  NACARA, 567
  relief from removal, 566
Immigration Court
  administrative closure, 546–549
  appeals from, 549–551
  asylum, 203
  case preparation, 529–531
  case proceedings, 531–532

change of venue, 544–546
closing argument, 532
continuances, 545
cross-examination, 532
decisions, 533
EOIR-33/IC, Alien's Change of Address Form/Immigration Court, 514, 545
evidence rules, 532–533
examination in chief, 531
G-639, Freedom of Information Act/Privacy Act Request, 521
hearings, 517–537
hearsay evidence, 532–533
immigration file, obtaining copy of, 521
individual hearings, 527–532
master calendar hearings, 517–527
minute orders, 534–535
motions, 543–546
Notice of Entry of Appearance as Attorney or Representative Before the Immigration Court, 518–519
Office of Chief Immigration Judge Practice Manual, 528, 543, 545
pleadings, 521–526
post-hearing Voluntary Departure, 533–537
post-order instructions for individuals granted relief from removal, 536
pre-hearing Voluntary Departure, 526–527
proffer of information or evidence, 529
proof of service, 530
reconsideration, 544
reopening of cases, 543–544
Immigration file, obtaining copy of, 521
Immigration Marriage Fraud Amendments Act of 1986 (IMFA), 10, 295
Immigration Reform and Control Act of 1986 (IRCA)
  adjustment of status, 287
  enactment of, 10
Immigration status
  defined, 2
  determination of, 36, 41
Immutable characteristics as grounds for asylum, 192
Imputed or perceived political opinion, asylum based on, 195

INA. *See* Immigration and Nationality Act of 1952
INA § 245(i). *See* Adjustment of status
In absentia orders in removal proceedings, 513
Inadmissibility
  generally, 11
  Accelerated Rehabilitative Disposition, 465
  adjustment of status, inadmissibility issues, 284–290
  agencies involved, 500–502
  aggravated felony crimes, 481
  aliens present without permission or parole, 476–477
  citizenship, ineligibility for, 480
  consulates and consular processing, 457, 469, 485, 488, 501
  controlled substances offenses, 469
  crimes of moral turpitude, 467–468
  criminal offenses, 464–472
  departing United States after unlawful presence, 481–487
  deportation compared, 496–500, 502
  documentation, 480
  drug addicts, 463
  drug offenses, 469
  Entered Without Inspection, 476, 486
  failure to attend removal proceedings, 477
  hardship, 471
  health-related grounds, 461–463
  I-192, Application for Advance Permission to Enter as Nonimmigrant, 488
  I-212, Application for Permission to Reapply for Admission into the United States After Deportation or Removal, 480, 486
  I-601, Application for Waiver of Ground of Inadmissibility, 463, 472, 480, 485
  illegal entrants, 476–480
  illness, 461–463
  ineligibility for citizenship, 480
  juvenile delinquency, 465
  labor certification, 475–476
  medical grounds, 461–463
  miscellaneous grounds, 487
  misrepresentation, 477–480
  multiple convictions, 469–472
  National Security Entry-Exit System, 473
  nonimmigrant waivers, 51

  overview, 455–456, 503
  petty offense exception, 468
  polygamous marriage, 487
  previous removal, 480–487
  public charges, 474–475
  security-related grounds, 472–473
  substance abuse, 463
  terrorism, 472–473
  unlawful presence, 481–487
  VAWA proceedings, 402–403
  voluntary departure, 482
  voting unlawfully, 487
  waiver to facilitate temporary admission of nonimmigrants, 487–488
India
  E-1/E-2 nonimmigrant visa, 97
  EB-2 nonimmigrant visa, 363
  family-sponsored immigration, 249
Indigent applicants for naturalization, 598
Indirect victims for U nonimmigrant visa, 409
Individual hearings
  asylum, 226
  case preparation, 529–531
  case proceedings, 531–532
  closing argument, 532
  cross-examination, 532
  defined, 527
  examination in chief, 531
  proffer of information or evidence, 529
  proof of service, 530
  removal proceedings, 527–532
Individuals with extraordinary ability in the sciences. *See* O-1B nonimmigrant status
Individuals with extraordinary ability in the arts, motion pictures, or television. *See* O-1A nonimmigrant status
Industrial workers for B-1 nonimmigrant visa, 68
Ineligibility for citizenship, inadmissibility for, 480
Initial consultation, 624–627
INS (former). *See* Immigration and Naturalization Service
Institutions of higher education, PERM process, 350–351
Intake, 624–627
Integration of refugees, 238

Intending immigrants, adjustment of status, 278
Inter-American Development Bank employees, 179
Interested government agency (IGA) waiver, 87–88
Internal relocation as alternative to asylum, 188
Internally displaced persons, asylum for, 183
International law, 20
International media,
Internationally recognized entertainment groups, 161–162. *See also* P-1B nonimmigrant visa,
International Marriage Broker Regulation Act of 2005 (IMBRA), 301–302
International Monetary Fund employees, 179
International organizations
   EB-4 immigrant visa, 368
   F-1/M-1 nonimmigrant visa, 78
   G nonimmigrant visa for employees of, 179
International Religious Freedom Act of 1998 (IRFA), 215–216
Intern programs, J-1 nonimmigrant visa for, 84–85
Interpreters, EB-4 immigrant visa for, 368
Intracompany transferee, 107–120. *See also* L-1A/L-1B nonimmigrant visa
Investor
   B-1 nonimmigrant visa, 68–69
   EB-5 immigrant visa, 375–380. *See also* EB-5 immigrant visa
Iran
   E-1/E-2 immigrant visa, 97
   Visa Waiver Program, 64
Iraq
   translators and interpreters, EB-4 immigrant visa, 368
   Visa Waiver Program, 64
IRCA (Immigration Reform and Control Act of 1986)
   adjustment of status, 287
   enactment of, 10
IRFA (International Religious Freedom Act of 1998), 215–216
Irrevocably committed funds for E-1/E-2 nonimmigrant visa, 100

J-1 nonimmigrant visa (Exchange visitors), 81–89
   children of, 89
   consulates and consular processing, 86–87
   cultural exchange program sponsors, 83
   DS-2019, Certificate of Eligibility for Exchange Visitor (J-1) Nonimmigrant visa, 83–84, 86, 89
   DS-7002, Training/Internship Placement Plan, 84
   exchange visitor programs, 81–82
   I-20, Certificate of Eligibility for Nonimmigrant Student Status, 84
   intern programs, 84–85
   overview, 81–83
   skills list, 86
   specific requirements, 83–85
   spouses, 89
   trainee programs, 84–85
   two-year home residency requirement, 85–87
   waivers
      exceptional hardship, 87
      Interested Government Agency (IGA), 87
      No Objection Statement, 87
      persecution, 87–88
Job description in PERM process, 330–336
Job flexibility in H-1B nonimmigrant visa, 130–131
Job Zones in PERM process, 331–334
Joint sponsors, adjustment of status, 279
Journalists (I nonimmigrant visa), 170–171
Judicial branch, authority of, 13
Judicial review, 11
Jus sanguinis, 570–571
Jus soli, 570
Juvenile courts, Special Immigrant Juveniles, 443
Juvenile delinquency, convictions and, 465

K-1/K-2 nonimmigrant visa (Fiancé(e)s and children), 298–303
K-3/K-4 nonimmigrant visa (spouses and children awaiting immigrant visas), 299–300, 302

L-1A/L-1B nonimmigrant visa (Intracompany transferees), 107–120
   affiliate, 109
   compiling the application, 118–119
   blanket nonimmigrant visa, 117–118
   branches, 109
   children of, 120
   Class A point of entry, 107
   consular officers and consular processing, 107–108, 115, 117–118
   control, 109
   dual intent, 115
   duration, 115–116
   employment abroad, 110–111
   functional manager, 113
   I-129, Petition for a Nonimmigrant Worker, 118
   L-1A positions, 111–113
   L-1B positions, 114–115
   managerial capacity, 111–112
   new offices, 117
   overview, 107
   premium processing service, 118
   qualifying employment, 110–115
   qualifying organizations, 108–110
   requirements, 108–115
   sources of law, 107–108
   spouses of, 120
   visa acquisition maps, 108
Labor certification, 329–364. *See also* PERM process
Labor Condition Application (LCA)
   H-1B nonimmigrant visa, 121, 125–128
Law enforcement certificate, 423
Law Enforcement Parole Unit (LEPU), 429
Lawful permanent residents (LPR)
   abandonment of status, 578
   adjustment of status. *See* Adjustment of status
   admission in, 458–459
   asylum, 203, 230
   cancellation of removal and, 556–558
   case assessment, 622
   conditional lawful permanent resident status, 295–298
   consular processing, 290–294
   defined, 3

Diversity Immigrant Visa Program, 380–381
EB-2 immigrant visa, 327–364. *See also* EB-2 immigrant visa
EB-3 immigrant visa, 327–362. *See also* EB-3 immigrant visa
EB-4 immigrant visa, 368–375. *See also* EB-4 immigrant visa
EB-5 immigrant visa, 375–380. *See also* EB-5 immigrant visa
employment-based immigration, 305–382. *See also* Employment-based immigration
family-sponsored immigration, 246–270. *See also* Family sponsored immigration
fiancé(e)s, 298–303
inadmissibility. *See* Inadmissibility
National Interest Waiver and, 365–367
naturalization, 574–576
nonimmigrants compared, 45
overview, 245–246
post-interview proceedings, 295–298
refugees, 240
relief from removal, 554, 556–558
Schedule A occupations, 367–368
Lawful status, 4
LCA. *See* Labor Condition Application
LEPU (Law Enforcement Parole Unit), 429
LIFE Act Amendments of 2000, 287–288
Limited liability entities and E-1/E-2 nonimmigrant visa, 98
Literacy Act of 1917, 7
Literacy requirement for naturalization, 587–588
Loss of citizenship, 611–614
LPR. *See* Lawful permanent residents

M-1 nonimmigrant visa (Vocational Student), 70–81. *See also* F-1 nonimmigrant visa
Magnuson Act of 1943, 6–7
Major League Baseball players, 156
Managers
intracompany transferees (L-1A nonimmigrant visa), 107–120. *See also* L-1A/L-1B nonimmigrant visa
managerial capacity for L-1A/L-1B nonimmigrant visa, 111–112
multinational, 322–324. *See also* EB-1C immigrant visa

Mandatory detention, 541–543
Mandatory recruitment in PERM process, 344–348
Marginal enterprises for E-1/E-2 nonimmigrant visa, 100
Marriage
Family sponsored immigration, validity for purposes of, 253–256
polygamous marriage, 386, 487
proxy marriages, 253
VAWA proceedings, validity for purposes of, 385–388
Marriage fraud, 10, 586
Master calendar hearings
asylum cases, 222
defined, 517–527
Immigration Court, 517–527
Material support, and inadmissibility, 472
McCarran-Walter Act of 1952. *See* Immigration and Nationality Act of 1952
Means-tested federal public benefits, 11
Media representatives (I nonimmigrant visa), 170–171
Medical conditions, relief from removal for, 560
Medical examinations, adjustment of status, 276–278
Medical grounds for inadmissibility, 461–463
Medically underserved areas, 88, 366
Membership in a particular social group. *See* Asylees and refugees
Mexico
family-sponsored immigration, 249
NAFTA status of professionals, 135–137. *See also* TN nonimmigrant visa
Military service
EB-4 immigrant visa, 368
naturalization, 575–576, 578
Militia as agents of persecution, 187
Minimum requirements in PERM process, 330–336
Ministers. *See* Religious workers
Minute orders in removal proceedings, 534–535
Misrepresentation, inadmissibility for, 477–480
Model Rules of Professional Conduct, 641–643, 645–646
Moral turpitude, crimes of deportation for, 490, 492

inadmissibility for, 467–468
Motion pictures, individuals with extraordinary ability in, 140–155. *See also* O-1B nonimmigrant visa
Motions
change of venue, 513, 544–546
Immigration Court, 543–546
reconsideration, 544
removal proceedings, 543–546
reopening of cases, 513, 543–544
Multinational corporations
executives and managers, 322–324. *See also* EB-1C immigrant visa
intracompany transferees, 107–120. *See also* L-1A/L-1B nonimmigrant visa
Multiple applications as bar to asylum, 202
Multiple convictions, inadmissibility for, 469–472

N-336, Request for a Hearing on a Decision in Naturalization Proceedings, 599
N-400, Application for Naturalization, 586–587, 589, 597–598, 615
N-426, Request for Certification of Military or Naval Service, 597
N-470, Application to Preserve Residency for Naturalization Purposes, 578–579
N-600, Application for Certificate of Citizenship
acquisition, citizenship by, 604
derivative citizenship, 603–604
N-600K, Application for Citizenship and Issuance of Certificate Under Section 322, 608
N-648, Medical Certification for Disability Exceptions, 589–595, 597, 599
NACARA. *See* Nicaraguan Adjustment and Central American Relief Act of 1997
NAFTA (North American Free Trade Agreement)
EB-4 immigrant visa, 368
professional status, 135–137. *See also* TN nonimmigrant visa
National Association of Legal Assistants, 640, 645
National Interest Waiver (NIW), 365–367
Nationality, asylum based on, 192

National Origins Act of 1924, 7
National Prevailing Wage Center (NPWC), 338, 343
National Security Entry-Exit System (NSEERS), 473, 507
National Visa Center (NVC)
  EB-2/EB-3 immigrant visa, 363
  family-sponsored immigration, 247–248
  immigrant visas, consular processing, 291–293
NATO (North Atlantic Treaty Organization)
  EB-4 immigrant visa, 368
  G nonimmigrant visa for employees of, 179
Naturalization
  generally, 571
  age requirements, 573
  armed forces members, 575–576, 578
  bars to, 596–597
  child support, nonpayment of, 585
  citizenship based on, 573–597
  civics requirement, 587–588
  compiling the application, 597–599
  conditional bars, 582–583
  continuous residency requirement, 576–579
  decision within 120 days, 599
  defined, 5
  denaturalization, 506, 613–614
  dependent support, nonpayment of, 585
  disability exception to requirements, 589–595
  examination, 599–600
  exemptions, 588–589
  final steps, 599–600
  G-28, Notice of Entry of Appearance of Attorney or Accredited Representative, 597, 599
  good moral character requirement, 580–588
  I-551, Permanent Resident Card, 597
  I-912, Request for Fee Waiver, 597–598
  I-912P, HHS Poverty Guidelines for Fee Waiver Request, 598
  indigent applicants, 598
  lawful permanent residents as prerequisite to, 574–576
  literacy requirement, 587–588
  marriage fraud, effect of, 586

marriage to USC, effect of,
military service, 575–576, 578
N-336, Request for a Hearing on a Decision in Naturalization Proceedings, 599
N-400, Application for Naturalization, 586–587, 589, 597–598, 615
N-426, Request for Certification of Military or Naval Service, 597
N-470, Application to Preserve Residency for Naturalization Purposes, 578–579
N-648, Medical Certification for Disability Exceptions, 589–595, 597, 599
name change, 600
oath of allegiance, 596–597
parole, effect of, 584
physical presence requirement, 579–580
probation, effect of, 584
process, 597–600
reasonable accommodation, 588–589
reexamination, 599
selective service, failure to register for, 584–585
statutory period, 573
  filing 90 days before, 575
taxes, nonpayment of, 585
VAWA proceedings, 574
voting unlawfully, effect of, 586
waivers, 588–589
Naturalization Act of 1790, 5
Naturalization Act of 1798, 5
Naturalization Clause, 16
New enterprise to qualify for EB-5 immigrant visa, 376
New office and L-1A/L-1B nonimmigrant visa, 117
Nicaragua, relief from removal for persons from, 567
Nicaraguan Adjustment and Central American Relief Act of 1997 (NACARA), 12, 554, 567
"90-day-rule," A-1/A-2 nonimmigrant visa, 178
NIW (National Interest Waiver), 365–367
Nobel Prizes, employment-based immigration of recipients, 314
Nolo contendere pleas, 464
Non-agricultural work of temporary or seasonal nature, 174–175

Non-governmental organizations (NGOs), refugees, 237
Nonimmigrant intent, defined, 45
Nonimmigrants, defined, 3
Nonimmigrant visas. *See also specific nonimmigrant visa*
  change of status, 54–60
  charts, 46–47, 91, 137–138
  checklist, 46–47
  comparison, 176–177
  consular processing, 20, 48
  consulates and consular processing, 20, 46, 48–53, 55
  defined, 3
  DS-160, Online Nonimmigrant Visa Application, 52
  extension of status, 54–60
  I-129, Petition for a Nonimmigrant Worker, 57–58
  I-539, Application to Extend/Change Nonimmigrant Status, 55, 57–58
  immigrant visas compared, 45–48
  nonimmigrant waivers, 50–51
  nunc pro tunc filings, 56
  overview, 20–22, 44–45, 92, 94, 138
  reciprocity fees, 52–53
  sources of law, 60–61
  stamps, 51–54
  unlawful presence, 59
  visa exempt status, 48–49
  visa types
    A-1/A-2, foreign government officials, 178
    B-1, business, 61–70
    B-2, tourists and visitors, 61–70
    C-1, transit, 70
    D, crew member, 70
    E-1, treaty trader, 95–100, 102–106
    E-2 treaty investor, 95–98, 100–102, 104–105,
    E-3, specialty occupation professionals from Australia, 134
    F-1, student, 70–81
    F-2, spouses and children of F-1 visa holders, 79
    G-1, employees of international organizations and NATO, 179
    H-1B, professional specialty occupations, 120–133
    H-1B1, specialty workers from Singapore and Chile, 133–134

H-2, temporary nonimmigrant workers, 171–176
H-2A, agricultural worker of temporary or seasonal nature, 171–174, 176
H-2B, non-agricultural worker of temporary or seasonal nature, 171–172, 174–176
H-3, cultural exchange or training, 90–91
H-4, spouses and children of H-1B visa holders, 133
I, media representative, 170–171
J-1, exchange visitors, 81–89
J-2, spouses and children of J-1 visa holders, 89
K-1, fiancé(e)s, 298–303
K-2, children of K-1 visa holders, 298, 300, 302
K-3, spouses and children awaiting immigrant visas, 299, 300, 302
K-4, children of K-3 visa holders, 299
L-1A/L1B, intracompany transferees of multinational corporations, managers and executives, 107–120
M-1, vocational student, 70–81
O-1A, individuals with extraordinary ability in the sciences, 140–149, 152–154
O-1B, individuals with extraordinary ability in the arts, motion pictures or television, 140–147, 149–151, 152–154
O-2, essential support of O1-A/O-1B, 154–155
O-3, spouses and children, 155
P-1, athletes, 156–160, 165
P-1B, internationally recognized entertainment groups, 161–163, 165
P-2/P-3, artists and entertainers, 156–160, 165
P-4, spouses and children, 165–166
Q, cultural exchange, 89–90
R-1, religious workers, 166–169
T, victims of human trafficking, 427–441
U, victims of certain enumerated crimes, 405–426

Visa Waiver Program, 48, 54–55
Nonimmigrant waivers, 50–51
Nonprofit organizations
  G-28, Notice of Entry of Appearance of Attorney or Accredited Representative, 619
  practice of law in, 618–620
  religious organizations, EB-4 immigrant visa, 370
Non-refoulement, 182
No Objection Statement, 87
North American Free Trade Agreement (NAFTA)
  EB-4 immigrant visa, 368
  professional TN nonimmigrant, 135–137. See also TN nonimmigrant visa
North Atlantic Treaty Organization (NATO)
  EB-4 immigrant visa, 368
  G nonimmigrant visa for employees of, 179
Notice of filing in PERM process, 345–347
Notice of hearing in removal proceedings, 514–516
Notice of Intent to Deny
  responding to, 638–639
  VAWA proceedings, 401
Notice of Intent to Offer Evidence
  defined, 528
  individual hearings, 528
  relief from removal, 562–563
Notice of Intent to Revoke, family-sponsored immigration, 264
Notice to Appear (NTA)
  generally, 460, 501
  removal proceedings, 507–514
NPWC (National Prevailing Wage Center), 338, 343
NSEERS (National Security Entry-Exit System), 473, 507
Numerical limitation on H-1B nonimmigrant visa, 129–130
Nunc pro tunc filings, 56
NVC. See National Visa Center

O-1A nonimmigrant visa (Individuals with extraordinary ability in sciences, education, business, or athletics), 140–155
  accompanying relatives, 155
  adjudications, 144
  agents as petitioners, 142

applications, 152–153
authorized entities, 140
changes in employment or permanent residency, 153
children, 155
compiling the application, 152–153
consultations or peer advisory opinions, 143–144
contact between petitioner and beneficiary, 145–146
contracts, 145–146
demonstrating extraordinary ability, 147–149
duration, 147
essential support, 154–155
evidentiary criteria, 142–143
extraordinary ability, defined, 142–143
I-129, Petition for a Nonimmigrant Worker, 142, 144, 152–153
I-907, Request for Premium Processing Service, 153
itineraries, 144–145
O-1B nonimmigrant visa, shared requirements, 141–142
overview, 140–141
P-1/P-2/P-3 visas compared, 165–166
peer groups, 141–142
published works, 148
requirements, 141–147
spouses, 155
O-1B nonimmigrant visa (Individuals with extraordinary ability in arts, motion pictures, or television), 140–155
  accompanying relatives, 155
  agents, 142
  authorized entities, 140
  changes in employment or permanent residency, 153
  children, 155
  compiling the application, 152–153
  consultations or peer advisory opinions, 143–144
  contracts, 145–146
  demonstrating extraordinary ability, 149–151
  duration, 147
  essential support, 154–155
  evidentiary criteria, 142–143
  extraordinary ability, defined, 142–143

I-129, Petition for a Nonimmigrant Worker, 142, 144, 152–153
I-907, Request for Premium Processing Service, 153
itineraries, 144–145
O-1A nonimmigrant visa, shared requirements, 141–142
overview, 140–141
P-1/P-2/P-3 visas compared, 165–166
peer groups, 141–142
requirements, 141–147
spouses, 155
O-2 nonimmigrant visa (Essential support of O-1A/O-1B Visa holders), 154–155
O-3 nonimmigrant visa (Spouses and children of O-1A/O-1B Visa holders), 155
Oath of allegiance, 596–597
Occupational Employment Statistics (OES), 338, 343
Occupational Information Network (O*Net), 123, 331–335, 338
Off-campus employment, when student has F-1/M-1 nonimmigrant visa, 77
Office of Refugee Resettlement (ORR)
overview, 13–14
refugees, 237
Special Immigrant Juveniles, 448–449
Office of Superintendent of Immigration, 7
Office of the Chief Immigration Judge (OCIJ) Practice Manual, 528, 543, 545
Olympic Medals, employment-based immigration of recipients, 314
On-campus employment, for students with F-1/M-1 nonimmigrant visa, 77
O*Net. *See* Occupational Information Network
One-year deadline for asylum applications, 198–199. *See also* Asylees and refugees
Optional Practical Training (OPT)
E-1/E-2 nonimmigrant visa, 106
F-1/M-1 nonimmigrant visa, 76, 78, 80
H-1B nonimmigrant visa, 122
Order of supervision, defined, 542
Organization of American States, G nonimmigrant visa for employees of, 179

ORR. *See* Office of Refugee Resettlement
Outlying possessions
citizenship, 572
defined, 572
Outstanding professors and researchers, 317–322. *See also* EB-1B immigrant visa
Overstayers, 222

P-1 nonimmigrant visa (Athletes), 156–166
applications, 165
children, 165–166
evidentiary criteria, 159–160
I-129, Petition for a Nonimmigrant Worker, 157–158, 165
multiple beneficiaries, 158
O-1A/O-1B nonimmigrant visa compared, 157–159
overview, 156–157
requirements, 157–159
spouses, 165–166
P-1B nonimmigrant visa (Internationally recognized entertainment groups), 161–162
P-2/P-3 nonimmigrant visa (Artists and entertainers), 156–166
children, 165–166
compiling the application, 165
culturally unique programs, 164–165
evidentiary criteria for P-2 nonimmigrant visa, 163
evidentiary criteria for P-3 nonimmigrant visa, 164–165
I-129, Petition for a Nonimmigrant Worker, 157–158, 165
multiple beneficiaries, 158
O-1A/O-1B nonimmigrant visa compared, 157–159
overview, 156–157
reciprocal exchange programs, 163
requirements, 157–159
spouses, 165–166
P-4 nonimmigrant visa (Spouses and children of P-1/P-2/P-3 Visa holders), 165–166
Paralegals
conflicts of interest, 644–646
ethical issues, 640–643
gathering evidence, 632–633
interviews by, 636
in private immigration law firms, 618

Paramilitary as agents of persecution, 187
Parents, VAWA proceedings, 391
Parole
generally, 3
aliens present without, 476–477
Central American Minors Refugee/Parole Program. *See* Central American Minors Refugee/Parole Program
defined, 476
naturalization, effect on, 584
Particularly serious crimes as bar to asylum, 200
Past persecution, 187–189
Peer advisory opinions for O-1A nonimmigrant visa, 143–144
Peer group and O-1A/O-1B nonimmigrant visa, 141–144, 157
Permanent research positions, 318–319
Permission, aliens present without, 476–477
PERM process, 329–364
applicant review, 349–350
audits, 334, 351-352
business necessity, 332–334
confirming satisfaction of minimum requirements, 336–337
denial, 352
determinations, 352–362
document retention, 351–352
drafting job description, 330–336
ETA 9141, Application for Prevailing Wage Determination, 338–342
ETA 9809, Application for Permanent Employment Certification, 330, 337, 345, 353–362
filing procedure, 351–352
I-140, Immigrant Petition for Alien Worker, 352
identifying minimum requirements, 330–336
institutions of higher education, 350–351
Job Zones, 331–334
labor certification application, 352
mandatory recruitment, 344–348
notice of filing, 345–347

O*Net, 331–335, 338
overview, 329–330
prevailing wage determination, 337–344
procedures, 363–364
professional recruitment, 348–349
recruitment, 344–351
specific vocational preparation, 331–334
Persecution, 184-186
agents of persecution, 187
enumerated grounds, 190–196
membership in a particular social group, 192–194
nationality, 192
political opinion, 195–196
past persecution, 187–189
persecution bar, 199–200
race,191
religion,191–192, 215–216
well-founded fear of future persecution, 189–190
Persecution waiver. See J-1 nonimmigrant visa
Persecutor bar to asylum, 199–200
Personal Responsibility and Work Opportunity Reconciliation Act of 1996, 11
Petitioner, defined, 94
Petition.
defined, 30
family sponsored immigration, 252–264. See also Family sponsored immigration
I-129, Petition for a Nonimmigrant Worker. See I-129, Petition for a Nonimmigrant Worker
I-129F, Petition for Alien Fiancé(e), 299
I-130, Petition for Alien Relative, 252, 269–270, 252, 284–285, 299–300
I-140, Immigrant Petition for Alien Worker, 312, 320, 325–327, 352, 363–5, 367, 382
I-360 Petition for Amerasian, Widow(er), or Special Immigrant, 267, 285, 312, 372–374, 445, 448
I-526, Immigrant Petition by Alien Entrepreneur, 379
I-730, Refugee/Asylee Relative Petition, 231, 234, 240, 242
I-751, Petition to Remove Conditions on Residence, 295–296
I-829, Petition by Entrepreneur to Remove Conditions, 380

I-918, Petition for U Nonimmigrant Status, 408, 410–413, 417, 423
relative petitions, 252–264. See also Relative petitions
VAWA self-petitions. See Violence Against Women Act
Petition for review, federal courts, 552
Petty offense exception to inadmissibility, 468
Philippines, family-sponsored immigration, 249
Photographs, adjustment of status applications, 284
Physical presence requirement for naturalization, 579–580
Pleadings in removal proceedings, 521–526
Political opinion, asylum based on, 195–196
Polygamous marriage
inadmissibility for, 487
VAWA proceedings, 386
Portability
EB-2/EB-3 immigrant visa, 364
H-1B nonimmigrant visa, 131
Post-hearing Voluntary Departure, 533–537
Poverty guidelines in relation to Affidavit of Support, 278
Practice of immigration law
accredited representatives, 618–620
case assessment, 620–624
case management, 638–639
conflicts of interest, 644–646
corporate offices, 618
criminal records, obtaining, 623–624
disciplinary actions, 647
engagement letters, 628–629
ethical issues, 640–644
evidence, gathering of, 632–635
examination of options, 636–637
filing systems, 640
Freedom of Information Act, 623
I-797C, Notice of Action Receipt Notice, 625
initial consultation, 624–627
intake, 624–627
nonprofit organizations, 618–620
Notices of Intent to Deny, responding to, 638–639
overview, 617, 649–650
payment of fees, 632
private immigration law firms, 618
representation agreements, 627

Requests for Evidence, responding to, 638–639
retainer agreements, 627
rules of conduct, 646–649
service fee agreements, 630–631
Predicate order and SIJ petitions, 443
Preemption, 17
Preference categories
chargeability, 250–251
cross-chargeability in family petitions, 250–251
family-sponsored petitions, 247–251
priority dates. 247–248
quotas,
family-sponsored immigrant visas, 249–250, 252
employment-based immigrant visas, 308, 312, 326, 363
Pre-hearing Voluntary Departure, 526–527
Premium processing service, 118
Prevailing wage
defined, 122
H-1B nonimmigrant visa, 127–128
PERM process, 337–344
Previous removal, inadmissibility for, 480–487
Prima facie eligibility in VAWA proceedings, 401
Primary sources of law, 17–18
Principal investors for E-1/E-2 nonimmigrant visa, 102–104
Priority 1 refugees, 238
Priority 2 refugees, 238
Priority 3 refugees, 238–239
Priority date
business-based immigration, 313, 363
family sponsored immigration, 247
Priority workers (EB-1 immigrant visa), 313–326. See also EB-1 immigrant visa
Private immigration law firms, 618
PRM. See Bureau of Population, Refugees, and Migration
Probation, effect on naturalization, 584
Productive work, B-1 nonimmigrant visa, 61, 63
Professional recruitment in PERM process, 348–349
Professionals
EB-2 immigrant visa, 327–364. See also EB-2 immigrant visa
EB-3 immigrant visa, 327–362. See also EB-3 immigrant visa

Professors, 317–322. *See also* EB-1B immigrant visa
Proffer of information or evidence in removal proceedings, 529
Proof of service in removal proceedings, 530
Proposed orders in removal proceedings, 547
Prosecutorial discretion in removal proceedings, 548–549
Pro se representation in removal proceedings, 517
Protocol Relating to the Status of Refugees (1967), 20, 182–183
Protocols, defined, 182
Proximate harm for U nonimmigrant status, 409
Proxy marriage, family-sponsored immigration, 253
Public access file, 126
Public charge
    affidavit of support, 474-475
    deportation, 495–496
    inadmissibility, 474–475

Q nonimmigrant visa (Cultural exchange), 89–90
Qualifying derivative family members. *See* Children; Derivative relatives; Spouses
Qualifying employment
    H-1B nonimmigrant visa, 122–123
    L-1A/L-1B nonimmigrant visa, 110–115
Qualifying organizations for L-1A/L-1B nonimmigrant visa, 108–110
Quotas
    generally, 7
        family-sponsored immigrant visas, 249–250, 252
        employment-based immigrant visas, 308, 312, 326, 363

R-1 nonimmigrant visa (Religious workers), 166–169. *See also* EB-4 immigrant visas
    bona fide non-profit religious organizations, 167
    children, 168
    compensation, 167
    compiling the application, 169
    duration, 168
    I-129, Petition for a Nonimmigrant Worker, 166, 169

I-539, Application to Extend/Change Nonimmigrant Status, 169
    ministers, 166–167, 169, 369–370, 372–373
    overview, 166
    religious occupation
    religious vocations, 166
    religious worker, 166–169, 368–375
    site inspections, 168
    spouses, 168
    types of religious workers eligible, 166–167
Race, asylum based on, 191
Rape as persecution, 185
REAL ID Act of 2005
    asylum requirements, 191, 197, 202
    overview, 13
Reasonable accommodation for naturalization, 588–589
Reasonable fear
    defined, 229
    interviews (for asylum), 229–230
Re-calendaring in removal proceedings, 546
Receipts, 30, 35–36
Reception and Placement Program, 241
Reciprocal exchange programs for P-2/P-3 nonimmigrant visa, 163
Reciprocity fees
    chart, 53
    defined, 52
Reciprocity tables, I nonimmigrant visa, 171
Reconsideration in removal proceedings, 544
Recruitment in PERM process, 344–351
Reentry after removal, consequences of, 480–481
Refugee Act of 1980, 9, 183, 237
Refugee Processing Center, 240
Refugees. *See* Asylees and refugees
Regional Centers and EB-5 immigrant visa, 375–379
Regulations as source of law, 18
Rehabilitation Act of 1973, 589
Reinstatement of F-1/M-1 nonimmigrant visa, 80–81
Reinstatement of removal, 485
Related cultural exchange
    H-3 nonimmigrant visa, 90–91
    Q nonimmigrant visa, 89–90

Relative petitions, 252–264. *See also* Adjustment of status
    Adam Walsh Child Protection and Safety Act, 259
    children. *See* Children
    Child Status Protection Act, 262–264
    defined, 247
    documentation, 260–262
    siblings, 257–259
    spouses, 253–256
    submission of, 269–270
Relief from removal, 552–556. *See also specific immigration benefits*
    adjustment of status, 553
    asylum. *See* Defensive asylum
    cancellation of removal, 553–556
    good moral character and, 559
    hardship and, 561
    I-130, Petition for an Alien Relative, 564
    I-140, Immigrant Petition for Alien Worker, 564
    INA § 212(c), 558
    inadmissibility and, 511, 526, 537-538, 556, 558, 563
    lawful permanent residents, 554, 556–558
    medical conditions, 560
    NACARA, 554, 567
    non-lawful permanent residents, 554, 558–561
    Notice of Intent to Offer Evidence, 562–563
    overview, 552–553
    post-order instructions for individuals granted relief from removal, 536
    VAWA proceedings, 554, 561–566
Religion, asylum based on, 191–192, 215–216
Religious worker
    EB-4 immigrant visa, 368–375. *See also* EB-4 immigrant visa
    R-1 nonimmigrant visa, 166–169. *See also* R-1 nonimmigrant visa
Relinquishment of citizenship, 612
Remand, 194
Removal period, 541
Removal proceedings. *See also* Deportation
    generally, 14, 456
    in absentia orders, 513
    accredited representatives, 517
    administrative closure, 546–549

appeals from, 549–551
asylum, defensive application, 221–226
authorized legal representatives, 517
battered spouses and children, 561–566
BIA. *See* Board of Immigration Appeals
bond. *See* Bond
burden of proof
  inadmissibility grounds, 511
  deportation grounds, 511–12
case preparation, 529–531
case proceedings, 531–532
change of venue, 513, 544–546
closing argument, 532
continuances, 545
counsel, right to, 515–516
cross-examination, 532
decisions, 533
de novo review, 221
detention, 539–543. *See also* Detention
due process in, 506
EOIR. *See* Executive Office for Immigration Review
EOIR-26, Notice of Appeal from a Decision of an Immigration Judge, 550
EOIR 27, Notice of Appearance as Attorney or Legal Representative, 550
EOIR-28, Notice of Entry of Appearance as Attorney or Representative Before the Immigration Court, 517
EOIR-33/BIA, Alien's Change of Address Form/Board of Immigration Appeals, 514
EOIR-33/IC, Alien's Change of Address Form/Immigration Court, 514, 545
evidence rules, 532–533
examination in chief, 531
expedited removal proceedings, 537–539. *See also* Expedited removal proceedings
failure to attend, 477
Federal Courts, appeals to, 551–552
Federal Rules of Evidence, 532-533
final order of removal, 541
G-28, Notice of Entry of Appearance of Attorney or Accredited Representative, 517

habeas corpus, 543
hearings, 517–537
hearsay evidence, 532–533
Immigration Court. *See* Immigration Court
inadmissibility for failure to attend, 477
individual hearings, 527–532
mandatory detention, 541–543
marriage during, 553
master calendar hearings, 517–527
minute orders, 534–535
motions, 543–546
naturalization and, 576, 578, 583, 586, 614, 615
notice of hearing, 514–516
Notice to Appear, 507–514
Office of Chief Immigration Practice Manual, 528, 543, 545
order of supervision, 542
overview, 505–507, 567
pleadings, 521–526
post-hearing Voluntary Departure, 533–537
post-order instructions for individuals granted relief from removal, 536
pre-hearing Voluntary Departure, 526–527
proffer of information or evidence, 529
proof of service, 530
proposed orders, 547
prosecutorial discretion, 548–549
pro se representation, 517
purpose of, 203
re-calendaring, 546
reconsideration, 544
relief from removal, 552–556. *See also* Relief from removal
reopening of cases, 513, 543–544
respondents, 506–507
statute of limitations, 203
stay of removal, 552
T nonimmigrant visa, 438–439
Temporary Protected Status, 548
U nonimmigrant visa, 421
withholding of removal, 231–234
Removal order, 513, 526-527, 535, 537, 542, 552
Reopening of cases in removal proceedings, 543–544
Reopening of removal proceedings, 513
Repatriation of refugees, 238

Representation agreement, 627
Request for Evidence
  form, 37–38
  overview, 36
  responding to, 638–639
  VAWA proceedings, 401
Researchers, 317–322. *See also* EB-1B immigrant visa
Resettlement program for refugees, 241
Residency requirements
  J-1 nonimmigrant visa, two-year home residency requirement, 85–87
  naturalization, continuous residency requirement, 576–579
  VAWA proceedings, 385–388
Resident Alien Card, 25–27
Respondent in removal proceedings, 506–507
Retainer agreement, 627
Returning resident, 458–459
Revocation, relative petition, 264–266
RSC (Refugee Support Centers), 238
Rules of conduct, 646–649
Russia, E-1/E-2 nonimmigrant visa, 97

Safe third country as bar to asylum, 201–202
Schedule A occupations, 367–368
Science, technology, engineering, and mathematics (STEM), 48, 76, 78
Sciences
  employment-based immigration of aliens with extraordinary ability in, 314–317. *See also* EB-1 immigrant visa
  individuals with extraordinary ability in, 140–155. *See also* O-1A nonimmigrant visa
Screen Actors Guild, 156
Seasonal nonimmigrant workers, 171–176. *See also* H-2 nonimmigrant visa
Second preference category, 247
Secondary Inspection, 53–54
Secondary sources of law, 18–20
Section 322 citizenship, 608–611
  generally, 571
  children born out of wedlock outside United States, 609–610
  N-600K, Application for Citizenship and Issuance of Certificate Under Section 322, 608

Security-related grounds
  as bar to asylum, 202
  deportation for, 495
  inadmissibility for, 472–473
Sedition Act of 1798, 5
Selective service, effect of failure to register on naturalization, 584–585
Self-sponsored immigration. *See* Employment-based immigration
Service fee agreements, 630–631
Severe form of human trafficking. *See* T nonimmigrant visa
SEVIS. *See* Student and Exchange Visitor Information System
SEVP (Student and Exchange Visitor Program), 71
Sexual orientation, asylum based on, 192–193
Siblings, family-sponsored immigration, 257–259
SIJ. *See* Special Immigrant Juveniles
Similar working conditions for H-1B nonimmigrant visa, 128–129
Singapore, H-1B1 nonimmigrant visa, 133–134
Site inspections of R-1 nonimmigrant visa religious workers, 168
Sixth Amendment, inadmissibility, 464
Skilled workers, professionals, and other workers, 327–362. *See also* EB-3 immigrant visa,
Skills list for J-1 nonimmigrant visa, 86
Slaves, citizenship of, 572
Social group membership, asylum based on, 192–194
Sources of law, 16–20
  agency guidance, 19
  asylum, 182–183
  casebooks, 20
  case law, 18, 60–61
  Constitution, 16–17
  E-1/E-2 nonimmigrant visa, 95–97
  family-sponsored immigration, 246–247
  H-1B nonimmigrant visa, 120–122
  international law, 20
  L-1A/L-1B nonimmigrant visa, 107–108
  nonimmigrant visas, 60–61
  primary sources, 17–18
  regulations, 18
  secondary sources, 18–20
  statutes, 17
  treatises, 20
  VAWA proceedings, 385
  websites, 19
Soviet bloc, relief from removal for persons from, 567
Special Immigrant Juveniles (SIJ), 443–449
  affirmative applications, 445–447
  compiling the application, 444–448
  defensive applications, 447–448
  dependency orders, 443–444
  G-325, Biographic Information, 445–446
  I-360, Petition for Amerasian, Widow(er), or Special Immigrant, 445, 448
  I-485, Application to Register Permanent Residence or Adjust Status, 445–446
  I-601, Application for Waiver of Ground of Inadmissibility, 445–446
  I-765, Application for Employment Authorization, 445–446
  I-912, Request for Fee Waiver, 445–446
  juvenile courts, 443
  Office of Refugee Resettlement, children in custody of, 448–449
  overview, 384, 443
  predicate order and, 443-444
  terrorism, 446
Special immigrants including religious workers, 368–375. *See also* EB-4 immigrant visa
Specialized knowledge
  defined, 114
  intracompany transferees, 107–120. *See also* L-1A/L-1B nonimmigrant visa
Specialty occupations
  H-1B nonimmigrant visa, 122
  H-1B1, nonimmigrant visas for specialty workers from Singapore and Chile
  professionals from Australia (E-3 nonimmigrant visa), 134
Specific vocational preparation in PERM process, 331–334
Sponsored immigrants, adjustment of status of, 278
Sports
  employment-based immigration of aliens with extraordinary ability in, 314–317. *See also* EB-1 immigrant visa
  O-1A nonimmigrant visa, 140–155. *See also* O-1A nonimmigrant visa
  P-1 nonimmigrant visa, 156–166. *See also* P-1 nonimmigrant visa
Spouses. *See also* Adjustment of Status, Marriage, Marriage fraud, VAWA relief
  asylees and refugees, 231, 239–240, 242
  asylum, 217
  E-1/E-2 nonimmigrant visa, 106
  F-1/M-1 nonimmigrant visa, 79
  Family-sponsored immigration, 253–256, 261
  H-1B nonimmigrant visa, 133
  J-1 nonimmigrant visa, 89
  L-1A/L-1B nonimmigrant visa, 120
  P-1/P-2/P-3 nonimmigrant visa, 165–166
  R-1 nonimmigrant visa, 168
  T nonimmigrant visa, 437–438
  U nonimmigrant visa, 417
Stamps for nonimmigrant visas, 51–54
Stateless persons
  generally, 8
  asylum, 183
Statute of limitations, 203
Statutes as source of law, 17
Statutory period, 573, 574–575, 577, 579–582, 584, 587, 598
Stay of removal, 552
STEM. *See* Science, technology, engineering, and mathematics
Step-children. *See* Children
Sterilization, involuntary, as persecution, 185
Stop-time rule, 555
Student and Exchange Visitor Information System (SEVIS), 71, 75, 79, 650
Student and Exchange Visitor Program (SEVP), 71
Students. *See* F-1, M-1 nonimmigrant visas
Sua sponte reopening of proceedings, 544
Substance abuse, inadmissibility for, 463
Substantial investments for E-1/E-2 nonimmigrant visa, 101

Substantial physical or emotional abuse for U nonimmigrant visa, 408–409
Sudan, Visa Waiver Program, 64
Supervisory employees and E-1/E-2 nonimmigrant visa, 102–104
Supremacy Clause, 17
SVP. *See* Specific Vocational Preparation
Syria, Visa Waiver Program, 64

T nonimmigrant visa (Victims of Human Trafficking), 427–441
　adjustment of status, 439–441
　applications, 430–438
　benefits of, 438
　children, 437–438
　compiling the application, 431–432
　consulates and consular processing, 437
　continued presence application, 429–430
　DNA testing, 438
　DS-160, Online Nonimmigrant Visa Application, 437
　eligibility, 428–429
　G-325, Biographic Information, 441
　I-192, Application for Advance Permission to Enter as Nonimmigrant, 432, 437, 440
　I-485, Application to Register Permanent Residence or Adjust Status, 439, 441
　I-912, Request for Fee Waiver, 432, 441
　I-914, Application for T Nonimmigrant Status, 431, 437
　I-914, Supplement A, Application for Immediate Family Member of T-1 Recipient, 432, 437
　I-914, Supplement B, Declaration of Law Enforcement Officer for Victim of Trafficking in Persons, 431–432
　law enforcement declaration, 430
　letter in support of application for adjustment of status, 432–436
　overview, 427–428
　protection for victims, 429–430
　public benefits, eligibility for, 429–430
　removal proceedings, 438–439
　spouses, 437–438
　U nonimmigrant visa compared, 441–442
Targeted employment area, EB-5 immigrant visa, 376
Taxes, effect of nonpayment on naturalization, 585
Television, individuals with extraordinary ability in (O-1B immigrant visa), 140–155. *See also* O-1B immigrant visa
Temporary nonimmigrant workers, 171–176. *See also* H-2 immigrant visa
Temporary Protected Status (TPS), generally, 4
　administrative closure, 548
　advanced parole, 235-236
　criminal convictions and, 235
　deferred enforced departure compared with, 237
　overview, 235–237
　removal proceedings, 58
Ten-year bar, 284–287, 482, 484, 486, 513, 535–537
Terrorism
　adjustment of status, 272
　as bar to asylum, 202
　detention, 539
　impact on immigration law, 12–13
　inadmissibility, 472–473
　Special Immigrant Juveniles, 446
　Visa Waiver Program, 64
Third preference category, 247
Three-year bar, 284–287, 482, 484, 486
Tickler system, 638–639
Title VII, nonimmigrant visas, 46
TN nonimmigrant visa (NAFTA professionals), 135–137
　applications, 136–137
　computer systems analysts, 135
　consulates and consular processing, 135
　duration, 136–137
　H-1B nonimmigrant visa compared, 136
　overview, 135
　requirements for classification, 135–136
Torture as persecution, 185, 194
Torture Convention. *See* Convention Against Torture and Other Cruel, Inhuman, or Degrading Treatment or Punishment
Tourists. *See* B-2 nonimmigrant visa
TPS. *See* Temporary Protected Status
Trafficking, 427–441. *See also* T nonimmigrant visa
Trainee programs for J-1 nonimmigrant visa, 84–85
Transit, 70. *See also* C-1 nonimmigrant visa
Travel considerations
　advanced parole, 235
　F-1/M-1 nonimmigrant visa, 79–80
Travel documents, 23
Treasury Department, 7
Treatises as source of law, 20
Treaty investor, 95–106. *See also* E-1/E-2 nonimmigrant visa
Treaty trader, 95–106. *See also* E-1/E-2 nonimmigrant visa
Troubled business and EB-5 immigrant visa, 376
TVPRA 2008. *See* William Wilberforce Trafficking Victims Protection Reauthorization Act of 2008
Two-year home residency requirement
　defined, 85
　J-1 immigrant visa, 85–87
　waiver, 87–88

U nonimmigrant visa (Victims of Certain Enumerated Crimes), 405–426
　adjustment of status, 422–426
　benefits of, 417–421
　children, 417
　compiling the U application, 410–417
　consulates and consular processing, 422
　direct harm, 409
　direct victims, 409
　eligibility, 405–406
　enumerated crimes, 406
　G-325, Biographic Information, 423
　I-192, Application for Advance Permission to Enter as Nonimmigrant, 411, 416–418, 422
　I-193, Application for Waiver of Passport and/or Visa, 411, 417
　I-485, Application to Register Permanent Residence or Adjust Status, 423
　I-539, Application to Extend/Change Nonimmigrant Status, 422–423

I-797C, Notice of Action Receipt Notice, 426
I-912, Request for Fee Waiver, 424
I-918, Petition for U Nonimmigrant Status, 413
I-918, Supplement A, Petition for Qualifying Family Member of U-1 Recipient, 417
I-918, Supplement B, Law Enforcement Certification Form, 408, 410–411, 413–414, 423
   identifying victim, 409–410
   indirect victims, 409
   law enforcement certification, 406–408
   overview, 405
   petitions, 410–417
   proximate harm, 409
   removal proceedings, 421
   spouses, 417
   substantial physical or emotional abuse, 408–409
   T nonimmigrant visa compared, 441–442
UACs. *See* Unaccompanied minors or children
Unaccompanied minors or children
   asylum, 198
   defined, 13
Undocumented or unauthorized, defined, 3
Uniform Limited Partnership Act, EB-5 immigrant visa, 377
United Kingdom
   E-1/E-2 nonimmigrant visa, 97
   EB-2 immigrant visa, 328
United Nations
   Convention Against Torture, 232–234. *See also* Convention Against Torture and Other Cruel, Inhuman, or Degrading Treatment or Punishment
   Convention Relating to the Status of Refugees, 20, 182–184, 191
   G nonimmigrant visa for employees of, 179
   Handbook and Guidelines on Procedures and Criteria for Determining Refugee Status Under the 1951 Convention and 1967 Protocol Relating to the Status of Refugees, 183, 185, 187, 191–192, 195

   High Commissioner for Refugees, 183, 192
   Protocol Relating to the Status of Refugees, 20, 182–183
United States citizen, defined, 2
United States Citizenship and Immigration Service (USCIS)
   Administrative Appeals Office. *See* Administrative Appeals Office
   agency guidance, 19
   authority of, 13–16
   authorized legal representatives, 517
   Field Offices, 270, 399, 447, 598, 600
   Fraud Detection and National Security Directorate, 48, 254–255
   Freedom of Information Act, 623
   immigration file, obtaining copy of, 521
   Notices of Intent to Deny, 638–639
   paralegals, 649–650
   Policy Manual and Memoranda, 307
   Request for Evidence, 36, 638–639
   website, 19
United States Refugee Admissions Program (USRAP), 237–238
Uniting and Strengthening America by Providing Appropriate Tools Required to Intercept and Obstruct Terrorism Act of 2001 (USA Patriot Act)
   generally, 12
   inadmissibility, 472–473
Unlawful presence
   adjustment of status, 284–287
   defined, 59
   exceptions, 484
   inadmissibility, 481–487
   three- and ten-year bar, 284–287, 482, 484, 486, 513, 535–537
   waivers, 485
Unskilled employees, 171
Uruguay, B-1 nonimmigrant visa, 65
U.S. Tennis Open Championship, P-1 nonimmigrant visa for, 160
U.S. workers, defined, 48
USA Patriot Act of 2001
   generally, 12
   inadmissibility, 472–473
USCIS. *See* United States Citizenship and Immigration Service
USRAP (United States Refugee Admissions Program), 237–238

Validity of marriage
   family-sponsored immigration, for purposes of, 253–256
   VAWA proceedings, for purposes of, 385–388
VAWA. *See* Violence Against Women Act
Veterans' Affairs Department, National Interest Waiver, 366–367
Victims of certain enumerated crimes
   T nonimmigrant visa, 427–441. *See also* T nonimmigrant visa
   U nonimmigrant visa, 405–426. *See also* U nonimmigrant visa
Victims of Trafficking and Violence Protection Act of 2000 (VTVPA), 12
   T nonimmigrant visa, 427–428
   U nonimmigrant visa, 405
Violence Against Women Act (VAWA)
   adjustment of status and, 401
   affirmative petitions, 403
   battery, 391–392
   cancellation of removal, 561–566
   children, petitions by, 389–391
   compiling the petition, 397–400
   confidentiality, 403
   criteria for relief, 391–397
   defensive applications, 403
   deferred action status, 401–402
   divorce, effect of, 386–387
   entry without inspection, effect of, 402
   evidence, gathering of, 633
   extreme cruelty, 391–392
   family sponsored immigration, 263
   good moral character, 392–394
   I-360, Petition for Amerasian, Widow(er), or Special Immigrant, 397–400, 402
   I-485, Application to Register Permanent Residence or Adjust Status, 398
   I-551, Permanent Resident Card, 404
   I-751, Petition to Remove Conditions on Residency, 404
   I-765, Application for Employment Authorization, 398
   I-912, Request for Fee Waiver, 404
   immigration status of abuser, 388
   inadmissibility, 402–403

marriage, petitions based on, 385–388
naturalization, 574
Notice of Intent to Deny, 401
overview, 384–385
parents, petitions by, 391
polygamous marriage, 386
prima facie eligibility, 401
processing of petition, 401–403
relief from removal, 554, 561–566
removal of conditions, 403–404
Request for Evidence, 401
residency requirements, 385–388
validity of marriage, 385–388
waiver of inadmissibility, 462, 471
Visa bulletin
employment-based immigration, 309–313
family-sponsored immigration, 247–250
Visa exempt status, defined, 49
Visas
defined, 4, 45
immigrant visas. *See* Immigrant visas
nonimmigrant visas. *See* Nonimmigrant visas
Visa Waiver Program (VWP)
B-1/B-2 nonimmigrant visa, 64–65
C-1 nonimmigrant visa, 70
changing or extending nonimmigrant status, 54–55
D nonimmigrant visa, 70
defined, 48
expedited removal proceedings, 538
visa applications, effect on, 48
Vocational education, F-1/M-1 nonimmigrant visa, 70–71
Volags (voluntary agencies), refugees, 240
Voluntary Departure
defined, 526
inadmissibility, 482
post-hearing, 533–537
pre-hearing, 526–527
Voting unlawfully
deportation for, 496
effect on naturalization, 586

inadmissibility for, 487
VTVPA. *See* Victims of Trafficking and Violence Protection Act of 2000
Vulnerable populations
Central American Minors Refugee/Parole Program, 451–453. *See also* Central American Minors Refugee/Parole Program
Deferred Action for Childhood Arrivals, 449–451. *See also* Deferred Action for Childhood Arrivals
overview, 384–385, 453
Special Immigrant Juveniles, 443–449. *See also* Special Immigrant Juveniles
T nonimmigrant visa, 427–441. *See also* T nonimmigrant visa
trafficking, 384
U nonimmigrant visa, 405–426. *See also* U nonimmigrant visa
VAWA proceedings. *See* Violence Against Women Act
VWP. *See* Visa Waiver Program

Wage and Hour Division, 48, 126
Waivers
adjustment of status, 284–290
defined, 456
INA § 212(a)(3)(A)(ii), 488
INA § 212(a)(3)(A)(iii), 488
INA § 212(a)(3)(E)(i), 488
INA § 212(a)(3)(E)(ii), 488
INA § 212(a)(3)(C), 488
INA § 212(a)(3)(D), 473
INA § 212(a)(3)(D)(iii), 473
INA § 212(a)(9)(B)(v), 488
INA § 212(a)(9)(C)(iii), 486
INA § 212(c), 493, 558
INA § 212(d)(3), 463, 469, 487–488
INA § 212(d)(11), 479
INA § 212(g)277, 462
INA § 212(h), 459, 469–470, 492, 549
INA § 212(i), 256, 271, 478
INA § 212(k), 476
INA § 237(a)(1)(H), 489
INA § 237(a)(2)(A)(iv), 491
INA § 237(a)(2)(B)(i), 493
INA § 245(e)(3), 256

INA § 216, 296–297
inadmissibility, waiver to facilitate temporary admission of nonimmigrants, 487–488
IGA or interested governmental agency waiver, 87–88
National Interest Waiver, 365–367
naturalization, 588–589
nonimmigrant waivers, 51
persecution waiver, 87–88
two-year home residency requirement, 87–88
unlawful presence, 485
VAWA, waiver of inadmissibility, 462, 471
Weapons offenses, deportation for, 493
Websites as source of law, 19
Welfare
deportation for public charge, 495–496
inadmissibility for public charge, 474–475
Well-founded fear of future persecution
asylum based on, 189–190
defined, 189–190
Widow(er)s, 266–269
"Widow's penalty," 267
William Wilberforce Trafficking Victims Protection Reauthorization Act of 2008 (TVPRA 2008)
Special Immigrant Juveniles, 444, 448
T nonimmigrant visa, 427, 430
Withholding of removal, 231–234
asylum and CAT reliefs compared, 233–234
defined, 231
Women. *See also* Violence Against Women Act
female genital mutilation, 184–185, 192–193
fiancées, 298–303
rape as persecution, 185
World Health Organization employees, 179
World Trade Organization employees, 179